Truth and Efficiency in Civil Litigation

Fundamental Aspects of Fact-finding and Evidence-taking in a Comparative Context

Editors:
C.H. van Rhee
A. Uzelac

Truth and Efficiency in Civil Litigation
Fundamental Aspects of Fact-finding and Evidence-taking in a Comparative Context

intersentia

METRO

Ius Commune Europaeum

Editors:
C.H. van Rhee
A. Uzelac

Truth and Efficiency in Civil Litigation:
Fundamental Aspects of Fact-finding and Evidence-taking in a Comparative Context

This book was published with the financial support of the Royal Netherlands Embassy, Zagreb, Croatia.

Intersentia Ltd
Trinity House | Cambridge Business Park | Cowley Road
Cambridge | CB4 0WZ | United Kingdom
Tel.: +44 1223 393 753 | Email: mail@intersentia.co.uk

ISBN 978-1-78068-133-7
D/2012/7849/80
NUR 822

Cambridge - Antwerp - Portland
www.intersentia.com | www.intersentia.co.uk

British Library Cataloguing in Publication Data. A catalogue record for this book is available from the British Library.

TABLE OF CONTENTS

EXPERIMENTAL APPROACH TO TRUTH-FINDING

LIST OF AUTHORS

G. Abolonin, PhD (Russia), Head of Legal Department for Russia, Linx Telecommunications CIS (Moscow), Russian Federation

V. Abolonin, PhD (Russia), LL.M. (Hanover/Lisbon), Associate Professor, Urals State Law Academy (Yekaterinburg), Russian Federation

M. Bina, Postdoctoral Researcher in civil procedural law, Milan University, Italy

R. Bloemink, Student, Utrecht University, The Netherlands

P.C.H. Chan, Teaching Fellow, City University of Hong Kong, People's Republic of China

S.P.W. van Dooren, Student, Maastricht University, The Netherlands

L.I.M. Entjes, Student, Maastricht University, The Netherlands

L.V. Fatkhullina, PhD student, Kazan (Volga Region) Federal University (Kazan), Russian Federation

F. Fernhout, Associate Professor of Civil Procedure, Maastricht University, The Netherlands

F. Ferrari, Aggregate Professor of Civil Procedure, Insubria University (Como-Varese), Italy

F. Ferraris, PhD (Milan), Research fellow in civil procedural law, University of Milan-Bicocca, Italy

S.A.H. van Gompel, Student, Maastricht University, The Netherlands

R. Jagtenberg, Associate Professor of Law, Erasmus University (Rotterdam), The Netherlands

T. Karlović, Assistant Professor of Roman Law, Zagreb University, Croatia

J.H. Langbein, Sterling Professor of Law & Legal History, Yale Law School (New Haven), USA

R.L. Marcus, Coil Chair in Litigation, University of California, Hastings College of the Law, USA; Associate Reporter, Advisory Committee on Civil Rules, Judicial Conference of the USA

I. Milotić, Research Assistant, Zagreb University, Croatia

M. Paleker, Associate Professor, Department of Private Law, University of Cape Town, South Africa

C.H. van Rhee, Professor of European Legal History and Comparative Civil Procedure, Maastricht University, The Netherlands

V. Rijavec, Head of the Institute for Civil, Comparative and International Private Law, University of Maribor, Slovenia

A. de Roo, Associate Professor of Law, Erasmus University (Rotterdam), The Netherlands

E. Silvestri, Associate Professor of Comparative Civil Procedure, University of Pavia, Italy

J. Sladič, Sladič Law Firm (Ljubljana), Slovenia, Associate Professor of International and European Law, University of Maribor, Slovenia

S. Spinei, Associate Professor of Law, University of Sibiu, Romania

A. Uzelac, Professor of Civil Procedure, Zagreb University, Croatia

D.Kh. Valeev, Professor of Civil Procedure, Kazan (Volga Region) Federal University (Kazan), Russian Federation

A. Valeeva, PhD student, Kazan (Volga Region) Federal University (Kazan), Russian Federation

R.R. Verkerk, Lawyer at Houthoff Buruma (Rotterdam), The Netherlands

LIST OF ABBREVIATIONS

AD	Anno Domini
ADR	Alternative Dispute Resolution
ALI/UNIDROIT	American Law Institute/Institut International pour l'Unification du Droit Privé
Art.	Article
BATNA	Best Alternative To a Negotiated Agreement
CCP	Code of Civil Procedure
CFI	Court of First Instance
CJEU	Court of Justice of the European Union
CJR	Civil Justice Reform
CPC	Commercial Procedure Code
CPR	Civil Procedure Rules
DNA	Deoxyribonuclein Acid
ECJ	European Court of Justice
EU	European Union
FCL	Federal Constitutional Law
FRCP	Federal Rules of Civil Procedure
GKAP	State Committee for Anti-Monopoly Policy
GPS	Global Positioning System
LEC	Ley de Enjuiciamiento Civil
MCR	Magistrates Courts Rules
NCPC	New Code of Civil Procedure
NPCSC	National People's Congress Standing Committee
OJ	Official Journal
PAIA	Promotion of Access to Information Act
RHC	Rules of the High Court
RSFSR	Russian Soviet Federative Socialist Republic
RUB	Ruble
SPC	Supreme People's Court
Stb.	Staatsblad (Dutch Official Journal)
TEU	Treaty on European Union
TFEU	Treaty on the Functioning of the European Union
UMA	Uniform Mediation Act

URC	Uniform Rules of Court
US	United States
USA	United States of America
ZPO	Zivilprozessordnung
ZPP	*Zakon o pravdnem postopku* (Civil Procedure Act)

INTRODUCTION

C.H. van Rhee
A. Uzelac

THE PURSUIT OF TRUTH IN CONTEMPORARY CIVIL PROCEDURE: REVIVAL OF ACCURACY OR A NEW BALANCE IN FAVOUR OF EFFECTIVENESS?

In the pursuit of justice, truth always plays a prominent role. Few if any legal systems are willing to waive the right to claim that the results of their legal processes are fair, just and above all based on the truth. In most legal systems, elaborate rules on the taking of evidence try to guarantee that an accurate, factual basis is used for the application of the law. Such rules are the core of most methods of adjudication.

There are, however, different approaches and even different procedural philosophies regarding the ways in which evidence should be selected, presented and evaluated in a court of law. These differences exist both between different legal traditions - e.g. between common law and civil law systems of civil justice - but also on local, regional and national levels. A question that needs to be addressed in this context is the place of truth-finding in the hierarchy of the values observed and respected by civil courts. Placing truth at the pinnacle of all procedural values (as is purportedly done by some systems of civil procedure) may have various detrimental consequences when balancing the core values of civil litigation and may not be justified.

Even if there is agreement on the systemic place of truth in a civil justice system, there are manifest and sometimes dramatic differences in the methods that are regarded as producing truthful results. At the level of procedural ideology, considerable differences may be noticed between traditions that rely on a strong judge, vested with inquisitorial powers and broad authorities, and traditions that prefer party presentation of evidence before a passive fact-finder.

John Henry Wigmore's statement in his 1904 *Treatise on the Anglo-American System of Evidence in Trials at Common Law* reflects the latter approach where he argues that 'cross-examination is beyond doubt the greatest legal engine ever invented for the discovery of truth'.[1] Starting from this background, the right to

1 This quote is often repeated in case law and contemporary legal publications. See e.g. *Lilly v Virginia*, 527 U.S. 116 (1999). See also Damaška 1975, p. 1103-1104.

party presentation of evidence, including the right to cross-examination, is regarded as so essential that it is considered to be of constitutional significance.[2]

The former approach may be noticed in modern Continental European civil procedure, especially in the twentieth and twenty-first centuries. One of the most influential modern procedural codifications in Europe, the Austrian Civil Procedural Code of 1895,[3] is based on the idea that the 'principle of party presentation should be superseded and the judge vested with the power to conduct the proceedings' since party presentation is considered to basically impede accurate fact finding and establishing the 'objective truth'.[4] The fundamental ideas of the author of that Code, Franz Klein, were directed against the concept of civil procedure as a 'war without the Red Cross',[5] in which the judge acts as a passive observer of the two fighting parties, each of which distorts reality for the benefit of its own cause.

The differences between the American and European approaches to the concept of truth and the corresponding method of presenting evidence in civil proceedings are still very prominent. In the era of globalisation it is only natural that the two approaches have been subject to comparative discussion, and some practitioners and individual dissident authors have occasionally argued for the adoption of an approach to evidence different from their own national approach. An example is Professor John Langbein, who has argued for assigning judges rather than lawyers the task to investigate the facts in the American legal system. In doing so, the author was at the time inspired by the legal system of West Germany which, in his opinion, would help reduce the problematic features of the adversarial process dominated by lawyers, who tend to distort evidence and add unnecessary complexity and expense to civil trials.[6] On the European Continent, we can meet voices inspired by American experiences that, on the contrary, ask for a more adversarial approach. In doing so, these voices promote gradually embracing evidentiary notions that were previously considered to be incompatible with fundamental principles of the national legal process.[7]

Yet, it is still too early to speak of 'harmonisation' as fact-finding practices are among the elements of procedural systems that are most difficult to amend by mere legislative action or any other method of reform. This may be explained not only by persisting contrasts in deeply rooted cultural perceptions about the truth and accuracy in civil litigation, or by a struggle between 'modernists' and 'traditionalists',[8] but also by the constant redefinition of these concepts in light of

2 In addition to the confrontation clause of the Sixth Amendment to the U.S. Constitution, 'innumerable cases insist that for a fair trial, civil litigants must have the right to cross-examine'. See Posner & Dodd 1993, p. 1.

3 See references in Verkerk 2010, p. 34.

4 More in Frodl 2012, p. 49.

5 See Klein 1891, p. 39.

6 Langbein 1985, p. 823-824.

7 Some popular Anglo-American procedural tools that are discussed in Europe are discovery, cross-examination and party-appointed expert witnesses.

8 Such national debates exist in almost any legal system. They can also be observed at an international level. The opposition between 'modernists' and 'traditionalists' may be nicely →

modern trends towards mediation and other means of dispute resolution as an alternative to litigation in a court of law.[9]

At a more pragmatic level, it should be noted that fact-finding practices greatly depend on the different procedural structures in particular jurisdictions, such as the participation of professional and/or lay fact-finders, the level to which rules of evidence are formalised, and the forms and organisation of trials (e.g. written or oral proceedings, concentration or 'deconcentration', case-management and time management). As long as procedural forms and structures remain different, approaches to evidence will also remain different.[10]

Nevertheless, at the European and global level some harmonisation of civil procedural forms and structures is taking place, and this also has an important impact on approaches to evidence.[11] The changes may be observed both in old and well-established legal systems such as, e.g., the English legal system, and in transition and post-transition countries. In particular, the latter countries have gone through a long and difficult period of transformation which is still not over. They share the common heritage of Socialist law, which puts great weight on the concept of the 'material truth', considered to be the key value in the hierarchy of procedural values. The 'material truth' was contrasted with the 'formal truth' as being the result of a formalistic and adversarial application of law that only pretended to ensure equality before the law, while at the same time essentially serving the interests of the ruling class or the bourgeoisie.[12] Instead of masking the class nature of judicial proceedings, Socialist law pretended to promote a truthful, correct ideology which had to be mirrored in litigation, displaying a 'Socialist legal consciousness', 'class instincts' and a 'Socialist legality'. The 'material truth' was considered to be a truth that resulted from a process in which judges, as agents of the ideology of the ruling Socialist elites, apply the law to facts established by these very judges on the basis of a free evaluation of evidence.

With the fall of Socialist regimes in Eastern Europe and the former Soviet Union, the transformation of the civil justice system of the former Socialist countries was put on the agenda. However, the process of transformation was neither fast nor straightforward. Some elements of the Socialist legal tradition managed to successfully survive the reform movement.[13] In particular, the central position of the

illustrated by the example of some forward-looking Dutch reforms (see the contribution of Verkerk in this volume) and the 'antiquarian approach' of Italian law (see the contribution of Silvestri in this volume).

9 More on truth in the context of mediation and litigation can be found in the contribution of Jagtenberg & De Roo in this volume. For an Asian perspective, see the contribution of Chan in this volume.

10 An exceptional jurisdiction in respect of the search for the truth in civil litigation is the United States of America. For more on American exceptionalism, see the contribution of Marcus in this volume. In contrast, the contribution of Langbein, also in this volume, highlights some areas where a modest convergence between American and European civil procedure is present.

11 Among recent works on the issue of harmonisation, see Kramer & Van Rhee 2012.

12 See Vyshinsky 1948, p. 73-76.

13 *Cf.* Uzelac 2010.

'material truth' and the strong, inquisitorial, paternalistic position of judges *vis-à-vis* the parties continued to be the hallmark of many post-Socialist states for a long period after the political changes. Some of the countries that decided to delete the 'material truth' from the list of key values in civil procedure soon after the fall of Communism (e.g. Hungary) later even had to face a certain revival of the old ideas. In addition, in various post-Socialist states ample opportunities to challenge final and binding judgments and to re-open the proceedings upon petition of the State Prosecutor or even by courts *ex officio* were preserved precisely with reference to the supremacy of the truth and the imperative to preserve substantive legality and accuracy. It is not clear how long this situation will continue to exist since many legislative reforms are in course or are about to be undertaken in a number of the post-Socialist states.[14] Some convergence may be observed between post-Socialist states and the rest of Europe where in various transition or post-transition countries the paternalistic inquisitorial tradition is traded for more responsibility for the parties and an enhanced collaboration between judge and parties.[15] On the other side, some of the old, established democracies are trading their tradition of more passive and reserved judges for an increase in the case-management powers of the judge and extended powers to order the taking of evidence *ex officio*.[16]

However, convergence does not mean that the debate about the fundamental principles underpinning the law of evidence and the practices of proof taking is over. More than ever before, we are witnessing intensive changes in approaches to evidence in civil litigation. The frequency of legislative changes at the national and international level, the internationalisation of the law of evidence through the jurisprudence of transnational tribunals[17] and also the variety of doctrinal views are unprecedented. Therefore, an effort to collect comparative information about the ways in which civil justice systems treat truth and fact finding is justified.

Consequently, in this volume we have tried to collect fresh, contemporary views on the various dimensions of truth and evidence taking in civil proceedings. A specific point of interest was the interplay between truth and evidence taking, on the one hand, and efficiency in civil proceedings, on the other. Efficiency is, in our opinion, a key issue to be discussed in a book on the pursuit of truth in civil litigation. Apart from the fact that a link between the pursuit of truth and efficiency has been emphasised since the time of ancient Rome,[18] all legal systems must find the right balance between the amount of time and money invested in the civil trial and the thoroughness of the proof-taking stage in litigation. Obviously, a system of proof that can produce trustworthy results is in need of considerable investment of

14 In the present volume, reforms in the following post-Socialist countries are discussed: Romania, Slovenia and the Russian Federation.

15 For instance, the Croatian Code of Civil Procedure was amended in 2003, limiting the powers of judges to order the taking of evidence *ex officio*.

16 The Netherlands is a good example of a jurisdiction displaying such a trend in Western Europe. On recent developments in this country, see the contribution of Verkerk in this volume.

17 See e.g. the situation at the Court of Justice of the European Union discussed by Sladič in this volume.

18 See the contributions of Milotić and Karlović in this volume.

time and resources, but the available amount of time and resources is not without limits. If a proper balance between truth and the necessary time and resources cannot be found, the whole process of litigation may be endangered.

Under the influence of the case law of the European Court of Human Rights, acceptable time-limits are a specific point of attention. From this case law it appears that many national legal systems have issues with securing legal protection within a reasonable time. The traditional, one-dimensional approach to civil procedure, according to which the use of any amount of time and money is justified if it results in accurate, legally correct judgments, is currently being superseded by a new, 'three-dimensional' concept under which keeping time and costs under strict control is equally important as producing a correct final decision.[19] In more and more jurisdictions, the truth in civil litigation is not an absolute goal anymore. As with most things in life, truth has its price, and this price should, according to many, be proportionate to the social importance of the case. Still, some procedural 'fundamentalists' argue the opposite, advocating a one-dimensional concept - i.e. truth at all costs - and unfortunately these fundamentalists are every now and then rather influential.

As stated above, in this volume we have made an effort to collect comparative information about the ways in which civil justice systems treat truth and fact finding. This information is presented in six parts.

In the first part, six authors address challenges in the area of truth and efficiency in Western Europe, more specifically in the Netherlands and in Italy. This part provides interesting contrasts, since obviously the two jurisdictions are each other's opposites: the Netherlands offering a no-nonsense approach to civil procedure and to truth and efficiency in which a clear balance between the two concepts seems to have been found,[20] and Italy providing a very learned approach with attention to every procedural detail without in practice being able to produce results acceptable to modern litigation standards (one of the contributors even speaks of the Antique Shop of Italian civil procedure).[21] In this part of the present volume not only litigation before a court of law, but also the role of truth in the area of alternative dispute resolution (mediation) is addressed.[22] Additionally, the following specific means of evidence are studied: oath and confession, expert testimony and court inspection.[23] Part 1 concludes with a contribution that studies the role of the truth in Italian summary proceedings.[24]

In Part 2, the common law perspective to the central issues of this volume is provided by studying developments in the United States and South Africa (in the procedural field, South Africa can rightly be classified as a common law jurisdiction even though in the area of substantive private law it is a so-called 'mixed jurisdiction'). The first contribution in Part 2 discusses the demise of the civil trial in

19 Zuckerman 2009, p. 49.

20 See the contribution of Verkerk.

21 See the contribution of Silvestri.

22 See the contribution of Jagtenberg & De Roo.

23 See the contributions of Silvestri, Ferraris and Bina.

24 See the contribution of Ferrari.

American civil litigation.[25] This is obviously of major importance for truth finding as it is a known fact that trial is (was) considered to be of primary importance for establishing the truth in common law systems. The author of this contribution also addresses the issue of (modest) convergence between American and European systems of civil procedure in the area of fact finding. Subsequently, American 'extremism' in the pursuit of the truth is discussed.[26] This 'extremism' may not always produce the right balance between truth and efficiency as discussed in the present volume, and the contribution may therefore serve as an example of an approach that from a European perspective raises some questions. Finally, the situation in South Africa is addressed.[27] The author of this contribution submits that South African civil procedure is still very much trial-centred and holds that this situation should change in the direction of what he calls 'a more nuanced continental European system'.

Part 3 of this volume discusses Socialist and post-Socialist perspectives on truth and efficiency. The contribution opening Part 3 forms a bridge between common law and civil law traditions, more specifically between the Socialist and post-Socialist variants of the latter, as it discusses developments in Mainland China and in Hong Kong.[28] Obviously, as a result of the existence of two systems of civil procedure within the People's Republic of China, interesting contrasts can be offered. Subsequently, Romania, Slovenia and the Russian Federation are the focus of attention.[29] These jurisdictions can be classified as post-Socialist members of the Civil Law family; the attentive reader may spot various interesting parallels between their (formerly Socialist) systems of civil procedure and that of mainland China. It should be noted that the contribution on truth and efficiency in the Russian Federation is preceded by a contribution discussing the jurisdiction of the various courts in Russia.[30] This contribution may be helpful for a better understanding of the subsequent contribution.

Part 4 of the present volume discusses taking and administering evidence before the Court of Justice of the European Union. Obviously, due to the nature of this court various issues in the field of truth and efficiency must be put in a different perspective than when these topics are studied within a purely national procedural context. The highly sophisticated means available at the CJEU to ensure truth and efficiency in judicial proceedings are discussed in depth in this part of the volume.

An historical Part 5 then follows in which Roman dispute resolution is the core issue. Truth and efficiency in Roman arbitration proceedings are discussed[31] next to the role of presumptions in the context of one of the major contracts of Roman law, the *stipulatio*.[32]

25 See the contribution of Langbein.
26 See the contribution of Marcus.
27 See the contribution of Paleker.
28 See the contribution of Chan.
29 See the contributions of Spinei, Rijavic and Abolonin & Abolonin.
30 See the contribution of Valeev, Fathkullina & Valeeva.
31 See the contribution of Milotić.
32 See the contribution of Karlović.

The final part of this volume (Part 6) discusses an experiment in the Netherlands aimed at rendering a judgment in civil proceedings immediately after the hearing before the cantonal section of the Dutch First Instance Court.[33] The authors show that the efficient approach in hearing civil cases discussed by them is very beneficial for quality. This may be considered a promising sign, since those who oppose reform often think that quality and efficiency are antagonists. Obviously, the contribution to the final part of the present volume is proof of the opposite which may, indeed, be reassuring for all those interested in the interplay between truth and evidence taking, on the one hand, and efficiency in civil proceedings, on the other.

Maastricht/Zagreb, November 2012

33 See the contribution of Bloemink, Van Dooren, Entjes, Van Gompel & Fernhout.

Bibliography

Damaška 1975
Damaška, M., 'Presentation of Evidence and Factfinding Precision', *University of Philadelphia Law Review*, 1975, Vol. 123, p. 1083-1106.

Frodl 2012
Frodl, S., 'The Heritage of the Franz Klein Reform of Austrian Civil Procedure', *Civil Justice Quarterly*, 2012, p. 43-68.

Klein 1891
Klein, F., *Pro Futuro*, Leipzig/Wien: Deuticke, 1891.

Kramer & Van Rhee 2012
Kramer, X.E. & Van Rhee, C.H. (eds.), *Civil Litigation in a Globalising World*, The Hague: T.M.C. Asser Press, 2012.

Langbein 1985
Langbein, J., 'The German Advantage in Civil Procedure', *University of Chicago Law Review*, 1985, Vol. 52, p. 823-866.

Posner & Dodd 1993
Posner, L.S. & Dodd, R.J., *Cross-Examination: Science and Technique*, Charlottesville: The Michie Company, 1993.

Uzelac 2010
Uzelac, A., 'Survival of the Third Legal Tradition?', *Supreme Court Law Review*, 2010, Vol. 49, p. 377-396.

Verkerk 2010
Verkerk, R.R., *Fact-finding in Civil Litigation*, Antwerp: Intersentia, 2010.

Vyshinsky 1948
Vyshinsky, A.J., *Theory of Court Evidence in Soviet Law* (*Teorija sudskih dokaza u sovjetskom pravu*), Beograd: Naučna knjiga, 1948.

Zuckerman 2009
Zuckerman, A., 'The Challenge of Civil Justice Reform: Effective Court Management of Litigation', *City University of Hong Kong Law Review*, 2009, Vol. 1, No. 1, p. 49-71.

TRENDS AND CHALLENGES IN WESTERN EUROPE: THE NETHERLANDS, ITALY

R.R. Verkerk

MORE FACTS, LESS EVIDENCE: THE GROWING IMPORTANCE OF FACT-GATHERING AND THE DEMISE OF THE TRADITIONAL PRESENTATION OF EVIDENCE IN COURTS IN THE NETHERLANDS

1. Introduction: The Ordinary Course of Litigation

According to the ALI/UNIDROIT Principles of Transnational Civil Procedure, a procedure normally consists of three phases (Principle 9). In the first phase, the parties exchange written pleadings in which they clarify their claims and defences and identify relevant facts in support of these claims and defences. In the interim phase, discovery mechanisms and hearings serve to gather information and evidence. The third and final phase consists of one concentrated hearing during which evidence is presented and the parties make their concluding arguments. This general structure in which three phases are identified more or less mirrors the practice in many jurisdictions.

This contribution argues that the significance of the final phase, during which the parties present their evidence, has decreased in the Netherlands. Section 2 provides an introduction to the ordinary course of litigation in the Dutch courts. Subsequently, the (little) empirical and anecdotal evidence will be discussed. In section 4, an explanation is provided for the demise of the traditional presentation of evidence. In the final section, the strengths and weaknesses of the new system are addressed.

2. The Ordinary Structure of Litigation in the Netherlands

The ordinary structure of litigation in the Netherlands somewhat resembles the phases identified in the Principles of Transnational Civil Procedure. In the pleading phase, the parties commonly exchange written pleadings in which they *inter alia* are required to provide an account of all relevant facts. It is common for parties to adduce documents along with their written pleadings. These documents serve to plead the case with sufficient particularity, but they also serve as evidence for the factual allegations in the pleadings. To the extent the parties have made use of their own experts, written expert reports are also commonly produced along with the written pleadings.

Other means of evidence, such as witness statements and court-appointed expert opinions, are normally only produced in the third and final phase of the litigation process. In essence, the presentation of evidence in the Dutch courts has a long history. Its fundamentals are clearly rooted in the Romano-canonical and French traditions. The presentation of evidence is normally preceded by an interim judgment that orders the production and examination of evidence (evidence order/*bewijsopdracht*). Subsequently, each of the parties may present witness evidence (*enquête* and *contra-enquête*). The presentation of evidence may take place during one uninterrupted hearing. Often, however, the final phase consists of a sequence of oral hearings scheduled several weeks or months apart.

In the Netherlands, the middle phase of litigation has changed over the last decades. An important milestone in the gradual process of change was the 2002 Reform Act.[1] A graphical representation of the ordinary structure of litigation in the Netherlands is depicted below. The graph certainly provides a simplification, in reality the system changed gradually from the early 1990s onwards. In addition, the structure of litigation is flexible and commonly adjusted to the specific needs of the case. Nevertheless, the graph provides an indication of the ordinary structure of litigation in the past and present.

Figure 1: Common Course of the Procedure

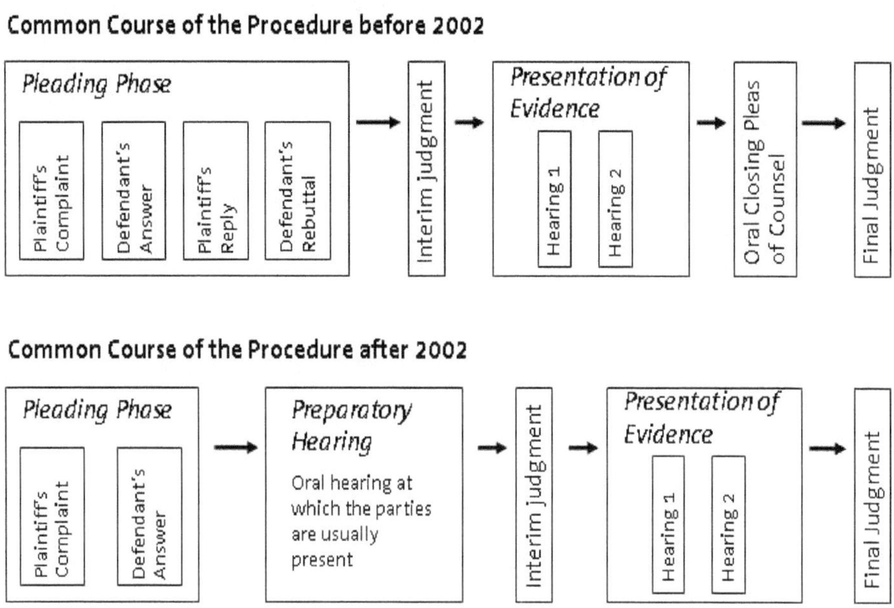

1 For an introduction to the Reform Act in English, see Jongbloed 2005, p. 69-95.

Most cases never reach the third and final phase of litigation during which evidence is presented. In roughly 40 per cent of all cases the defendant fails to defend himself or herself and the judge renders a default judgment. If the parties settle the case before the judge renders a judgment, there is no need to examine evidence. Mutual settlement has always been a reasonable alternative to resolve the dispute.

Many cases are resolved by means of a summary judgment. In essence this implies that, if the judge determines that there is no genuine dispute of fact, the judge may establish the facts without ordering either one of the parties to present evidence. Article 149(1) of the Dutch Code of Civil Procedure states that 'facts or rights that have been alleged by one party and have not been denied or ... adequately denied by the other party, shall be considered true by the court'. This rule is frequently used in cases where a party denies the allegations of his or her adversary without any further motivation. A mere denial of the other party's statement rarely suffices. If a party is not sufficiently forthcoming in his or her written pleading or during the oral hearing, the judge may very well decide on matters of fact to that party's detriment. In the Dutch legal system, one has to plead one's case with sufficient particularity. If one fails to do so, it is very possible that the judge will render an unfavourable final judgment. In essence, Article 149 of the Dutch Code enables the court to decide matters of fact without examining any evidence. The provision grants the judge a fair amount of discretion to determine whether or not a factual allegation is 'adequately denied' or put forward in sufficient detail.

3. Fewer Judicial Orders to Produce Evidence

Both now and in the past a large number of cases are resolved by means of a default judgment or a mutual settlement. It has always been the situation that most cases do not reach the third and final phase in the litigation process. Many experienced litigators have noticed that over the last decades there has been a decline in the proportion of cases in which witnesses are heard. Unfortunately, there is little empirical evidence that confirms this observation. The only empirical evidence I have found was gathered by Ahsmann at the District Court of Rotterdam. Ahsmann counted judgments rendered by the commercial section of the District Court (*sector civiel, handelszaken*) in 1997, 1998, 2007 and 2008. She counted both dispositive judgments (i.e. final judgments, including summary judgments that dispose of the case) and interim judgments in which the court had ordered the presentation of evidence (evidence orders).[2] The table below summarises her findings.

2 Ahsmann 2010, p. 23. Unfortunately, Ahsmann provides only very few details on the applied methodology. I assume that the number of dispositive judgments does not include default judgments.

Table 1: Number of Judgments, District Court of Rotterdam

Year	Dispositive judgments	Evidence orders
1997	627	350
1998	790	418
2007	705	175
2008	799	200

The table shows that in 2007 and 2008 judges rendered significantly fewer interim judgments ordering the presentation of evidence than they did in 1997 and 1998. In my opinion, these data justify the conclusion that a much smaller proportion of cases than before reaches the third and final phase of litigation.

It seems to be more common for judges to render summary judgments than roughly fifty to sixty years ago. In the early twentieth century, a simple denial would require the court to render an evidence order.[3] In addition, there are now much stricter rules that require the parties to identify the evidence they wish to adduce (*specificeren van het bewijsaanbod*).[4] Today, the court has much wider discretion to render summary judgments instead of evidence orders. From my own experience, I know it often happens, even in relatively complex cases, that a final decision is rendered by a district court or a court of appeal without hearing a single witness. Practitioners note that one of the most common complaints in proceedings before the Dutch Court of Cassation is that the courts of appeal have wrongly denied the parties their right to present witness evidence.[5] It seems that judges render more summary judgments and fewer evidence orders than before.

More empirical research is needed before one can conclude with a reasonable level of certainty that the number of cases that reach the third and final phase in the process of litigation is decreasing nationwide. Nevertheless, anecdotal evidence suggests that the Rotterdam findings represent a broader national trend.

4. Demise of the Traditional Presentation of Evidence: An Explanation

The decrease in the traditional taking of evidence never was a part of the government policies that were introduced during the past decades to reform the justice system. Nevertheless, it seems the many changes to the justice system have caused judges and parties to avoid the taking of evidence in court. I believe a number of recent innovations have contributed to the decline in the number of evidence orders and evidentiary hearings. In my view, the decline of evidentiary hearings is, at least in part, an unintended side effect of a number of government policies.

3 See Verkerk 2010, p. 70-72.

4 Thoe Schwarzenberg 2011, § 31-33.

5 For a recent example, see HR 28 January 2011, LJN BO 6106.

4.1. *The New Middle Phase in the Structure of Litigation: Frontloading*

As depicted in Figure 1, the Dutch system traditionally focused on the first and the last phases in the litigation process. The parties first exchanged two written pleadings, after which the court would render a judgment. Very often, the court would render an evidence order enabling the parties to present their evidence in court. In the Dutch system today, written pleadings still play a vital role. The possibilities to gather and exchange factual information after the pleading phase have, however, been significantly extended. Most significant in this respect are (*a*) the rise of oral preparatory hearings, (*b*) the rise of document discovery and (*c*) the wider possibilities to examine evidence prior to litigation.

The Growing Significance of Oral Preparatory Hearings

In the 1960s and 1970s, local courts experimented with the increased use of oral hearings after the defendant had filed his or her answer. In the early 1990s, such a hearing was scheduled in only 15 per cent of the defended cases nationwide.[6] Large differences between the district courts existed in the 1980s and 1990s.[7] In the District Court of Breda, for example, the personal appearance of the parties was ordered in 44 per cent of all cases concluded in 1989.[8] Since the early 1990s, the number of cases in which hearings were scheduled has increased.

The 2002 Reform Act further encouraged the use of oral hearings and specified that the personal appearance of the parties should ordinarily be scheduled right after the defendant filed his or her answer. Data from cases handled by 10 out of the 19 district courts, between 1 May and 31 August 2002, show that the personal appearance of the parties was scheduled in 60 per cent of all defended cases. Differences between the 10 district courts were fairly large, ranging from 29 to 100 per cent.[9] Data from the District Courts of Utrecht and 's-Hertogenbosch in 2006 and 2007 indicate that in these courts the personal appearance of the parties was scheduled in 90 to 95 per cent of all cases.[10]

Before 2002 parties would generally be allowed to exchange additional pleadings after the oral hearing. Since 2002, judges more often render a (dispositive) judgment after the personal appearance of the parties.[11] Data based on 150 personal appearances before the District Courts of Utrecht and 's-Hertogenbosch in 2006 and 2007 show that in 32 per cent of all cases a settlement was reached during the personal appearance of the parties. In 60 per cent of all cases, the judge rendered a(n) (interim) judgment after this appearance of the parties. Only in the remaining 8 per cent of cases were other steps taken pursuant to the hearing, such as a

6 Groeneveld & Klein 2002, para 1.1.

7 Also see Eshuis 2007, p. 125, on the differences between courts in 1994-1996 and 2003.

8 Duin, Warnaar & Leijten 1990, p. 405.

9 Groeneveld & Klein 2002, para 1.1.

10 Van der Linden 2008, para 1.5.

11 Surveys reveal that a personal appearance is now more often followed by a judgment; see Groeneveld & Klijn, para 2.1.

continuation of the hearing at a later point in time or the exchange of additional written pleadings.[12]

A 2004 survey of Dutch judges showed that most Dutch courts scheduled ninety minutes for the personal appearance of the parties.[13] This shows that judges take a fair amount of time to discuss the case with the parties.

Increased Number of Motions for Document Discovery

Legislative changes in 1989, 1991 and 2002 further amplified the judicial power to order the parties, *ex officio*, to produce case-related documents. At the same time, in 1988 and 2002 the provision that enabled the party-driven discovery of documents was substantially broadened (Article 843a, Code of Civil Procedure). Currently, legislation is being proposed to further enable the parties to obtain a judicial order compelling their adversaries to produce documents.[14] These changes certainly have increased the possibilities for parties and judges to request the production of documents. Sijmonsma counted only seventeen published cases on the provisions that enabled party-driven document discovery between 1925 and 1988.[15] This figure illustrates that document discovery was essentially non-existent before 1988. If one searches for recently published case law on Article 843a of the Code of Civil Procedure, one finds hundreds of published cases.

Examination of Witnesses and Expert Investigations Prior to Litigation

Traditionally in the Netherlands, one could only hear witnesses (or request the court to appoint experts) prior to the commencement of the action for the purpose of avoiding loss of information. Article 876 of the 1838 Code of Civil Procedure restricted the possibility to examine witnesses prior to litigation to exceptional cases, for example when the witness was very old or seriously ill.[16]

Gradually, the possibilities to hear witnesses prior to litigation have been widened. A 1951 Act[17] allowed parties to request an examination of witnesses prior to litigation if this was needed to make informed decisions about settlement or initiating a procedure. The 1988 Civil Evidence Act further widened the possibilities for the provisional examination of evidence prior to the commencement of the action or during (the early phases of) litigation. This Act widened the existing possibilities for hearing witnesses before the initiation of the action. The Act also introduced provisions that enable investigations by a court-appointed expert and a local visit to a scene of the dispute prior to the commencement of the proceedings. In recent case law, the Dutch Court of Cassation held that judges must in principle grant a request for the pre-action examination of evidence.[18] Especially when it

12 Van der Linden 2008, para 3.7.

13 'Handleiding Regie vanaf de Conclusie van Antwoord', 2008, para 16, available at: <www.rechtspraak.nl>, last consulted in February 2010.

14 Parliamentary Papers (Kamerstukken) No. 33079.

15 Sijmonsma counted cases published in the *Nederlandse Jurisprudentie*, Sijmonsma 2010, p. V.

16 See e.g., Court of Cassation, 16 January 1928, W. 11786, *NJ* 1928, 329.

17 Act of 18 July 1951, *OJ* (Stb.), 302.

18 See, for an overview of this case law, Thoe Schwartzenberg 2011, § 44.

concerns the appointment of an expert, the dominant strategy often is to ask the court to appoint the expert prior to litigation. Once the action is pending, the judge may freely refuse to appoint an expert. These changes have certainly widened the possibilities to gather information and to obtain evidence at a much earlier point in time.

4.2. *The Organisation of the Judiciary: Financing the Courts*

The 2002 Reform Act formed one part of a major overhaul of the system of civil justice between 1996 and 2003. Other changes included nationwide programmes to decrease significant backlogs, the expansion of the jurisdiction of the county courts, an increase in the staff and budget of the district courts and the introduction of a new mechanism to finance the courts. Beyond doubt these changes all affected the operation of the machinery of justice.

The new system of financing the courts essentially implied that courts were to be paid on the basis of the number of cases resolved rather than on the basis of the number of incoming cases. The system basically makes use of a table that sets standards for the amount of time that is appropriate for each 'product' that the Judiciary 'produces'. For example, one contested labour case equals 385 'standard minutes' of judge time and 275 'standard minutes' of time for the paralegal staff. A contested commercial case handled by the district court should on average consume 940 minutes of judge time and 760 minutes of time for the paralegal staff (*Lamicie-normen*).[19] In the end, this system implies that courts that do not meet these averages are likely to face deficits. The system was introduced between 2002 and 2005. Since 2005, this 'output'-based system of financing the courts has been fully in place.

It is widely acknowledged that the new system has its benefits; on the other hand, it is believed the system has serious drawbacks.[20] There is some survey evidence available on the effects of the new system of financing the courts. One survey, for example, revealed that judges perceived much more work pressure in 2008 than they did in 2003.[21]

An extensive report published in 2007 showed that the efficiency measured in 'standard minutes' increased between 2001 and 2005.[22] Surveys showed that a large proportion of the judges who were interviewed believed that efficiency played a greater role in the Judiciary than before. Nevertheless, a large majority of judges believed they had sufficient time to handle standard cases. Roughly half the judges, however, believed they had insufficient time to handle special/exceptional cases. On average, judges were of the opinion that the quality of their work had remained unchanged. Another interesting aspect of the study is that several interviews with judges were conducted, including with those who played a more managerial role in the court. Although the surveys had not shown that judges believed the quality of their work was worse since the introduction of the new system, judges often

19 These are 2002 figures. *OJ* (Stb.) 2002, 390.

20 For a recent example, see Van der Wilt 2011, p. 120-126.

21 Weimar 2008.

22 Boone 2007, Chapter 5.

indicated in interviews that the new system increased work pressure. Judges experienced a tension between efficiency, on the one hand, and quality, on the other. Some judges admitted that they would limit the time they spent on fact-finding in civil litigation, for example, by trying to avoid rendering evidence orders. A senior judge who led a division of a district court admitted the system was vulnerable to manipulation. In a clear-cut case in which the court lacked jurisdiction, a judge could render a summary judgment straight away, and the case would not generate much revenue for the court. If, however, the court first ordered a (brief) oral hearing, the court would receive a much larger revenue for doing only little additional work.[23]

4.3. *The Likely Causes of the Decline of the Traditional Presentation of Evidence*

It is not easy to untangle cause and effect in a system that witnessed so many changes in so little time. Many factors that have not been discussed so far, such as an increase in the number of incoming cases, undoubtedly influenced the machinery of justice. Empirical evidence is not as widely available as one would hope, so to some extent my argument below is a hypothesis rather than a properly tested theory.

One likely cause for the waning importance of evidentiary hearings is the introduction of a variety of effective mechanisms to gather evidence and information at a much earlier point in time. In essence, much of the fact-finding has been shifted from the third and final phase to the middle phase of litigation. If one examines a key witness prior to litigation, if one hears the parties at an oral hearing or if relevant documents are produced, one is much better informed about the facts of the case. Judges may have good reasons not to examine further evidence. Often, there is limited evidence available for each material contention of fact. If more information has been gathered in the early phases of litigation, it may well be the case that virtually all relevant information on a particular factual issue has already been examined. It may also become clear, for example during an oral hearing, that apparent contradictions in the written pleadings are not genuine disputes of fact. Judges may have good reasons to render more summary judgments if more information was gathered in the early phases of litigation. In short: a likely cause for fewer cases reaching the third and final phase of litigation is that much of the work that was traditionally done in the third phase is now shifted to the earlier phases of the litigation process.

In addition, there may be reasons to believe that judges have incentives to avoid the examination of evidence in the third and final phase of litigation. The greater emphasis on the middle phase of litigation had forced judges to shift their attention from writing judgments and examining evidence to other activities, such as attending oral hearings and ruling on motions that request the production of documents. In essence, the new middle phase created new judicial tasks. Ahsmann

23 Boone 2007, Chapter 5, p. 172.

argues that the hearing of witnesses is very time-consuming for judges.[24] Often evidentiary hearings are scheduled quite some time after the judge has rendered his or her interim judgment. Essentially this means that the judge is required to reread much of the case file prior to the (largely court-driven) examination of witnesses. The examination itself and the drafting of a summary of the witness statement take at least sixty to ninety minutes per witness. Often, the opposing party also wishes to present witness evidence, which generally requires the judge to schedule another evidentiary hearing for that purpose. Ahsmann claims that the time to examine witnesses exceeds the number of 'standard minutes' in the administrative financial system of the courts. From a revenue perspective, examining witnesses is not attractive. This implies that judges who are faced with much work pressure have strong incentives to render dispositive summary judgments rather than evidence orders: it reduces their future workload and positively affects the budget of the courts.

Settlement may also be an alternative to the presentation of evidence. It is clear that the Judiciary promotes settlement. In particular, during the personal appearance of the parties the judge will encourage settlement. A recent empirical study shows that 19.1 per cent of the litigants agreed or fully agreed with the statement that 'the behaviour of the judge forced us to settle'.[25] Another study showed that preparatory hearings do not lead to more settlements but do cause settlements to be reached at an earlier point in time.[26]

Parties may also be more willing to avoid the third and final phase of litigation. The middle phase of litigation, in particular the oral hearing, increases the information available to the parties and their lawyers. If more information is available, parties are able to make a more accurate estimation of the odds of winning the case. On average, they will be more willing to settle.[27] The middle phase of litigation has become more time-consuming and costly for the parties. Once the parties have been heard in court, they may no longer have the desire to present evidence. After all, the presentation of evidence is costly for the parties as well: if the parties have been served several starters, they may be more inclined to skip the main dish.

It is likely that the changes described above are fuelled by technological changes. In my view, we should bear in mind that fact-finding processes in our everyday lives have changed as much as they have in the courtroom. The third and final phase in the litigation process in the Netherlands is in essence still the same as it was many decades ago. Much of our legal tradition, however, predates computers, video cameras, photocopiers and cloud computing. In the Netherlands, as well as in common law jurisdictions, the third and final phase of the litigation process was designed to accommodate the oral examination of witnesses. Today,

24 Ahsmann 2010, p. 13-27, p. 25.

25 Van der Linden 2010, p. 82, '... er is door het gedrag van de rechter sprake van een dwangschikking'.

26 Eshuis 2007, p. 214-216.

27 If more information is available to both parties, this will promote settlement; see Priest & Klein 1984.

data can be stored and processed in large amounts and at low costs. Electronic documents are widely available. We may now produce three e-mail messages in cases where we would previously summon a witness. Modern means of evidence probably have gained a fair share of the market whilst the traditional oral examination of evidence has lost ground. Given these circumstances, it is no surprise that the focus shifts away from the traditional examination of evidence towards fact-gathering and (e-)discovery. To a large extent, technical innovations may have caused much of the changes described above. The function performed by the third and final phase of litigation, that is, the oral examination of witnesses, is less important today than it was seventy years ago.

5. The Demise of the Traditional Presentation of Evidence: An Appraisal

Fewer cases reach the third and final phase in the litigation process. Is this development a favourable one? Or is reform needed in order to preserve (elements of) the traditional presentation of evidence?

On the one hand, it should be noted that the multitude of changes brought about in the Dutch legal system have had a very positive impact. Empirical studies have shown that, for instance, the introduction of preparatory oral hearings has had a positive effect on the litigants' perception of the fairness of the legal process.[28]

Another upside of the new system is that the greater emphasis on efficiency also seems to have had a positive effect. Taxpayers may demand that the budget of the courts be allocated efficiently. To what extent the litigants' costs of being involved in procedures have been affected by the many changes in the Dutch legal system is - to my knowledge - unclear. There is convincing empirical evidence which reveals that the time to disposition has decreased since the early 1990s.[29]

On the other hand, although it is widely accepted that efficiency is of great importance, there may be a tension between efficiency and other values of the justice system. As noted before, Dutch judges indicated that in their experience there is a tension between efficiency and the pursuit of truth. Fact-finding in civil litigation is important to promote the rectitude of judicial decisions. In addition, if a judge renders a decision without examining all relevant facts and evidence, this may negatively affect the litigants' perception of fairness. It must be noted that the demise of the third and final phase of the litigation process does not imply that judges render decisions on a narrower factual basis. To a large extent there has been a tendency to 'frontload' the process of fact-finding. Facts are now gathered through different means and at a different point in time.

Designing a procedural system remains a balancing act. If one aims to design a system that treats litigants fairly, operates efficiently and generates correct outcomes, one has to make tough choices. Granting the parties an absolute right to

28 Van der Linden 2010. Eshuis 2009, Section 7.1, Table 20, p. 84, p. 88. Verkerk 2010, Chapter 6.2.

29 Eshuis 2007, p. 157-160.

present witness evidence may have a positive effect on the litigants' perception of fairness; on the other hand, this may be very inefficient. It seems reasonable that one designs a system that allows the judge some discretion to avoid or discourage the presentation of evidence in court if this would lead to disproportionate costs.

It is my impression that the diminishing significance of the third and final phase in the litigation process is a trend that can be perceived in many jurisdictions. In common law jurisdictions, the demise of trial has been a well-documented and much-discussed development. In virtually all common law jurisdictions, the percentage of cases that actually reach the third and final phase of litigation has declined. Often this trend is caused by developments similar to those described above. In common law jurisdictions, for example, there has also been a tendency, over the last seventy years or so, to expand the available pre-trial fact-finding mechanisms.[30] The rise of e-discovery in the United States and the introduction of pre-action protocols in England provide recent examples of such developments. This supports the observation mentioned earlier that these changes may well be fuelled by technological changes that have partly undermined the functions of the traditional presentation of evidence. It is not unlikely that modern fact-finding processes, whereby e-mails are produced in the early phases of litigation and witnesses are seldom heard, provide for a more accurate and possibly less costly fact-finding procedure.

30 Verkerk 2010, p. 130 *et seq.*

Bibliography

Ahsmann 2010
Ahsmann, M.J.A.M., 'Bewijs: verschuiving van "bewijzen" naar "stellen"', in: Ahsmann, M.J.A.M. *et al.* (eds.), *Bewijs*, Den Haag: Boom Juridische uitgevers, 2010, p. 13-27.

Boone 2007
Boone, M. *et al.*, *Financieren en verantwoorden*, Den Haag: Boom Juridische uitgevers, 2007.

Duin, Warnaar & Leijten 1990
Duin, S.C., Warnaar, C.M. & Leijten, J.P., 'Het rendement van de ambtshalve bevolen comparitie na antwoord', *Trema*, 1990, Vol. 13, p. 401-407.

Eshuis 2007
Eshuis, R.J.J., *Het Recht in Betere Tijden*, Onderzoek en Beleid, 254, Meppel: Boom, 2007.

Eshuis 2009
Eshuis, R.J.J., *De daad bij het woord. Het naleven van rechterlijke uitspraken en schikkingsafspraken*, Research Memoranda No. 1, The Hague: SDU, Raad voor de Rechtspraak, WODC, 2009.

Groeneveld & Klijn 2002
Groeneveld, J.P. & Klijn, A., *Nieuwe Burgerlijke Rechtsvordering*, Amsterdam: NIPO, 2002.

Jongbloed 2005
Jongbloed, A.W., 'The Netherlands, 1838-2005', in: Van Rhee, C.H. (ed.), *European Traditions in Civil Procedure*, Antwerp: Intersentia, 2005, p. 69-95.

Priest & Klein 1984
Priest, G.L. & Klein, B., 'The Selection of Disputes for Litigation', *Journal of Legal Studies*, 1984, Vol. 13, p. 1-55.

Sijmonsma 2010
Sijmonsma, J., *Het inzagerecht*, Deventer: Kluwer, 2010.

Thoe Schwartzenberg 2011
Thoe Schwartzenberg, H.W.B., *Civiel bewijsrecht voor de rechtspraktijk*, Apeldoorn: Maklu, 2011.

Van der Linden 2008
Van der Linden, J., *Zitten, luisteren en schikken*, Research Memoranda No. 5(4), The Hague: Raad voor de Rechtspraak, 2008.

Van der Linden 2010
Van der Linden, J., *De civiele zitting centraal: informeren, afstemmen en schikken*, Deventer: Kluwer, 2010.

Van der Wilt 2011
Van der Wilt, C.J., 'De mammon in de rechtszaal', *Trema,* 2011, Vol. 4, p. 120-126.

Verkerk 2010
Verkerk, R.R., *Fact-finding in Civil Litigation*, Antwerp: Intersentia, 2010.

Weimar 2008
Weimar, A.M., 'Rechters, Raadsheren en prestatiegerichte bekostiging', *Trema,* 2008, Vol. 9, p. 384-389.

A. de Roo
R. Jagtenberg

THE RELEVANCE OF TRUTH: THE CASE OF MEDIATION VERSUS LITIGATION

1. Introduction

It has been argued that in today's world there is too much information rather than a lack of information, and one no longer knows what to believe or who to trust. As a corollary, people have lost confidence in the capacity of judges and other traditional authorities to determine 'the truth'.[1] Disputants thus increasingly choose to exercise control over *what* information is used in settling disputes, and over *who* uses it and for what purposes. This desire is thought to explain why disputants increasingly trade in formal litigation for alternative methods of dispute resolution (ADR) such as mediation and arbitration. This observation has been made with regard to the USA, where trial-centred litigation is even said to be vanishing, a process largely attributed to the rise of ADR.[2] Whether this observation holds true for Europe as well is not entirely clear - although today, the European Court of Justice (ECJ) wholeheartedly endorses schemes for mandatorily re-routing litigants away from the courts and into ADR schemes.[3] At any rate, control over information or facts or 'the truth' is perceived as a defining issue in the relationship between litigation, on the one hand, and ADR methods such as mediation, on the other.

This contribution therefore starts by indicating briefly what can be understood by 'truth', 'fact' and 'information', and how these concepts relate to each other and to the key notion in mediation: 'interests' (Part 2). Next, the array of dispute resolution methods is summarily portrayed (Part 3) before proceeding to address (Part 4) the aforementioned central issue of what information is used and who uses it and for what purposes, whereby litigation in various traditions and domains is compared to mediation. The process of assembling facts differs as between litigation and mediation in view of the different *aims* of these two methods, as will be illustrated through a fictitious case. Next follows (Part 5) a comparison of the

1 Bingham 2006; also Hogan & Loeb 2011.
2 Galanter 2004.
3 Case C-317/08 *Rosalba Alassini v Telecom Italia SpA* (ECJ judgment of 18 March 2010).

mechanisms in litigation and mediation that aim to compel parties to disclose particular facts (and penalise them for not disclosing), or exactly the other way around: to compel them not to disclose facts (and penalise them for disclosing). Mechanisms for excluding particular facts or for replacing facts by (legal) fiction - even mandatorily - are discussed in Part 6. Finally, the issue is considered of how disputants and neutrals (mediators, judges) alike perceive facts, or the truth (Part 7), and what mechanisms exist in litigation and in mediation to correct perceptions that are likely erroneous. The contribution concludes (Part 8) by hinting at some unintended effects that financing mechanisms (and the drive for efficiency) may have on dealing with facts and information in litigation and in mediation. Two proposals are presented, one for improving litigation and one for improving mediation with regard to the assessment of facts.

2. Truth, Facts and Information

One could easily fill a library with theoretical and philosophical treatises on the concept of 'truth' alone. The present contribution, however, leans much more on the *practice* of dispute resolution. Just a simplified scheme is introduced to clarify roughly what is understood by 'truth', 'facts' and 'information' for the purpose of the analysis that follows here.

In the introduction, the concept of information was mentioned. This is a fairly broad and neutral concept that may encompass fiction, advertising, infotainment and of course factual information as well, varying from a timetable of train departures to an in-depth report by investigative journalists uncovering the 'truth' about, for example, sub-prime mortgages. In this meaning, information is a container concept. It exists where human beings experience something through their senses and brain activities, no matter whether it is a picture of the Marlboro Man or an exchange of views between Wittgenstein exegetes.

By contrast, the concept of 'truth' conveys that something, usually a statement, is in accordance with a (verifiable) fact, or - broader - with reality. In common parlance, reality will encompass more than just a single isolated fact, and often even more than a whole pattern of facts: emotions or values - which are normally distinguished from facts, strictly speaking - may all belong to 'reality'. *Classical theories* have it that there is such a thing as 'external' or 'objective' reality that exists independent of a human observer. This classical view has, however, been challenged in numerous ways.

Constructivism claims that 'truth' is created by historical and cultural processes and shaped particularly through power struggles within a community. *Consensus theory* posits that truth is whatever is agreed upon by a particular group of human beings, and in the extreme this could be just two persons acting together. *Pragmatism* emphasises that whatever is verified by putting one's concepts into actual practice can be regarded as truth.

There are thus many perspectives on what constitutes truth, and within the confines of this contribution the foregoing simplified and far from complete overview is all that can be offered.[4] Moreover, two further concepts need to be dealt with briefly: facts and interests.

Of all four concepts reviewed here, 'fact' arguably has the strongest legal connotation. In the sciences, facts are distinguished from assumptions or mere speculation, and in the social sciences particularly (positive) facts are contrasted with norms or values. A fact is mostly taken to be something provable, a reference to an event that can be, or has been, verified. In law, allegations of fact have to be stated to demonstrate a cause of action. This implies a selection: only those facts that support the legal action are relevant. Where, as a next step in the legal process, the law is correctly applied to the relevant true facts, rectitude of decision is procured. This ideal of rectitude, which dates back to Bentham, is no longer regarded as an absolute, paramount ideal today. In his seminal work *Civil Justice in Crisis*, Adrian Zuckerman concludes on the basis of a multi-country comparison that each system of in-court procedural law must find a balance between three dimensions. Procuring rectitude of decision is just one dimension; competing dimensions are constituted by the requirement that courts have to decide within a reasonable time and the requirement that the costs of the legal process must be reasonable.[5] If perfection could be attained at all in legal decision-making, the sacrifices that would then have to be made in terms of time and money spent would likely be intolerable.

In mediation, the ADR method focused on throughout this contribution, 'interests' rather than 'facts' are central. A dispute is understood in mediation as a process that starts once a party perceives its interests to be negatively affected by another party's behaviour. Interests are, of course, important in litigation, too, but only to the extent that the law protects the interests. Usually, a party alleging a legal norm has been violated must be able to demonstrate that the norm addressed a genuine and real interest of the claimant personally. Otherwise such a party may not pass the threshold of *recevabilité* or (procedural) admissibility. Conversely, facts also play their role in mediation. But as will be demonstrated below, facts that are relevant in mediation are by no means identical to the facts relevant in litigation.

4 For more extensive references, see, *inter alia*, Audi 1999.

5 Zuckerman 1999.

Figure 1: Information, Facts, Reality and Truth

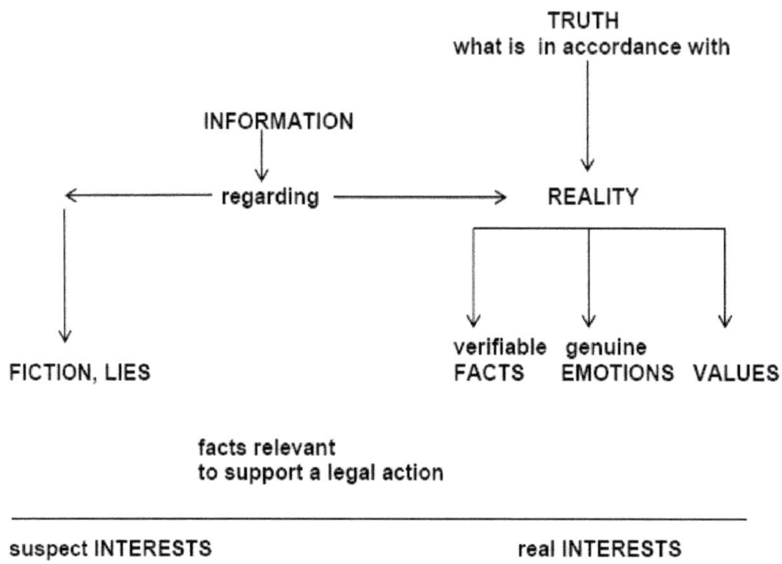

3. Dispute Resolution Strategies: From Flight to Fight

It is important to realise that for disputants going to court is just one of many options and often only the option of last resort. This appears, for instance, from the results of a survey conducted in the Netherlands between 1998 and 2003.[6] In this survey a large number of private citizens were asked what their course of action had been to handle legal disputes they had confronted. Less than 4 per cent indicated they had ended up in a court of law. An equally small percentage had submitted their dispute to some informal, quasi-judicial agency, of which there are many in the Netherlands. But the overwhelming majority had either negotiated a solution (45 per cent) or just lumped their case (47 per cent).

Social psychologists have proposed that human response to a conflict situation has developed out of what can be seen in nature, where animals have to choose between 'fight' or 'flight'. In human relations, flight has become distinguished into 'avoiding' the whole conflict or into 'yielding' to the wishes or demands of the other side. Since about half of all private citizens will opt for avoiding or yielding, even if the law might be on their side, these options and the 'why's' are apparently very important and ought to be covered therefore in any serious legal textbook.

The remaining options are known in social psychology as 'solving' and 'confronting'. Solving implies that parties discuss together the real causes of their problem and try to negotiate a common, acceptable solution. Confronting means

6 Van Velthoven & Ter Voert 2004.

that one tries to get one's way one-sidedly, overriding one's opponent: this strategy includes suing the other side in a court of law, or using yet other resources apart from the law, such as physical violence – a remnant of 'fight' in the animal world.

The focus of this contribution is on mediation and litigation. There is a linear relationship between negotiation, mediation, arbitration and litigation in that these methods imply an ever-decreasing amount of control on the part of disputants. At negotiation, there is full party autonomy. It is the primary tool for a 'solving' strategy. Negotiation usually implies we must give up something in order to get something else in return. Mediation refers to a process of negotiation but this time under the guidance of a neutral, the mediator.

Mediation as a generic process has been with us for ages and has been practised traditionally by a wide variety of people, usually as a side activity. Such traditional mediation is still practised today by judges in local and first instance courts. There is also modern mediation, emanating from the USA and rapidly proliferating throughout Europe, which – by contrast – is practised on a professional basis by neutrals who are usually registered with a provider agency, and who have mastered a body of professional mediator knowledge. This professional knowledge has been accumulated through research, initially conducted at Harvard University.

The gist of this research is that a mediator should try to instil more effective negotiation skills in disputants who have become stuck in their dispute. More effective negotiation will free the disputants from the positions they have taken – digging their heels in the ground – and take them back to what it was really all about: a perceived clash of interests.

Harvard negotiation theory predicts that opportunities for truly resolving a conflict will improve if disputants are willing to abandon their legal positions and disclose their real underlying interests. Then, a search may commence to see whether both their interests cannot be served at the same time, through a so-called 'win win' solution. Parties in a dispute will often have become very emotional and convinced that a court will fully sympathise with them. It has been demonstrated that in court cases *both* parties estimate their chance of winning at around 80 per cent. In order to restore the dynamics in a stalemate ensuing from such unrealistic expectations, it is helpful to make parties think over quietly what their best alternative to a negotiated agreement ('BATNA') really is.

Although the presence of a mediator requires more commitment of the parties in mediation than in direct negotiations, mediation is still understood as a voluntary process, at least with regard to reaching an agreement. The entire process of negotiating under the guidance of the mediator is to be kept confidential by all persons involved. This is important in the event the disputants have been frank and disclosed their real interests and made concessions at the mediation table, whereupon the mediation fails. It would be detrimental if then the case still ends in court and one party were to refer to the concessions that the other party was actually willing to make. That party would then be penalised for his frankness, the very frankness which is necessary for getting deadlocked negotiations back on track.

For completeness' sake: at arbitration and litigation, disputants have given up partial or full control over their dispute. Now there is a third party imposing his decision on the disputants. Still, at arbitration the parties largely control *who* will be deciding, and they may also exercise some control over the rules of evidence and the standards by which an arbitrator will decide.

4. Control over the Use of Facts: Litigation and Mediation Compared

The fundamental difference between mediation and litigation as methods is fully reflected in the role reserved for 'facts' and 'the truth'.

The parties involved in litigation and mediation alike will realise they have (seemingly) opposing interests. These interests will appear from a variety of facts.

If the parties opt for litigation, they will first turn to a lawyer. The lawyer will cut off a party who starts to vent feelings and elaborate on everything that irritates him about his opponent. After all, the lawyer has to filter out just those facts that are needed in support of the legal positions that will be taken.

Conversely, in addition to obviously relevant facts, the lawyer may consider the need for collecting evidence on facts that seem less relevant to the party, but which may help to fortify the legal position taken.

One could say that thus in this process of transforming the conflict into a legal case, the disputant is gradually alienated from his dispute. For the lawyer, by contrast, the facts needed to prove his client's case before a court of law will be predictable at an early stage.

In mediation the situation is different. Here, each party will be encouraged by a mediator to tell his own story in full detail. Emotions will be considered relevant too, although at a further stage the mediator will try to make the parties give their emotions a place where they will not hamper a solution.

It is not directly clear, even to the mediator, which facts - if any - will be relevant. First, both parties must tell their story, and the mediator will try to uncover together with the parties, possibly by having side-meetings with each of them, what their genuine interests and top priorities are. The mediator will then try to let the parties themselves discover that there may be scope for a solution that will serve the interests of both of them. The facts that have relevance for such a solution will be selected by the parties jointly and will become part of their new, joint-story-in-the-making. These facts may differ significantly from the facts that are relevant in litigation. There, facts dating back to a situation in the past that could support a legal position will be selected. In mediation, it is mostly the facts that are relevant to the (common) future interests of the parties that will be in the forefront.

4.1. *The BRICK and ROOF Case*

An example may illustrate this.[7] Two companies - BRICK and ROOF - are located next to each other at an industrial park. BRICK is a wholesale business in building materials, and ROOF is a specialist in roofing and has a showroom. Both companies

7 The example of BRICK and ROOF has been based on Pel 2001, and has been slightly modified by the present authors. On the role of facts in litigation generally, see *inter alia*: De Bock 2012.

also refer clients to each other regularly. Only a small strip of land, divided into two equal parts by a shared brick wall, separates the buildings. The directors have informally agreed to build a warehouse at the back of the existing buildings, thereby connecting the two buildings at the same time. A common entrance door is to be constructed at the front, and this door will be made accessible through a driveway. For this to be possible, the brick wall has to be removed.

On the agreed day, BRICK had arranged for the construction materials and for personnel to assist. It appeared, however, that the director of ROOF had cancelled the contractor he had called in. The reason was that he had found out two days before that the building permit was not in order. The director of ROOF prefers to act in accordance with the law. The director of BRICK, however, is annoyed that ROOF did not stick to the agreement. The dispute soon escalated, and BRICK and ROOF ceased to communicate. After some weeks, BRICK manages to obtain a building permit by itself and wants to build a warehouse for its own use. BRICK's lawyer had checked the land register and found that BRICK is the rightful owner not only of the land on its side of the brick wall, but also of a strip of one meter in width on ROOF's side of the wall. The wall, therefore, is not shared property after all.

ROOF seeks to stop this plan, and takes legal advice as well.

At this stage the facts that will be concentrated on will differ depending on which avenue the disputants are preparing for: litigation or mediation.

The Litigation Avenue

ROOF's lawyer selects the facts he thinks may have legal relevance. The legal action envisaged will be to ask the judge to declare that ROOF has become the owner of the disputed land strip by reason of prescription: BRICK did not bring a legal claim to terminate ROOF's possession in time. BRICK in turn is advised to respond that ROOF has not *de facto* secured possession of the land strip. So, in this procedure the central issue has now become: the prescription of BRICK's claim to terminate ROOF's possession of half of the land strip. Legally relevant facts thereto are, for instance, the cadastral registration, when and how ROOF has *de facto* secured possession, the facts establishing that ROOF was a possessor in good faith and so on.

The Mediation Avenue

If the director of ROOF turns to a lawyer skilled in mediation advocacy with the question of how to prevent BRICK from building the warehouse, this lawyer would ask the director *why* he has this wish and what exactly are his worries. ROOF's director then tells the whole story. It appears he essentially wants to prevent the building activities if he cannot take part himself. He also feels cheated by the director of BRICK. Following further probing questions from the lawyer, the director explains there is a bad atmosphere now, unlike in the old days, and he fears he might have to move eventually; financially, that would be a disaster. So the real interests of ROOF are not in the prescription of claims terminating possession, but in the commercial consideration of continuation of the company at the same location, (re-)develop a good relationship with BRICK and other neighbours, and a swift solution to the problem.

Unlike in litigation, where a lawyer will have a clear expectation of the questions a judge will likely ask, it is not yet clear at all which questions a mediator will ask. Possibly, a mediator will try to find out how shared decisions were taken in the past, before the conflict arose; what the reason is for the parties' inability to resolve the dispute themselves; what the trigger was for the escalation of the dispute. And he may ask hypothetical questions, such as: If you do not settle the case, what will your alternative be? The purpose of such questions will be to facilitate communication and to search for and establish common interests. Eventually a story may develop in which the perspectives of both parties will be incorporated, and here the parties will decide which facts are relevant to their story and to the resolution of their dispute.

4.2. *The Role of Facts in View of the Aims of Litigation and Mediation*

The overall aim against which to assess whether mediation has been successful is that the solution (if any) must have the approval of the parties involved. Private customer satisfaction is thus the sole criterion. There is no ambition to serve 'the objective truth' in any way. Here, the consensus theory of truth, discussed above, may apply. Naturally, if many parties partake in a mediation effort, as has happened in some Truth and Reconciliation projects, such as those in South Africa, the facts that are shared may approximate a kind of collective 'truth' indeed.[8] It is important to note that truth in mediation definitely comprises values and emotions that will have to be recognised by all involved, and is thus wider than a collection of facts, strictly speaking. There is a good reason for that. Neurobiologists have demonstrated that when the part of our brain where emotions are seated (the limbic system, notably the amygdale) is very active, we do not listen very well. As mediation will usually start out to improve communication first, it will be necessary to recognise emotion and to deal with it. Once emotions have been given a proper place, the upper part of the brain, the neo-cortex, where our ability is seated to understand and to balance interests, will take charge enabling parties to really listen to each other, which in turn is a prerequisite for a genuine solution.[9]

When litigating a court decision, the role of emotions tends to be limited to those situations where emotions amount to severe suffering that the law recognises as damage. This may be the situation where such severe suffering can be associated with an undisputed clinical picture or trauma in a victim, for which the opposing party can be held liable. Different types of emotions, such as grief or agony over the loss of a child, may not qualify as a category of damage that must be compensated under the law.[10] In litigation, ascertaining truth (common law lawyers might prefer 'the most probable version of truth') is always limited to facts needed in support of a legal action. Differences of degree exist between, for example, criminal procedure - where the aim is to ascertain objective reality within the confines of a particular

8 Hayner 2010.

9 See, e.g., Rolls 1999.

10 For example, the Dutch Supreme Court did not allow such a claim, except under very strict conditions: HR 22 February 2002, LJN AD 5356.

crime a suspect is charged with – and civil procedure, where consensual elements of truth have a place. 'Truth' here encompasses those facts (relevant to demonstrate a cause of action) that have not been contradicted by the other side. A leaning towards objective, external truth appears in civil procedure where facts were contradicted, and thus have to be established on the basis of applicable standards of proof.

4.3. *The Relevance of Legal Traditions*

The importance that is attached to ascertaining facts and truth in litigation may vary according to legal tradition (common law versus civil law) but also within each jurisdiction, depending on the particular subject area.

As far as legal traditions are concerned, an elucidating example drawn from practice concerns a dismissal case that was first litigated in the Netherlands and then shortly after again in England. In the Netherlands, the parties had to send in all documents they sought to rely on beforehand to the court. According to the Dutch court-planning rules, for a case like this (an employment dispute with a multinational enterprise) one hour was allotted to the hearing. At the outset the judge made it quite clear (as is customary) that he had read all pieces and the lawyers should thus restrict their pleadings to ten minutes each, leaving some time for the judge to ask questions. From the judge's questions it soon became clear what his judgment would likely be, but at the end of the hearing the parties were asked whether they would like to participate in a judicial conciliation attempt after lunch (an invitation emphatically declined by the American lawyers representing the multinational).

The case was then brought before an English court. There, two full days were first spent discussing how to proceed with the case, and particularly with the hearing of the witnesses: in all, some twenty-five witnesses were proposed, and sufficient time had to be allotted for their examination and cross-examination. A period of five consecutive days was finally reserved to this end in all agendas. The files pertaining to the case had to be rolled into the courtroom every morning on a trolley, in accordance with the tradition that dictates a judge should only form an opinion on the basis of direct observation.

Both courts rendered judgment: the Dutch judgment counted three pages – no witnesses were heard here, the Dutch lawyer, familiar with the one-hour time slot, had not even dared to ask for this. The English judgment counted seventy-one pages giving an accurate description of the (contradictory) witness statements and a weighing of the credibility of all evidence presented. Interestingly, what came out was that in respect of three or four factual circumstances, the Dutch judge had made assumptions which the English court had refuted after careful weighing of the evidence.

This double case provides a life illustration of how two neighbouring jurisdictions struck a different balance with regard to the key factors of 'rectitude of decision', 'time' and 'costs', as identified by Zuckerman.

Unlike in litigation, modern mediation does not reflect any substantial difference as to how facts are treated in the civil law and common law traditions. The modern mediator is, after all, not a judge but (ideally) a facilitator whose focus will be, not on legal positions, but on the real interests underlying such positions. Hence, the mediator is not bound by the historically differing technical rules of evidence either.[11]

4.4. *The Relevance of Domains*

In litigation, the treatment of facts differs greatly as between areas, also within a single jurisdiction. In the Netherlands for example, court-planning models allot on average one minute per case for criminal law bulk matters such as minor traffic offences. It pays to observe a session of the cantonal judge deciding such cases *à gogo* in a large amphitheatre in the court building. The parties are invited to come forward one by one to plead their case. If one listens carefully, one will notice that the judge, who nearly always runs out of time, increasingly makes assumptions or deploys formulae to get the case over with, such as in the case where a driver had changed lanes: 'You may think that the police did not investigate the skid marks of the car that bumped into your back, but they usually do, you know, so I must assume there was nothing indicating an unauthorized high speed of the car bumping into you. I thus endorse the fine. Next please'.

Much time, by contrast, will be spent on collecting and discussing evidence in high-profile criminal trials. Thus it has been calculated that the trial of the well-known gang leader Willem H. (accused of several brutal murders and extortion) cost the Dutch taxpayer millions of Euros, with the only result that Mr. H. was acquitted, since the prosecution did not succeed in having the charges meet the strict rules of evidence in criminal law that were now applied much more seriously than in the aforementioned bulk cases.[12]

In civil litigation, employment disputes constitute an interesting area. Another example drawn from practice illustrates the importance of the array of dispute resolution methods discussed above in Part 3. In a secretariat, the chief secretary engaged in bullying all three secretaries who were employed there. The bullying practices made the secretaries feel sick, but they did not dare to complain to the director, as he was known to be a close friend of the bully. One secretary collapsed under the pressure mounted on her and decided to resign. The secretary who then became a target of the bully collapsed when the bullying reached a new climax. This was exactly at a time a dear relative died. This secretary suffered a nervous breakdown that lasted several years, and the employer terminated her contract. For the purpose of challenging this termination in court, it would be extremely important to hear the other secretaries as witnesses. When asked, however, it appeared that none of them dared to testify, either because they feared repercussions from the employer, or because the stress involved in testifying was considered too high. The secretary whose employment was terminated did not want to subpoena her former colleagues, as this was thought likely to increase tensions

11 Evidentiary rules may, however, play a role in communicating the mediation process to the outside world; see Part 5 below.

12 More detailed information can be found on, e.g., the site <Elsevier.nl> (the Holleeder file) (last accessed in October 2012).

even more. Lacking the witness testimony, the court agreed with the employer who argued that the employee's breakdown was just a consequence of the death of her relative, for which the employer was not to blame. So here, the 'avoiding' or 'yielding' strategy of some had a defining effect on the confrontational strategy of a colleague - a phenomenon quite common in the domain of employment disputes. This is all the more worrying as within a relatively short period of time a total of eight secretaries had come and gone as a result of the chief secretary's workplace bullying practices (with major financial consequences for the organisation).[13]

The focus on interests in modern mediation implies that here no significant differences in the treatment of facts are to be expected between different subject areas. It is noticeable though that increasingly mediators will be appointed for reasons of personal expertise in the subject area at stake. Obviously, expertise may help the mediator to recognise which technical details may be important in a particular area such as, for example, construction and engineering.

In the employment dispute area, the power differences that gave rise to the avoiding and yielding strategies discussed above can leave their mark in mediation, too. A powerful employer may require the mediation to be conducted by a mediator who is familiar with - and loyal to - the company, ideally an internal mediator on the company's payroll. Such a mediator may be tempted to rely on facts and evidence provided mainly by the employer and/or not to reveal particular facts to the employee that might keep the employee from signing a disadvantageous settlement agreement. Here the interrelationship between the independence of the 'neutral' and 'truth' comes into play.[14]

5. (Non-)disclosure - Obligations, Penalties

In ascertaining facts and truth in mediation and in litigation a further question is, to what extent may a party decide to withhold facts vis-à-vis his opponent, and vis-à-vis the neutral (judge or mediator)? A special variety concerns the status of facts that were disclosed during a mediation that eventually failed; what of the disclosure of such facts before a judge in a subsequent court procedure?

Litigation

The concept of 'disclosure' itself is a common law concept. The general duty of disclosure, enforceable through discovery orders, is only suspended where privilege exists. On the European continent, the responsibility of the judge to ascertain 'the material truth', with a corresponding right for particular categories of witnesses to excuse themselves, comes close to the common law model in practice. Is a party to a civil dispute allowed to withhold material facts, or even to make a false statement? In most continental legal systems, it seems a party has some room to manoeuvre, unlike a witness who will be testifying under oath and who will thus

13 De Roo 2008.

14 Guidelines are occasionally drafted for internal mediators to cope with such dilemmas: Kousen 2006.

commit perjury if 'the whole truth' is not being shared with the court. Moreover, where documentary evidence appears to have been withheld, a judge may draw inferences adverse to the party concerned. In most common law jurisdictions a party may face more severe sanctions in the event it is found that a discovery order was not complied with.

But every time, the crucial issue is whether such behaviour is detected at all, and whether it can be proved that the withholding of facts took place intentionally. An American expert, discussing the special responsibility of the party's lawyer in such matters, points out that a lawyer's mere suspicion that evidence is false does not require him to take further action, nor is a lawyer required to act if the evidence is not material.[15] These provisos already imply considerable latitude. Furthermore, an incorrect factual statement might have been made 'inadvertently' instead of knowingly.

Once a case has become *res judicata* it may be extremely difficult to redress the harm caused.

Mediation

It may be helpful to recall that in modern mediation disputants will mostly select a mediator who is registered with a particular provider institution. They will entrust their case (and the mediator will accept the case) by all of them signing an agreement to mediate, through which the provider's rules of professional conduct will also be made to apply. In mediation then, again, how much information they are willing to share with the other side is up to the parties. Particularly in sensitive cases, the parties may request side-meetings (caucuses) with the mediator and tell him exactly which facts he is allowed to convey to the other side and which facts will have to remain strictly confidential for the time being.

When a mediation is drawing to a close, however, a mediator might feel that for a settlement to stand in the long run, it might be necessary for a party to disclose more facts to the other side, as these may be crucial to the other side's final consent. When one of the parties, or both, is a one-shotter, such as in family cases, the mediator might even be obliged through his rules of conduct to ensure that all parties have agreed on the basis of informed consent - consent referring here to all relevant facts *and* applicable mandatory legal provisions.

Moreover, by signing an agreement to mediate at the outset, the parties will have taken it upon themselves to use their best endeavours to negotiate a settlement, which rules out - in our view - any concealment of material facts. This may imply proper negotiation behaviour. But 'best endeavours' do not imply a rock-solid guarantee, and in commercial disputes, particularly, this remains a somewhat grey area.

From Mediation to Litigation

While agreements to mediate more or less oblige the parties in a mediation to disclose material facts *to each other* eventually, the same agreements normally

15 Mogill 2011.

prevent all participants in a mediation from disclosing anything that surfaced during the process of negotiation *to the outside world* - and to the court particularly, in the event the mediation fails and litigation is resorted to next. Within the European Union (EU), until recently it was entirely up to the courts in each jurisdiction to give priority either to such contractually secured secrecy or to its own duty to ascertain the material truth.

EU Directive 2008/52 on mediation in civil and commercial matters, which had to be implemented by 21 May 2011, has changed this situation in that it requires Member States to ensure that *mediators* shall not be compelled to give evidence in subsequent judicial proceedings, unless this would be necessary for overriding considerations of public policy, notably the protection of children or to prevent harm to the physical or psychological integrity of a person.[16]

The directive thus introduces a professional privilege for mediators where such a privilege hitherto did not exist in most jurisdictions within the EU; at the same time, the directive does not extend privilege to the disputants themselves - a curious blank spot.

Meanwhile, this duty of secrecy or confidentiality makes it all the more important for a mediator to verify during the mediation that all the facts that really matter for a settlement have been disclosed and understood. For it will not be easy for a party that signs too hastily to void the settlement later on, pleading a defect of consent such as error. After all, it is exactly this duty of secrecy that would prevent the party from reconstructing before a court of law the events that resulted in his alleged defective consent.

6. Excluded Facts, Prescribed Fictions

As stated earlier, in several jurisdictions judges in litigation following a failed mediation have developed a standing practice of honouring the secrecy contracted through the agreement to mediate. The legal basis for this practice is that in these jurisdictions the law of procedure tends to allow litigants to exclude particular types of evidence, such as evidence pertaining to a mediation. An interesting exercise would be to compare at the international level any differences in the precise ambit of such provisions.

Apart from the litigants themselves, judges and legislators may also decide to disregard certain facts, or may even substitute an investigation into the real facts for a mere fiction. Judicial fictions may be found in many jurisdictions and in several areas ranging from assuming fictitious contractual relationships with professionals to apportioning liability in multiple causation traffic accidents.[17] The most notorious examples of statutory fictions arguably can be found in (Dutch) revenue law, where we came across a provision that parking one's car free of charge at one's employer's premises will be monetised as taxable income according to a pre-set calculation

16 Art. 7 of the Directive.

17 E.g. the House of Lords in *White v Jones* [1995] AC 207; and the Arnhem Court of Appeal on 20 January 1998, as referred to by the Netherlands Supreme Court, HR 12 March 2010, LJN BK 9158.

standard.[18] Incidentally, such fictions never seem to work in reverse to the benefit of private citizens.

Rebuttable presumptions - though fundamentally different from fictions - can work out sometimes as near-fictions. A good example is the presumption that the management of a company will use its prerogative to direct the company affairs only to the best interest of that company (and not to serve any manager's private interests). For other stakeholders, be they employees or minority shareholders, this presumption in practice constitutes an almost insurmountable threshold, partly as judges seem fearful to be otherwise accused of occupying the manager's chair.[19]

In mediation, by contrast, fictions and presumptions are not used if only because it is not the (facts determinant of) legal positions which are at the centre, but the underlying interests, as narrated in full by the participants.

7. Perceptions of Truth and Corrective Mechanisms

Facts are not twisted or eliminated only through the intermediary of the law. Human beings tend to twist facts in their own mind, and memory. Fascinating case studies are available providing insight into how people come to believe in what at the end of the day was only made up by themselves, or by others. Two examples mentioned here are investigative journalist Gitta Sereny's in-depth interviews with former Nazi leader Albert Speer, who became completely entangled in the story he made up before the Nuremberg Tribunal; and the analysis of well-known examples of miscarriage of justice in our home country (the Netherlands), the Putten and the Lucia de B. murder cases, where suspects, due to police interrogation tactics, were made to believe (and confess) they had committed a murder in which they were in no way involved.[20] Cognitive psychologists searching to understand this phenomenon have elaborated theories and concepts, such as 'belief perseverance', on the basis of intriguing experiments.

We would like to raise two issues here: Are *disputants'* perceptions verified in litigation and in mediation, and are the *neutral's* perceptions verified in litigation and in mediation? In litigation, one disputant's perception of the facts, and the truth, is normally extensively tested against the perception of the opposing party through the cross-examination of witnesses or (as on the Continent usually) more summarily by comparing written statements of claim and defence, and by the judge asking questions, particularly questions based upon lacunae or inconsistencies noted. The facts are - again - just those which are relevant to support the legal positions taken.

In mediation, the subtle work of a mediator largely consists in helping parties to change their perception of reality or 'truth', often from a position of bias against the other side personally to one focused on the real problem that needs to be solved.

18 Niessen 2002.

19 Interview by Dr. Nobelen on 18 August 2009 with the President of the Enterprise Section of the Amsterdam Court of Appeal, which entertains requests for inquiries into corporate policy, in: 'Kritiek op Ondernemingskamer', *Management Scope Magazine,* 2009.

20 Sereny 1999; Derksen 2010.

A major part of the professional training of modern mediators is concerned with recognising personal perceptions of reality that stand in the way of a solution and assisting disputants in putting different, more creative labels on reality as experienced. Thus the verification of perceptions in mediation extends over a much larger area than in litigation.

But what of the neutral's own perceptions? As officials vested with authority, judges are hardly ever challenged to critically re-assess their own perceptions.[21] As one highly experienced Dutch judge observed recently:

> 'I catch myself frequently trying to bend and shape parties' account of (in their view) material facts into the decision making scheme that is already in the back of my mind. I must remain aware here, that in doing so I might give a decisive twist to the truth reasoning backwards from what is going to be my final decision'.[22]

A former university lecturer who attended a vocational training programme for prospective judges was appalled when during an experiment to test *listening skills* it became evident that the participating judges could not clearly recall what other people had told or asked them, since they had been concentrating too much on formulating their own statements.[23]

In the training of mediators, the ability to listen well is rated the most important of all skills. What a judge might learn from a mediator then is how to ask good searching questions that do not betray a particular point of view, but are really instrumental in getting useful information out into the open.

This does not mean that a mediator would never make a mistake in helping to re-state perceptions of facts, or in ascertaining that crucial facts are at the basis of a mediated settlement agreement. However, when a party suffers serious damage as a consequence of a mediator's negligence in this respect, it is possible in at least some jurisdictions, notably within the USA, to sue a mediator for professional negligence. Unlike the EU directive, the American Uniform Mediation Act (UMA) has explicitly limited privilege and secrecy where a disputant seeks to assert mediator negligence in a court of law. In a number of other jurisdictions, complaint procedures with disciplinary review boards may be available to this end. In this respect, a mediator may thus be held accountable. Judges, by contrast, can hardly ever be held accountable, as immunity will accrue to them in most Western jurisdictions.[24] This despite a first crack in the immunity wall following the ECJ's *Köbler* and *Traghetti* judgments.[25]

21 Or as Barendrecht puts it: '... courts do not have many outside incentives to do their job well'; Barendrecht 2010, p. 7.

22 Asser 2010.

23 Compare Zweigert & Kötz 1998, who summarise the common law approach of the umpire-judge as follows, at p. 273: 'The judge who opens his mouth closes his mind'.

24 Even if they supervise a settlement.

25 ECJ cases C-224/01 *Köbler v Austria* [judgment of 30 September 2003] and C-173/03 *Traghetti del Mediterraneo SpA v Italy* [judgment of 13 June 2006].

8. Truth and the Financing of Litigation and Mediation

Truth requires resources. As Zuckerman observed in *Civil Justice in Crisis*, the ideal of rectitude of decision has to be balanced against the ideals of reasonable costs and time. Costs are increasingly a major problem in these times when public expenditure has to be curbed. As has been argued elsewhere, the efforts of many Western governments today are aimed at influencing both the demand side and the supply side of judicial services: the demand side by increasingly prescribing mediation mandatorily; and the supply side by imposing increasingly stringent output requirements on the Judiciary.[26] Such requirements are conducive to strategic behaviour among judges, and this behaviour becomes particularly manifest when it comes to an independent judicial assessment of disputed facts (or rather, the *lack* of any such assessment). This is after all one of the most time-consuming aspects of judicial work, and time is money.[27]

The European Court in Strasbourg has reproached national judiciaries time and again for refraining from such an independent assessment where this was nevertheless required under Article 6 of the Convention.[28] Such judicial inertia may negatively affect weaker parties in the first place, and hence contribute to undermining judicial independence in the slightly longer run.

But output requirements may corrupt the professionalism and independence of mediators as well. Mediators may be prone to strategic behaviour of a different kind. Since most of them are self-employed and have to bill by the hour, they will try to secure clients who may provide them with multiple assignments. The effect of these tendencies may be remarkably similar in litigation as well as in mediation: an unconscious bias may creep in in favour of the large institutional repeat player to the detriment of an opposing individual one-shotter.

Put briefly: judges will attune their output to fit their fixed salary or budget; mediators will attune their output so as to maximise their income.

The concept of 'demand adjustment' was mentioned above as part of the drive for curbing public expenditure on the courts. Here we have the larger policy framework underlying court-ordered mediation before us. In order to alleviate the publicly funded court system, governments across Europe are referring litigants to privately funded mediation schemes, increasingly mandatorily. Quite a few scholars, though, have pointed out the risk for society if legal disputes are removed en masse from the public realm to the seclusion of a private conference room.

26 Jagtenberg & De Roo 2009.

27 This reflects a desire for one particular of efficiency, that is: productive efficiency, which refers to production units maximising output while minimising input.
Although productive efficiency may be commendable to strive for in environments that suffer from irresponsible, sloppy behaviour, it may give rise to irresponsible strategic behaviour exactly where stringent quality requirements need to be met and productivity pressure is already high.

28 *Inter alia*: ECtHR 17-12-1996 *Terra Woningen v the Netherlands*, Appl. No. 20641/92 at para 54.

Defining rights and duties in many areas publicly fuels public debate and thus fortifies the social texture that holds society together.[29]

Moreover, there is the 'shadow of the law effect' that may remind even the more powerful entities in the world that there are limits to what they can do. In that sense, there may be a dark side to the arrows signposting cases from litigation on to mediation.[30]

9. Concluding Observations

In the foregoing analysis quite a number of observations have been made, often with reference to day-to-day litigation practice, and the gist of these observations may strike some readers as perhaps too critical and pessimistic. A well-known strategy to tackle critics is to ask them how they then would solve the problems they signalled.

Just two very modest proposals are submitted here. The first regards the tendency of courts not to assess disputed facts independently, due to limited resources.

It might be worthwhile to experiment in litigation with a two-stage procedure, that is: a preliminary fact-finding procedure (another member of the ADR family) resulting in a provisional statement of the facts on which the parties may then comment. Subsequently, the court will just apply the law to the facts, as these will have been established clearly during the first stage. The additional time this two-step procedure may take may be offset by a higher compliance rate with the final court judgment.

The second proposal relates to mediation: the barrier that the duty of confidentiality/secrecy constitutes for the parties to whom facts have been misrepresented and who then seek in vain to annul the settlement should be lifted, for one-shotters particularly. The EU could take the UMA arrangement as a starting point. A specialised judge might be appointed to hear and assess such complaints in order to retain the useful firewall between mediation and adjudication.

29 Fiss 1984.

30 Jagtenberg & De Roo 2011.

Bibliography

Asser 2010
Asser, W.D.H., 'Burgerlijk (proces-) recht: bewijs in het spanningsveld tussen rechter en partijen', in: Asser, W.D.H., Nijboer, J.F. & Schuurmans, Y. (eds.), *Bewijsrecht: het bewijs geregeld?* Preadviezen voor de Nederlandse Vereniging voor Rechtsvergelijking, Nijmegen: Wolf Legal Publishers, 2010, p. 1-37.

Audi 1999
Audi, R. (ed.), *The Cambridge Dictionary of Philosophy*, 2nd edn., Cambridge: Cambridge University Press, 1999.

Barendrecht 2011
Barendrecht, M., 'Courts, Competition and Innovation, Inaugural Lecture as Hague Visiting Chair on the Rule of Law', 27 September 2011, on-line publication by HiiL, the Hague Institute for the Internationalisation of Law, 2011.

Blomgren Bingham 2006
Blomgren Bingham, L., 'When we hold no Truths to be self-evident: Truth, Belief, Trust and the Decline of Trials', *Journal of Dispute Resolution*, 2006, p. 131-154.

De Bock 2012
De Bock, R.H., *Tussen waarheid en onzekerheid: over het vaststellen van feiten in de civiele procedure*, Deventer: Kluwer, 2012.

Derksen 2010
Derksen, A.A., 'Valkuilen van de alledaagse Waarheidsvinding in de strafrechtcontext', *Rechtsgeleerd Magazijn Themis*, 2010, Vol. 5/6, p. 217-224.

Fiss 1984
Fiss, O., 'Against Settlement', *Yale Law Journal*, 1984, p. 1073-1090.

Galanter 2004
Galanter, M., 'The Vanishing Trial', *Journal of Empirical Legal Studies*, 2004, p. 459-501.

Hayner 2010
Hayner, P., *Unspeakable Truths: Transnational Justice and the Challenge of Truth Commissions*, 2nd edn., London: Routledge, 2010.

Hogan & Loeb 2011
Hogan, C.A. & Loeb, H.A., 'The Negotiability of Truth in the digital age', *The Practical Lawyer*, 2011, p. 37-41.

Jagtenberg & De Roo 2009
Jagtenberg, R. & De Roo, A., 'From Traditional Judicial Style to Verdict Industries Inc.', in: Huls, N., Adams, M. & Bomoff, J. (eds.), *The Legitimacy of Highest Courts' Rulings*, The Hague/Cambridge: T.M.C. Asser and Cambridge University Press, 2009, p. 301-322.

Jagtenberg & De Roo 2011
Jagtenberg, R. & De Roo, A., 'Frame for a Dutch Portrait on Mediation', in: *Judiciary Quarterly, special issue on Customized Conflict Resolution*, The Hague: Netherlands Council for the Judiciary, 2011, p. 7-23.

Kousen 2006
Kousen, F., *De interne mediator – Interne mediation en beroepsethiek*, Rotterdam: Nederlands Mediation Instituut, 2006.

Mogill 2011
Mogill, K., 'What to do when the Client or Witness lies?', *The Practical Lawyer*, 2011, p. 53-59.

Niessen 2002
Niessen, R.E., 'Belastingheffing op basis van ficties', *Weekblad Fiscaal Recht*, 2002, Vol. 6465, p. 28-30.

Pel 2001
Pel, M., 'Feiten zijn Feiten?', in: Brand, I. *et al.* (eds.), *Recht(er) en Belang*, BW-krant, Jaarboek 17, Deventer: Kluwer, 2001, 91-104.

Rolls 1999
Rolls, E.T., *The Brain and Emotion*, Oxford: Oxford University Press, 1999.

De Roo 2008
De Roo, A., 'Arbeid en Conflictmanagement', *TMD Nederlands Vlaams Tijdschrift voor Mediation en Conflictmanagement*, 2008, Vol. 3, p. 48-66.

Sereny 1996
Sereny, G., *Albert Speer: His Battle with Truth*, New York: A. Knopf, 1996.

Van Velthoven & Ter Voert 2004
Van Velthoven, B.C.J. & Ter Voert, M., *Geschilbeslechtingsdelta 2003*, Den Haag: WODC, 2004.

Zuckerman 1999
Zuckerman, A., *Civil Justice in Crisis: Comparative Dimensions of Civil Procedure*, Oxford: Oxford University Press, 1999.

E. Silvestri

THE ANTIQUE SHOP OF ITALIAN CIVIL PROCEDURE: OATH AND CONFESSION AS EVIDENCE

1. Introduction

I love antique shops. For me, crossing the threshold of an antique shop is like entering a magical world. In an antique shop you can find what is left of a time long gone, and imagine, for instance, which kinds of embarrassing letters were hidden in a beautifully carved *trumeau* or what pressing clothes with a cast-iron ironer was like. Antiques are fascinating; those who collect them appreciate their value, whether it is the value of a real masterpiece or a mere symbolic one. Nobody cares if the *trumeau* is not safe as a hiding place or if the ironer is likely to make a mess of the clothes in need of pressing. Nobody expects antiques to be practical, useful implements good at making our everyday lives simpler. They must satisfy our sense of beauty, of good taste in home decor, of curiosity for a life-style belonging to the past: that is what antiques are for, and that is all we ask of them.

In Italy you can find many antique shops stuffed with furniture, paintings, lamps, china, and so on. But in Italy we also have a special kind of virtual antique shop, that is, our codes that display a collection of old and obsolete legal rules. The Civil Code and the Code of Civil Procedure are antique shops of such a kind, at least with reference to some of the rules governing the law of evidence applicable to civil and commercial litigation. The two oldest and most outdated items one can come across while browsing the antique shop of Italian civil procedure are the party oath and the confession: two relics of a time when adjudications were solemn and mysterious rites performed by the high priests of the law.

Nowadays, no reasonable person (whether a lawyer or a layman) would contend that an oath or a confession could advance the cause of an efficient fact-finding in litigation; by the same token, law reports show that both the oath and the confession have drifted away as evidence offered by the parties and taken into account by the courts to ascertain the factual issues in dispute. Still, some scholars as well as the Legislator seem to consider the party oath and the confession the true *pièces de résistence* of Italian evidentiary law, and no imminent reforms aimed at abolishing them or changing at least their probative value are in sight. We Italians do like our antiques.

2. Italian Law of Evidence in a Nutshell

Let me begin with a brief overview of the Italian law of evidence. The rules and regulations applicable to civil and commercial proceedings are consistent with what has been for a long time the law in force in many continental European countries. The difference is that while from the last decades of the nineteenth century onwards many legal systems belonging to the civil law tradition have modernized their law of evidence, Italy has kept its unconditional allegiance to the approach adopted by the Napoleonic codes, that is, the Civil Code of 1804 and the Code of Civil Procedure of 1806. These codes have been highly influential for the Italian codification movement,[1] to the point that even the codes still in force (the Civil Code and the Code of Civil Procedure, both enacted in the early 1940s) show a clear continuity with the French codes of the early nineteenth century.[2]

In Italy, just as in France, the law of evidence is split into two groups of rules, according to the much debated theory on the true 'nature' of evidentiary rules, that is, the theory according to which these rules can be classified as either 'substantive' or strictly 'procedural'.[3] The rules governing what is called the 'substance' of evidence can be found in the Civil Code. These rules identify the evidence that is admissible, state which kind of evidence can be offered as to demonstrate certain facts, allocate the burden of proof, and, most of all, determine the probative value of each piece of admissible evidence. The rules dealing with this last subject are very significant, since they bring about a distinction of paramount importance, that is, the distinction between the so-called 'legal proof' (meaning the evidence whose value is determined *a priori* by law) and the evidence that can be weighed by the court according to the principle known as 'free evaluation of the evidence by the court', meaning that the court enjoys wide latitude as to making its own evaluation

1 On the French codes as milestones of the continental European codification model, see Van Rhee 2007, p. 41.

2 As far as the discipline of evidence is concerned, the *trait d'union* connecting the Code of Civil Procedure of 1940 to the French codification is the first Code of Civil Procedure of the unified Kingdom of Italy, enacted in 1865. The former Code and the latter one are virtually identical. In the Report accompanying the text of the Code of 1940, reference is made to the 'profound reasons' justifying the choice of following the arrangement of the previous Code as regards the law of evidence: see *Relazione alla Maestà del Re Imperatore del Ministro Guardasigilli (Grandi) presentata nell'udienza del 28 ottobre 1940-XVIII per l'approvazione del testo del Codice di procedura civile,* available at: <http://unifi.academia.edu/remocaponi/Books/137149/Relazione_al_re_per_lapprovazione_del_testo_del_codice_di_procedura_civile>, last consulted in October 2011, at § 6. Such 'profound reasons', though, are not expanded upon, leaving the impression that modernizing the law of evidence was not a priority of the Legislators. On the continuity between the Codes, see the critical remarks by Taruffo 1980, p. 270-272.

3 The distinction between 'substance' and 'procedure' is applied in different legal systems to diverse areas of law, and this very fact, by itself, makes it impossible to offer a list of useful references on the topic, whether in Italian or in other languages. In any event, an effective summary of the Italian scholarly approach to the distinction, in its prong affecting the law of evidence, can be found in Denti 1983, p. 263-294.

of the evidence presented by the parties.[4] Even though this principle is supposed to be the rule according to which the trier of fact evaluates the evidence with a view to deciding which party will prevail in the case, the importance of 'legal proofs' is still great, for reasons that I will explain soon.

The rules governing the procedural aspects of evidence can be found in the Code of Civil Procedure; essentially, these rules provide for the various steps to be followed by the parties as well as by the court in the process that can be defined in general terms as the presentation of evidence (meaning the evidence that is both admissible according to the law and relevant for the case at stake, according to the court's evaluation).

Another distinction interlaces the one I mentioned above when I talked about 'substance' and 'procedure' in the law of evidence. It is the distinction between written and oral evidence. The Italian legal system sticks to the civil law tradition, and relies heavily upon written evidence. It is interesting to point out that nowadays the reliance on documents as the evidence on which the fate of a case can depend is not really a consequence of a deeply-rooted distrust toward the testimony given orally by a witness (or, even worse, by a party to a case). Actually, the reliance on documents has much to do with the way adjudication is organized in Italy. The presentation of evidence does not take place in a concentrated trial, but rather develops through a sequence of piecemeal hearings, often set months apart and spread over a period so long that it can be numbered in years. Frequently, the judge presiding over the hearings in which the evidence is presented is not the same judge entrusted with the task of rendering the final judgment, or he is just one member of the panel bearing the responsibility of weighing the evidence presented and deciding the case. I think that explains why documents are still the evidence that is likely to tip the scales of justice in favour of the party who is able to offer them to demonstrate his own theory of the case. Besides, even when witnesses are heard, what is taken into account by the court is a written record (by the way, not even a *verbatim* one) of their testimony, since the time-factor makes it impossible to rely on something other than a written (and often old) record. The Legislator himself was forced to acknowledge that when the court is expected to weigh the probative value of statements made by witnesses who probably were deposed when their recollection of the events had already begun to fade away, it is better and more practical to dispense with the oral examination of witnesses: since 2009, Italian courts can authorize witnesses to render a 'written testimony',[5] that is, something half-way between affidavits and other kinds of written statements witnesses sometimes are allowed to render in other European legal systems, namely those in France, Spain and Germany.

The prevailing probative weight of written evidence over oral evidence also depends on other reasons: first of all, certain transactions can be proved only by written evidence; in addition, specific types of documents amount to what I called

4 On the concept of 'legal proof' as opposed to the free evaluation of evidence, see Taruffo 2010, § 89-91.

5 See Fabiani 2011; Crevani 2010, p. 325.

previously 'legal proofs', whose demonstrative value is predetermined by law and cannot be nullified by any other evidence. But - and this may come as a surprise - the catalogue of 'legal proofs' also lists two very peculiar kinds of oral evidence that only the parties to a dispute can give: the party oath and the confession. If certain requirements are met, the truth of the statement on which the oath was taken or that was uttered as a confession cannot be contradicted by any other evidence.

One might say there is something wrong with a system that, on the one hand, prevents the parties from being heard as witnesses on the assumption that they are biased by definition, and, on the other hand, grants the statements they make by way of oath or confession the highest possible probative value. Actually, the historical development of the law of evidence in Continental Europe offers a sound justification for such an awkward arrangement, which was not an exclusive feature of Italian civil procedure.[6] On the contrary, the same feature could be found, for instance, in Germany, Austria, the Netherlands and Spain: what marks the difference between Italy and the other countries listed is that while these countries have either repealed both the party oath and the confession, or at least have reduced their probative value so that they have lost their nature as sources of irrebuttable evidence, in Italy the pompous and redundant rules on party oath and confession are still in force. Since - as they say - trouble shared is trouble halved, I must admit that things are not so different in France, where scholars seem quite at ease with a system in which the catalogue of admissible evidence is still organized in a sort of hierarchical order, with 'legal proofs' towering above the evidence that can be weighed by the judge according to his *intime conviction*: after all - it is argued - the advantage of 'legal proofs' is *d'assurer une plus grande sécurité juridique*.[7]

3. The Confession and the Party Oath

A quick overview of the Italian rules governing the party oath and the confession seems in order. I will follow the arrangement of the Civil Code, and therefore I will start from the confession. I use the term 'confession' even though in English the Italian word '*confessione*' is often referred to as 'admission'. For instance, the Book I still consider the best comprehensive treatise written in English on Italian civil procedure (I mean, *Civil Procedure in Italy*, authored by Mauro Cappelletti and Joseph Perillo, and published in the early 1960s) talks about 'admission' and never uses the word 'confession'.[8] The term 'admission', in my opinion, is too broad to define the true meaning of what I call 'confession'. Parties can make various types of admissions in civil proceedings, even without making the kind of statement that could amount to a confession: for instance, failure to deny an allegation made by the opposing party is deemed to be an admission as to the facts asserted, facts that become - as we say in Italy - undisputed.[9]

6 On this subject, see, for instance, Lévy 1965, p. 9; Lepointe 1963, p. 141; Storme 1963, p. 211.
7 Cadiet, Normand & Amrani Mekki 2010, p. 853.
8 Cappelletti & Perillo 1965, p. 199.
9 See Art. 115(1) of the Code of Civil Procedure, as modified in 2009. On the rule according to which each party to a lawsuit bears the burden of denying specifically the allegations made →

According to the Civil Code, the confession is a statement made by a party as to the truth of facts that are adverse to the party himself, and favourable to his opponent.[10] A confession can be made in court or out of court; if made in court, it can be either an oral statement made by the party spontaneously or a statement made by the party in response to the so-called formal interrogatory. Detailed rules provide for the confession made in a document, whether it is a pleading or a different kind of document, such as a will; another set of rules takes care of the confession received by third parties; other rules clarify what happens if, in case of necessary joinder of parties, the confession is rendered by one party only; yet more rules control the situation arising from a complex confession, that is, when the adverse statement made by the party is followed by another statement whose purpose is precisely to nullify the unfavourable effects of the former (statement). I think this sample of the law governing the confession can give one at least a vague idea of what I consider a small masterpiece in the art of drafting legal rules in such an extravagant way as to make them hardly understandable.

If the confession meets certain requirements, it is conclusive evidence as to the facts stated by the party: in other words, the court is bound to regard the same facts as indisputably true. It is often said that a confession amounts to a 'full proof': no contrary evidence can contradict it, and in principle no room is left to the court for an independent appreciation of the facts at issue. The rationale supporting the highest probative weight ascribed to the confession is nothing but a rule of thumb: someone is inclined to state facts that are unfavourable to his own interests only if those facts are true.

If the party confession deserves the attribute of 'full proof', one can say that the party oath is 'the fullest proof of all': if a judgment is rendered on the basis of a statement made by the party under oath, the judgment stands even though the party is later convicted for perjury. The Italian Civil Code regulates the party oath as solemn and very formal evidence:[11] solemnity and a high degree of formalism make the statement of the party as to the truth of facts favourable to the party himself so reliable that such a statement counts as conclusive and irrebuttable evidence.

There are two main types of party oath. The first is the decisory oath, which is tendered by one party to the other. The oath may concern any relevant facts that are deemed to be decisive, that is, facts upon which the case can be disposed of. There are elements of challenge as well as compulsion in the mechanics of the decisory oath: the party to whom the oath is tendered is not forced to take the oath, but if he refuses to appear in court and take the oath, the party is bound to lose the case. For the party, the only way to escape such a predicament would be to tender the oath back to his adversary, but that is possible only under restrictive circumstances.

by the adverse party in order to avoid that the alleged facts are considered undisputed by the court, see Rota 2010, p. 181.

10 The rules governing confession are Arts. 2730-2735 of the Civil Code and Arts. 228-232 of the Code of Civil Procedure. See Segatti 2012, p. 523; Comoglio 2010, p. 677; Silvestri 1988, p. 422.

11 On the party oath, see Arts. 2736-2739 of the Civil Code and Arts. 233-243 of the Code of Civil Procedure. See Gamba 2012, p. 435; Comoglio 2010, p. 715; Balena 1993, p. 105.

The second type of oath provided for by the Italian Civil Code is called suppletory (or, according to a different translation, supplementary) oath. The court may tender this oath *ex officio* to either party when the evidence presented up to that point in the development of the adjudication bears some weight, but is not conclusive. One can say that if a party has offered enough evidence as to make his allegation at least probable, then the court can tender this very party the oath in order to afford him an opportunity to supplement the missing portion of the proof. Finally, a sub-species of the suppletory oath is the oath of estimation, whose purpose is to allow the court to determine the amount of the sum one party is supposed to recover. It implies, first, that the court has already established that the party to whom the oath is tendered is entitled to receive monetary compensation and, second, that there is no other way to determine the amount of such compensation.

What I just described is a sketchy outline of a set of complex and quite obscure rules that include the rules dealing, for instance, with various oath impediments relating to the party's capacity to take the oath, with the kinds of facts that cannot be stated under oath, with the probative value of the oath taken by one party only in case of necessary joinder of parties, and so on. In short, the regulation of the party oath is a legal conundrum even more disheartening than the one that is likely to challenge the sanity of those who try to untangle the strands of the confession.

Does it still make any sense in 2012 to retain the party oath as a source of irrebuttable evidence? Confronted with this question, some authors say that the party oath still performs a useful function as an extreme measure whenever no other evidence is available and the court could reach a judgment only by a blind reliance on the principle governing the burden of proof.[12] Other authors emphasize the alleged strategic role the oath (I mean the decisory oath) can play, when party A wants to corner party B and has good reasons to believe that party B will fail to take the oath and is in no position to tender the oath back to party A.[13] Yet another argument that could be advanced in support of the oath and its reliability is the fact that no party can volunteer to take the oath, since only his opponent or the court can tender it.

Any attempts at justifying the survival of the party oath as evidence conducive to the truth take for granted that in modern societies the solemn commitment undertaken with the oath has the same meaning it had when one took the oath calling God as his witness, fearing in good faith that perjury would be punished by the 'vengeance of Heaven'. Maybe I am too cynical, but I am inclined to believe that in the world we live in to accept the idea that the outcome of a case could depend upon a solemn commitment is quite naïve, and my opinion does not change even if I take into account that perjury can bring about criminal sanctions instead of divine punishment.

12 Comoglio 2010, p. 718; Consolo 2010, p. 171.

13 Luiso 2011, p. 154.

4. Final Remarks

As I mentioned earlier, the confession and the party oath have disappeared from many continental European legal systems. I will not expand on the subject since what happened in the Netherlands, Germany and Austria has been analyzed thoroughly by Remme Verkerk in his outstanding book *Fact-finding in Civil Litigation*, and I am sure I would not be able to add anything original to the results of his study.[14] I only want to mention that recently Spain, too, changed its attitude toward the statements of fact made by the parties. For a long time, the Spanish arrangement of the law of evidence was the same as in France and in Italy, with rules spread across the Civil Code and the Code of Civil Procedure. The new Code of Civil Procedure (LEC, *Ley de Enjuiciamiento Civil*, enacted in 2000) has brought about a true revolution in many features of civil proceedings. As far as evidence is concerned, it is worth mentioning that confession and party oath have been abolished, and that according to the new law in force the parties to a case can be examined in court the same way as third parties may be heard as witnesses. No statements made by the parties are granted the status of 'legal proofs'; each and every statement is weighed by the court to determine what probative value it deserves.[15]

By contrast, Italy, the land of the never-ending reform of civil procedure, is still quietly cherishing the party oath and the confession. The last attempts at getting rid of them date back to the 1970s,[16] and no reforms of the evidentiary law as regards the probative value of the parties' statements are expected any time soon. So, why is this so? Is the Italian Legislator so absent-minded as not to realize that confession and party oath are not precious antiques, worth keeping? Do we owe so much to the French tradition that we must keep pretending that someone still believes a solemn oath or a confession deserves the rank of *preuve parfaite* (perfect proof), as the French say?

I think the explanation is different. The resilience of the confession and the oath as evidence, and – more generally – the resilience of 'legal proofs' at large is still connected with the reasons that centuries ago gave rise to the system of legal proof. When non-rational and religious proofs were abolished, the decision-maker

14 See Verkerk 2010, p. 212.

15 See Arts. 301-316 of the *Ley de Enjuiciamiento Civil*. There is only one exception to the rule according to which the court can determine freely the probative value of the parties' statements: if the facts asserted are personal to the party and run against his interests, the same facts must be taken as 'certain' (that is, established), provided that no other evidence disproves such 'certainty' (Art. 316(1) of the *Ley de Enjuiciamiento Civil*). See Armenta Deu 2010, p. 182. Some authors remark that such a rule is the only vestige left of the traditional approach to the confession as a means of legal proof: see, for instance, Gómez de Liaño Gonzáles 2000, p. 372.

16 An important project for the reform of civil procedure (the so-called Liebman project, that is, the project prepared by a group of Italian scholars, led by the late professor Enrico Tullio Liebman) contemplated substituting a sworn interrogatory of the parties for the confession, allowing the court to establish the probative weight of the parties' statements, regardless of their contents: on this project, see Montesano 1979, p. 33; Liebman 1977, p. 452.

was no longer God, but the judge, a human being. The judge is fallible: he must be protected from undue influence, and his discretion must be limited. One very efficient way to reach such a goal is to establish a system of evidence according to which the judge is relieved from the responsibility of weighing by himself the evidence offered by the parties.[17]

If a legal system does not trust its own judges, it may not be very inclined to get rid of 'legal proofs': even though the black letter law governing the evaluation of evidence is said to be inspired by the principle of free evaluation, legal proofs still provide for a safe harbour against judicial discretion. In Italy, a substantial portion of the political class shows a clear lack of confidence in the Judiciary; this attitude is exposed more openly toward the judges assigned to criminal courts, but it is equally noticeable in the field of civil justice. Step by step, with an array of reforms apparently aimed at reducing the dramatic backlog of the courts, the Legislator is pursuing the goal of privatizing civil justice. Therefore, it makes perfect sense that the soundness of 'legal proofs' in a legal system allegedly aspiring to grant an efficient administration of justice is an issue not even touched on by the law reformers.

In conclusion, I think there are good reasons to believe that the party oath and the confession are going to survive for a while still. So, welcome to the antique shop of Italian civil procedure: it is open for business.

17 On the development of 'legal proofs' and their rationale, see Lévy 1965, p. 37; Merryman 1969, p. 125.

Bibliography

Armenta Deu 2010
Armenta Deu, T., *Lecciones de Derecho Procesal Civil (Proceso de Declaración, Proceso de Ejecución y Procesos Especiales)*, 5th edn., Madrid/Barcelona/Buenos Aires: Marcial Pons, 2010.

Balena 1993
Balena, G., 'Giuramento', in: *Digesto delle discipline privatistiche*, Sezione civile, III, Torino: Utet, 1993, p. 105-120.

Cadiet, Normand & Amrani Mekki 2010
Cadiet, L., Normand, J. & Amrani Mekki, S., *Théorie générale du procès*, Paris: Thémis/PUF, 2010.

Cappelletti & Perillo 1965
Cappelletti, M. & Perillo, J., *Civil Procedure in Italy*, The Hague: Nijhoff, 1965.

Comoglio 2010
Comoglio, L.P., *Le prove civili*, 3rd edn., Torino: Utet, 2010.

Consolo 2010
Consolo, C., *Spiegazioni di diritto processuale civile, III, Il processo di primo grado e le impugnazioni delle sentenze*, Torino: Giappichelli Editore, 2010.

Crevani 2010
Crevani, R., 'L'istruzione probatoria', in: Taruffo, M. (a cura di), *Il processo civile riformato*, Torino: Zanichelli Editore, 2010, p. 325-376.

Denti 1983
Denti, V., 'La natura giuridica delle norme sulle prove', in: Denti, V., *Dall'azione al giudicato. Temi del processo civile*, Padova: Cedam, 1983, p. 263-294.

Fabiani 2011
Fabiani, E., 'Note sulla nuova figura di testimonianza (c. d. scritta) introdotta dalla legge n. 69 del 2009', *Rivista trimestrale di diritto e procedura civile*, 2011, p. 823-844.

Gamba 2012
Gamba, C., 'I giuramenti', in: Taruffo, M. (a cura di), *La prova nel processo civile*, Milano: Giuffrè Editore, 2012, p. 435-521.

Gómez de Liaño Gonzáles 2000
Gómez de Liaño Gonzáles, F., *Ley de Enjuiciamiento Civil (Ley 1/2000)*, Oviedo: Editorial Forum, 2000, p. 372-373.

Lepointe 1963
Lepointe, G., 'La preuve judiciaire dans les codes napoléoniens', in: *Recueils de la Societé Jean Bodin pour l'histoire comparative des institutions, La preuve, XIX, Quatrième partie: Période contemporaine,* Bruxelles: Éditions de la Librairie Encyclopédique, 1963, p. 141-186.

Lévy 1965
Lévy, J.-P., 'L'évolution de la preuve, des origines à nos jours. Synthèse générale', in: *Recueils de la Societé Jean Bodin pour l'histoire comparative des institutions, La preuve, XVII, Deuxième partie: Moyen Age et temps modernes,* Bruxelles: Éditions de la Librairie Encyclopédique, 1965, p. 9-70.

Liebman 1977
Liebman, E.T., 'Proposte per una riforma del processo civile di cognizione', *Rivista di diritto processuale,* 1977, p. 452-454.

Luiso 2011
Luiso, F.P., *Diritto processuale civile, II, Il processo di cognizione,* 6th edn., Milano: Giuffrè Editore, 2011.

Merryman 1969
Merryman, J.H., *The Civil Law Tradition,* Stanford, CA: Stanford University Press, 1969.

Montesano 1979
Montesano, L., 'Le prove', in: *Quaderni dell'Associazione italiana fra gli studiosi del processo civile, Incontro sulla riforma del processo civile. Il progetto Liebman sul processo di cognizione (Milano, 20-21 maggio 1978),* Milano: Giuffrè Editore, 1979, p. 33-45.

Rota 2010
Rota, F., 'I fatti non contestati e il nuovo art. 115', in: Taruffo, M. (a cura di), *Il processo civile riformato,* Torino: Zanichelli Editore, 2010, p. 181-221.

Segatti 2012
Segatti, M., 'La confessione', in: Taruffo, M. (a cura di), *La prova nel processo civile,* Milano: Giuffrè Editore, 2012, p. 523-571.

Silvestri 1988
Silvestri, E., 'Confessione nel diritto processuale civile', in: *Digesto delle discipline privatistiche,* Sezione civile, III, Torino: Utet, 1988, p. 422-431.

Storme 1963
Storme, M., 'L'influence des codifications napoléoniennes hors de France, dans le domaine de la preuve', in: *Recueils de la Société Jean Bodin pour l'histoire comparative des institutions, La preuve, XIX, Quatrième partie: Période contemporaine,* Bruxelles: Éditions de la Librairie Encyclopédique, 1963, p. 212-217.

Taruffo 1980
Taruffo, M., *La giustizia civile in Italia dal '700 a oggi*, Bologna: Il Mulino, 1980.

Taruffo 2010
Taruffo, M., 'Evidence', in: Cappelletti, M. (ed.), *Civil Procedure, Chapter 7, International Encyclopedia of Comparative Law*, Tübingen/Dordrecht/Boston/Lancaster: Mohr Siebeck/Martinus Nijhoff Publishers, 2010, p. 1-120.

Van Rhee 2007
Van Rhee, C.H., 'Public Justice: Some Historical Remarks', in: Uzelac, A. & Van Rhee, C.H. (eds.), *Public and Private Justice. Dispute Resolution in Modern Societies*, Antwerp/Oxford: Intersentia, 2007, p. 31-54.

Verkerk 2010
Verkerk, R., *Fact-finding in Civil Litigation: A Comparative Perspective*, Cambridge/Antwerp/Portland: Intersentia, 2010, p. 212-217.

F. Ferrari

THE JUDGMENT ON FACTS IN ITALIAN SUMMARY PROCEEDINGS

1. Introduction: The Judgment on Facts

Giving full meaning to what is clearly stated in Article 24 of the Italian Constitutional Charter,[1] the law assigns to the judge the obligation to 'decide on the entire claim, but not beyond its limits'.[2] In providing tangible content to the right to take action, the Italian Code of Civil Procedure sets forth the judge's so-called duty to decide. Therefore, the judge is institutionally required to 'decide', or, in general terms, to provide an answer in the form of a legal decision to the party - whether claimant or defendant - as the promoter of a petition addressed to him.

This duty to decide and therefore to render judgment is traditionally understood in its bi-phasic structure as consisting of a *de facto* judgment and a *de jure* judgment, the major and minor premises, respectively, of the so-called judicial syllogism.[3]

It is precisely this judgment, and mainly its major premise, that will be examined in this contribution; this examination, however, shall be made not according to the rules of ordinary proceedings, but rather within the context of the summary proceedings governed by the Italian Code of Civil Procedure: specifically,

1 Where it is stated that 'everyone can take action in court for the purpose of safeguarding his own rights'.

2 Art. 112 of the Italian Code of Civil Procedure. On this issue, see Cerino Canova 1980; Grasso 1973; Comoglio, Ferri & Taruffo 1998; Verde 1989.

3 Such clear-cut distinction was criticised because of its rigidity: it was observed that 'the moment the facts are ascertained, the judge prepares to become aware not of the pure and simple historical truth, but of the juridical significance of the facts themselves', so that the final decision becomes the 'conclusion of a complex process, characterised by the mutual conditioning of *de facto* verifications and *de jure* qualifications that are only abstractly distinguishable' (Nasi 1967, p. 972). As one can see, even those who conform to the traditional syllogistic reconstruction of the decision-making process do not fail to caution the reader from an inflexible reading of the dogmatic distinction between the *de facto* and the *de jure* judgment, since it is a 'diagram, in other words a suitable simplification of a series of much more complex mental operations' (Mandrioli 2011, p. 93).

in the context of the summary proceedings recently introduced by the Italian legislator in Article 702-*bis* and following.[4]

2. The Heterogeneous Category of Summary Proceedings and the Different Meanings of Summariness

In Italian civil procedure, summary proceedings include both the above-mentioned summary proceedings on the merits (aiming at obtaining the ascertainment that is typical of the ordinary trial on the merits) and the so-called ascertainment proceedings mainly having an enforcement function. But it also includes provisional measures proceedings.[5] Therefore, the category of summary proceedings includes injunction proceedings, eviction proceedings, seizures, proceedings to report new works and feared damage, preventive inquiry proceedings, urgency proceedings, summary proceedings on the merits pursuant to Article 702-*bis*, as well as possession proceedings, to which Article 669-*bis* and following of the uniform provisional measures proceedings apply.

So, although referring to these proceedings, intrinsically and genetically different one from the other, as an *unicum* is consistent with their position within the civil procedure legal framework,[6] this, however, can only be done based on a rather variegated conception of summariness. The adjective 'summary' must be necessarily understood by the reader - as it must have been understood by the legislator - as having a different meaning whenever it is used with reference to specific proceedings referred to in Title I, Volume IV of the Italian Code of Civil Procedure.

The different meanings of summariness are clearly linked to the different purposes of the different proceedings: while provisional measures are 'instrumental to the decision on the merits', summary non-provisional proceedings are 'anticipatory and perhaps "substitutive" for the effects of the decision on the merits'.[7] So, if the rationale that requires a summarisation of certain areas of the judicial protection made available to the citizens by the state is different, the forms in which the summarisation is achieved are also different. In other words, while the aim pursued by the proceedings has imposed that a summary protection be achieved, the ways through which such summariness is achieved result in different meanings of summariness.

4 Summary proceedings on the merits represent one of the changes made to the Italian Code of Civil Procedure by Law No. 69 of 18 June 2009.

5 Thus, Carratta 2008, p. 877.

6 This is understood to refer to proceedings governed by Title I, Vol. IV of the Italian Code of Civil Procedure.

7 Carratta 2008, p. 878, where it is pointed out that prior to the adoption of the Code of 1942 scholars had acknowledged the existence 'in the context of litigations, of provisional summary proceedings in light of the principle for which the trial must provide, insofar as it is possible to those who are entitled, all that to which they are entitled to pursue at a substantial level', as well as the existence of non-provisional summary proceedings, this time 'in light of the principles for which the duration of the ordinary trial on the merits should not be detrimental to the claimant who has the law on his side'.

The key to understanding the meaning of summariness was provided by the early scholars,[8] who identified it in both the simplification of the forms of the proceedings and in the temporary, partial or superficial nature of the ascertainment of the facts of the case. While the simplification of the forms of proceedings was a typical feature of the summary proceedings introduced by the Code of Civil Procedure of 1865, as opposed to the ordinary ones, the partial, superficial or temporary ascertainment of the facts is *vice versa* a typical feature also of the ascertainment proceedings carried out for enforcement purposes and of the measures having a provisional nature.[9]

Consequently, two different definitions of summariness were provided - summary (in the sense of simplified) proceedings and summary (in the sense of not on the merits)[10] proceedings - without considering that these distinct kinds of summarisation may actually combine with each other, and in abstract terms result in the creation of different summary proceedings, each one with its own extent of summariness.

With specific reference to the case of 'summariness-simplification', it is clear that we can speak of simplification only if there is a term of comparison. This term is actually the ordinary proceedings on the merits, the forms of which are the only ones that can be defined as 'ordinary'.

In this context, scholars[11] have made a further distinction between summary proceedings all details of which are regulated by law, and summary proceedings in which much of the procedure is left to the judge's discretion. In respect of the first type of summary proceedings, the legislator has defined all details. For the second type of summary proceedings simplification is only contemplated in abstract terms by the law, while the proper determination of the procedural forms is left to the judge. More cautious scholars have also pointed out that simplification is not *per se* an indicator of summariness. Actually, proceedings can only be defined as summary if the deviation from the forms of ordinary trials is such as to establish limitations to the position of the parties to the trial by subtracting certain powers ordinarily available to them; otherwise, the procedure may simply be one of the possible alternatives to the ordinary proceedings.[12]

Turning now to summary (not on the merits) proceedings, the focus switches from the procedural forms to the manner in which the judge investigates the case. His investigation of the facts is simplified according to the law which governs summary proceedings. Compared to ordinary litigation on the merits, in summary proceedings the judicial investigation is quantitatively or qualitatively limited. This limitation may result in excluding any evidence-taking phase whenever the judge is entrusted with checking merely the existence of admissibility requirements, and is not allowed to carry out any additional ascertainment; furthermore, summary (not on the merits) proceedings may involve a limitation on the number or kinds of facts

8 Chiovenda 1960, p. 93.

9 Carratta 2008, p. 878.

10 *Ibidem.*

11 Chiovenda 1960, p. 93.

12 Carratta 2008, p. 886.

subject to ascertainment by the judge, the types of evidence available to the parties and to the judge may be reduced, and lastly, a deviation may be established from the methods by which evidence is acquired. In these cases, scholars identify the procedure as summary (not on the merits) proceedings without any evidence-taking phase, with a partial evidence-taking phase, or with an atypical or informal evidence-taking phase, respectively.[13]

A first conclusion may be drawn from the above: summary proceedings may have different meanings when juxtaposed with the ordinary proceedings on the merits as regulated by Volume II of the Italian Code of Civil Procedure. If the procedural rules are simplified, one may shortly speak of summary proceedings. However, if the judge's investigation on the facts is simplified, we should speak of summary (not on the merits) proceedings.

Due to the different terminology used by scholars,[14] the reader has to then deal with the additional difficulty of understanding the meaning of the expression 'on the merits'.[15]

Only based on 'the instrument used to gain knowledge of the facts of the case' not being confused with 'the outcome of the evidence taking phase' or the 'ascertainment',[16] will we be able to disagree with the statement of traditional scholars, according to whom procedural forms different from those of the ordinary proceedings result in a merely superficial ascertainment and, therefore, are not suited for proceedings on the merits.[17]

In light of the above, we can agree that when one talks of summary (in the sense of simplified) proceedings, one means that the procedural forms through which the judge arrives at the judgment are simplified, but the proceedings are on the merits. Consequently, in summary (in the sense of simplified) proceedings,

13 The classification listed in the text is presented by Carratta 2008, p. 886.

14 See, for example, Luiso 2009, p. 105. For a different opinion, see Besso 2010, p. 723.

15 See Satta 1960.

16 Taruffo 1992, p. 470, n. 190, where it is stated that the 'two levels – the "cognisance" level ... and the "ascertainment" level – ... must not be confused, since it may happen "that the fact is known in a way that is anything but superficial, albeit [ascertained] through methods that are totally or partially different from the ordinary methods"'; Carratta 2008, p. 886, where reference is made to Taruffo, as well as Carratta 2010, p. 728, according to whom 'it is advisable to try and avoid falling into the misunderstanding of confusing "cognisance" intended as *modus procedendi* with "cognisance" intended as outcome of ascertainment'.
In this context, see Ricci 1987, p. 20 *et seq*., where the author points out that although generally speaking 'the term "judicial ascertainment" may be used to describe the activity through which the judge ascertains whether the requirements for the measure to be issued from time to time are met' – and in this sense we speak of cognisance as *modus procedendi* – 'according to the civil procedure scholars the term "judicial ascertainment" also has a different meaning ... In fact, this expression is used to describe an effect of the ruling on the controversial situation: and precisely the effect consisting in verifying the existence (or non-existence) of the situation, as declared by the judge'.

17 See Carratta 2010, p. 728; Proto Pisani 1990, Vol. I, p. 411; Taruffo 1992, p. 470, n. 190, according to whom we cannot exclude that 'the fact is known in a way that is not in the least superficial, albeit with methods in all or in part different from the ordinary ones'.

while the *modus procedendi* is simplified, the judicial ascertainment is not and cannot be simplified.

3. The Introduction of Summary Proceedings on the Merits ex-Article 702-bis and following of the Code of Civil Procedure

By Law No. 69 of 18 June 2009, the Italian legislator, in order to reform certain aspects of the civil trial system, *inter alia* added a new paragraph III-*bis*, dealing with the so-called summary proceedings on the merits to Title I of Volume IV of the Code of Civil Procedure. Articles 702-*bis*,[18] 702-*ter*[19] and 702-*quater*[20] regulate

18 Article 702 *bis* - Form of the claim. Filing of appearance by the parties
[1] In the controversies in which *Tribunale* decides as a single judge, the claim may be filed by motion to the *Tribunale* which is the proper venue for the action. The motion, signed pursuant to Article 125, shall contain the indications under Article 163, third paragraph, numbers 1, 2, 3, 4, 5 and 6 and the warning under number 7.
[2] Following the filing of the motion, the court clerk prepares the judge's docket and, without delay, gives it to the president of *Tribunale*, who designates a magistrate in charge of the trial of the proceeding.
[3] By decree, the designated judge schedules the hearing for the parties' appearance, assigning a time-limit for the defendant's filing of appearance, which shall be accomplished no later than 10 days before the hearing: the motion, together with the decree for scheduling the hearing, shall be served upon the defendant at least 30 days before the date scheduled for the defendant's filing of appearance.
[4] The defendant shall file his appearance by filing with the clerk office his answer in which he shall indicate all his defence and take a position with respect to the facts o which the movant based his motion, indicate the means of evidence which he intends to offer and the documents which he exhibits, and indicate his conclusions. Under penalty of waiver, the defendant shall file any counterclaim and raise any procedural objection or objections on the merits of the case, which objections be raised by the judge, *sua sponte*.
[5] If the defendant intends to file an impleader claim, to call a third party join to proceeding in order to be guaranteed by this latter, he shall declare such intention in his answer and ask the designated judge to adjourn the hearing. By decree communicated by the court clerk to the parties who filed their appearance, the judge proceeds to schedule the date of the new hearing, assigning a final time-limit to the defendant to summon the third. The third party files his appearance pursuant to the fourth paragraph.

19 Article 702 *ter* - Proceeding
[1] If the judge deems that he is not the proper venue for the action, he states so by order.
[2] If the judge finds that the claim does not fall among those under Article 702 *bis*, by unchallengeable order, he declares the claim inadmissible. Similarly, the judge decides the counterclaim.
[3] If the judge deems that the defence filed by the parties require a nonsummary evidentiary phase by unchallengeable order, he schedules the hearing under Article 183. In this event, the provisions of Book II shall apply.
[4] When the case concerning the counterclaim requires a nonsummary evidentiary phase, the judge orders the separation of the actions.
[5] If the judge does not proceed pursuant to the previous paragraph, at the first hearing, after hearing the parties, omitted any formality not indispensable for complying with the principle of parties' equal opportunity to defence, he proceeds in the way he deems more proper to accomplish the evidentiary activities which are relevant in relation to the object of the requested decision and, by order, he grants or denies the claims.

→

proceedings that compete, as an alternative, with the ordinary proceedings on the merits set forth in Volume II of the Code.[21] Claimants can opt for this procedure, as long as the requirements set out by the law are met,[22] namely that a single-judge court has jurisdiction to render a judgment in the case at issue and that the judge, recipient of the claim pursuant to Article 702-*bis*, believes that the parties' statements do not require an ordinary evidence-taking phase. Scholars state that the claimant is not 'entitled to a pre-selected procedural model'.[23] This is, in fact, a direct consequence of granting the judge the power to order the continuation of the trial according to the ordinary procedural forms, upon the outcome of an initial review as to the possibility to proceed with a summary evidence-taking phase.[24]

It has to be pointed out that although the decision concluding the summary proceedings on the merits pursuant to Article 702-*bis* and following is in the form of an order and not of a judgment, it is not only temporarily enforceable and able to be recorded, but also 'produces the effects of *res iudicata* as referred to in Article 2909 of the Civil Code'. Such effects may be avoided only if the losing party files an appeal pursuant to Article 702-*quater*. This means that the legislator intended to grant the order concluding the proceedings precisely the same effects as the judgment concluding the ordinary proceedings.

This last consideration is crucial in underscoring, in its wide breadth, the gap between the institute at issue and the summary proceedings referred to in Article 19 of Legislative Decree No. 5 of 17 January 2003.

This law, since then abrogated by Law No. 69 of 2009, regulated commercial litigation and, in this context, provided for summary proceedings, whose outcome was also an enforceable order, likewise subject to appeal, however - and this is by far a significant difference - this order was not able to produce *res judicata* pursuant

[6] The order is temporarily enforceable and is titled for the registration of the judicial mortgage and for the transcription.

[7] In any event, the judge decides on the expenses of the proceeding pursuant to Articles 91 and following.

20 Article 702 *quater* - Appeal

[1] The order issued pursuant to Article 702 *ter*, sixth paragraph, has the effects under Article 2909 of the civil code, if it is not challenged by 30 days running from its communication or service. New means of evidence and new documents are admitted when the panel of judges considers them relevant to decide the case, or the party proves that he could not offer them during the summary proceeding due to a cause not attributable to him. The president of the panel may delegate the admission of the means of evidence to one of the members of the panel.

21 See Dittrich 2009, p. 1582; Consolo 2009a, No. 7, p. 882. With reference to the relationship with the special labour procedure, see Vidiri 2010, p. 1377 *et seq.*; see also Lombardi 2010, p. 477, as well as Luiso 2009, p. 112.

22 See Lombardi 2010, p. 474, where it is noted that 'these are two prerequisites that become significant separately, at different moments of the proceedings, and the first one defines the second one'. Therefore, it would be more correct to avoid speaking of 'prerequisites', as underlined by Porreca 2010, p. 825. See also Dittrich 2009, p. 1587.

23 Lupoi 2010, p. 1225 *et seq.*

24 Menchini 2009b, p. 1025.

to Article 2909 of the Italian Civil Code.[25] Therefore, the above-mentioned summary proceedings[26] were intrinsically and definitely different in their essence from the current summary proceedings on the merits.

4. Systematic Position and Juridical Nature

Scholars have been engaged in a careful 'definition campaign' of the institute introduced by the legislator in June 2009. Although no interpretation capable of earning the unanimous support of scholars can be traced, it is possible, however, to categorise their reflections into two opposing interpretations.

According to some scholars, the new proceedings fall within the category of not on the merits proceedings aimed at quickly obtaining, based on a superficial ascertainment of the facts, a decision that can be immediately enforced.

According to the other interpretation, the new institute constitutes an alternative with respect to the ordinary proceedings on the merits that, although characterised by a simplified *modus procedendi*, nevertheless presupposes a full ascertainment by the judge.[27]

The arguments submitted by scholars to support their theses range from the name that the legislator assigned to the institute at issue to its placement within the Code of Civil Procedure; other scholars take into account the (partial) correspondence between the text of Article 702-*ter*, 5th paragraph, and the text of Article 669-*sexies*, 1st paragraph,[28] which govern the provisional measures procedure.[29] In any event, these arguments all seem quite weak.

As for the name 'summary proceedings on the merits', it coincides with the title given to paragraph III, Title II, of Italian Legislative Decree 5/2003, that, no doubt, was not on the merits.[30] But it is also the same name that the Code of Civil Procedure of 1865 had assigned to the simplified proceedings on the merits

25 See Basilico 2010, p. 739; Menchini 2009b, p. 1025.

26 It is at least its most recent predecessor. See Arieta 2009. Subsequent to the summary proceedings referred to in Art. 19 of the Italian Legislative Decree 5/2003, we find the proposal contained in the so-called Mastella Bill – Art. 46 of Bill No. 1524/S/XV – and in the Bill furthered by Proto Pisani 2009. However neither of them became law.

27 Besso 2010, p. 722, to which we owe the recognition of positions taken by scholars little by little and the consequent synthesis. The first group includes Carratta 2009, p. 160; Luiso 2009, p. 1568; Mandrioli 2011b, p. 364; Menchini 2009b, p. 1031; Proto Pisana 2009, p. 223. The second group, on the other hand, includes Arieta 2009; Balena 2009, p. 329; Biavati 2010; Caponi 2009, p. 337; Chiarloni 2009, p. 32; Dittrich 2009, p. 1582; Porreca 2010, p. 825. As for case law, note Court of Varese 18 November 2009, in *Guida al diretto*, 2009, No. 50, 46.

28 Article 669 *sexies* – Proceeding
[1] After hearing the parties, omitting any formality which is not necessary to comply with the principle of parties' equal opportunity to defence, the judge proceeds in the way he deems more proper to the accomplishment of the evidentiary activities which are indispensable in relation to the requirements and the ends of the decision requested and, by order, he grants or denies the motion.

29 Besso 2010, p. 723.

30 On corporate summary proceedings, see, among others, Caponi 2004, p. 1359 *et seq.*; Volpino 2007, p. 67 *et seq.*; Saletti 2003, p. 467 *et seq.*

regulated therein as an alternative to the ordinary trial.[31] As for the position within the Code of Civil Procedure, it is to be pointed out that it is criticised by the same authors who use it as an argument to support the juridical qualification which they put forth:[32] therefore, this element loses its already weak persuasive strength. Lastly, with regard to the parallelism between Article 702-*ter*, 5th paragraph and Article 669-*sexies*, 1st paragraph, the profound differences actually between the two rules are self-evident and they operate also at the level of the inspiring rationale governing the evidence-taking phase in the two contexts.

In any event, what is most worthy of being contradicted is the premise itself of the first interpretation, namely the argument based on the so-called summariness of the ascertainment that allegedly characterises the proceedings as not on the merits.[33] In this context, the debate concerning summariness reveals all its utility. Therefore, the remarks provided above when speaking in general terms of the 'summary' nature can be rightly transposed herein, with the effect that the legislator's naming it as summary first and then including it in Title I of Volume IV does not necessarily render the proceedings pursuant to Article 702-*bis* and following summary not on the merits proceedings. Better yet, a similar assumption can be agreed upon only to the extent that we can subscribe to the view that proceedings can be summary as to their nature due to their being only simplified.[34]

Starting from the clarification given above, we come to agreement with those scholars according to whom the summary proceedings on the merits pursuant to Article 702-*bis* are characterised as summary inasmuch as the forms are simplified. However, as one can see, this does not mean entirely rejecting the opposite thesis. As a matter of fact, of the first 'interpretation' referred to above, we can appreciate the perspective, the point of view from which scholars have felt it necessary to start from for their qualification investigation; and in fact the focus on the 'acceleration purpose' of the summary proceedings can be agreed upon as a key to the text.[35] It cannot be denied that the objective of the introduction of the summary proceedings on the merits in the Code was that of providing suitable protection quickly, or at least within a shorter time span, compared to the lengthy one, due to which the ordinary trial is at risk of being in conflict with the very principle of fair trial referred to in Article 111 of the Constitution.[36]

31 See Carratta 2008, p. 878.

32 See Mandrioli 2011b, p. 361.

33 See Besso 2010, p. 723.

34 See Section 2.

35 With regard to 'acceleratory purpose', see Mandrioli 2011b, p. 361, advocate of the first doctrinal interpretation, who deems that the (contested) placement in the Code of the rules governing summary proceedings on the merits, which are located after the regulation of provisional measures proceedings, is due to the 'general acceleration purpose typical of this new proceedings'. See Olivieri 2009, p. 37; Menchini 2009a, p. 1103; Biavati 2010, p. 185; Carratta 2010, p. 726, according to whom 'its purpose, then, seems to be ... granting the parties the possibility that the object of the litigation quickly becomes *res judicata*'.

36 See Bina 2010, p. 120, where the author links the 'granting to the judge of discretionary powers of trial management and the identification of the procedural forms best suited to the complexity of the case' for the purpose of 'maximising the effectiveness of the jurisdictional →

In conclusion, we are faced with summary proceedings on the merits, alternative to, and in competition with, the ordinary proceedings, being simplified as to the *modus procedendi*, where the summariness-simplification is left to the judge, and aimed at obtaining a decision able to achieve *res judicata*, but more quickly. This institute, on the one hand, pursues the same purpose as the ordinary trial, offering protection not only in terms of a judge's order, but also in terms of a decision establishing a new juridical status;[37] on the other hand and at the same time, it '[strives to] answer the society's need for quick justice, in a political context in which the resources available are not likely to increase, or are even reduced'.[38]

5. The Summariness of the Evidence-taking Phase: The quid and quomodo of this Phase of the Proceedings

As highlighted above, for the purpose of applying the summary (on the merits) proceedings, the law postulates that particular prerequisite be satisfied, among others: that the statements of the parties do not require an ordinary evidence-taking phase.[39]

We have already mentioned that the summary nature typical of the summary proceedings at issue must be identified in its simplified *modus procedendi*.[40] The essence of such simplification is clear in the wording of the 5th paragraph of Article 702-*ter*, titled 'proceedings', according to which 'the judge, after hearing the parties and omitting any formalities except those to be complied with in the adversarial system, proceeds in the manner he considers to be most suitable to the relevant evidence-taking means in connection with the object of the requested decision, and issues an order granting or rejecting the petitions'.

The de-formalisation becomes evident first in that the judge can disregard any formalities the omission of which, in the judge's opinion, does not affect the basic principle referred to in Article 101 of the Code of Civil Procedure, an explicit limit set by the law in order to safeguard the ordinary procedural forms.[41] Moreover, the mere fact of speaking of evidence-taking means (*atti di istruzione*) authorises one to deem that the legislator - in describing the activity that the judge is entitled to

protection, at the same time ensuring a trial of a reasonable duration'; Consolo 2009b, p. 743. On the judges' being unable to ensure jurisdictional protection in a reasonable time, see Chiarloni, Gottwald & Zuckermann 1999.

37 See Olivieri 2009, p. 37; Lombardi 2010, p. 484, where it is said that 'the new model of summary proceedings has the same function as the full trial on the merits and grants the same type of protection'.

38 Biavati 2010, p. 185.

39 This prerequisite appears when interpreting the wording of the law where (Art. 702-*ter*, 3rd para) it sets the obligation for the judge, who feels 'that the statements of the parties require a non-summary evidence-taking phase', to 'schedule a hearing as referred to in Article 183', thus ordering to move from summary proceedings to ordinary proceedings.

40 Lupoi 2010, para 1. As a further and final confirmation of the concept of the summariness of this procedure as de-formalisation, reference is made to the statement made by the legislator himself (Carratta 2010, p. 729).

41 Porreca 2010, p. 844.

perform – intended to refer not only to the evidence-taking means of the ordinary proceedings, but also to a 'variant' of them.[42] All this contributes to outline the summariness typical of the proceedings at issue.[43]

The implicit yet obvious reference to Article 669-*sexies* – whose language is quite similar – should not mislead the reader, who should not be led to draw a naïve juxtaposition between the evidence-taking phase of the uniform provisional measures proceedings and the one referred to in Article 702-*ter*.[44] Actually, if the rule on summary proceedings on the merits talks of 'relevant' evidence activities, Article 669-*sexies*, 1st paragraph, on the other hand, recalls only the 'indispensable' ones; moreover, while Article 702-*ter* makes reference to evidence activities in relation to the 'object of the requested measure', Article 669-*sexies*, 1st paragraph, considers the evidence activities indispensable in relation to 'the prerequisites and purposes' of the requested provisional measure. Hence, keeping in mind that the object, broadly speaking, of the protection requested through the claim pursuant to Article 702-*bis* consists in 'ascertaining the subjective rights, dictating the rule of conduct for the case at issue, providing certainty to juridical relationships regarding anything being an object of rights (*bene della vita*)'[45] – and not in 'obviating any dangers that, during the time that it takes to obtain jurisdictional protection, may jeopardise its outcome'[46] – one will be able to acknowledge the profound gap that separates the two evidence-taking phases, so similar to each other as to the appearance of legislative formulas, but so different from each other in substance.[47]

Going straight into detail, we have to investigate the *quid* and *quomodo* of the evidence–taking phase to which Article 702-*ter* refers.

As for the first aspect, it is of paramount importance to decide whether a general principle, as on the limited, pre-defined number of evidentiary means, can be accepted. It is clear that the answer being searched for within the limited scope of the summary proceedings on the merits is strictly associated with, and intrinsically

42 Carratta 2010, p. 729.

43 See Proto Pisani 1991, p. 19, recalled by Carratta 2010, p. 729.

44 Lupoi 2010, p. 7; Biavati 2010, p. 190.

45 Menchini 2009a, p. 1103: see Section 4, final para, above, n. 39. See Bove 2010, p. 441; Lombardi 2010, p. 484, where it is stated that in the provisional measures procedure 'the prerequisite for issuing the measure (in addition to the danger in the delay) is the *fumus bonis iuris*, in other words the likelihood that the right exists … therefore, the ascertainment of facts that the judge must carry out consists in allowing access to evidence aimed at representing the likelihood but not the certainty of a fact'. From this last consideration, Dittrich 2009, p. 1588, draws the conclusion that, in connection with summary proceedings, we should think of 'a different concept of summariness that can be described in terms of structural simplicity of the controversy and consequently of limited quantity (and not quality) of the evidence required for purposes of the decision'.

46 These are the words of Mandrioli 2011a, p. 23. On the function of the provisional measures procedure, see Tarzia 2011, p. XXVIII, where it is explained that the latest scholars link provisional measures to a 'function of preservation of the *de facto* and *de jure* situation; a function of temporary regulation of the situation, by means of innovative measures, intended to last only until the achievement of ordinary protection; an anticipatory function (in full or in part) of the effects of the final measure'.

47 See Lupoi 2010, para 7; Caponi 2009, p. 336; Volpino 2010, p. 552.

dependent on, the one that is accepted in the law governing civil procedure generally.[48] In other words, one can claim that Article 702-*ter* intends to gain some room for atypical evidence-taking means only in the event that this is deemed admissible in the ordinary proceedings: a generic prohibition of atypical evidence-taking means would preliminarily resolve the matter in a negative sense also for the summary proceedings.[49]

At this point, it is useful to endorse what has been stated with reference to the almost identical legislative provision mentioned above, although in a totally different context, namely in the context of the uniform provisional measures proceedings. The reference here is to Article 669-*sexies*, 1st paragraph, according to which 'the judge, after hearing the parties and omitting any formalities except those to be complied with in the adversarial system, proceeds in the manner he considers to be most suitable to the indispensable evidence-taking means' was in fact interpreted as an opening, not so much to evidence-taking means, but rather to employing typical evidence-taking means according to atypical methods.[50] Basically, as for the amount of evidence that the judge can use to form his opinion, nothing would change, at least nothing that is likely to be more permissive.

Moving on to the second aspect, it is precisely the *modus procedendi* that marks the distance between the summary proceedings at issue and the ordinary ones; in fact, while the evidence-taking means admissible in abstract terms are the same,

48 See Lupoi 2010, para 7, n. 161; Porreca 2010, p. 846.

49 As one can see, if on the one hand the debate over the principle of typicality of the evidence is useful for the purposes of this discussion, on the other hand it seems advisable to acknowledge what is stated by scholars under another perspective: Cavallone 1991c, p. 336 *et seq*. In fact, scientific unjustifiability and practical needlessness has been claimed in respect of a debate on the topic of atypical evidence set 'in terms of obligatoriness or exemplification of the legal collection of evidence-taking means' (p. 345); and this statement, along with the criticism 'of the most accredited theory of atypical evidence' – as claimed by the same author – 'does not want to start the construction of a different theory but instead, if anything, the conclusion that we can advantageously draw without any theory of atypical evidence'. This can be claimed in light of the fact that 'the heterogeneous phenomena usually traced back to that notion do not lend themselves to being subject to a unitary regulation, neither from the (pre-trial) point of view of their admissibility and/or usability for trial purposes, nor from the (subordinated and possible) point of view of their effectiveness. Each of them should instead be carefully and rigorously evaluated, from both points of view, in connection to the legal discipline of the evidence phase' (p. 401). On this issue, we may refer to Ferrari 2004, p. 347 *et seq*., where 'we can observe that one cannot speak of the category of atypical evidence as a whole, contrasting two opposing as well as abstract alternatives (admissibility/-inadmissibility) since the reader's job should instead be carried out at the level of admissibility/inadmissibility of the individual and tangible pieces of evidence that are reviewed from time to time'. The inadequacy of the positions taken by case law did not fail to show itself, as highlighted by Cavallone 2008, p. 947 *et seq*.

50 Carratta 2008, p. 888; Carratta 2003, p. 46; Salvaneschi 2011, p. 414; Ricci 1999, p. 447. With specific reference to the summary proceedings on the merits: Lombardi 2010, p. 486; Dittrich 2009, p. 1596, who states that 'all admissibility limits of evidence, just like, obviously, all rules concerning documentary evidence, remain valid'; Volpino 2010, p. 554. In the same sense, Consolo 2009a, p. 885; Consolo 2009b, p. 743. Contra, Bove 2010, p. 441; Porreca 2010, p. 846.

'what changes are the ways in which they are employed'.[51] The law allows the judge to establish, from time to time and in connection with the actual case, the most appropriate methods for employing the relevant evidence-taking means.[52]

In this sphere of liberty granted to the jurisdictional authority in light of the law not dictating *ex ante* the detail of the procedure to be followed, the judge, however, does not enjoy full and unconditional discretion. A first obstacle is identified by Article 702-*ter* itself, where it affirms the intangible nature of the mandatory principle of the adversarial system. Observance of this principle is pre-eminent here compared to other interests the protection of which is implicit in the procedural forms, and which are sacrificed together with such procedural forms.[53] In the second place, the principle of the *onus probandi* as established by Article 2697 of the Italian Civil Code must be complied with, as well as the principles of party presentation and party prosecution of the case, principles according to which the parties are the only 'masters' of the judicial proceedings,[54] and the principle of non-contestation, recently formally introduced in Article 115[55] of the Code of Civil Procedure.[56] We should further mention a thesis according to which Article 702-*ter* determines an enlargement of the evidence-taking powers of the judge.[57]

That said, it is true that the aforementioned statements add nothing to the debate over what the judge can actually do within the context of the evidence-taking phase of the summary (on the merits) proceedings. To speak of simplification in fact means to rely on a metaphor. With the intention of establishing the tangible

51 Salvaneschi 2011, p. 414.

52 See Dittrich 2009, p. 1587.

53 Among others, Bove 2010, p. 445; Balena 2009, p. 329.

54 Here, reference is made to the traditional perspective, which sees in Art. 115 of the Italian Code of Civil Procedure (only) the codification of the rule according to which the judge's decision has to be exclusively founded on the evidence offered by the parties, without the judge being allowed to exercise any power of evidence-related initiative. In any event, this reference is justified as a mere terminological custom: in fact, it has been demonstrated that the rule at issue instead provides the basis for (also and above all) the fundamental prohibition of the judge's 'private knowledge': in other words the basic 'prohibition of initiatives by the judge aimed at finding outside the trial topics and sources of proof other than the ones indicated by the parties'. Cavallone 1991b, p. 322; Ferrari 2004, p. 287 *et seq*. In this context, around the debate on the contents of Art. 115, see Ricci 1974, p. 380 *et seq.*; Taruffo 2011, p. 202 *et seq.*; Cavallone 2008, p. 947 *et seq.*; Cavallone 2009, p. 861 *et seq.*; Picó I Junoy 2007, p. 1457 *et seq.*

55 Article 115 – Availability of evidence
[1] Save where otherwise provided by the applicable law provisions, the judge shall base his decision on the evidence offered by the parties or by the public prosecutor, as well as on the facts which have not been specifically contested by the party who filed his appearance.
[2] However, the judge may, without the need of any evidence, base his decision on facts of common experience.

56 Lupoi 2010, para 7, n. 161; Lombardi 2010, p. 487.

57 So,Volpino 2010, p. 555, according to whom the 'summariness of the evidence phase seems … to lend itself to determining a widening of evidence-gathering powers that can be exercised by the judge, although in compliance with Art. 112, in other words within the limits defined by the allegations of the parties'. *Contra*, Porreca 2010, p. 845; Lombardi 2010, p. 486, n. 28, who refers to Olivieri 2009, p. 43.

meaning of the simplification, and consequently pinpointing the procedural formalities that can be omitted, it is necessary that the purpose of the simplification be taken into account, which consists in savings in terms of time compared to the ordinary proceedings. Summariness, then, means, in the specific case at issue, full yet simplified ascertainment of facts for the purpose of reaching the end of the litigation as quickly as possible. In this perspective, we can think of witness evidence 'purified' of the requirement of summoning the witnesses (perhaps replaced by a simple convocation to be sent by the parties), of the prior indication of their names and of the specific drafting of the questions to be asked. Then, court-appointed expertise may be arranged for without applying the provisions of Article 195 of the Code of Civil Procedure as reformed, but in any event in compliance with the mandatory rules of the adversarial system. For example, we can hypothesise that the court-appointed expert is simply requested to verbally report at the hearing in the presence of the parties' experts.[58] Making the most of what has been said concerning the evidence-taking powers of the judge, as well as the rules referred to in Articles 257[59] and 281-*ter*,[60] which identify the judge's powers of evidence taking, we can also hypothesise the possibility for the judge to order *ex officio* the disclosure of documents to which the parties have made reference in their statements of case.[61] Given that the legislator has not defined the contents of the evidence phase in summary proceedings and that the judge has to evaluate whether the parties' statements are suitable for the summary evidence phase or need the ordinary evidence phase, it is clear that the judge finds himself faced with a rather important as well as difficult task.[62]

Certainly, there are cases in which the choice appears to be, if not obvious, at least easy. For example, we could justifiably presume that where the evidentiary means requested by the parties are limited to the category of documents only, the judge will not be led to arrange for the continuation of the proceedings in the ordinary forms. And the same can be said in reference to the situation in which the case submitted to the judge's evaluation appears to be ready for decision (where there is absolutely no need for an evidence-taking phase).[63]

But there are also situations in which the issue is much more complex: and this is when it seems advisable that a careful analysis of the complexity of the evidence phase as presented by the parties be carried out. This analysis may avail itself of conceptual categories already focused on by scholars,[64] such as the concept of

58 Porreca 2010, p. 845; Lupoi 2010, para 7; Ricci 2009, p. 110; Dittrich 2009, p. 1595; Court of Varese 18 November 2009, in *Guida al diritto*, 2009, No. 50, 46.

59 Pursuant to which 'if one of the witnesses refers, for knowledge of the facts, to other people, the judge can issue a court order to the effect that the said individuals are called to testify'.

60 Which grants the judge the power 'to order *ex officio* that witness evidence be taken, formulating the questions to be asked, when the parties in submitting the facts refer to individuals who seem likely to know the truth'.

61 On this topic, see Cavallone 1991a, p. 669.

62 Bina 2010, p. 123.

63 See Bina 2010, p. 124, and the doctrine mentioned in n. 19.

64 The necessity of a screening that is as 'thought out' as possible is clear in the statements by Bina 2010, p. 127, according to which 'the seriousness of the result of the summary trial (the →

'prompt solution evidence' referred to in Article 648 of the Italian Code of Civil Procedure.

Not excluding any evidence-taking means from the number of those in abstract terms admissible in summary proceedings does not mean, in fact, levelling the difference between the evidence phase typical of summary proceedings and the one typical, on the other hand, of the ordinary proceedings to solely 'de-formalisation':[65] the latter does indeed characterise the entire evidence-taking process pursuant to Article 702-*ter*, yet it does not represent the only distinguishing element; on the contrary, de-formalisation would represent a consequence, and not a defining trait. Rather, once the road is open even to the evidentiary means that require a certain activity to be taken on by the judge, the distinction between statements of case that require an 'ordinary' evidence phase and those that, on the other hand, are 'satisfied' with just a 'summary' evidence-taking phase seems to be the degree of complexity of the statements: in other words, 'the prompt solution' allowed by the evidence.[66]

This statement leads us to outline two additional profiles that distinguish the evidence phase of the summary proceedings on the merits and the one typical of other summary (in their own way) proceedings, that is, the uniform provisional measures proceedings.[67]

First, we should exclude that in summary proceedings the judge may resort to the tool of 'summary information' envisaged by the legislator in the provisional measures proceedings *ex parte*. This conclusion is supported by the wording of the law itself: in fact, this expression is used by Article 669-*sexies* - the rule whose affinity with Article 702-*ter* has already been discussed[68] - but only in its second paragraph[69] and, namely, where the proceedings *ex parte* are regulated.

application of Art. 2909 of the Italian Civil Code) suggests that the institute should be limited to ... cases that can be readily solved ...[,] those in which the opposing party is defaulting, or ... those in which the validity, or invalidity of the claim is obvious'. On the need for caution, see also Consolo 2009a, p. 883.

65 As seems to be supported by Ferri 2010, p. 99.

66 A quick solution is also discussed by Bina 2010, p. 127, although he refers to the case generally and not to the state of the evidence.

67 The uniform provisional measures proceedings were introduced by Italian Law No. 353 of 26 November 1990 in the new Art. 669-*bis* and following for the purpose of governing all proceedings specifically mentioned in Art. 669-*quaterdecies*, titled 'field of application'. Art. 669-*sexies* deals with the 'proceedings' in a strict sense, and the first two paragraphs set forth two alternative procedural models: one, taken as a model for the preparation of the summary procedure on the merits, defines a streamlined and de-formalised procedure compared to the one typical of the ordinary trial on the merits; the other, concerning the rendering of the order *inaudita altera parte*, should be followed when 'the calling of the opposing party may prejudice the implementation of the measure'. On the provisional measure procedure, see Tarzia 2011, p. XXVIII.

68 See Section 5.

69 [2] When summoning the opposing party might prejudice the execution of the granted precautionary measure, the judge decides by ex parte motivated decree collecting, where necessary, summary information. In this event the judge, by the same decree, schedules the hearing for the parties' appearance before him by a time-limit not longer than 15 days, assigning to the movant a final time-limit of no more than 8 days for serving the motion and →

Secondly, and lastly, during the summary proceedings on the merits the so-called balancing of opposing interests, a permitted criterion which is advisable to be used by the judge in the provisional measures proceedings, should not be taken into consideration. Such balancing - in imposing on the judge to take into account the impact that granting or denying of protection would have, in terms of damages - partly affects the ordinary evidence-taking rules and, namely, the principle of the *onus probandi* set out in Article 2697 of the Civil Code.[70] This exception to the general precepts of the law governing civil procedure, clearly associated with the traits of temporariness and instrumentality typical of the provisional measures procedure,[71] is not justified within the scope of a proceedings that, just like the ordinary proceedings, are to end in a decision suitable to become *res judicata* pursuant to Article 2909 of the Italian Civil Code.

6. Final Remarks

Having underscored that in our view the purpose of simplification in the summary proceedings on the merits consists in savings in terms of time and costs compared to the ordinary proceedings, we believe also to have pointed out that simplification does not mean the abandonment of the rules of evidence in such a context or the refusal of the regular *onus probandi* principle. It means rather the acceptance by the judge to continue the debate in the procedural form chosen by the plaintiff only if he can envisage that the evidentiary needs of the case may be satisfied within certain time and cost limits.

Actually, we believe that no specific evidentiary means can be considered, from an abstract point of view, time- or cost-consuming. Such an evaluation has to be achieved by the judge, taking into consideration not only the relevance of the evidence request, but also another criterion, namely, the compatibility of such a request, and/or of the evidentiary needs of the case, with the purpose of simplification as identified above. Thus the judge - within the summary proceedings - shall not only examine the relevance of a certain item of evidence, taking into consideration the fact the party wishes to use the evidence to prove in order to determine whether the evidence tends to make the existence of the fact more likely,[72] but shall also evaluate the impact of the evidence in terms of time and costs.

the decree upon the defendant. At this hearing, by order, the judge confirms, amends, or revokes the decisions previously adopted by decree.

70 This was highlighted by Cavallone 1998, p. 174.

71 These assumptions are still valid, in light of the peculiarities undeniably typical of the provisional measures procedure, also following the reform introduced by Italian Law No. 80 of 14 May 2005, converting Italian Law Decree No. 35 of 14 March 2005. This is a legislative act that, for certain provisional measures, has deleted the requisite of initiating the relevant subsequent ordinary proceedings so that we have come to speak of 'reduced instrumentality'. See Saletti 2011, p. 293 *et seq*.

72 The definition of relevancy chosen is the one given by James 1941, p. 690: 'Relevancy, as the word itself indicates, is not an inherent characteristic of any item of evidence but exists as a →

This means that the Italian judge in summary proceedings on the merits has to exercise case-management powers in admitting evidence due to the fact that certain items of evidence could be relevant, but could imply - if admitted - the need to leave out the procedural form at issue. In a certain way, within summary proceedings on the merits the evaluation concerning the admissible and relevant evidence to actually be admitted has to be performed aggregately and will affect the procedure to be followed. This specific task placed upon the Italian judge marks the difference between our summary proceedings on the merits and the proceedings similarly named in the English[73] or U.S. systems.[74]

Finally, the above conclusion demonstrates that the evidentiary rules and principles - as already identified by legal scholars[75] - are clearly and heavily influenced by their procedural environment, and this is true not only when comparing different systems, but also when comparing different proceedings belonging to the same system.

relation between an item of evidence and a proposition sought to be proved. If any item of evidence tends to prove or to disprove any proposition, it is relevant to that proposition'.

73 In the English system in fact the summary judgment proceedings are regulated by CPR 24.2, according to which such a streamlined procedure is available only if one of the parties may show that the opponent's claim or defence lacks a real prospect of succeeding. As clarified by the rules as well as by the case law the only admissible evidentiary means are written statements and statements of truth, and the summary judgment hearings should not become mini-trials so as not to distort the function of the proceedings (Andrews 1998, p. 52 and Andrews 2012, p. 71-72 quoting Lord Wolff in *Swain v Hillman* (2001)).

74 In the U.S., summary judgments are regulated by FRCP 56, according to which a party may move for summary judgment, identifying each claim or defence - or the part of each claim or defence - on which summary judgment is sought. But 'the court shall grant summary judgment' only if 'the movant shows that there is no genuine dispute as to any material fact and the movant is entitled to judgment as a matter of law. The court should state on the record the reasons for granting or denying the motion'.

75 Damaška 1997.

Bibliography

Andrews 1998
Andrews, N., 'The New English Civil Procedure Rules (1998) ', in: Van Rhee, C.H. (ed.), *European Tradition in Civil Procedure*, Antwerp: Intersentia, 2005, p. 161-181.

Andrews 2012
Andrews, N., *The Three Paths of Justice: Court Proceedings, Arbitration and Mediation in England*, Cambridge: Springer, 2011.

Arieta 2009
Arieta, G., 'Il rito "semplificato" di cognizione', available at: <www. Judicium.it>.

Balena 2009
Balena, G., 'Il procedimento sommario di cognizione', *Foro italiano*, 2009, V, p. 324-334.

Basilico 2010
Basilico, G., 'Il procedimento sommario di cognizione', *Giusto processo civile*, 2010, p. 737-770.

Besso 2010
Besso, C., 'Il nuovo rito ex art. 702-bis c.p.c.: tra sommarietà del procedimento e pienezza della cognizione', *Giurisprudenza italiana*, 2010, p. 722-726.

Biavati 2010
Biavati, P., 'Appunti introduttivi sul nuovo processo a cognizione semplificata', *Rivista trimestrale di diritto e procedura civile*, 2010, p. 185-196, available at: <www.fondazioneforensebolognese.it>.

Bina 2010
Bina, M., 'Il procedimento sommario di cognizione', *Rivista di diritto processuale*, 2010, p. 117-133.

Bove 2010
Bove, M., 'Il procedimento sommario di cognizione', *Giusto processo civile*, 2010, p. 431-454.

Caponi 2004
Caponi, R., 'La tutela sommaria nel processo societario in prospettiva europea', *Rivista trimestrale di diritto e procedura civile*, 2004, p. 1359-1392.

Caponi 2009
Caponi, R., 'Un modello ricettivo delle prassi migliori: il procedimento sommario di cognizione', *Foro italiano*, 2009, V, p. 334-338.

Carratta 2003
Carratta, A., 'Prova e convincimento del giudice nel processo civile', *Rivista di diretto processuale*, 2003, p. 27-64.

Carratta 2008
Carratta, A., 'Processo sommario (dir. proc. civ.)', *Enciclopedia del diritto*, Vol. II, Milano: Giuffrè, 2008, p. 877-893.

Carratta 2010
Carratta, A., 'Le "condizioni di ammissibilità" del nuovo procedimento sommario di cognizione', *Giurisprudenza italiana*, 2010, p. 726-730.

Cavallone 1991a
Cavallone, B., 'Esibizione delle prove nel diritto processuale civile', *Digesto delle Discipline Privatistiche, Sezione Civile*, VII, Torino: Utet, 1991, p. 664-683.

Cavallone 1991b
Cavallone, B., 'Crisi delle *Maximen* e disciplina dell'istruzione probatoria', in: *Il giudice e la prova nel processo civile*, Padova: Cedam, 1991, p. 289-322.

Cavallone 1991c
Cavallone, B., 'Critica della teoria delle prove atipiche', in: *Il giudice e la prova nel processo civile*, Padova: Cedam, 1991, p. 335-410.

Cavallone 1998
Cavallone, B., 'Les mesures provisoires et les règles de preuve', in: Van Compernolle, J. & Tarzia, G. (eds.), *Les Mesures provisoires en droit belge, français et italien. Étude de droit comparé*, Bruxelles: Bruylant, 1998, p. 163-174.

Cavallone 2008
Cavallone, B., 'Riflessioni sulla cultura della prova', *Rivista italiana di diritto e procedura penale*, 2008, p. 947-986.

Cavallone 2009
Cavallone, B., 'Il divieto di utilizzazione della scienza privata del giudice', in: *Rivista diritto processuale*, Padova: Cedam, 2009, p. 861-873.

Cerino Canova 1980
Cerino Canova, A., 'La domanda giudiziale e il suo contenuto', in: Allorio, E., *Commentario del Codice di procedura civile*, Book II, Tome I, Torino: Utet, 1980, p. 5-480.

Chiarloni, Gottwald & Zuckermann 1999
Chiarloni, S., Gottwald, P. & Zuckermann, A.S., *Civil Justice in Crisis: Comparative Perspectives of Civil Procedure*, Oxford: Oxford University Press, 1999.

Chiarloni 2009
Chiarloni, S., *Le principali novità introdotte nel codice di procedura civile con la L. 69/2009*, Bologna/Rome: Zanichelli, 2009.

Chiovenda 1960
Chiovenda, G., *Istituzioni di diritto processuale civile*, Vol. I, 2nd edn, repr., Napoli: Jovene, 1960.

Comoglio, Ferri & Taruffo 1998
Comoglio, L.P., Ferri, C. & Taruffo, M., *Lezioni sul processo civile, Vol. I, Il processo ordinario di cognizione*, 2nd edn., Bologna: Il Mulino, 1998.

Consolo 2009a
Consolo, C., 'La legge di riforma 18 giugno 2009, No. 69: altri profili significativi a prima lettura', *Corriere Giuridico*, 2009, 7, p. 877-890.

Consolo 2009b
Consolo, C., 'Una buona "novella" al c.p.c.: la riforma del 2009 (con i suoi artt. 360-bis e 614-bis) va ben al di là della sola dimensione processuale', *Corriere Giuridico*, 2009, 6, p. 737-743.

Damaška 1997
Damaška, M.R., *Evidence Law Adrift*, New Haven: Yale University Press, 1997.

Dittrich 2009
Dittrich, L., 'Il nuovo procedimento sommario di cognizione', *Rivista di diritto processuale*, 2009, p. 1582-1600.

Ferrari 2004
Ferrari, F., *La prova migliore. Un'indagine di diritto comparato*, Milano: Giuffrè, 2004.

Ferri 2010
Ferri, C., 'Il procedimento sommario di cognizione', *Rivista di diritto processuale*, 2010, I, p. 92-101.

Grasso 1973
Grasso, E., 'Dei poteri del giudice', in: Allorio, E., *Commentario del Codice di procedura civile*, Book I, Tome II, Torino: Udet, 1973, p. 1254-1345.

James 1941
James, G.F., 'Relevancy, Probability and the Law', *California Law Review*, 1941, Vol. 29, p. 689-705.

Lombardi 2010
Lombardi, R., 'Il procedimento sommario di cognizione generale', *Giusto processo civile*, 2010, p. 473-494.

Luiso 2009
Luiso, F.P., 'Il procedimento sommario di cognizione', *Giurisprudenza italiana*, 2009, p. 1568-1570.

Lupoi 2010
Lupoi, M.A., 'Sommario (ma non troppo)', *Rivista trimestrale di diritto e procedura civile*, 2010, p. 1225-1260. Available at: <www.judicium.it>.

Mandrioli 2011a
Mandrioli, C., *Diritto processuale civile, Vol. I, Nozioni introduttive e disposizioni generali*, 21st edn., Torino: Giappichelli, 2011.

Mandrioli 2011b
Mandrioli, C., *Diritto processuale civile, Vol. IV, L'esecuzione forzata, i procedimenti sommari, cautelari e possessori, il nuovo procedimento sommario cognitorio, la giurisdizione volontaria*, 21st edn., Torino: Giappichelli, 2011.

Menchini 2009a
Menchini, S., 'Il rito semplificato a cognizione sommaria', *Giusto processo civile*, 2009, p. 1101-1113.

Menchini 2009b
Menchini, S., 'L'ultima "idea" del legislatore per accelerare i tempi della tutela dichiarativa dei diritti: il processo sommario di cognizione', *Corriere giuridico*, 2009, 8, p. 1025-1034.

Nasi 1967
Nasi, A., 'Giudizio di fatto (dir. proc. civ.)', *Enciclopedia del diritto*, Vol. XVI, Milano: Giuffrè, 1967, p. 967-987.

Olivieri 2009
Olivieri, G., 'Al debutto il rito sommario di cognizione', *Guida al diritto*, 2009, 28, p. 37-51.

Picó I Junoy 2007
Picó I Junoy, J., 'Judex judicare debet secondum allegata et probata, non secundum coscientiam: storia della erronea citazione di un brocardo nella dottrina tedesca e italiana', *Rivista di diritto processuale*, 2007, p. 1497-1518.

Porreca 2010
Porreca, P., 'Il procedimento sommario di cognizione: un rito flessibile', *Rivista trimestrale di diritto e procedura civile*, 2010, p. 823-858.

Proto Pisani 1990
Proto Pisani, A., 'Usi e abusi della procedura camerale ex art. 737 ss. c.p.c.', *Rivista di diritto processuale*, 1990, Vol. I, p. 393-458.

Proto Pisani 1991
Proto Pisani, A., 'Procedimenti cautelari', *Enciclopedia giuridica Treccani*, Vol. XXVII, Roma: Treccani, 1991.

Proto Pisani 2009
Proto Pisani, A., 'La riforma del processo civile: ancora una legge a costo zero', *Foro italiano*, 2009, Vol. V, p. 221-227.

Ricci 1974
Ricci, E.F., 'Il principio dispositivo come problema di diritto vigente', *Rivista di diritto processuale*, Padova: Cedam, 1974, p. 380-389.

Ricci 1987
Ricci, E.F., 'Accertamento giudiziale', *Digesto delle Discipline Privatistiche*, Torino: Utet, 1987, Vol. 1, p. 16-27.

Ricci 1999
Ricci, G.F., *Le prove atipiche*, Milano: Giuffrè, 1999.

Ricci 2009
Ricci, G.F., *La riforma del processo civile. Legge 18 giugno 2009*, No. 69, Torino: Giappichelli, 2009.

Saletti 2003
Saletti, A., 'Il procedimento sommario nelle controversie societarie', *Rivista di diritto processuale*, 2003, p. 467-483.

Saletti 2011
Saletti, A., 'Le misure cautelari a strumentalità attenuata', in: Tarzia, G. & Saletti, A. (eds.), *Il processo cautelare*, 4th edn., Padova: Cedam, 2011, p. 293-324.

Salvaneschi 2011
Salvaneschi, L., 'La domanda e il procedimento', in: Tarzia, G. & Saletti, A. (eds.), *Il processo cautelare*, 4th edn., Padova: Cedam, 2011, p. 389-444.

Satta 1960
Satta, S., 'Cognizione', *Enciclopedia del diriritto*, Vol. VII, Milano: Giuffrè, 1960, p. 306-307.

Tarzia 2011
Tarzia, G., 'La tutela cautelare', in: Tarzia, G. & Saletti, A. (eds.), *Il processo cautelare*, 4th edn., Padova: Cedam, 2011, p. XXIII-XXXIX.

Taruffo 1992
Taruffo, M., 'La prova dei fatti giuridici. Nozioni generali', in: *Trattato di diritto civile e commerciale*, Vol. III, Tome II, Section III, Milano: Giuffrè, 1992.

Taruffo 2011
Taruffo, M., *Per una rilettura dell'art. 115 del Codice di procedura civile, in La disponibilità della tutela giurisdizionale (cinquant'anni dopo)*, Milano: Giuffrè, 2011.

Verde 1989
Verde, G., 'Domanda (principio della), Diritto processuale civile', *Enciclopedia Giuridica Treccani*, Vol. XII, Roma: Treccani, 1989.

Vidiri 2010
Vidiri, G., 'Procedimento sommario di cognizione e rito del lavoro tra "provvedimenti presidenziali" ed "osservatori sulla giustizia civile"', *Corriere giuridico*, 2010, No. 10, p. 1377-1384.

Volpino 2007
Volpino, D., 'Cognizione e decisione nel procedimento sommario societario', *Rivista trimestrale di diritto e procedura civile*, 2007, p. 67-95.

Volpino 2010
Volpino, D., 'Il procedimento sommario di cognizione e la delega sulla riduzione e semplificazione dei riti', in: Taruffo, M. (ed.), *Il processo civile riformato*, Bologna: Zanichelli Editore, 2010, p. 525-568.

F. Ferraris

EXPERT TESTIMONY IN THE ITALIAN JUDICIAL SYSTEM: CHARACTERISTICS, QUESTIONS AND COMPARATIVE VIEWS

1. Introduction

Science and knowledge continue to advance and to become more complex and specialised. It is clear that this development, although it carries certain benefits and contributes to society's progress, also involves the achievement of results which are equally complex and often difficult to fully understand, especially for those who are not provided with certain abilities or technical and specific skills.

This disadvantage enters into the trial. Frequently, parties submit to the court complex facts which cannot be properly understood in their essence but by means of specialised knowledge. The problem, in particular, is of two types: how to introduce - and to demonstrate - this kind of information about events in legal proceedings; and, how to successfully make this information about events clear to a person - the judge - traditionally considered *peritus peritorum* but, actually, devoid of the necessary abilities to fully understand what goes beyond the knowledge and comprehension of the average person.

Of course, the Italian system of evidence - like the systems of all other Western countries - provides for certain tools which allow the court to obtain the technical knowledge necessary to approach certain facts. One tool, certainly, is technical advice, whose function is precisely to help the judge in understanding particular information about events that cannot be adequately comprehended without the technical skills of an advisor.

However, in addition to this tool, academics have long suggested the possibility that, under certain conditions, some 'technical' elements may also be introduced through witness testimony, a reference to so-called 'technical testimony', that is to say, testimony where the witness uses a specific - technical - language.

The aim of this paper is to describe this particular means of proof in the Italian judicial system as well as to highlight some critical issues, especially those related to the position of Italian courts, which are not inclined to consider technical testimony admissible. Moreover, the analysis of this issue will take into account other perspectives, too - in particular, the experience of criminal case law and the comparative law experience - in order to investigate how these systems and experiences have developed such a particular evidentiary means.

2. Technical Testimony as a Hybrid between Witness Testimony and Technical Advice

In order to reach a clear perception of what exactly is meant by technical testimony, we first have to define the two kinds of evidence - namely, witness testimony and technical advice - that, more than any types of evidence, share with technical testimony certain characteristics.

As is well known, witness testimony is a report - made by a third party uninterested in the dispute - about facts relevant for deciding the case.[1] Therefore, the relevant aspects of this evidence are based on the independence and impartiality of the witness, and on his statement of facts the understanding of which is useful - if not necessary - in order to achieve a proper assessment of the facts at issue.

In contradistinction, through technical advice courts are provided with the specialised knowledge necessary for a complete understanding of certain events (e.g. the course of an illness). Strictly speaking, from the Italian perspective, this tool is not a means of evidence since it would not, at least directly, determine the court's decision on the truth of certain facts, but rather it would simply stand as a special kind of help offered to a judge anytime he needs it.[2]

Technical testimony can be placed somewhere in the middle between witness testimony and technical advice. As with the former, it is available if the parties request it and remains within the scope of a clear reconstruction of some relevant facts; as with the latter, it is 'specialised/technical knowledge' possessed and used by the witness to clarify and explain a certain fact.

In particular, academics refer to technical testimony to identify 'witness testimony, qualified by technical profiles, in which the perceptions of the witness and his assessments cannot find other suitable means of expression outside a language necessarily specialised'.[3] So, by way of example, a doctor - when called upon to elucidate a fact connected to his profession - would give 'technical' testimony that is characterised by the use of the skills (and language) pertaining to this particular knowledge.

The use of the conditional verb form in the previous sentence is not accidental, since one of the most debated issues related to the admissibility of this kind of evidence in the Italian legal system deals with the object of witness testimony: that is, the witness is expected to report facts only and not personal opinions, and this because, otherwise, he would bring into the evidence phase subjective elements that cannot be checked by the court.

Prevailing case law includes in this prohibition even a 'technical opinion' regarding the facts: the concern is that through scientific language the witness might transition too easily from a mere statement of the facts to their diagnostic and prognostic evaluation.

1 Many Italian scholars have analysed witness testimony: *cf.*, among others, Carnelutti 1957; Cappelletti 1962; Gibiino 1971; Marzocchi 1977; Spiazzi 1986; Chiarloni 1994; Comoglio, Ferri & Taruffo 2008; Mandrioli 2009; Comoglio 2010.

2 On technical advice, see Franchi 1959; Dones 1962; Cavallone 1991; Molfese 2003; Bove 2011.

3 Comoglio 2010, p. 580.

While this last concern seems understandable, nevertheless we can agree with those statements made by academics that the dichotomy 'fact-opinion', which should guide any testimony, would really be something as difficult to be made in practice as it is clear in theory. Indeed, speaking of a 'reference to the facts' necessarily requires a reconstruction by the person who makes this reference: 'the mnemonic reconstruction and statement of facts - state Italian scholars - always involve a series of complex and diverse opinions [and] the witness always report[s] an opinion of truth or falsity of the factual propositions'.[4] Hence 'the impracticality of a rigid separation between purely descriptive and evaluative aspects in the context of witness statements'.[5]

Of course, here I do not want to argue that witness testimony should always contain opinions, but simply that the 'limitation to the facts only' for witness testimony should not be considered as absolute. There are, instead, situations when knowledge (before) and exposition (after) necessarily carry with them a certain evaluation of the facts by the witness. Among these there can also be detailed technical matters that can be properly comprehended only through specialised knowledge which should be used even for their presentation in a judicial proceeding.

3. Case Law on Technical Testimony

According to the above definition, the testimony is technical when it consists of an assessment of the facts made by a third party with special skills.

Looking at the decisions of the Italian Supreme Court (*Corte di Cassazione*), however, one can hardly find a special definition of this kind of witness testimony or any practical applications: in fact, on many occasions the Court has upheld the principle that the testimony 'shall not consist in an entirely subjective interpretation or in technical or legal evaluations of the facts', thereby (apparently) closing the door to the admissibility of any technical testimony.[6]

Many reasons support this position. In addition to the concern mentioned previously, it is reasonable to assume that there is also another concern regarding, on the one hand, the real competence of the witness in a particular field[7] and, on the other hand, the effective impartiality of the witness; and connected to this last concern is the stronger reason used by the courts, namely, that in the Italian system there is already an instrument - technical advice - through which specialised knowledge can enter a legal proceeding whenever the court considers it necessary in order to understand particular facts.

Therefore, the advisor should satisfy all the requirements for the performance of his duties: he is an auxiliary of the court, and so he is required to be impartial and independent; and, the effectiveness of his expertise is guaranteed by the special

4 Taruffo 1988, p. 729.

5 Dondi 1996a, p. 44.

6 *Cf.* Cass., 10.4.1999, No. 3505.

7 *Cf.* the relevant problem of the general acceptance of scientific evidence; on this, see Lombardo 2007.

register of technical consultants kept by the court.[8] Moreover, the advisor is appointed 'when it is necessary',[9] so the judge will be able to check in advance whether he understands a certain phenomenon before deciding to appoint him.

However, this position must not be considered rigid.

In fact, it must be emphasised that the complexity of the world today has led the courts to the conclusion that technical advice is often useful, not only for the understanding of certain facts the parties have advanced, but also for the reconstruction of historical facts, or even for the quantification of damages. In all these cases, the court 'does not just apply ... criteria and parameters for assessing the evidence already offered by the parties through other means, but use[s] them in terms of evidence to acquire direct knowledge of a relevant fact that would otherwise be impossible to ascertain'.[10]

Thus, the purpose of this 'revised' technical advice becomes basically the same as the one scholars attribute to technical testimony: both these means, in fact, share the importance (and the necessity, of course) of appointing a person provided with a specific expertise in order to ascertain certain facts that otherwise would escape the understanding of the average person, as well as to report them in the trial.[11]

Yet, the same decisions that expressly exclude technical opinions regarding the facts seem to provide a saving clause where they say that 'although opinions may not be the subject of witness evidence ..., where the opinion is of an absolute immediacy, almost inseparable from the perception of the same historical facts, they may contribute to the judge's opinion on the facts'.

In particular, the Supreme Court specifies that the 'immediate opinion' would be admissible when the witness refers to objective data and detailed specifications of the actual situation which show that the opinion is not of a subjective type, but that it pertains directly to the event.[12]

It is possible to assume, then, that the immediacy of the opinion may also be referred to as a technical approach with regard to a fact that cannot be understood but through specialised knowledge, and that the explicit reference to 'objective data' could provide the basis for such a working hypothesis.

To be sure, a more solid basis for this interpretation can be found in the Italian Code of Criminal Procedure.

8 Rules governing the special register of technical consultants are well explained in Protetti & Protetti 1999.

9 *Cf.* Art. 61 Italian Code of Civil Procedure.

10 Comoglio 2010, p. 888; with regard to case law, see, among others, Cass., 23.2.2006, No. 3990; Cass., 19.1.2006, 1220.

11 Notwithstanding such *eadem ratio*, there is at least one difference in using each one of these two means of proof. While it is true that the scope of technical advice is undoubtedly more extensive than that of technical testimony, it is no less true that opting for advice at the expense of testimony may have some negative consequences (at least in cases where a third 'expert' party has assisted with defining the fact to be stated) on the right of the parties to bring evidence since the testimony is a measure available upon request of the parties (of course, if relevant), while the advice is available *ex officio* at the discretion of the court.

12 *Cf., inter alia,* Cass., 22.4.2009, No. 9526.

In particular, Article 194, paragraph 3, of the Code states that 'the witness ... cannot give evidence about public rumours or express personal opinions unless it is impossible to separate them from the testimony he gives on the facts'. Now, the Supreme Court has consistently interpreted this prohibition in the sense that it does not apply if the witness, who is qualified by special professional training, is called to report facts related to his profession and his special activities. In this case, technical opinions become inseparable from the facts, since the opinions were necessarily perceived through the filter of the technical and professional knowledge of the witness.[13] Therefore, 'the witness takes, basically, almost a dual role of witness and expert, even if the final evaluation of the facts and their development always belongs to the court'.[14]

Thus, criminal law provides for a special 'technical witness'.[15] This helps to make a first, useful distinction between technical testimony and technical advice, a distinction which may clarify the issue discussed here and avoid confusion. The Supreme Court clarifies, in particular, that while the particular knowledge of the witness can certainly be used to report facts, the same principle does not work with testimony containing assessments of facts connected to subjective opinions of the witness, which could become part of the evidence only through technical advice. Therefore, according to the Court, the technical witness is just required to report the facts perceived, and he must avoid going too far beyond that, for example by evaluating the causes, by formulating hypotheses regarding the development of the situation.

4. The Dispute among Italian Academics on Technical Testimony

Without any doubt, the growth of independent technical testimony is due to Italian scholars, who first tried to define the characteristics and the boundaries of such evidence.

Of particular importance is a paper written by a prominent Italian scholar in the 1960s which first talked about technical testimony.[16] It is interesting to note the focus it places on the obstacle that - more than others - seems to hinder the full usability of technical testimony, and it is not the fact that witness testimony should be free of opinions.[17] The real reason for exclusion of technical testimony seems to lie in the language used by the witness: in other words, according to the Italian Code of Civil Procedure, the witness should use ordinary, non-specialised

13 Cass., 21.12.1998, *Crispolti*; see also Cass., 29.9.2004, *Comberlato*; Cass., 12.12.1995, *Vazzolo*; Cass., 9.9.1985, *Gengotti*; Cass., 29.10.1984, *Megliali*.

14 Nappi 2007, p. 99.

15 *Cf.* Cass., 19.9.2007, *Ranieri*, which clearly states that 'the testimony of a technical witness, i.e. a witness particularly skilled in a specific field, that reports facts perceived using his own experience is admissible'.

16 Denti 1962.

17 It is worth remembering that 'any knowledge of the past is always and only inferential, based on certain assumptions and causal laws' and 'cognitive activity necessarily presupposes the attribution of certain categories to the observed facts': Denti 1962, p. 14.

language. This principle can be found in Article 61 of the Code which allows the court - whenever it appears necessary - to avail itself of technical advice: this follows because judges are non-specialists and, this being the case, since they 'will evaluate the evidence', the witness testimony should be provided 'normally on the basis of a common understanding'.[18]

Therefore, the general rule is that of simplicity. However, sometimes there are situations in which 'the witness cannot adequately report the facts in any other way. Only in this case may he use specialised or technical language'.[19] So, the distinction between 'ordinary' and 'technical' testimony would not rely on the technical preparation of the witness - in fact there could be cases where an 'expert' witness is called to give evidence about circumstances that do not require the use of his skills - but, precisely, on the nature of the language, necessarily 'technical' in order to explain certain phenomena.

Another theory focuses on the value of the statement.[20] In particular, while the ordinary witness reports facts to the court in an analytical way, the technical witness does something more: he provides the court not with mere observations (and an analytical statement) but with a synthesis of what he observed, a synthesis made possible by his particular knowledge. Therefore, the two kinds of testimony differ 'with regard not to the object, which is the same, but to the value of the testimony, which in the first case makes reference to a common experience, while in the second to a specific experience'.[21]

Other scholars, instead, are more interested in the results of technical testimony than in the problem related to its admissibility:[22] the problem, in particular, arises when the court is faced with the uneasy task of rightly and properly assessing the outcome of technical testimony. In other words, the risk is that the court may not fully grasp the meaning of the testimony. In this case, it would not be unreasonable to expect that it will ask for the assistance of a technical advisor: 'this assistance can certainly be used for a correct understanding of witness statements, where the use of technical language by the witness was essential and the court is not able to understand the appropriate meaning of it'.[23]

Now, it seems there are reasonable grounds to support the theory according to which the technical language is the distinctive characteristic of the evidence in question. In order to explain a fact correctly, the language of the witness, it should be stressed, has to be related not just to its utility but also to its indispensability.

Therefore, the filter of 'expert knowledge' must become a real *conditio sine qua non* without which the facts cannot be adequately understood.

18 Denti 1962, p. 17.
19 Denti 1962, p. 18.
20 Franchi 1959.
21 Franchi 1959, p. 55.
22 Patti 2001, p. 8, clearly states that 'when the subject of the case necessarily involves the use of technical language, the witness can certainly use his skill in his testimony'.
23 Patti 2001, p. 8.

5. A Comparison between Technical Testimony and Technical Advice

After having described the principal characteristics of technical testimony, it is now important to outline the features distinguishing that evidence from technical advice. As will be seen shortly, although both types of evidence share the element of technical knowledge, there are still many differences.

The first distinction has to do with the object of the evidence. A comparison between the two rules that govern, respectively, witness testimony and technical advice (namely, Articles 244 and 194 of the Code of Civil Procedure) shows that the former relates to 'facts', and the latter to 'investigation'. Therefore, as mentioned earlier, the testimony, though technical, is required to report only facts (as they are complex) without going into personal assessments with regard to possible future developments or into hypothetical reconstructions of causes.[24]

The other significant distinction regards the nature of the testimony, which is a means of evidence at the discretion of the parties, while the advice (may be sought by the parties, but) remains a discretionary option for the court.[25]

Additional elements of the distinction can be identified in the different relationship between the person and the fact (to explain/investigate). While the witness is necessarily a predetermined person (that is, the person who has been present at a particular event which has to be proven), the advisor would rather be a 'fungible' person, who is chosen *a posteriori* and only with regard to his specific skills within the relevant scientific community, without any connection, therefore, with the specific fact to be investigated.[26]

Finally, also the liability of the witness/advisor may be used to distinguish the two types of evidence: in fact, while the technical witness does not assume any responsibility for the 'rightness' of the technique he used, not so the consultant who, instead, pursuant to Article 64 of the Code of Civil Procedure, is liable in the event of serious misconduct, both in criminal and in civil fields, for the damages caused to the parties.[27]

6. A Comparative View: The Introduction of Expert Knowledge in the American and English Legal Systems

The theme related to expert knowledge and its use in a legal proceeding is particularly debated in the common law systems, traditional precursors of new ideas and trends; but although both the United States and England provide specific rules for the introduction of expert knowledge in a trial, there are nevertheless significant differences in regard to the person appointed to be an expert: while the U.S. refers expressly to an 'expert witness', in England the expert has quite a different role.

24 *Cf.* Mandrioli 2009, p. 275, which affirms that 'while the technical consultant is called to evaluate certain facts, the witness shall only report facts'; Giudiceandrea 1961, p. 532.

25 Taruffo 1988, p. 735.

26 Andrioli 2008, p. 137; Beghini 1997, p. 7.

27 Laudisa 1991, p. 2.

As for the American system, in particular, testimony can be divided into simple testimony (i.e. lay testimony) and technical testimony (i.e. testimony by experts). On the latter, Rule 702 of the Federal Rules of Evidence expressly states that 'if scientific, technical, or other specialized knowledge will assist the trier of fact to understand the evidence or to determine a fact in issue, a witness qualified as an expert by knowledge, skill, experience, training, or education, may testify thereto in the form of an opinion or otherwise, if (1) the testimony is based upon sufficient facts or data, (2) the testimony is the product of reliable principles and methods, and (3) the witness has applied the principles and methods reliably to the facts of the case'.

So if, for the understanding of a certain fact, special skills are required, a technical witness may be called by the parties as long as the statement of the witness is based on clear facts and he makes use of reliable methods and theories.

The development of this evidence in the American system is justified, first and foremost, by the constant specialisation of knowledge.[28] It is not by chance that scholars have defined recent years as 'the age of experts'[29] to emphasise the fact that, increasingly, the ability to understand certain events necessarily involves the use of a set of special skills.

Moreover, the success of 'expert testimony' is also due to two further factors: within the rules on evidence, it is hard to find a means of evidence that can be compared to the Italian technical advice; and, in the United States the parties are faced with a judge (in most cases) completely devoid of expert knowledge (a so-called 'generalist'). What is true of judges is even more the case with respect to the jury, whose members are chosen, as a rule, from among the lists of driver license holders.

Therefore, the ordinary way to introduce expert knowledge in a trial is by testimony, but, certainly, a kind of testimony that is far away from the Italian technical one: in fact, the American expert witness is able to express technical evaluations of the facts, to test hypotheses, and he may even go so far as to offer up a prognostic evaluation of the same.

Certainly, such a tool - which is essential, and has become 'ubiquitous in American courtrooms'[30] - did not fail to raise doubts and concerns about its use. In essence, two issues have emerged over the years: first, the problem of the (in)dependence of the witness and, second, the real scientific contribution given by the expert witness.

28 It may be of interest to report what one academic said: 'We surrender our car to the auto-repair expert, we surrender our children to the education specialist, we surrender our marriages to the sex therapist, our diet to the health experts, our beaches to the oil-spill experts, our defence to the military and foreign-policy experts in the Pentagon, our tax policy to the corporate-supported economic experts, and the administration of justice to the expert witness in the courtroom'. *Cf.* Laughlin 1992, p. 72.

29 Brint 1994.

30 Browne, Williamson & Barkacs 2002, p. 67.

As to the first issue, some scholars underscore that expert witnesses are only 'ideally' impartial observers of external events, but in reality they are 'partisan rhetors whose opinions are for sale'.[31]

As to the second issue, the risk is to introduce in trials a kind of knowledge defined, in a particularly colourful way, as 'junk science':[32] in other words, the problem is related not only to the actual reliability of the witness's knowledge, but also to the question whether the witness can be considered an expert or, more simply, a person adequately 'hired' to 'simply create evidence that coincides with the case of [his] customer'.[33] The two problems are closely related in the sense that the less 'scientific' the witness is, the more 'party connected' he is.

It should also be pointed out that other scholars believe that the system already provides for some mechanisms to prevent access to spoiled expert testimony. These mechanisms are, on the one hand, the power of gate keeping of the court, either in admitting the witness or when assessing his scientific contribution, and, on the other hand, the techniques of cross-examination - the heart of the adversary model.[34]

In particular, along the same lines the court would still have the last word in admitting the witness, both in terms of relevance and, especially, in terms of reliability and quality of the knowledge used. On this issue, the severe screening role played by the judge - which is a well-known important development in case law that occurred in the 1990s - marked a real turning point in the introduction of expert knowledge in the trial.[35]

In fact, before the U.S. Supreme Court overruled the decision rendered in *Frye*, the admissibility of scientific evidence was subject to prior verification as to the general acceptance of the theory used in the relevant scientific community.[36] Today

31 *Ibidem*. On this, *cf.* also Jensen 1993. This is the same concern that has led the Italian legislator to provide for a separate - and independent - figure (the advisor), chosen by the court, and covered with all the provisions on challenge and waiver as provided by the Code of Civil Procedure.

32 This expression was first used in a 1985 report by the Department of Justice (Report of the Tort Policy Working Group on the Causes, Extent and Policy Implications of the Current Crisis in Insurance Availability and Affordability, which can be found at the website <www.eric.ed.gov/PDFS/ED274437-.pdf>, last consulted in June 2012; it became commonly accepted after its use in the *General Electric Company v Robert K. Joiner* case, 522 U.S. 136, 1996, where Justice Stevens stated that 'an example of "junk science" that should be excluded under the *Daubert* standard as too unreliable would be the testimony of a phrenologist who would purport to prove a defendant's future dangerousness based on the contours of the defendant's skull'.

33 Browne, Williamson & Barkacs 2002, p. 66; see also Alcorn 2006, p. 25, which underscores that the parties that want to use an expert witness will always be faced with a 'conflict between an advocate's duty to make the best possible arguments supporting a client's case and the advocate's duties to the court'.

34 *Cf.* Sundby 1997; Gross 1991.

35 The reference goes to the well-known leading case of the U.S. Supreme Court *Daubert v Merrell Dow Pharmaceuticals., Inc.*, 509 U.S. 579, 1993; on this, *cf.* Imwinkelried 1993; Dondi 1996b; Ansanelli 2009.

36 See *Fryre v United States*, 293 F. (D.C. Cir.), 1923, 1013 *et seq.*: '[J]ust when a scientific principle or discovery crosses the line between the experimental and demonstrable stages is difficult to →

the Supreme Court, with its decision in *Daubert*, has established a detailed 'catalogue' of the checks the court should first try, with a view to ensuring the adequacy of the knowledge that the parties intend to use.[37]

However, as noted by academics, even though the framing of the problem is undoubtedly correct, the result obtained seems doubtful for several reasons.

First of all, the provided catalogue of tests appears hardly applicable to real data. Secondly, *Daubert* has tended to bring inside the trial also that knowledge (perhaps experimental, so-called 'novel evidence') not yet endorsed by the entire scientific community of reference; but the subsequent applications of the catalogue show that courts have begun to admit expert witnesses in a much more rigorous and, above all, limited way than in the past.

With regard to the argument related to cross-examination, it is held that this tool is 'the greatest legal engine ever invented for the discovery of truth': in particular, in this case, the examination by the party would be an effective way to show, on the one hand, the lack of competence of the witness and, on the other hand, his possible biased attitude.

Finally, it should be recalled that some other measures have been proposed in order to obtain, as far as possible, a statement based both on impartiality and rigorous technique. First, a greater use of Rule 706, which authorises the court to appoint expert witnesses *ex officio*. Second, the progressive development of professional associations that provide appropriate forms of accountability and disciplinary powers against their members when they make partial (if not scientifically false or inconsistent) statements. Finally, the training of judges so as to make them specialists in different areas in which they will be called to work.

Compared to the American system, English rules on evidence provide for a different way of introducing expert knowledge in a trial. In particular, there are two figures that can bring in their professional skills: assessors and experts.

define. Somewhere in this twilight zone the evidential force of the principle must be recognized, and while courts will go a long way in admitting expert testimony deduced from a well recognized scientific principle or discovery, the thing from which the deduction is made must be sufficiently established to have gained general acceptance in the particular field in which it belongs'.

37 The parameters followed by the Court in order to verify expert knowledge are: (1) *testability* ('Ordinarily, a key question to be answered in determining whether a theory or technique is scientific knowledge that will assist the trier of fact will be whether it can be (and has been) tested. "Scientific methodology today is based on generating hypotheses and testing them to see if they can be falsified; indeed, this methodology is what distinguishes science from other fields of human inquiry"'); (2) *peer review* ('[S]ubmission to the scrutiny of the scientific community is a component of "good science", in part because it increases the likelihood that substantive flaws in methodology will be detected'; even if 'publication (which is but one element of peer review) is not a *sine qua non* of admissibility', because 'some propositions, moreover, are too particular, too new, or of too limited interest to be published'); (3) *rate of error* ('[I]n the case of a particular scientific technique, the court ordinarily should consider the known or potential rate of error'); (4) *maintenance of standards*; and, (5) *general acceptance* ('[W]idespread acceptance can be an important factor in ruling particular evidence admissible').

The assessor plays a role that is quite similar to the Italian technical advisor: he is appointed by the judge whenever it is necessary to make use of expert knowledge.[38]

The experts are (in general) previously identified and appointed by the parties. This aspect has persuaded the legislator to ensure, as far as possible, their independence and impartiality. Thus, in the Civil Procedure Rules, reading the rules that explicitly refer to the experts, we find, first, that the duty of experts - that is, to 'help the court on matters within their expertise' - 'overrides any obligation to the person from whom experts have received instructions or by whom they are paid'; that 'expert evidence should be the independent product of the expert uninfluenced by the pressure of litigation'; and finally that 'experts ... should not assume the role of an advocate'.

Moreover, the Rules provide for at least three types of powers of the court in the use of experts, namely, a preventive-type and two concurring ones. The first power refers to the necessary authorisation from the court regarding the use of such experts, a 'permission' which is justified in relation to the increased powers of case-management of the courts, even in the evidence-taking phase.

With the second, the court may order that if both parties wish to appoint an expert, the advice is given by a single expert, identified by the parties, if they agree on the appointment, or by the court.

Regarding the third, the court may give precise instructions to the 'single joint expert', with reference to the payment of the costs relating to any inspection, any examination or experiment that the expert proposes to undertake.

In this context it is important to emphasise the fact that the appointed expert may, at any time, request from the court specific instructions for the execution of his duties, even bypassing the party that has appointed him.

Therefore, independence, impartiality, autonomy and competence are the typical features of the English expert: characteristics that make the English expert very similar to the Italian technical consultant; it is not a coincidence that the Rules do not speak of 'testimony', but always and only of 'expert evidence' or an 'expert report'.

If these elements are not surprising for lawyers of the Civil Law tradition, certainly two elements sound peculiar from the standpoint of lawyers of the Common Law tradition: the morphology of the expert report in a system still dominated by the principle that the trial 'is in the hands of the parties'.

38 Indeed, the terminology, used by the Civil Procedure Rules as well as by the Practice Directions, seems to make possible a similarity of roles between the assessor and the *amicus curiae*. This figure (at least in its original form), which has been developed in the common law system, is a 'helper' of the court, whose duty consists in making elements - of fact or of law - clear to the court: it is a 'bystander, who without having an interest in the cause, of his own knowledge makes suggestions on a point of law or of fact for the information of the presiding judge': *cf.* Krislov 1962, p. 694.

7. Conclusion

Once the usefulness of expert testimony even in the Italian legal system is accepted, the above-mentioned comparative perspective makes one wonder whether the common law expert should be considered more helpful – in terms of effectiveness of the results – than the civil law expert.

In this regard, both systems analysed present at least one weak point: the American expert witness, even if particularly well-skilled, has been defined as a 'hired gun', in the sense that in most cases he lacks the independence necessary to provide a correct service to the court, while the Italian system of taking expert evidence fails in the end because, as we have seen, the presiding judge, usually not provided with the skills necessary to understand the specific facts, can on his own motion evaluate the results of an expert activity and decide whether they can be accepted as reliable.

Probably the right answer lies somewhere in the middle: a good evidence system that aims to be effective should ensure both the independence of the expert it relies upon and the binding character of the results brought about by the activity performed by the expert.

Bibliography

Alcorn 2006
Alcorn, R., 'Ethics and Expert Witnesses', *Arizona Attorney*, 2006, Vol. 43, p. 24-32.

Andrioli 1960
Andrioli, V., 'Comments to Articles 244-257', in: Aa.Vv., *Commento al codice di procedura civile*, Napoli: Jovene, 1960, p. 190-213.

Andrioli 2008
Andrioli, V., *Studi sulle prove civili*, Milano: Giuffrè, 2008.

Ansanelli 2009
Ansanelli, V., 'Comparazione e ricomparazione in tema di expert witness testimony', *Rivista di diretto processuale*, 2009, p. 713-723.

Beghini 1997
Beghini, R., *La prova per testimoni nel rito civile*, Padova: Cedam, 1997.

Bove 2011
Bove, M., *Il sapere tecnico nel processo civile*, available at: <www.judicium.it>.

Brint 1994
Brint, S., *In an Age of Experts: The Changing Role of Professionals in Politics and Public Life*, Princeton: Princeton University Press, 1994.

Browne, Williamson & Barkacs 2002
Browne, M.N., Williamson, C.L. & Barkacs, L.L., 'The Perspectival Nature of Expert Testimony in the Unites States, England, Korea and France', *Connecticut Journal of International Law*, 2002, Vol. 18, p. 55-102.

Cappelletti 1962
Cappelletti, M., *La testimonianza della parte nel sistema dell'oralità*, Milano: Giuffrè, 1962.

Carnelutti 1957
Carnelutti, F., 'Il testimonio, questo sconosciuto', *Rivista di diretto processuale*, 1957, p. 177-185.

Cavallone 1991
Cavallone, B., *Il giudice e la prova nel processo civile*, Padova: Cedam, 1991.

Chiarloni 1994
Chiarloni, S., 'Per la chiarezza di idee in tema di analisi comparata dei testimoni', *Rivista di diretto processuale*, 1994, p. 382-394.

Comoglio 2010
Comoglio, L.P., *Le prove civili*, Torino: Utet, 2010.

Comoglio, Ferri & Taruffo 2008
Comoglio, L.P., Ferri, C. & Taruffo, M., *Lezioni sul processo civile*, Bologna: Il Mulino, 2008.

Denti 1962
Denti, V., 'Testimonianza tecnica', *Rivista di diretto processuale*, 1962, p. 9-18.

Dondi 1996a
Dondi, A., 'Prova testimoniale (c.p.c.)', in: Aa.Vv., *Digesto delle Discipline privatistiche - Sezione civile.*, XVI, Torino: Utet, 1996, p. 40-64.

Dondi 1996b
Dondi, A., 'Paradigmi processuali ed "expert witness testimony" nel diritto statunitense', *Rivista trimestrale di diritto procedura civile*, 1996, p. 261-285.

Dones 1962
Dones, C., *Struttura e funzione della consulenza tecnica*, Milano: Giuffrè, 1962.

Franchi 1959
Franchi, G., *La perizia civile*, Padova: Cedam, 1959.

Gibiino 1971
Gibiino, S., *La prova testimoniale nel processo civile*, Napoli: Jovene, 1971.

Giudiceandrea 1961
Giudiceandrea, N., 'Consulente tecnico', in: Aa.Vv., *Enciclopedia del Diritto*, Milano: Giuffrè, 1961, p. 531-540.

Gross 1991
Gross, S.R., 'Expert Evidence', *Wisconsin Law Review*, 1991, p. 1113-1232.

Imwinkelried 1993
Imwinkelried, E., 'The Daubert Decision and the Admissibility of Scientific Evidence: The Supreme Court Chooses the Right Piece for All the Evidentiary Puzzles', *St. John's Journal of Legal Commentary*, 1993, Vol. 9, p. 5-22.

Jensen 1993
Jensen, E.G., 'When "Hired Guns" Backfire: The Witness Immunity Doctrine and the Negligent Expert Witness', *University of Missouri at Kansas City Law Review*, 1993, p. 185-207.

Krislov 1962
Krislov, S., 'The Amicus Curiae Brief: From Friendship to Advocacy', *Yale Law Journal*, 1962, Vol. 72, p. 694-721.

Laudisa 1991
Laudisa, L., 'Prova testimoniale, I Diritto processuale civile', in: Aa.Vv., *Enciclopedia Giuridica Treccani*, XXVIII, Roma: Istituto della Enciclopedia Italiana, 1991, p. 1-12.

Laughlin 1992
Laughlin, S., 'When Students Confront the Experts: Toward Critical Thinking', *English Journal*, 1992, Vol. 81, p. 72-75.

Lombardo 2007
Lombardo, L., 'La scienza e il giudice nella ricostruzione del fatto', *Rivista di diretto processuale*, 2007, p. 35-62.

Mandrioli 2009
Mandrioli, C., *Diritto processuale civile*, II, Torino: Giappichelli, 2009.

Marzocchi 1977
Marzocchi, P., 'La prova testimoniale', *Rivista trimestrale di diritto procedura civile*, 1977, p. 410-480.

Molfese 2003
Molfese, G., *Il consulente tecnico in materia civile*, Padova: Cedam, 2003.

Nappi 2007
Nappi, A., 'Comments to Article 194', in: Lattanzi, G. & Lupo, E. (eds.), *Codice di procedura penale - Rassegna di giurisprudenza e di dottrina*, Milano: Giuffrè, 2007, p. 97-100.

Patti 2001
Patti, S., 'Prova testimoniale. Presunzioni, Artt. 2721-2729', in: Scialoja, A. & Branca, G. (eds.), *Commentario al codice civile*, Bologna: Zanichelli, 2001, p. 1-149.

Protettì & Protettì 1999
Protettì, E. & Protettì, M., *La consulenza tecnica nel processo civile*, Milano: Giuffrè, 1999.

Spiazzi 1986
Spiazzi, D., 'Prova testimoniale (dir. proc. civ.)', in: Aa.Vv., *Novissimo Digesto Italiano*, App., VI, Torino: Unione Tipografico-Editrice Torinese, 1986, p. 84-85.

Sundby 1997
Sundby, S.E., 'The Jury as Critic: An Empirical Look at How Capital Juries Perceive Expert and Lay Testimony', *Virginia Law Review*, 1997, Vol. 83, p. 1109-1187.

Taruffo 1988
Taruffo, M., 'Prova testimoniale, a) diritto processiale civile', in: Aa.Vv., *Enciclopedia del Diritto*, XXXVII, Milano: Giuffrè, 1988, p. 729-758.

M. Bina

INSPECTION BY THE COURT AS A MEANS OF EVIDENCE IN ITALY AND THE *NOTORIUM FACTI PERMANENTIS*: A BALANCE BETWEEN EFFICIENCY AND DUE PROCESS OF LAW

1. Introduction

This contribution discusses the problems relating to the efficiency of fact-gathering, the quality of adjudication and due process of law. Article 111 of the Italian Constitution (as modified in 2001) addresses the principle of due process of law (*giusto processo*). It provides that 'justice has to be administered by a fair trial regulated by the law'. Various academics have stated that this article should be interpreted in such a way that it encompasses the right to a fair and public hearing within a reasonable time before an independent and impartial court established by law.[1] Others, however, are of the opinion that due process of law in relation to Article 111 only implies that the court must seek the truth, and establish the facts relevant for the judgment.[2]

The latter reading of Article 111 fuels the controversy between 'truth-lovers' and 'veriphobes' in the theory of civil procedure,[3] and raises it onto a constitutional level. The truth-lovers are in the majority. They explain their reading of Article 111 by asserting that litigation has to be a truth-finding tool. Consequently, according to them, due process of law requires a limitation of exclusionary rules regarding evidence, and an increase of the court's powers to take evidence on its own motion.

In this chapter the relationship between truth and due process of law will be studied in relation to inspection by the court (*l'ispezione*). As a matter of fact, such inspection is a means of evidence which allows us to clarify this relationship better than by studying oral or documentary evidence.

1 Comoglio 2002, p. 702-758; Aa.Vv. 2003; Proto Pisani 2000, col. 241 *et seq.*; Lanfranchi 2001; Tarzia 2001, p. 1 *et seq.*; Bove 2002, p. 495 *et seq.*

2 See Chiarloni 2009, p. 403-417; Taruffo 2009, p. 116 *et seq.*

3 Among the truth-lovers, see Taruffo 2009; Taruffo 2010, p. 995-1011. Among the veriphobes, see Cavallone 2008, p. 947-983; Cavallone 2010a; Dittrich 2011.

2. Articles 115 and 118 of the Italian Code of Civil Procedure

In Italy, the judge can order a inspection by the court *ex officio*, which is a typical feature not only of continental European civil procedure,[4] but also of procedure in common law countries.[5] An inspection has various characteristics that differentiate it from other means of evidence.

In the Italian Code of Civil Procedure (CCP), court inspection[6] is governed by Article 118(1), which states:

> 'The court may order the parties or a third party to allow the inspection of their body or the things in their possession when this is absolutely necessary in order to have full knowledge of the facts of the case, as long as the inspection can be carried out without causing serious damage to the parties or to a third party, and without forcing them to violate one of the privileges covered by Articles 351 and 352 of the Code of Criminal Procedure'.[7]

Articles 258 to 262 govern the technical procedural features of court inspection, such as: the content of the order for inspection and the discretionary powers of the court to order it (Article 258); the right to request that inspection be carried out by another court or by an expert who may replace the court (Articles 259 and 260);[8] the way the results of the inspection are recorded (Article 261); the powers of the court regarding the way an inspection is executed, in particular powers aimed at ensuring the effectiveness of the order for inspection and the completeness of the results of the inspection (Article 262).

4 In Germany, §144 ZPO provides that the court may order a visit to the scene; see Walter 2005; Caponi 2007, p. 265 *et seq.* More clearly, see § 368 of the Austrian ZPO. In France, Arts. 179-183 *Code de procédure civile* govern the *vérifications personelles du juge:* the court can order an inspection when it thinks that it is necessary; see Cadiet & Jeuland 2009, p. 418 *et seq.*; Vincent & Guinchard 2003, p. 824 *et seq.*; Couchez 2008, p. 350 *et seq.* In Spain, Arts. 353-359 *Ley de Enjuiciamiento Civil* 1/2000 govern the *Reconocimiento judicial*: Art. 354(2), gives the court a discretionary power to order an inspection which is necessary or desirable (Art. 354(1)). See for a comparative study: Taruffo 2006, p. 431 *et seq.*; Fabiani 2008, p. 349-522; Nagel 1967, p. 356 *et seq.*

5 On the inherent power of the court to order an inspection, see Wigmore 1940, IV, p. 268 *et seq.*; Cleary 1972, p. 537 *et seq.*; Nokes 1962, p. 449 *et seq.*; Weinstein *et al.*, 1988, p. 131 *et seq.*; Dunn 1965, p. 36, 142 *et seq.*; Wendorf 1963, p. 392; Malek 2005, p. 271 *et seq.*

6 For a general overview on the inspection in Italian legal scholarship, see Taruffo 2011a; Comoglio 2010, p. 813-838; Trisorio Liuzzi 1993, p. 118 *et seq.*; Balena 1990, p. 1-8; Finocchiaro 1972; Massari 1963; Cavallone 1991b, p. 197 *et seq.*

7 Author's translation. Today, after the new Italian Code of Criminal Procedure of 1988 repealed Arts. 351 and 352, references to privileges can be found in Arts. 200, 201 and 202.

8 For the purposes of this text, there are no practical differences between the inspection carried out by an expert charged by the court, or by a single member of the tribunal, and an inspection performed by the court, as is underscored by Cavallone 1991b, p. 199 *et seq.*, n. 41. The issue is discussed by Satta 1959-1962, II, 1, p. 288; D'Onofrio 1957, p. 438; Luiso 2007, p. 161 *et seq.*; Massari 1963, p. 196. See also Cass. 3.2.1993, n. 1318, in *Giur. it.* 1993, I, 1, 1431.

Another important rule can be found in Article 115 CCP, entitled 'Party presentation of evidence':[9]

> '1. Unless provided by the law, the court shall base its judgment on the evidence submitted by the parties or by the public prosecutor,[10] as well as on the facts which are not specifically denied by the opposing party.
> 2. However, the court may also base its judgment on notorious facts, without the need to take any evidence'.

Comparing Article 118 CCP with Article 115 CCP, the first aspect which deserves attention is that Article 118 gives the court the power to order an inspection of persons, places and things on its own motion, which is an important exception to Article 115 and the principle of party presentation of evidence, which is traditionally considered, by case law and scholars, as one of the formative principles of Italian civil procedure. This exception will be examined in more detail below.

3. The Meaning of Party Presentation According to Article 115 CCP

Italian academics argue over whether Article 115(1) CCP, as presently formulated, should be interpreted as containing the principle of party presentation of evidence (*disponibilità delle prove,* party presentation of evidence). These academics traditionally assert that this provision actually transposes the Roman principle *iudex iudicare debet iuxta allegata et probata* into the law, interpreted by modern doctrine with the added reference to *probata partium,* and the omission of the final part of the principle *non secundum conscientiam.*[11] According to Italian doctrine,[12] the rule of Article 115 corresponds to the German *Verhandlungsmaxime,* which is one of the formative principles of the *Dispositionsmaxime.*[13] This principle comes together with the principle of party prosecution[14] – *ne procedeat iudex ex officio* – in Article 99 CCP formulated as *principio della domanda,* and the principle that the judge may not go

9 See further in Taruffo 2011c, p. 447-519; Fabiani 2008, p. 228-345. For the history of this rule, see Cavallone 1991a.

10 See Arts. 60 and 70 CCP, which give the public prosecutor some powers in civil matters involving public interest, such as the power to intervene in civil proceedings.

11 For a historical study of the principle and its mistaken interpretation, see Nörr 1967; Picó i Junoy 2007a, p. 35 *et seq.*; Picó i Junoy 2007b, p. 1497 *et seq.*

12 In spite of the differences between the authors, usually two independent principles are distinguished: the first principle implies that the parties have full control over their substantive rights, and the power to exercise them or not; the second principle is technical in nature and concerns the parties' power in matters of evidence. The distinction coincides with that between the *Verhandlungmaxime* and the *Untersuchungsmaxime.* See Carnacini 1951, p. 695 *et seq.*; Cappelletti 1962, Vol. I, p. 303 *et seq.*; Benvenuti 1953, p. 19 *et seq.* See also Millar 1923, p. 9 *et seq.*

13 The *Prozessmaximen* originate with Gönner (Gönner 1804). They had an unlucky history in the theory of civil procedure on the European Continent. See, for a general survey, Cavallone 1991a, p. 22 *et seq.* (German scholarship), and p. 29 *et seq.* (Italian scholarship).

14 *Ibidem,* p. 19.

beyond the statements of case of the parties - *ne eat iudex ultra petita partium* - in Article 112 CCP formulated as *corrispondenza tra il chiesto e il pronunciato*.

Italian scholars have not reached consensus on the true meaning of Article 115 CCP, both on the level of principles[15] and on the level of its strict legal meaning.[16] Some claim that Article 115 grants the parties the right to take evidence;[17] others state that this rule acknowledges the prohibition of considering evidence that was not submitted by the parties[18] (the prohibition for the judge to use his private knowledge).[19]

Regardless of the reading of the Article 115, it should be stressed that case law uniformly recognizes the principle of party presentation of evidence. The Italian courts strictly apply the Roman principle *iudex iudicare debet iuxta allegata et probata partium*: Italian judges, in fact, rarely make use of their powers to introduce evidence, preferring to leave it to the initiative of the parties.[20] This is primarily due to cultural reasons, as judges consider that their powers to take evidence on their own motion could possibly conflict with their impartiality. There are also more practical reasons, related to the inefficiency of the rules on the presentation of evidence.[21] Thus, judges prefer using alternative avenues to influence the evidentiary stage, e.g. by way of the burden of proof rules (see Article 2697 of the Italian Civil Code) or the 'principle of not objecting', recently codified in Article 115(1), which allows the court to justify a decision by stating that a particular statement was 'not specifically denied' (*relevatio ab onere probandi*).[22] Moreover, case law follows a strict reading of the rules on preclusion in the proceedings,[23] which are regarded as inflexible and not adaptable to the particulars of the case. On the one hand, these rules state that the parties should introduce evidence only in specific stages of the proceedings; on the other hand, they state that the powers of the judge to order the taking of evidence *ex officio* cannot be used to circumvent deadlines imposed by the law[24] or to fill in a gap in the available evidence.[25]

15 The fallacies in the theory of the *Prozessmaximen* are demonstrated by Cavallone 2001a; Cavallone 2001c, p. 289-322; Bomsdorf 1971. See also Fabiani 2008, p. 525 *et seq*.

16 For a critical approach from the perspective of hermeneutics and logic, see Taruffo 2011b, p. 101-139.

17 Ricci 1974, p. 380 *et seq*.; differently, Cavallone 2001c.

18 Cavallone 2010b, p. 861 *et seq*.; Cavallone 1991c, p. 297 *et seq*.; Cavallone 1991a, p. 85 and 95, who joins Liebman's ideas expressed in Liebman 1960, p. 551 *et seq*. Liebman holds that the rationale of the principle of party presentation of evidence can be found in the need to assure the court's impartiality as a universal procedural value. Traditional scholarship criticises Liebman's views; see Montesano 1978, p. 191; Denti 1965, p. 30 *et seq*.; Taruffo 2011b.

19 See, in general, Cavallone 2010b, p. 861-871; Stein 1893; Radin 1932, p. 506 *et seq*.; Morgan 1944, p. 269 *et seq*.

20 See Denti 1968.

21 See Dittrich 2011, p. 108 *et seq*.

22 Patti 2011, p. 101-139; Tedoldi 2011, p. 76-96.

23 See Attardi 1985, p. 893 *et seq*.; Proto Pisani & Tombari Fabbrini 1995.

24 An exception is the rule that gives to the parties that do not respect a deadline the power to ask the court to fix another deadline to exercise their power. The 2009 Reform of Civil Procedure shifted the rule stated in Art. 184 bis CCP to the new Art. 153(2) CCP.

25 For a general survey, see Laudisa 2006, p. 227 and Dittrich 2011, § 6.

A rational explanation of the court's power to order an inspection on its own motion cannot disregard the approach discussed above. There is definitely a compatibility problem between the usual interpretation of the principle of party presentation in case law, and the powers of the court to order an inspection on its own motion, i.e. regardless of the parties' wishes.

In procedural scholarship different attempts were made to resolve this conflict: most scholars[26] simply hold that the relationship between Article 115 and Article 118 can be viewed as a general rule (Article 115) and an exception (Article 118); but some scholars[27] try to further explore the issue, arguing that Article 118 is a rational extension of the principle of party presentation, grounded on logical and practical reasons. Both theories will be briefly presented.

4. The Court's Power to Order an Inspection

According to one theory the court's power to order an inspection *ex officio* was introduced due to a political decision made by the Legislature.[28] This power is considered to be an exception to the principle of party presentation of evidence.[29] It may therefore only be used as a measure of last resort for proving a disputed fact, namely if other evidence is not available. Consequently, court inspection would be an example of a *best evidence rule* in an *exclusionary* way.[30]

Another theory assumes that the power of the court to order an inspection may be exercised independently and not linked to the principles of party presentation and the court's power to take evidence *ex officio*. This theory is rooted in the criticisms launched at the *Maximen* method.[31] As a matter of fact, finding an explanation for the court's power to order an inspection on its own motion unrelated to the principles would be proof of the uselessness of the *Maximen* method.

As far as the *pars destruens* is concerned, the common interpretation of the requirement that the inspection should be 'absolutely necessary' is not convincing. Historical research shows that the introduction of this requirement had a contingent nature: its aim was to limit the practice of judges ordering an inspection in order to profit from the available subsistence allowance[32] (at least, this is the reason

26 For details and quotations of views of individual scholars, see Cavallone 1991b, p. 184 *et seq.*

27 See Cavallone 1991b, p. 197 *et seq.*; Ferrari 2002, p. 314 *et seq.*

28 For a different decision see Art. 244 CCP, which rules witness testimony; or Art. 210 CCP, which rules the Court's power to order the production of documents. Notwithstanding, the academics try to read this rule giving to the Court the power to order the production of documents *ex officio*. See Graziosi 2003; Cavallone 1991e, p. 664 *et seq.*; La China 1989, p. 2 *et seq.*; La China 1966, p. 706; La China 1960.

29 Andrioli 1957, Vol. I, p. 346; Carnelutti 1956, I, p. 216, n. 226; Finocchiaro 1972, p. 951; Massari 1963, p. 190; Trisorio Liuzzi 1993, § 3; Comoglio 2010, p. 825; Taruffo 2011a, p. 583.

30 See Ferrari 2002, p. 315.

31 For a critical approach to the *Maximen* method, see the fundamental work by Cavallone 1991. In Germany, see Bomsdorf 1971.

32 See Cavallone 1991b, p. 199 *et seq.*; Lessona 1927, p. 9 *et seq.*, for a general survey of the old procedural legislation.

mentioned in the text of the French Code Louis or 1667 Ordinance, Title XXI, Article 1).[33] In addition, comparative analysis shows that the requirements that needed to be met before an inspection would be allowed, were introduced in order to avoid abuses, not for reasons linked to the inquisitorial powers of the court.[34] This seems to be confirmed by the praxis of the Italian courts: the inspection is ordered without paying particular attention to the requirement that it is 'absolutely necessary' - the court usually entrusts an officer to carry out the inspection without specifying why such an inspection is 'absolutely necessary' (although it must be admitted that this is different where the inspection of persons is concerned due to reasons linked to the protection of their privacy). This being the case, a different reason has to be assigned to the existence of the requirement that the inspection is 'absolutely necessary'. Most likely its reason of existence should be linked to the idea that the court cannot order an inspection if the parties involved would suffer a 'serious harm'; when the harm is insignificant or non-existent an inspection may take place.[35]

After having examined the requirement that an inspection should be 'absolutely necessary', another possible link between the principle of party presentation of evidence and court inspection can be studied. The analysis of the historical background of court inspection may help us to reveal a different relationship, namely between court inspection and so-called notorious facts[36] or *notorium facti permanentis*.[37] Facts are notorious because they are part of common knowledge. These facts are simple, clear and evident to the community where the litigation is situated. As demonstrated in literature,[38] in Roman law the court would

33 Cavallone 1991b, p. 199 *et seq.*; Lessona 1927, p. 9 *et seq*. See also Art. 295 of the old French Code of Civil Procedure, which preferred an inspection by an expert to a court inspection: Vincent & Guinchard 2003, p. 824 *et seq.*; Garsonnet & Cezar-Bru 1912, T. 2, p. 2, Vol. I, p. 596 *et seq*. and n. 5.

34 In common law jurisdictions, ordering an inspection is at the court's discretion. This power is motivated by the wish to avoid abuses. See Wigmore 1940, p. 277; Cleary 1972, p. 537; Jones 1972, p. 55 *et seq.*; Wendorf 1963, p. 389 *et seq.*

35 See Liebman 2007, p. 388; Balena 1990, p. 4; Cavallone 1991b, p. 199; Ferrari 2002, p. 316.

36 On the doctrine of *notoria*, see F. Stein's seminal book *Das Private Wissen des Richters*, (Stein 1893, p. 74 *et seq.*); Tiranti 1903; Calamandrei 1925; Allorio 1933; Mazzarella 1934; Ferrara 1940; De Stefano 1947; De Stefano 1967, p. 999-1013; Micheli 1945; Montesano 1947; Denti 1947; Leone 1954; Carnelutti 1959, p. 639; Bertolino 1965; Taruffo 1967, p. 438 *et seq.*; Dittrich 2005. For the history of the doctrine on notorious facts, see Levy 1939, III, 5, p. 33 *et seq.*; Levy 1965, p. 160 *et seq.*; Ghisalberti 1957; Ghisalberti 1967.

37 The doctrine on notorious facts originates in Canon law (see Ghisalberti 1967, p. 885 *et seq.*). It goes back to the first letter of Saint Paul's to the Corinthians (5.1.5) aiming at punishing a public scandal (see Levy 1939, p. 33). According to Levy's reconstruction (Levy 1939, p. 41 *et seq.*), the subdivision between *notorium facti* and *notorium iuris* is due to Tancredus; it was refined by Giovanni Teutonico, *Glossa Manifesta* ad col. 15, C.II, q. 1, who added a sort of *notorium praesumptionis*. The authors, then, usually distinguished *notorium facti* in *notorium facti permanentis sive continui*, a continuously and persistently existing fact; *notorium facti actu transeunti sive momentanei*, which belonged to collective memory; and *notorium facti interpolati*, a continuous repetition of an act.

38 See Levy 1939, p. 25 *et seq.*, 43 *et seq.*; Cavallone 1991b, p. 202 *et seq.*; Leone 1954, p. 68; Ferrari 2002, p. 309 *et seq.*; Pertile 1900, Vol. VI, 1, p. 408.

have access to places for inspection in specific actions (e.g. in the *actio sacramenti in rem* the *vindicatio* had to take place at the site were the property was situated). Inspection was also indispensable in actions to ascertain boundaries.[39]

During the *ius commune* period court inspection came to be referred to as *inspectio ocularis.* By way of this inspection, the court could verify the physical characteristics of an object.[40] Once they were classified as *notoria,* such facts no longer needed proof, and the court could ground its judgment on them.

These considerations are still valid today: Articles 118 and 258 CCP,[41] referring to 'persons', 'places' and 'things', embrace a wide range of situations - from which, it seems, we can only exclude documents.[42] Court inspection may be used to prove all the existing facts that may be alleged by the parties[43] and perceived by the judge in an out-of-court situation.[44] Therefore, it seems that the fundamental characteristics of court inspection have remained the same, although the present rules have widened its field of application compared to the historical *inspectio ocularis,* or to the rules on access to places for inspection.[45] The court's power to

39 Cavallone 1991b, p. 204 *et seq.;* Lessona 1927, p. 5 *et seq.;* Keller 1966, VI, p. 57 *et seq.*

40 The theory is grounded on two arguments: (1) in the Middle Ages evidence could not be provided by *inspectio ocularis* nor by access to places; these types of proof were regulated differently in the broader classification of *evidentia rei* or *aspectus corporis;* (2) the definition of notorious facts given by medieval authors coincided with the object of the inspection. See the authors mentioned in n. 39.

41 In the old Italian Code of Civil Procedure, the relation between court inspection and the *notorium facti permanentis* was stricter. The 1865 CCP did not have a general rule for court inspection; Arts. 271-281 only governed access to places ordered by the court on its own motion when this was 'necessary to inspect places or things'. See Andrioli 1937, p. 77 *et seq.;* Chiovenda 1965, p. 841 *et seq.*

42 See Cavallone 1991b, p. 218, 224 *et seq.;* Balena 1990, p. 4; Comoglio 2010, p. 824, n. 45; Satta 1959-1962, p. 472; La China 1960, p. 163-164; Verde 2008, p. 123. Different, Finocchiaro 1972, p. 952; Massari 1963, p. 194; Besso 2004, p. 174-175; Andrioli 1957, Vol. I, p. 345; Grasso 1973, p. 1331; Graziosi 2003, p. 88. The Supreme Court rules out the possibility of a court inspection of documents: Cass., 5.3.1970, n. 540, in *Repertorio Foro it.* 1970, I, 2117; Cass., 16.4.1997, n. 3260, in *Rep. Foro it.* 1997, item *Esibizione delle prove,* n. 3; Cass., 19.11.1994, n. 9839, in *Rep. Foro it.* 1994, item *Prova civile in genere,* n. 22; Cass., 3.12.1994, n. 10411, in *Rep. Foro it.* 1994, item *Ispezione giudiziale,* n. 1.

43 In Italy, Art. 112 Code of Civil Procedure governs the burden of the presentation of *facta probanda* (or facts in issue), stating that these facts have to be presented by the parties. A party's burden of presentation of *facta probantia* (or facts relevant to the issue) is probably governed by Art. 115, moderated by the so-called *acquiring powers* of the court. See Cavallone 2001d, p. 145-154; Cavallone 2001b, p. 221, who criticises the theory of Cappelletti 1962, vol. I, p. 351. Cappelletti asserts that the court has the power to find and to acquire notorious facts relevant to the issue because these are outside the field of application of Art. 112.

44 This is the background of the doctrine which distinguishes *Beweismittel* (*mezzi di prova*), regarding historical facts, from *Erkenntnissmittel* (*accertamenti*), regarding facts existing at the time of the proceedings. See Heusler 1879, p. 237 *et seq.;* Satta 1959-1962, Vol. I, p. 454; for a global view, see Cavallone 1991b, p. 210 *et seq.*

45 We can read Art. 261(2) CCP, which governs the judicial reconstruction of the events (*esperimento giudiziale*) in the same manner. This rule gives the court the power to order *ex officio* a reconstruction of the facts or events when this is necessary to determine whether something has taken place in a certain way (also allowing the use of film or photographic reproduction). In this case, also, the aim is to prove a fact presented by the parties but, unlike →

order an inspection of places, of people, of physical characteristics, or of objects is practical and appropriate, because as a result the court may immediately perceive these facts; an attempt to verify them through oral evidence or other evidence would be illogical. As the facts to be established, i.e. the target of the court inspection, have to be argued by the parties, the inspection ordered by the court may only complete the proof-taking and does not add anything new to the facts already presented by the parties.[46] In this way, court inspection seems to implement the rule of completeness, which follows the best evidence principle.[47]

Another argument for our theory is drawn from a comparative perspective: in the American adversarial system the court may order an inspection on its own motion, both in jury and non-jury trials.[48] Therefore, we can assume that the court's power to take evidence *ex officio*, which exists both in the common law and the civil law, has an extra-legal ground which surpasses the current law or policy options. Assuming that different procedural law families know the same rule, the ground of that rule must be found on a more fundamental level. The court's power to order an inspection seems to be a useful way to avoid a contrast between the facts as reflected by the judgment and notorious facts, as, most probably, the community would not accept a judgment which is in conflict with easily verifiable facts.[49]

In short: the court's power to order an inspection *ex officio* is not an exception to the principle of party presentation. It is a consequence of logical and practical reasoning: an inspection of physical evidence is preferred to witness testimony describing the physical characteristics of a material object. It also has an anthropological background: the community would not accept a decision which would conflict with facts that everyone can readily verify.

5. Court Inspection and Respect for Procedural Fairness

After having explained court inspection as a way to verify notorious facts and, today, as a way to verify an existing extra-procedural fact which can be perceived by everyone (including the judge), we can inquire whether in this matter the Lawmaker has found a right balance between efficiency and due process of law. In other words, we have to establish whether court inspection is an efficient and necessary means of evidence. Moreover, we will have to deal with the issue whether court inspection denies the traditional principle *notoria non sunt probanda*, which teaches us that notorious facts do not need to be supported by evidence.

court inspection, in which the perception is static, judicial reconstruction gives a dynamic perception of the fact. See Andrioli 1960, p. 852; Comoglio 2010, p. 837 *et seq.*; Pasquali 1980, p. 174 *et seq.*; Massari 1963, p. 187; Balena 1990, p. 6; Ferrari 2002, p. 320. Differently, Luiso 2009, Vol. II, p. 162, who underscores that judicial reconstruction is only a simulation of the facts to be proven.

46 See Cavallone 1991b, p. 221.

47 In this way, Ferrari 2002, p. 315.

48 See the authors quoted in n. 5 above.

49 Levy-Bruhl 1964, p. 29; Nesson 1985.

To begin with, when someone affirms that notorious facts do not require to be proven,[50] he holds that the court does not need to take evidence to demonstrate the truth of the notorious facts. Assuming that notorious facts are facts that belong to public knowledge (i.e. to verified knowledge available to all), proof of the truth of notorious facts is an out-of-court proof and is based on the fact itself.[51] The court's duty, therefore, is to check the notorious fact; but once the notoriety of the fact is verified (i.e. when its notorious nature is confirmed) it must be treated as a formal, definitive proof which the court cannot freely evaluate. It remains to be explained why court inspection is different - why it may still be necessary to have court inspection as proof of facts that are obvious.

It is pointed out that the *inspectio ocularis* was in the Middle Ages used to reach a compromise between the needs of logic and psychology on one side, and of the needs which are subject to the principle of party disposition on the other side. In other words, court inspection may be defined as a middle ground between the prohibition of personal knowledge, and the ratification of the judgment by the community. The court's power to take notorious facts into consideration *ex officio* is a principle which only emerged over time. The court's power to order an inspection on its own motion appeared to be in history the most useful instrument for finding facts which, otherwise, could not have been used as the basis for the decision-making.[52] Today, after accepting the principle that the court can freely consider notorious facts, court inspection still appears to be a mediated solution between the anthropological and cultural reasons outlined above, and the need to observe procedural fairness, which is one of the key elements of the due process of law concept. We are referring here to the necessity to take evidence in the proceedings and to the right of a party to be heard and to have an opportunity to challenge all factual inferences. The judge cannot base his findings solely on its personal, private observations; he cannot carry out the inspection of physical evidence without notifying the parties or without facts introduced by the parties.[53]

The parties' right to take part in the inspection seems to be *a fortiori* supported by the fact that parties have the right to be heard when the judge takes notice of a question of law on his own motion. This is confirmed by a recent amendment to Article 101 of the Code of Civil Procedure,[54] asserting that the judge has to inform the parties and allow them to challenge his conclusions every time he intends to pass a judgment grounded on legal provisions relied on *ex officio*. Assuming that the

50 This rule originates in Canon law, although this is disputed by some scholars, see Ghisalberti 1957, p. 437 *et seq*.

51 See De Stefano 1967, p. 1007 *et seq*.

52 Cavallone 1991b, p. 203, n. 46; Cavallone 2010b, p. 862 *et seq*., who interprets the use of notorious facts as an exception to the prohibition against the use of personal knowledge.

53 See Wigmore 1940, p. 282 *et seq*.; Jones 1972, p. 64 *et seq*. See also among French academics Cadiet & Jeuland 2009, p. 418 *et seq*.; Couchez 2008, p. 351; Le Foyer de Costil & Le Foyer de Costil, 1986; Chevallier 1962, p. 5 *et seq*.

54 Art. 101 CCP acknowledges a rule from case law that forbids the judge to pass a so-called 'third way judgment' (*decisione della 'terza via'*): if the judge intends to justify his decision by a legal point raised *ex officio*, he has to set a deadline for the parties to deposit briefs containing observations on this legal point.

court has to observe the formalities of procedural fairness in the *iura novit curia* field, an area which is, as official knowledge, traditionally extraneous to the court's personal knowledge, it is indisputable that the same applies to notorious facts, which also cannot be established without allowing the parties the opportunity to be heard. Finally, in the case of another type of notorious facts, so-called historical notorious facts, the situation is the same. Again, it is necessary that the judge observes procedural fairness, and allows the parties to challenge his findings before a fact is declared common knowledge.[55] This is obvious when the fact is (co-) perceived by a party; but when the court takes notice of such facts on its own motion, it has to invite the parties to challenge its conclusions and inferences. The purpose of this is both to ensure the active participation of the parties in the process of decision-making, and to ensure the possibility of review of the judgment before a higher court.[56]

It follows that the court has to order an inspection even if the judge is able to verify certain matters through his own personal perception, because only in such a way can due process of law be guaranteed.

6. Conclusions: Court Inspection and Due Process of Law

From the point of view of procedural fairness, court inspection strikes a balance between due process of law and the efficiency of the civil proceedings. The inspection is the best means available to verify physical evidence which cannot be brought before the court. The provisions of law which insist on the parties' right to be heard and to be present at the inspection assure impartiality of the court by forbidding the use of the personal knowledge and views of the judge.
However, from a fact-finder's point of view, the author of the chapter cannot concur with the statement that the power to order a court inspection *ex officio* is aimed at seeking the truth regarding the facts relevant to the case. The historical origins of the inspection, which emerged as a way to verify the *notorium facti permanentis* in previous centuries, shows that court inspection was introduced as a useful way to make sure that the local community would accept the judgment. An indiscriminate use of the court's power to order an inspection *ex officio* could violate the prohibition of the use of personal knowledge. Pursuant to Article 118 CCP, the court's power to order an inspection has to be limited to the facts presented by the parties. The court cannot use its powers to circumvent the limitations regarding facts that may be proved by evidence, not even by invoking the necessity of truth-finding.

55 See Dittrich 2011, p. 108 *et seq.*, especially § 7, referring to knowledge acquired using the Internet.

56 In the U.S. this duty is called *Judicial Notice*, and is regulated by Rule 201 of the Federal Rules of Evidence. The common law, forbidding the use of personal knowledge by the court (or by the members of the jury), allows the court to take notice of some facts that are not in dispute, after having invited the parties to challenge these facts. The facts that the court can take notice of are considered to be notorious facts. See Weinstein *et al.* 1988, p. 1266 *et seq.*; Morgan 1944, p. 57, p. 269 *et seq*. See also, for England, Malek 2005, p. 65 *et seq*.

Bibliography

Allorio 1933
Allorio, E., 'Osservazioni sul fatto notorio', *Rivista di diritto processuale civile,* 1933, Vol. II, p. 3-17.

Andrioli 1937
Andrioli, V., 'Accesso giudiziale', in: *Nuovo digesto italiano,* Vol. I, Torino: Utet, 1937.

Andrioli 1957
Andrioli, V., *Commento al codice di procedura civile,* 3rd edn., Napoli: Jovene, 1957.

Andrioli 1960
Andrioli V., 'Esperimento giudiziario', in: *Novissimo digesto italiano,* Vol. I, Torino, Utet, 1960.

Attardi 1985
Attardi, A., 'Preclusione (principio di)', in: *Enciclopedia del diritto,* Vol. XXXIV, Milano: Giuffrè, 1985.

Balena 1990
Balena, G., 'Ispezione giudiziale. I) Diritto processuale civile', in: *Enciclopedia giuridica,* Vol. XVII, Roma: Treccani, 1990.

Benvenuti 1953
Benvenuti, F., *L'istruzione nel processo amministrativo,* Padova: Cedam, 1953.

Bertolino 1965
Bertolino, R., *Il notorio nell'ordinamento giuridico della Chiesa,* Torino: Giappichelli, 1965.

Besso 2004
Besso, C., *La prova prima del processo,* Torino: Giappichelli, 2004.

Bomsdorf 1971
Bomsdorf, F., *Prozessmaximen und Rechtswirklichkeit: Verhandlungs- und Untersuchungsmaxime im deutschen Zivilprozess: vom gemeinen Recht bis zur ZPO,* Berlin: Duncker & Humblot, 1971.

Bove 2002
Bove, M., 'Art. 111 Cost. e "giusto processo civile"', *Rivista di diritto processuale,* 2002, p. 479-522.

Cadiet & Jeuland 2009
Cadiet, L. & Jeuland, E., *Droit judiciaire privé,* Paris: Litec, 2009.

Calamandrei 1925
Calamandrei, P., 'Per la definizione del fatto notorio', *Rivista di diritto processuale civile*, 1925, Vol. I, p. 273-304. Also in: Cappelletti, M. (ed.), *Opere Giuridiche*, Vol. V, Napoli: Morano, 1965, p. 425-451.

Caponi 2007
Caponi, R., 'Note in tema di poteri probatori delle parti e del giudice nel processo civile tedesco dopo la riforma del 2001', in: Aa.Vv., *Atti del XXV convegno nazionale dell'Associazione italiana fra gli studiosi del processo civile tenutosi in Cagliari 7-8 ottobre 2005*, Milano: Giuffrè, 2007, p. 265-301.

Cappelletti 1962
Cappelletti, M., *La testimonianza della parte nel sistema dell'oralità*, Milano: Giuffrè, 1962.

Carnacini 1951
Carnacini, T., 'Tutela giurisdizionale e tecnica del processo', in: Carnelutti, F. *et al.* (eds.), *Studi in onore di E. Redenti nel 40° anno del suo insegnamento*, Vol. II, Milano: Giuffrè, 1951, p. 695-772.

Carnelutti 1956
Carnelutti, F., *Istituzioni del processo civile italiano*, 5th edn., Roma: Società editrice del Foro italiano, 1956.

Carnelutti 1959
Carnelutti, F., 'Massime d'esperienza e fatti notori', *Rivista di diritto processuale*, 1959, p. 639-640.

Cavallone 1991a
Cavallone, B., 'I poteri di iniziativa istruttoria del giudice civile. Premessa storico-critica', in: Cavallone B., *Il giudice e la prova nel processo civile*, Padova: Cedam, 1991, p. 1-98.

Cavallone 1991b
Cavallone, B., 'Le iniziative probatorie del giudice: limiti e fondamento. Ispezione giudiziale e consulenza tecnica', in: Cavallone, B., *Il giudice e la prova nel processo civile*, Padova: Cedam, 1991, p. 179-261.

Cavallone 1991c
Cavallone, B., 'Crisi delle Maximen e disciplina dell'istruzione probatoria', in: Cavallone, B., *Il giudice e la prova nel processo civile*, Padova: Cedam, 1991, p. 289-323.

Cavallone 1991d
Cavallone, B., 'Principio dispositivo, fatti secondarii e fatti "rilevabili d'ufficio"', in: Cavallone, B., *Il giudice e la prova nel processo civile*, Padova: Cedam, 1991, p. 99-179.

Cavallone 1991e
Cavallone B., 'Esibizione delle prove nel diritto processuale civile', in: *Digesto discipline privatistiche, sezione civile,* Vol. VII, Torino: Utet, 1991.

Cavallone 2008
Cavallone, B., 'Riflessioni sulla cultura della prova', *Rivista italiana di diritto e procedura penale,* 2008, p. 947-983.

Cavallone 2010a
Cavallone, B., 'In difesa della Veriphobia (considerazioni amichevolmente polemiche su un libro recente di Michele Taruffo)', *Rivista di diritto processuale,* 2010, p. 1-26.

Cavallone 2010b
Cavallone, B., 'Il divieto di utilizzazione della scienza privata del giudice', *Rivista di diritto processuale,* 2010, p. 861-873.

Chevallier 1962
Chevallier, J., 'Remarques sur l'utilisation par le juge de ses informations personelles', *Revue trimestrielle de droit civil,* 1962, p. 5 *et seq.*

Chiarloni 2009
Chiarloni, S., 'Giusto processo', in: *Enciclopedia del diritto,* Annali II, Tome I, Milano: Giuffrè, 2009.

Chiovenda 1965
Chiovenda, G., *Principii di diritto processuale civile,* 3rd edn., Napoli: Jovene, repr. 1965.

Civinini & Verardi 2001
Civinini, M.G. & Verardi, C.M. (eds.), *Il nuovo articolo 111 della Costituzione e il giusto processo civile: atti del convegno dell'Elba, 9-10 giugno 2000,* Milano: F. Angeli, 2003.

Cleary 1972
Cleary, E.W., *McCormick's Handbook of the Law of Evidence,* 2nd edn., St. Paul Minn.: West Publishing, 1972.

Comoglio 2002
Comoglio, L.P., 'Il "giusto processo" civile nella dimensione comparatistica', *Rivista di diritto processuale,* 2002, p. 702-758.

Comoglio 2010
Comoglio, L.P., *Le prove civili,* 3rd edn., Torino: Utet giuridica, 2010.

Couchez 2008
Couchez, G., *Procédure civile,* 15th edn., Paris: Sirey, Dalloz, 2008.

Denti 1947
Denti, V., 'Ancora sulla nozione di fatto notorio', *Giurisprudenza completa della corte suprema di cassazione sezioni civili*, 1947, p. 264-267.

Denti 1965
Denti, V., 'L'evoluzione del diritto delle prove nei processi civili contemporanei', *Rivista di diritto processuale*, 1965, p. 31-70.

Denti 1968
Denti, V., 'Una ricerca sulle prove nel processo civile', *Giurisprudenza italiana*, 1968, IV, col. 143 *et seq*.

De Stefano 1947
De Stefano, G., *Il notorio nel processo civile*, Milano: Giuffrè, 1947.

De Stefano 1967
De Stefano, G., 'Fatto notorio. b) Diritto privato', in: *Enciclopedia del diritto*, Vol. XVI, Milano: Giuffrè, 1967.

Dittrich 2005
Dittrich, L., 'Appunti per uno studio del fatto notorio giudiziale', in: Aa.Vv., *Studi di diritto processuale civile in onore di Giuseppe Tarzia*, Milano: Giuffrè, 2005, p. 819-841.

Dittrich 2011
Dittrich, L., 'La ricerca della verità nel processo civile: profili evolutivi in tema di prova testimoniale, consulenza tecnica e fatto notorio', *Rivista diritto processuale*, 2011, p. 108-125.

D'Onofrio 1957
D'Onofrio, P., *Commento al codice di procedura civile*, 4th edn., Torino: Utet, 1957.

Dunn 1965
Dunn, S., 'View by Court and Jury', *Mississipi Law Journal*, 1965, 36, p. 142-154.

Fabiani 2008
Fabiani, E., *I poteri istruttori del giudice civile. I. Contributo al chiarimento del dibattito*, Napoli: Edizioni scientifiche italiane, 2008.

Ferrara 1940
Ferrara, L., 'Relatività del notorio', *Foro italiano*, 1940, section I, col. 966 *et seq*.

Ferrari 2002
Ferrari, F., *La 'prova migliore'. Un'indagine di diritto comparato*, Milano: Giuffrè, 2002.

Finocchiaro 1972
Finocchiaro, A., 'Ispezione giudiziale. a) Diritto processuale civile', in: *Enciclopedia del diritto*, Vol. XXII, Milano: Giuffrè, 1972.

Garsonnet & Cezar-Bru 1912
Garsonnet, E. & Cezar-Bru, Ch., *Traité théorique et pratique de procédure civile et commerciale en justice de paix et devant les conseils de prud'hommes*, 3rd edn., Paris: Libr. de la société du Recueil général des lois et arrêts, 1912-1925.

Ghisalberti 1957
Ghisalberti, C., 'La teoria del notorio nel diritto comune', *Annali di storia del diritto*, 1957, Vol. I, p. 403-451.

Ghisalberti 1967
Ghisalberti, C., 'Fatto notorio. a) Premessa storica', in: *Enciclopedia del diritto*, Vol. XVI, Milano: Giuffrè, 1967.

Gönner 1804
Gönner, N.T., *Handbuch des deutschen gemeinen Prozesses*, Erlangen: Johann Jacob Palm, 1804.

Grasso 1973
Grasso, E., 'Dei poteri del giudice', in: Allorio, E. (ed.), *Commentario al codice di procedura civile*, Vol. I, Torino: Utet, 1973, p. 1328-1337.

Graziosi 2003
Graziosi, A., *L'esibizione istruttoria nel processo civile italiano*, Milano: Giuffrè, 2003.

Heusler 1879
Heusler, A., 'Grundlagen des Beweisrechts', *Archiv für die Civilistische Praxis*, 1879, p. 237 *et seq*.

Jones 1972
Jones, B.W., *The Law of Evidence: Civil and Criminal*, San Francisco: Bancroft-Whitney, 1972.

La China 1960
La China, S., *L'esibizione delle prove nel processo civile*, Milano: Giuffrè, 1960.

La China 1966
La China, S., 'Esibizione delle prove (diritto processuale civile)', in: *Enciclopedia del diritto*, Vol. XV, Milano: Giuffrè, 1966.

La China 1989
La China, S., 'Esibizione delle prove', in: *Enciclopedia giuridica*, Vol. XIII, Roma: Treccani, 1989.

Lanfranchi 2001
Lanfranchi, L., 'Giusto processo. I) Processo civile', in: *Enciclopedia Giuridica*, Roma: Treccani, 2001.

Laudisa 2006
Laudisa, L., 'Preclusioni e ricerca della verità', *Il giusto processo civile*, 2006, p. 227 *et seq*.

Le Foyer de Costil & Le Foyer de Costil 1986
Le Foyer de Costil, H. & Le Foyer de Costil, G., 'Les connaissances personnelles du juge', *Revue internationale de droit comparé*, 1986, Vol. 38, p. 517-527.

Leone 1954
Leone, C., 'Contributo allo studio delle massime d'esperienza e dei fatti notori', *Annali della Facoltà giuridica dell'Università di Bari*, 1954, Vol. XIII, p. 3-86.

Lessona 1927
Lessona, C., *Trattato delle prove in materia civile, Vol. V. Accesso giudiziale, intervento istruttorio, presunzioni*, 3rd edn., Torino: Utet, 1927.

Levy 1939
Levy, P.H., *La hiérarchie des preuves dans le droit savant du Moyen Age depuis la renaissance du droit romain jusqu'à la fin du 14e siècle*, Paris: Librairie du Recueil Sirey, 1939.

Levy 1965
Levy, P.H., 'Le problème de la preuve dans les droits savants du Moyen Age', in: Aa.Vv., *Recueils de la société Jean Bodin pour l'histoire comparative des institutions, Vol. XVII La preuve. Moyen age et temps modernes*, Bruxelles: Éditions de la librairie encyclopédique, 1965, pp. 137-167.

Levy-Bruhl 1964
Levy-Bruhl, H., *La preuve judiciaire*, Paris: Librairie Marcel Rivière, 1964.

Liebman 1960
Liebman, E.T., 'Fondamento del principio dispositivo', *Rivista diritto processuale*, 1960, p. 551 *et seq*.

Liebman 2007
Liebman, E.T., *Manuale di diritto processuale civile. Principi*, 7th edn., Milano: Giuffrè, 2007.

Luiso 2007
Luiso, F.P., *Diritto processuale civile*, Milano: Giuffrè, 2007.

Malek 2005
Malek, H.M., *Phipson on Evidence*, London: Sweet & Maxwell, 2005.

Massari 1963
Massari, A., 'Ispezione giudiziale', in: *Novissimo digesto italiano*, Vol. IX, Torino: Utet, 1963.

Mazzarella 1934
Mazzarella, G., 'Appunti sul fatto notorio', *Rivista di diritto processuale civile*, 1934, Vol. II, p. 66-74.

Micheli 1945
Micheli, G.A., 'Sulla nozione di fatto notorio', *Giurisprudenza completa della corte suprema di cassazione sezioni civili*, 1945, Vol. II, p. 286 *et seq*.

Millar 1923
Millar, R.W., 'The Formative Principles of Civil Procedure', *Illinois Law Review*, 1923, Vol. XVIII, p. 1-36, 94-117, 150-168.

Montesano 1947
Montesano, L., 'Osservazioni sui fatti notori', *Giurisprudenza completa della corte suprema di cassazione sezioni civili*, 1947, p. 223-229.

Montesano 1978
Montesano, L., 'Le prove disponibili d'ufficio e l'imparzialità del giudice civile', *Rivista trimestrale di diritto e procedura civile*, 1978, p. 189-206.

Morgan 1944
Morgan, E.M., 'Judicial Notice', *Harvard Law Review*, 1944, Vol. 57, p. 269 *et seq*.

Nagel 1967
Nagel, H., *Die Gründzuge des Beweisrechts im europäischen Zivilprozess: eine rechtsvergleichende Studie*, Baden-Baden, Nomos, 1967.

Nesson 1985
Nesson, C., 'The Evidence or the Event? On Judicial Proof and the Acceptability of Verdicts', *Harvard Law Review*, 1985, p. 98 *et seq*.

Nokes 1962
Nokes, G.D., *An Introduction to Evidence*, 3rd edn., London: Sweet & Maxwell, 1962.

Nörr 1967
Nörr, K.W., *Zur Stellung des Richters im gelehrten Prozess der Frühnzeit: Iudex secundum alligata non secundum conscientiam iudicat*, München: Beck, 1967.

Pasquali 1980
Pasquali, A., 'L'esperimento giudiziario in materia di circolazione stradale', *Diritto e giurisprudenza*, 1980, p. 169-177.

Patti 2011
Patti, S., 'La disponibilità delle prove', in: Aa.Vv., *La disponibilità della tutela giurisdizionale (cinquant'anni dopo)*, Milano: Giuffrè, 2011, p. 101-139.

Pertile 1900
Pertile, G., *Storia del diritto italiano dalla caduta dell'Impero romano alla codificazione, Vol. VI - Storia della procedura*, 2nd edn., Torino: Unione tipografico-editrice, 1900.

Picó i Junoy 2007a
Picó i Junoy, J., *El juez y la prueba. Estudio de la errónea recepción del brocardo iudex iudicare debet secundum allegata et probata, non secundum conscientiam y su repercusión actual*, Barcelona: Bosch, 2007.

Picó i Junoy 2007b
Picó i Junoy, J., 'Judex judicare debet secundum allegata et probata, non secundum conscientiam: storia della erronea citazione di un brocardo nella dottrina tedesca e italiana', *Rivista di diritto processuale*, 2007, p. 1497-1518.

Proto Pisani 2000
Proto Pisani, A., 'Il nuovo art. 111 cost. e il giusto processo civile', *Foro italiano*, 2000, Section V, cols. 241-250.

Proto Pisani & Tombari Fabbrini 1995
Proto Pisani, A. & Tombari Fabbrini, G., 'Preclusioni', in: *Enciclopedia giuridica*, Vol. XXIII, Roma: Treccani, 1995.

Radin 1932
Radin, M., 'The Conscience of the Court', *Law Quarterly Review*, 1932, Vol. 48, p. 506-520.

Ricci 1974
Ricci, E.F., 'Il principio dispositivo come problema di diritto vigente', *Rivista di diritto processuale*, 1974, p. 380 *et seq*.

Satta 1959-1962
Satta, S., *Commentario al codice di procedura civile*, Milano: Vallardi, 1959-1962.

Stein 1893
Stein, F., *Das Private Wissen des Richters*, Leipzig, 1893 (Aalen: Scientia Verlag, 1969).

Taruffo 1967
Taruffo, M., 'Il giudice e lo storico: considerazioni metodologiche', *Rivista di diritto processuale*, 1967, p. 438 *et seq*.

Taruffo 2006
Taruffo, M., 'I poteri del giudice in europa', *Rivista trimestrale di diritto e procedura civile*, 2006, p. 451-482.

Taruffo 2009
Taruffo, M., *La semplice verità. Il giudice e la costruzione dei fatti*, Bari: Laterza, 2009.

Taruffo 2010
Taruffo, M., 'Contro la Verifobia', *Rivista di diritto processuale*, 2010, p. 995-1011.

Taruffo 2011a
Taruffo, M., 'Sub art. 118', in: Taruffo, M. & Carratta, A. (eds.), *Art. 112-120. Dei poteri del giudice. Commentario del Codice di Procedura civile*, Bologna: Zanichelli, 2011, p. 580-589.

Taruffo 2011b
Taruffo, M., 'Per una rilettura dell'art. 115 c.p.c.', in: Aa.Vv., *La disponibilità della tutela giurisdizionale (cinquant'anni dopo)*, Milano: Giuffrè, 2011, p. 101-139.

Taruffo 2011c
Taruffo, M., 'Sub art. 115', in: Taruffo, M. & Carratta, A. (eds.), *Art. 112-120. Dei poteri del giudice. Commentario del Codice di Procedura civile*, Bologna: Zanichelli, 2011, p. 447-519.

Tarzia 2001
Tarzia, G., 'L'art. 111 Cost. e le garanzie europee del processo civile', *Rivista di diritto processuale*, 2001, p. 1-22.

Tedoldi 2011
Tedoldi, A., 'La non contestazione nel nuovo art. 115 c.p.c.', *Rivista di diritto processuale*, 2011, p. 76-96.

Tiranti 1903
Tiranti, E., *L'opinione pubblica nei suoi rapporti con la prova*, Pisa: Spoerri, 1903.

Trisorio Liuzzi 1993
Trisorio Liuzzi, G., 'Ispezione nel processo civile', in: *Digesto discipline privatistiche, sezione civile*, Vol. IV, Torino: Utet, 1993.

von Keller 1966
von Keller, L.F., *Der römische Zivilprozess und die Aktionen in summarischer Darstellung*, 6th edn., Leipzig, 1883 (Aalen: Scientia, 1966).

Verde 2008
Verde, G., *Profili del processo civile*, Napoli: Jovene, 2008.

Vincent & Guinchard 2003
Vincent, J. & Guinchard, S., *Procédure civile*, 27th edn., Paris: Dalloz, 2003.

Walter 2005
Walter, G., 'The German Civil Procedure Reform Act 2002: Much Ado about Nothing?', in: Trocker, N. & Varano, V. (eds.), *The Reforms of Civil Procedure in Comparative Perspective*, Torino: Giappichelli, 2005, p. 67-89.

Weinstein *et al.* 1988
Weinstein, J.B., Mansfield, J.H., Abrams, N. & Berger, M.A., *Evidence. Cases and Materials*, 8th edn., New York: Westbury, 1988.

Wendorf 1963
Wendorf, H.D., 'Some Views on Jury Views', *Baylor Law Review*, 1963, Vol. 15, p. 379-402.

Wigmore 1940
Wigmore, J.H., *A Treatise on the Anglo-American System of Evidence*, 3rd edn., Boston: Little Brown and Company, 1940.

COMMON LAW PERSPECTIVE:
USA, SOUTH AFRICA

J.H. Langbein

THE DEMISE OF TRIAL IN AMERICAN CIVIL PROCEDURE: HOW IT HAPPENED, IS IT CONVERGENCE WITH EUROPEAN CIVIL PROCEDURE?*

1. Introduction

A striking trend in the administration of civil justice in the United States in recent decades has been the virtual abandonment of the centuries-old institution of trial. As late as 1936, a fifth of all civil cases that were filed in the federal courts were resolved at trial.[1] The rest terminated either in the pleading and motions phase for failure to state a cause of action, or were settled before trial. That one-fifth trial rate was 'a minority, but a very substantial minority. Civil practice was still in significant measure a trial practice'.[2]

By 1940 the proportion of cases tried declined to 15.2 per cent.[3] By 1952, the figure was 12 per cent;[4] in 1972, 9.1 per cent; in 1982, 6.1 per cent; and in 1992, 3.5 per cent.[5] By the year 2002, only 1.8 per cent of federal civil filings terminated in trials of any sort, and only 1.2 per cent in jury trials.[6] At the state level, where most civil litigation takes place,[7] jury trials in 2002 constituted less than one per cent (0.6 per cent) of all state-court dispositions.[8] Thus, American civil justice has gone from a world in which trials, typically jury trials, were routine, to a world in which trials

* An earlier version of this article was presented at the 2011 Conference on Public and Private Justice, Inter-University Center, Dubrovnik, Croatia, May 2011. The article draws upon a more extensive historical account being published in the 2012 *Yale Law Journal*.

1 Yeazell 2001, p. 185, n. 9; Yeazell 1994, p. 633, n. 3.

2 Yeazell 2001, p. 185.

3 Galanter 1983, p. 44 (table 2).

4 Galanter 2005a, p. 1258.

5 Galanter 2004, p. 462-463 (table 1).

6 *Ibidem.*

7 Galanter reports that 98 per cent of all trials in the U.S. take place in state courts. Galanter 2006, p. 9.

8 Ostrom 2004, p. 768.

have become 'vanishingly rare'.[9] How and why did this movement away from trial occur?

In functional terms, from the perspective of the litigants,[10] a civil procedure system has two connected objectives: investigating the facts of the case, and adjudicating disputed issues of law or fact. Of these functions, investigating is far more important than adjudicating. Sir William Blackstone, the English jurist who wrote in the 1760s, underscored the centrality of fact issues in an arresting passage: '[E]xperience will abundantly show', he said, 'that above a hundred of our lawsuits arise from disputed facts, for one where the law is doubted of'.[11] Was the traffic light red or green? Was the signature forged or genuine? Ascertain the facts in such a dispute, and the law is usually easy - so easy, indeed, that the parties will commonly settle the case, or the court will be able to dismiss it as groundless. Thus, the better that a civil procedure system is at investigating and clarifying the facts, the less it will need to take cases to adjudication.

Alas, investigating the facts was for centuries a critical weakness of common law civil procedure in England and the United States, for reasons connected to the central role of the jury system. Section 4 of this essay emphasizes that, apart from pleading, the Anglo-American common law provided no means other than trial to probe matters of fact, and pleading was preoccupied with other objectives - keeping order among the writs, and circumscribing the role of the jury. Common law procedure offered the litigant no means to locate or force production of documentary evidence in the hands of an opponent or a third party, no opportunity other than trial to examine an uncooperative or adverse witness, and no opportunity whatever to obtain the sworn testimony of an opposing party.

Responding to the shortcomings of common law procedure, the English legal system developed an alternative civil procedure system, known as equity procedure, which was located in a separate court, Chancery. The judge in this court was known as the chancellor. The early chancellors were bishops. Having been keepers of ecclesiastical courts in their dioceses, they were experienced in Roman-canon civil procedure.[12] They patterned Chancery civil procedure on the Roman-canon model, although with significant departures.[13] Chancery procedure (described below in Section 3 of this essay) was jury-free, as in European civil procedure systems. The chancellor alone decided any case that went to adjudication. Being a nonjury court, Chancery procedure was also non-trial. Equity courts[14] gathered evidence not in a single concentrated oral proceeding as in a

9 The term originates with Gross & Syverud 1996, p. 51. Galanter's important empirical study has popularized the concept of the vanishing trial. Galanter 2004.

10 Of course, providing an effective dispute resolution system serves a variety of larger social purposes.

11 Blackstone 1765-1769, Vol. 3, p. 330 (spelling modernized).

12 Some of the early chancellors had formal training in canon law. For biographical detail, see Haskett 1996, p. 311-313.

13 For authority supporting the view that the English 'courts of equity [were] fundamentally civilian in their proof procedure and concepts', see Macnair 1999, p. 14 *et seq*.

14 Regarding the so-called lesser courts of equity, including the palatinate courts and the court of Requests, see Jones 1967, p. 348-389; regarding Exchequer equity, see Bryson 1975.

common law jury trial, but in the course of an investigative process that transpired over as many evidence-gathering sessions as were needed. The English division of civil procedure into separate systems of common law and equity was largely absorbed in American civil procedure at the time of American independence and thereafter.

Section 4 of this essay explains that in the United States, the merger of the systems of law and equity that took place in the Federal Rules of Civil Procedure of 1938[15] was the precipitating event in what we now see as the movement from trial to non-trial procedure. The Federal Rules and state procedure codes patterned on the Federal Rules now govern most civil litigation in the United States.[16] The drafters of the Federal Rules had two dominant and connected objectives: to consolidate the previously distinct procedures and courts of common law and equity into a single system;[17] and to redirect pre-trial procedure away from pleading and toward discovery, a system of litigant-conducted investigation, derived from the evidence-gathering practices of Chancery procedure, featuring the sworn interrogation of parties and witnesses, and compulsory disclosure of documents (and now electronic records). Relatedly, the Federal Rules made liberal provision for summary judgment in cases in which discovery showed that there was no material dispute of fact requiring trial. The discovery regime of the Federal Rules and the associated practices of judicial case-management, ostensibly directed at enabling the litigants to prepare for trial, have had the effect of displacing trial in most cases, causing ever more cases to be resolved in the pre-trial process, either by settlement or by pre-trial adjudication. Pre-trial civil procedure has become non-trial civil procedure.

I conclude this essay in Section 5 with a glance at the grand question of comparative civil procedure, the potential convergence of the Anglo-American and European traditions in civil procedure. Should the virtual disappearance of civil trial in the United States be understood as convergence toward the characteristically non-trial procedures of European legal systems? I express the view that, despite large differences from European practice, the American development of a prevailingly non-trial civil procedure can be seen in historical perspective as evidencing a sort of Europeanization. The core failing of the trial-centered Anglo-American common law was a pre-trial process that made virtually no provision for rational investigation of witness testimony and documentary evidence. The new, discovery-driven American civil procedure, embodying a commitment to rational investigation of witness testimony and documentary evidence, traces to the

15 The Federal Rules of Civil Procedure, as amended to December 2010, are available at <www.uscourts.gov/uscourts/RulesAndPolicies/rules/2010%20Rules/Civil%20Procedure.pdf>, last consulted in June 2012.

16 Regarding the absorption of the Federal Rules into the procedural systems of the states, see *infra*, text at n. 91.

17 As promulgated in 1938, Rule 1 announced that '[t]hese rules govern procedure ... in all suits of a civil nature whether cognizable as cases at law or in equity ...'. Federal Rules of Civil Procedure 1.

influence that the European-derived procedures of English equity gained over common law when the Federal Rules finally merged the two systems.

2. Common Law Civil Trial: Origins and Attributes

2.1. *The Shaping Role of the Jury System*

The main features of the Anglo-American civil trial developed in the practice of the English common law courts[18] in medieval and early modern times, as a consequence of the jury system, in which panels of lay persons were used to decide cases.[19] Legal professionals - judges and lawyers - operated the initial pleading stage of the procedure, which was meant to identify and to narrow the dispute between the parties. If the dispute turned on a matter of law - that is, on a question such as whether the complaint stated a legally actionable claim, or whether some particular legal rule governed - the professional judges decided the case on the pleadings.[20] If, however, the case as pleaded turned on a disputed question of fact, that question was sent for resolution at trial by a jury composed of citizens untrained in the law.[21] So tight was the linkage between trial and jury that *there was no such thing as nonjury trial at common law*.[22] In any case involving a disputed issue of fact, bench trial (adjudication by the judge sitting without a jury) was unknown until the nineteenth century.[23]

In the early days of the jury system, in the twelfth and thirteenth centuries, jurors were drawn from the immediate vicinity in which the events giving rise to the dispute had occurred, in the expectation that the jurors would have knowledge of the events, or if not, that jurors so selected would be able to investigate the matter on their own in advance of the trial.[24] Medieval jurors came to court mostly to speak

18 For a capsule historical account, see Baker 2002, p. 17-20, 37-39.

19 '[T]he common law trial, as we know it, is a direct result of the use of the jury. Without the common law jury, there would be no common law trial'. Goldstein 1996, p. 170. The defining role of the jury in shaping the Anglo-American trial has been a central theme of historical and comparative scholarship since James B. Thayer; see Thayer 1898.

20 For an historical overview of the pleading system, see Plucknett 1956, p. 399-418.

21 Regarding the composition of medieval juries, see Masschaele 2008, p. 89-156.

22 'Until 1854, trial by jury was the only form of trial used in any court of common law'. Zuckerman 2006a, p. 343 n. 14; *accord*, Jolowicz 2000, p. 29.

23 In England the Common Law Procedure Act of 1854 first authorized the parties in certain circumstances to waive jury trial. 17 & 18 Vict., c. 125, § 1 (1854). In American practice, the right of civil litigants to waive jury trial was recognized slightly earlier than in England, but the history is 'obscure'. Millar 1952, p. 260-261. For the American federal system, Clark and Moore identify legislation enacted in 1865 as '[t]he first general act authorizing parties to dispense with a jury, and try the issue of fact before the court ...'. Clark & Moore 1935, p. 412.

24 For discussion of the workings of the self-informing jury, see Oldham 2006, p. 115-126. The expectation that jurors would form their verdict in advance of trial is made explicit in a statute of 1427 that provided that in certain civil cases the sheriffs were, on demand of a litigant, to furnish the names of the prospective jurors to the litigants at least six days before the convening of the trial court, a step that would enable the litigants 'to inform them [the jurors] of their right and title before the day of the sessions ...'. 6 Hen. 6, c. 2 (1427), remarked in Thayer 1898, p. 92.

rather than to listen - not to hear evidence, but to report a verdict that they had agreed upon in advance.[25] Across the later Middle Ages, the jury ceased to function in this way - for complex reasons, including cataclysmic demographic dislocations following the Black Death (the great plague) of the 1340s,[26] and the effects of urbanization[27] in producing more impersonal social relations. By early modern times, as jurors ceased to come to court supposedly knowing the facts, the trial changed character and became an instructional proceeding to inform the jurors about the matter they were being asked to decide.[28]

This instructional form of trial came to have six distinguishing features, all of which were shaped by the special problems of using jurors, unlearned in the law, as triers of fact.

1. *Concentration.* In the parlance of comparative law, the Anglo-American trial is said to be concentrated, meaning that it transpires as a single continuous meeting of the court. This proceeding may now adjourn for the evening or the weekend, but it is otherwise uninterrupted. At this continuous proceeding, the court hears all the evidence and all the legal submissions, after which the judge instructs the jurors regarding the relevant legal principles and the jurors then deliberate and render judgment.

The principle of concentration arose from the challenges of assembling, informing, and controlling a group of twelve lay judges. If you let jurors go home and tell them to return three weeks later, some of them may not show up.[29] Moreover, during any such interval, jurors would be at risk of being intimidated, bribed, or otherwise tampered with. 'It is quite impractical, if not completely impossible, to reconvene a jury of laymen for a number of short hearings held over an extended period of time'.[30]

In jury-free Continental legal systems, based on the Roman-canon tradition,[31] civil proceedings are discontinuous, taking place across as many hearings as the court, staffed exclusively with professional judges, thinks necessary. At these hearings the court hears testimony and the submissions of the parties' lawyers.[32]

25 It was the duty of the jurors 'so soon as they have been summoned, to make inquiries about the facts of which they will have to speak when they come before the court. They must collect testimony; they must weigh it and state the net result in a verdict'. Pollock & Maitland 1898, Vol. 2, p. 624-625.

26 For detail, see Langbein, Lerner & Smith 2009, p. 224-227.

27 Dyer reckons 'a fivefold rise in the urban population between 1086 and 1300, ... culminating in a total of about a million town dwellers by 1300'. Dyer 1997, p. 39.

28 Regarding the emergence of the instructional trial, see Langbein, Lerner & Smith 2009, p. 238-248.

29 Regarding the burden of jury service and the difficulty of obtaining jurors, see Klerman 2003, p. 146-148. Regarding the unpleasantness of jury service in late medieval and early modern times, see Seipp 2002, p. 86-89 (discussing the practice of confining jurors without food, water, heat, or light until they returned a verdict).

30 Goldstein 1996, p. 171; *accord*, Damaška 1997, p. 60.

31 Regarding the Roman-canon origins of the European tradition, see Merryman & Pérez-Perdomo 2007, p. 112-124; van Caenegem 1973, Vol. 16, § 2-13/19, p. 16-23.

32 Damaška contrasts the Anglo-American 'day-in-court' with Continental-style 'piecemeal trial'. Damaška 1986, p. 51-53, 57, 62.

The court records evidence and party submissions in an official file or dossier, which the court will draw upon when writing its judgment if the case does not settle. For efficiency reasons, there has been an effort in modern times in various European systems to encourage the courts to conduct civil proceedings in a single, well-prepared hearing, but this *Konzentrationsmaxime*[33] is at most a managerial aspiration. If the proceedings in a case cannot be so arranged, the case will transpire across as many discontinuous hearings as the circumstances require. In an Anglo-American jury trial, by contrast, the principle of concentration is structural.[34]

2. *The pre-trial/trial division*. The principle of concentration makes the danger of surprise in an Anglo-American trial acute, because a trial once underway cannot be interrupted and adjourned to a further hearing. In a system of concentrated trial, there is no tomorrow. Contrast Continental procedure: If one party raises an issue of law or fact or offers a significant item of evidence that the opposing party has not anticipated, the surprised party simply motions the court to schedule a further hearing, which will allow time to explore the new matter and, if need be, to identify further responsive evidence.[35]

Because the danger of surprise in Anglo-American procedure has been so consequential, the system has had to institute some sort of procedure in advance of trial to identify and to limit what the trial will be about. For most of the history of the common law, this pre-trial procedure was largely confined to pleading - that is, the opening phase of litigation in which the litigants were meant to disclose their respective positions. 'Indeed, pleadings were nearly the only device that common law procedure afforded for the pre-trial disclosure of the parties' claims and evidence'.[36] Common law pleading had the further function of controlling the jury, by severely narrowing - to a single issue - the question that the jury would be asked to decide.[37]

The common law made no provision for the pre-trial examination of opposing parties or non-party witnesses; nor did the common law provide any means[38] to compel the production of documents. This inattention to gathering evidence traces to the foundational period of the common law, in which the self-informing jury was expected to know the facts or to investigate on its own. By treating the jurors as already knowing the facts when they arrived in court, the common law happily dispensed with the need to develop procedures to investigate fact. In later times, when the trial became an instructional proceeding to educate jurors who no longer

33 See Willman 2004.

34 Regarding the relationship between the principle of concentration and the law of evidence, see Damaška 1997, p. 58-73.

35 '[I]n systems where the trial is not concentrated ... the problem of surprise at the trial stage can be handled by simply allowing a further appearance before the court at a later date'. von Mehren 1982, p. 364.

36 James, Hazard & Leubsdorf 2001, § 3.1, p. 181.

37 Regarding the single-issue pleading requirement, see *infra* text at notes 150-152. 'The logic of medieval pleading was directed to the possible misleading of juries'. Milsom 1981, p. 79.

38 There was one exception: the rare circumstance in which a separate common law action of replevin (to recover personal property) could be brought in respect of documents alleged to belong to the demandant.

had knowledge of the matter in dispute, the pre-trial phase remained confined to pleading. Investigation by means of witness testimony occurred only at trial.[39] Moreover, because the parties were disqualified from testifying on account of interest until the middle of the nineteenth century,[40] the common law wholly suppressed party testimony.

This impoverishment of the investigative function was perhaps the greatest weakness of common law civil procedure in the centuries before the fusion of law and equity.[41] A litigant was powerless to locate or force production of documentary evidence that was in the hands of an opponent or a third party. There was no opportunity to examine an uncooperative or adverse witness in advance of trial,[42] and no opportunity to examine an opposing party either in the pre-trial or at trial. In American civil procedure before the Federal Rules, 'trial was often the only real way to do discovery, and some of the trials in this earlier era can be seen as in-court efforts to seek information'.[43]

3. *Bifurcation and jury control.* The jury system resulted in a division of adjudicative responsibility within the first-instance court, expressed clumsily in the slogan that the judge decides questions of law, and the jury decides matters of fact.[44] This division of function within the common law court, which is without counterpart in the jury-free Continental tradition, is known in comparative law as the principle of bifurcation.[45]

Bifurcation required rules allocating the powers of judge and jury - in function, a law of jury control.[46] In the formative era of the common law, the pleading process carried the main work of jury control, by specifying and limiting to a single issue the question to be put to the jury. In later times, as the instructional trial developed to inform the jurors about the facts and the law, the judges were

39 Not until 1563 did civil litigants obtain the right of compulsory process, that is, the power to require a witness to appear at trial. 5 Eliz. I, c.9, § 6 (1563).

40 Regarding the impact of the disqualification rule on doctrinal development, see Abraham 2009; Langbein 1996, p. 1178-1179, 1184-1186. Regarding the movement to abolish the rule, see Fisher 1997, p. 656-662, 709-711.

41 I have emphasized elsewhere that English criminal procedure exhibited a similar impoverishment of investigative capacity into the nineteenth and twentieth centuries, on account of the resistance to professionalizing police and prosecution. From the late Middle Ages, detective work and prosecuting functions had been left to amateur constables and justices of the peace. Langbein 2003; Langbein 1974.

42 'Witnesses had no role in the traditional pre-trial process'. Zuckerman 2006b, § 19.1, p. 697. Blackstone regarded '[t]he want of a complete discovery by the oath of the parties' and 'the want of a compulsive power for the production of books and papers belonging to the parties' as among the 'principal defects' of common law procedure. Blackstone 1765-1769, Vol. 3, p. 381-382.

43 Yeazell 2004, p. 951.

44 *'Ad questionem facti non respondent judices ...; ad questionem juris non respondent juratores'.* Coke 1628, Bk. 2, Ch. 12, § 234, p. 155(b). Coke's formulation neglects the law-applying role of the jury.

45 For detail, see Langbein 2012.

46 In Damaška's formulation, 'a body of procedural and evidentiary law to regulate the internal relationships between [the] two parts' of the trial court. Damaška 2010, p. 7.

able to devise far-reaching practices of trial-level jury control, including (1) judicial comment on the merits of the evidence, (2) the exclusionary apparatus of the law of evidence, (3) ever more detailed instructions on the law, and (4) the quashing or pre-empting of a verdict by ordering a new trial or a directed verdict.[47] The development of these trial-level controls, by relieving the pleading process of the need to serve the function of jury control, was an important precondition for the redesign of pre-trial procedure in the Federal Rules (discussed in Section 4 of this essay), in which discovery came to be substituted for the disclosure function of pleading.

4. *Orality, immediacy, and public access.* The connected set of values known as orality, immediacy, and public access was another defining aspect of the Anglo-American trial. Medieval English jurors were commonly illiterate. The only way to inform people who cannot read is by talking to them. Jury trial had to be oral. When trial became an instructional proceeding to educate the jurors about the dispute, it took the form of having the parties' lawyers and the fact witnesses speak to the jurors at the trial.[48]

Jury trials took place in public.[49] Spectators as well as participants could attend, in contrast to the secrecy[50] of evidence-gathering both in European civil procedure and in the European-derived procedures of the English equity courts. The public character of trial was thought to deter false testimony,[51] and to restrain

47 Regarding the history of the law of jury control in England and the United States from medieval to modern times, see Langbein, Lerner & Smith 2009, p. 415-456. The story of how the practice of jury control led in England to the suppression of civil jury trial across the later nineteenth and twentieth centuries is told in Hanly 2005.

48 Sir John Fortescue, who had been chief justice of the Court of King's Bench, described the course of a civil trial *circa* 1470: '[E]ach party shall declare in the presence of the court, either by himself or by his counsel, and explain to these jurors all and singular of the matters and evidence which he believes may show them the truth of the issue in question. And then either party may produce before the justices and jurors all and singular witnesses whom he desires to produce ...'. Fortescue (Chrimes ed.) 1942, Ch. 26, p. 61.

49 Purpose-built courthouses were uncommon in England before the eighteenth century. Under the assize system of sending itinerant trial courts into the shires, trials took place in any one location for only a few days a year. See Graham 2003, p. 66-67. Writing *circa* 1565, Sir Thomas Smith depicted criminal trials as taking place '[i]n the town house [i.e., the town hall], or in some open or common place'. Smith (Dewar ed.) 1982, Bk. 2, Ch. 23, p. 111 (spelling modernized).

50 Regarding the rationale for secrecy in Chancery proceedings, see Kessler 2005, p. 1216-1217.

51 Describing criminal trials of the mid-sixteenth century, Sir Thomas Smith hinted at this point: 'All ... is done openly in the presence of the Judges, ... the inquest [jury], the prisoner, and so many as will or can come so near as to hear it, and all depositions and witnesses given aloud, that all men may hear from the mouth of the depositors and witnesses what is said'. Smith (Dewar ed.) 1982, Bk. 2, Ch. 23, p. 114. Writing in the 1760s about civil trials, Blackstone voiced a similar view: 'This open examination of witnesses *viva voce*, in the presence of all mankind is much more conducive to the clearing up of truth, than the private and secret examination' characteristic of civilian courts. Blackstone 1765-1769, Vol. 3, p. 373.

misbehaviour by judges.[52] Secrecy would in any event have been impractical to implement in trial courts staffed with dozens of local jurors.

Guarantees of openness in trial proceedings are found in many American state constitutions[53] and are no longer particularly associated with jury proceedings. In modern circumstances, commentators regard these measures as serving monitoring and legitimating functions.[54]

Contrast the European systems (and the English equity courts), in which the practice was for judges or examiners to question witnesses and to summarize their testimony in writing for the court file.[55] The judge or the court that decided the case based judgment on reading the file, often not having seen or heard the witnesses. Accordingly, the procedure gave no weight to so-called demeanour evidence, or to the confrontation of witness and litigant.[56] In the German system of *Aktenversendung* (sending away the court file), it was routine for some distant court (or a university law faculty serving as a court) to render the decision, based on reading the file that had been assembled at the local level.[57] It is in this sense that the unreformed European procedure is said to have lacked immediacy (*Unmittelbarkeit*).[58]

The orality of trial procedure has declined precipitously in modern England, where civil jury trial has been largely suppressed. Since 1985, in a case that goes to trial, witness testimony ('evidence in chief') is submitted by affidavit, but the witness may be called for oral cross-examination.[59]

5. *Partisan investigation and presentation of fact; cross-examination.* In striking contrast to the European tradition of judicially conducted fact-gathering, the common law judge took no responsibility for investigating the facts of a case. This concept of the judicial role, distancing the judge from investigating the facts, developed in England in medieval times, when the jurors were expected to come to court already knowing the facts. Later, however, when the jurors ceased to be self-informing, and the trial became an instructional proceeding to educate them about

52 Bentham wrote: 'Publicity is ... the surest of all guards against improbity. It keeps the judge himself, while trying [the case], under trial'. Bentham 1843, p. 115, cited by Andrews 1994, p. 24.

53 Resnik cites 18 state constitutions that require that 'all courts shall be open'. Resnik 2011, p. 104 and n. 136.

54 *Ibidem*, p. 87-90.

55 Regarding the centrality of this practice in Continental procedure, and its tension with the orality of common law trial, see Damaška 1986, p. 50-51, 61.

56 Writing sometime before 1676, Sir Matthew Hale, the preeminent common law judge of his age, praised the 'Excellency' of common law trial, especially the 'Opportunity of confronting the adverse Witnesses, ... [by which] great Opportunities are gained for the true and clear Discovery of the Truth'. Hale (Gray ed.) 1971, p. 163-164. Hale linked confrontation to cross-examination, but he did not see cross-examination solely as the work of counsel. '[T]here is Opportunity for all Persons concerned, *viz.* The Judge, or any of the Jury, or Parties, or their Counsel or Attorneys, to propound occasional Questions, which beats and bolts out the Truth much better than when the Witness only delivers a formal [statement] without being interrogated ...'. *Ibidem*, p. 164.

57 See Dawson 1968, p. 196-213.

58 See Merryman & Pérez-Perdomo 2007, p. 114-115.

59 See Zuckerman 2006b, § 19.1-19.49, p. 696-712.

the facts, the judges did not materially alter their role; they still took no hand in the work of investigating the facts.[60] That work fell to the litigants, which in practice meant their lawyers. Both in pre-trial investigation[61] and at trial, the lawyers came to dominate the process of gathering, selecting, and presenting evidence about the facts.[62] As the instructional trial developed, the lawyers took charge of examining and cross-examining witnesses and presenting any documentary evidence, as well as addressing the jurors.[63]

The practice of lawyer-conducted cross-examination of witnesses, which is 'unknown to systems of trial other than the common-law system',[64] took hold in early modern times.[65] By the nineteenth century cross-examination had come to be seen as the central safeguard in the common law trial. An American commentator writing in 1857 called cross-examination 'the most perfect and effectual system for the unravelling of falsehood ever devised by the ingenuity of mortals'.[66] This reliance upon cross-examination as the guarantor of truth is puzzling, because contemporaries knew that cross-examination could as easily be put to truth-defeating ends.[67]

The movement to non-trial civil procedure in the later twentieth century has necessarily entailed an abandonment of cross-examination, although (as remarked below in connection with discovery practice under the Federal Rules) the pre-trial deposition serves a somewhat comparable function, allowing counsel to probe the projected testimony of adverse witnesses.

60 Remarked in Damaška 1997, p. 58.

61 Already in medieval times, hence before the instructional trial, the attorney (forerunner of today's solicitor) investigated fact in order to supply the serjeant (forerunner of today's barrister) with the information that the serjeant needed in order to select the correct writ and plead the case. See Brand 2000, p. 101-103.

62 The surviving historical sources about the development of trial procedure are better for criminal than for civil justice. Regarding the former, see Langbein 2003, p. 180-190; Langbein 1983, p. 3-30.

63 Regarding the significance of partisan control over the investigation and presentation of facts in the development of Anglo-American procedure, see Morgan 1937. I have elsewhere pointed to some of the shortcomings of this partisanship. Langbein 1985.

64 Morgan 1956, p. 113.

65 The historical sources thus far identified bearing on the emergence of the practice and theory of lawyer-conducted cross-examination are slender. Hale's discussion is reproduced *supra*, n. 56. Morgan pointed to a case as early as 1668 in which the objection was raised that the testimony of a hearsay declarant escaped cross-examination. Morgan 1948, p. 182 and n. 7. Working from the published law reports and treatise literature, Gallanis found a significant increase in the frequency of hearsay objections in civil litigation in the 1780s and 1790s. Gallanis 1999, p. 533. The earliest mention of cross-examination as the basis for excluding hearsay in the criminal trials reported in the *Old Bailey Sessions Papers* (contemporary published reports of London trials) appears to have been a case heard in 1789. See Langbein 2003, p. 245 and n. 289.

66 Anon. 1857, p. 262, cited in Bodansky 1981-1982, p. 96.

67 Compare Wigmore's panegyric, that cross-examination is 'the greatest legal engine ever invented for the discovery of truth', Wigmore 1940, Vol. 5, § 1367, p. 29, with his admission that cross-examination was 'almost equally powerful for the creation of false impressions'. *Ibidem*, Vol. 1, § 8, p. 237.

6. *Opacity of the verdict: results without reasons.* Like the rest of jury trial, the jury's judgment - the verdict - was and commonly still is rendered orally, usually unsupported by any statement of reasons. This opacity of the verdict - the failure to disclose the reasons for decision - underlies another notable feature of the common law, that for centuries there was no effective appellate review of first-instance judgments. It is very hard for a superior court to review a judgment that is unsupported either by a written statement of reasons[68] or by a court-compiled dossier of written evidence. Commencing in the mid-seventeenth century, the common law judges began to develop the remedy of new trial, that is, quashing a verdict and retrying the case to a new jury, as a means for correcting a jury verdict that appeared contrary to the weight of the evidence or to the law.[69] By contrast, in jury-free European civil procedure, liberal appellate review of first-instance proceedings has been an enduring trait.[70]

3. Equity: Non-trial and Nonjury Civil Procedure

Jury procedure made it awkward for common law courts to administer specific remedies, such as the injunction (cease this) or the decree of specific performance (do that). Specific relief often requires continuing supervision and modification as circumstances change, but a jury dissolves once it has delivered its verdict.[71] Accordingly, the early common law courts largely confined themselves to awarding money damages[72] except in cases involving ownership or possession of real property.[73] But no society can long tolerate a legal system that lacks the power to

68 One technique of jury control used in the seventeenth and eighteenth centuries effectively overcame this attribute of jury verdicts. The trial judge could refuse to accept a proffered verdict, require the jury to explain its thinking, then reinstruct the jury and send it out to re-deliberate. For detail regarding this practice, see Langbein, Lerner & Smith 2009, p. 433-438.

69 A jury verdict 'can only be set right by a new trial, which is no more than having the cause more deliberately considered by another jury, when there is a reasonable doubt, or perhaps a certainty, that justice has not been done'. *Bright v Enyon*, 1 Burr. 390, 393, 97 Eng. Rep. 365, 366 (K.B. 1757) (Lord Mansfield). Regarding the origins of the new trial remedy in England, see Langbein, Lerner & Smith 2009, p. 439-447; for the development in colonial and early national America, see *ibidem*, p. 522-529; Pound 1941, p. 76-80.

70 See van Caenegem 1973, § 2-15, p. 18-19.

71 'Tailoring specific relief requires factual investigation and raises issues of supervision and adjustment of the decree that are beyond the administrative capability of a jury of laypersons convened for a one-time sitting ...'. Langbein, Lerner & Smith 2009, p. 274.

72 The early common law did experiment with granting specific performance, but ceased doing so by the fourteenth century, in part because of the difficulty of enforcing such relief by distraint, which was the common law mode of process. The chancellor, by contrast, could order a defendant imprisoned for defiance. See Plucknett 1956, p. 678-680. Plucknett thought that 'there is no very great reason in the nature of things why common law should confine itself to an action for damages ...'. *Ibidem*, p. 678. As explained in text, I think this view is mistaken. Juries cannot supervise specific performance.

73 Regarding the recovery of possession under the medieval real actions, see Holdsworth 1927, p. 10-16. In a successful action of *novel disseisin*, 'the sheriff would restore the plaintiff to seisin in the presence and "by the view" of the jurors', who 'would point out exactly what properties they had awarded to the plaintiff'. Sutherland 1973, p. 74. The ejectment writ was →

grant specific remedies. The English solved this dilemma in the later fourteenth and fifteenth centuries by creating the nonjury court of Chancery. The chancellor exercised the power to order specific relief,[74] based upon his power to imprison a person who disobeyed his decree.[75]

Beyond remedy law, Chancery's other great contribution to English civil procedure was to enable the use of witness testimony and documentary evidence. As previously remarked, common law civil procedure had been shaped at a time when the supposition was that a jury of the vicinity of the events already knew the facts. In consequence, the early common law developed virtually no means for investigating the facts. 'The common law made no provision for the interrogation of adverse parties on oath as a means of proof',[76] nor for the examination of non-party witnesses, nor for the production of a document not already in the possession of the party seeking it. Chancery, by contrast, drawing on the Roman-canon tradition, developed procedures that enabled a litigant (1) to obtain sworn responses from an opposing litigant;[77] (2) to require a non-party witness to answer interrogatories on oath;[78] and (3) to compel either to produce relevant documents.[79] In a Chancery case, proceedings were discontinuous rather than concentrated; witness testimony was collected in closed sessions and reduced to writing rather than heard orally.[80] In a case that went to adjudication, the chancellor based judgment on the evidence in the court file. Chancery developed the ability to handle multi-issue and multiparty litigation,[81] which the common law courts had been largely unable to entertain,[82] both for fear that such cases were too complex for jurors, and because such cases did not fit within the bipolar pleading process.

Thus, by early modern times, the English were operating two distinct civil procedure systems, the common law system, rooted in jury trial, and the supplementary system of equity, which employed nonjury and non-trial procedure. The common law courts had jurisdiction over most of the law of property and obligations, but even in those fields, a common law litigant had to bring a parallel action in Chancery to obtain documents needed in a common law trial,[83] or to

manipulated to displace *novel disseisn* in the fifteenth and sixteenth centuries. See Wonnacott 2011, p. 129-130.

74 For the mature practice, see Fry 1858; Kerr 1867.

75 See Yale 1965, p. 48.

76 Macnair 1999, p. 58.

77 See Yale 1965, p. 53, 99-100; Jones 1967, p. 214-215; Dawson 1960, p. 148-149, 158-159; Spence 1846, p. 372-373.

78 Jones 1967, p. 236, describing the resulting examinations as 'the principal way in which the court could find out the facts'.

79 See Story 1838, § 311-325, p. 252-264.

80 On the differences between common law and Chancery procedure, see Langbein, Lerner & Smith 2009, p. 289-299.

81 See Story, 1838, § 72, p. 74.

82 Multiparty actions are to be distinguished from representative actions, in which a single party pleaded on behalf of an entity or group such as a village or a parish. See Yeazell 1987.

83 'The common law ... had no power of compelling litigants to disclose what documents in their possession threw a light upon the dispute, or to answer interrogatories before the trial. →

enforce a judgment by means of an injunction or a decree of specific performance. Bringing that second lawsuit was costly; sequencing the two actions was complex;[84] and because a litigant seeking discovery of documents was required to 'describe them with reasonable certainty',[85] he had to know in advance what he was looking for.

The Americans absorbed this dual system of civil procedure, with jury trial at common law and nonjury proceedings in equity. Some states, such as New York and Delaware, replicated the English system of separate courts of law and equity. In other states, notably Massachusetts and Pennsylvania, and in the federal courts, one court administered both systems with varying degrees of distinctness.[86]

Dissatisfaction with the complexity and expense of running two distinct civil justice systems led in the nineteenth century to efforts to merge law and equity, notably in the Field Code in New York in 1848,[87] and then in a series of legislative measures in England across the years from 1852 to 1875.[88] The fusion movement culminated in 1938 in the Federal Rules of Civil Procedure.

4. The Federal Rules: The Pre-trial Becomes the Non-trial

Beginning in the 1930s, the Americans have devised what amounts to a new civil procedure system. This system is called pre-trial procedure, in the sense of procedures whose purpose is to allow the litigants to prepare for trial, but that term is now a misnomer. The more candid term - in a system that takes only one or two per cent of its cases to trial[89] - would be non-trial procedure.

The precipitating event in the creation of this new system was the promulgation in 1938 of the Federal Rules of Civil Procedure.[90] The Federal Rules were devised for use in the federal courts, but most of the American states have chosen to emulate the Federal Rules,[91] with the result that the Federal Rules and state codes patterned on them now govern most civil litigation in the United States.

The Federal Rules sound no clarion call for the suppression of trial. Far from it: Rule 38(a) declares that '[t]he right of trial by jury as declared by the Seventh

In all such cases the suitor was driven into equity to assist him even in the prosecution of a legal claim'. Bowen 1907, p. 518.

84 Discussed in Story 1838, § 317-319, p. 258-260.

85 *Ibidem*, § 320, p. 261.

86 The patterns as developed in colonial times are discussed in Katz 1971, p. 262-283.

87 New York Code of Procedure, 1848 New York Laws 497; regarding the objectives of the Field Code, see Subrin 1988.

88 Summarized in Langbein, Lerner & Smith 2009, p. 376-377, 384-385. Regarding the background to the English reforms, see Lobban 2004.

89 Galanter 2004, p. 462-463 (table 1).

90 Regarding the origins of the Federal Rules, see Marcus 2010; Subrin 1987; Burbank 1982.

91 See Oakley & Coon 1986, updated in Oakley 2003. Some proponents of what would become the Rules Enabling Act of 1934, authorizing the drafting of what became the Federal Rules, anticipated that the states would emulate the resulting federal code. See Subrin 1998, p. 693 and n. 13.

Amendment' to the Constitution is to be 'preserved to the parties inviolate'.[92] What the Federal Rules have largely done is to create conditions in which litigants have found it not in their interests to exercise that right.

The drafters of the Federal Rules had two main objectives: fusion, that is, merging law and equity into a single system in which one court administers a shared regime of procedure; and reforming the pleading practices that had grown up at common law, in part by substituting for pleading other techniques of pre-trial disclosure.

4.1. *The Flight from Pleading*

By the early twentieth century, many observers had come to the view that pleading did serve its notice and disclosure poorly, because the pleading process allowed too much latitude for an artful pleader to conceal or mislead. Edson Sunderland, a civil procedure scholar at the University of Michigan Law School whose central role in drafting the Federal Rules is discussed below, wrote in 1933: '[A] pleader may allege many things that he knows may or cannot be proved ... The other party has no way of determining from the pleadings what facts will actually become the subjects of proof and what will be merely ignored at the trial'.[93] Each pleader strains, Sunderland observed, 'to give himself the widest freedom of action at the trial and at the same time convey as little information as possible to his adversary'.[94]

Responding to this view that pleading was structurally defective for the task of pre-trial clarification, the drafters of the Federal Rules instituted two major and interconnected reforms. The Rules debased the pleading function, providing in Rule 8 for mere notice pleading ('a short and plain statement of the claim'[95]) that ceased to require the pleading of supporting facts.[96] As a functional substitute for pleading,[97] the Rules instituted a regime of broad pre-trial discovery, discussed below, which derived to some extent from former equity practice.

4.2. *Party-Conducted Discovery: Overcoming the Investigation Deficit*

In Section 2 of this essay, discussing the origins of the pre-trial/trial distinction, I have emphasized the impoverishment of the investigative function in the pre-trial process of the common law courts. A common law litigant had no means of

92 Federal Rules of Civil Procedure 38(a).

93 Sunderland 1933a, p. 864. 'The same double uncertainty inheres ... in the denials which the pleader employs'. *Ibidem*.

94 Sunderland 1933b, p. 73-74.

95 Federal Rules of Civil Procedure 8.

96 Regarding the drafters' critique of fact pleading, see Marcus 2010, p. 490-491 and sources there cited.

97 'In the United States, the pure pleading approach has largely been supplanted by ... arrangements that permit each party to familiarize himself before trial with the details of all positions that the other party may advance when the controversy is ultimately presented to the adjudicator. This solution requires elaborate pre-trial interrogatory and discovery procedures'. von Mehren 1982, p. 363.

compelling the production of documents, no opportunity before trial to examine adverse witnesses, and no opportunity whatever to examine opposing parties.

Equity, by contrast, enabled a litigant to obtain discovery of documents; equitable pleading could be manipulated to obtain what amounted to sworn evidence from an opposing party; and interrogatories requiring sworn responses directed to non-party witnesses were a staple of equitable procedure. In equitable causes of action, these techniques of investigation were not pre-trial procedures; rather, they were modes of investigation and proof for an adjudicative process in which there would be no trial in the common law sense - that is, no concentrated public proceeding for the oral examination and cross-examination of witnesses. Equity courts collected witness proofs in the form of written summaries of responses to party-propounded interrogatories. The judge decided a case in equity by examining those summaries and any documentary evidence, but not by hearing witnesses testify and be cross-examined at a concentrated trial. Thus, equity's techniques of investigation had been devised to serve non-trial procedure.

It was long understood, however, that in the hands of a common law litigant, equity's investigative procedures could in some circumstances be made to function in a pre-trial dimension, by means of what came to be known as equity's supplemental or auxiliary jurisdiction.[98] A common law litigant could bring a parallel lawsuit in equity, usually in the form of a bill of discovery, for the purpose of compelling the production of a document important to the common law case. Equity also permitted a common law litigant to obtain a decree permitting the taking and preserving of witness testimony for a common law proceeding, in circumstances in which it was feared that the witness would be unavailable at the time of the trial on account of ill health or distance.[99]

1. *The regime*. The drafters of the Federal Rules routinized the practice of using equity-derived investigative techniques as pre-trial discovery procedures. The Federal Rules make available three main forms of discovery: documents (now including electronic records), interrogatories, and depositions. A party may demand the production of documents 'relevant to any party's claim or defence'.[100] A party may propound interrogatories, that is, written questions directed to another party, which that party must answer 'fully in writing under oath'.[101] And a party may conduct an oral deposition, that is, an out-of-court examination of 'any person, including a party',[102] under oath and stenographically recorded. Whereas some

98 In Story's phrase, 'the auxiliary or assistant Jurisdiction'. Story 1836, Vol. 2, § 1480, p. 699.

99 *Ibidem*, Vol. 2, § 1505-1516, p. 718-730.

100 Federal Rules of Civil Procedure 26(b)(1).

101 Federal Rules of Civil Procedure 33(b)(3).

102 Federal Rules of Civil Procedure 30(a)(1). Taking the pre-trial deposition of a party in order to prepare for that party's testimony at trial would scarcely have occurred to anyone before the middle of the nineteenth-century, when legislation in England and the United States overcame the testimonial disqualification of civil parties and other persons deemed interested in the outcome of the case. Regarding the timing and circumstances of the movement to abolish the disqualification, see Fisher 1997, p. 659, 709-711; Bodansky 1981-1982.

documentary discovery[103] and some use of interrogatories had been known in prior equity practice, the oral deposition was in major respects a creation of the Federal Rules.[104]

The 1938 discovery regime has been altered on several subsequent occasions. An amendment in 1946 broadened the scope of discovery to include material that would be inadmissible 'at the trial if the discovery appears reasonably calculated to lead to the discovery of admissible evidence'.[105] Amendments promulgated in 1970 made insurance policies discoverable, eliminated the requirement of advance judicial approval for conducting discovery, and allowed follow-up discovery.[106] Further amendments have been made in efforts to restrain discovery abuse[107] and to guide electronic discovery.[108]

In past centuries, the term 'deposition' was used to refer to written testimony of all sorts. In modern American usage, the term has lost any meaning other than the counsel-conducted pre-trial examination[109] - an indication of how important that device has become. Deposition procedure allows the lawyers for each side to question opposing parties and potential witnesses under oath. No judge is present, but counsel for both sides (all sides in a multiparty case) attend and may examine or cross-examine the deponent.[110] In this way cross-examination, the talismanic safeguard of common law trial procedure, is projected into the pre-trial process. A stenographer[111] records the testimony. If the case goes to trial, the stenographic transcript is not ordinarily admissible in evidence, but can be used to impeach a

103 Judith Resnik has observed that the discovery rules were devised 'before photocopying and computers were commonplace, [and] did not envision the massive amounts of information that could be generated, stored, or hidden'. Resnik 2003, p. 183. Prior to the spread of photocopying in the 1960s and thereafter, the practice of discovering documents had been largely limited to inspection and note-taking on site.

104 Writing in 1933, Edson Sunderland, who would become the principal drafter of the discovery regime of the Federal Rules, referred to 'oral examination by deposition' as 'a new method, unknown to the [historic English] chancery practice', but found by then in one form or another in some American state procedure systems. Sunderland 1933b, p. 874. Regarding practice in the states in which some type of deposition predated the Federal Rules, see Ragland 1932, pp. 62-91. These state practices exhibited various limitations or restrictions that the Federal Rules would relax or abandon. See Subrin 1998, p. 698-706. 'Probably the most important change made by the Federal Rules ... was to permit parties to take oral depositions of both parties and witnesses as a matter of right ...'. *Ibidem*, p. 703 (observing that such provision was at the time found in only seven states).

105 Federal Rules of Civil Procedure 26(b)(1).

106 See Advisory Committee 1970.

107 See Beisner 2010, p. 561-563, 577-581.

108 *Ibidem*, p. 581-584.

109 See Kessler 2005, p. 1206.

110 'The examination and cross-examination of a deponent proceed as they would at trial ...'. Federal Rules of Civil Procedure 30(c)(1).

111 There was a technological dimension to the emergence of the deposition, in the development and widespread use of stenography in legal proceedings. I am not aware of legal historical scholarship regarding this phenomenon.

witness whose trial testimony varies from what was said at the deposition,[112] or in circumstances in which the witness has died, or is otherwise unavailable for trial.[113]

Having dispensed with the participation of the judge or judge-equivalent officer, the pre-trial deposition effectively displaces much of the law of evidence, a body of law that presupposes trial-stage judicial rulings on admissibility or exclusion. Likewise, in the realm of documentary discovery, Rule 26(b)(1) allows a party to 'obtain discovery of any non-privileged matter that is relevant to any party's claim or defence', and provides that the information sought need not be admissible at trial 'if reasonably calculated to lead to the discovery of admissible evidence'.[114]

In many relatively simple cases, little or no formal discovery takes place;[115] in some such cases, the facts are evident; in others, no discovery is needed beyond the 'initial disclosures' respecting potential witnesses and records that each party is required to make 'without awaiting a discovery request ...'.[116]

In theory, the discovery system of the Federal Rules is a branch of pre-trial procedure designed to assist a litigant to prepare for trial, both by gathering evidence to support that litigant's case, and by ascertaining the positions and the likely evidence that the opposing party or parties might present were the case to advance to trial. However, precisely because discovery allows such far-reaching disclosure of the strengths and weaknesses of each side's case, discovery often has the effect of facilitating settlement. In such cases, discovery serves to displace rather than to prepare for trial. Indeed, part of the rationale that motivated the drafters of the Federal Rules to prefer discovery over pleading was the expectation that the change would promote settlement. On the eve of the drafting of the Federal Rules, Sunderland, the architect of the discovery regime, wrote that 'one of the greatest uses of judicial procedure is to bring parties to a point where they will seriously discuss settlement'.[117] Part of what was wrong with the pleading-centeredness of the received common law, Sunderland thought, was that 'the pleadings seldom disclose a basis upon which a settlement can be reached. It is not what a party asserts, but what he can establish by proof'[118] that shapes settlement. 'Many a case would be settled, to the advantage of the parties and to the relief of the court, if the true situation could be disclosed before the trial begins'.[119]

2. *Paper and electronic trails: the changing character of evidence.* A background factor of some importance in the decline of trial has been the changing character of

112 Federal Rules of Civil Procedure 32(a)(2).

113 Federal Rules of Civil Procedure 32(a)(4).

114 Federal Rules of Civil Procedure 26(b)(1).

115 A five-state empirical study conducted in the early 1990s by the National Center for State Courts found that no discovery took place in 42 per cent of the cases. Keilitz *et al.* 1993.

116 Federal Rules of Civil Procedure 26(a)(1)(A) requires each party to disclose without demand the names of persons 'likely to have discoverable information', and also to disclose documents and electronic records in the party's possession that the party 'may use to support its claims or defences ...'.

117 Sunderland 1933a, p. 864.

118 *Ibidem.*

119 *Ibidem*, p. 865.

the evidence. In earlier times, when the procedures of oral trial took shape, evidence in contested cases was more likely than today to take the form of witness testimony - about what the witness saw or heard or said or did - as opposed to the writings and electronic records[120] characteristic of much modern transactional life. Documentary evidence often 'speaks for itself' (as a common phrase has it), and is usually less in need of the probing that occurs at trial. The centrality of documentary discovery in non-trial procedure reflects this change in the character and reliability of evidence. (The growing use of summary judgment, discussed below, also reflects the trend toward documents and other proofs more reliable than witness testimony.[121])

A main factor underlying the trend toward documentary evidence is the ever greater role of large institutions such as corporations and government agencies in the transactions and activities that give rise to litigation.[122] Record generation and record retention are essential to the work of such organizations. I have had occasion elsewhere, in discussing the growth of corporate trust companies, to point to the way that

> 'the needs of ordinary business practice incline institutional trustees toward good record keeping. A bank trust department or other institutional fiduciary is an intrinsically bureaucratic entity. Performing trust functions necessarily involves the conduct of many persons deliberating and acting over time - account officers, investment officers, accountants, information technology personnel, supervisors, review committees. Internal coordination requires that transactions, authorizations, and committee decisions be documented. The data processing revolution has reinforced these tendencies by lowering the cost of creating and retaining many kinds of records'.[123]

In place of witnesses being asked 'to recall conversations lost to memory or recalled only through a prism of self-interest',[124] today's lawsuit is ever more likely to turn on well-preserved transactional documentation.

The discovery-based processes of modern litigation have been conducive to the growth of large law firms and hourly billing.[125] American litigators incline 'to leave no stone unturned, provided of course that they can charge by the stone'.[126]

120 See, e.g., *Scott v Harris*, 550 U.S. 372 (2007), basing summary judgment on video evidence.

121 The greater reliability of a particular form of evidence bears on whether that evidence satisfies the summary judgment standard of Federal Rules of Civil Procedure 56(a), that there be 'no genuine dispute as to any material fact'.

122 For empirical study of the shift in lawyers' work across recent decades from personal to institutional clients such as corporations and other business organizations, nonprofits, labour unions, and governments, see Galanter 2005b; Galanter 1998, p. 718-719.

123 Langbein 2005, p. 948.

124 Davidson 2007, p. 3.

125 For the view that the discovery system of the Federal Rules influenced the emergence of large law firms dependent on hourly billing, see Shepherd & Cloud 1999; Subrin 1998, p. 741; Galanter 2004, p. 502-504. Subrin points out that the Advisory Committee that drafted the Federal Rules was composed mostly of lawyers 'associated with what was then considered large firm practice ...'. Subrin 1987, p. 971-972.

126 Rhode 1985, p. 635.

A similar change in the character of evidence can be observed in criminal justice, in which the movement towards non-trial criminal procedure has been associated with the growing importance of forensic evidence such as DNA and fingerprints.[127] Damaška speaks of this trend (and the related growth of expert evidence) as 'the scientization of proof'.[128] As with civil justice, this change in the character of evidence in criminal cases has been associated with the growth of complex bureaucratic institutions specializing to some extent in generating and preserving evidence - police forces, crime labs, and prosecutorial corps.

3. *Displacing trial.* In a procedural system ever more oriented to pre-trial resolution, the deposition has in important respects replaced the trial as the primary occasion for probing sworn testimony about matters of fact. In combination with what the litigants learn from discovery of documents and from disclosures in response to interrogatories, deposition testimony provides the litigants a detailed advance view of what the issues and the evidence would be (on both or all sides) were the case to go to trial. In this way the discovery system has transferred into the pre-trial process much of the work of eliciting facts and refining legal issues that had formerly been the function of trial. Having seen the dress rehearsal, today's litigants often find that they can dispense with the scheduled performance.

4. *The drawbacks to the discovery revolution: expense and abuse.* There are serious downsides to discovery as practiced in the United States. Discovery is costly, so costly that the prospect of having to bear those costs can dissuade a potential litigant from advancing a meritorious claim or defence. The perverse incentives of the adversary system intensify the problem, because each party's discovery activities are conducted in large part at the expense of the opposing litigant(s).[129] '[I]t is almost invariably cheaper to ask for materials than to produce them', which tempts litigants 'to seek costly information of marginal relevance ...'.[130] The prospect of bearing these costs pressures 'the parties continually to recalculate the comparative advantages of settlement and trial'.[131] The greater the investment that either side has made in pre-trial investigation, the greater is the incentive to avoid the risk of total loss that can result at trial.[132]

Accordingly, American-style litigant-conducted discovery has two inseparable dimensions: investigating the facts and inflicting costs on the other side. A party

127 See Weigend 2006, p. 210. Relatedly, there has been a growing awareness in criminal justice circles of the potential unreliability of witness testimony, especially eyewitness identifications. Garrett 2011; Loftus & Doyle 1997. DNA evidence has revolutionized the proof of paternity in civil cases, even in cases in which the alleged father is deceased when the issue arises. An Ohio court observed in one such case: 'Science has developed a means to irrefutably prove the identity of an illegitimate child's father. No longer are we dependent upon fallible testimony, nor are we concerned that the decedent cannot be present to defend himself. The accuracy and infallibility of the DNA test are nothing short of remarkable'. *Alexander v Alexander*, 537 N.E.2d 1310, 1314 (Oh. Probate Ct. 1988).

128 Damaška 1997, p. 147.

129 For discussion, see Maxeiner *et al.* 2011, p. 147-150; Easterbrook 1989.

130 Issacharoff 2010, p. 44-45.

131 Yeazell 2004, p. 951.

132 *Ibidem*, p. 958-964.

receiving a discovery demand needs to engage counsel to study and interpret the demand (and sometimes to institute proceedings to resist it). The producing party must locate the documents, then pay counsel to examine them for relevance and privilege. The trend toward electronic documents has exacerbated the expense, because 'the costs of producing electronic documents far exceed those of producing paper documents'.[133] When depositions are demanded of parties or witnesses, the complying side is put to the expense and distraction of preparing the deponents for the deposition, usually with the aid of counsel. When a deposition takes place, even in a relatively simple case, '[at] least two lawyers are normally present, in addition to the witness and the court reporter, and questioning moves slowly'.[134] Thereafter, counsel will study and evaluate the transcripts. When a case entails the use of expert witnesses, they must be paid for preparation and deposition time and for expenses.

The broad scope of permitted discovery together with the failure of the Federal Rules to institute a 'loser pays' cost-shifting regime invites cost-inflicting abuse.[135] Although cases of abuse are thought to be infrequent,[136] when they occur, they transform discovery from a truth-serving to a truth-impairing device.

4.3. *Judicial Case-Management*

1. *The pre-trial conference.* In part to compensate for the weakened role of pleading in the Federal Rules,[137] the drafters made provision in Rule 16 for 'the court ... in its

[133] Beisner 2010, p. 565, observing that electronic records tend to be created in greater number and, that such records are commonly more difficult for the producing party's counsel to review for responsiveness and privilege; for discussion of the cost factors, see *ibidem*, p. 565-570.

[134] Hazard, Leubsdorf & Bassett 2011, § 8.16, p. 357.

[135] Among the practices regarded as abusive are 'discovery beyond what the rules require or what is necessary to prove the proponent's case; discovery of information not needed by the proponent but having potential for coercing the respondent to settle because of its confidential or embarrassing nature; discovery taken primarily to impose expense and delay on the respondent rather than to obtain information for the lawsuit; discovery for purposes unrelated to the litigation in which it is sought (such as obtaining access to protected and otherwise unavailable intellectual property); propounding discovery requests to which the costs of responding exceed the anticipated increase in value of the proponent's claim or defence; withholding discoverable information or materials on the basis of groundless boilerplate objections; and unjustifiable or bad faith assertions of privilege'.
Beckerman 2000, p. 507.

[136] For empirical studies to the effect that such abuse does not occur 'in the great bulk of cases', see James, Hazard & Leubsdorf 2001, § 5.2, p. 288 n. 7, and sources there cited. Empirical studies canvassed in Mullenix 1998, p. 684, indicate that no discovery occurs in as many as half of all cases, and that abusive discovery is most likely to occur in 'complex, high stakes litigation, handled by big firms with corporate clients ...'. *Ibidem*, p. 685.

[137] Rule 16 was 'designed to substitute for formal pleadings the less formal processes of discussion and exchange as ways of narrowing issues for trial and of expediting proof'. Shapiro 1989, p. 1981. Donald Elliott has argued that managerial judging incident to Rule 16 'is a response to a fundamental design flaw in the Federal Rules of Civil Procedure: the lack of incentives for litigants to narrow issues for trial ...'. Elliott 1986, p. 308. '[T]he problem that →

discretion [to] direct the attorneys for the parties to [attend] ... a conference to consider' matters including 'simplification of the issues', amending the pleadings, and 'obtaining admissions of fact and of documents which will avoid unnecessary proof ...'.[138] This so-called 'pre-trial conference' can take the form of an off-the-record conversation in the judge's chambers, or a formal hearing at which the judge, sitting without a jury, hears counsel and resolves pre-trial issues.[139]

In the pleading-centered pre-trial procedure that prevailed before the Federal Rules, the litigants exchanged written pleadings by filing them with the court, but the judge had little or no contact with the case before the trial commenced. The discovery revolution,[140] by shifting so much activity into the pre-trial, effectively required that the Rules make provision for judicial determinations before trial – for example, in disputes about the scope of discovery.[141] Granting the lawyers for the parties 'unprecedented authority to obtain sworn testimony and to compel the other party to disclose information' required that there be 'judicial oversight' to keep order and to restrain abuse and delay.[142]

An important change in judicial administration, which took root in the federal courts in the late 1960s and thereafter, facilitated case-management: A system of 'continuous' or 'individual' case assignment was introduced, in which the same judge oversees all proceedings in the case, pre-trial and trial.[143]

As judicial involvement in the pre-trial increased, Rule 16 was amended in 1983 to expand the range of matters that the judge was empowered to resolve in such hearings. The amended rule directs the judge to 'establish[] early and continuing control so that the case will not be protracted because of lack of management ...'.[144] Among the topics that the revised rule identifies as appropriate for resolution at such hearings are the sequencing of discovery[145] and of pre-trial motions;[146] and 'adopting special procedures for managing potentially difficult or

managerial judging aims to solve is, at base, structural: it results from a fundamental imbalance in the Rules between the techniques available for developing and expanding issues and those for narrowing or resolving them prior to trial.' *Ibidem*, p. 319.

138 Federal Rules of Civil Procedure 16(1)-(3) (1938). In the drafting process Sunderland was again the moving figure. See Shapiro 1989, p. 1978. Sunderland pointed to prior Michigan practice as the model. Sunderland 1937, p. 225.

139 Regarding the range of issues that can be the subject of pre-trial conferences, see Hazard, Leubsdorf & Bassett 2011, 10.3, p. 392-394.

140 Armistead Dobie, dean of the University of Virginia Law School and a member of the Federal Rules drafting committee, wrote at the time that the discovery provisions were 'revolutionary' in their importance. Dobie 1939, p. 275.

141 'A party or any person from whom discovery is sought may move for a protective order in the court where the action is pending ...'. Federal Rules of Civil Procedure 26(c)(1).

142 Damaška 2010, p. 11.

143 Regarding the ways that continuous case assignment promotes judicial case-management, see Gensler 2010, p. 674-675; Resnik 2000, p. 939-943.

144 Federal Rules of Civil Procedure 16(a)(2).

145 Federal Rules of Civil Procedure 16(b)(3).

146 Federal Rules of Civil Procedure 16(b)(2).

protracted actions that may involve complex issues, multiple parties, difficult legal questions, or unusual proof problems ...'.[147]

2. *Managerial judging and complex cases.* The special sensitivity toward the managerial problems of complex cases voiced in the 1983 revision of Rule 16 underscores that the trend toward greater judicial management in the pre-trial process ('managerial judging'[148] in Judith Resnik's apt term) had causes beyond the weakening of pleading and the profusion of discovery. The Federal Rules brought over from equity and expanded not only liberal discovery but also liberal joinder of parties and claims.[149] The pleading rules at common law, especially the single-issue requirement,[150] greatly restricted multiparty and multi-issue litigation.[151] 'Single issue pleading allowed only one contested issue of fact to reach the jury for decision, no matter how complex the facts of the case. Single issue pleading was a way to restrict and simplify the jury's task, but often at the heavy cost of oversimplifying and distorting the case'.[152] The nonjury equity courts, freed from the need to package cases for decision by lay triers, had been able to entertain multiparty and multi-issue cases, which is why substantive fields characterized by multiparty relations such as account,[153] business associations,[154] and estate administration[155] developed in equity rather than at common law.[156]

Amendments to the Federal Rules in 1966 further promoted large-scale litigation by facilitating class actions.[157] In the 1980s, the *Agent Orange* case became a

147 Federal Rules of Civil Procedure 16(c)(2)(L).

148 The widely accepted term coined by Resnik 1982. Resnik understood the term to embrace not only the growing involvement of judges in the pre-trial process, but also the expanded judicial role in fashioning remedial decrees in post-trial proceedings, notably in complex public-law litigation concerning prison conditions and racial desegregation of schools. *Ibidem*, p. 393-394.

149 Federal Rules of Civil Procedure 18-25. Provisions of the Federal Rules promoting 'free joinder of parties, of claims, and of counterclaims, free amendment, and extensive impleader of new parties' were features that Charles Clark advertised at the outset 'as among the most important'. Clark 1936, p. 448.

150 Under single-issue pleading, 'the parties pleaded back and forth until one side either demurred, resulting in a legal issue, or traversed, resulting in a factual issue'. Subrin 1987, p. 916.

151 'Pleading to a single issue meant no joinder of claims or defences, extraordinarily limited joinder of parties, and no pleading in the alternative. Equity took the opposite position – that all interested parties should be joined so that complete justice could be done in every case'. Laycock 1993, p. 65.

152 Langbein 2012, p. 71.

153 See Devlin 1983, p. 1623-1633; Devlin 1980, p. 65-72.

154 Regarding equity's effective capture of jurisdiction over partnership matters, see Story 1836, Vol. 1, § 659-683, p. 612-633.

155 Spence 1846, p. 578-586.

156 A study of all reported English civil cases for the years 1789-1791 found that cases of any complexity or large value were prevailingly allocated to and resolved by equity courts rather than by jury trial in common law courts. King 1984, p. 590-608.

157 See Kaplan 1967-1968; for the practice as it has since developed, see American Law Institute 2010.

celebrated example,[158] 'consolidat[ing] more than 600 separate actions' that sought damages for toxic harm on behalf of a purported plaintiff class of 2.4 million persons.[159]

The absorption and expansion of equity's multiparty and multi-issue practice in the Federal Rules coincided with and encouraged the development of fields of substantive law that depended upon such procedures - notably antitrust,[160] securities regulation,[161] international trade law,[162] products liability and other mass torts,[163] and various public-law causes of action.[164]

The proliferation of complex cases led to the development across the 1950s and 1960s of case-management techniques, which the organized federal Judiciary endorsed in a handbook,[165] subsequently revised several times and now known as the *Manual for Complex Litigation*.[166] In a case involving dozens or indeed thousands of parties, leaving each party free to conduct discovery and make pre-trial and trial motions according to that party's convenience and strategic advantage would result in duplication, delay, avoidable expense, and in some circumstances chaos. Accordingly, the *Manual* provides for extensive use of pre-trial conferences to identify and refine issues, as well as to plan (and limit) discovery and the use of experts.[167] Another initiative in this vein was the legislation dealing with multidistrict litigation, enacted in 1968,[168] which provides a process for consolidating in a single federal district court all the discovery and other pre-trial activity arising from cases that involve 'common questions of facts',[169] for example, products liability suits concerning the same product.

3. *Promoting settlement*. The *Manual* emphasizes the responsibility of the judge to whom a case is assigned to promote settlement,[170] a theme that the 1983 revision of Rule 16 governing pre-trial conferences endorsed for all cases. The revision made

158 Recounted in detail in Schuck 1987; for citation to the various published opinions in the litigation, see Schuck 1986, p. 337-338 n. 6.

159 Schuck 1986, p. 341-342.

160 'Complex litigation became a catalytic force with the electrical equipment antitrust cases in the 1950s ...'. Burbank 1997, p. 224. Regarding those cases, see Neal & Goldberg 1964.

161 E.g., *In re U.S. Financial Securities Litigation*, 609 F.2d 411 (9th Cir. 1979) (reversing the district court's finding that the case was too complex for jurors to understand).

162 E.g., *In re Japanese Electronics Product Antitrust Litigation*, 611 F.2d 1069 (3d Cir. 1980). The case alleged antitrust and tariff violations and was projected to require a year of trial time, following nine years of discovery that had 'produced millions of documents and over 100,000 pages of depositions'. *Ibidem*, 611 F.2d 1073.

163 Regarding the 'steady evolution toward a more collectivist, functional, and managerial tort law', see Schuck 1987, p. 12.

164 For an overview of the expansion of federal regulatory activity from the later nineteenth century into the 1970s, see Rabin 1986.

165 Manual 1960.

166 Manual 2004.

167 *Ibidem*, § 11.11-13, p. 32-34; 11.2-23, p. 36-42; 11.33, p. 44-46.

168 28 U.S.C. § 1407, creating the Judicial Panel on Multidistrict Litigation.

169 *Ibidem*. Regarding the work of the panel, see Herr 2011.

170 Manual 2004, § 13.1-24, p. 167-182.

'facilitating the settlement of the case'[171] an express objective of pre-trial conferences. Managerial judging thus expanded 'from a set of techniques for narrowing issues to a set of techniques for settling cases'.[172] Geoffrey Hazard has remarked that, by acquainting a neutral observer with the evidence, judicial case-management can function as 'mediation by another name'.[173]

The danger, however, is that the judge may know less than he or she thinks; the judge may have only 'a generalized understanding'[174] of the case. Pressing for settlement in such circumstances risks denying adequate opportunity for a litigant to develop his or her case. In *Agent Orange*, Judge Jack Weinstein promoted settlement by a variety of means, some of which remain highly controversial, including imposing severe time-limits on pre-trial investigation ...'.[175]

Caseload pressures incline judges toward settlement, even though empirical study indicates that, at least in the federal system, judicial resources have largely kept pace with caseloads across the past half century.[176] Judge Weinstein has spoken of the link between caseload pressures and settlement pressures. 'Federal judges tend to be biased toward settlement. We are the kitchen help in litigation. We clean the dishes and cutlery so they can be reused for the long line of incoming customers. Settlements are the courts' automatic washer-dryers'.[177] Weinstein's theme is that in processing any one case, the judge must take into account the rest of the court's caseload. This concern with cross-caseload efficiency has become particularly prominent in England, where the Woolf Reforms of the 1990s[178] established the policy of using aggressive judicial case-management to diminish the incidence of trials.[179]

The disposition to promote settlement found in the 1983 revision of Federal Rule 16 is also evidenced in federal legislation enacted in 1998, requiring each federal district court to devise and implement a program 'to encourage and promote the use of alternative dispute resolution ...'.[180] So-called court-connected

171 Federal Rules of Civil Procedure 16(a)(5); *accord*, Federal Rules of Civil Procedure 16(c)(1), 16(c)(2)(I).

172 Elliott 1986, p. 323.

173 Geoffrey C. Hazard Jr., in an email to the author, 22 November 2011.

174 Schuck 1986, p. 349-350.

175 *Ibidem*, p. 344. Promoting settlement spared Weinstein not only a trial that was projected to last a year, but also '[t]he prospect of having either to direct a verdict for the chemical companies or to reverse a jury verdict in favour of the [plaintiffs] ...'. *Ibidem*, p. 343.

176 See Galanter 2004, p. 500-504.

177 Weinstein 2009, p. 1265.

178 An official study conducted in the mid-1990s by Lord Harry Woolf resulted in a new civil procedure code, called the Civil Procedure Rules (CPR). The recommendations leading to the CPR appear in Woolf 1996; Woolf 1995. The current text is CPR 2012.

179 Case-management powers are scheduled in CPR § 1.4(2); for discussion, see Andrews 2000. Hazel Genn reads the 'message' of the Woolf reforms to be that 'diversion and settlement is the goal, [and] that courts exist only as a last resort and, perhaps, as a symbol of failure'. Genn 2010, p. 53.

180 28 U.S.C. § 651(b). Congressional findings accompanying the legislation declare that 'alternative dispute resolution ... in a program adequately administered by the court, has the potential to provide a variety of benefits, including greater satisfaction of the parties, →

mediation programs, in which litigants are required to attempt settlement with the assistance of a neutral mediator, have become widespread.[181] (Alternative dispute resolution programs of various sorts, notably arbitration and mediation, also operate apart from the civil courts.[182])

Settlement of a civil dispute has material advantages over adjudication: Settlement is usually cheaper and faster, the court is spared the labour of adjudication, each party is spared the risk of a less favourable outcome, and neither party is stigmatized as the loser. The parties to a civil suit appropriately seek private advantage, and can be expected to 'bargain in the shadow'[183] of what they know about the facts, the law, and the litigation costs. Cases that resist settlement are typically those in which there is material uncertainty about the relevant legal rules, or in which the facts remain doubtful despite discovery.[184] Thus, so long as adjudication is preserved as a viable alternative, the litigants' choice to settle a case is voluntary, and facilitating settlement is sound public policy.[185] In law-and-economics terms, the parties' decision to settle a civil case in the pre-trial is a Coasean[186] determination to contract around the costs and risks of trial.

The trend to recast the judicial role to include the objective of encouraging settlement was contrary to the design of the original drafters of the Federal Rules, several of whom had opposed it.[187] Charles Clark, chair of the drafting committee, thought that '[c]ompelled settlement negotiations are dangerous', because they induce doubt about 'the impartiality of the tribunal.'[188] Later commentators have emphasized that concern. Albert Alschuler has referred to pre-trial conferences as 'Cajolery Conferences',[189] and he has cautioned that 'a judge who has gained familiarity with the facts of a case during his pre-trial activities is unlikely to relish the prospect of hearing the evidence again at trial'.[190] Judith Resnik has pointed to the danger that, in a judicially supervised settlement negotiation, 'litigants who

innovative methods of resolving disputes, and greater efficiency in achieving settlements.' Pub. L. 105–315, § 2, Oct. 30, 1998, 112 Stat. 2993.

181 Regarding the varieties, see Wissler 2010.

182 Regarding mandatory arbitration programs arising from consumer sales and from contracts of employment, see Resnik 2006, p. 1134-1139 (2006); regarding the tendency of major federal administrative agency proceedings to displace civil jurisdiction, see *ibidem*, p. 1130-1131.

183 The celebrated term coined in Mnookin & Kornhauser 1979.

184 The theme of Priest & Klein 1984.

185 But see Fiss 1984, p. 1076-1078, 1085, observing that settlement may be unfair when the parties have unequal resources to conduct litigation; and that settlement prevents the generation of precedent. For the view that subsequent changes in the plaintiffs' bar (discussed in Yeazell 2001) have rendered resources more equal in many categories of case, see Issacharoff & Klonoff 2009, p. 1179-1184.

186 Coase 1960.

187 See Bone 2008, p. 1578.

188 Clark 1962, p. 456, cited by Shapiro 1989, p. 1980.

189 Alschuler 1986, p. 1828.

190 *Ibidem*, p. 1835.

incur a judge's displeasure may suffer judicial hostility or even vengeance with little hope of relief'.[191]

4.4. *Summary Judgment*

For cases in which pre-trial proceedings do not result in consensual resolution, the Federal Rules provide for adjudication without trial in two distinct ways. One is ancient: the motion to dismiss the opponent's case at the pleading stage, on the ground that the pleaded allegations do not state an actionable claim.[192] The other mode of involuntary termination without trial is the motion for summary judgment. Under Rule 56(a), the court must grant judgment 'as a matter of law' in circumstances in which 'there is no genuine dispute as to any material fact ...'.[193] Summary judgment is 'the primary procedure used to avoid unnecessary civil trials ...'.[194]

Summary judgment entered mainstream Anglo-American civil procedure remarkably late, in an English statute enacted in 1855.[195] That act provided a creditor's remedy for collecting liquidated debts arising from bills of exchange or promissory notes. Further legislation in the 1870s extended the procedure to a few other types of case.[196] Writing in 1925, Sunderland, who would become the main architect of the summary judgment provision of the Federal Rules,[197] observed that summary judgment in England was 'in essence ... nothing but a process for the prompt collection of debts'.[198] The English legislation, which was limited to plaintiffs, was the apparent model for most of the summary judgment provisions found in those American states (about 20)[199] that had any such procedure before the promulgation of the Federal Rules.[200] Federal Rule 56(a), drafted by Sunderland and somewhat based on an earlier Michigan statute that Sunderland had championed, constituted a drastic expansion, because it made summary judgment available in

191 Resnik 1982, p. 425. Regarding the difficulty of obtaining appellate review of judicial determinations made in the pre-trial process, see Yeazell 1994, p. 651-653.

192 Federal Rules of Civil Procedure 12(b).

193 'The court shall grant summary judgment if the movant shows that there is no genuine dispute as to any material fact and the movant is entitled to judgment as a matter of law. The court should state on the record the reasons for granting or denying the motion'. Federal Rules of Civil Procedure 56(a).

194 Brunet & Redish 2006, § 1.1, p. 1.

195 Summary Procedure on Bills of Exchange Act, 18 & 19 Vict., c. 67 (1855), also known as Keating's Act, named after Sir Henry Keating, the MP (later judge of Common Pleas) who sponsored the bill. Regarding the act, see Bauman 1956, p. 337-338. Regarding earlier impulses toward summary judgment in legislation in some American states, see Millar 1928.

196 For practice under the English legislation, see Clark & Samenow 1929, p. 424-435.

197 Regarding Sunderland's role, see Burbank 2004, p. 596-603.

198 Sunderland 1925, p. 111.

199 Discussed in Clark & Samenow 1929, p. 440-471.

200 Bauman 1956, p. 343. 'Summary judgment prior to the Federal Rules was in fact a collection of very different tools of very different (and usually very limited) scope: as to the types of cases in which they could properly be invoked, the parties who could invoke them, and the purposes for which they could be used'. Burbank 2004, p. 595.

any type of case, and to any party. Under the Federal Rule, summary judgment lies if the moving party can show that 'there is no genuine dispute as to any material fact ...'.[201] The Supreme Court liberalized the interpretation of this standard in three prominent cases decided in 1986,[202] but whether that development has affected summary judgment rates is disputed.[203]

There is an intimate connection between the discovery revolution and summary judgment. Litigants who seek summary judgment commonly do so after discovery has taken place. Rule 56(c) contemplates that, in deciding whether there is genuine dispute regarding a material fact, the court may rely upon elements of the discovery product, 'including depositions, documents, ... [and] interrogatory answers ...'.[204] Many litigators now 'believe that discovery's primary use is to develop evidence for summary judgment, not to prepare for trial'.[205] In many cases in which a motion for summary judgment is denied, the denial exercises a shaping influence on settlement. In such a case, the judge who has 'review[ed] a substantial factual record ... send[s] a signal that the judge thinks the claim has some merit'.[206] Such cases commonly lead to settlement.[207]

Summary judgment has preserved adjudication on issues that ostensibly present no material fact dispute, but has transferred adjudication into the pre-trial. In consequence, as Judge Patricia Wald has written, '[f]ederal jurisprudence is largely the product of summary judgment'.[208]

4.5. *Why Civil Trial Vanished*

To summarize: Although the Federal Rules of Civil Procedure preserve the right to civil trial, since the promulgation of the Rules in 1938 the incidence of civil trial has declined precipitously in the United States. In this essay I have offered a functional account, historically rooted, of how this great transformation occurred. Build a better mousetrap, said Ralph Waldo Emerson, and the world will beat a path to your door.[209] The Federal Rules built a better mousetrap, a pre-trial procedure centered in discovery. Litigants no longer go to trial because they no longer need to.

201 Federal Rules of Civil Procedure 56(a).

202 *Anderson v Liberty Lobby, Inc.*, 477 U.S. 242 (1986); *Celotex Corp. v Catrett*, 477 U.S. 317 (1986); *Matsushita Elec. Indus. Co. v Zenith Radio Corp.*, 475 U.S. 574 (1986). For discussion, see Brunet & Redish 2006, § 5.6-9, 9.6, 9.9, p. 100-119, 322-335, 347-351; Issacharoff & Lowenstein 1990.

203 For the view that the 1986 Supreme Court decisions have materially increased the reach of summary judgment, see Miller 2003, p. 1048-1057 (reviewing empirical studies and judicial opinions). For the contrary view, see Eisenberg & Lanvers 2009 (empirical study finding no material increase in summary judgment in post-1986 cases).

204 Federal Rules of Civil Procedure 56(c). For discussion of the evidentiary materials used in summary judgment proceedings, Brunet & Redish 2006, § 8.1-12, p. 205-279.

205 Wood 2010, p. 245 (reporting survey data).

206 Rave 2006, p. 894.

207 Schneider 2010, p. 540.

208 Wald 1998, p. 1897.

209 Oxford 1955, p. 201.

The core function of civil trial is to facilitate the investigation and resolution of disputes that cannot be resolved otherwise. Still as in Blackstone's day,[210] most civil cases concern matters of fact - what happened in the past. In the early decades of the twentieth century, a consensus emerged that the inherited system for investigating and resolving such disputes at common law was deeply deficient. That inherited system consisted of a pre-trial process largely limited to pleading, and a trial procedure reliant on lawyer-conducted selection, preparation, examination, and cross-examination of witness testimony.

In the 1930s, the drafters of the Federal Rules devised a system of discovery that was meant largely to substitute for pleading. They did not foresee that the package of discovery techniques that they devised - interrogatories, documentary discovery, and sworn depositions - would constitute a truth-revealing process so powerful that it would ultimately displace not only the older pleading-based pre-trial, but also the trial. By so enhancing the information available to litigants about the evidence likely to be presented were trial to occur, discovery promoted settlement in place of trial. Clarification promoted pacification.

The other innovations of the Federal Rules that have contributed to the demise of trial are importantly connected to the discovery revolution. The driving force behind the pre-trial conference and the associated growth of judicial case-management was the need to manage discovery, that is, to sequence discovery and the discovery-based pre-trial motions, and to resolve disputes concerning the permitted scope of discovery. The discovery revolution also underlies the displacement of trial in cases resolved by means of summary judgment, because the showing that a party seeking summary judgment needs to make - that 'there is no genuine dispute as to any material fact'[211] - is routinely based on discovery product.[212]

The substitution of non-trial for trial procedure to which the Federal Rules gave rise took place gradually, across the last two-thirds of the twentieth century, as evidenced in the statistics on declining trial rates canvassed above.[213] The discovery rules underwent important changes in 1946 and in the 1970s that made them even more permissive.[214] The continuous case assignment system of judicial administration did not develop until the 1960s.[215] The modern class action rules were put in place in 1966 and thereafter.[216] The procedure for consolidating multidistrict cases dates from 1968.[217] In 1983 Rule 16 was revised to reconceptualise

210 *Supra*, n. 11.

211 Federal Rules of Civil Procedure 56(c).

212 'A party asserting that a fact cannot be or is genuinely disputed must support the assertion by ... citing to particular parts of materials in the record, including depositions, documents, electronically stored information, affidavits or declarations, stipulations (including those made for purposes of the motion only), admissions, interrogatory answers, or other materials ...'. Federal Rules of Civil Procedure 56(c)(1)(A).

213 *Supra*, text at notes 1-9.

214 *Supra*, text at notes 105-106.

215 *Supra*, text at n. 143.

216 *Supra*, text at n. 157.

217 *Supra*, text at n. 168-169.

the pre-trial conference as a forum for encouraging settlement[218] and in 1998 Congress made it federal policy to promote alternative dispute resolution, including court-connected mediation.[219]

Although the central dynamic in the disappearance of trial has been the substitution of discovery-induced settlements and dismissals, other factors have also been at work. The growth of the regulatory state and the growth in scale of private enterprise have led to growth in the size and complexity of some modern lawsuits - the phenomenon sometimes called the Big Case.[220] Big Cases have bred 'Big Law', that is, the litigation departments of large law firms. Large law firms that bill by the hour have thrived on the discovery-based processes of modern litigation.[221] In the field of tort law, large defence-side law firms have provoked plaintiff-side adaptations such as litigation consortia that share expertise and in some cases discovery product and discovery costs.[222] With sophisticated counsel on both sides, the paradigm of modern tort litigation consists of discovery to establish the facts, followed by settlement.

Judges have welcomed the case-management role, which has enhanced judicial authority both in promoting settlement[223] and in pre-trial (non-trial) adjudication.[224] Non-trial procedure has transformed the judicial role, from courtroom umpire to office-bound caseload manager.[225]

The movement to non-trial procedure has inevitably undermined the civil jury, because the civil jury has always been a trial-phase institution. Discovery and its associated techniques of case-management, which derive from the jury-free procedures of equity, can be seen as an 'implicit attack on the jury'.[226] The civil jury has indeed been a casualty, but more in the nature of collateral damage than as target. The right to civil jury trial remains protected in the federal and state constitutions,[227] and in the Federal Rules.[228] Only when discovery and related pre-

218 *Supra*, text at n. 147.

219 *Supra*, text at n. 180.

220 *Supra*, text at n. 157-169.

221 *Supra*, text at n. 125-126.

222 See Issacharoff & Witt 2004, p. 1622-1624. For the view that changes in the organization and capitalization of the plaintiffs' bar have inclined plaintiff-side law firms to seek more to settle than to try cases, see Yeazell 2004, p. 954-964.

223 *Supra*, text at notes 171-177.

224 In a discovery dispute, 'the trial judge enjoys enormous discretionary power to shape what may be the only significant stage of litigation. The broad language of most of the key discovery rules gives the judge wide latitude. Moreover, [the abuse-of-discretion standard of review renders] the trial judge, when acting on a discovery dispute, ... in most cases virtually immune to appellate supervision ...'. Yeazell 1994, p. 651.

225 Federal District Judge Brock Hornby describes himself spending his days 'using a computer and court administrative staff to monitor the entire caseload and individual case progress; conferring with lawyers (often by telephone or video conference) in individual cases to set dates or limits;' and researching and writing judgments on pre-trial motions. Hornby 2007, p. 462.

226 Subrin 1987, p. 1000.

227 U.S. Constitution, Amendment VII. '[N]early every state constitution contains a similar guaranty'. Hazard, Leubsdorf & Bassett 2011, § 12.1, p. 529.

trial motions reveal a case to be meritless do the Federal Rules preclude jury trial (by means of summary judgment) in circumstances in which pre-Rules procedure would mostly have allowed jury trial. Apart from such cases, the main reason that the jury is disappearing is that litigants who are entitled to demand trial decide to settle, either because they no longer need trial, or because they cannot afford it.

American civil procedure is unique among the major Western legal systems in failing to have some form of loser-pays regime for the allocation of litigation costs, both pre-trial and trial.[229] This so-called 'American rule' long predates the discovery revolution,[230] but the interaction of discovery with the American rule has become a main shortcoming of the new discovery-based civil procedure.

Common law trial was never a particularly good way of resolving fact disputes, because the common law was never able to overcome the mistake that hobbled it from the outset in the Middle Ages, the failure to devise suitable means of investigating the facts. The discovery revolution of the Federal Rules, by overcoming that investigation deficit, set in motion changes that have made trial obsolete.

5. Convergence?

The institution of trial was the root difference that for centuries separated Anglo-American civil procedure from European. In this essay I have emphasized that into the nineteenth century in both England and the United States, jury trial was the only method of resolving a common law case that turned on a dispute of fact. The pre-trial processes of the common law were largely confined to pleading, and thus grievously deficient in facilitating the investigation of potential evidence. Trial was the common law's crude effort at investigating fact. European civil procedure systems, by contrast, were and remain non-trial systems, in which courts staffed by professional judges gather evidence (and when necessary adjudicate) in proceedings that span as many hearings as are convenient for the case. Thus, the virtual disappearance of civil trial in the United States in recent decades has brought American civil procedure into an alignment of sorts with the non-trial tradition of European systems.

I have emphasized that the driving force behind the movement toward non-trial procedure in the United States has been the development of a system of discovery so effective at investigating the facts and encouraging informed settlement that it has rendered trial largely obsolete. But American discovery differs from European practice, in ways that seem to resist a convergence account. The vast

228 Federal Rules of Civil Procedure 38(a).

229 'In almost all other countries, except Japan and China, the winning party, whether plaintiff or defendant recovers at least a substantial portion of litigation costs'. ALI/Unidroit 2006, p. 6 and sources cited *ibidem*, n. 8.

230 See Leubsdorf 1984.

scope[231] and the partisanship of American-style litigant-conducted discovery are without counterpart in European practice.[232] Beneath these differences, however, is a profoundly important point of convergence: the commitment to rational investigation of the relevant evidence. This was what the pleading-dominated pre-trial process of the common law lacked. The discovery regime of the Federal Rules of Civil Procedure traces back to the practice of the English court of Chancery,[233] although greatly refined and expanded. Like modern European civil procedure, English Chancery procedure had been based on Roman-canon civil procedure, and had absorbed from the Roman-canon tradition the commitment to basing adjudication upon rational investigation of relevant witness testimony and documentary evidence. The fusion of common law and equity in the Federal Rules injected equity-derived techniques for investigating fact into the common law pre-trial process. Although litigant-conducted rather than court-conducted as in Europe,[234] the American discovery process operates under the oversight of judicial case-management. In this way, American civil procedure has come to acquire an eerie resemblance to the European. Both systems now entail a jury-free, judge-supervised process, in which the gathering of witness proofs and documentary evidence leads in most cases to settlement.

231 *Supra,* text at n. 114, pointing to the rule allowing a litigant to seek discovery of information known to be inadmissible at trial 'if reasonably calculated to lead to the discovery of admissible evidence'. Federal Rules of Civil Procedure 26(b)(1).

232 Regarding German resistance to litigant-conducted American discovery, see Gerber 1986.

233 Regarding the equity-preferring orientation of the Federal Rules, see especially Subrin 1987, summarizing that message in the subtitle, 'How Equity Conquered Common Law'.

234 See John Dawson's account of the origins of this divergence, in the failure of the early English court of Chancery to establish a staff of judges or examiners commensurate with the extent of the subject-matter jurisdiction that the court was developing. Dawson 1960, p. 150-159. Into the nineteenth century, Chancery was a one judge court, and in consequence, largely delegated the work of investigating matters of fact to the parties and their counsel. For detail, see Langbein, Lerner & Smith 2009, p. 291-298, 371-376.

Bibliography

Abraham 2009
Abraham, K.S., 'The Common Law Prohibition on Party Testimony and the Development of Tort Liability', *Virginia Law Review*, 2009, Vol. 95, No. 3, p. 489-515.

Advisory Committee 1970
Advisory Committee, 'Explanatory Statement Concerning Amendments of the Discovery Rules', *Federal Rules Decisions*, 1970, Vol. 48, p. 487-545.

ALI/Unidroit 2006
ALI/Unidroit, *Principles of Transnational Civil Procedure*, Cambridge: Cambridge University Press, 2006.

Alschuler 1986
Alschuler, A.W., 'Mediation with a Mugger: The Shortage of Adjudicative Services and the Need for a Two-Tier Trial System', *Harvard Law Review*, 1986, Vol. 99, No. 8, p. 1808-1859.

American Law Institute 2010
American Law Institute, *Principles of the Law: Aggregate Litigation*, St. Paul, MN: American Law Institute Publishers, 2010.

Andrews 1994
Andrews, N., *Principles of Civil Procedure*, London: Sweet & Maxwell, 1994.

Andrews 2000
Andrews, N., 'A New Civil Procedural Code for England: Party-Control "Going, Going, Gone"', *Civil Justice Quarterly*, 2000, Vol. 19, p. 19-38.

Anon. 1857
Anon., 'Of the Disqualification of Parties as Witnesses', *American Law Register*, 1857, Vol. 5, No. 5, p. 257-268.

Baker 2002
Baker, J.H., *An Introduction to English Legal History*, 4th edn., London: Butterworths, 2002.

Bauman 1956
Bauman, J.A., 'The Evolution of the Summary Judgment Procedure: An Essay Commemorating the Centennial Anniversary of Keating's Act', *Indiana Law Journal*, 1956, Vol. 31, p. 329-355.

Beckerman 2000
Beckerman, J.S., 'Confronting Civil Discovery's Fatal Flaws', *Minnesota Law Review*, 2000, Vol. 84, p. 505-587.

Beisner 2010
Beisner, J.H., 'Discovering a Better Way: The Need for Effective Civil Litigation Reform', *Duke Law Journal*, 2010, Vol. 60, p. 547-596.

Bentham 1843
Bentham, J., *Benthamiana, or, Select Extracts from the Works of Jeremy Bentham*, (Burton, J.H. (ed.)), Edinburgh: W. Tait, 1843.

Blackstone 1765-1769
Blackstone, W., *Commentaries on the Laws of England*, Oxford: Oxford University Press, 1765-1769 (4 Vols.).

Bodansky 1981-1982
Bodansky, J.N., 'The Abolition of the Party-Witness Disqualification: An Historical Survey', *Kentucky Law Review*, 1981-1982, Vol. 70, p. 91-130.

Bone 2008
Bone, R.G, '"To Encourage Settlement": Rule 68, Offers of Judgment, and the History of the Federal Rules of Civil Procedure', *Northwestern University Law Review*, 2008, Vol. 102, p. 1561-1621.

Bowen 1907
Bowen, C., 'Progress in the Administration of Justice during the Victorian Period', in: *Select Essays in Anglo-American Legal History*, Boston: Little Brown, 1907, Vol. 1, p. 516-557 (3 vols., 1907-1909).

Brand 2000
Brand, P., 'Inside the Courtroom: Lawyers, Litigants and Justices in England in the Later Middle Ages', in: Coss, P. (ed.), *The Moral World of the Law*, New York: Cambridge University Press, 2000, p. 91-112.

Brunet & Redish 2006
Brunet, E. & Redish, M.H., *Summary Judgment: Federal Law and Practice*, 3rd edn., St. Paul, MN: Thomson/West, 2006.

Bryson 1975
Bryson, W.H., *The Equity Side of the Exchequer: Its Jurisdiction, Administration, Procedures and Records*, Cambridge: Cambridge University Press, 1975.

Burbank 1982
Burbank, S.B., 'The Rules Enabling Act of 1934', *University of Pennsylvania Law Review*, 1982, Vol. 130, p. 1015-1197.

Burbank 1997
Burbank, S.B., 'Implementing Procedural Change: Who, How, Why, When', *Alabama Law Review*, 1997, Vol. 49, p. 221-250.

Burbank 2004
Burbank, S.B., 'Vanishing Trials and Summary Judgment in Federal Civil Cases: Drifting Toward Bethlehem or Gomorrah', *Journal of Empirical Legal Studies*, 2004, Vol. 1, p. 591-626.

Clark 1936
Clark, C.E., 'The Proposed Federal Rules of Civil Procedure', *American Bar Association Journal*, 1936, Vol. 22, p. 447-451, 491.

Clark 1962
Clark, C.E., 'To an Understanding Use of Pre-Trial', *Federal Rules Decisions*, 1962, Vol. 29, p. 454-461.

Clark & Moore 1935
Clark, C.E. & Moore, J.W., 'The New Federal Civil Procedure: I. The Background', *Yale Law Journal*, 1935, Vol. 44, p. 387-435.

Clark & Samenow 1929
Clark, C.E. & Samenow, C.E., 'The Summary Judgment', *Yale Law Journal*, 1929, Vol. 38, p. 423-471.

Coase 1960
Coase, R., 'The Problem of Social Cost', *Journal of Law & Economics*, 1960, Vol. 3, p. 1-44.

Coke 1628
Coke, E., *The First Part of the Institutes of the Laws of England*, 16th edn., London: Society of Stationers, 1823 (1st edn. 1628).

CPR 2012
Civil Procedure Rules, <www.justice.gov.uk/courts/procedure-rules/civil/rules>.

Damaška 1986
Damaška, M., *The Faces of Justice and State Authority*, New Haven: Yale University Press, 1986.

Damaška 1997
Damaška, M., *Evidence Law Adrift*, New Haven: Yale University Press, 1997.

Damaška 2010
Damaška, M., 'The Common Law/Civil Law Divide: Residual Truth of a Misleading Distinction', in: Walker, J. & Chase, O. (eds.), *Common Law, Civil Law and the Future of Categories*, Dayton, OH: LexisNexis, 2010, p. 3-22.

Davidson 2007
Davidson, G.A., 'Who Killed the Civil Trial?', *New York Law Journal Magazine*, 2007, p. 1-3.

Dawson 1960
Dawson, J.P., *A History of Lay Judges*, Cambridge, MA: Harvard University Press, 1960.

Dawson 1968
Dawson, J.P., *The Oracles of the Law*, Ann Arbor: University of Michigan Law School, 1968.

Devlin 1980
Devlin, P., 'Jury Trial of Complex Cases: English Practice at the Time of the Seventh Amendment', *Columbia Law Review*, 1980, Vol. 80, p. 43-107.

Devlin 1983
Devlin, P., 'Equity, Due Process and the Seventh Amendment: A Commentary on the *Zenith* Case', *Michigan Law Review*, 1983, Vol. 81, p. 1571-1638.

Dobie 1939
Dobie. A., 'The Federal Rules of Civil Procedure', *Virginia Law Review*, 1939, Vol. 25, p. 261-315.

Dyer 1997
Dyer, C., 'How Urban Was Medieval England?', *History Today*, 1997, p. 37-43.

Easterbrook 1989
Easterbrook, F., 'Discovery as Abuse', *Boston University Law Review*, 1989, Vol. 69, p. 635-648.

Elliott 1986
Elliott, E.D., 'Managerial Judging and the Evolution of Procedure', *University of Chicago Law Review*, 1986, Vol. 53, p. 306-336.

Eisenberg & Lanvers 2009
Eisenberg, T. & Lanvers, C., 'Summary Judgment Rates Over Time, Across Case Categories, and Across Districts: An Empirical Study of Three Large Federal Districts', in: Haung, K.-C. (ed.), *Empirical Studies of Judicial Systems*, Taipei: Institutum Jurisprudentiae, 2009, p. 1-34.

Fisher 1997
Fisher, G., 'The Jury's Rise as Lie Detector', *Yale Law Journal*, 1997, Vol. 107, p. 575-713.

Fiss 1984
Fiss, O.M., 'Against Settlement', *Yale Law Journal*, 1984, Vol. 93, p. 1073-1090.

Fortescue (Chrimes ed.) 1942
Fortescue, J., *De Laudibus Legum Anglie* [On the Laws and Governance of England] (c. 1470), Chrimes, S.B. (ed.) & transl., Cambridge: Cambridge University Press, 1942.

Fry 1868
Fry, E., *A Treatise on the Specific Performance of Contracts*, London: Butterworths, 1858.

Galanter 1983
Galanter, M., 'Reading the Landscape of Disputes: What We Know and Don't Know (And Think We Know) About Our Allegedly Contentious and Litigious Society', *UCLA Law Review*, 1983, Vol. 31, p. 4-71.

Galanter 1998
Galanter, M., 'An Oil Strike in Hell: Contemporary Legends about the Civil Justice System', *Arizona Law Review*, 1998, Vol. 40, p. 717-752.

Galanter 2004
Galanter, M., 'The Vanishing Trial: An Examination of Trials and Related Matters in Federal and State Courts', *Journal of Empirical Legal Studies*, 2004, Vol. 1, p. 459-570.

Galanter 2005a
Galanter, M., 'The Hundred-Year Decline of Trials and the Thirty Years War', *Stanford Law Review*, 2005, Vol. 57, p. 1255-1274.

Galanter 2005b
Galanter, M., 'Planet of the Aps: Reflections on the Scale of Law and Its Users', *Buffalo Law Review*, 2005, Vol. 53, p. 1369-1417.

Galanter 2006
Galanter, M., 'A World Without Trials?', *Journal of Dispute Resolution*, 2006, Vol. 1, p. 7-33.

Gallanis 1999
Gallanis, T.P., 'The Rise of Modern Evidence Law', *Iowa Law Review*, 1999, Vol. 84, p. 499-560.

Garrett 2011
Garrett, B.L., *Convicting the Innocent: Where Criminal Prosecutions Go Wrong*, Cambridge, MA: Harvard University Press, 2011.

Genn 2010
Genn, H., *Judging Civil Justice*, Cambridge: Cambridge University Press, 2010.

Gensler 2010
Gensler, S.S., 'Judicial Case-Management: Caught in the Crossfire', *Duke Law Journal*, 2010, Vol. 60, p. 669-744.

Gerber 1986
Gerber, D., 'Extraterritorial Discovery and the Conflict of Procedural Systems: Germany and the United States', *American Journal of Comparative Law*, 1986, Vol. 34, p. 745-788.

Goldstein 1996
Goldstein, S., 'The Anglo-American Jury System as Seen by an Outsider (Who Is a Former Insider)', in: *The Clifford Chance Lectures: Bridging the Channel*, New York: Oxford University Press, 1996, p. 165-191.

Graham 2003
Graham, C., *Ordering Law: The Architectural and Social History of the English Law Court to 1914*, Aldershot: Ashgate, 2003.

Gross & Syverud 1996
Gross, S. & Syverud, K.D, 'Don't Try: Civil Jury Verdicts in a System Geared to Settlement', *UCLA Law Review*, 1996, Vol. 44, p. 1-64.

Hale (Gray ed.) 1971
Hale, M., *The History of the Common Law of England* (Gray, C.M. (ed.) 1971) (1st edn. 1713) (posthumous publication, Hale died in 1676).

Hanly 2005
Hanly, C., 'The Decline of Civil Jury Trial in Nineteenth-Century England', *Journal of Legal History*, 2005, Vol. 26, p. 253-278.

Haskett 1996
Haskett, T.S., 'The Medieval English Court of Chancery', *Law & History Review*, 1996, Vol. 14, p. 245-313.

Hazard, Leubsdorf & Bassett 2011
Hazard, G.C., Jr., Leubsdorf, J. & Bassett, D.L., *Civil Procedure*, 6th edn., New York: Foundation Press, 2011.

Herr 2011
Herr, D.F., *Multidistrict Litigation Manual: Practice before the Judicial Panel on Multidistrict Litigation*, St. Paul, MN: Thomson/West, 2011.

Holdsworth 1927
Holdsworth, W., *An Historical Introduction to the Land Law*, Oxford: Clarendon Press, 1927.

Hornby 2007
Hornby, D.B., 'The Business of the U.S. District Courts', *Green Bag 2d*, 2007, Vol. 10, p. 453-468.

Issacharoff 2010
Issacharoff, S., 'Facts, Investigation, and the Role of Discovery', in: Gottwald, P. (ed.), *Litigation in England and Germany*, Bielefeld: Gieseking-Verlag, 2010, p. 39-50.

Issacharoff & Klonoff 2009
Issacharoff, S. & Klonoff, R.F., 'The Public Value of Settlement', *Fordham Law Review*, 2009, Vol. 78, p. 1177-1202.

Issacharoff & Lowenstein 1990
Issacharoff, S. & Lowenstein, G., 'Second Thoughts about Summary Judgment', *Yale Law Journal*, 1990, Vol. 100, p. 73-126.

Issacharoff & Witt 2004
Issacharoff, S. & Witt, J., 'The Inevitability of Aggregate Settlement: An Institutional Account of American Tort Law', *Vanderbilt Law Review*, 2004, Vol. 57, p. 1571-1636.

James, Hazard & Leubsdorf 2001
James, F., Hazard, G.C., Jr., & Leubsdorf, J., *Civil Procedure*, 5th edn., New York: Foundation Press, 2001.

Jolowicz 2000
Jolowicz, J., *On Civil Procedure*, Cambridge: Cambridge University Press, 2000.

Jones 1967
Jones, W.J., *The Elizabethan Court of Chancery*, Oxford: Clarendon Press, 1967.

Kaplan 1967-1968
Kaplan, B., 'Continuing Work of the Civil Committee: 1966 Amendments of the Federal Rules of Civil Procedure', *Harvard Law Review*, 1967-1968, Vol. 81, p. 356-416, 591-623.

Katz 1971
Katz, S.N., 'The Politics of Law in Colonial America: Controversies over Chancery Courts and Equity Law in the Eighteenth Century', in: Fleming, D. & Bailyn, B. (eds.), *Law in American History*, Boston: Little Brown, 1971, p. 257-284.

Keilitz *et al.* 1993
Keilitz, S. *et al.*, 'Is Civil Discovery in State Trial Courts Out of Control?', *State Court Journal*, 1993, p. 8-17.

Kerr 1867
Kerr, W.W., *A Treatise on the Law and Practice of Injunctions in Equity*, London: W. Maxwell & Son, 1867.

Kessler 2005
Kessler, A.D., 'Our Inquisitorial Tradition: Equity Procedure, Due Process, and the Search for an Alternative to the Adversarial', *Cornell Law Review*, 2005, Vol. 90, p. 1181-1275.

King 1984
King, D., 'Complex Civil Litigation and the Seventh Amendment Right to a Jury Trial', *University of Chicago Law Review*, 1984, Vol. 51, p. 581-614.

Klerman 2003
Klerman, D., 'Was the Jury Ever Self-Informing?', *Southern California Law Review*, 2003, Vol. 77, p. 123-149.

Langbein 1974
Langbein, J.H., *Prosecuting Crime in the Renaissance,* Cambridge, MA: Harvard University Press, 1974.

Langbein 1983
Langbein, J.H., 'Shaping the Eighteenth-Century Criminal Trial: A View from the Ryder Sources', *University of Chicago Law Review*, 1983, Vol. 50, p. 1-136.

Langbein 1985
Langbein, J.H., 'The German Advantage in Civil Procedure', *University of Chicago Law Review*, 1985, Vol. 52, p. 823-866.

Langbein 1996
Langbein, J.H., 'Historical Foundations of the Law of Evidence: A View from the Ryder Sources', *Columbia Law Review*, 1996, Vol. 96, p. 1168-1202.

Langbein 2003
Langbein, J.H., *The Origins of Adversary Criminal Trial,* Oxford: Oxford University Press, 2003.

Langbein 2005
Langbein, J.H., 'Questioning the Trust Law Duty of Loyalty: Sole Interest or Best Interest?', *Yale Law Journal*, 2005, Vol. 114, p. 929-990.

Langbein 2012
Langbein, J.H., 'Bifurcation and the Bench: The Influence of the Jury on English Conceptions of the Judiciary', in: Brand, P. & Getzler, J. (eds.), *Judges and Judging in the History of the Common Law and Civil Law: From Antiquity to Modern Times,* Cambridge: Cambridge University Press, 2012, p. 67-82.

Langbein, Lerner & Smith 2009
Langbein, J.H., Lerner, R.L. & Smith, B.P., *History of the Common Law: The Development of Anglo-American Legal Institutions,* New York: Aspen Publishers, 2009.

Laycock 1993
Laycock, D., 'The Triumph of Equity', *Law & Contemporary Problems*, 1993, Vol. 56, p. 53-82.

Leubsdorf 1984
Leubsdorf, J., 'Toward a History of the American Rule on Attorney Fee Recovery', *Law & Contemporary Problems*, 1984, Vol. 47, p. 9-36

Lobban 2004
Lobban, M., 'Preparing for Fusion: Reforming the Nineteenth-Century Court of Chancery', *Law & History Review*, 2004, Vol. 22, p. 389-427, 565-599.

Loftus & Doyle 1997
Loftus, E.F. & Doyle, J.M., *Eyewitness Testimony: Civil and Criminal*, 3rd edn., Charlottesville: Lexis Publishing Co., 1997.

Macnair 1999
Macnair, M.R.T., *The Law of Proof in Early Modern Equity*, Berlin: Duncker & Humblot, 1999.

Manual 1960
'Handbook of Recommended Procedures for the Trial of Protracted Cases', *Federal Rules Decisions*, 1960, Vol. 25, p. 351-451.

Manual 2004
Federal Judicial Center, *Manual for Complex Litigation, Fourth*, St. Paul, MN: Thomson/West, 2004.

Marcus 2010
Marcus, D., 'The Federal Rules of Civil Procedure and Legal Realism as a Jurisprudence of Law Reform', *Georgia Law Review*, 2010, Vol. 44, p. 433-510.

Masschaele 2008
Masschaele, J., *Jury, State, and Society in Medieval England*, New York: Palgrave Macmillan, 2008.

Maxeiner *et al.* 2011
Maxeiner, J.R. *et al.*, *Failures of American Civil Justice in International Perspective*, Cambridge: Cambridge University Press, 2011.

Merryman & Pérez-Perdomo 2007
Merryman, J.H. & Pérez-Perdomo, R., *The Civil Law Tradition*, 3rd edn., Stanford, CA: Stanford University Press, 2007.

Millar 1928
Millar, R.W., 'Three American Ventures in Summary Civil Procedure', *Yale Law Journal*, 1928, Vol. 38, p. 193-224.

Millar 1952
Millar, R.W., *Civil Procedure of the Trial Court in Historical Perspective*, New York: National Conference of Judicial Councils, 1952.

Miller 2003
Miller, A.R., 'The Pretrial Rush to Judgment: Are the "Litigation Explosion", "Liability Crisis", and Efficiency Clichés Eroding Our Day in Court and Jury Trial Commitments?', *New York University Law Review*, 2003, Vol. 78, p. 982-1134.

Milsom 1981
Milsom, S.F.C., *Historical Foundations of the Common Law*, 2nd edn., London: Butterworths, 1981.

Morgan 1937
Morgan, E., 'The Jury and the Exclusionary Rules of Evidence', *University of Chicago Law Review*, 1937, Vol. 4, p. 247-258.

Morgan 1948
Morgan, E.M., 'Hearsay Dangers and the Application of the Hearsay Concept', *Harvard Law Review*, 1948, Vol. 62, p. 177-219.

Morgan 1956
Morgan, E.M., *Some Problems of Proof under the Anglo-American System of Litigation*, New York: Columbia University Press, 1956.

Mnookin & Kornhauser 1979
Mnookin, R.H. & Kornhauser, L., 'Bargaining in the Shadow of the Law: The Case of Divorce', *Yale Law Journal*, 1979, Vol. 88, p. 950-997.

Mullenix 1998
Mullenix, L.S., 'The Pervasive Myth of Pervasive Discovery Abuse: The Sequel', *Boston College Law Review*, 1998, Vol. 39, p. 683-689.

Neal & Goldberg 1964
Neal, P.C. & Goldberg, P., 'The Electrical Equipment Antitrust Cases: Novel Judicial Administration', *American Bar Association Journal*, 1964, Vol. 50, p. 621-628.

Oakley 2003
Oakley, J.B., 'A Fresh Look at the Federal Rules in State Courts', *Nevada Law Journal*, 2003, Vol. 3, p. 354-387.

Oakley & Coon 1986
Oakley, J.B. & Coon, R.F., 'The Federal Rules in State Courts: A Survey of State Court Systems of Civil Procedure', *Washington Law Review*, 1986, Vol. 61, p. 1367-1434.

Oldham 2006
Oldham, J., *Trial by Jury: The Seventh Amendment and Anglo-American Special Juries*, New York: New York University Press, 2006.

Ostrom 2004
Ostrom, B.J. *et al.*, 'Examining Trial Trends in State Courts: 1976-2002', *Journal of Empirical Legal Studies*, 2004, Vol. 1, p. 755-782.

Oxford 1955
Oxford Dictionary of Quotations, 2nd edn., Oxford: Oxford University Press, 1955.

Plucknett 1956
Plucknett, T.F.T., *A Concise History of the Common Law*, 5th edn., Boston: Little Brown, 1956.

Pollock & Maitland 1898
Pollock, F. & Maitland, F.W., *The History of English Law before the Time of Edward I*, 2nd edn., Cambridge: Cambridge University Press, 1898 (2 Vols.).

Pound 1941
Pound, R., *Appellate Procedure in Civil Cases*, Boston: Little Brown, 1941.

Priest & Klein 1984
Priest, G. & Klein, B., 'The Selection of Disputes for Litigation', *Journal of Legal Studies*, 1984, Vol. 13, p. 1-56.

Rabin 1986
Rabin, R., 'Federal Regulation in Historical Perspective', *Stanford Law Review*, 1986, Vol. 38, p. 1189-1326.

Ragland 1932
Ragland, G., Jr., *Discovery before Trial*, Chicago: Callaghan, 1932.

Rave 2006
Rave, D.T., 'Questioning the Efficiency of Summary Judgment', *New York University Law Review*, 2006, Vol. 81, p. 875-910.

Resnik 1982
Resnik, J., 'Managerial Judges', *Harvard Law Review*, 1982, Vol. 96, p. 374-448.

Resnik 2000
Resnik, J., 'Trial as Error, Jurisdiction as Injury: Transforming the Meaning of Article III', *Harvard Law Review*, 2000, Vol. 113, p. 924-1037.

Resnik 2003
Resnik, J., 'For Owen M. Fiss: Some Reflections on the Triumph and the Death of Adjudication', *University of Miami Law Review*, 2003, Vol. 58, p. 173-200.

Resnik 2006
Resnik, J., 'Whither and Whether Adjudication?', *Boston University Law Review*, 2006, Vol. 86, p. 1101-1154.

Resnik 2011
Resnik, J., 'Fairness in Numbers: A Comment on *AT&T v Conception, Wal-Mart v Dukes*, and *Turner v Rogers*', *Harvard Law Review*, 2011, Vol. 125, p. 78-170.

Rhode 1985
Rhode, D., 'Ethical Perspectives on Legal Practice', *Stanford Law Review*, 1985, Vol. 37, p. 589-652.

Schneider 2010
Schneider, E.M., 'The Changing Shape of Federal Civil Pretrial Practice: The Disparate Impact on Civil Rights and Employment Discrimination Cases', *University of Pennsylvania Law Review*, 2010, Vol. 158, p. 517-570.

Schuck 1986
Schuck, P.S., 'The Role of Judges in Settling Complex Cases: The Agent Orange Example', *University of Chicago Law Review*, 1986, Vol. 53, p. 337-365.

Schuck 1987
Schuck, P.S., *Agent Orange on Trial: Mass Toxic Disasters in the Courts*, enlarged edn., Cambridge, MA: Harvard University Press, 1987.

Seipp 2002
Seipp, D.J., 'Jurors, Evidences and the Tempest of 1499', in: Cairns, J. & McLeod, G. (eds.), *'The Dearest Birth Right of the People of England': The Jury in the History of the Common Law*, Oxford: Hart, 2002, p. 75-92.

Shapiro 1989
Shapiro, D.L., 'Federal Rule 16: A Look at the Theory and Practice of Rulemaking', *University of Pennsylvania Law Review*, 1989, Vol. 137, p. 1969-1998.

Shepherd & Cloud 1999
Shepherd, G.B. & Cloud, M., 'Time and Money: Discovery Leads to Hourly Billing', *University of Illinois Law Review*, 1999, p. 91-179.

Smith (Dewar ed.) 1982
Smith, T., *De Republica Anglorum*, c. 1565, Dewar, M. (ed.), Cambridge: Cambridge University Press, 1982.

Spence 1846
Spence, G., *The Equitable Jurisdiction of the Court of Chancery*, London: V. & R. Stevens/G.S. Norton, 1846.

Story 1836
Story, J., *Commentaries on Equity Jurisprudence as Administered in England and America*, Boston: Hillard, Gray, 1836 (2 Vols.).

Story 1838
Story, J., *Commentaries on Equity Pleadings*, Boston: Little Brown, 1838.

Subrin 1987
Subrin, S.N., 'How Equity Conquered Common Law: The Federal Rules of Civil Procedure in Historical Perspective', *University of Pennsylvania Law Review*, 1987, Vol. 135, p. 909-1002.

Subrin 1988
Subrin, S.N., 'David Dudley Field and the Field Code: A Historical Analysis of an Earlier Procedural Vision', *Law & History Review*, 1988, Vol. 6, p. 311-373.

Subrin 1998
Subrin, S.N., 'Fishing Expeditions Allowed: The Historical Background of the 1938 Federal Discovery Rules', *Boston College Law Review*, 1998, Vol. 39, p. 691-745.

Sunderland 1925
Sunderland, E.R., 'An Appraisal of English Procedure', *Michigan Law Review*, 1925, Vol. 24, p. 109-129.

Sunderland 1933a
Sunderland, E.R., 'Scope and Method of Discovery before Trial', *Yale Law Journal*, 1933, Vol. 42, p. 863-877.

Sunderland 1933b
Sunderland, E.R., 'Improving the Administration of Civil Justice', *Annals of the American Academy of Political & Social Science*, 1933, Vol. 167, p. 60-83.

Sunderland 1937
Sunderland, E.R., 'The Theory and Practice of Pre-Trial Procedure', *Michigan Law Review*, 1937, Vol. 36, p. 215-226.

Sutherland 1973
Sutherland, D.W., *The Assize of Novel Disseisin*, Oxford: Clarendon Press, 1973.

Thayer 1898
Thayer, J.B., *Preliminary Treatise on Evidence at the Common Law*, Boston: Little Brown, 1898.

van Caenegem 1973
van Caenegem, R.C., 'History of European Civil Procedure', in: M. Capelletti (ed.), *International Encyclopedia of Comparative Law*, Tübingen: Mohr, 1973, p. 3-79.

von Mehren 1982
von Mehren, A.T., 'The Significance for Procedural Practice and Theory of the Concentrated Trial: Comparative Remarks', in: Horn, N. *et al.* (eds.), *Europäisches Rechtsdenken in Geschichte und Gegenwart: Festschrift für Helmut Coing*, München: Beck, 1982 (2 Vols.), Vol. 2, p. 361-371.

Wald 1998
Wald, P.M., 'Summary Judgment at Sixty', *Texas Law Review*, 1998, Vol. 76, p. 1897-1945.

Weigend 2006
Weigend, T., 'Why Have a Trial When You Can Have a Bargain?', in: Duff, A. *et al.* (eds.), *The Trial on Trial*, Vol. 2, Oxford: Hart, 2004-2006 (3 Vols.), p. 207-222.

Weinstein 2009
Weinstein, J.B., 'Comments on Owen M. Fiss, *Against Settlement* (1984)', *Fordham Law Review*, 2009, Vol. 75, p. 1265-1272.

Wigmore 1940
Wigmore, J.H., *A Treatise on the Anglo-American System of Evidence in Trials at Common Law*, 3rd edn., Boston: Little Brown, 1940 (10 Vols.).

Willman 2004
Willman, P., *Die Konzentrationsmaxime: Eine Untersuchung heutigen und früheren Rechts*, Berlin: Duncker & Humblot, 2004.

Wissler 2010
Wissler, R.L., 'Court-Connected Settlement Procedures: Mediation and Judicial Settlement Conferences', *Ohio State Journal of Dispute Resolution*, 2010, Vol. 26, p. 271-325.

Wonnacott 2011
Wonnacott, M., *The History of the Law of Landlord and Tenant in England and Wales*, Clark, NJ: Lawbook Exchange, 2011.

Wood 2010
Wood, D.P., 'Summary Judgment and the Law of Unintended Consequences', *Oklahoma City University Law Review*, 2010, Vol. 36, p. 231-252.

Woolf 1995
Woolf, H., *Access to Justice: Interim Report to the Lord Chancellor on the Civil Justice System in England and Wales*, London: HMSO, 1995.

Woolf 1996
Woolf, H., *Access to Justice: Final Report to the Lord Chancellor on the Civil Justice System in England and Wales*, London: HMSO, 1996.

Yale 1965
Yale, D.E.C., *Lord Nottingham's 'Manual of Chancery Practice' and 'Prolegomena of Chancery and Equity'*, Cambridge: Cambridge University Press, 1965.

Yeazell 1987
Yeazell, S.C., *From Medieval Group Litigation to the Modern Class Action*, New Haven: Yale University Press, 1987.

Yeazell 1994
Yeazell, S.C., 'The Misunderstood Consequences of Modern Civil Process', *Wisconsin Law Review*, 1994, Vol. 1994, p. 631-678.

Yeazell 2001
Yeazell, S.C., 'Re-Financing Civil Litigation', *DePaul Law Review*, 2001, Vol. 51, p. 183-218.

Yeazell 2004
Yeazell, S.C., 'Getting What We Asked For, Getting What We Paid For, and Not Liking What We Got: The Vanishing Civil Trial', *Journal of Empirical Legal Studies*, 2004, Vol. 1, p. 943-971.

Zuckerman 2006a
Zuckerman, A., 'From Formalism to Court Control of Adjudication', in: Cadiet, L. & Canivet, G. (eds.), *De la commémoration d'un code à l'autre: 200 ans de procédure civile en France: 1806-1976-2006*, Paris: Lexis Nexis/Litec, 2006, p. 339-362.

Zuckerman 2006b
Zuckerman, A., *Zuckerman on Civil Procedure: Principles of Practice*, 2nd edn., London: Sweet & Maxwell, 2006.

R.L. Marcus

EXTREMISM IN THE PURSUIT OF TRUTH IS OUR 'VIRTUE': THE AMERICAN INFATUATION WITH BROAD DISCOVERY

I take my title from Barry Goldwater. When he accepted the Republican nomination for President of the United States in 1964, Goldwater said: 'I would remind you that extremism in the defence of liberty is no vice! And let me remind you that moderation in the pursuit of justice is no virtue!' A similar attitude pervades the American approach to discovery; for a long time, it seemed that a 'leave no stone unturned' attitude prevailed.

At first blush, that attitude seems to fly in the face of efficiency. Certainly it seems that most (or all) of the rest of the world has been repelled by the American embrace of broad discovery. A number of countries have adopted 'blocking' statutes to prevent American discovery from occurring on their soil.[1] Most permit nothing of the sort in cases before their courts. And even though American courts will make U.S. discovery available to produce evidence for use in the tribunals of other nations,[2] many nations will not use the fruits of that discovery.[3]

1 Born 1996, p. 856-871.

2 See 28 U.S.C. Paragraph 1782(a) provides that a U.S. district court may order anyone found within the United States to give testimony or provide documents 'for use in a proceeding in a foreign or international tribunal'. The Supreme Court has taken a broad view of what is a 'tribunal' under the statute, including proceedings before the Directorate-General for Competition of the Commission of the EC. See *Intel Corp. v Advance Micro Devices, Inc.*, 542 U.S. 241 (2004).

3 Lower courts in the U.S. had disagreed about whether it was necessary to show that the foreign tribunal would accept the evidence. One view was that there is no point in authorizing American discovery - and much potential mischief - if the non-U.S. tribunal will not even use the resulting material. Another view, however, was that it is inefficient to expect the U.S. court to guess whether the foreign court will accept or reject the evidence. See Wright, Miller & Marcus 2010, § 2005.1, p. 82-84. The Supreme Court has stated that there is no requirement that the American court worry about whether the information would be subject to judicial discovery in the other country; '[w]here the foreign tribunal would readily accept relevant information discovered in the United States, application of a foreign-discoverability rule would be senseless'. *Intel Corp. v Advanced Micro Devices, Inc.*, 542 U.S. 241, 260-62 (2004).

To varying degrees, the prevailing attitudes toward fact-gathering in the rest of the world seem to be variants of 'Do it yourself' (i.e., without court assistance) or 'Leave it to the judge'.[4] Those alternatives may achieve efficiency because those who must do it themselves can only trouble others moderately in their efforts, and because judges who control the process may inherently behave reasonably, or at least do not often engage in wasteful wild goose chases.

This paper explores the American romance with broad discovery to evaluate whether it is wasteful. Much as it seems easy to prove that Americans go to excess, the reality is more nuanced. For more than a generation, American discovery rules have emphasized the concept of 'proportionality', stressing that the amount of discovery should be proportional to the stakes in the litigation.[5] During that same time, discovery rules have been changed to limit excessive discovery, and some voluntary disclosure has been required without formal discovery at all.[6]

Considerable empirical research shows that over-discovery is not nearly as large a problem as might be expected from the attention it receives. Extremism in the pursuit of truth - at least through discovery - turns out to be a rare thing. Calculated evidence-gathering that corresponds to the needs of the case seems much more common. And discovery does frequently reveal important - sometimes crucial - evidence. Particularly in view of the American reliance on private enforcement of public laws through litigation,[7] it can be said that the level of discovery is generally fairly efficient. Of course, one may argue against the entire project of private enforcement, but in efficiency terms there are very respectable points in favour of it.

The alternative arrangements in the rest of the world are not obviously better in producing truthful outcomes, and perhaps not even more efficient. Clearly the U.S. and Europe have - at a general level - divergent attitudes toward privacy, at least when it comes to revealing evidence for use in civil litigation. Partly as a consequence, as Professor Damaška has observed, the European willingness to permit civil litigation to be resolved on a very thin evidentiary basis is baffling to Americans.[8] It may be 'efficient' in reducing the efforts expended on litigation, but it seems less efficient in terms of ensuring that legal outcomes correspond with the law they supposedly enforce, in other words, in serving the truth.

4 Indeed, Professor Hazard has written that 'recognizing in a party a *right* to require production of evidence, as distinct from a party's right to ask the *court* to require production of evidence, violates the constitutional principle of adjudication in a civil law system'. Hazard 1998a, p. 1017.

5 See Federal Rules of Civil Procedure 26(b)(2)(C)(iii), directing the court to limit the discovery if 'the burden or expense of the proposed discovery outweighs its likely benefit, considering the needs of the case, the amount in controversy, the parties' resources, the importance of the issues at stake in the action, and the importance of the discovery in resolving those issues'.

6 See Marcus 1998.

7 See Farhang 2010 for an extended analysis of the extent and importance of private enforcement in the American political structure.

8 Damaška 1997, p. 843, noting that Continental Civil Procedure exhibits 'a considerable degree of tolerance - almost an insouciance, to common law eyes - for the incompleteness of evidentiary material'.

The American reality, meanwhile, does not normally correspond to the caricature prevalent in some quarters. The concept of proportionality did not immediately take hold, but seems increasingly important.[9] The advent of E-Discovery has magnified discovery and reportedly also its costs. But there is also reason to suspect that it could be cheaper and much more complete than traditional hard-copy discovery. That outcome would serve interests of truth-finding *and* efficiency.

Altogether, then, it is at least possible to regard the American adversarial method of fact-gathering as efficient and preferable to others. This is not an argument that it is perfect. To the contrary, efforts to constrain and contain American discovery have preoccupied the American rule makers since the mid 1970s, and they do not seem likely to leave center stage soon. But despite those reform efforts, America's core commitment to broad discovery (compared to the rest of the world) persists.

1. The Promise

Discovery has long held out a promise for American litigants that few others could hope to emulate. Even before the 'revolution' in discovery wrought by the Federal Rules of Civil Procedure in 1938, the availability of court-ordered evidence production in the U.S. had ruffled foreign feathers. In the 1870s, American discovery efforts provoked formal German diplomatic protests.[10] But the American discovery of that era was a pale imitation - if even an imitation - of the regime introduced by the Federal Rules and gradually expanded for three decades after the rules went into effect.

It's important to recognize that the adoption of the Federal Rules really produced a revolution. As described by Professor Subrin: 'If one adds up all the types of discovery permitted in individual [American] state courts, one finds some precursors to what later became discovery under the Federal Rules, but ... no one state allowed the total panoply of devices. Moreover, the Federal Rules, as they became law in 1938, eliminated features of discovery that in some states had curtailed the scope of discovery and the breadth of its use'.[11]

The framers of the Federal Rules recognized that their new system broke new ground, and worried that it would be rejected as out of control.[12] But the Supreme Court embraced it, and within a decade proclaimed: 'No longer can the time-honoured cry of "fishing expedition" serve to preclude a party from inquiring into the facts underlying his opponent's case. Mutual knowledge of all the relevant facts gathered by both parties is essential to proper litigation'.[13] One might almost say

9 As I have written recently, although the proportionality requirements were not enforced vigorously for more than a decade after they were added, they are being invoked much more frequently. See Wright, Miller & Marcus 2010, § 2008.1, p. 155-167.

10 Born 1996, p. 849.

11 Subrin 1998, p. 719.

12 See Subrin 1998, p. 717-729.

13 *Hickman v Taylor*, 329 U.S. 495, 507 (1947).

that the Court was announcing that the pursuit of truth - perhaps even extremism in pursuit of truth - was the new credo.

The original rules seemed to invite the most aggressive discovery. Indeed, to counter any temptation to resist broad discovery, they insisted that unless the court entered a protective order against discovery (which was difficult to obtain) 'the frequency and use of these methods is not limited'.[14] Meanwhile, the march of technology made a much larger fund of information obtainable through discovery. The invention and widespread use of the photocopier meant that the volume of documents subject to discovery expanded exponentially. And in 1970, the prior requirement that parties seek court approval for document production requests was removed; instead, the rules permitted any party to demand any 'relevant' documents from another party or (by subpoena) from a non-party without any prior approval by a judge. Judges got involved only if the responding party sought protection from the court, and then the burden was on the party resisting discovery, not the one seeking production.[15]

This expansion of fact-gathering could readily be seen as furthering the interests of truth-finding. Certainly it permitted litigants who had limited information at the time the case began to use discovery to obtain what they lacked without it. That opportunity even expanded the legal grounds for relief in our common law system, according to Professor Friedenthal:

> '[O]ver the years developments in many areas such as products liability, employment discrimination, and consumer protection have been the result at least partly of broad-ranging discovery provisions. For example, lawyers would not have pushed in the courts and in the Legislatures for expanded causes of action hinged on proof that defendants knew or should have known of a product's danger, if such proof were normally unavailable. The ability of plaintiffs' attorneys to obtain a corporate defendant's records, to depose corporate employees, and to send searching interrogatories has had a substantial impact in particular areas of law, and is one important factor in the dramatic increase in cases filed'.[16]

Indeed, this existence of broad discovery could be regarded as serving truth in the most desirable manner by deterring potential wrongdoers from pursuing courses of conduct forbidden by the law. In the words of Dean Carrington:

> 'Every day, hundreds of American lawyers caution their clients that an unlawful course of conduct will be accompanied by serious risk of exposure at the hands of some hundreds of thousands of lawyers, each armed with a subpoena power by which misdeeds can be uncovered'.[17]

Often, discovery would reveal the smoking gun that proved liability; striking to the eyes of the uninitiated, American defendants really would produce harmful information.

14 Federal Rules of Civil Procedure 26(a) (1970 version).
15 For details on these developments, see Marcus 1998, p. 748-53.
16 Friedenthal 1981, p. 818.
17 Carrington 1997, p. 54.

Courts came to accept that discovery was essential to the truth-seeking goal even when there was no smoking gun. For example, a federal appellate court in a discrimination case explained:

> 'Because employers rarely leave a paper trail - or 'smoking gun' - attesting to a discriminatory intent, disparate treatment plaintiffs often must build their cases from pieces of circumstantial evidence which cumulatively undercut the credibility of the various explanations offered by the employer'.[18]

As Professor Hazard put it, the confluence of broad discovery and evolving grounds of legal relief enshrined discovery as a value unto itself: 'Broad discovery is thus not a mere procedural rule. Rather, it has become, at least in our era, a procedural institution perhaps of virtually constitutional foundation'.[19] Some courts even seemed to embrace the idea of filing a lawsuit mainly or solely to obtain discovery: '[C]ertain civil suits may be instigated for the very purpose of gaining information for the public. ... Civil Litigation in general often exposes the need for governmental action or correction'.[20] One might view broad discovery and truth as intertwined and interdependent.

2. The Caricature

Applause for this vision of broad discovery was never universal even in America, however; one did not have to look abroad for those who found the vision actually to be a caricature. Beginning in the 1970s, and increasing since, broad discovery has come under attack as subverting rather than seeking truth. There was surely something to this criticism.

Efficiency: As a starting point, it could hardly be said that discovery was always an efficient way of developing information. Carried on in an atmosphere of fairly extreme adversarialism (because the stakes were high), it invited inefficiency. Litigants could not ask the other side to provide the 'most important' documents, because that would not be a proper discovery request. Instead, they had to make more objective requests, based partly on guesswork about what might or should exist since they would often not know what did exist. This was *discovery*, after all.

In an atmosphere of trust, efficiency might not suffer too much. Each side might be able to determine informally what materials the other side had and tailor its discovery requests accordingly. Although discovery could be used (among other things) to determine the existence and whereabouts of records and witnesses, this sort of informal exchange was not common. Indeed, it might even be regarded as inconsistent with the American adversarial tradition.

In an atmosphere of extreme mistrust, efficiency is the first victim. Responding parties may parse discovery requests in the most remarkable way to avoid turning over harmful information. Requesting parties therefore shun rifle-shot requests

18 *Hollander v American Cyanamid Co.*, 895 F.2d 80, 84-85 (2nd Cir. 1990).

19 Hazard 1998b, p. 1694.

20 *Chicago Council of Lawyers v Bauer*, 522 F.2d 242, 258 (7th Cir. 1975).

narrowly targeting crucial information because they understandably fear that they will not get what they need unless they make very broad requests that make narrow readings impossible. So discovery requests tend to be extremely expansive. Plaintiff lawyers admit that 'We make overbroad requests because we know that we can only get the material we want by asking for a huge amount of additional material we don't want'.

The responding parties then tend to move in the opposite direction from withholding items based on an unduly narrow reading of a discovery request. If there is no way to parse the request to exclude the items the responding party really does not want to disclose, the alternative is to honour it literally, or even go beyond it, producing with a vengeance. Thus was born the idea of 'dump truck' responses to document discovery. The dump truck would deliver a huge mound of material to the requesting party, which then had to sort through myriad items of little or no importance to find the few items that really mattered. Efficiency went out the window.

A further element of waste was introduced by the right of the responding party to make and defend objections to the document requests. Litigation about those objections could be extremely time-consuming, but sometimes after it was finally resolved with a court order to produce, the outcome was that the producing party then would reveal that actually nothing had been withheld on the basis of that objection. The entire effort resolving the objection was therefore a waste.

This sort of contretemps underscores a long-term reality for American civil litigation: Discovery is often the main battlefield. Merits decisions (judicial decisions about who wins and loses the case on the merits) were rarely possible on the pleadings, and usually could not be made at summary judgment until discovery had been entirely or largely completed. Moreover, merits litigation is extremely risky. For defendants, we are told, going to trial is often too risky. For plaintiffs, the stakes at summary judgment may raise similar risks. Better, perhaps, to fight discovery fights; then even a loss only means that one has to release some additional material, or one does not obtain some additional material that might be useful (or might not even exist).

Burden: As should be obvious, this activity was costly. For a responding party that was honouring its obligations, the task of finding all the responsive items it has within its 'possession, custody, or control' could be monumental. The larger the entity, the larger the burden.

The extent of this burden, it should be clear, depends a great deal on the inherent inefficiencies of the adversarial stance of the parties in relation to discovery. The vehemence brought to litigation of discovery disputes has long repelled the American courts. For more than 40 years, the Federal Rules have instructed the judge to impose on the losing party the cost of a discovery motion unless it finds that the losing party's position was 'substantially justified'.[21] For more than 25 years, the rules have also required the parties to confer before approaching the court with a discovery dispute in an effort to negotiate a resolution

21 Federal Rules of Civil Procedure 37(a)(5).

without the court's intervention.[22] Courts, as well as parties, can be burdened by discovery.

Indeed, as a renowned magistrate judge observed in the 1980s, the entire judicial system depends on non-judicial resolution of discovery issues: 'The courts, sorely pressed by demands to try cases promptly and to rule thoughtfully on potentially case-dispositive motions, simply do not have the resources to police closely the operation of the discovery process. The whole system of civil adjudication would ground to a virtual halt if the courts were forced to intervene in even a modest percentage of discovery transactions'.[23] A recent case involving sanctions for failure to preserve electronic information provides a vivid example. The judge, in her long opinion imposing sanctions on plaintiffs, noted in a footnote that she and her law clerks spent over 300 hours working on this one discovery dispute.[24] Admittedly, this was an important discovery dispute, but spending 300 hours of court time to resolve it cannot be regarded as efficient.

The burden on the parties can dwarf the burden on the courts. The recurrent complaint is from what might be called the 'producer' side – usually the defence – that must gather and produce the material sought through discovery. But there is at least some basis for believing that the burdens are at least as great for those seeking information. It takes a lot of effort to paw through all the material that comes off the dump truck and identify the few genuinely important items.

These burdens compare unfavourably with what seems to be the cost of similar litigation preparation in the rest of the world. A study done in 2010 probed this question by gathering data on the litigation costs of multinational corporations by comparing their revenues from given countries with the litigation cost they incurred defending cases in the courts of those countries. According to this study, the cost of American litigation far outstripped the cost of litigation in any other country, measured as a proportion of the business done by the companies surveyed in the countries in question.[25] For any one concerned about burden (or efficiency) it offers a sobering contrast.

22 Federal Rules of Civil Procedure 37(a)(1).

23 *In re Convergent Technologies Securities Litigation*, 108 F.R.D. 328, 331 (N.D. Cal. 1985).

24 *The Pension Committee of the University of Montreal Pension Plan v Bank of America Securities, LLC*, 685 F.Supp.2d 456, 471-72 n. 56 (S.D.N.Y. 2010).

25 See 'Litigation Cost Survey of Major Companies', available in the Library at <http://civilconference.uscourts.gov>, last consulted in June 2012. This research effort collected data on legal expenditures (not including amounts paid to satisfy judgments or settle cases) by Fortune 200 companies for the period 2004 to 2008. It contrasted the amounts paid for U.S. litigation costs and non-U.S. litigation costs. The comparison presented those legal costs as percentages of revenue – U.S. legal costs as a percentage of U.S. revenue, and non-U.S. legal costs as a percentage of non-U.S. revenues.
Figure 9, on p. 13 of the study, presents those comparisons, and they are striking:

	U.S. costs	Non-U.S. costs
2004	0.48%	0.11%
2005	0.48%	0.06%
2006	0.56%	0.07%
2007	0.53%	0.06%
2008	0.51%	0.06%

→

The collateral purpose temptation: Another disagreeable feature of discovery in some cases is what might be called the collateral purpose temptation. Discovery is justified only to the extent it provides information that is relevant to the lawsuit and, hopefully, information that will advance the case toward resolution. But the actual motivation for discovery may go beyond such goals.[26]

As the world increasingly understands, information itself has a value. Governmentally-required information revelation (as occurs due to discovery) may, therefore, be very attractive to those who want to use the information for a variety of purposes besides the one for which government intends it be used. And there certainly have been examples of collateral purposes that seem to influence discovery efforts.

As noted above, some courts have said they are receptive to the prospect of litigation filed primarily to reveal information, not to seek other relief in court. More frequently, particularly in intellectual property litigation, there are serious concerns that material sought through discovery may be used to obtain a competitive advantage in the marketplace. It has even been suggested that discovery of certain intellectual property without suitable protections against misuse would constitute an illegal taking of private property for a 'public' purpose (ostensibly of resolving litigation).[27] There have even been instances of parties marketing the fruits of discovery.

Obviously, such marketing efforts bring us no closer to the 'truth' that discovery supposedly serves. Indeed, for those seeking the truth in terms of vindication in court, one might even criticize the costs of discovery as a sort of tax on getting to the truth.

Subverting the truth: If the promise of broad discovery is that it will provide the means to determine the truth, the reality, according to some, is that it subverts the truth. In large measure this asserted effect results from the two features just considered. The inefficiency of discovery makes litigation extremely expensive and quite unpredictable. The burden of responding to discovery, particularly for large organizational litigants, may seem to outstrip the actual stakes in the case.

At some point, these pressures may cause some parties to settle with justice undone, producing the opposite of the truth we are seeking. To the extent that is true, one could conclude that the American way of discovery actually installs a regime in which the truth is frustrated, not furthered. Some defence-side lawyers argue that plaintiff lawyers pursue broad discovery precisely to prevent resolution of cases on their merits; knowing they have weak claims, they want to catch the

As the study points out, measured in this manner the U.S. costs range from four times as much to nine times as much. It suffices to emphasize that they are much higher. The survey was administered and the data were compiled by the Searle Center on Law, Regulation, and Economic Growth of Northwestern University School of Law.

26 The risk of collateral purposes has long been recognized. For example, as the Supreme Court put it in a leading case, 'when the purpose of a discovery request is to gather information for use in proceedings other than the pending suit, discovery is properly denied'. *Oppenheimer Fund, Inc. v Sanders*, 437 U.S. 340, 352 n.17 (1978). When the purpose of discovery appears designed for use in business rather than in any proceedings, the case is even clearer.

27 Gelfand 1988.

defendant in a discovery mistake and ask the court to declare them victors on the basis of that mistake – by imposing the sanction of default or some similar disadvantage – in cases they could not win on the relevant evidence.

3. The Reality

As is often (perhaps always) true, the actual situation lies somewhere between the extremes, such as those set forth above. For some time, as a result, American academics have poured scorn on the hyperbolic attacks on broad discovery that have recurred for the last forty years.[28]

Hard data on discovery are not easy to obtain, In the 1960s, while considering pervasive revisions of the Federal Rules, the rules makers commissioned a comprehensive study of the way the federal discovery provisions had worked for their first quarter century. That period had begun with forecasts that broad discovery would destroy the American adversary system, and also that it would produce a utopia with total sharing of essential information. The study showed that the actual effect had been in between: 'By means of discovery and other reforms of recent centuries, the adversary system has been altered but not transformed. Deeply rooted in tradition, in the rules, and in the interests of litigants, the adversarial method of conducting civil suits has determined how discovery has worked in practice. Basically, it is used by each side to strengthen its own case. ... Most lawyers use it for the information purposes anticipated by the rules and not for the tactical purposes condemned by the authorities. Most lawyers use discovery successfully, with gains in evidence, names of witnesses, awareness of new issues, and other information useful in settlement negotiations and at trial. Discovery enables each side to learn more about the other's position, but each is still motivated to conceal as much as possible, particularly evidence or witnesses that will have a dramatic effect at trial. Many lawyers continue to be surprised by their adversaries at trial, despite their own use of discovery'.[29]

More recent research has produced somewhat similar results. In particular, case-based studies by the American Federal Judicial Center in 1997[30] and 2009[31] both showed that in most cases lawyers found that the amount of discovery done before the case was resolved was about right. Among those who thought the amount was not quite right, there was a fairly even split between those who felt that there was too little discovery and those who believed there was too much discovery. The caricature, in other words, was not accurate. Perhaps unexpectedly, there was some indication that discovery is costlier for plaintiffs than for defendants. Also somewhat different from the normal complaints about discovery, it appeared that deposition discovery was costlier than document discovery, even though the strongest criticism was directed at document discovery. In the 2009 survey, it was striking that lawyers who reported that the level of discovery in their individual

28 See, e.g., Mullenix 1994.
29 Glaser 1968, p. 234.
30 Willging *et al.* 1997.
31 Lee & Willging 2009.

cases was about right also said that they believed that discovery in most litigation, or in general, was unduly extensive and expensive. This divergence could be seen as the difference between rumour and actual knowledge; the lawyers had actual knowledge of their own cases, and relied on rumour about the general conditions in litigation.

One feature of the caricature is the claim that discovery costs far outstrip the stakes in litigation. That attitude may be reinforced by the conclusion, reported above, that multinational companies found that American litigation was far costlier (measured as a proportion of revenues from various countries) than litigation in other countries. That finding seems to be contradicted by the finding of the Federal Judicial Center studies that discovery costs are almost always a small and seemingly reasonable proportion of the stakes involved in the litigation.[32] Yet multinational corporations find their litigation costs so much higher in the U.S. as a percentage of revenue from the country than in other industrialized countries.

But this contradiction is probably illusory. The reality is that litigation in the U.S. regularly involves higher stakes than litigation elsewhere. Unlike most of the rest of the world, the U.S. often permits large damage recoveries for pain and suffering or emotional distress. As a leading treatise acknowledged long ago, '[b]ecause pain and suffering damages are not compensatory, at least in the ordinary sense, there is no clear method of measuring them; indeed, there is almost no method at all'.[33] Although some decry that sort of award,[34] the reality is that it increases the heft of litigation.

Punitive damages claims also can significantly raise the stakes in a variety of kinds of litigation. But this effect may be overstated. As a recent study reported,

> '[c]ontrary to public belief, juries rarely award punitive damages, and award them especially rarely in products liability and medical malpractice cases. Rather, juries tend to award punitive damages in intentional misconduct cases. When juries do award punitive damages, they do so in ways that relate strongly to compensatory awards'.[35]

Notwithstanding, some American academics vigorously challenge the use of punitive damages; one recent article characterized them as 'the legal version of vigilantism and blood feuds'.[36]

Another feature of American litigation that may contribute to the higher litigation expenses multinational corporations reportedly experience in the U.S. is that large organizations often face litigation that involves pro-plaintiff attorney fee-shifting statutes that vary the American Rule requiring each party to pay its own

32 See Willging *et al.* 1997, p. 548-549. Table 6 shows that, at the median, discovery expenses were 3 per cent of the stakes in litigation. At the 95th percentile, they were about a third of the stakes.

33 Dobbs 1973, p. 545.

34 See Niemeyer 2004.

35 Eisenberg *et al.* 2004, p. 745. These conclusions have been disputed. See Hersch & Viscusi 2004, reporting that juries award punitive damages more frequently than judges, and that jury awards correlate less with compensatory damages.

36 Redish & Mathews 2004, p. 2.

lawyer. Those provisions are commonplace in many environmental and consumer protection statutes, and sometimes fee awards in such cases could outstrip compensatory recoveries.[37] But more generally, the American Rule on attorney fees requires each side to pay its own, so American plaintiffs are not deterred by the prospect of having to pay their opponents' fees, and multinational corporations in the U.S. cannot look forward to collecting their attorneys' fees from the other side if they win.

Other rules can have different effects. The prospect of recovering attorneys' fees can itself magnify the cost of litigation. At least in England, before the Woolf Reforms Professor Zuckerman reported that the prospect of full indemnity for attorneys' fees could (and often did) prompt all parties to increase their expenditure on litigation:

> '[O]nce it is clear that a dispute is destined to go all the way to trial, the indemnity principle tends to erode resistance to costs. ... Indeed, a point may come where the parties would have reason to persist with investment in litigation, not so much for the sake of a favorable judgment on the merits as for the purpose of recovering the money already expended in the dispute, which may well outstrip the value of the subject-matter at issue'.[38]

Finally, American plaintiffs almost always have the right to a jury trial,[39] a factor that introduces additional uncertainty. Although judges can cut back large awards, they can only do so in very remarkable circumstances; extremely substantial jury awards often survive judicial review.

Altogether, what these features of American litigation can mean is that some regard litigating all the way to a final decision is too risky because the outcome could be too crushing. In such a setting, particularly with insurance companies to fund substantial settlements with money that does not come out of the settling defendants' pockets, it is not surprising that there are accusations that litigation can have a value that far outstrips the value of the underlying claim, that 'the merits don't matter'. As one study of American securities fraud class actions put it, '[w]ith adjudication before trial unavailable as a practical matter and adjudication at trial a virtually unthinkable alternative, settlement becomes a foregone conclusion'.[40] In that sense, some urge, truth is frustrated. But even if that critique has some justification, it is difficult to conclude that evidence-gathering itself is the driving force. Instead, discovery seems in general to be calibrated to the (admittedly high) stakes involved in American litigation.

And that calibration is no accident. For one thing, given the American Rule that parties must usually pay their own attorney fees, the investment in litigation

37 See *City of Riverside v Rivera*, 477 U.S. 561 (1986), in which the Supreme Court upheld a fee award of $245,000 even though plaintiffs' compensatory recoveries totalled only $33,000.

38 Zuckerman 1996, p. 778.

39 See, e.g., U.S. Const. Amend VII, guaranteeing a right to jury trial in federal court for suits at law seeking more than $20. All, or almost all, states also have constitutional provisions guaranteeing the right to jury trial.

40 Alexander 1991, p. 567. This conclusion has been questioned. See Seligman 1994.

may tend toward being proportional to the stakes. As Professor Zuckerman observed (quoted above), the reverse rule of full indemnity in England tended often to prompt excessive expenditure on litigation as a way of recouping the sums already spent on litigation. Beyond that, the American rules themselves seek to constrain discovery and make it proportional. Although until the 1980s the Federal Rules invited almost unlimited discovery,[41] that invitation eventually was removed and rules insisting on proportionality were installed in its place.[42] Numerical limitations were also placed on the use of various discovery devices.[43] And a moratorium was placed on initiation of formal discovery to require the parties first to confer about a discovery plan and, hopefully, to exchange some basic information up front.[44] Judges, meanwhile, were prodded to take a more prominent role in regulating discovery, providing some 'adult supervision' for this adversary process.[45]

Ideally, these rule changes should fortify the existing and understandable urge toward discovery that fits the case. Ideally, then, the trend should be towards both truth and efficiency. Operating in the real world, we must admit that we have not reached that happy medium. And there surely are U.S. cases that fit the caricature. But on balance the American approach has not rejected the broad discovery path that was chosen seventy years ago.

4. The Alternative

Since the U.S. is an outlier, and perhaps unique, it is worthwhile to compare alternatives. In terms of truth and efficiency, they might be clearly preferable.

In terms of truth production, there are certainly many complaints that American discovery operates as a bludgeon that deprives parties - particularly defendants - of a true outcome. Given the repeated reports that American discovery ordinarily involves expenditures that are actually proportional to the stakes in the litigation, that argument seems less compelling. Of course, one could argue that the stakes themselves defeat some versions of the truth, but the panoply of features of American law that permit large recoveries (e.g., pain and suffering recoveries, punitive damages, and jury trial) ought to be appreciated to be features of the 'truth' embraced by American litigation.

41 Prior to 1983, Federal Rules of Civil Procedure 26(a) said: 'Unless the court orders otherwise under subdivision (c) of this rule [dealing with protective orders, which were difficult to obtain], the frequency of use of these methods is not limited'. This sentence was removed at the same time the proportionality idea was inserted into the rule. See Wright, Miller & Marcus 2010, § 2008.1.

42 See Federal Rules of Civil Procedure 26(b)(2)(C).

43 See Federal Rules of Civil Procedure 30(a)(2)(A)(i) (limit of 10 depositions); 33(a)(10 (limit of 25 interrogatories). See also Federal Rules of Civil Procedure 26(b)(2)(A) (authorizing alterations of these limits on depositions and interrogatories by court order, and imposition of a numerical limitation on requests for admission by local rule).

44 Federal Rules of Civil Procedure 26(d).

45 See Federal Rules of Civil Procedure 16(b)(3) (on contents of scheduling order for each case).

This American 'truth' seems to differ from the 'truths' embraced elsewhere. But the procedures used elsewhere don't, to American eyes, seem to serve even their 'truth'. Most of the rest of the world, for example, takes a much more exacting attitude toward what a plaintiff must include in a complaint. The proposed Transnational Rules of Civil Procedure illustrate this point and insist that the plaintiff include detailed facts in the complaint and attach or describe the evidence that will be used to support those claims.[46] Although such requirements may serve sometimes to deter groundless claims, they must also deter well-grounded claims of plaintiffs who lack the ability to obtain the evidence needed to prove their cases.

In terms of the 'truth' of any legal system, then, there is at least a valid basis for something more like the American willingness to accept rather loose 'notice' pleading and permit fairly considerable discovery as a way of exploring the evidentiary foundation of the claims thus stated. Even if the 'truth' is the more restrictive version accepted in the rest of the world, this technique would seem to have merit. Claims would at least get through the front door of litigation, although they might be disposed of through the side door of summary judgment or by other pre-trial means if the evidentiary support were not forthcoming. In this way, the promise of broad discovery might be realized.

At least in a significant number of American cases, the promise is probably realized. Parties do disclose damaging information through discovery, and their opponents are able to use that information to support claims (or defences) they could not have proved without it. In at least some cases, the process reveals that claims are not supportable, and many cases settle for small amounts. Some are even abandoned.

But that vision would be deceptive if the process itself defeated the truth, as the caricature suggests it might. Though assertions abound that expensive discovery has prompted litigants, particularly corporate litigants, to capitulate when they have perfectly good defences, hard proof of those assertions is difficult to produce. That is not surprising. Defendants would not much want to self-identify as patsies who could be pressured into settlement by aggressive discovery tactics. More significantly, however, such third-party research as we have shows that such cases are almost nonexistent, or at least fairly rare.

So one can conclude that the American practice of broad discovery - at least when measured by the American version of 'truth' - is fairly successful in a number of instances. The ever-declining trial rate[47] makes us uneasy about what exactly should be regarded as 'truth'. Without a trial, there is at least an argument that the 'truth' has not been determined in the way the system prefers that it be determined. That decline in trial rate could be attributed to the money and time consumed by broad discovery; perhaps that it is an obstacle to attaining truth. But another goal of discovery is to permit the parties to settle with sufficient knowledge of the evidence, so discovery may provide the parties with an agreed 'truth' in light of what they can obtain through discovery.

46 See ALI/UNIDROIT 2006, p. 111-112.

47 Galanter 2004.

As noted, trial is not the only possible method of deciding the case based on the evidence. Indeed, summary judgment has become considerably more frequent, particularly in some categories of cases. A prime example is employment discrimination litigation, where defendants frequently succeed in defeating plaintiffs' claims on summary judgment, normally occurring only after substantial discovery. That statistic might be cited to show that American laxity in pleading defeats the truth because it permits these cases to progress to this point. But that sort of argument disregards the multitude of cases in which summary judgment is *denied.* Assuming that plaintiffs lacking discovery would be unable to proceed in such cases, there is a valid argument that the American method is serving the truth by enabling those cases to proceed, and that other approaches that would prevent the cases from being prosecuted are frustrating the truth. And even in those cases in which defendants are granted summary judgment, there could be a 'truth' value in the process by which they were exonerated when that is compared to the suspicions of wrongdoing that might fester were pursuit of the truth through discovery not permitted.

Whether party-controlled discovery is necessary to achieve truthful results can be debated. As we have seen, giving the parties control of discovery introduces incentives to misuse it for improper purposes. Professor Langbein thus proposed, famously, that evidence gathering could be left to judicial officers instead of the parties; he called it 'the German advantage' in civil procedure.[48] But according to Professor Damaška, we can, at a minimum, be sceptical about that alternative. As he observes, continental civil procedure exhibits 'a considerable degree of tolerance - almost an insouciance, to common law eyes - for the incompleteness of evidentiary material'.[49] Leaving this task to the judge often will not do, because 'the protagonist who tends to monopolize fact gathering - the judge - is not really very energetic or resolute in his probing. His exercise of his near-monopoly power to develop evidence seems lazy'.[50] As Professor Damaška recognized, the American method was different: 'Because processes of proof are propelled by the parties self-interest, there is no lack of incentive to energetic evidentiary action'.[51] So there may be reason to fear for the truth if the parties themselves are not empowered to gather the evidence, perhaps even to be uneasy about whether all judges would be as vigorous in pursuit of truth as German judges.

Indeed, in Professor Fuller's view, the adversary method is the only way to overcome the tendency of even the most assiduous judicial officer to adopt and pursue an early 'hunch', causing her to disregard evidence that the adversary system would require her to consider:

> '[F]ailure generally attends the attempt to dispense with the distinct roles traditionally implied in adjudication. What generally occurs in practice is that at some early point a familiar pattern will seem to emerge from the evidence; an accustomed label is

48 Langbein 1985.

49 Damaška 1997, p. 843.

50 *Ibidem,* p. 844.

51 Damaška 1986, p. 122.

> wanting for the case and, without awaiting further proofs, this label is promptly assigned to it. It is a mistake to suppose that his premature cataloguing must necessarily result from impatience, prejudice or mental sloth. Often it proceeds from a very understandable desire to bring the hearing into some order and coherence, for without some tentative theory of the case there is no standard of relevance by which testimony may be measured. But what starts as a preliminary diagnosis designed to direct the inquiry tents, quickly and imperceptibly, to become a fixed conclusion, as all that confirms the diagnosis makes a strong imprint on the mind, while all that runs counter to it is received with diverted attention'.[52]

Perhaps even a German judge could not resist this tendency.

If our coordinate concern is efficiency, we may be inclined to reject party-controlled evidence-gathering because it is not efficient, even if it may be more reliable to get out the full story. Beyond a doubt, it may be prone to wastefulness. Parties seeking evidence are likely to ask for too much. Parties resisting disclosure are likely to fight too hard, and perhaps to contrive to provide too much chaff along with the wheat. Litigants who can see that the evidence proves they will lose have incentives to delay and obfuscate. Costs and delays will mount up.

It could be that judicial control of fact-gathering would be an antidote to these problems. But it could also be that the antidote is only as good as the judges and the system on which they rely. Actually, at least in terms of litigation duration (sometimes called 'delay'), American litigation seems reasonably efficient. Whether that is due to the model or other factors is uncertain. At least some countries that employ a model that seems like the German model (Italy comes to mind) seem to suffer from chronic problems of delay and, one suspects, litigation cost. Those problems have even prompted rulings by the European Court of Justice holding that the delays deny citizens their basic rights to a prompt resolution of their cases.

In sum, when measured in terms of serving the truth and in terms of efficiency, the American method seems to stand up fairly well compared to the apparent alternatives despite its bad reputation.

5. The Future

Even if the basic American format is likely to continue to prevail for U.S. litigation for the foreseeable future, it could be modified to be more effective in achieving truth and/or efficiency. As noted, many changes to the American rules have been adopted to prevent and confine perceived discovery overkill. The Supreme Court recently signalled that pleading scrutiny should also be tightened up due, in part, to the cost of discovery,[53] and that development has sparked an intense debate about whether this tightening should be loosened by either legislation or a rule change.

Nonetheless, actual or possible changes under consideration in the U.S. might begin to serve interests of accuracy or efficiency.

Disclosure: In some countries, it is said, parties can be relied upon to disclose evidence without the need for costly and intrusive discovery forays. Certainly that

52 Fuller 1978, p. 383.

53 See *Bell Atlantic Corp. v Twombly*, 550 U.S. 544 (2007).

sort of exchange could be more efficient than vigorous disputes about discovery and huge efforts to find the relevant needle in a haystack of largely irrelevant material. In the U.S., we have for nearly a half century recognized that the prosecution in a criminal case has a constitutional obligation to turn over certain exculpatory material.[54] Perhaps a similar directive for civil cases could improve the search for truth and reduce the high discovery costs that arise in many cases.

Twenty years ago, the federal rules makers attempted to introduce something of the sort - an obligation that each side turn over 'core information' at the beginning of the case, and before formal discovery began.[55] Some even suggested that this new procedure might make formal discovery unnecessary in most cases. The proposal encountered a firestorm of opposition, and was made voluntary instead of binding, so each district court could decide for itself whether to adhere to the national disclosure rule. Even with that opt-out provision, Justice Scalia of the Supreme Court dissented from adoption of the new disclosure rule on the ground, essentially, that it was un-American:

> 'The proposed new regime does not fit comfortably within the American judicial system, which relies on adversarial litigation to develop the facts before a neutral decision-maker. By placing upon lawyers the obligation to disclose information damaging to their clients - on their own initiative and in a context where the lines between what must be disclosed and what need not be disclosed are not clear but require the exercise of considerable judgment - the new Rule would place intolerable strain upon lawyers' ethical duty to represent their clients and not to assist the opposing side'.[56]

The actual result of this experiment was a patchwork of disclosure regimes in the federal courts across the country. In 2000, the disclosure rule was made nationally binding but changed to require disclosure only of witnesses and documents that the disclosing party might use to support its claim or defence in the action.[57] In a sense, then, it provided for something that in many countries is a part of pleading - a statement by the party about what evidence it has to support its case. But if one assumes that vigorous pursuit of the truth calls also for inquiry into information a party possesses that helps its opponent, the revised disclosure provision could hardly supplant formal discovery. Even this somewhat toothless disclosure provision is regularly criticized, often for being ineffective. So for the present the disclosure route does not seem to hold promise in the American federal courts. Some American states - most notably Arizona - have more forceful disclosure regimes, but those state-court provisions do not seem likely to sweep the nation.

Electronic information and the CSI effect: American jurors increasingly are said to exhibit the 'CSI effect', named after the American television show 'Crime Scene Investigation'. In the TV show, crime scene investigators use a variety of high-

54 See *Brady v Maryland*, 373 U.S. 83 (1963).

55 See Marcus 1993, p. 805-812.

56 Scalia, J., dissenting from adoption of amendments to Federal Rules of Civil Procedure, 146 F.R.D. at 511 (1993).

57 See Federal Rules of Civil Procedure 26(a)(1).

technology devices to solve crimes. Often (perhaps always) they are able to come up with indisputable evidence of guilt, often including surveillance video pictures of the culprit at the scene of the crime. The reality is that surveillance is increasingly an almost constant feature of daily life, or at least daily urban life. Not only are there thousands of digital cameras focused on myriad public spaces, there are also such things as GPS features of cellular phones that permit very accurate tracking of where a person has been.[58]

This material is the stuff of civil litigation as well as TV crime dramas. For more than a decade, electronic discovery has been the Brave New World of American civil litigation.[59] It has grown rapidly into a major business, supposedly generating over $4 billion in revenue for American E-Discovery providers in 2009.

On one level, this information permits more accurate and 'truthful' determinations than could be had without it. Indeed, the Supreme Court has recently held that video footage of a police pursuit established as a matter of law that the police were justified in ramming the car they were pursuing even though the driver claimed he was in control of the car.[60] In other cases, parties have relied on such evidence to argue that their cases should be decided by courts based on digital evidence alone.[61] At least 'truth' might be said to get a boost from this prospect.

The variety of proof possibilities is illustrated from a recent article in a trial lawyers' magazine about the 'black boxes' in automobiles. For decades, the black boxes in airliners have been important to determining the reasons why they have crashed. Many modern cars have 'event data recorders' that record and retain a variety of data. GPS readings may be so precise that the location of vehicles can be analyzed by experts who can use it to reconstruct accidents. Consider the author's description of the use of this sort of data in a case in which a critical question was

58 For discussion of these developments, see Marcus 2009, p. 298-301.

59 For discussion, see Marcus 2006.

60 *Scott v Harris*, 550 U.S. 372 (2007).

61 In *Cameron v City of New York*, 598 F.3d 50 (2d Cir. 2010), plaintiff claimed that police officers had violated her civil rights by arresting her for complaining about police incompetence. The officers testified, however, that they had arrested plaintiff only after she reached violently into the police vehicle and tried to hurt the officer who was driving. The jury returned a verdict for defendants, which the appellate court overturned due to errors in the admission of evidence. It remanded for a new trial. Plaintiff claimed there was no need for a new trial because surveillance photographs taken by a security camera at the scene so strongly contradicted the officers' story that judgment should be entered against them. The appellate court rejected this argument because the photos, which were taken at two-second intervals, were blurry and it was 'difficult, if not impossible, to decipher from the photographic footage what is happening'. Although the court conceded that it seemed unlikely that plaintiff had reached inside the police car, but concluded that the photos 'do not rule out [the officers'] interpretation, as they would need to do' to justify entry of judgment for plaintiff. The court was cautious to leave open the possibility that in other cases there would be no need for a jury verdict: 'This is not to say that still photographs can never belie a party's interpretation of events so definitively that judgement as a matter of law is warranted. We hold only that *these* photographs, especially when viewed in light of the testimony and the record in this case, do not provide the level of certainty requisite to negate the jury's verdict'. *Idem* at 61.

where a given vehicle (called the 'bullet vehicle') was travelling at the time of the crash:

> 'While the plotted GPS data was not refined enough to define the specific distance between the vehicle and the edge line or centerline [of the highway], it was sufficient to show that the bullet vehicle was in the left westbound lane for about 22 seconds and that about 10 seconds before the collision, it moved into the right westbound lane. ... By defining the lane where the collision occurred, the credibility of both vehicle operators' testimony could be gauged on scientific evidence'.[62]

Surely this sort of detail promises greater 'truth' than the alternatives formerly available.

Whether reliance on digital data would result in efficiency is another matter. Many decry E-Discovery as hugely expensive and mainly wasteful. But coming up with a substitute is not easy. Increasingly, many or most organizations rely mainly or solely on electronic storage and transmission for their data. Often there are no other records, so E-Discovery must occur. Because this information is so important, potential litigants in America may often feel obliged to retain huge quantities of it, perhaps at great cost. Today, the question whether this preservation situation calls for further rulemaking about E-Discovery is under active review.

But the news is not all bad. For one thing, the increasing reliance on email may obviate some costly discovery activities. Depositions, for example, can be very costly. But the tendency of witnesses to commit so much to 'writing' via email may make them unnecessary to effective cross-examination at trial. Consider the views of an experienced trial lawyer on the possibility of a 'blind' cross-examination – one done without the benefit of a prior deposition of the witness:

> 'The advent and indeed overuse of e-mails has made blind cross-examination through the use of documents even simpler, and the use of depositions almost superfluous. Witnesses do not talk to each other anymore. They merely e-mail each other. Hundreds of e-mails. Thousands of e-mails. We are drowning in a flood of e-mails, and they are all part of e-discovery. The overuse of e-mails has made blind cross a much less risky task. Each witness's testimony is set forth in his or her own words through a series of 'instant messages' and endless e-mail exchanges. ... All you have to do for effective blind cross is to have the witness repeat what he or she wrote and then merely ask if the witness believes it to be a true statement at the time he or she wrote it'.[63]

Moreover, new technology may provide valuable solutions to the problems caused by the abundance of electronically stored information. A new technique called TREC may soon be ready, and it holds promise of using digital techniques to extract the pertinent information from huge masses of digital information.[64] Presently the most costly part of the document discovery process is the review of this material for responsiveness by attorneys (at high billing rates), so this technology may provide an inexpensive alternative to that activity. Coupled with a recent rule change that

62 Schorr & King 2011, p. 34.
63 Neubauer 2009, p. 25.
64 Grossman & Cormack 2011.

permits parties to avoid the risk of waiver of the attorney-client privilege,[65] this process could actually shorten the document review effort and save large sums of money. Thus might efficiency interests be served.

Whether the interests of truth will be served is arguably less clear. For a long time, American lawyers have looked for 'hot documents', the inculpatory materials that support a claimant's case. For centuries, courts have submitted the question whether to treat these hot documents as overcoming myriad witnesses who claim that the defendant never would consider the wrongful conduct plaintiff claims occurred.

The advent of email and text messaging greatly multiplies the chance that the plaintiff will be able to find some documents in the records of a large organization that support her theory of culpability. Whether that really provides a greater confidence that the adjudicated result will serve the truth could be debated, however. Because email and other digital communication seem to include myriad offhand comments, treating a few of those as sufficient to show that the organization acted for a bad motive is dubious. Not only could the search for those stray comments undermine efficiency by costing huge amounts of money, then, it might be seen as undercutting the accuracy interest as well.

But perhaps it would be possible to use digital information in context, improving the search for truth. Assume an employment discrimination case, for example, in which the plaintiff claims she was passed over for promotion because she is a woman. Discovery might unearth a couple of comments suggesting gender bias among her superiors, but if it also revealed a mountain of commentary lacking any such taint, that mountain might be treated as overcoming the probative value of the couple of inappropriate comments. Although the 'truth' is often somewhat elusive in such cases, one could argue that such a 'total recall' approach would permit a more accurate assessment whether the comments on which the plaintiff relies really support her theory.

'Simplified' procedure: For as long as people have thought about procedure as a distinct topic, there have been complaints about cost and delay. Often, the solution has been said to depend on simplifying unduly complicated procedures.

Actually, there is a fair argument that procedures are often complicated because the problems they seek to solve are themselves complicated. Those who endorse simple answers often turn against simplicity when they do not like the answers, and ask instead for more thorough methods to resolve problems.

In the U.S., there are recurrent efforts to achieve simplicity, at least in cases that do not have stakes that warrant more complicated procedures. In the California state courts, some low-stakes civil cases may be governed by simplified procedures.[66] More recently, California has also introduced a 'fast track' simplified trial option that depends on parties waiving a variety of procedural incidents that would otherwise slow the case down. Around a decade ago, the federal courts

65 See Federal Rules of Evidence 502.

66 See California Code of Civil Procedure § 90-99, providing 'economic litigation' procedures for certain cases.

considered the possibility of developing some simplified procedure techniques also.[67]

But for the present, simplified procedure seems largely to depend on party agreement, and quite often at least one party will not agree. Indeed, one feature of arbitration that has frustrated some is that even though it is supposed to be simpler and faster than litigation it often gets encrusted by procedures that are just as daunting as formal civil litigation.

6. Conclusion

Focusing on truth and efficiency looks to the right things. But too often it seems to involve tradeoffs - one can get an improvement in truth-seeking only by enduring an efficiency cost.

The American version may seem to emphasize truth-seeking as the sole consideration, to say that extremism in the pursuit of truth is a virtue, not a vice, and that the costs of that pursuit are insignificant compared to the importance of the goal. But the reality of U.S. litigation is much more nuanced, and the reforms of the last 30 years have certainly pushed efficiency to the fore.

The alternative 'efficient' model of the rest of the world is not uniform, but also does not seem clearly to have struck a better balance between truth and efficiency. To the contrary, it seems too often to give truth short shrift. Perhaps in systems that regard civil litigation as an entirely private matter, that orientation makes sense. In the U.S., 'private' civil litigation is an important method of enforcing important public laws. In that atmosphere, extremism in pursuit of truth may further public goals.

At the same time, even the American attitude is sufficiently nuanced to resist overkill in pursuit of truth. The caricature of American litigation is just that - a caricature. Even if there are actual cases that seem to exemplify the worst aspects of American litigation, they are not the norm. An other systems generate caricatures as well; Dickens' *Jarndyce v Jarndyce* is just one illustration.

So ultimately each nation is likely to strike its own balance between truth and efficiency. To some extent, that balance will depend heavily on the role civil litigation plays in that society. At the same time, however, national systems can learn important lessons for other nations. Not only is harmonization a desirable goal, but experience is an extremely valuable source of ideas for innovation. Extremism in pursuit of desirable innovations is surely a virtue.

[67] See Cooper 2002.

Bibliography

Alexander 1991
Alexander, J., 'Do the Merits Matter? A Study of Settlements in Securities Class Actions', *Stanford Law Review*, 1991, Vol. 43, p. 497-598.

ALI/UNIDROIT 2006
ALI/UNIDROIT, *Principles of Transnational Civil Procedure*, Cambridge: Cambridge University Press, 2006.

Born 1996
Born, G., *International Civil Litigation in United States Courts*, 3rd edn., Boston: Kluwer, 1996.

Carrington 1997
Carrington, P., 'Renovating Discovery', *Alabama Law Review*, 1997, Vol. 49, p. 51-78.

Cooper 2002
Cooper, E., 'Simplified Rules of Federal Procedure', *Michigan Law Review*, 2002, Vol. 100, p. 1794-1820.

Damaška 1986
Damaška, M., *The Faces of Justice and State Authority*, New Haven: Yale University Press, 1986.

Damaška 1997
Damaška, M.R., 'The Uncertain Fate of Evidentiary Transplants', *American Journal of Comparative Law*, 1997, Vol. 45, p. 839-852.

Dobbs 1973
Dobbs, D., *Law of Remedies: Damages, Equity, Restitution*, St. Paul: West Publishing Co., 1973.

Eisenberg *et al.* 2004
Eisenberg, T., LaFountain, N., Ostrom, B., Rottman, D. & Wells, M., 'Juries, Judges, and Punitive Damages', *Cornell Law Review*, 2004, Vol. 87, p. 743-782.

Farhang 2010
Farhang, S., *The Litigation State*, Princeton/Oxford: Princeton University Press, 2010.

Friedenthal 1981
Friedenthal, J., 'A Divided Supreme Court Adopts Discovery Amendments to the Federal Rules of Civil Procedure', *California Law Review*, 1981, Vol. 69, p. 806-820.

Fuller 1978
Fuller, L., 'The Forms and Limits of Adjudication', *Harvard Law Review*, 1978, Vol. 92, p. 353-409.

Galanter 2004
Galanter, M., 'The Vanishing Trial: An Examination of Trials and Related Matters in Federal and State Courts', *Journal of Empirical Legal Studies*, 2004, Vol. 1, p. 459-570.

Gelfand 1988
Gelfand, G., '"Taking" Informational Property Through Discovery', *Washington University Law Quarterly*, 1988, Vol. 66, p. 703-744.

Glaser 1968
Glaser, W., *Pretrial Discovery and the Adversary System*, New York: Russell Sage Foundation, 1968.

Grossman & Cormack 2011
Grossman, M. & Cormack, G., 'Technology-Assisted Review in E-Discovery Can be More Effective and More Efficient Than Exhaustive Manual Review', *Richmond Journal of Law and Technology*, 2011, Vol. 17, p. 11-38.

Hazard 1998a
Hazard, G., 'Discovery and the Role of the Judge in Civil Law Jurisdictions', *Notre Dame Law Review*, 1998, Vol. 73, p. 1017-1028.

Hazard 1998b
Hazard, G., 'From Whom No Secrets Are Kept', *Texas Law Review*, 1998, Vol. 76, p. 1665-1694.

Hersch & Viscusi 2004
Hersch, J. & Viscusi, K., 'Punitive Damages: How Judges and Juries Perform', *Journal of Legal Studies*, 2004, Vol. 33, p. 1-36.

Langbein 1985
Langbein, J., 'The German Advantage in Civil Procedure', *University of Chicago Law Review*, 1985, Vol. 52, p. 823-866.

Lee & Willging 2009
Lee, E. & Willging, T., 'National Case-Based Civil Rules Survey', available at: <www.fjc.gov/public/pdf.nsf/lookup/FJC_Report_Sept._2009.pdf>.

Marcus 1993
Marcus, R., 'Of Babies and Bathwater: The Prospects for Procedural Progress', *Brooklyn Law Review*, 1993, Vol. 59, p. 761-825.

Marcus 1998
Marcus, R., 'Discovery Containment Redux', *Boston College Law Review*, 1998, Vol. 39, p. 747-784.

Marcus 2006
Marcus, R., 'E-Discovery and Beyond: Toward *Brave New World* or *1984*?', *Federal Rules Decisions*, 2006, Vol. 236, p. 598-638.

Marcus 2009
Marcus, R., 'The Electronic Lawyer', *DePaul Law Review*, 2009, Vol. 58, p. 263-310.

Mullenix 1994
Mullenix, L., 'The Pervasive Myth of Pervasive Discovery Abuses and the Consequences for Unfounded Rulemaking', *Stanford Law Review*, 1994, Vol. 46, p. 1393-1446.

Neubauer 2009
Neubauer, M., 'Mastering the Blind Cross-Examination', *Litigation Magazine*, 2009, Vol. 35, p. 23-26.

Niemeyer 2004
Niemeyer, P., 'Awards for Pain and Suffering: The Irrational Centerpiece of Our Tort System', *Virginia Law Review*, 2004, Vol. 90, p. 1401-1421.

Redish & Mathews 2004
Redish, M. & Mathews, A., 'Why Punitive Damages are Unconstitutional', *Emory Law Journal*, 2004, Vol. 53, p. 1-53.

Schorr & King 2011
Schorr, S. & King, R.S., 'Beyond Black Boxes', *Trial Magazine*, 2011, p. 32-35.

Seligman 1994
Seligman, J., 'The Merits Do Matter', *Harvard Law Review*, 1994, Vol. 108, p. 438-457.

Subrin 1998
Subrin, S., 'Fishing Expeditions Allowed: The Historical Background of the 1938 Federal Discovery Rules', *Boston College Law Review*, 1998, Vol. 39, p. 691-746.

Willging *et al.* 1997
Willging, T., Stienstra, D., Shapard, J. & Miletich, D., 'An Empirical Study of Discovery and Disclosure Practice Under the 1993 Federal Rules Amendments', *Boston College Law Review*, 1997, Vol. 39, p. 525-596.

Wright, Miller & Marcus 2010
Wright, C., Miller, A. & Marcus, R., *Federal Practice & Procedure*, 3rd edn., Vol. 8, Rochester, N.Y.: West Publishing Co., 2010.

Zuckerman 1996
Zuckerman, A., 'Lord Woolf's Access to Justice: Plus Ca Change ...', *Modern Law Review*, 1996, Vol. 59, p. 773-796.

M. Paleker

FACT- AND TRUTH-FINDING IN SOUTH AFRICAN CIVIL PROCEDURE

1. Introduction

A critical engagement with truth- and fact-finding mechanisms in the civil justice system is considered important in many jurisdictions. Sadly, this has received scant attention in South Africa. It is not an exaggeration to say that the overwhelming majority of civil cases are settled either on the doorsteps of the court or during the course of litigation. This comes at great emotional and financial expense to litigants, who are expected to endure the slings and arrows of litigation for many months, and often, years.[1] One can only wonder if the situation would be any better if there was more emphasis on how the rules of procedure support fact- and truth-finding. Experience has shown that where facts and evidence are revealed earlier rather than later, parties have a greater chance of arriving at the truth sooner. This may provoke early settlement and prevent needless litigation.

This chapter will look at the issue of fact- and truth-finding in South African civil procedure. Existing procedural mechanisms will be examined with a view to determining the extent to which civil procedure rules cater for fact- and truth-finding.

It should be noted that South African civil procedure is somewhat of a unique oddity for it boasts features of both the civil law (on account of seventeenth and eighteenth century Roman-Dutch law influence[2]) and the common law (on account of nineteenth century English law influence[3]) traditions. This amalgam makes for an

* I would like to thank Messrs Michael Crystal, Andrew Surgey and Ernst Muller for their assistance with the preparation of the final draft of this Chapter. Their comments proved to be extremely valuable. Any mistakes are entirely my own doing.

1 Former Chief Justice of South Africa, Judge S.S. Ngcobo, made the following statement: 'When it takes five, four, three or two years to get a civil case to trial, judges cannot escape the charge that a system that functions so slowly has defeated one of its primary objectives at the very threshold of the judicial process'. See Ngcobo 2003, p. 688.

2 Fagan 1996, p. 33-64. See also *Spies v Lombard* 1950 (3) SA 469 (A) at 482; *Du Plessis v Strauss* 1988 (2) SA 105 (A) at 149 *et seq.*

3 Erasmus 1996, p. 146-150; Botha 1923, p. 396-406; Erasmus 1991, p. 266; Taitz 1979, p. 470 *et seq.*

interesting blend of procedural rules, which can appear rather confusing to an outsider.

2. The Role of the Judge

With the exception of the Small Claims Courts,[4] where proceedings are 'inquisitorial',[5] in all other courts the procedure is adversarial. The parties are responsible for taking charge of and driving litigation forward. They formulate cases and present evidence in court. During trial, the judge simply sits as a neutral umpire who does not descend into the litigation arena. The judge may, from time to time, ask a witness who has been called to the stand a question for the sake of clarification, but the judge does not have an investigative role *per se*. The judge has no discretion about which witness comes to court. This is a matter for the parties to decide. The key function of the judge at trial is to ensure that courtroom decorum is maintained, that parties keep to the rules of evidence and procedure and that the court process is not abused. Thus, when it comes to fact- and truth-finding, the judge has a very limited role to play. The judge relies on facts alleged in pleadings and patiently waits for the appropriate evidence to be tendered during trial.[6]

Because of the adversarial system, practitioners are known to play a tactical game of cat-and-mouse. Too much openness and transparency is regarded as strategic suicide. Simulating a poker game, practitioners are known to hold their 'evidential cards' face down and will only expose the 'aces' up their sleeves when it is necessary or opportune to do so. Since the parties are responsible for preparing and presenting evidence in court, the judicial officer has very little chance of knowing what evidence will be led in advance. Even where evidence is exposed in pleadings and in the pre-trial stage through the process of discovery, the judge cannot know for sure what stratagem counsel will use to lay the evidence before the court and what direction the case will follow. To the judge and the parties, everything is very much up in the air at the opening of the trial. As the trial progresses, things become more apparent.

4 Small Claims Courts are governed by the Small Claims Courts Act 61 of 1984 and the Rules Regulating Matters in Respect of Small Claims Courts Government Notice R1893 in *Government Gazette* 9909 of 30 August 1985 as amended by GN R851 in *Government Gazette* 13178 of 19 April 1991.

5 Small Claims Courts Act 61 of 1984, s 26(3). The legislation makes reference to proceedings being 'inquisitorial' so as to distinguish the processes of fact-finding and evidence-gathering in the Small Claims Courts, where the presiding officer takes an active role, from the adversarial nature of proceedings in all the other courts. The notion of 'inquisitorial' proceedings in a civil suit is, of course, terminologically incorrect as the term is more apposite in the arena of criminal justice to explain the distinction between inquisitorial versus accusatorial systems: see, Merryman & Pérez-Perdomo 2007, p. 115-116.

6 The adversarial litigation system was adopted in South Africa in the early part of the nineteenth century. See Erasmus 1996, p. 149-150. For an instructive analysis of the differences between the common law and civil law procedural styles see Von Mehren 1982, p. 361-371; see also Merryman & Pérez-Perdomo 2007, p. 112 *et seq*.

Cases are not assigned to a judge until a few days before trial. On that occasion, the judge peruses pleadings, discovery schedules and expert witness statements. From the court file the judge gets a pretty good idea of the cause of action and the issues in dispute. Because of very particular pleading requirements,[7] the judge will acquire information about some evidential facts, but not all. At the conclusion of the case, the judge weighs all the evidence presented by the parties and determines whether, according to law, the plaintiff has made out a case on a balance of probabilities.[8] The judge's duty is discharged once a reasoned decision is delivered.[9]

In light of the non-investigative role of the judge in the civil justice process, it is perhaps incorrect to continue talking about fact and truth-finding in South African civil procedure. Maybe it is more correct for this contribution to make reference to the potential which litigants have for fact- and truth-*determination*. Be that as it may, for the sake of aligning this contribution with the general theme of the book of which it forms a part, the phrase 'fact- and truth-finding will be used' even when what is meant is 'fact- and truth-determination'.

3. The Role of Pleadings

Unlike many other legal systems, South African civil procedure distinguishes between two distinct procedures for initiating a civil suit: the *application procedure* and the *action procedure*. The form, function and content of pleadings are fundamentally different depending on which procedure is utilised.

While no one has ever considered these procedures in terms of their fact- and truth-finding potential, research for this contribution has revealed that that the application procedure scores much better as it naturally lends itself to an early determination of both fact and evidence. In theory, it affords the parties greater opportunity to enter into early negotiation with a view to settlement without the court's intervention. The practicalities are, however, very different. The application, by its very nature, also enables the judge to be conversant with the facts and evidence before a matter is even heard. This may explain why decisions in applications are rendered more quickly than in actions.

7 The pleadings requirements are set out in the Rule 6 of the Rules Regulating the Conduct of the Proceedings of the Magistrates' Courts of South Africa GN R740 *Government Gazette* 33487 of 23 August 2010, as amended (hereinafter referred to as the 'MCR') and Rule 18 of the Rules Regulating the Conduct of Proceedings of the Several Provincial and Local Divisions of the High Court of South Africa, Government Notice R48, in *Government Gazette* 999 of 12 January 1965, as amended (hereinafter referred to as the Uniform Rules of Court or simply as the 'URC' in abbreviated form).

8 Cilliers, Loots & Nel 2009, p. 895.

9 On the merits of a reasoned judgment, see *Stuttafords Stores (Pty) Ltd v Salt of the Earth Creations (Pty) Ltd* 2011 (1) SA 267 (CC); *Mphahlele v First National Bank of SA Ltd* 1999 (2) SA 667 (CC) at para 12; *Strategic Liquor Services v Mvumbi NO* 2010 (2) SA 92 (CC) at para 17. See also Corbett 1998, p. 118 and 123.

(i) The Application Procedure

As noted, the format, function and content of pleadings differ in the application procedure when compared to the action procedure. In the application procedure, the pleadings, which consist of the *notice of motion*[10] and affidavits, contain not only an exposition of the material facts (the *facta probanda*), but also all the relevant evidential facts (the *facta probantia*).[11] The application procedure is characterised by just two stages: the pleading stage and the hearing stage. Because of the general rule that there is no *viva voce* evidence in an application, the parties must take care to meticulously present all their evidence on paper. The role of the attorney or advocate[12] at the hearing is to clarify issues raised in the papers, to argue legal principles, to answer questions posed by the judge and to motivate for the relief sought in the notice of motion.

In an application, the parties are limited to three sets of affidavits: the *founding affidavit* by the applicant, which is attached to the notice of motion,[13] the *answering affidavit* by the respondent[14] and the *replying affidavit* by the applicant.[15] The time for delivering these affidavits is strictly controlled.[16] If any of the parties wish to file

10 The notice of motion contains administrative information such as time periods for the filing of papers and more importantly, the relief sought by the applicant. The present distinction between motion and trial proceedings is attributed to the first rules of procedure of the Supreme Court of the Cape of Good Hope promulgated in open court on 1, 24, 31 January 1828 and 27 and 31 March of that year. Proceedings by way of motion imitated a common practice before the Court of Chancery in so far as they were mainly on paper and 'little adapted for the determination of controversial issues of fact': see Lord Bowen 1907, p. 517.

11 *Valentino Globe BV v Phillips* 1998 (3) SA 775 (SCA) at 779; see also Van Blerk 1998, p. 49; Marnewick 2003, p. 171 *et seq.*

12 Following the English tradition of having a split legal profession comprising of barristers and solicitors, the legal profession in South Africa is split into the advocates' profession governed by the Admission of Advocates Act 74 of 1964 and the attorneys' profession governed by Attorneys Act 53 of 1979. The Legislature has embarked on a process of re-evaluating the legal professions and to this extent has been deliberating the Legal Practice Bill: for more information see <http://www.lssa.org.za/>, last consulted on 1 September 2011. When passed into law, the proposed Legal Practice Act will repeal the Attorneys Act of 1979 and the Admission of Advocates Act of 1964. It is quite clear, however, from the latest draft legislation that the split bar system is going to remain.

13 URC 6(1); MCR 55(1)(a).

14 URC 6(5)(d)(ii); MCR 55(1)(g)(ii).

15 URC 6(5)(e); MCR 55(1)(h).

16 The founding affidavit must be served with the notice of motion when the matter is initiated. The answering affidavit, which contains the respondent's answer to the applicant's founding affidavit, must be delivered within 15 court days of when the respondent has filed its notice of intention to oppose the application. The applicant's reply must be delivered within 10 court days of receipt of the respondent's answer. Failure to deliver the relevant documents within the prescribed time periods will automatically bar a litigant from being able to file that document. To lift the bar, a party will have to bring an interlocutory application requesting condonation from the court on good cause shown. See generally URC 6 and MCR 55; see also *James Brown and Hamer (Pty) Ltd (Previously Gilbert Hamer & Co Ltd) v Simmons NO* 1963 (4) SA 656 (A) at 660F.

additional affidavits, the permission of the court is required.[17] This will entail an interlocutory application for leave of court to file further papers.[18]

The founding affidavit of the applicant is the key and requires careful preparation. The courts have said that a case is made or broken by the founding affidavit.[19] Material facts and evidential facts must be fully canvassed. To this extent, the applicant is permitted to annex supporting evidence to the affidavit, for example, contracts, reports, photographs, tape recordings and of course, confirmatory affidavits deposed by third parties etc.[20]

The courts will not permit the applicant to use its replying affidavit to bolster an initially weak case or to raise an issue which has not been raised in the founding affidavit.[21] The purpose of the reply, the courts hold, is to simply address what the respondent has stated in his or her answering affidavit.[22] The level of exactitude required of the applicant in the founding affidavit prevents the applicant from using the founding affidavit to make out a *prima facie* case, hoping to draw the defendant into litigation, and then to embark on a fishing expedition for evidence or for causes of action. Of course, this places quite a large burden on the applicant. Not only is the applicant expected to be fairly certain about the merits of his or her case, but he or she must also frame the cause of action correctly by relying on the appropriate evidence.

17 URC 6(5)(e); MCR 55(1)(i).

18 For factors the courts will consider when exercising its discretion to permit further affidavits, see *Afric Oil v Ramdaan Investments CC* 2004 (1) SA 35 (N) at 381; *Parow Municipality v Joyce & McGregor (Pty) Ltd* 1973 (1) SA 937 (C); *Gibb v Du Toit (2)* 1938 (1) PH F64 (W); *Hersman v Jacobz Brothers Ltd* 1931 EDL 134 (C).

19 *Bayat v Hansa* 1955(3) SA 547 (N) at 553; C-E; *Mauerberger v Mauerberger* 1948 (3) SA 731 (C) at 732; *Coffee, Tea and Chocolate Co Ltd v Cape Trading Company* 1930 CPD 81 at 82; *Joseph and Jeans v Spitz and Others* 1931 WLD 48.

20 Cilliers, Loots & Nel 2009, p. 443. In *Swissborough Diamond Mines (Pty) Ltd v Government of the Republic of South Africa* 1999 (2) SA 279 (T) the court stated at 324F-H:
'Regard being had to the function of affidavits, it is not open to an applicant or a respondent to merely annexe to its affidavit documentation and to request the Court to have regard to it. What is required is the identification of the portions thereof on which reliance is placed and an indication of the case which is sought to be made out on the strength thereof. If this were not so the essence of our established practice would be destroyed. A party would not know what case must be met. See *Lipschitz and Schwarz NNO v Markowitz* 1976 (3) SA 772 (W) at 775H and *Port Nolloth Municipality v Xahalisa and Others; Luwalala and Others v Port Nolloth Municipality* 1991 (3) SA 98 (C) at 111B-C'.

21 *Poseidon Ships Agencies (Pty) Ltd v African Coaling and Exporting Co (Durban) (Pty) Ltd* 1980 (1) SA 313 (D) at 316A; *Union Finance Holdings Ltd v I S Mirk Office Machines II (Pty) Ltd* 2001 (4) SA 842 (W) at 847G-848E.

22 In *Bayat v Hansa* 1955(3) SA 547 (N) at 553C-E the court held:
'[A]n applicant for relief must (save in exceptional circumstances) make his case and produce all the evidence he desires to use in support of it, in his affidavits filed with the notice of motion, whether he is moving *ex parte* or on notice to the respondent, and is not permitted to supplement it in his replying affidavits (the purpose of which is to reply to averments made by the respondent in his answering affidavits), still less make a new case in his replying affidavits'.

Depending on the complexity of the matter, it is not uncommon for a founding affidavit to run into hundreds of pages. Fortunately, the courts take a dim view of litigants who are repetitive and whose affidavits contain irrelevant or malicious information which is inserted only to vex the other party and to increase costs.[23]

In the respondent's answering affidavit, the respondent is expected to admit, deny, confess and avoid or to plead no knowledge to all of the allegations contained in the applicant's founding affidavit.[24] A bare denial by the respondent of all the allegations contained in the founding papers is inadmissible and will be considered insufficient.[25] It is important for the respondent when denying material allegations to state facts and evidence which explain the basis of the respondent's denial.[26] The idea is to enable a court to weigh a case simply on what has been stated in the three affidavits, without recourse to extrinsic evidence.

When material disputes of fact and evidence arise, a court is not obligated to dismiss the matter.[27] The court can apply the so called 'Plascon-Evans rule' evinced

23 URC 6(15) and MCR 55(9)(a) provides: 'The court may on [interlocutory] application order to be struck out from any affidavit and matter which is scandalous, vexatious or irrelevant, with an appropriate order as to costs, including costs as between attorney and client'. As to the interpretation of these provisions see *Vaatz v Law Society of Namibia* 1991 (3) SA 563 (Nm). In *Minister of Environmental Affairs and Tourism v Bato Star Fishing (Pty) Ltd; Minister of Environmental Affairs and Tourism v Phambili Fisheries (Pty) Ltd* 20003 (6) SA 407 (SCA) at 439 G-H the court held: 'There is one other matter that I am compelled to mention – replying affidavits. In the great majority of cases the replying affidavit should be by far the shortest. But in practice it is very often by far the longest – and the most valueless. It was so in these reviews. The respondents, who were the applicants below, filed replying affidavits of inordinate length. Being forced to wade through their almost endless repetition when the pleading of the case is all but over brings about irritation, not persuasion. It is time that the courts declare war on unnecessarily prolix replying affidavits and upon those who inflate them'. In *Van Zyl v Government of the Republic of South Africa* 2008 (3) SA 294 (SCA) at 307 G-H the court stated: 'A reply in this form is an abuse of the court process and instead of wasting judicial time in analysing it sentence by sentence and paragraph by paragraph such affidavits should not only give rise to adverse costs orders but should be struck out as a whole ... mero motu ...'.

24 Marnewick 2003, p. 176-179. See also See also *Moosa v Knox; Paruk v Knox* 1949 (3) SA 327 (N).. See, for example, *United Methodist Church of South Africa v Sokufundumala* 1989 (4) SA 1055 (O) at 1059A; *Ebrahim v Georgoulas* 1992 (2) SA 151 (B) at 153D.

25 *Peterson v Cuthbert & Co Ltd* 1945 AD 420 at 428-9; *Room Hire Co (Pty) Ltd v Jeppe Street Mansions (Pty) Ltd* 1949 (3) SA 1155 (T) at 1163 and 1165; *Associated South African Bakeries (Pty) Ltd v Oryx Vereinigte Bäckereien (Pty) Ltd* 1982 (3) SA 893 (A) at 923G-924B; *Plascon-Evans Paints Ltd v Van Riebeeck Paints (Pty) Ltd* 1984 (3) SA 623 (A) at 634I-635A; *South African Veterinary Council v Szymanski* 2003 (4) SA 42 (SCA) at 51A-C; *Fakie NO v CCII Systems (Pty) Ltd* 2006 (4) SA 326 (SCA) at 347G-H; *Malan v Law Society, Northern Provinces* 2009 (1) SA 216 (SCA) at 222C; *National Director of Public Prosecutions v Zuma* 2009 (2) SA 277 (SCA) at 290F.

26 Van Blerk 1998, p. 64-65.

27 URC 6(5)(g); MCR 55(1)(k); see also *Room Hire Co (Pty) Ltd v Jeppe Street Mansions (Pty) Ltd* 1949 (3) SA 1155 (T) at 1162, 1168; *Adbro Investments Co Ltd v Minister of the Interior,* 1956 (3) SA 345 (A) at 349-350; *Pressma Services (Pty) Ltd v Schuttler,* 1990 (2) SA 411 (C) at 419C-I.

by the Appellate Division in *Plascon-Evans Paints (TVL) Ltd v Van Riebeeck Paints (Pty) Ltd:*[28]

> 'It is correct that, where in proceedings on notice of motion disputes of fact have arisen on the affidavits, a final order, whether it be an interdict or some other form of relief, may be granted if those facts averred in the applicant's affidavits which have been admitted by the respondent, together with the facts alleged by the respondent, justify such an order. The power of the court to give such final relief on the papers before it is, however, not confined to such a situation. In certain instances the denial by respondent of a fact alleged by the applicant may not be such as to raise a real, genuine or *bona fide* dispute of fact (see in this regard *Room Hire Co (Pty) Ltd v Jeppe Street Mansions (Pty) Ltd* 1949 (3) SA 1155 (T) at p. 1163-1165; *Da Mata v Otto NO* 1972 (3) SA 585 (A) at p. 882 D-H). If in such a case the respondent has not availed himself of his right to apply for the deponents concerned to be called for cross-examination under Rule 6(5)(g) of the Uniform Rules of Court (*cf. Petersen v Cuthbert & Co Ltd.* 1945 AD 420, at p. 428; *Room Hire* case, *supra*, at p. 1164) and the court is satisfied as to the inherent credibility of the applicant's factual averment, it may proceed on the basis of the correctness thereof and include this fact among those upon which it determines whether the applicant is entitled to the final relief which he seeks (see e.g., *Rikhoto v East Rand Administration Board* 1983 (4) SA 278 (W) at p 283 E-H). Moreover, there may be exceptions to this general rule, as, for example, where the allegations or denials of the respondent are so far-fetched or clearly untenable that the Court is justified in rejecting them merely on the papers (see the remarks of Botha AJA in the *Associated South African Bakeries* case, *supra*, at p. 924 A)'.

As is evident from the *Plascon-Evans dictum,* a court can hear oral evidence in application proceedings. However, such indulgence is granted only if this would be 'convenient', where the issues are 'clearly defined', the dispute is 'comparatively simple', and a 'speedy determination of a dispute is desirable'.[29] In the absence of these *indicia* the proposition stands that all the facts must be disclosed in the papers, failing which the court has no other choice except to dismiss the application or to make a ruling of absolution from the instance.

While the application procedure places quite a heavy burden on the applicant to make out a good case *ab initio* and on the respondent to actively and decisively engage with the claims and allegations raised in the applicant's founding papers, from the point of view of fact- and truth-finding, the application procedure is quite effective. Each party knows exactly what evidence the other party has at its disposal, what the precise factual arguments are and what evidential burdens it

[28] 1984 (3) SA 623 (A) at 634-I.

[29] *Standard Bank of SA Ltd v Neugarten* 1987 (3) SA 695 (W) at 699D-E. Van Loggerenberg 2011, at 55-19 makes the following comment: 'In resolving to refer a matter to evidence a court has a wide discretion. In every case the court must examine an alleged dispute of fact and see whether in truth there is a real dispute of fact which cannot be satisfactorily determined without the aid of oral evidence; if this is not done a respondent might be able to raise fictitious issues of fact and thus delay the hearing of the matter to the prejudice of the applicant. Vague and insubstantial allegations are insufficient to raise the kind of dispute of fact that should be referred for oral evidence. If a respondent genuinely intends to raise a serious matter such as corruption as an issue, it must be based on fact not rumour, innuendo or inference based only on speculation'.

should meet. This also makes it relatively simple for a judge to prepare for a case and to address direct questions to the parties' representatives at the hearing on the most pertinent issues. It thus allows a judge to get to the heart of the argument much earlier than would be the case in an action. Since parties are not expected to regurgitate all the trite facts and evidence in court and can simply refer the court to the most pertinent aspects of their argument, the duration of the hearing is significantly shorter than a trial. Needless to say, this translates into fewer costs for the litigants.

A possible drawback of the application procedure is that there is no discovery process *per se*. Parties are expected to be in possession of relevant evidence and cannot ask for disclosure of evidence, other than the evidence which is mentioned in the three affidavits. Aside from the mechanisms contained in the Promotion of Access to Information Act of 2000[30] (discussed later) there is no other mechanism by which parties to an application can obtain pre-litigation discovery. It is generally accepted that the discovery mechanisms contained in the rules of court[31] (also discussed later) are relevant to actions only.

The absence of a formal discovery process in the application procedure is not considered insurmountable, because a party is always at liberty to institute an action and to seek discovery of documentary and other discoverable evidence as part of the pre-trial action procedure. However, this argument is based on two false assumptions. The first is that the action procedure is an efficient procedure. The second is that the discovery protocols in the action procedure adequately safeguard the interests of litigants. As will be noted later, the action procedure is time-consuming, expensive, plagued by incredible delay and is, by and large, trial-dependent for the determination of the truth. Because pre-trial discovery protocols are firmly embedded within the action procedure, these are negatively affected by the problems associated with the procedure in general. It is submitted that to defer problems experienced in the application procedure to the action procedure is, therefore, unwise. There is thus a case to be made for a limited discovery process in the application procedure. This, it is submitted, will bolster the already strong fact- and truth-finding characteristic of the application procedure.

Another seemingly negative aspect of the application procedure is that there is no reference to law and legal principles in the affidavits. The affidavits are crafted with the law in mind. There may be trite references here and there to some or other legal principle but, as a general rule, law is not alleged in the affidavits.[32] Legal arguments and principles are addressed in *heads of argument*. These are usually filed at court and exchanged between the parties a few days before the hearing. With regard to the higher courts, filing heads of arguments is mandatory in some courts, but optional in other courts.[33] In the Magistrates' Courts, the process is entirely optional. In practice, if a matter is complicated, the parties are more likely to file heads of argument, even where it is optional to do so.

30 Act 2 of 2000.
31 URC 35; MCR 23.
32 L.T.C. Harms *Civil Procedure in the Supreme Court* (loose-leaf binder) B6.27.
33 L.T.C. Harms *Civil Procedure in the Supreme Court* (loose-leaf binder) B6.41.

Heads of argument must not be confused with a brief or an opinion. Heads of argument are staccato in form and style. They outline the nature of the parties' legal arguments in skeletal format and the authorities that will be relied on in support of those arguments. During the hearing, legal arguments will be fleshed out more fully.[34] The idea of filing truncated arguments may seem arbitrary, but the system works well. Nine out of ten times, on a simple reading of the heads, one will be able to figure out the nature of the legal argument to be tendered. Heads of argument are carefully drafted, because parties know that not to deal with an aspect of the law will result in the court being unwilling to countenance the argument at the hearing.[35] To this extent, the process can be a bit formalistic and counterintuitive to the extrapolation of the truth. But on the other hand, formalism demands of practitioners to be on top of their game, to frame arguments clearly and carefully, to conduct comprehensive research, and not to come to court unprepared. It must be remembered that South African law is an uncodified legal system. The courts are thus reliant on counsel to identify and to discuss applicable legal principles in detail.

As is the case with affidavits, there are some practitioners who abuse the system by filing lengthy heads of argument. When the practitioners are admonished, the argument is made that the matter is simply too complex for concision. However, lengthy heads inflate costs, tend to encroach on limited judicial time[36] and from a tactical point of view, seek to intimidate the opposition. It is for

34 Van Blerk 1998, p. 49. In *Caterham Car Sales & Coachworks Ltd v Birkin Cars (Pty) Ltd* 1998 (3) SA 938 (SCA) the Supreme Court of Appeal, per Harms J.A., stated at paras 37-38: 'There also appears to be a misconception about the function and form of heads of argument. The Rules of this Court require the filing of main heads of argument. The operative words are 'main', 'heads' and 'argument'. 'Main' refers to the most important part of the argument. 'Heads' means 'points', not a dissertation. Lastly, 'argument' involves a process of reasoning which must be set out in the heads. A recital of the facts and quotations from authorities do not amount to argument. By way of a reminder I wish to quote from *Van der Westhuizen NO v United Democratic Front* 1989 (2) SA 242 (A) at 252B-G: 'There is a growing tendency in this Court for counsel to incorporate quotations from the evidence, from the Court a quo's judgment and from the authorities on which they rely, in their heads of argument. I have no doubt that these quotations are intended for the convenience of the Court but they seldom serve that purpose and usually only add to the Court's burden. What is more important is the effect which this practice has on the costs in civil cases. ... Superfluous matter should therefore be omitted and, although all quotations can obviously not be eliminated, they should be kept within reasonable bounds. Counsel will be well advised to bear in mind that Rule 8 of the Rules of this Court requires no more than the main heads of argument. ... The heads abound with unnecessary quotations from the record and from the authorities. They reveal, moreover, another disturbing feature which is that the typing on many pages does not cover the full page. ... Had the heads been properly drawn and typed I do not think more than 20 pages would have been required. The costs cannot be permitted to be increased in this manner and an order will therefore be made to ensure that the respondent does not become liable for more than what was reasonably necessary'. Practitioners should note that a failure to give proper attention to the requirements of the practice note and the heads might result in the disallowance of part of their fees'.

35 Van Blerk 1998, p. 80.

36 See Rozenberg 1994, p. 41.

this reason that the courts have expressed displeasure with the practice,[37] and in some instances the rules of court have been amended to limit the length of heads of argument.[38]

Whenever the rules of procedure are abused in an application, or for that matter in an action, to gain an unfair advantage or to gain some perverse pleasure, the courts have the residual power to impose costs orders.[39] Depending on the type of infraction, even a winning party[40] may be prevented from recovering costs either *in toto* or in part, or the costs order may require the guilty party to pay wasted costs.[41] In extreme cases, an attorney or an advocate can be saddled with an order *de bonis propriis,* which effectively prevents the practitioner from recovering fees from his or her client, and the practitioner may even be required to pay the costs of the opposition.[42]

It is thus axiomatic from the above that when it comes to fact- and truth-finding, the application procedure has advantages. By the time pleadings close, the parties will be fully *au fait* with the material facts and the evidence. As the hearing

37 See dicta in *Van der Westhuizen NO v United Democratic Front* 1989 (2) SA 242 (A) at 252B-G cited in n. 34 above.

38 According to Rule 8 of the Practice Directives of the Eastern Cape Division of the High Court of South Africa practitioners are cautioned that heads of argument:
'(i) Shall consist of a concise and succinct statement of the main points which will be argued and should not contain unnecessary elaboration;
(ii) In particular, shall not contain lengthy quotations from either the record or from authorities to which reference will be made;
(iii) Are not to refer in general to the record and authorities but to specific pages and paragraphs of relevance;
(iv) Shall be accompanied by the list of the authorities to be quoted in support of the argument;
(v) Shall, if such authority is not readily available, be further accompanied by copies of the text to which reference is made - particularly in the case of unreported decisions, where a copy of the entire judgment should be attached.
Rule 9.8 of the South Gauteng Practice Directives provide that heads of argument should be 'rarely longer than 5 pages'. Virtually every one of the thirteen divisions of the High Court as well the Supreme Court of Appeal and the Constitutional Court circumscribe the length of heads of argument by either placing page limit guidelines or by requiring brevity in form and style.

39 See the court's statement in *Van Zyl v Government of the Republic of South Africa* 2008 (3) SA 294 (SCA) at 307 G-H referred to in n. 23 above.

40 The general rule is that the winning party is entitled to recover legal costs: *Pretoria Garrison Institutes v Danish Variety Products (Pty) Ltd* 1948 (1) SA 839 (A) at 863; *Union Government v Gass* 1959 (4) SA 401 (A) at 413C; *Gamlan Investment (Pty) Ltd v Trilion Cape (Pty) Ltd* 1996 (3) SA 692 (C) at 700E. However, the courts have discretion to deviate from this rule if there is a good reason to do so: *Hollywood Curl (Pty) Ltd v Twins Products (Pty) Ltd (I)* 1989 (1) SA 236 (A); *Poverini v General Accident Insurance Co South Africa Ltd* 1998 (3) SA 546 (W) at 555; *Strauss v Strauss* [1998] 4 All SA 137 (C); *Treatment Action Campaign v Minister of Health* 2005 (6) SA 363 (T).

41 MCR 33(12) and the commentary thereto in Van Loggerenberg 2011.

42 *David v Naggyah* 1961 (3) SA 4 (N); *Webb v Botha* 1980 (3) SA 666 (N); *Philotex (Pty) Ltd v Snyman; Braitex (Pty) Ltd v Snyman* 1998 (2) SA 139 (SCA) at 186J-187C; *Makuwa v Poslson* 2007 (3) SA 84 (T); *Schneider NO v AA* 2010 (5) SA 203 (WCC) at 223E-F.

approaches, heads of argument will lay bare principles of law and legal contentions. At the hearing itself, counsel will address the court on the pertinent issues and deal with the disputes that have arisen on the papers. The court will address questions to the parties on the basis of the papers before it. It is thus very unlikely that anyone will be able to pull the proverbial 'rabbit out of the hat'.

One would assume that since the application procedure exposes the material facts and evidence at such an early stage, the parties would be more inclined to engage in settlement negotiations. However, this is not the case. Far too often, cases are left pending and are settled on the doorsteps of the court on the hearing day. A major reason for this has to do with the enormous delay in assigning a court date for the hearing of an application. In the High Courts, parties can wait up to two years for a hearing date after the close of pleadings. In the Magistrates' Courts, depending on the administrative efficiency of the court concerned,[43] and the court's workload, it can take a couple of weeks to a year before an application is heard.[44] The time delay between when pleadings close and the date of hearing encourages many litigants to stall resolution of a matter in the hope that the other side will throw in the towel due to emotional and/or financial pressure. The result is that the application procedure, whilst perhaps a relatively effective fact- and truth-finding mechanism, is not as potent as to encourage early settlement and cost-effective dispute resolution.

43 In the attorneys' magazine, *De Rebus* (December 2010) 5, an attorney writes: ' I read the letter of a Sandton attorney in *De Rebus* (October 2010) 7 regarding the state of the High Court with feelings, *inter alia*, of sorrow, anger, disappointment, embarrassment, frustration, annoyance, helplessness and not an inch of surprise. The writer quite rightfully points out the dismal state of the South Gauteng High Court in Johannesburg. Even on writing this I feel a sense of annoyance that the Department of Justice apparently felt it helpful to change the name of the court from the former "Witwatersrand Local Division" to the "South Gauteng", yet, as with so many other things in this sunny country nobody bothers with making sure anything underneath the pretty new name works. ... It is indeed not only the South Gauteng High Court that suffers from this infectious, ravaging disease, but most of the courts, including the lower courts around the country. Although I cannot speak for many courts in other provinces, I certainly have experience in and around most of the courts in Gauteng and from what I hear from my colleagues elsewhere, the situation in other provinces is not much better. ... By far the worst court I have ever set my foot in is the Johannesburg Magistrates' Court. Not only are the staff exceedingly unpleasant, rude and unhelpful, but they are also probably the laziest, most incompetent people I have ever come across. The so-called admin "system" (system? where?) is an absolute farce'. The views of this writer is echoed by an attorney writing in *De Rebus* (January-February 2011) at 6 who says: 'Our profession, and more importantly, the public are frustrated and prejudiced by the long delays caused by the failure of administrators of many magistrates' courts to carry out their duties properly. ... The shambles is a serious indictment on the administration of justice in South Africa. If it is not reversed South Africa could be regarded as not a good place to do business'. See also Whittle 2011, p. 17; Welgemoed 2011, p. 4.

44 See for example, *Investec Bank Ltd v Mutemeri* 2010 (1) SA 265 (GSJ) at para 2 where Trengrove A.J. makes reference to the fact that the respondents, who made application to the Magistrates' Court for a debt review in terms of s 86 of the National Credit Act 34 of 2005, launched their application on 15 May 2009, but the application was only enrolled for hearing on 11 August 2010.

(ii) The Action Procedure

Despite the positive and more pronounced fact- and truth-finding attributes of the application procedure, it may be surprising to note that in the overwhelming number of cases the action procedure is utilised. There are several reasons for this. There are times when the common law or statute precludes a plaintiff from instituting proceedings using the application procedure.[45] For example, it is trite that divorce proceedings may only be brought by action, and not by application.[46] Claims for unliquidated[47] damages cannot be brought by application. This means that contract and delict (tort) cases are more often than not brought by action.[48] Even when the common law or statute permits the use of the application procedure, the plaintiff is obliged to use the action procedure if he or she foresees the possibility of a material dispute of fact arising that will be difficult to resolve on the papers.[49] Furthermore, and as mentioned earlier, even when a matter may be ripe for resolution by way of application, a dearth of available evidence will oblige the plaintiff to use the action procedure so that he or she can utilize the pre-trial discovery protocols to obtain evidence in support of a claim.

The action procedure is characterized by three stages: the pleadings stage, the pre-trial stage, and the trial. On account of English law influence and adversarialism, evidence in an action is lead at trial and is generally not exposed in pleadings. The nature and content of pleadings in the action procedure is thus considerably different to pleadings in applications, which as noted before contain an exposition of both fact and evidence.

Since time immemorial, the principle has been that pleadings in actions should only contain the material facts (*facta probanda*) that are necessary to sustain the cause of action.[50] The general principles of pleading were explained in the 1917 case of *Benson & Simpson v Robinson*:[51]

> 'The plaintiff must not set out the evidence upon which he relies, but he must state clearly and concisely on what facts he bases his claim and he must do so with such exactness that the defendant will know the nature of the facts which are to proved

45 *Room Hire Co (Pty) Ltd v Jeppe Street Mansions (Pty) Ltd* 1949 (3) SA 1155 (T) at 1161; Cilliers, Loots & Nel 2009, p. 292.

46 *Ex parte Inkley & Inkley* 1995 (3) SA 528 (C).

47 Unliquidated damages refer to those claims which are not capable of speedy and prompt ascertainment and in respect of which the claimant has to lead evidence on the quantification of damages.

48 *Room Hire Co (Pty) Ltd v Jeppe Street Mansions (Pty) Ltd* 1949 (3) SA 1155 (T) at 1161; Cilliers, Loots & Nel 2009, p. 292.

49 *Room Hire Co (Pty) Ltd v Jeppe Street Mansions (Pty) Ltd* 1949 (3) SA 1155 (T) at 1161.

50 It would appear that the present pleading style emanate from rules of procedure dating back to 1828 promulgated in open court by William Westbrooke Burton second puisne judge of the Cape Supreme Court from 1828 to 1832. These rules subsequently came to be firmly entrenched throughout the territory of South Africa by the time that the Union of South Africa was declared in 1910. See Erasmus 1996, p. 147-148; Erasmus 1991, 265-276; Girvin 1990.

51 1917 WLD 126.

> against him so that he may adequately meet him in court and tender evidence to disprove the plaintiff's allegations'.

Determining how exactly to plead the material facts of a case can be quite difficult, for it does not simply require one to plead facts, but to plead the facts in such a way such as to complete the cause of action.[52] Sometimes even experienced practitioners are confounded by what the material facts of a case are, and how to distinguish between fact and evidence.[53] Fortunately, precedent books[54] and judicial precedent[55] make the task somewhat easier and less scientific. But woe betide the party who fails to plead all the *facta probanda*, for failure to do so will render a summons[56] or a plea[57] susceptible to exception[58] for being 'vague and embarrassing',[59] or for failing to disclose a cause of action. This will require the defaulting party to amend the pleading so as to state the necessary fact that was omitted.

Although there is nothing precluding the parties from pleading evidence in an action, this seldom happens. In fact, practitioners will go out of their way to ensure that evidence is omitted. The motivation for this is to prevent the opposition from gaining a tactical advantage by gaining knowledge of what should essentially be trial-led *viva voce* evidence.[60]

Just like with applications, in actions legal rules and principles are also not pleaded. However, by pleading material facts the cause of action and legal defences will immediately become discernable, even to a layperson with average abilities. Where a layperson may experience difficulty is to understand the underlying legal

52 Daniels 2002, P. 47. See also *Romoff v Union Castle SS Co Table Bay Harbour Board and McKenzie & Co* 18 SC 177; and see *Grobbelaar v Minister for Agriculture* 1913 EDL 203; *Mayor and Town Council of East London v Williams and Others* 1882 2 EDC 179; *Feathers v The London Trading Association* 1922 CPD 253; *Lavery & Co Ltd v Jungheinrich* 1931 AD 156; *Graham v McGee* 1949 (4) SA 770 (D); *Wessels v Badenhorst* 1939 TPD 465; *Hanford v Springbok Pools (Pty) Ltd* 1939 TPD 76.

53 The following statement of Barry J. in *Jones v Hamilton & Haw* 1886 5 EDC 222 at 228 explains the position: 'There is distinction between giving evidence of a fact and stating that fact. ... Stating that a thing was done is stating a fact; giving the details of how it was done would be giving evidence of it. Sometimes it is very difficult to state concisely, without stating it, indicating the evidence of it. ... Under the present rules of pleading you may not only state the necessary facts, but you are required to state all material facts relied on. So that if a fact which, not absolutely necessary but material either in aggravation or mitigation, is within your knowledge and you intend to lay it before the court, you are invited and it is certainly your privilege to plead it'.

54 Daniels 2009.

55 *Jones v Hamilton and Haw* 1886 5 EDC 222 at 228.

56 An action is initiated when the plaintiff serves a summons on the defendant.

57 The plea is the document in which the defendant sets out the defence to the plaintiff's claim. It is also acceptable for a defendant to incorporate its counterclaim in the plea document.

58 The 'exception' is akin to what was called the 'demurrer' in English law. Today, of course, under the new English civil procedure rules the demurrer is called an 'objection in point of law'.

59 URC 23(1); MCR 19(1). For a very good analysis of when a pleading will be considered 'vague and embarrassing' see *Jowell v Bramwell-Jones* 1998 (1) SA 836 (W) at 899-903. See also Cilliers, Loots & Nel 2009, p. 634 *et seq.*

60 See *Staples v Marquard* 1919 CPD 181; *Cumes v Estate Cumes* 1950 (2) SA 15 (C).

premises around which the facts are constructed, for this is rarely stated in pleadings. Legal arguments are usually delivered after all the evidence has been adduced at trial and after each party has exchanged heads of argument.[61]

As a basic proposition then, in the action procedure, pleadings have limited value in terms of fact- and truth-finding. Of course, they provide the necessary information to crystallize the cause of action and the defences to the claim, but in terms of discovering the truth, and all the facts behind the action, and the defences thereto, they have limited value. They do not assist the parties or a judicial officer to weigh the probabilities of success. In fact, pleadings have a *limiting effect* because they preclude parties from adducing evidence to prove a fact which has not been specifically pleaded, or from invoking a rule or principle of law not supported by the facts as pleaded.[62]

On average, from the time when a defendant receives a summons to the moment when pleadings close (*litis contestatio*) a better part of a year can pass in the High Courts and many months in the Magistrates' Courts. Although the rules of court stipulate strict time periods for filing pleadings, practitioners are not averse to dragging their feet. The rules are generally reluctant to automatically bar parties from filing late pleadings, and so they require the innocent party to first place the defaulting party on terms.[63] Practitioners are also not reticent to institute interlocutory challenges to pleadings. Often the validity of pleadings or their content is disputed or some or other technical or substantive defence is raised. This delays resolution of the matter. No matter how drawn out a matter becomes, the court has no truth-finding powers. The court is expected to sit back and to watch the matter unfold. The only time the court intervenes is when it feels that a party is abusing the court process.[64] Intervention (usually at the behest of one of the parties) entails restraining the guilty party as the court deems necessary and imposing an appropriate costs order.[65]

So, for a considerable period of time in the action, the truth is unknown and the facts are scant. Facts are limited to what is absolutely necessary. The first opportunity for some semblance of the truth to come to the fore and for more facts to be exposed arises in the pre-trial stage by way of the discovery protocols.

61 Heads of argument in an action are drafted on the same lines as heads of argument in applications. For a discussion of heads of argument see what was stated under 'applications'.

62 *Mutual & Federal Insurance Co Ltd v SMD Telecommunications* CC 2011 (1) SA 94 (SCA) at para 23; *Presidency Property Investments (Pty) Ltd v Patel* 2011 (5) SA 432 (SCA) at paras 19-21; 24.

63 See Peté *et al.* 2011, p. 211.

64 *Beinash v Wixley* 1997 (3) SA 721 (SCA) at 734C-H.

65 *Beinash v Wixley* 1997 (3) SA 721 (SCA) at 739I-J.

4. Discovery

The importance of discovery for the manifestation of the truth was confirmed in a rather hyperbolic statement in *The MV Urgup: Owners of the MV Urgup v Western Bulk Carriers (Australia) (Pty) Ltd*[66] in which it was held:

> 'Discovery has been said to rank with cross-examination as one of the two mightiest engines for the exposure of the truth ever to have been devised in the Anglo-Saxon family of legal systems. Properly employed where its use is called for it can be, and often is, a devastating tool. But it must not be abused or called into aid lightly in situations for which it was not designed or it will lose its edge and become debased'.

While the above statement is indeed correct in so far as it links discovery to uncovering the truth, the cautious approach evinced by the court must be questioned. The court does not explain how discovery can be 'abused' or in what situations it can be said to be 'called into aid lightly'. Although the above dictum has been cited on numerous occasions, no court has ever defined the meaning of the circumscriptive language employed by the court. One must in any event question whether the court was correct to take a cautious approach to discovery, for as noted by the learned authors of *Herbstein & van Winsen: The Civil Practice of the High Courts of South Africa*, 'Discovery is obligatory in all trial actions and has not lost its edge and has not become debased'.[67]

It is also interesting to note that discovery as a concept was not a unique English invention; discovery dates back to Roman law.[68] While there is little doubt that current South African discovery rules, on account of the historical evolution of South African civil procedure, owe their origin to English influence, discovery as a concept was also known in Roman-Dutch Law,[69] and may have been applied in some or other form by early South African courts practising the Roman-Dutch system of procedure.[70]

(i) Pre-trial Discovery in Terms of the Promotion of Access to Information Act

In the past, there was considerable debate as to whether discovery could be ordered prior to instituting proceedings. The general rule was that discovery could only be ordered after legal proceedings were initiated. This debate has to a certain extent been laid to rest by the Promotion of Access to Information Act of 2000 (PAIA)[71] which was enacted by the Legislature so as to comply with the Constitution.[72]

66 1999 (3) SA 500 (C).

67 Cilliers, Loots & Nel 2009, p. 785. Van Loggerenberg 2011, opines at 23-4: '[Discovery] is not a tool designed to put a party in a position to draw the battle lines and establish the legal issues. Rather, it is a tool used to identify factual issues once legal issues are established'.

68 Code of Justinian, Book 2, Title 1.

69 Voet 1704, Book 2, Title 13, § 16-26. As noted earlier, the common law of South Africa is essentially Roman-Dutch.

70 As noted earlier, the common law of South Africa is essentially Roman-Dutch.

71 Act 2 of 2000.

72 Constitution of the Republic of South Africa Act, 1996.

Section 32(1) of the South African Constitution provides that everyone has the right to access to (a) information held by the state; and (b) any information that is held by another person and that is required for the exercise or protection of any rights. Subsection 2 provides that national legislation must be enacted to give effect to this right.

The PAIA was the legislative answer to the constitutional imperative. Section 9 makes it quite clear that the Act has both vertical and horizontal application.[73] In terms of the PAIA one can request information not only for the purposes of exercising or protecting a constitutional right, but also a proprietary right.

While there are not many reported cases dealing with the PAIA, the case of *Unitas Hospital v Van Wyk*[74] is instructive to appreciate the ambit of the legislation. In this case, the first respondent intended to institute action against the appellant hospital for damages arising from the death of her late husband while he was a patient. She contended that his death was as the result of negligence on the part of the hospital's nursing staff.[75] With a view to instituting proceedings, the first respondent brought an application in the High Court against the appellant and the second respondent under s 50 of the PAIA. She sought access to a report that had been compiled by the second respondent on general nursing conditions in the intensive care and high-care units at the hospital. She claimed to be entitled to access to the report on the ground that, without access to it, her right to claim damages from the appellant would be affected.[76]

Section 50(1)*(a)* of the PAIA provides that a requester of information must be given access 'to any record of a private body if that record is *required* for the exercise or protection of any rights'. The appellant and second respondent resisted the request on the ground that the first respondent had not shown, as was stipulated by s 50(1)*(a)* of the Act, that the information sought was 'required' for the exercise or protection of any right.[77] It was contended that the respondent already had access to whatever information her experts required, such as the deceased's hospital records, clinical notes and medical reports, in order to be able to advise her on the formulation and assessment of her claim. Significantly, she also had access to the second respondent, who was the author of the report.[78] The first respondent retaliated, claiming that the report would assist her in establishing whether she had a reasonable prospect of success in the action she intended instituting against the appellant.[79] The Western Cape High Court granted the order sought against both

73 Section 9(1) of the Promotion of Access to Information Act 2 of 2000 provides:
The objects of this Act are:
(a) to give effect to the constitutional right of access to-
(i) any information held by the state; and
(ii) any information that is held by another person and that is required for the exercise or protection of any rights...'.

74 *Unitas Hospital v Van Wyk* 2006 (4) SA 436 (SCA).

75 At para 1.

76 At para 11.

77 At para 6.

78 At para 11.

79 At para 13.

the appellant and the second respondent. It found that the first respondent reasonably required the report in order to establish whether she should pursue her claim. The Court *a quo* made the following important observation:

> '(I)t seems to me that having access to the [second respondent's] report will assist the applicant in either proceeding with or abandoning the claim against the first respondent. It is in the interest of *bona fide* litigation that the parties should take this critical decision on the basis of essential information where such is available. In the words of Cameron J [in *Van Niekerk v Pretoria City Council* 1997 (3) SA 839 (T) at 848G]:
>
> > "Either way, disclosure will promote an early settlement of the dispute and bring the envisaged litigation, by settlement or abandonment, to a short, sharp end. In this sense, the applicant can in my view be said reasonably to require the report."
>
> Such is indeed the view I hold in the present case'.

The Court went on to state:

> 'While the applicant may arguably be in possession of some information on the basis of which she may issue summons against the first respondent, there can be no doubt that, the less the information she has, the higher the risk she runs of either formulating her claim incorrectly or even of proceeding with the litigation when, with a fuller picture, she might decide not to.... Another advantage of assessing information early is that, if, indeed, based on the available information, the applicant does not have a case against the first respondent, the applicant will be placed in the position to know this early and therefore avoid unnecessary litigation. This, as I understand the position, is precisely part of the driving notion behind the ideals of promoting access to information. Access to information must limit prejudice and encourage or facilitate early or timeous resolution of disputes. It is a fitting philosophical approach to dispute resolution in an open and democratic society'.[80]

The appellant hospital appealed the ruling of the court *a quo*.

The Supreme Court of Appeal held that in order for information to be considered 'required' within the meaning of s 50(1)*(a)* of the Act, it had to be information that would be of assistance for the respondent's stated purpose. However, the mere fact that it would be of 'assistance' did not mean that it was 'required'.[81] The Court stated that it was inappropriate to formulate a positive and generally applicable definition of 'require', because ultimately, whether or not information is 'required' depends on the facts of a case.[82] The furthest the court was willing to go was to say that 'reasonably required' connoted 'a substantial advantage or an element of need'.[83]

The PAIA, held the court, was not intended to have any impact on the discovery procedure in civil cases and therefore, did not supplant the normal court

80 Quoted at para 14.
81 At para 17.
82 At para 18.
83 *Ibidem.*

rules relating to discovery.[84] Once proceedings commenced, the rules of discovery took over and the provisions of the PAIA would no longer apply between the parties.[85] For the first respondent, once she instituted her action against the appellant, and if the report became relevant to the issues raised on the pleadings, the appellant would be obliged to discover the report in terms of the normal civil procedure discovery rules.

The Supreme Court of Appeal was at pains to point out that pre-action discovery under s 50 of the Act had to remain the exception rather than the rule. Consequently, its availability is restricted to the requester who has shown the 'element of need' or 'substantial advantage'. A requester is *not* entitled, as a matter of course, to all information that might assist him or her in evaluating his or her prospects of success against a potential defendant.[86] As the first respondent, by her own admission, had a number of alternative sources of information, including the second respondent, she failed to indicate what further knowledge and benefit she could hope to gain from the report.[87] The Court concluded that the application ought to have been dismissed by the High Court,[88] because the first respondent had failed to meet even the threshold requirement that the report would be of assistance to her in the action. By implication therefore the 'element of need' or 'substantial advantage' was absent.

Cameron JA dissented. His dissent was based on three principled arguments, which can be summarised as follows. First, he noted that it was too narrow to focus on the relevance of the information for formulating a damages claim against the hospital. The second respondent's claim against the hospital, in the mind of the judge, involved issues not only of individual conduct and responsibility; it scrutinised how the hospital's systems functioned, and whether institutional procedures and protocols were adhered to. The report was instrumental in determining whether accepted procedures were followed. Second, even though the hospital was not a public body under the PAIA - it was a private hospital - the statute's approach to private bodies was no different when compared to public bodies. The declared objects of the PAIA suggested that, where appropriate, courts should 'encourage transparency, accountability and effective governance in private

84 Section 7 of the PAIA declares:
'7 (1) This Act does not apply to a record of a public body or a private body if:
(a) that record is requested for the purpose of criminal or civil proceedings;
(b) so requested after the commencement of such criminal or civil proceedings, as the case may be; and
(c) the production of or access to that record for the purpose referred to in paragraph (a) is provided for in any other law.
(2) Any record obtained in a manner that contravenes subsection (1) is not admissible as evidence in the criminal or civil proceedings referred to in that subsection unless the exclusion of such record by the court in question would, in its opinion, be detrimental to the interests of justice'.

85 At para 19.

86 At para 22.

87 At para 23.

88 At para 25.

institutions'. Large private institutions like the hospital performed vital public functions and therefore fell plainly within the generous scope of the statutory objective. Thirdly and most significantly, '[p]re-discovery disclosure is important and helpful in assisting a litigant - and, thereby, also the opponent - to determine whether litigation should commence at all, or whether it should proceed'. The PAIA recognised the importance of post-commencement access procedures; but its novel dimension lay in the fact that it created pre-commencement access. The judge opined that courts should be slow to stifle access to information. Litigation, it was noted, 'involves massive costs, time, personnel, effort and risks. Where access to a document can assist in avoiding the initiation of litigation, or opposition to it, the objects of the statute suggest that access should be granted'.[89]

The *ratio* in the *Unitas* case has been confirmed in a subsequent decision of the Supreme Court of Appeal.[90] The case has also attracted favourable legal comment.[91] Favourable comment notwithstanding, the case can be criticised for uncritically trying to reconcile the PAIA with the traditional adversarial system. The Court initially considers the purpose of the Act, but in the interpretation of its provisions it emphasises the 'ordinary and literal interpretation' of words when it could so easily have adopted a 'purposive approach' to statutory interpretation.[92]

A purposive approach would not have been misplaced if one keeps in mind the remedial, moral and constitutional motivations behind the legislation.[93] Furthermore, there is simply an assumption, in so far as the PAIA falls short of affording unrestricted access to information, that the normal rules of discovery will complete the picture. As will be discussed below, the normal rules of discovery are fraught with delay and other limitations. The case also raises other critical questions such as: why should a litigant not be entitled to information that would enable him or her to determine the probabilities of success at the outset? Why should a litigant only be entitled to information as is necessary to frame his or her cause of action? What difference would it have made if the report in the *Unitas* case was made available before proceedings were instituted, as opposed to after proceedings were instituted as part of the normal discovery process? For one thing, permitting early access to discoverable information could save time and costs as it would prevent the institution of proceedings in cases where the merits are weak. What possible sense can there be in running a cause of action which may be weak in prospects, but which is nonetheless initiated only because the plaintiff was unable to get her hands on relevant information which she *knew* existed, and which she would eventually get her hands on through the normal rules of discovery?

89 At 448G-449F.

90 *Claase v Information Officer, South African Airways (Pty) Ltd* 2007 (5) SA 469 (A) at 473G-H.

91 July 2006 *De Rebus* 37.

92 *Bank of Lisbon and South Africa Ltd v Tandrien Beleggings (Pty) Ltd* 1983 (2) SA 621 (W) at 624H-625C endorsed a purposive approach when interpreting discovery rule 35(8).

93 See the Preamble to the Act.

(ii) Discovery in Terms of the Rules of Court

Discovery in terms of the rules of court is said to 'exclude the element of surprise in the interests of a proper ventilation of disputes'.[94] Unless leave of court has been obtained, discovery under both the Magistrates' Courts Rules as well as the Uniform Rules of the High Court may not take place before the close of pleadings.[95]

Discovery is usually prompted when the opposing party sends a *notice of discovery*. The party receiving the notice must make discovery within court 20 days[96] of receiving the notice. A 'discovery affidavit' is filed and served on the opposing party.[97] In it, the party must on oath list all the documents that he or she requires to discover.[98] A party is expected to discover all documents and tape recordings which relate to 'any matter in question' in the action and also all the documents which the party has in its possession or control, or which it had 'at any time in the past' in its possession.[99]

The word 'documents' bears its ordinary and literal meaning, but includes a 'tape recording' which in turn is wide enough to cover 'a sound track, film, magnetic tape, record or any other material on which visual images, sound or other information can be recorded'.[100] Compact disks, computer discs, computer hard drives, videotapes and photographs fall within the meaning of 'tape recording'. A document will be considered under the 'control' of a party even if it is in the possession of his or her attorney.

A notable, but not an insurmountable, shortcoming is that a party cannot, as a general rule, require the opposing party to discover documents in the hands of third parties. For the party to have sight of those documents, the third party must be served with a subpoena *duces tecum* to produce the documents.[101] The Latin phrase does not reflect the practical realities of the subpoena in the High Courts. The reality is that the party serving the subpoena does not have to wait until trial to have sight of the documents. In terms of the rules of court, the document must be produced by the witness for inspection within a reasonable time after having been served with the subpoena.[102] In the Magistrates' Courts, however, all that can be required of a third party upon whom a subpoena *duces tecum* has been served is to bring the documents to the trial. The documents cannot be inspected until the third party is

94 *Bank of Lisbon and South Africa Ltd v Tandrien Beleggings (Pty) Ltd* 1983 (2) SA 621 (W) at 624B.

95 URC 35(1); MCR 23(1)(b); See also *Wiese v Mostert* 1893 10 SC 137; *Ehlers v Malmesbury Board of Executors* 1909 26 SC 406; *Teperson v Hoffman* 1910 20 CTR 88; *Cremhold's Estate v Cohen Bros* 1923 OPD 125; *Unterhalter v Minkowitz* 1951 (2) SA 125 (W).

96 Court days are reckoned by excluding Saturdays, Sundays and public holidays. When something has to be performed *within* a particular time period one excludes the first day from when a particular period starts to run and counts the consecutive number of days after that, excluding of course all Saturdays, Sundays and public holidays.

97 URC 35(2); MCR 23(2(a).

98 The format of the affidavit must correspond to Form 11 of the First Schedule of the URC in the High Court, and Form 13, Annexure 1 of the Magistrates' Courts Rules.

99 URC 35(2); MCR 23(2)(a) read with MCR 23(2)(c).

100 URC 35(15); MCR 23(16).

101 URC 38(1)(a). There is no analogous provision in the Magistrates' Courts. In the Magistrates' Courts the *subpoena duces tecum* can be issued in terms of the common law.

102 URC 38(1)(b).

called as witness and asked to produce the document at trial.[103] It is uncertain why the Magistrates' Courts rules differ on this aspect to the rules of the High Courts. It seems rather inefficient for a party to have first sight of a document in the hands of a third party at trial. Aside from obscuring the truth for much longer than is necessary, it also makes it rather difficult for a party to prepare adequately for trial. It is, therefore, submitted that for purposes of truth- and fact-finding and also for the purposes of efficiency and convenience, the Magistrates' Courts Rules should be amended to be consonant with the Uniform Rules of Court applicable in the High Courts.

As regards the content of documents and tape recordings which must be discovered, the courts have said that the party making discovery must discover *all* documents which relate to 'any matter in question in the action'. This places a positive obligation to discover all documents which are directly or indirectly relevant to the case. As the courts have noted, a document will be indirectly relevant if it 'fairly' leads a party 'to a train of enquiry' that may advance his case or damage that of his opponent.[104] Whether or not a document is relevant will be determined by the issues in dispute as reflected in the pleadings.[105]

It is surprising to note that South African courts[106] still apply the former English law rule that a document is privileged and need not be produced if it is part of the evidence supporting the case of the party in possession of the document, and does not support or tend to support the opponent's case. In other words, the party calling for discovery is not entitled to see documents that do not help to advance his or her own case or damage the case of the party making discovery. The rationale for the non-disclosure was explained in the English decision of *Brooks v Prescott* (cited as authority by South African courts):[107]

> 'A party is entitled to get inspection of any documents relating to his own case. He is not entitled to see documents relating exclusively to his opponent's case in order that he may prepare means of meeting it or try to discover flaws in it. ... In England it is considered contrary to the interests of justice to compel a litigant to disclose to his opponents before trial the evidence to be adduced against him ... it is considered that it would give him unfair advantages for cross-examination and lead to endless side

103 Van Loggerenberg 2011, p. 23-3.

104 *Rellams (Pty) Ltd v James Brown and Hamer Ltd* 1983 (1) SA 556 (N) at 564A.

105 *Swissborough Diamond Mines (Pty) Ltd v Government of the Republic of South Africa* 1999 (2) SA 279 (T) at 311A.

106 *Bilborough v Mutual Life Insurance Co of New York* 1906 TH 53; *Robinson v Farrar* 1907 TS 740; *Power v Wilson* 1909 TH 254; *Freeman v Freeman* 1921 WLD 1; *Maxwell v Rosenberg* 1927 WLD 1; *Northern Assurance Co Ltd v Rosenthal* 1927 WLD 209; *Caravan Cinemas (Pty) Ltd v London Film Productions* 1951 (3) SA 671 (W); *Lenz Township Co (Pty) Ltd v Munnick* 1959 (2) SA 567 (W); *Lenz Township Co (Pty) Ltd v Munnick* 1959 (4) SA 567 (T); *Ferreira v Endley* 1966 (3) SA 618 (E) at 622A; *Tractor & Excavator Spares (Pty) Ltd v Groenedijk* 1976 (4) SA 359 (W) at 362B-E; *Rellams (Pty) Ltd v James Brown and Hamer Ltd* 1983 (1) SA 556 (N) at 564A; *Carpede v Choene NO* 1986 (3) SA 445 (O) at 452; *Quintessence Co-ordinators (Pty) Ltd v Government of the Republic of Transkei* 1991 (4) SA 214 (Tk) at 216D.

107 *Lenz Township Co (Pty) Ltd v Munnick* 1959 (4) SA 567 (T) at 575D-F; *Tractor & Excavator Spares (Pty) Ltd v Groenedijk* 1976 (4) SA 359 (W) at 362C-F.

> issues; and would enable witnesses to be tampered with, and give unfair advantage to the unscrupulous'.

The rule stated in *Brooks* was of course abolished in English law in 1968.[108] However, South African courts continue to apply this relic from its colonial past, and it would even appear that the Legislature has extended the rule to the Magistrates' Courts. It is trite that in the past the rule stated in *Brooks* did not form part of the practice of the Magistrates' Courts.[109] In 2010 the Rules Board[110] introduced a new set of rules for the Magistrates' Courts.[111] The new discovery rules[112] in some respects mirror the discovery rules in the High Courts.[113] The consequence of this is that the rule stated in *Brooks* has been extended to the Magistrates' Courts. One can only assume that the extension was inadvertent. The lament by the learned writers of *Herbstein & Van Winsen: The Civil Practice of the High Courts of South Africa* is correct when they state:

> 'A serious reconsideration of this rule [the rule stated in *Brook's* case] is necessary. Not only does it fly in the face of the stated function of discovery, namely to provide parties with the relevant documentary or recorded material before the hearing so as to assist them in appraising the strength or weakness of their respective cases, but it also allows an opponent to decide subjectively whether a particular document, although relevant, would impeach his or her own case or support or tend to support the case of the opponent'.

It is submitted that the *Brook's* rule does violence to the pursuit of truth which lies at the heart of discovery. It may also be the case that the rule is unconstitutional. As has been mentioned above, the Constitution[114] grants a right of access to all documents which are 'required'[115] for the exercise or protection of any right. To this extent, the Promotion of Access to Information Act[116] seeks to give effect to the constitutional right to information. However, it will be recalled that the Act[117] specifically excludes its operation when legal proceedings have been initiated. The exclusion carries an implicit assumption that the rules of procedure (civil and criminal) will adequately safeguard the constitutional right of litigants to access information and that the procedural rules will be consonant with constitutional

108 Civil Evidence Act, 1968, s 16(1) and (2).

109 Rule 23 of the Magistrates' Courts rules required the discovery of 'books and documents ... which tend to prove either party's case'. See also Cilliers, Loots & Nel 2009, p. 801 fn 149.

110 The Rules Board has delegated authority in terms of s 6 of the Rules Board for Courts of Law Act 107 of 1985 to make rules, with the approval of the Minister of Justice and Constitutional Development for, *inter alia*, the Magistrates' Courts.

111 Rules Regulating the Conduct of the Proceedings of the Magistrates' Courts of South Africa GN R740 *Government Gazette* 33487 of 23 August 2010.

112 MCR 23.

113 MCR 35.

114 Constitution of the Republic of South Africa, 1996, s 32.

115 See the discussion pertaining to the case of *Unitas Hospital v Van Wyk* 2006 (4) SA 436 (SCA) above.

116 Act 2 of 2000.

117 Act 2 of 2000, s 7.

norms and values. Since the rule stated in *Brooks* has the potential of curtailing one's constitutional right to information, it does mean that information seekers will be subject to disparate treatment.[118] The disparity of treatment is attributed to the fact that if a litigant were to seek information in terms of the PAIA the *Brooks* rule would not apply, but the moment litigation is instituted, thereby rendering the PAIA inapplicable, the *Brooks* rule would apply. This difference in treatment must surely be ground for a constitutional challenge.

Documents which fall within the rubric of attorney-client privilege,[119] marital privilege[120] or which are injurious to the public interest[121] need not be discovered. Furthermore, documents containing a written offer made *without prejudice* with the intention of settling a matter may also be excluded.[122] The privilege against self-incrimination[123] is also seen as an excuse for non-discovery of documents in civil proceedings. However, the existence of this privilege is open to doubt.

118 In *Ingledew v Financial Services Board: In re Financial Services Board v Van der Merwe* 2003 (4) SA 584 (CC) at para 29 the Constitutional Court referred to the possibility of 'anomalies' arising between the discovery rules in terms of the rules of court and the access to information provision (s 32) of the Constitution. The court, however, refrained from speculating what these anomalies might be as the issue was strictly speaking not before the court for consideration. It is submitted that the Brook's rule is indeed an example of such an anomaly.

119 Attorney-client privilege was recognized by the common law (*S v Safatsa* 1988 (1) SA 868 (A) at 885H-886H) and is also constitutionally protected (*Jeeva v Receiver of Revenue, Port Elizabeth* 1995 (2) SA 433 (SE) at 453C-457B, 459G-460C; *Nortje v Attorney-General, Cape* 1995 (2) SA 460 (C) at 480E-I. See also Klaaren 1996, p. 24-27.

120 Civil Proceedings Act 25 of 1965, s 10 and 10A:
'10 (1) No husband shall be compelled to disclose any communication made to him by his wife during the marriage and no wife shall be compelled to disclose any communication made to her by her husband during the marriage.
(2) Subsection (1) shall also apply to a communication made during the subsistence of a marriage or a putative marriage which has been dissolved or annulled by a competent court'.
10A Any customary marriage or customary union, concluded under the indigenous law and custom of any of the indigenous peoples of the Republic of South Africa or any marriage concluded under any system of religious law, shall be regarded as a valid marriage for the purposes of the law of evidence'.

121 *Van der Linde v Calitz* 1967 (2) SA 239 (A) at 259; and see *Conway v Rimmer* [1968] AC 910, [1968] 1 All ER 874. On the rationale of public interest as a ground for non-disclosure of documents or information, see *D v National Society for the Prevention of Cruelty to Children* [1977] 1 All ER 589 (HL). This common law rule is of course subject to the s 32 of the Constitution of the Republic of South Africa, 1996 and the tenets of the Promotion of Access to Information Act 2 of 2000.

122 Van Loggerenberg 2011 holds: 'The rationale of the rule is public policy: parties to disputes are encouraged to avoid litigation by resolving their differences amicably in full and frank discussions without the fear that, if the negotiations fail, any admissions made by them during such discussions will be used against them in ensuing litigation'. See also *Kapeller v Rondalia Versekeringskorporasie van SA Bpk* 1964 (4) SA 722 (T) at 728; *Naidoo v Marine and Trade Insurance Co Ltd* 1978 (3) SA 666 (A) at 677; *Tshabalala v President Versekeringsmaatskappy Bpk* 1987 (4) SA 72 (T) at 76.

123 See Peté *et al.* 2011, p. 230. The learned writers at fn 425 refer to s 14 of Civil Proceedings Evidence Act 25 of 1965. However, the s 14 refers to oral witness statements and not to documentary disclosure.

The dictum in *R v Camane*[124] is often cited as confirming the privilege against self-incrimination. In this case Chief Justice Innes stated:

> 'It is an established principle of our law that no one can be compelled to give evidence incriminating himself. He cannot be forced to do that either before the trial, or during the trial. The principle comes to us through English law, and, its roots go back far in history ... What the rule forbids is compelling a man to give evidence which incriminates himself'.

Critics argue that this dictum is inapplicable to documentary discovery. They argue that the privilege against self-incrimination should only extend to verbal testimony.[125] They also argue that when a person discovers a document it cannot be said that he or she admits to anything. The party is not required to say anything about the authenticity of the documents or their truth.[126] In the face of these common sense criticisms, time is indeed ripe to reconsider the privilege.

On the surface it sounds easy to say that parties are required to discover *all* relevant documents, but it is quite another thing to see how the rule is applied in practice. While many parties exercise good faith when complying with the rule, a considerable number of litigants exhibit selective amnesia when making discovery. They often omit, conceal and sometimes destroy evidence which may be prejudicial to their case. It is, therefore, not surprising that the courts are faced, on a daily basis, with many interlocutory applications in which an order for full discovery is sought. In these applications the onus falls on the applicant to indicate to the court what evidence they think should have been discovered, but which was not. Needless to say, this can be a very difficult exercise when one keeps in mind that none of the parties can investigate the evidence held by the other party. It thus all comes down to logical deduction and rational reasoning, which in itself is not very useful when one simply does not know what evidence the other side possesses. It is difficult to propose a solution to this problem save to perhaps suggest that maybe South African law should move towards a system of witness depositions. Interviewing witnesses at an early stage may be a way of determining the kinds of evidence which the other party has, but which has not been discovered.

If a party believes that the opposition or a third party is in possession of sensitive information which may be destroyed so as to prevent it from being adduced at court, the party can apply to court for an 'Anton Piller order'.[127] This

124 1925 AD 570 at 575.

125 Cilliers, Loots & Nel 2009, p. 809. See also *Ex parte Minister of Justice: In re Matamba* 1941 AD 75.

126 See Cilliers, Loots & Nel 2009, p. 808. See also the views of Zuckerman 2007, p. 403.

127 The name of the procedural remedy 'Anton Piller' derives from the English case *Anton Piller KG v Manufacturing Processes Ltd* [1976] 1 All ER 779 (CA). The remedy came be judicially accepted in *Roamer Watch Co SA v African Textile Distributors also t/a M K Patel Wholesale Merchants & Direct Importers* 1980 (2) SA 254 (W). It was subsequently accepted by the Appellate Division *Universal City Studios Inc v Network Video (Pty) Ltd* 1986 (2) SA 734 (A). In all of these cases the Court gave recognition to the inherent jurisdiction of the Supreme Court of South Africa (now High Court) to develop the common law by arrogating procedural remedies when the interests of justice so required. The 'Anton Piller order' passed →

order will entitle the applicant to direct the Sheriff[128] of the court to search the premises where the evidence is kept, to seize it, and to hold it in safe custody until trial.

When making discovery it is obligatory to list documents in chronological order. This prevents an attorney from 'burying' a document. In *Copalcor Manufacturing (Pty) Ltd v GDC Hauliers (Pty) Ltd (formerly GDC Hauliers CC)*[129] it was held that it is not 'sufficient for a party in custody of a large volume of documentation to point to a storeroom and give access thereto to his adversary with an injunction to inspect and to copy to his heart's content'. Documents relevant to the action must be identified and described with a degree of specificity. This, it is submitted, is a positive feature of the South African discovery procedure. In the United States for example, parties constantly lament the unwieldy nature of the discovery process. Parties are expected to wade through a morass of paperwork to identify what is sometimes a needle in a haystack. The South African courts take a dim view of such practices. Where one does refer to a bundle of documents, such as invoices or statements, the rules relating to discovery provide that in lieu of itemizing each document, a party can discover the documents by describing them 'as being one of a bundle of documents of a specified nature, which have been initialled and consecutively numbered'.[130] Documents may, therefore, be individually identified, or identified as a bundle, initialled and consecutively numbered.

(iii) Failure to Discover

Failing to discover a discoverable document will generally mean that the defaulting party will be unable to rely on that document in court, unless of course, if that document is discovered as part of the opposing party's case.[131]

constitutional muster in *Dabelstein v Hilderbrandt* 1996 (2) SA 42 (C). The 'Anton Piller order' is currently known as 'search order' in English law.

128 Sheriffs are not police officials. They are synonymous with bailiffs in other legal systems. They are appointed in terms of the Sheriffs Act 90 of 1986 and are responsible for executing all sentences, decrees, judgments, writs, summonses, rules, orders, warrants, commands and processes of court.

129 2000 (3) SA 181 (W) at 194B-195C.

130 URC 35(2).

131 The case of *Ottowa (Rhodesia) (Pvt) Ltd v Highams Rhodesia (1969) (Pvt) Ltd* 1975 (3) SA 77 (R) is authority for the proposition that the ethical duty to disclose all information to the court sometimes trumps the principle that one is unable to rely on documents that were not discovered. In this case, plaintiff's counsel was placed in an ethical quandary by the defendant's failure to discover documents which exposed the plaintiff's main witness as a liar and effectively demolished the plaintiff's case. Goldin J. held that in the circumstances plaintiff's counsel had correctly not invoked the Rhodesian rule to the effect that counsel is unable to rely on undiscovered documents, for although the rule entitled the plaintiff to object to the use of the undiscovered documents, to do so would have amounted to a deception of the court. Even though the decision of the Rhodesian High Court is not binding in South Africa, decisions of this court are considered persuasive on account of the fact that Rhodesia (now Zimbabwe) shares the same common law as South Africa. The adjectival laws of the two countries are also similar, mostly based on South African law.

When a party fails to discover, a notice can be sent to him or her to make discovery within the requisite time period.[132] Failure to do so will ground an application to court to compel discovery with an appropriate costs order.[133] Noncompliance with a court order obliging discovery may result in the dismissal of the plaintiff's claim or the striking out of the defendant's defence. It is uncommon for the courts to make such order as the overwhelming majority of litigants try to comply with the obligation to discover. In most instances, however, it is not the failure to discover *at all* that is the problem, but the failure to discover adequately and in accordance with the rules of court. For this reason the courts are more inclined to impose costs orders as opposed to striking out a matter.[134]

Where a party makes discovery but the discovery is inadequate, the rules of court provide that before rushing off to court to obtain an order compelling discovery, a notice should be served on the opposing party to make undiscovered documents or tape recordings (or copies of them) available for inspection. The opposing party is also informed that if the documents are no longer in its possession, the whereabouts of such documents must be stated. Failure to comply with this notice will then ground an application to court to compel discovery.[135]

The rules of court compelling a party to discover work well when a party knows about evidence which the other party has or ought to have. Obviously, where the rules fall flat is where a party is unaware of the kinds of evidence held by the other side and which might be advantageous to its case and prejudicial to the other party's case. South African law, as is the case in many other legal systems, places an ethical and moral duty on attorneys to discover all discoverable documents in their possession or in their clients' possession. However, anecdotal evidence suggests that there are unscrupulous practitioners who turn a blind eye to less-than-complete discovery.

A particularly worrying feature has emerged with regard to discovery. In terms of the rules of court, parties are entitled to request discovery once pleadings have closed. However, it would appear that the courts (especially the High Courts) are reluctant to make orders compelling discovery at such an early date. The argument is often made that, on account of the time delay between when pleadings close and the actual trial date, discovery is not urgent. The reasoning is hard to understand. It is incorrectly assumed that discovery is only relevant for the purpose of preparing for trial. What is ignored, however, is that discovery is an incredibly useful tool to measure the quality of evidence and consequently, the probabilities of success in an action. Instead of exploring opportunities to eradicate frivolous, time-consuming and expensive litigation, the courts are inadvertently perpetuating negative adversarialistic conduct by precluding early discovery. Some may argue that early discovery will prejudice a party if the opposing party comes into

132 URC 35(3); MCR 25(3).

133 URC 55(7); MCR 23(8).

134 *Stanley Motors Ltd v Administrator Natal* 1959 (1) SA 624 (D); *Sandy's Construction Company v Pillai* 1965 (1) SA 427 (N); *Tractor & Excavator Spares (Pty) Ltd v Groenedijk* 1976 (4) SA 359 (W) at 263G-364A.

135 URC 35(3); MCR23(3).

possession of further documents after the process is concluded. This is a nonsensical argument, because it is trite that one is obliged to make supplementary discovery the moment new and relevant documents come to hand.

(iv) Inspection

Parties are entitled to *inspect* all discovered documents. The party seeking to inspect must send the opposition a notice calling on it to produce the documents for inspection.[136] The opposing party must reply to that notice and indicate a date not more than 5 court days from when it replies as to when the documents can be inspected.[137] The inspecting party must inspect the documents at the offices of the attorneys for the opposition; alternatively, if the documents are of such a nature that the attorney cannot take custody thereof, such as banker's books, or accounting records, the documents may be inspected at the place where they are kept.

Documents may be inspected during normal business hours for five consecutive court days. During this period copies and transcriptions may be made.[138] Failure to produce a document for inspection will result in the defaulting party being unable to use that document at trial. The aggrieved party may also make an application to court requesting an order to compel the opposing party to produce particular documents for inspection.

Although the general rule is that the litigant and his or her attorney may inspect the document concerned, the courts have on occasion permitted an expert to inspect documents where the documents were of a technical nature.[139]

While the initial process of seeking and obtaining discovery remains a formal process, many attorneys do not follow the formal procedure when inspecting documents. Practice has grown whereby attorneys simply contact each other informally and request the documents which they wish to see. These are then photocopied by the opposing side.

(v) The Specification Rule

The rules of court also make provision for a further discovery mechanism, which must be complied with 15 court days before the trial. This mechanism supplements the discovery rules mentioned above. It permits a party to send the opposing party a notice calling on the opposing party to specify the dates of, the parties to, and the general nature of documents or tape recordings which are in his or her possession and which are intended for use at trial. Furthermore, the opposing party is also called to specify the particulars of all documents and tape recordings which are not in his or her possession, but which he or she intends to use at trial.[140] The name and

136 URC 35(6); MCR 23(6).

137 URC 36(6); MCR 23(6)(b).

138 For limitations on what may be copied see *Crown Cork & Seal Co Inc v Rheem South Africa (Pty) Ltd* 1980 (3) SA 1093 (W).

139 *Supervisors of Bethelsdorp Institute v Port Elizabeth Salt Pan Co* 1918 EDL 261; *Mackenzie v Furman & Pratt* 1918 WLD 62 at 66.

140 URC 35(8); MCR 23(9).

address of the persons in whose possession the documents and tape recordings are must also be stated.

Some attorneys think that the 'specification' rule is a duplication of the discovery rules mentioned above. However, there is a technical difference. Whereas the preliminary discovery rules require parties to discover documents *currently in their possession or under their control and documents which they formerly had in their possession or under their control*, the 'specification' rule requires parties to specify documents they *intend to use at trial*. This means that they must also specify those documents which are in the hands of third parties whom they intend to call as witnesses at trial. Attorneys who comply with the 'specification' rule in a cursory manner by simply stating that they intend to use all the documents disclosed in the preliminary discovery affidavit may[141] be surprised to learn that the opposition has a tactical advantage, because the latter will be permitted to object at trial to the use of documents in the hands of third parties, which were not part of the initial discovery process.[142]

On the one level the specification rule introduces an additional element of formalism, but from a practical viewpoint it gives litigants an opportunity to focus on those documents which will be specifically used at trial and in this way prevents them from having to prepare cross-examination on each and every possible document that formed part of the initial discovery process. Parties who abuse the specification rule by declaring all documents applicable at trial, and then only refer to some documents, will be penalized when the eventual bill of costs is taxed by the taxing master.[143]

(vi) Production at Trial

A party who wishes to make absolutely certain that a document discovered by the opposition will surface at court in support of its case can serve a notice on the opposition to bring such document to court. The effect of producing a document is that the document can be tendered into evidence without calling any witnesses to introduce it at trial.[144]

The technical limitation of the rule lies in the fact that a party is not obliged to produce a document at court that is in the hands of a third party. As noted earlier, the third party must be subpoenaed to bring the document to court.

141 The word *may* is used because the specification rule does not have a specific sanction for non-compliance with the rule. However, some commentators have argued that non-compliance or improper compliance gives the opposition a tactical advantage.

142 See Peté *et al.* 2011, p. 235.

143 A taxing master is a court official who is appointed to check a bill of costs once this has been drafted. On finalisation of a matter, the parties must appear before the taxing master to prove the work that was done in a particular matter. The taxing master can disallow costs for wasted expenses. A decision of the taxing master can be taken on review.

144 URC 35(10); MCR 23(11).

(vii) Admission of Documents for the Purposes of Evidence

The discovery rules also make provision for the possibility of a party sending a notice to the opposition requesting the latter to admit that certain documents or tape recordings were properly executed and that they are what they purport to be. After receiving the notice the opposing party has 10 court days to decide whether it intends to make the admission. The effect of an admission is that the party requesting the admission can rely on documents in court without having to call a witness to identify them.[145] Thus where an extraneous contract is going to be used in a trial, the party in whose favour the admission operates will not be required to call the parties to the contract to testify that they are indeed contracting parties. This will be accepted as a given. However, an admission does not deny the party who admits to the document to challenge the veracity or accuracy of the document, as it is the identity of the document, not its contents, which is admitted.[146]

(viii) Thoughts on Discovery

It is axiomatic from the above that discovery in South Africa hardly attracts the involvement of the court. The only time the court is involved is when it has to enforce discovery rules. It is up to the parties to initiate discovery and to take the discovery process to its conclusion. The court has no investigative powers. The parties are saddled with the duty to exercise good judgment and make full and complete discovery. It also falls to each party to take the initiative to identify evidence which it believes is in the hands of the opposition or in the hands of third parties, and to request such evidence if not discovered.

In South Africa there is a massive backlog of trials, especially in the higher courts. It is not uncommon to wait for two to five years for a trial date.[147] As noted earlier, it is for this reason that the courts are often inclined to take the attitude that early discovery is not urgent or essential. It is submitted that the stance of South African courts is counterintuitive to fact- and truth-finding as well as to efficiency. Early discovery is important and necessary because it enables the parties to have critical knowledge of some types of evidence. This may spark negotiation and early settlement.

It is submitted that a way of securing early discovery is to have judicial case-management. A judge will *inter alia* take charge of the discovery process as soon as pleadings close and oblige parties to comply as soon as possible. At present, discovery is left in the hands of the parties, and only reaches the court when there is a dispute regarding compliance.

5. Medical Examinations and Technical Inspections

For some odd reason the rules of court relating to discovery do not make reference to medical examinations and technical inspections. These are treated separately.

145 URC 35(9); MCR 23(10).

146 *Selero (Pty) Ltd and Another v Chauvier and Another* 1982 (2) SA 208 (T) at 216. See also Peté *et al.* 2011, p. 235.

147 See n. 1 above.

Consequently, many civil procedure textbooks are careful not to lump medical examinations and technical inspections as part of the discovery process. Following that tradition, this chapter also maintains that distinction - although it is conceded that the distinction may be artificial and that the subject at hand should be treated as part of the discovery process.

(i) Medical Examinations, Reports, Records and X-rays

Aside from documentary evidence and tape recordings, pre-trial procedures also permit parties to have sight of plans, diagrams, photographs, medical evidence and other forms of physical evidence.[148]

Where a plaintiff claims damages for physical injury, the defendant may require him or her to submit to an independent medical examination.[149]

The party calling for the examination must ensure that a full written report is compiled by the person who carries out the examination. The report must detail the 'results of the examination' as well as 'opinions formed' by the person who conducted the examination.[150] The report must be made available to any party to the litigation who requests it.

Aside from physical examinations the rules also stipulate that medical reports, hospital records, x-rays, or similar documentary information may be requested.[151]

The rules do not stipulate at what point in the litigation process a medical examination and records may be requested. Practice has grown whereby such examinations and records are requested during the pre-trial stage. However, there is nothing in principle which precludes a plaintiff from requiring a defendant to submit to a medical examination after a summons or counterclaim is served. The rules even make provision for a second medical examination where this is necessary. The fact that one can request a medical examination and medical reports at any stage of proceedings is a positive feature as it could assist in limiting the issues between the parties, foster negotiation and provoke early settlement.

(ii) Technical Inspection

The rules of court also permit the 'inspection or examination' of any object, if its 'state or condition' is relevant to an action. This includes both movable and immovable property.[152] A technical inspection may be undertaken at any stage of the proceedings, including the pleadings stage.

An interesting feature of an inspection is that it is not limited to visual inspection. If necessary, and where possible, the inspecting party may test, experiment or even dismantle the item.[153] If there is a dispute between the parties about the extent of an inspection, the matter can be referred to a judge in chambers for an appropriate order. A report on the inspection must be compiled by the party

148 URC 36; MCR 24.
149 URC 36(1); MCR 24(1).
150 URC 36(8); MCR 24(8).
151 URC 36(4); MCR 24(4).
152 URC 36(6); MCR 24(6).
153 *Caltex Oil Rhodesia (Pvt) Ltd v Perfecto Dry Cleaners (Pvt) Ltd* 1970 (2) SA 44 (R).

carrying out the inspection. The report must be made available to any party to the action on request.

It is interesting to note that medical examinations and technical inspections may be undertaken very early on in proceedings. This provides the parties wide latitude when it comes to truth-finding. But like the general discovery procedure discussed, a court is not involved in the process. The entire process is at the behest of the parties. Of course a judge will come to know of the results of an inspection or a medical examination when he or she peruses the bundle of court documents in preparation for trial.

6. Special Evidence

(i) Expert Witnesses

While parties are obliged to discover documentary evidence and to permit the examination of physical evidence, ordinarily there is no obligation on a party to reveal the nature and content of oral testimony that their witnesses will present in court. However, an exception to this rule is expert testimony.

A party who intends to call an expert witness must give notice of his or her intention to do so not less than 15 days before the trial, and must deliver not less than 10 days before the trial a summary of the expert's opinion, which must state the basis upon which the opinion was formed.[154]

The rationale behind the rule is to enable the opposing party to prepare a counterargument to the expert's testimony. This usually entails the opposing party calling his or her own expert. The rule is thus useful because it allows experts to exchange reports and views, and possibly to eliminate unnecessary points in dispute between themselves before the matter reaches trial.

Some would argue that the rule makes serious inroads to the common law right of a party to call a witness.[155] It also places a party at the disadvantage of having to intimate in advance what the expert is going to say. However, the rule is clearly designed to prevent the parties from being taken by surprise. From the point of view of truth-finding and efficiency, the rule is clearly beneficial to disputing parties. The rule saves time and costs. In the past when the rule was nonexistent the testimony of experts caused serious delays in trials. Practitioners who were not versed with the technical nature of evidence often had to seek postponement so that they could consult other experts before cross-examining an expert witness.[156]

In line with the Woolf reforms in England and Wales, there are currently plans afoot to rationalise the production of expert reports. In 2008 the South Gauteng High Court, for example, issued a practice directive requiring experts to meet in an attempt to settle or define differences of opinion with greater precision and clarity.

154 URC 36(9); On the nature of the opinion see *Coopers (South Africa) (Pty) Ltd v Deutsche GesellsChauft für Schädlingsbekämpfung mbH* 1976 (3) SA 352 (A) at 371 A-B.

155 *Boland Construction Co (Pty) Ltd v Lewin* 1977 (2) SA 506 (C) at 508H.

156 See *Coopers (South Africa) (Pty) Ltd v Deutsche GesellsChauft für Schädlingsbekämpfung mbH* 1976 (3) SA 352 (A) at 371 C-D.

One of startling features of the rules dealing with expert witnesses must surely be the time constraints within which practitioners are expected to work. The fifteen-day and ten-day time periods are far too short. Given the delay in the allocation of court dates for trial, the parties spend a significant portion of time doing absolutely nothing. Why then is it necessary to stipulate compliance with the rule so near to the trial date? Surely, these matters can be dealt with way in advance, thereby giving parties more time to evaluate the merits of their case.

(ii) Photographs, Plans, Models and Diagrams

Although photographs and plans may be covered by the other rules of discovery, the rules of court permit a party who wishes to rely on a photograph, plan, model or diagram to give notice of intention to do so. On receiving the notice, the opposing party must either admit or reject the authenticity of the photograph, plan, model or diagram. If authenticity is admitted the party wanting to introduce the evidence at trial will be able do so without having to lead evidence as regards its origin or its physical attributes.[157] If authenticity is rejected, then evidence will have to be led at trial to prove origin and physical attributes.

7. Request for Further Particulars for the Purposes of Trial

A further truth-finding opportunity available to parties is to request further particulars which are 'strictly necessary' to enable a party to prepare for trial.[158] What exactly may be asked during this process is quite open-ended. Galgut J in *Thompson v Barclays Bank, DCO*[159] held that the purpose of further particulars for trial is:

> '*(a)* to prevent surprise; *(b)* that the parties should be told with greater precision what the other party is going to prove in order to enable his opponent to prepare his case to combat counter allegations …; *(c)* having regard to the above nevertheless not to tie the other party down and limit his case unfairly at the trial'.

To this extent, it has been said that further particulars may be requested from sources other than pleadings; one may ask limited questions about the opposing party's sources of evidence that go beyond discovery or examination. Although pleadings may be a starting point for framing the request for further particulars, other portions of the record such as expert summaries and evidence from earlier hearings may also be requested.[160] What further particulars definitely do not entail is information about the exact nature of the evidence the other side is going to lead at trial or the evidential information that will be adduced by cross-examination.[161]

157 URC 36(10)(a)-(b).
158 URC 21(2); MCR 16.
159 1965 (1) SA 365 (W) at 369C-E.
160 *Schmidt Plant Hire (Pty) Ltd v Pedrelli* 1990 (1) SA 398 (D) at 402-403.
161 *Von Gordon v Von Gorden* 1961 (4) SA 211 (T) at 213.

Pleadings must have closed before a party can request further particulars. The notice requesting further particulars must not be served less than 20 court days before trial.[162] The 20 day time period is an inflexible period. On receiving a notice to furnish further particulars, the recipient has 10 court days to respond.[163] Failure to do so can ground an application to court to compel compliance with the request for further particulars.[164]

In the greater scheme of things, the request for further particulars has very limited opportunities for truth-finding.

8. Pre-trial Conferences

The rules of court also make provision for pre-trial conferences, but these have limited value in terms of truth-finding. They are designed to encourage the parties to meet so that they can discuss the possibility of limiting issues and reaching settlement. Witnesses are not permitted to attend these conferences and in most cases not even the litigants themselves will appear. This is the domain of advocates and attorneys. Once the conference is over, the parties must record the decisions reached at the conference in *minutes*. The minutes must be signed by each party and filed at court.

In the High Courts, judges are rarely involved in pre-trial conferences. However, the rules of court do provide for a judge to order a conference to be held in his or her chambers. In the Magistrates' Courts (unlike the High Courts where such conferences are mandatory) pre-trial conferences are optional. For a conference to be held, the magistrate has to specifically make an order in this regard. Alternatively, one of the parties has to address a request to the magistrate for a pre-trial conference to be held.

The conclusion to be drawn from the way in which pre-trial conferences are dealt with in the rules of court and from anecdotal evidence as regards what happens at these conferences, is that it is incontrovertible that pre-trial conferences do not play a significant role in fact- or truth-finding. They do not give the judge an opportunity to investigate the case. They also do not give the parties an opportunity to examine or to discuss evidence held by the other side and which has not been discovered already.

9. The Holy Grail: The Adduction of Evidence at Trial

One of the characteristics of adversarial systems, and to this extent South Africa is no exception, is the centrality of holding a trial to the determination of the truth. The idea of adducing evidence by examination, cross-examination and re-examination of witnesses[165] is the holy grail of truth-finding.

162 URC 21(2); MCR 16(2)(a).
163 URC 21(2); MCR 16(2)(b).
164 URC 21(4); MCR 16(4).
165 URC 39(5)-10.

Because South Africa does not subscribe to a jury system, the eventual determination of the truth falls to the judge. It is on the basis of a trial that a judge is expected to weigh and measure evidence to arrive at the truth. In *Stellenbosch Farmers' Winery Group Ltd v Martell et Cie*[166] the Supreme Court of Appeal summarized the technique generally employed by the courts in resolving factual disputes where there are two irreconcilable versions:

> 'The technique generally employed by courts in resolving factual disputes of this nature may conveniently be summarised as follows. To come to a conclusion on the disputed issues a court must make findings on (a) the credibility of the various factual witnesses; (b) their reliability; and (c) the probabilities. As to (a), the court's finding on the credibility of a particular witness will depend on its impression about the veracity of the witness. That in turn will depend on a variety of subsidiary factors, not necessarily in order of importance, such as (i) the witness's candour and demeanour in the witness-box, (ii) his bias, latent and blatant, (iii) internal contradictions in his evidence, (iv) external contradictions with what was pleaded or put on his behalf, or with established fact or with his own extracurial statements or actions, (v) the probability or improbability of particular aspects of his version, (vi) the calibre and cogency of his performance compared to that of other witnesses testifying about the same incident or events. As to (b), a witness's reliability will depend, apart from the factors mentioned under (a) (ii), (iv) and (v) above, on (i) the opportunities he had to experience or observe the event in question and (ii) the quality, integrity and independence of his recall thereof. As to (c), this necessitates an analysis and evaluation of the probability or improbability of each party's version on each of the disputed issues. In the light of its assessment of (a), (b) and (c) the court will then, as a final step, determine whether the party burdened with the onus of proof has succeeded in discharging it. The hard case, which will doubtless be the rare one, occurs when a court's credibility findings compel it in one direction and its evaluation of the general probabilities in another. The more convincing the former, the less convincing will be the latter. But when all factors are equipoised probabilities prevail'.

The above dictum reflects the role of the judge in an adversarial litigation system. A judge, in the face of irreconcilable evidential differences, does not engage in fact- and truth-finding. He or she simply works within the framework of what has been presented by the parties and applies various substantive law considerations and principles from the law of evidence to decide in whose favour the probabilities are more weighted.

South African law makes no provision for prior witness depositions. It is thus at trial when the parties and the court will for the first time become conversant with witness testimony in a case. Unsurprisingly, it is not uncommon for the most experienced lawyer to be caught completely off guard by the evidence that is adduced in court. Up to this point he or she may think that a client has a clear and strong case, only to discover what the truth really is. This is perhaps one of the most uncomfortable features of the South African adversarial litigation system.

Another harrowing aspect, which is perhaps a hallmark of adversarial systems in general, is the manner in which witnesses and their testimony are treated at trial. Despite what textbooks say about how to run trials or the purpose of trials, anyone

166 2003 (1) SA 11 (SCA) at 14-15.

who has ever practised law will confess to the recurring theme pervading coffee shops frequented by practitioners, namely, how a particular lawyer (usually the person relating the story) tore a witness to pieces in the witness box. Witnesses are creatures to be discredited. Their memories, observations, opinions, and conclusions must be negated. Evidence must be declared irrelevant or inadmissible. In this environment, the truth comes second to winning a case.

To its credit South African law makes provision for securing the testimony of a witness who is unable to attend trial. The rules of procedure, following English law, allow for the parties to secure the evidence of the witness on commission.[167] However, the courts have consistently refused to allow experts to give evidence on commission,[168] unless the best experts are overseas.[169] If the witness is in South Africa, a magistrate can be appointed to preside over proceedings. If the witness is in a foreign country, an attorney, solicitor, advocate or barrister can be appointed to preside. The legal representatives of both parties will orally examine the witness under oath. Keeping with the adversarial process, the presiding officer is not expected to take an active part in proceedings. He or she merely ensures that the basic rules of evidence are adhered to.

If a litigating party is unable to attend cross-examination of a witness on commission, he or she may elect to take evidence by means of interrogatories.[170] This entails drafting a set of questions called *interrogatories,* which is then put to the witness by the presiding officer. The person presiding cannot supplement the questions, nor can he or she deviate from the manner in which the questions are put to the witness.

The rules of court do not set a deadline by which evidence by commission may be obtained. It would appear that evidence may be acquired before the trial begins or even during trial. Of course, all the parties to proceedings must have sight of the transcript of the evidence and may *ex post facto* challenge the evidence of a witness in court. The court, however, loses the advantage of observing the demeanour of the witness, and is unable to put clarifying questions to him or her.

10. Conclusion

In this chapter I have tried to show that South African law takes a very different approach to fact- and truth-finding to many other jurisdictions. Within the interstices of the procedural rules there are fact- and truth-finding mechanisms, but these are by no means complete. With the exception of the limited application procedure, to a large extent, the South African litigant is still dependent on the trial as the prism through which the truth will be unveiled. By virtue of pleadings some facts become apparent and through discovery some more aspects of the truth will be revealed, but never all. The South African civil litigation system is still very much

167 URC 38(3)-(8).

168 *Hill v Hills (II)* 1933 NPD 293 at 294.

169 *Gough v Woolley* 1912 EDL 39.

170 URC 38(5).

trial-centred. This is in keeping with a traditional adversarial approach to resolving disputes.

It is submitted that South Africa needs a new set of rules of engagement where there are greater opportunities for parties to unearth aspects of the truth very early on in the litigation process. If this entails that we jettison the current adversarial legal system for a more nuanced continental European system affording judges more investigative powers, then so be it. It may also be the case that a judicial case-management system would serve as an effective tool for unearthing evidential facts resulting in the early determination of the truth. It would seem that there is already momentum for change.[171] Only time will tell how strong and committed the forces of change really are.

171 In an *Address by the Minister of Justice and Constitutional Development Mr Jeff Radebe, on the Occasion of the Access to Justice Conference on Friday 8 July 2011, Sandton, Johannesburg*, the Minister of Justice quoted from a communiqué which he received from Judge Professor Erasmus who said: 'Our civil justice system suffers from a number of weaknesses: it is expensive, it is slow, it is complex, it is fragmented and overly adversarial. These weaknesses combine to produce a system that is gradually becoming inaccessible to the average person. In a country like South Africa where there are gross disparities of wealth and education, the system becomes unequal for those who are wealthy and those who are poor and the result it produces is similarly unequal. ... Citizens have a right of access to vindicate their constitutional rights. The civil justice system in a constitutional state is therefore to facilitate that access and not to obstruct it ... My efforts [at law reform on the invitation of the government] have led me to a conclusion that the development of a set of rules within the parameters of existing legislation and rules (i.e. the existing "infrastructure") is an impossible task. What is required is comprehensive and wholesale review of the system in all its underlying elements. ... In evaluating the civil justice system and in recommending change, it would be important to bear in mind that it is part of a larger system. Thus for example, the total cost of litigation embraces more than the cost to the parties. There are also infrastructural costs provided by the state in the form of the provision of a court room, officials and a judge. The wasteful use of time of the court and judged is an abuse of an expensive resource which has an adverse effect on the allocation of judicial resources. An inefficient civil justice system may, for example, adversely affect the allocation of resources in criminal cases. The economics of civil justice, a largely neglected topic in South Africa, should receive attention when an overview of the system is undertaken'.

Bibliography

Botha 1923
Botha, C.G., 'The Early Influence of the English Law upon the Roman-Dutch Law in South Africa', *South African Law Journal,* 1923, Vol. 40, p. 396-406.

Cilliers, Loots & Nel 2009
Cilliers, A.C., Loots, C. & Nel, H.C., *Herbstein & Van Winsen. The Civil Practice of the High Courts of South Africa,* 5th edn., Vol. 1, Cape Town: Juta and Co, 2009.

Corbett 1998
Corbett, M.M., 'Writing a Judgment', *South African Law Journal,* 1998, Vol. 115, p. 116.

Daniels 2002
Daniels, H., *Beck's Theory and Principles of Pleadings in Civil Action,* Durban: Butterworths, 2002.

Erasmus 1991
Erasmus, H.J., 'Historical Foundations of the South African Law of Civil Procedure', *South African Law Journal,* 1991, Vol. 108, p. 265.

Erasmus 1996
Erasmus, H.J., 'The Interaction of Substantive Law and Procedure', in: Zimmerman, R. & Visser, D. (eds.), *Southern Cross - Civil Law and Common Law in South Africa,* Oxford: Oxford University Press, 1996, p. 146-150.

Fagan 1996
Fagan, E., 'Roman-Dutch Law in its South African Historical Context', in: Zimmerman, R. & Visser, D. (eds.), *Southern Cross - Civil Law and Common Law in South Africa,* Oxford: Oxford University Press, 1996, p. 33-64.

Girvin 1990
Girvin, S.D., *The Influence of British Legal Education and Practice at the Bar on the Judges appointed to the Supreme Courts of Southern Africa 1827-1910* (unpublished PhD thesis), University of Aberdeen, 1990.

Klaaren 1996
Klaaren, J., 'Access to Information', in: Chaskalson, M., Kentridge, J., Klaaren, J., Marcus, G., Spitz, D. & Woolman, S. (eds.), *Constitutional Law of South Africa,* Cape Town: Juta and Company Limited, 1996, p. 24-27.

Lord Bowen 1907
Lord Bowen, 'Progress in the Administration of Justice during the Victorian Period', in: *Select Essays in Anglo-American Legal History,* Vol. 1, Boston: Little, Brown and Company, 1907, p. 516.

Marnewick 2002
Marnewick, C.G., *Litigation Skills for South African Lawyers,* Durban: Lexisnexis Butterworths, 2002.

Merryman & Pérez-Perdomo 2007.
Merryman, J.H. & Pérez-Perdomo, R., 'Civil Procedure', in: *The Civil Law Tradition – An Introduction to the Legal Systems of Europe and Latin America,* Stanford: Stanford University Press, 2007, p. 1.

Ngcobo 2003
Ngcobo, S.S., 'Delivery of Justice: Agenda for Change', *South African Law Journal,* 2003, Vol. 120, p. 688.

Peté *et al.* 2011
Peté, S., Hulme, D., du Plessis, M., Palmer, R. & Sibanda, O., *Civil Procedure – A Practical Guide,* Cape Town: Oxford University Press (Southern Africa), 2011.

Rozenberg 1994
Rozenberg, J., *The Search for Justice –An Anatomy of the Law,* London: Hodder & Stoughton, 1994.

Taitz 1979
Taitz, J., 'A further Tribute to the Charter of Justice', *South African Law Journal,* 1979, Vol. 96, p. 470.

Van Blerk 1998
Van Blerk, P., *Legal Drafting: Civil Proceedings,* Cape Town: Juta and Company Ltd, 1998.

Van Loggerenberg 2011
Van Loggerenberg, D.E., *Jones & Buckle The Civil Practice of the Magistrates' Courts in South Africa, Vol. II, The Rules,* 10th edn., Cape Town: Juta and Company Ltd, 2011, loose-leaf binder service.

Voet 1704
Voet, J., *Commentarius ad Pandectas,* Book 2, Lugduni Batavorum: apud Johannem Verbessel, 1704.

Von Mehren 1982
Von Mehren, A.T., 'The Significance for Procedural Practice and Theory of the Concentrated Trial: Comparative Remarks', in: Horn, N. (ed.), *Europäisches Rechtsdenken in Geschichte und Gegenwart: Festschrift für Helmut Coing,* Vol. II, Munich: Beck, 1982, p. 361-371.

Welgemoed 2011
Welgemoed, H., 'Echoing "Enough is Enough"', *De Rebus,* August 2011, p. 4.

Whittle 2011
Editor, 'Law Society of South Africa Speaks Out on Conditions in Johannesburg and on Errant Magistrates', *De Rebus,* January-February 2011, p. 17.

Zuckerman 2007
Zuckerman, A., 'The Privilege Against Self-incrimination may not Confer a Right to Refuse Disclosure of Incriminating Documents that came into Existence Independently of the Disclosure Order', *Civil Justice Quarterly,* 2007, Vol. 26, p. 395.

SOCIALIST AND POST-SOCIALIST PERSPECTIVES: CHINA, ROMANIA, SLOVENIA, RUSSIA

P.C.H. Chan

EFFICIENCY AND TRUTH IN CIVIL FACT-FINDING: THE EVOLVING ROLE OF THE JUDGE IN MAINLAND CHINA AND HONG KONG AND THE EFFECT OF THE POLICY PREFERENCE FOR COURT MEDIATION ON FACT-FINDING IN THE PEOPLE'S COURTS

1. Introduction

1.1. *Efficiency and Fact-finding: Two Jurisdictions, Different Approaches*

Fairness in adjudication is premised on accurate facts. Constructing a sophisticated and efficient regime for fact-finding is therefore an imperative for civil justice.

China's attempt to enhance efficiency was mainly effected by devolving the responsibilities of fact-finding from the judge to the parties and strengthening the adversarial principle in its civil procedure.[1] Parties are playing an increasingly crucial role in fact-finding. As a general duty, a party is required to produce evidence in support of the facts on which the party's allegations are based. However, it would be a misconception to view fact-finding in China as purely a party driven exercise. In fact, the judge retains extensive powers in shaping the landscape of fact-finding.[2] The extent to which the judge should be allowed to participate in the fact-finding process is worth close academic scrutiny, particularly given that procedural reforms in China are intended to confer greater autonomy to parties in proceedings.

In Hong Kong, a converse development has been witnessed. The Civil Justice Reform substantially expanded the court's powers in case-management. The court

1 In this regard, China is not alone given similar experiences of transitional (or former socialist) legal systems. Uzelac described the strengthening of the adversarial principle as 'an attempt to empower judges to use the right to decide on the basis of burden of proof rules, instead of allowing endless, unsuccessful attempts to find certainty based on the evidence that is taken *sua sponte*'. *See* Uzelac 2010, p. 392.

2 The judge is empowered to look beyond the pleadings in determining the material facts of the case. The court has the power to investigate and collect evidence on its own account. The judge is also given extensive discretion to determine the burden of proof in cases where the evidentiary rules are silent on the subject. See Zhong & Yu 2004, p. 401.

is now equipped with greater discretionary powers to enforce procedural deadlines, limit discovery and administer the litigation timetable. These powers have immense implications for the fact-finding process in Hong Kong, particularly in enhancing efficiency in fact-finding.

1.2. *The Policy Preference for Court Mediation in China: A Cause for Concern*

The Chinese Government's promotion of a harmonious society (*he xie she hui*) since 2002 has immense influence over China's civil justice reform. In recent years, court mediation has been identified by the Chinese Judiciary as the preferred method for civil dispute resolution. This is a clear shift away from the old policy of promoting and formalizing civil adjudication in the 1990s. Pressing social circumstances are responsible for the change of policy. Minzner observed, 'Chinese leaders face increasing social unrest generated by civil conflicts between citizens, and between citizens and the state'.[3] In response to mounting social tension, the state has turned to court mediation as the 'artificial panacea for social stability'.[4] Furthermore, the way in which the performance of the judge is assessed encourages the judge to resort to court mediation and avoid adjudication.

Court mediation can be an effective alternative dispute resolution method if the decisions to mediate and to settle are made out of the independent will of the parties. But when there is a strong policy preference for court mediation, it will no longer be a genuine 'alternative' dispute resolution method.[5] Court mediation then loses its original ADR function and creates serious problems for fact-finding. The policy preference creates an artificial settlement culture in the courts. From the judge's perspective, the primary goal in a civil lawsuit is dispute resolution, rather than the enforcement of rights. The need to fairly enforce the rights of the parties necessitates a thorough fact-finding process that assists the judge in ascertaining the truth. Overemphasizing court mediation would inevitably result in the laxity of the fact-finding process as the focus shifts from the enforcement of rights to pure dispute resolution.

3 Minzner 2011b, p. 938.
4 Minzner 2011b, p. 963.
5 *Ibidem.*

2. The Evolving Role of the Judge in Civil Fact-Finding - Mainland China and Hong Kong

2.1. The Evolving Role of the Judge in Civil Fact-Finding: Mainland China

2.1.1. Background

In the past, the Chinese judge wields monolithic powers in civil litigation. The Ma Xiwu style of adjudication in the past (which emerged in communist controlled areas in China before 1949) required the judge to be extremely active in the fact-finding process. The judge would visit the community in which the dispute arose, ascertain the actual situation by interviewing the persons involved in the dispute and actively collecting evidence, and reach a decision in the best interest of the community and in line with government policy.[6] Judicial mediation was the main method for dispute resolution.[7] The Ma Xiwu style of adjudication greatly influenced the construction of China's modern civil justice system. Although it is no longer the adjudicatory approach in China, some academics are calling for its revival in rural areas. Jiang argued that the Ma Xiwu style of adjudication fits well with the contemporary reality in rural China where parties have very limited resources to conduct fact-finding on their own.[8]

A ground-breaking development in Chinese civil fact-finding was the promulgation by the Supreme People's Court (SPC) of the *Some Provisions of the Supreme People's Court on Evidence in Civil Procedure* (Civil Evidence Rules).[9] The Civil Evidence Rules consist of 83 articles and remain the most comprehensive legal instrument regulating civil fact-finding to date. It is important to read the Civil Procedure Law of the People's Republic of China (*Code*)[10] in conjunction with the Civil Evidence Rules in order to fully understand Chinese civil fact-finding.[11]

6 Huang 2010, p. 115.

7 Consider Huang's summary of the fundamental principles of the Ma Xiwu style of adjudication: 'The entire process was summed up in a three-clause formula: "rely on the masses" (*yikao qunzhong*), "investigate and do research" (*diaocha yanjiu*), and "mainly use mediation" (*tiaojie weizhu*)'. See Huang 2010, p. 115.

8 Jiang 2010, p. 154.

9 Note that there are some discrepancies in the English translation of the rules. It is sometimes translated as Specific Provisions on Evidence in Civil Actions of the Supreme People's Court or Several Rules of Evidence Concerning Civil Litigation.

10 The Code (which came into effect on 9 April 1991) has been revised twice, in 2007 and 2013 respectively. The second amendment was passed on 31 August 2012 (by way of the *Decision of the Standing Committee of the National People's Congress on Amending the Civil Procedure Law of the People's Republic of China (2012)*) and will come into effect on 1 January 2013. References in this article are made to the latest version of the Code (i.e. the 2013 version).

11 The Code must be read in conjunction with the judicial opinions and interpretations of the SPC. The SPC is at the apex of the Chinese court system and supervises the work of lower courts. It also performs a regulatory role in that the judicial opinions and interpretations of the SPC (on matters relating to civil justice and procedure) are *de facto* 'statutory instruments'. From the judge's perspective, these opinions and interpretations are as important as the →

There is clear devolution of fact-finding responsibilities from the judge to the parties since the Code and the Civil Evidence Rules came into force.[12] The fact-finding function of the judge has (in principle) turned from collecting evidence to reviewing and checking evidence.[13]

However, commentators have warned that the enhanced role of the parties in fact-finding must not be interpreted to mean that the inquisitorial nature of civil adjudication has changed once and for all.[14] The principle of party presentation does not apply and the judge still retains extensive discretionary powers in fact-finding.[15]

On a general procedural level, efforts were made to promote the principle of party disposition. However, as Fu argued, the court still retains the authority to decide certain adversarial matters *ex parte* (e.g. the filing of additional claims).[16] This remains a major obstacle for China to fully entrench the principle of party disposition.

2.1.2. Evidence Collection: Party Responsibility System and Judicial Intervention

Article 64 of the Code provides, 'A party shall have the responsibility to provide evidence in support of its own propositions'. Article 2 of the Civil Evidence Rules provides, 'The parties concerned shall be responsible for producing evidences to prove the facts on which their own allegations are based or the facts on which the allegations of the other party are refuted'. The Code establishes a party responsibility system under which the parties have the primary role of evidence collection while the judge's role becomes secondary.[17] However, Article 64 of the Code retained the judge's *ex officio* powers of investigation and evidence collection

Code, as they provide concrete operational rules and guidance. Simply referring to the Code without understanding the SPC's opinions and interpretations is seriously inadequate.

12 Apart from evidence collection, party participation extends to the exchange of evidence (Arts. 32 to 46 of the Civil Evidence Rules), and the cross-examination of evidence and witnesses (Art. 68 of the Code; Arts. 47-62 of the Civil Evidence Rules).

13 Fu & Cao 2010, p. 12.

14 *See* Zhang & Zwier 2003, p. 455. It is fair to say that fact-finding under Chinese civil procedure has moved from a strict inquisitorial system to a mixed regime with inquisitorial and adversarial traits.

15 Consider the views of Zhong & Yu 2004, p. 401:
'Chinese judges have more extensive powers than their U.S. counterparts. In common law jurisdictions, judges will only consider the issues raised, the objections mentioned, and the points made in the pleadings. The issues that the parties do not raise are usually waived. Therefore, the judge's determination is limited to the pleadings the parties have filed. As the judge "sits solely to decide" the dispute, she will not make an independent inquiry into the merits of the case, let alone independent investigation. Under the Chinese system, however, a judge's adjudication is not limited to the pleadings and arguments, but focuses on actual investigation and study. The adjudication system and the style of work of Chinese courts are intended to be convenient to, maintain close ties with, and serve the masses. Only after the court has discovered the whole truth of the case and collected sufficient evidence can it make its judgment.'

16 Fu & Cao 2010, p. 11.

17 Woo & Wang 2005, p. 932.

in two situations:[18] (1) when the parties cannot independently obtain the evidence for some realistic or objective reasons (the parties may request the court to collect the evidence); and (2) when the court considers the evidence necessary for adjudicating the case.[19] For the first situation, an example is where the evidence is archived at a public security authority (or when the evidence relates to land or bank deposits),[20] it is impossible (or very difficult) for parties to collect such evidence on their own accord. Upon application from the party, the court may collect the evidence on the party's behalf.[21] In the second situation, 'necessity' is elaborated in Article 15 of the Civil Evidence Rules, which tends to give it a restrictive definition, limiting the exercise of the court's *ex officio* power of investigation and evidence collection to matters relating to state/public interests and non-substantive disputes only.[22] It is further stated in the rules that, unless provided in Article 15 of the Civil Evidence Rules, 'the investigation upon and collection of evidences by the People's court shall be based on the application of the parties concerned'.[23] However, in practice, 'necessity' has sometimes been interpreted widely to encompass any matters that the court in its discretion believes to be necessary for the adjudication of the case. An example is where the case involves complex issues such that the parties are unlikely to be able to provide adequate evidence. Under these circumstances, the court will collect evidence on its own initiative to obtain first-hand knowledge of the relevant facts.[24] A discrepancy between the legislative intent and actual practice seems to arise here. On the one hand, it has been argued that the Civil Evidence Rules were intended to give Article 64 of the Code a narrow interpretation with the view of weakening the *ex officio* power of the court in evidence collection.[25] On the other hand, as a matter of practice, a wide interpretation can be given to the concept of 'necessity'.[26]

18 Zhang and Zwier argued that the Civil Evidence Rules gave Art. 64 of the Code a narrow interpretation with the view of weakening the *ex officio* powers of the court in evidence collection. *See* Zhang & Zwier 2003, p. 441.

19 Art. 64 of the Code provides, 'For the evidence that cannot be obtained by any parties or their litigation representatives because of some realistic reasons or for the evidence that the people's court considers necessary for adjudicating the case, the people's court shall investigate and collect such evidence'; Art. 3 of the Civil Evidence Rules provides, 'Any party who cannot independently collect evidence due to objective reasons may request the People's court to collect after investigations'.

20 NPCSC Publication 2007, p. 219.

21 Art. 17 of the Civil Evidence Rules sets out three circumstances under which the parties concerned may request the court to investigate or collect evidence on their behalf.

22 Art. 15 of the Civil Evidence Rules reads, 'The "evidences deemed as necessary by the People's court for hearing the case" as mentioned in Article 64 of the Civil Procedure Law of the People's Republic of China shall refer to the following: (1) The facts that may injure the interest of the state, the public interest of the society or the lawful interest of other people; (2) The procedural maters that have nothing to do with the substantial dispute, such as adding parties concerned, suspending the litigation, ending the litigation, withdrawing, etc. on the basis of authority of the courts.'

23 Art. 16 of the Civil Evidence Rules.

24 NPCSC Publication 2007, p. 112.

25 Zhang & Zwier 2003, p. 441.

26 NPCSC Publication 2007, p. 112.

As a general principle of fact-finding, the parties and the court are positioned to work hand in hand to discharge the evidentiary responsibilities in a civil action.[27] A possible reason for the retention of the judge's *ex officio* powers of investigation and evidence collection is the parties' relative lack of resources to conduct fact-finding (as compared with litigants in Western jurisdictions).[28] With the exception of large commercial cases, an average Chinese party may not have the economic resources to conduct a comprehensive evidence collection exercise. Another hurdle of implementing a full party-driven evidence collection regime is the administrative red tape in China. Nothing really gets done without good connections. Again, an average party may find it very difficult to collect evidence when the source is a government body, a state-owned enterprise or entities backed by powerful individuals. The judge's intervention in the evidence collection exercise does sometimes alleviate these difficulties.

In addition to its investigatory powers, the court retains extensive authority in a number of other areas relating to evidence collection and preservation.[29]

Despite the retention of the court's *ex officio* powers to intervene, the attempt to move to a party responsibility system in evidence collection is already a significant step forward in promoting greater judicial impartiality in fact-finding (it is at least arguably successful as a legislative design).[30] The past practice of collecting evidence *sua sponte* by judges (without any restrictions) bears the danger of the judge forming premature views on the merits of the case (e.g. favouring one side over the other) during the process of evidence collection, thereby negatively affecting the impartiality of the court.[31] However, the ease with which judges may intervene with evidence collection today (even in the absence of application from the parties) suggests that the same danger is still very much present under the current fact-finding regime.[32] An inappropriate exercise of judicial activism will result in unwarranted encroachment on what is supposed to be a party responsibility system of evidence collection.

27 *Ibidem.*

28 Jiang 2010, p. 153-155.

29 The following are a few examples of these powers (as provided in the Code):
Art. 67 states that the court has the authority to obtain evidence from any relevant units or individuals, and such units and individuals may not refuse to provide evidence. The court shall then verify and determine the validity of documentary evidence provided by the relevant unit.
Art. 71 states that the court shall authenticate audio and visual materials and decide whether they can be admitted as a basis for finding the facts after examining them and comparing them with other evidence of the same case.
Art. 75 states that the court has the authority to examine the statements of the parties in connection with other evidence of the case to decide whether such statements can be taken as a basis for finding the facts. The refusal of a party to make a statement shall not prevent the court from finding the facts of a case based on other evidence.
Art. 81 states that the court may preserve evidence on its own initiative where there is a likelihood that the evidence may be destroyed or become too difficult to obtain later on.

30 Woo & Wang 2005, p. 932.

31 Zhang & Zwier 2003, p. 430.

32 Fu & Cao 2010, p. 12-13.

The way in which the court exercises its powers of investigation and evidence collection also deserves attention. Under the current evidence collection regime, judges are still allowed to contact the parties and witnesses individually without a formal hearing or without the participation of the opposing party. This practice contradicts the principle of open trial, potentially taints the reliability of evidence (as a witness testimony may be influenced by the exchange between the judge and the witness) and assaults judicial impartiality.[33] Another concern is the power of the Chinese judge to take both real and documentary evidence *ex officio*.[34] As Zhong and Yu argued, an arbitrary exercise of judicial powers of investigation and evidence collection negatively affects the reliability of evidence gathered and places 'extra-evidentiary influences on judgments'.[35]

Empirical research shows that judges still exercise their powers of investigation and evidence collection to 'varying degrees, depending on judicial temperament, philosophy and ability'.[36] Another factor that determines the degree of judicial evidence collection is the caseload of the court. A court struggling with a heavy caseload usually has no time to actively investigate, thus allowing greater party autonomy in evidence collection.[37]

2.1.3. Civil Burdens of Proof – A Big Step Forward?

The issue of civil burdens of proof is closely intertwined with the devolution of evidence collection responsibilities to the parties. These elements form the building blocks of the party responsibility system in Chinese civil fact-finding. The foundational provision for civil burdens of proof is Article 2 of the Civil Evidence Rules:

33 Fu & Cao 2010, p. 11.

34 This is contrasted with the judges in certain continental European jurisdictions (e.g. Austria) who are only able to take real evidence *ex officio*. In these jurisdictions, documentary evidence is only admissible if at least one of the parties has referred to the document in question. *See* Oberhammer & Domej 2005, p. 304.
The extent to which the court uses its investigatory power also varies with jurisdictions. For example, in France, the preparatory judge (*le juge de la mise en état*) 'in practice seldom uses the statutory powers to investigate, and so controls more than directs factual investigation in the pretrial phase'. See Clermont & Sherwin 2002, p. 248.

35 Consider the views of Zhong & Yu 2004, p. 436:
'Formal procedure is often perfunctorily applied. Because the judge conducts an extensive investigation and collects evidence before he hears the case, he has an understanding of the likely result of the litigation before adjudication commences. In some instances, the judge will make a decision about the outcome of a case before hearing any argument, making the trial essentially a "show trial". Further, in the course of investigation, the judge inevitably has frequent, often ex parte, contacts with both litigants. All of these extra-evidentiary influences on judgments are problematic. Frequent contacts between the judge and litigants facilitate judicial corruption because they are not subject to any procedural requirements.'

36 Woo & Wang 2005, p. 933.

37 *Ibidem*.

> 'The parties concerned shall be responsible for producing evidences to prove the facts on which their own allegations are based or the facts on which the allegations of the other party are refuted.
>
> Where any party cannot produce evidence or the evidences produced cannot support the facts on which the allegations are based, the party concerned that bears the burden of proof shall undertake unfavourable consequences'.

Articles 4, 5 and 6 of the Civil Evidence Rules allocate specific burdens of proof in tortuous, contractual and other forms of disputes. Under Article 7 of the Civil Evidence Rules, where specific burdens of proof are not explicitly provided and it is not possible to define who shall be responsible for producing evidence according to the Civil Evidence Rules or other judicial interpretations, the court may determine the burden of proof in accordance with the principle of fairness and the principle of honesty and credit, and taking factors such as the ability to produce evidence into consideration.[38]

There are obvious gaps in the current rules governing burden of proof. Firstly, the standard of proof has not been expressly delineated. Secondly, there is no provision governing the shifting of burden of proof in specific situations. Thirdly, greater procedural guidance is warranted when the court exercises its wide discretion in determining the burdens of proof when encountered with the situation under Article 7 of the Civil Evidence Rules. Fourthly, some commentators have criticised the overly serious consequence when a party fails to provide adequate evidence in support of its allegations, which usually results in the party losing the case. Jiang observed that China should develop its own evidence production regime based on the joint effort of the parties and the judge (inferring that the second paragraph of Article 2 of the Civil Evidence Rule should be repealed).[39]

The first two problems have been partially addressed in Articles 133 to 142 of the *Uniform Provisions of Evidence of the People's Court: Proposal for Judicial Interpretations* (Proposal).[40]

In practice, the question is whether the courts truly subscribe to the burdens of proof requirements as a fundamental premise for decision-making. An empirical study shows that judges generally view burdens of proof as relevant in the decision-making process. Burdens of proof tend to be 'decisive in close decisions'.[41]

2.1.4. The Paradox of Party Responsibility in the Absence of the Principle of Party Presentation

Paradoxically, the devolution of fact-finding responsibilities to the parties and the introduction of adversarial elements to the fact-finding regime proceeded without

38 Art. 7 of the Civil Evidence Rules.

39 Jiang 2010, p. 154-155.

40 Zhang 2008, p. 94-100. Currently, the Proposal is adopted in pilot programmes of a number of local courts in China. If the trial run is satisfactory, it is possible that the Proposal would replace the Civil Evidence Rules.

41 Woo & Wang 2005, p. 933-934.

implementing the principle of party presentation (*Verhandlungsmaxime*).[42] The follow-up question must be whether the reform to enhance party participation in fact-finding was intended only to achieve efficiency rather than promoting overall justice through true party empowerment.[43]

Examples that demonstrate the operation of this paradoxical fact-finding philosophy are numerous. Firstly, statements made by parties are a specific class of evidence.[44] While performing a similar function as pleadings (i.e. setting out the party's claim), the status of party statements is nothing close to that of common law pleadings. Article 75 of the Code provides that the court shall examine the statements of the parties in connection with other evidence of the case to decide whether such statements can be taken as a basis for finding the facts. The refusal of a party to make a statement shall not prevent the court from finding the facts of the case based on other evidence. In other words, party statements may not be taken as a basis for fact-finding if the judge decides it is inappropriate to do so (having also considered other evidence). In any event, party statements may only form part of the basis for fact-finding and the court is at liberty to depart from the remits of the statements.[45] In case a party refuses to make a statement, the court can do away with the party statement requirement altogether and rely on other evidence as the basis for fact-finding.[46] Secondly, while parties are entitled to engage in debate in a court session,[47] the debate only serves as a fraction of the fact-finding procedure. As with party statements, the court has no obligation to render judgment on the basis of party debates. This is known as the non-binding principle of debate.[48] Thirdly, judicial evidence collection may go well beyond the factual remits set out by the parties under circumstances explained above.

Without entrenching the principle of party presentation, the remit of fact-finding becomes nebulous. Despite positive developments in the Civil Evidence Rules[49] in the direction of abandoning the doctrine of factuality,[50] the backdoor for active judicial investigation invites the reincarnation of the doctrine. If determined

42 Lenhoff observed (when discussing the principle of party presentation), 'Since it is for the parties to initiate the proceedings, it is left to them to present the facts in support of their demands and defences'. *See* Lenhoff 1954, p. 313.

43 The Proposal still retained the *ex officio* powers of the judge to collect evidence under certain circumstances (e.g. facts involving a person's identity and relationships) or where it is 'necessary to collect evidence...to verify evidence of significant importance to a case or evidence having material doubts'. *See* Article 110 of the Proposal.

44 Art. 63 of the Code.

45 Fu & Cao 2010, p. 13; also see Zhong & Yu 2004, p. 401: 'Under the Chinese system, however, a judge's adjudication is not limited to the pleadings and arguments, but focuses on actual investigation and study.'

46 Fu & Cao 2010, p. 13.

47 Under Arts. 12 and 49 of the Code, parties are entitled to engage in debate. Arts. 127 and 128 of the Civil Evidence Rules set out the procedures for court debate.

48 Fu & Cao 2010, p. 7.

49 Art. 63 of the Civil Evidence Rules.

50 Zhang & Zwier 2003, p. 451. The doctrine of factuality concerns the judicial pursuit of the material truth.

to be 'necessary for adjudicating the case',[51] the judge may go beyond the evidence presented by the parties and engage in his own train of evidential enquiry *ex officio*, causing delay and other problems.[52] Without the entrenchment of the principle of party presentation, party participation in fact-finding may reduce (in the extreme case) to a mere nominal exercise under which parties spend considerable time delineating the facts, producing evidence and debating the facts only to find that their participation had very limited influence over the court's ultimate fact-finding determination. Paradoxically, as a result of the absence of the principle of party presentation, the increased adversarial elements in Chinese civil procedure (which were introduced partly to achieve procedural efficacy) have the potential of causing greater delay due to the formal requirements of party participation. On a substantive level, the lack of entrenchment of the principle of party presentation is contrary to the objective of party empowerment, which is supposed to be one of the main themes in the Chinese civil justice reform.

There are two main reasons for the continued rejection of the principle of party presentation in Chinese civil procedure. Firstly, the Chinese legal historical experience in civil litigation was about the empowerment of the magistrate (or the judge) and not the parties. In magisterial civil adjudication in imperial China, unrestrained fact-finding powers were conferred to the magistrate.[53] While parties were allowed to be involved in presenting evidence, the magistrate was the ultimate arbiter in determining the factual scope of the case. The Ma Xiwu style of adjudication was also premised on the notion of an all-powerful investigatory judge. Secondly, the obsession for material truth in Chinese legal culture nurtured an adjudicative philosophy that is hostile to the principle of party presentation.[54] Under this jurisprudential view, which in some ways is revealed in the Code,[55] party-presented facts can only form the legal truth of a case. The partisan predispositions of the litigants almost certainly cannot ensure that a fact-finding process premised on the principle of party presentation can ever reveal the material truth. This view necessitates the court to go one step further to ascertain the material truth. The Maoist instrumentalist approach to legal procedure (which focuses on material truth) still has a lingering effect on the contemporary civil justice system.[56] Indeed, the obsession with material truth has been identified as a characteristic feature of former socialist or transitional civil justice systems.[57] While Article 63 of the Civil Evidence Rules is said to have repealed the doctrine of factuality,[58] the traditional preference for material truth and the retention of the

51 Art. 64 of the Code.

52 Fu & Cao 2010, p. 13.

53 Zhong & Yu 2004, p. 433.

54 For academic support of the doctrine of factuality, *see* Jiang 2010, p. 155. For criticism of the judicial preference for material truth, *see* Zhang & Zwier 2003, p. 431-432; also see Zhong & Yu 2004, p. 433-436.

55 Under Art. 64 of the Code, 'The people's court shall, in accordance with the procedure prescribed by law, collect and examine evidence comprehensively and objectively'.

56 Zhong & Yu 2004, p. 433-436.

57 Uzelac 2010, p. 390.

58 Zhang & Zwier 2003, p. 451.

judge's *ex officio* powers of investigation and evidence collection suggest that the doctrine of factuality still exerts considerable influence over contemporary civil adjudication in China.

2.1.5. Judicial Clarifications in Chinese Civil Fact-finding

Article 3 of the Civil Evidence Rules provides, 'The People's court shall inform the parties concerned of the requirements for producing evidences and of the corresponding legal liabilities so that the parties concerned may produce evidence actively, completely, correctly and honestly within the reasonable time period'. In the context of judicial clarifications (*Richterliche Aufklarung*), it is clearly inadequate if the court only provides general clarifications on the evidentiary requirements. Zhang observed that any direction from the court must be made after carefully considering the party's allegations made.[59] The clarifications should preferably be concrete and specific. In practice, the lack of clarification has caused parties to omit evidence resulting in the failure to establish the facts on which their allegations were based.[60] Unclear clarification would also result in delay in evidence production. However, it is unrealistic (and objectionable from a procedural efficacy perspective) to require the judge to micromanage the parties' evidence production exercise. A balance needs to be struck.

Another example is Article 35 of the Civil Evidence Rules. Under the rule, 'If, in the process of litigation, the nature of the legal relations alleged by the parties concerned or the validity of the civil acts are inconsistent with the findings of fact made by the People's court on the basis of the facts of the case, the provisions of Article 34 of the present Provisions shall not be applicable, and the people's court shall inform the parties concerned that the allegations [of the] litigation may change'.[61] For instance, if the contract that forms the basis of the plaintiff's claim for the repayment of a loan was determined to be invalid by the court, the court will notify the plaintiff and the plaintiff would need to decide whether to amend his claim (e.g. from a contractual claim to a proprietary claim).[62] Inconsistency between an allegation and the facts would only lead the litigation to a dead end causing undue delay. The rule allows some leeway for the plaintiff to modify his claim and saves time and cost.

These examples illustrate the importance of judicial clarifications in Chinese civil fact-finding.

2.1.6. Evidence Exchange and Management with Efficiency in Mind

An example of evidence management is the regulation of production of new evidence. Under Article 139 of the Code, parties may present new evidence during trial (first instance hearing) or on appeal (second instance hearing). This rule has

59 Zhang 2006, p. 142.
60 *Ibidem*.
61 Zhang 2006, p. 143.
62 Zhang 2006, p. 144.

been criticised for causing undue delay.[63] However, if one looks at Article 139 of the Code in conjunction with Articles 40 to 45 of the Civil Evidence Rules, the parties' right to present new evidence is not unrestricted.[64] In the case of *Guo Chun Xuan v Liu Zong Lai*,[65] the plaintiff applied to the Zhengzhou City Intermediate Court to produce supplemental evidence. The court rejected the application on the basis that the supplemental evidence was not 'new evidence', as it is already in 'objective existence' (and in the custody of the plaintiff) during the time period for producing evidence.[66] The 'objective existence' test[67] is contrasted with the more sophisticated test in Hong Kong for adducing new evidence on appeal pursuant to the principles in *Ladd v Marshall*.[68]

A second example is the introduction of time-limits for producing evidence. As a general principle under the Civil Evidence Rules, parties are required to produce evidence 'actively, completely, correctly and honestly within the reasonable time period'.[69] On this basis, the Chinese Judiciary is determined to establish the normative effect of time-limits by providing a severe 'sanction' for non-observance of time-limits. Failure to submit evidence within the time period shall be deemed as giving up the right to produce evidence.[70] The position on time-limits has been further clarified since the promulgation of the *Notice of the Supreme People's Court on Applying the Provisions on Time-Limits for Producing Evidence of Some Provisions on Evidence in Civil Procedures*,[71] which provides for detailed regulations on time-limits for different types of procedures (e.g. summary procedure and jurisdictional challenge).

63 Zhang and Zwier noted, 'It is very common that a party refuses to produce or exchange evidence before the trial, but presents the evidence to the court during the trial by surprise, or even on appeal. Even where a party has presented no evidence during the trial, he could present to the appellate court "new" evidence in his favour.' See Zhang & Zwier 2003, p. 430-431; also see Uzelac 2010, p. 392.

64 'New evidence' is clearly defined. For instance, in relation to the first instance hearing, Art. 41 of the Civil Evidence Rule states, 'The new evidences of the first instance hearing include: the evidences newly found by the parties concerned after the expiration of the time period for producing evidences in the first instance court hearing; the evidences which the parties concerned cannot provide during the time period for producing evidences due to objective reasons and still cannot provide during the extended time period approved by the People's court.'

65 (2008) *zheng min san chu zi* (No. 99) [reported civil judgment of the Zhengzhou Intermediate People's Court, Henan Province]. It is a first instance hearing.

66 *Ibidem.*

67 Art. X of the Notice of the Supreme People's Court on Applying the Provisions on Time-Limits for Producing Evidence of Some Provisions on Evidence in Civil Procedures.

68 [1954] 1 WLR 1489, 1491. For the Hong Kong test, consider Wilkinson, Cheung & Booth 2009, p. 953: 'The Court of Appeal has power to receive further evidence on questions of fact, but no such further evidence (other than evidence as to matters which have occurred after the date of the trial or hearing) shall be admitted except on special grounds [as set out in *Ladd v Marshall*].'

69 Art. 3 of the Civil Evidence Rules.

70 Art. 34 of the Civil Evidence Rules.

71 Promulgated by the SPC on 11 December 2008; effective since 11 December 2008.

A third example is the exchange of evidence. Article 39 of the Civil Evidence Rules provides that the court shall manage the process of exchange of evidence and '[in] the process of exchanging evidences, the judges shall record in the case files the facts and evidences to which the parties concerned have no objection'. The evidence not subject to objection is deemed to be 'affirmed' or 'admitted' by the parties. Such evidence would be taken as the basis for affirming the facts of the case without cross-examination.[72] Where there are any objections, the objecting party must provide reasons. Having satisfied with the reasons, the judge will record such evidence in accordance with the classified facts that need to be provided. By managing the exchange of evidence, it is intended that the major factual issues of the case are determined in advance of trial.[73] There is a statutory limit on the exchange of evidence: there can be no more than two rounds of exchange of evidence, unless the case is very important or very complicated and the court believes it is necessary to have another round of exchange of evidence.[74]

2.2. *The Evolving Role of the Judge in Civil Fact-Finding: Hong Kong*

The Chinese system of civil fact-finding shifted from a judge-dominated process to a party responsibility system in which the judge and the parties each play a role in fact-finding. With the devolution of fact-finding responsibilities from the judge to the parties, the function of the judge has (in principle) turned from collecting evidence to reviewing and checking evidence.[75]

In Hong Kong, a very different development was seen. Reform in the system of civil fact-finding was premised on empowering the court to take an active role in case-management. It was identified that the traditional non-interventionist role of the judge has made litigation very inefficient, both in terms of time and cost. Armed with extensive case-management powers, the judge today is expected to manage proceedings in a way that gives effect to the underlying objectives of the reform, including the objectives to promote procedural expediency and increase cost-effectiveness. This development has great implications for the fact-finding process in Hong Kong, particularly in the enhancement of efficiency in fact-finding.

2.2.1. Underlying Objectives and the Surge of Judicial Power in Fact-finding

There has been a significant shift of case-management powers from the parties to the judge in Hong Kong with the implementation of the Civil Justice Reform (CJR) since 2 April 2009. The exercise of these powers by the judge has significant

72 Art. 47(2) of the Civil Evidence Rules; also see Zhang & Zwier 2003, p. 448.
Under Art. 68 of the Code, cross-examination is a prerequisite to admission of evidence (with the exception of evidence 'admitted' by the parties). The purpose is to ensure that the evidence is reliable and avoid discrepancies in the fact-finding process. Also see Arts. 47-62 of the Civil Evidence Rules on cross-examination.

73 Art. 39 of the Civil Evidence Rules.

74 Art. 40 of the Civil Evidence Rules.

75 Fu & Cao 2010, p. 12.

implications for fact-finding. Civil procedure in Hong Kong is governed by the Rules of the High Court (Cap 4A)(RHC). The RHC have been amended to effect the changes of the CJR.[76]

The CJR not only conferred extensive procedural case-management powers to the judge but also substantive case-management powers. For instance, RHC Order 1A, rule 4(2)(c) provides that 'Active case-management includes ... deciding promptly which issues need full investigation and trial and accordingly disposing summarily of the others' and RHC Order 1B, rule 1(2)(j) provides that the court may 'exclude an issue from consideration'.

The CJR does not seek to transform the adversarial system into an inquisitorial one. Parties are still actively involved in a civil lawsuit. The principle of party presentation is securely entrenched and the court has no *ex officio* power to investigate. What the CJR has done is to curtail the excesses of the adversarial system and concurrently retain the best features of the adversarial system.[77]

On the whole, the CJR was regarded as a success, at least in its first year of implementation.[78]

2.2.2. Statement of Truth and Restrictions on Amendment of Pleadings

The CJR introduced the requirement that all pleadings must be verified by a statement of truth.[79] The effect of the statement of truth is that the pleader believes that the facts stated in the pleadings are true.[80] The statement of truth may be signed by the pleader or his legal representative.[81] The court may, by order, strike out a

76 The amendments were set out in the Rules of the High Court (Amendment) Rules 2008 (L.N. 152 of 2008).

77 First Year Report 2010, p. 1 (para 3(a)).
An example of this philosophy at work is discovery, which is still fundamentally a party-driven exercise. Consider the Working Party's recommendation that a modified regime of discovery should focus on improving case-management instead of narrowing the scope of discovery: *see* Final Report 2004, p. 246 (para 478).

78 Consider the views expressed in the First Year Report 2010, p. 2 (para 5): 'the implementation of CJR had on the whole been smooth in the first year ... [and based on the feedback received] no major problems were identified; all issues raised were minor and operational in nature'.
This is supported by the statistics in the report, in which the average time from commencement to trial in the Court of First Instance has been reduced from more than 1000 days (pre-CJR) to 167 days (post-CJR). However, the statistics should not be over-read given the post-CJR sample (number of hearings) was substantially less than the pre-CJR sample. In relation to the average time from commencement to trial in the Court of First Instance, three scenarios were reported: (1) where both date of commencement and date of trial were on or before 1 April 2009, the average time was 1,013 days (totalling 212 hearings); (2) where the date of commencement was on or before 1 April 2009 and the date of trial was on or after 2 April 2009, the average time was 1,132 days (totalling 251 hearings); and (3) where both date of commencement and date of trial were on or after 2 April 2009, the average time was 167 days (totalling 16 hearings). *See* First Year Report 2010, p. 10 (Table 6.1).

79 RHC O. 41A, r. 2.

80 RHC O. 41A, r. 4.

81 RHC O. 41A, r. 3.

pleading that is not verified by a statement of truth.[82] Proceedings for contempt of court may be brought against a person if he makes a false statement in a document verified by a statement of truth without an honest belief in its truth.[83]

The verification requirement serves two important functions that are conducive to efficient fact-finding. Firstly, if a party 'is required to certify his belief in the accuracy and truth of the matters put forward' in the pleadings, he is 'less likely to include assertions that are speculative'.[84] Secondly, the requirement (coupled with another new rule) limits the pleader's ability to allege inconsistent alternative sets of facts (unless there are reasonable grounds).[85] The case of *Tong Kin Hing v Autron Mauritius Corporation*[86] confirmed this point.[87]

In addition to the verification requirement, new restrictions have been implemented by the CJR on amending pleadings. While a party may still amend his pleadings once without leave before the close of pleadings,[88] any further amendments must obtain leave from the court.[89] The court must not order a pleading to be amended unless it is of the opinion that the amendment is necessary either for disposing fairly of the cause or matter or for saving costs.[90]

82 RHC O. 41A, r. 6(1).

83 RHC O.41A, r. 9(1).

84 Final Report 2004, p. 111 (para 221), quoting the English White Book 2003, 22/0/2.

85 RHC O.18, r. 12A; also see White Book 2011, p. 415 (18/20A/2).

86 [2010] 1 HKLRD 77.

87 Consider the following judgment of Rogers VP in *Tong Kin Hing v Autron Mauritius Corporation* [2010] 1 HKLRD 77, 82-83:
'Hence the seriousness of the statement of truth cannot be brushed aside. It may not be an affidavit or an affirmation but the Rules themselves treat the statement with similar seriousness. The requirement of a statement of truth is important. Its purpose is to focus the mind of the relevant party and to deter sloppy or speculative pleadings and prevent dishonest cases being put forward…the requirement serves to help the Court and the parties to achieve the underlying objectives which are set out in Order 1A Rule 1 of the Rules of the High Court … In my view, when faced with a situation where a pleading has been verified in circumstances where it has been demonstrated that the verification should never have been made, the Court should be very slow to permit any amendment to that pleading. If the part of the pleading that is defective is the central part of a claim then the Court may well consider that the pleading should be struck out and the party left to whatever course is open to him in bringing new proceedings. It is a matter of discretion and in exercising that discretion the Court recognises that the primary aim in exercising its powers is to secure the just resolution of disputes in accordance with the substantive rights of the parties. Hence, there can be no hard and fast rule, but the onus lies heavily on the party in default. In this case I consider that the pleading was so defective that it is not a matter of simple amendment; it is a matter of reconstituting any claim.'

88 RHC O. 20, r. 3(1). The opposite party may apply to the court within 14 days after being served with the amended pleadings to disallow the amendment: RHC O. 20, r. 4(1).

89 See RHC O. 20, r. 5, which must be read subject to RHC O. 20, r. 8. Under RHC O. 20, r. 8(1), for the purpose of determining the real question in controversy between the parties, or of correcting any defect or error in any proceedings, the court may at any stage (either of its own motion or on the application of parties) order a pleading to be amended.

90 Under O. 20, r. 8(1A). Consider the views of Wilkinson, Cheung & Booth 2009, p. 302:
'The courts have, therefore, been less prepared to permit substantial amendments for which last-minute applications are made than in the past. Leave is especially likely to be refused →

From a practical point of view, the verification requirement coupled with the new restrictions on amendments encouraged the pleader to advance his whole case with minimal amendments and be as forthcoming and honest as possible in the pleadings. The CJR conferred greater powers to the judge with regards to pleadings. It allows the court to identify the issues at an early stage of the proceedings and take proactive steps to ensure that this initial stage of fact-finding (i.e. the pleadings stage) is carried out expediently and appropriately. The serious consequences of making false statements without honest belief promotes the truthfulness of the cases pleaded, which contribute to the search for truth in civil fact-finding.

The mandatory verification requirement does not lower the cost of fact-finding. In the light of Rogers VP's judgment in *Tong Kin Hing*, parties are now required to make full investigation of their cases before pleadings, which inevitably involves thorough fact-finding at an early stage of the proceedings (even before commencement in the case of a plaintiff). As such, while the cost of fact-finding has been frontloaded, it has not been lowered in any significant way.

An advantage of frontloading the fact-finding exercise is that parties would be better informed of the case to explore settlement at an earlier stage of the proceedings, thus saving time and costs. Chief Justice Ma observed:

> 'A just settlement for the right reasons involves a timely settlement. Prior to the CJR, many settlements of course took place but the majority of these did not occur until the eve of the trial itself. There were many reasons for this, chief among them a realization only at a late stage of the real strengths and weaknesses of one's own and the other side's case'.[91]

2.2.3. Efficiency in Discovery

The Chief Justice's Working Party on Civil Justice Reform (Working Party) commented that 'there was a broad consensus that the excesses of discovery ought to be tackled by appropriate case-management by the courts'.[92] Following this view, a major change was implemented in the regime for discovery by conferring extensive powers to the judge in limiting discovery. For the purposes of case-management and furthering the underlying objectives, the judge may make an order to limit the discovery of documents under RHC Order 24, rule 15A. Such orders can be made of the court's own motion without application by any party. The default position is that the parties should decide their discovery regime

where an adjournment would be necessitated involving the change of a milestone date or where, if the amendment were allowed, the trial would have to be adjourned to allow the other party time to prepare a revised case.'

91 Ma 2010, p. 5.

92 Final Report 2004, p. 259 (para 500). The Working Party considered whether to limit the scope of automatic discovery set out in *Compagnie Financière du Pacifique v Peruvian Guano Co* (1882) 11 QBD 55 to only those documents directly relevant: see Final Report 2004, p. 242 (Proposal 25). However, the Working Party reached the conclusion that the *Peruvian Guano* principles should be retained as the primary benchmark for discovery and be taken as the starting point for case-management.

appropriate for the action. But if they do not do so, or if the court considers a different regime to be more appropriate, the court may exercise its power to limit discovery. This new rule also allows the judge to order the manner of discovery and the time for inspection.[93] The new rule provides an avenue for judicial intervention when faced with the excesses of discovery. The court should be guided by the underlying objectives in exercising its powers under this new rule.[94] It is questionable whether the rule will be frequently invoked, as any judicial decision to limit discovery may become a point for appeal. For instance, if the rule is invoked to exclude marginally relevant documents in the name of speeding up the discovery, the party requesting the document may challenge the court's decision arguing that its case-management powers must not override the party's rights to discovery under the principles in *Compagnie Financière du Pacifique v Peruvian Guano* Co[95] (or *Peruvian Guano* principles).

Whether it is discovery by parties without order,[96] or when discovery is ordered by the court,[97] the court may (upon application) order for the determination of issues or questions before discovery under RHC Order 24, rule 4. This rule (which came into effect before the CJR) can effectively limit the scope of discovery when the court directs that particular issues have to be determined in advance of discovery. This would ensure the discovery to be more focused and avoid undue delay caused by the ambiguities with what the issues are. In practice, however, this rule is rarely invoked.[98] This is because lawyers are usually able to identify the issues unless the case is very complicated. But after the CJR, the situation is likely to be different given the judicial mandate of case-management and the sanctions parties may face for undue delay.

Another effective fact-finding tool (which was also available before the CJR) is the party's right to inspect documents referred to in pleadings and affidavits under RHC Order 24, rule 10. The party requesting inspection must satisfy the court that inspection is necessary either to dispose fairly of the matter or to save costs.[99] The documents must be specifically referred to (or directly alluded to) in the pleadings or affidavits. Mere inference is insufficient.[100] The advantage of RHC Order 24, rule 10 is that it allows parties to better prepare for their case at an earlier stage. For instance, a defendant may request to inspect documents referred to in the statement of claim to assist the preparation of the defence. This rule was underutilized before

93 White Book 2011, p. 561 (24/15A/1).

94 Consider the examples of case managing discovery in the Final Report 2004, p. 245 (para 475): 'where appropriate, that discovery should take place in stages or in relation to particular issues first; or that it should be limited to particular classes of documents; or that documents need not be listed individually but by bundle or by file in certain categories.'

95 (1882) 11 QBD 55.

96 RHC O.24, r. 2.

97 RHC O.24, r. 3.

98 White Book 2011, p. 531 (24/4/1).

99 RHC O.24, r. 13.

100 White Book 2011, p. 555-556 (24/10/1); also see *Alexina Investments Ltd & Anor v Keysberg Ltd & Ors* (HCA 6359/1992, 27 March 2002).

the CJR because it was easier to amend pleadings then. After the CJR, given the restrictions on amendment of pleadings, parties are more likely to rely on this rule.

2.2.4. Amplification of Witness Statements

After the CJR, it is possible to amplify a witness statement or for the witness to give evidence relating to new matters when testifying in court. Order 38, rule 2A(7)(b) provides:

> '(b) the witness may with the leave of the Court –
>
> (i) amplify his witness statement; and
>
> (ii) give evidence in relation to new matters which have arisen since the witness statement was served on the other party'.

Order 38 rule 2A(7A) further provides:

> 'The Court may grant leave under paragraph (7)(b) only if it considers that there is good reason not to confine the evidence of the witness to the contents of his witness statement'.

The Working Party explained the rationale behind this new rule:

> 'This [rule] maintains the basic position that a witness is generally to be confined to the contents of his witness statement. However, the court has a general discretion to allow him to go beyond such contents if there is "good reason" to do so. The court's discretion would no longer be restricted to the narrow categories set out in O 38 r 2A(7)(b). Where, for instance, the amplifying or supplementary evidence would take the other side by surprise, the court could be expected to disallow it unless there was good reason to do otherwise, in which case it would be likely to let in the evidence on terms designed to avoid prejudice to the other side'.[101]

On an operational level, commentators observed, 'Circumstances in which a witness may be permitted to amplify his or her evidence include where events occur, or matters are discovered, after the statement was served, or where a response to matters dealt with in a witness statement of another party's witness is required'.[102] The party seeking to amplify a witness statement must do so in a timely fashion to avoid undue delay or being seen as taking the other side by surprise.[103]

101 Final Report 2004, p. 312 (para 589).

102 Rogers 2009, p. 186-187.

103 *Ibidem*.

2.2.5. Appeals from Certain Decisions of Masters to a Judge in Chambers

Under the RHC Order 58, rule 1(5),[104] the court should only allow new evidence to be adduced for an appeal from Masters on special grounds being shown.[105] Before the introduction of this provision, there was no limitation for a party appealing against a Master's decision to adduce new evidence.[106] Such old practice, inevitably, escalated time and expenses incurred by the parties since new round(s) of affirmations would have to be filed, which RHC Order 58, rule 1(5) aims to defeat.

2.2.6. Practice Direction 5.2 and the Listing Questionnaire

At the pre-trial stage, while discovery and the exchange of witness statements are completed, a further mechanism is available to manage the scope of issues to be tried. While this mechanism does not directly affect the cost and time of fact-finding as such (as most of the facts would have been gathered by this stage), it directly affects *whether* and *how* the facts gathered would be used and presented at trial. Paragraph 6 of Practice Direction 5.2 provides that parties should focus on the relevant issues. Proliferation of efforts on irrelevant factual or legal disputes should be avoided.[107] The Listing Questionnaire to be filed before Case-Management Conference or Pre-trial Review (Appendix C to Practice Direction 5.2) requires the solicitor or counsel to attach a one-page summary of the issues to be tried. It is queried whether the summary of issues cannot be introduced at a much earlier stage, for instance at the time when the Timetabling Questionnaire is filed.[108] Given the bulwark of the fact-finding work has been frontloaded to the pleading stage the parties should be in a good position to ascertain what the key issues of the litigation are by the close of pleadings.

3. The Policy of Giving Priority to Court Mediation: A Roadblock to Fairness in Civil Fact-finding in the People's Courts (in Mainland China)

An overly strong policy preference for court mediation distorts the original ADR function of mediation[109] and creates severe problems for fact-finding. A fair judgment is premised on meticulous and accurate fact-finding. But when an artificial settlement culture is created through policy, fact-finding becomes less of a priority. This section explores how overemphasizing court mediation could result in the deterioration of the fact-finding regime in Mainland China.

104 RHC O. 58, r.1(5) is a new provision introduced by the CJR.

105 *Aggressive Construction Company Limited v Yick Wai Cheong* (HCA 1889/2008, 29 June 2009).

106 Such appeal was therefore, in substance, a rehearing of the same application.

107 Para 6(2), PD 5.2.

108 The requirement of producing a summary of the issues is currently not included in the Timetabling Questionnaire (Appendix A to Practice Direction 5.2), which should be filed after close of pleadings and way before the Case-Management Conference.

109 Minzner 2011b, p. 963.

3.1. *The Origins of the Rise of Court Mediation: Social Instability, Policy Preference for Court Mediation and Judicial Fear of Decision-making in Adjudication*

The Central People's Government's emphasis on the need to construct a harmonious society (*he xie she hui*) since 2002 has immense influence over China's civil justice reform. In response to the proliferation of 'citizens petition' (also known as 'letters and visits' (*xinfang* and *shangfang*))[110] resulting from social discontent, the state has turned to court mediation as the 'artificial panacea for social stability'.[111] In recent years, the old policy to promote and formalize civil adjudication (in the 1990s)[112] gave way to the momentous rise of court mediation.[113] In the *Notice of the Supreme People's Court on Issuing Several Opinions on Further Implementing the Work Principle of 'Giving Priority to Mediation and Combining Mediation with Judgment'* (SPC 2010 Notice),[114] the SPC made it its official position that court mediation is the preferred method for resolving civil and commercial disputes.[115] Article 2 of the SPC 2010 Notice calls for 'Firmly establishing the idea of "mediation first"' and requires courts to 'take mediation as the first choice of handling cases'. Article 2 further notes, 'We shall conduct mediation wherever it works, and shall not miss any opportunity of mediation emerged in litigation and each stage before and after litigation so as to grasp all opportunities of settling a case through mediation as much as possible'.

Minzner explained that the promotion of court mediation had everything to do with curbing social instability in mind:

> 'Consistent with increased concerns about social instability, central Chinese authorities have ratcheted up pressure on lower-level Party and government officials to prevent instances of citizens petitioning (*shangfang*) to higher levels of the bureaucracy ... This

110 Note Art. 2 of the *Regulations on Letters and Visits, Decree of the State Council of the People's Republic of China, No. 431* (effective as of 1 May 2005):
'The term "letters and visits" in these Regulations means that citizens, legal persons or other organizations give information, make comments or suggestions or lodge complaints to the people's governments at all levels and the relevant departments of the people's governments at or above the county level through correspondence, E-mails, faxes, phone calls, visits, and so on, which are dealt with by the relevant administrative departments according to law.'

111 Minzner 2011b, p. 963.

112 The 1990s saw a decline in the use of court mediation. One of the reasons for this phenomenon was the promotion of adjudication and procedural formalism by the leadership of the Chinese Judiciary at that time, most notably, Xiao Yang, the former president of the SPC.

113 Legal elites in the 1990s called for the separation of mediation and adjudication (*tiao shen fen li*). However, they are losing the battle recently as the prevailing policy promotes the further integration of mediation with adjudication.

114 No. 16 [2010] of the SPC (effective since 7 June 2010).

115 The Chinese Judiciary's emphasis on court mediation also has budgetary and case-management reasons. The SPC and the Ministry of Justice were concerned that the proliferation of civil appeals would overburden the courts and add insurmountable cost on China's judicial system. *See* Peerenboom & He 2009, p. 26.

> also extends to the courts. Judges are being held individually liable for decisions they issue that generate petitions by disgruntled litigants to higher officials. Increased mediation targets are simply one component of this broader shift. Party institutions are issuing comprehensive orders to courts and other institutions instructing them to both keep petitioners away from higher authorities at all costs, and to successfully resolve massive percentages of disputes through mediation'.[116]

Unlike a civil judgment, a court-mediated settlement cannot be challenged by citizens petition. By giving priority to court mediation (and thereby implicitly discouraging adjudication), the state is hoping to lower the overall petitioning rate.

Apart from the policy preference for court mediation stemming from social circumstances, the rise of court mediation is also explainable by the way in which the performance of the individual judge is assessed. The performance of a judge is partly assessed on the basis of his or her ability to avoid mistakes (including to minimise reversals of judgments on appeal). Adjudication is therefore a 'risky business' for a judge from a career perspective given the possibility of reversals of judgments on appeal.[117] Court mediation becomes a very attractive option for judges.[118] This is because parties cannot appeal against a court-mediated settlement.[119] Furthermore, by resorting to court mediation, the judge is absolved from the responsibility to render a fact-finding determination. Issues of facts remain the main ground for appeal in China[120] and therefore judges who are uncertain with their factual determinations are exposed to the imminent risk of having their judgments reversed on appeal.[121]

The state believes that giving priority to court mediation in civil dispute resolution promotes social harmony.[122] Scholars, however, have questioned the alleged link between social harmony and the state's policy towards court mediation.[123] In many Chinese courts today, settling a dispute by court mediation has become an end in itself, rather than a genuine alternative means for resolving disputes.[124] This phenomenon is worrying as it encroaches upon the litigants' right

116 Minzner 2011b, p. 958.

117 Peerenboom and Scanlon noted that judges 'are assessed, in part, on how many of their judgements are overturned on appeal'. See Peerenboom & Scanlon 2005, p. 40.

118 While party consent is stipulated to be the prerequisite to court mediation under statute (*see* Art. 93 of the Code), there is a noticeable discrepancy between the law and actual practice. Parties sometimes find themselves persuaded, induced or pressured into mediation by the judge. A foreign party may find itself engaging in court mediation even if it had no intention to mediate in the first place.

119 Note, however, that parties are allowed to challenge a mediation agreement on narrow grounds of coercion or violation of the law.

120 Zhang & Walton 2010, p. 110.

121 The fear of making an improper fact-finding determination is one of the reasons for judicial procrastination and undue delay in many transitional (or ex-socialist) jurisdictions. *See* Uzelac 2010, p. 392-393.

122 Consider Art. 2 of the SPC 2010 Notice: 'Mediation is conducive to the elimination of social conflicts and the realization of the resolution of all disputes upon close of a case, conducive to the restoration of the relations among the parties concerned and the realization of harmony.'

123 Zhang 2007, p. 24.

124 Minzner 2011b, p. 963.

to be heard. This section critically examines the rise of court mediation in China (with a particular focus on judicial conciliation, which is a type of court mediation) and the ramifications for civil fact-finding.

3.2. *The Chinese Concept of Mediation: The Traditional Legal Culture at Work*

Confucianism projected the ideal society as one free from litigation (*wu song*). Disputes should be resolved through mediation to preserve social harmony. This cultural predisposition is still very much alive today and impacts the conduct of court mediation.

The fundamental principles of party autonomy, the neutrality of the mediator and mediation confidentiality in modern mediation do not fit well with the Chinese traditional legal culture. Mediation in imperial China had strong didactic functions. Mediators had the inherent mandate to educate the people on Confucian morals and the law. In this regard, traditional Chinese mediation differed from modern mediation in that the Chinese mediator was not an impartial and neutral third party, but rather a conciliator with a quasi-official mandate to advance the objectives of the governing discourse and value system. It remains to be seen how this facet of Chinese legal tradition affects contemporary court mediation.

3.3. *Court Mediation in China: A Critical Appraisal*

Court mediation is an integral part of contemporary Chinese civil procedure.[125] Two basic principles underscore court mediation in China: legality and voluntariness (of the parties).[126] Respecting voluntariness of the parties in court mediation is an observance of the principle of party disposition. It also promotes the enforcement of a mediated settlement.[127] Unfortunately, as a result of the policy of giving priority to court mediation, voluntariness is hanging by the thread.

Court mediation may be conducted at various stages of a civil lawsuit (first instance proceedings, appeal or retrial). The procedural rules for court mediation are set out in the *Provisions of the Supreme People's Court about Several Issues Concerning the Civil Mediation Work of the People's Court* (SPC 2004 Provisions).[128] Reference should also be made to the *Several Opinions of the Supreme People's Court on Establishing a Sound Conflict and Dispute Resolution Mechanism that Connects Litigation and Non-litigation* (SPC 2009 Opinion). The court may invite other entities (or individuals) that have a special relationship with the parties or are connected with the case to assist in court mediation.[129] The parties as well as the 'presiding

125 Alexander 2009, p. 139.

126 Art. 9 of the Code. Also see Arts. 93 and 96 of the Code.

127 NPCSC Publication 2007, p. 155.

128 Effective since 1 November 2004.

129 Art. 3 of the SPC 2004 Provisions. Also see Art. 95 of the Code.

staff over the mediation' (i.e. the mediator) may present a settlement proposal.[130] When a settlement is reached through court mediation, the court shall draw up a written 'mediation agreement'. A mediation agreement shall clearly set out the claims of the action, the facts of the case, and the result of the mediation. The mediation agreement shall then be signed by the judge and the court clerk, sealed by the court and served on both parties. Once the mediation agreement is signed and exchanged by both parties, it becomes legally binding.[131] If either party fails to perform the mediation agreement, the other party can apply to the court to enforce the mediation agreement.[132]

Court mediation generally includes two distinct procedures: pre-trial mediation and judicial conciliation. Pre-trial mediation takes place at the docketing stage. It is usually conducted by a judge or judicial officer.[133] The judge conducting the mediation must be different from the trial judge.[134] Judicial conciliation takes place after the case is transferred from the docketing court to the trial court. In judicial conciliation, the trial judge acts as the conciliator. If conciliation fails, the same judge will continue with the adjudication of the case. This practice is likely to threaten the without prejudice nature of the conciliation process (particularly given the judge is allowed to meet *ex parte* with parties).[135] It also affects the judge's impartiality in the adjudication that follows. Judicial conciliation may occur at the closing phase of the trial right before the rendering of a judgment so long as parties consent to mediation.[136] While party autonomy is emphasized under the law,[137] the judge (or judicial officer) sometimes dominates the mediation process and steers the settlement negotiation along its adjudicative agenda.[138]

As a result of the policy of giving priority to court mediation, parties of a civil dispute are sometimes forced to mediate their case and become 'victims' of a compelled settlement.[139] When a party enters into a settlement against its will, it is more likely that it will not honour the settlement agreement. This leads to enforcement problems. It will be fallacious to conclude that court mediation of civil disputes in China has been successful by simply looking at the rising court mediation settlement rate. If mediated settlements are frequently subject to court enforcement, the necessary conclusion must be that the mediation in the first place

130 Art. 8 of the SPC 2004 Provisions. Indeed, this particular rule carries an element of conciliation given its directive and interventionist nature (i.e. the mediator may present a settlement proposal).

131 Art. 97 of the Code.

132 Art. 13 of the SPC 2004 Provisions.

133 Art. 15 of the SPC 2009 Opinion.

134 Art. 16 of the SPC 2009 Opinion.

135 Art. 7 of the SPC 2004 Provisions.

136 Art. 1 of the SPC 2004 Provisions.

137 The question of party autonomy must be addressed not simply from the perspective of whether party consent to mediate had been obtained. Party autonomy is a core principle of ADR that should permeate the whole mediation process ranging from the definition of issues to the methods employed for reaching settlement.

138 Fu & Cullen 2011, p. 51.

139 Wang 2009, p. 71-73.

was not effective.[140] The enforcement of settlement agreements reached by court mediation has been increasingly problematic.[141] While the court mediation settlement rate has arisen during the period between 2002 and 2009, court enforcement rate of the same period also skyrocketed.[142] This suggests that a considerable number of mediated settlements did not conclusively resolve disputes and parties had to resort to the court for enforcement. The situation is particularly serious in basic-level people's courts.[143]

Conflict of interest arises inevitably when the judge acts as both the conciliator and the adjudicator (in the case of judicial conciliation). The question of mediation confidentiality was a subject widely discussed in international academia. China is underdeveloped in the area of mediation confidentiality.

The civil court performs important public functions, namely the enforcement of rights and the declaration of norms.[144] Court mediation is designed to settle disputes only and not to enforce rights and declare norms. Overemphasizing court mediation risks the civil court losing its public functions.[145]

3.4. *The Onslaught of Judicial Conciliation on Fact-finding*

The policy of giving priority to court mediation detrimentally affects the fairness of civil fact-finding. The situation is particularly serious in the case of judicial conciliation, as the judge wears the hats of both conciliator and adjudicator. There are at least three problem areas that deserve attention.

The policy preference for judicial conciliation creates an artificial settlement culture in the courts. From the judge's perspective, the primary goal in a civil lawsuit is dispute resolution, rather than the enforcement of rights. The need to fairly enforce the rights of the parties necessitates a thorough fact-finding process that assists the judge in ascertaining the truth (whether legal or objective truth). Overemphasising judicial conciliation will inevitably result in the laxity of the fact-finding process as the focus shifts from the enforcement of rights to pure dispute resolution. The laxity in fact-finding deteriorates the public function of the court, which involves the delivery of justice to parties, both in the form of rights enforcement, as well as in the form of ascertaining the truth. The search for the truth through fact-finding is a core and indispensable component of public justice. Overemphasizing judicial conciliation (at the expense of adjudication) compromises this core value of public justice.

140 Pan & Liu 2010, p. 75.

141 Peerenboom & He 2009, p. 25-26.

142 Pan & Liu 2010, p. 75.

143 Pan & Liu 2010, p. 76.

144 Zuckerman observed, 'The civil court provides a law enforcement service. The role of the civil court is not merely to mediate disputes but to give effect to our rights and enforce them'. See Zuckerman 2009, p. 53.

145 Overemphasizing court mediation will result in the deterioration of the adjudicatory function of the court (especially in fact-finding) as the focus is shifted from the enforcement of rights to pure dispute resolution. See Wang 2009, p. 72.

Apart from being an integral part of adjudication, the fact-finding process also assists parties in assessing their positions in settlement negotiations (ADR function of fact-finding). For instance, when parties reach a stage at which they have obtained enough facts that reflect their relative positions, they would be more likely to engage in settlement negotiations. This is only possible if the principle of voluntariness is strictly observed (i.e. parties genuinely consent to conciliate and may terminate the conciliation process at anytime). As judicial conciliation is given priority as a matter of policy, the principle of voluntariness is endangered. As a result, the parties may be induced or pressured into judicial conciliation without sufficient facts on which to base their settlement process. Even where the parties agree to conciliate, it is possible that the decision is made on the basis of what they believe the judge prefers, rather than on the basis of their genuine interests. This obscures the ADR function of fact-finding. A policy-driven settlement culture endangers the deliberative process in which parties are free to assess the facts and evidence in considering their ADR options.

When judicial conciliation fails and adjudication resumes, there is always the risk of the judge inappropriately utilizing the facts ascertained in the conciliation process for adjudicative purposes. In the ensuing adjudication, the judge may be swayed or affected by the facts revealed in the conciliation process. This gives rise to an apparent bias on the part of the judge and in turn affects the quality of justice.

Proper fact-finding is the basis for the fair disposal of a lawsuit. The court, through fact-finding determinations, performs an important norm-declaring function.[146] The institutional bias in favour of court mediation creates a policy-driven settlement culture that reduces the court's norm-declaring function.

4. Conclusion

In relation to civil fact-finding in Mainland China, the next stage of reform must involve the entrenchment of the principle of party presentation, without which there can be no true party empowerment. Noting the relatively weak positions of the parties in rural China, such reform efforts may proceed in stages based on geographical differentiation.

[146] In theory, court mediation must be conducted on the basis of clear and accurate facts (*see* Art. 93 of the Code). However, there are simply no procedural rules to ensure the facts established in court mediation are clear and accurate. Settlement, unlike adjudication, is based on the interests of the parties and not entirely on facts. Overemphasizing court mediation as a matter of policy diminishes the functional role of fact-finding in civil justice. While China does not embrace the principle of *stare decisis*, the SPC publishes 'guiding cases' to provide direction to lower courts. While not being binding, the guiding cases are expected to be referred to by lower courts. The guiding cases are (supposedly) based on sound fact-finding. As such fact-finding determinations in guiding cases possess enormous normative force. *See* <http://news.stanford.edu/news/2012/february/china-guiding-cases-020612.html>, last consulted in July 2012.

The individual Chinese judge is institutionally weak. External interference with the adjudicatory process is the norm, rather than the exception.[147] Wang has warned that the 'bureaucratization of the court', a widespread phenomenon in China, has stripped every opportunity to develop adjudicatory independence in China. The collective decision of the court organization trumps the decision of the individual judge, despite the individual judge having superior knowledge and understanding of the case.[148] The individual judge's deference to the court leadership (coupled with external interferences with adjudication) makes it almost impossible to construct a fair fact-finding regime. Factors completely unrelated to the adjudication of the case could affect the fact-finding process. Unfortunately, recent reform efforts in relation to fact-finding focused on minor technicalities without due consideration on how to promote fundamental principles in this area.[149]

For Hong Kong, the task going forward is to test the effectiveness of the new tools introduced by the CJR (such as the power of the court to limit discovery)[150] designed to enhance efficiency in fact-finding.[151]

The policy preference for court mediation obscures the function of fact-finding in the Chinese courts. Under the artificial settlement culture in China, court mediation is at risk of losing its function as an alternative dispute resolution method as parties no longer truly voluntarily submit to mediation.[152]

147 A noteworthy example is the existence of an adjudicative committee in every court in China. In certain important and complex cases, the judge must first refer such cases to the adjudicative committee for discussion. The judgment must implement the decision/opinion of the adjudicative committee. See Chen 2011, p. 186.
Another example is the system of advisory requests (*qingshi*). Consider the views of Minzner 2011a, p. 58-59: 'To avoid appellate reversal, lower Chinese courts and judges rely on an ill-defined system of advisory requests (*qingshi*) to solicit the views of higher courts and judges on how to decide pending cases.'

148 Wang 2011, p. 1.

149 *Ibidem.*

150 RHC O. 24, r. 15A.

151 The CJR emphasizes on identification of the issues at an early stage of the proceedings so that the court can take proactive steps to ensure this initial step of fact-finding is carried out expediently and appropriately. This is envisaged, for example, under RHC O.24, r. 15A. There is no reported or unreported case, which illustrates how this power is exercised at this point. It is therefore unknown at this stage whether or how the said intention of the CJR has been achieved, especially in relation to discovery of documents between parties under RHC O.24, rr. 1 and 2.

152 Minzner noted, 'Alternative dispute resolution succeeds when it truly represents an "alternative" to litigation... But that is not the case when alternative dispute resolution becomes an artificial panacea for social stability'. See Minzner 2011b, p. 963.

Bibliography

Alexander 2009
Alexander, N., *International and Comparative Mediation: Legal Perspectives*, Alphen aan den Rijn: Kluwer Law International, 2009.

Chen 2011
Chen, A.H.Y., *An Introduction to the Legal System of the People's Republic of China*, 4th edn., Hong Kong: LexisNexis, 2011.

Clermont & Sherwin 2002
Clermont, K.M. & Sherwin, E., 'A Comparative View of Standards of Proof', *The American Journal of Comparative Law*, 2002, Vol. 50, No. 2, p. 243-276.

Final Report 2004
Chief Justice's Working Party on Civil Justice Reform, *The Final Report of the Chief Justice's Working Party on Civil Justice Reform*, Hong Kong, 3 March 2004.

First Year Report 2010
Legislative Council Panel on Administration of Justice and Legal Services, *The First Year's Implementation of the Civil Justice Reform from 2 April 2009 to 31 March 2010*, Hong Kong, LC Paper No. CB(2)591/10-11(06), December 2010.

Fu & Cao 2010
Fu, Y.L. & Cao, Z.X., 'The Position of the Judges in Civil Litigation in Transitional China: Focusing on Judicial Mediation and Case-Management for Trial' (unpublished), Conference Paper, *Towards a Chinese Civil Code: Historical and Comparative Perspectives*, international conference organized by the School of Law, City University of Hong Kong, Hong Kong, 22-23 October 2010.

Fu & Cullen 2011
Fu, H.L. & Cullen, R., 'From Mediatory to Adjudicatory Justice: The Limits of Civil Justice Reform in China', in: Woo, M.Y.K. & Gallagher, M.E. (eds.), *Chinese Justice: Civil Dispute Resolution in Contemporary China*, New York: Cambridge University Press, 2011, p. 25-57.

Huang 2010
Huang, P.C.C., *Chinese Civil Justice, Past and Present*, Lanham, MD: Rowman & Littlefield Publishers Inc., 2010.

Jiang 2010
Jiang, W., 'Min shi su song fa qian yan li lun wen ti' [Frontiers of the theoretical issues of the Civil Procedure Law], *Journal of National Prosecutors College*, 2010, Vol. 18, No. 2, p. 152-160.

Lenhoff 1954
Lenhoff, A., 'The Law of Evidence: A Comparative Study Based Essentially on Austrian and New York Law', *The American Journal of Comparative Law*, 1954, Vol. 3, No. 3, p. 313-344.

Ma 2010
Ma, G., 'Efficiency at all Costs - True or Bluff?', in: Meggitt, G. (ed.), *Civil Justice Reform - What Has It Achieved?*, Hong Kong: Sweet & Maxwell/Thomson Reuters, 2010, p. 3-9.

Minzner 2011a
Minzner, C.F., 'Judicial Disciplinary Systems for Incorrectly Decided Cases: The Imperial Chinese Heritage Lives On', in: Woo, M.Y.K. & Gallagher, M.E. (eds.), *Chinese Justice: Civil Dispute Resolution in Contemporary China*, New York: Cambridge University Press, 2011, p. 58-90.

Minzner 2011b
Minzner, C.F., 'China's Turn Against Law', *American Journal of Comparative Law*, 2011, Vol. 59, No. 4, 935-984.

NPCSC Publication 2007
Office for Civil Law of the Legislative Affairs Commission of the National People's Congress Standing Committee (ed.), *Zhonghua Renmin Gongheguo min shi su song fa tiao wen shuo ming, li fa li you ji xiang guan gui ding* [The Civil Procedure Law of the People's Republic of China: annotated provisions, legislative reasoning and related regulations], Beijing: Peking University Press, 2007.

Oberhammer & Domej 2005
Oberhammer, P. & Domej, T., 'Germany, Switzerland and Austria', in: Van Rhee, C.H. (ed.), *European Traditions in Civil Procedure*, Oxford/Antwerp: Intersentia, 2005, p. 295-305.

Pan & Liu 2010
Pan, J.F. & Liu, Z.W., 'Lun fayuan tiaojie yu jiufen jiejue zhi guanxi - cong goujian hexie shehui de jiaodu zhankai' [The Relationship Between Court Mediation and Dispute Resolution - From the Perspective of Constructing A Harmonious Society], *Journal of Comparative Law*, 2010, Vol. 4, p. 70-81.

Peerenboom 2003
Peerenboom, R., 'The X-Files: Past and Present Portrayals of China's Alien "Legal System"', *Washington University Global Studies Law Review*, 2003, Vol. 2, p. 37-95.

Peerenboom & He 2009
Peerenboom, R. & He, X., 'Dispute Resolution in China: Patterns, Causes and Prognosis', *East Asia Law Review*, 2009, Vol. 4, p. 1-61.

Peerenboom & Scanlon 2005
Peerenboom, R. & Scanlon, K., 'An Untapped Dispute Resolution Option: Mediation Offers Companies Distinct Advantages in Certain Cases', *The China Business Review*, 2005, Vol. 32, No. 4, p. 36-41.

Rogers 2009
Rogers, M. (ed.), *Hong Kong Civil Justice Reform Practice Manual*, Hong Kong: Sweet & Maxwell/Thomson Reuters, 2009.

Uzelac 2010
Uzelac, A., 'Survival of the Third Legal Tradition?', in: Walker, J. & Chase, O.G. (eds.), *Common Law, Civil Law and the Future of Categories*, Markham: LexisNexis, 2010, p. 377-396.

Wang 2009
Wang, L.M., 'Characteristics of China's Judicial Mediation System', *Asia Pacific Law Review*, 2009, Vol. 17, No. 2, Supp. (Special Issue on Mediation), p. 67-74.

Wang 2011
Wang, Y.X., 'The Preinstall Premises to Understand the Differences Between the Current Chinese Civil Litigation Practice and Western Legal Tradition' (unpublished), Expert Meeting Paper, *The Role of the Judge and the Parties in Civil Litigation: Towards an Efficient Procedure under the Rule of Law in China and the EU*, Maastricht, 12-14 September 2011 (research project funded by the China-EU School of Law at the China University of Political Science and Law, 2011-2012).

White Book 2011
Chan, P. (Permanent Judge of the Court of Final Appeal of Hong Kong) & Rogers, M. (ed.), *Hong Kong Civil Procedure 2011*, Vol. 1, Hong Kong: Sweet & Maxwell, 2011.

Wilkinson, Cheung & Booth 2009
Wilkinson, M., Cheung, E.T.M. & Booth, C.N. (eds.), *A Guide to Civil Procedure in Hong Kong (Incorporating the New Civil Justice Reform Rules)*, 3rd edn., Hong Kong: LexisNexis, 2009.

Woo & Wang 2005
Woo, M.Y.K. & Wang, Y.X., 'Civil Justice in China: An Empirical Study of Courts in Three Provinces', *American Journal of Comparative Law*, 2005, Vol. 53, No. 4, p. 911-940.

Zhang 2006
Zhang, W.P., 'On the Concept of Aufklarung in Civil Procedures', *Peking University Law Journal*, 2006, Vol. 18, No. 2, p. 129-146.

Zhang 2007
Zhang, W.P., 'Su song tiao jie: shi xia shi tai de fen xi yu si kao'[Court mediation: an analysis of the contemporary situation], *Legal Science*, 2007, Vol. 5, p. 18-27.

Zhang 2008
Zhang, B.S., *Uniform Provisions of Evidence of the People's Court: Proposal for Judicial Interpretations and Drafting Commentary*, Beijing: China University of Political Science and Law Press, 2008.

Zhang & Walton 2010
Zhang, N.N. & Walton, D., 'Recent Trends in Evidence Law in China and the New Evidence Scholarship', *Law, Probability & Risk*, 2010, Vol. 9, p. 103-129.

Zhang & Zwier 2003
Zhang, M., & Zwier, P.J., 'Burden of Proof: Developments in Modern Chinese Evidence Rules', *Tulsa Journal of Comparative & International Law*, 2002-2003, Vol. 10, No. 2, p. 419-471.

Zhong & Yu 2004
Zhong, J.H., & Yu, G.H., 'Establishing the Truth on Facts: Has the Chinese Civil Process Achieved This Goal?', *Journal of Transnational Law & Policy*, 2004, Vol. 13, p. 393-445.

Zuckerman 2009
Zuckerman, A., 'The Challenge of Civil Justice Reform: Effective Court Management of Litigation', *City University of Hong Kong Law Review*, 2009, Vol. 1, No. 1, p. 49-71.

S. Spinei

RULES OF EVIDENCE IN ROMANIAN CIVIL PROCEDURE AND THEIR IMPACT ON TRUTH AND EFFICIENCY

1. Interrelations

There is an unconcealed, intense correlation between Justice and Truth. The natural function of the justice system is that of *ius dicere*, which means 'to dictate', 'to say' or 'to tell the law'. This sounds notably akin to the expression 'to tell the truth', at the very least because justice actually does this, even if this truth may sometimes come as a mere 'judicial' one. Finding the substantive or material truth, the 'real' truth, is a paradigm - strongly asserted in some legal theories,[1] not always achievable in reality. However, in court, every truth requires a proof. As a consequence, rules of evidence hold central importance in procedural law. Such connections are discernible in fundamental legal precepts: ... *suum cuique tribuere; ex facto oritur jus; da mihi factum ...; secundum allegata ...*, and others.

2. Current Developments

For several decades now, in many parts of the world, warnings have been issued regarding the state of justice. According to various sources (press reports, opinion polls, professional legal literature, official government documents), a state of crisis existed in numerous justice systems.[2] In one location, the court system was said to be 'on the brink of a heart attack'.[3] In another, civil justice was said to belong to 'another century'.[4] 'Disaster', 'disease', 'evil' were also words used to describe the situation.[5] The difficulties justice encountered were almost everywhere the same - a growing number of cases, delays, increasing costs, insufficient resources and

1 See 'Principle of truth' in Section 3.1.
2 Fix-Fierro 2003, p. 1-2.
3 *Ibidem*, p. 1.
4 *Ibidem*.
5 Fix-Fierro 2003, p. 1-2.

ineffective organisation.[6] The answer to this predicament was the undertaking of justice reforms[7] and, in particular, the development of the notion of judicial efficiency[8] (and the actual implementation of instruments designed to improve the efficiency of justice). In this context, finding how rules of evidence impact on efficiency, and where the right balance between truth and efficiency stands, seems an acutely legitimate engagement.

3. Romanian Experience

3.1. *Principle of Truth*

The principle of truth was always professed in modern Romanian civil procedure.[9] Moreover, the Socialist legal system proclaimed the principle of the substantive, material or objective truth under which the court is capable, from a philosophical perspective, of knowing the truth and legally compelled or assigned 'to establish the facts of the case in such a way as to ensure a complete concordance between the reality of the circumstances of the case and the conclusions of the court regarding those circumstances'.[10] In close connection with this principle, the court was supposed to act in a particularly active manner.[11] Today, it is still said that truth must represent the goal of the judicial activity[12] and, in effect, a valid or correct judgment is deemed to be the one that is *well founded* (i.e., one which establishes the facts accurately, according to the truth) and *lawful* (one in which the law is correctly interpreted and applied). According to the Romanian Code of Civil Procedure (henceforth, also CPC), 'the judge [still] has the duty to persist ... [in] preventing any error in finding the truth in the case',[13] but neither the 'principle of truth' nor the 'active role' any longer implies the exorbitant (asserted) features of the Socialist period.[14]

6 In other systems, additional issues were identified - corruption, politicisation and inadequate training of legal professionals (Fix-Fierro 2003, p. 2); see also Leş 2004, p. 19: 'Romanian justice passes through an identity, efficiency and morality crisis'.

7 Shetreet 2011, p. 3: 'the court system' developed 'three main models' of coping with the situation. 'The first model is to make the judicial system and the judicial process more efficient, thus saving resources. The second model is to introduce reforms which reduce the number of cases that come into the court. The third model is to increase the resources allotted to the court system'.

8 Judicial efficiency was seen as designating 'speed in processing cases, decrease of delays and costs, for a better use of public resources' (Jean 2007, p. 35).

9 See, e.g., Leş 2002, p. 21; Ciobanu 1997, p. 133-134 (he mentions the duty of the judge to discover the truth, etc. The principle can also be found in Cădere 1928, p. 198-199, in connection with the evidentiary activity.

10 Hilsenrad & Stoenescu 1957, p. 38, 43-44.

11 See, 'Adversarial principle' in Section 3.4.

12 Leş 2005, p. 39.

13 Art. 129(5) CPC.

14 See 'Adversarial principle' in Section 3.4, on the way recent case law comprehends the active role of the judge and fact-finding.

3.2. *Efficiency*

When compared to the principle of truth, in Romania the complex notion of 'efficiency' represents today a rather marginal concept, being a topic in recent official documents[15] or statements by Romanian officials confronted with European Union requirements, but seldom, if ever, in the legal literature.[16] Nevertheless, almost constantly, some essential components of this notion were either frequently referred to (the term 'proper rendering/distribution of justice' is a traditional one)[17] or downright stated as guidelines of civil procedure, as is the case with the concept of 'celerity' (i.e., swiftness, speed). The necessity of expeditious litigation is a prevalent notion in recent years, but one also having quite a consistent history.

3.2.1. Modifications of the Code of Civil Procedure. Acceleration Laws

The Romanian 1865 Code of Civil Procedure[18] was significantly modified in 1900, when the first serious reform took place, followed by a series of modifications - the 1925, 1929 and 1943 laws 'for the Acceleration of Litigation'.[19] This sequence of reforms demonstrates the constant preoccupation, in those times, with improving the administration of justice. It also shows modern themes on the agenda of the

15 For example, the Explanatory Memorandum for the New Code of Civil Procedure.

16 Still, one can notice concern for efficiency and implementation of adequate instruments in early times. An *avant la lettre* example of creating 'infrastructure for avoiding litigation' (see Fix-Fierro 2003, p. 123) can be found in the 1830s 'Organic Regulations' of Valachia and Moldova (see Spinei 2012). Once the fact that the setting of landed property borderlines as one of the most frequent types of lawsuit of the time was acknowledged, the solution for reducing the number of such lawsuits was to provide for charging the Administration with the task of establishing the limits of all landed property in the country. Interestingly enough, a somewhat similar situation occurred in 1991, when the task of restoring state-confiscated land to the previous owners was assigned to the local administrations through a non-judicial procedure. What happened this time was that those administrations performed in such a faulty manner that a tremendous number of motions and petitions eventually came before the courts.

17 The concept refers sometimes to the efficiency (see, e.g., Art. 128(3) of the Constitution, or the theoretical justifications of the *lis pendens* exception) and sometimes to the quality of justice (see, on the significance of the duty of the court to state reasons for its decision, Romanian Court of Cassation (Î.C.C.J., Secția contencios administrativ şi fiscal), Decision No. 1540 of 17 March 2010, <www.scj.ro/SCA%20rezumate%202010/SCA%20dec%20r%201540%202010.-htm>, last consulted 15 October 2011.

18 Its sources were the Civil Procedure Rules of Geneva and the 1842 version of the French Code of Civil Procedure.

19 All these modifications were inspired by the 1898 Austrian reforms initiated by Franz Klein. This influence is certainly attributable to the fact that until 1918 some regions of modern Romania (Transylvania and Bucovina) were parts of Austria-Hungary. The Austrian *Zivilprozessordnung* was directly in force in Bucovina (situated in the north-eastern part of present-day Romania, also spelled *Bukowina*). Transylvania had its own law of procedure - Law No. I of 1911, which was preceded by several laws in 1868, 1881, 1893 and 1907 (see Cădere 1928, p. 40-41). See, on Franz Klein and the reforms instituted by him, Van Rhee 2008a.

epoch: '[A] country cannot be built if not based on right decisions - but also swift ones. Delayed justice means, most of the time, true injustice', stated the Minister of Justice in his 1943 Report to the Head of State, regarding the Acceleration Law. This 1943 law was perhaps the most important amongst the three Acceleration Laws, and it proved to be extremely influential.[20] It introduced (or reinforced)[21] a number of principles and rules,[22] such as:

- the principle of the active role of the judge;[23]
- the institution of the 'first day of appearance' as a major phase in litigation;[24]
- the rule of raising exceptions (preliminary/procedural defences) and submitting evidence *in limine litis* only;[25]
- the rule of mentioning the name of proposed witnesses in the introductory claim or in the statement of defence;
- the rule that evidence can be admitted only if it is conclusive;
- the rule according to which the court can limit the number of witnesses that are going to be heard;
- new rules on questioning parties who live abroad or cannot appear in court due to illness or other reasons;[26]
- the rule that witnesses can be brought to court by police agents, following an order issued by the judge;
- the rule that if the exception of lack of jurisdiction is admitted, the evidence already presented will be used by the competent court instead of being administered once again;

20 Not only that, most provisions of this law are still in force, and maintained also by the New Code, but a 2010 law (Law No. 202/2010, which introduces some legal rules of the future New Code of Civil Procedure into the existing one) was even named 'Law for the Acceleration of Litigation', following the previous model.

21 Elements of judicial activism were already introduced by the Laws of 1900 (see Art. 95 of the modified Code), 1925 (Arts. 9, 22, 23, 26) and 1929 (Arts. 21-26).

22 See Păduraru *et al.* 1943, *passim*.

23 See Arts. 16-30 of the 1943 Acceleration Law.

24 *Prima zi de înfățișare*. It is defined currently by Art. 134 CPC as the first court session when the parties are properly (legally) summoned and able to argue the case (on any of its aspects, but primarily, in this stage, on preliminary issues; being 'able' means the party is not prevented by a justifiable circumstance - e.g., illness, retention). It was inspired by the Austrian institution of *der ersten Tagsatzung* (see van Rhee 2008a, p. 2-3; Oberhammer & Domej 2008, p. 65) via the procedural rules of Transylvania and Bucovina (see Cădere 1928, p. 63 on 'the introduction [in Romanian procedure] of the formal preparation of the trial'; see also n. 19 above). When first introduced by the 1925 Acceleration Law it was called 'the preliminary hearing' (*ședința preliminară* - Art. 9). It bears the current name since 1929. It has an important procedural significance, being the last occasion for the parties to amend their pleas, submit evidence requests and raise 'public order' exceptions (*exceptions d'ordre public*). The closing arguments can also be made at this hearing.

25 In the written pleadings (see 'Written phase of the lawsuit' in Section 3.2.3.1.) or on the first day of appearance.

26 In such cases, the court will not postpone the hearing, but the questioning will be carried out by way of written documents.

- the obligation of the court to decide on an exception before examining the merits of the case;
- the possibility of awarding a partial (and enforceable) decision upon a partial recognition of the claim, etc.

3.2.2. Socialist and Early 'Transition' Period

Almost no mention of the concept of 'celerity' is made between 1948 and 2000. Under the Socialist regime, the omission may be understandable, since a certain degree of immobility or inactivity marks the period. The absence of many types of social and legal relations (related to private property, business, trade, public bodies, etc.) naturally led to the incidence of a smaller number of cases in courts, hence there was no sense of pressure for and no theoretical preoccupations with the idea of expediting the procedures.

3.2.3. Ordinance No. 138/2000

A law that introduced significant amendments to the Code of Civil Procedure was adopted in the year 2000. This law brought important measures for accelerating judicial (and enforcement) procedures.[27] Its proposed objectives were to ensure celerity, to save time and money for the parties, to remove the possibilities of abusive exercise of procedural rights and tendencies of the parties to cause delays, and to sanction such actions.[28] In order to attempt to implement these objectives, different methods were engaged.

3.2.3.1. Written Phase of the Lawsuit

The first method of accelerating the administration of justice was the readjustment of the structure of the written phase of the lawsuit. Its importance and relevance were reinforced by (re-)introducing[29] the obligatory character of the statement of defence.[30]

In the written preparatory phase of the lawsuit the introductory claim, the statement of defence and, if it is the case, the counterclaim are filed. These documents establish the issues to be decided by the court, they 'build' or 'aggregate' the case: the claim and the counterclaim indicate the demands of the parties, identify the grounds for the demands (the facts that occurred and the applicable legal rules) and propose the evidence that is going to be produced to support the alleged facts. Through the written statement of defence, the defendant answers the claims and raises his defences and exceptions. The evidence for the defendant must also be proposed. All the written introductory documents must mention the names

27 As regards judicial proceedings, it can be noted, though, that the ordinance reinstituted many principles and solutions provided by the Acceleration Laws.

28 Ciobanu *et al.* 2001, p. 3

29 Over the years, the rule was consecutively introduced and removed a number of times.

30 The answer or response of the defendant to the introductory claim.

and addresses of the witnesses. The role of the statement of defence is to ensure the equality of means between the parties (both being able to know from the beginning of the lawsuit each other's claims,[31] defences and evidence); furthermore, the judge is aware of the structure of the case and his future activity in the earliest stage of the trial,[32] the limits of the trial are set from the early beginning, and future adjournments may be avoided. The statement of defence must be submitted at least five days before the first court session. If the defendant does not present the statement of defence, he will lose the right to submit evidence and raise exceptions (apart from those pertaining to 'public order' - i.e., those indicating a violation of imperative legal rules, considered to be ordered for the general/public interest).

In this manner, the expected preoccupation of the parties with having more chances to win in court (by being able to prove their allegations or to try to quickly provoke a dismissal of the claim) was turned by the Legislator into an instrument for stimulating efficiency. There is also a corrective to this rule: on the 'first day of appearance', the judge will advise the party that is not assisted by a lawyer to formulate exceptions and defences and to submit evidence. Upon request, an adjournment can be granted for preparing the defence and for submitting the statement of defence.

3.2.3.2. *Taking of Evidence by Lawyers*

Ordinance No. 138/2000 also proposed the introduction of an (optional) procedure regulating the taking of evidence by lawyers. The intended purpose of this procedure was the disencumbrance of the courts from the task of taking evidence themselves. Instead, the lawyers of the parties would have the case file prepared. The judge's function would be only to examine the evidence and decide the case. The procedure was approved in July 2005, being also maintained by the New Code of Civil Procedure (henceforth, also NCPC).[33] Unfortunately, it is a procedure that is seldom (if ever) used. The justification for this circumstance appears to be a complex one, with a number of reasons being evoked - the conflict of this instrument with Romanian 'legal tradition' or 'legal culture',[34] and the 'psychology' of the participants (reciprocal distrust between the lawyers of the opposing parties, the mistrust of the judges towards the lawyers).[35] Problems with the lawyers

31 No other additional allegations or claims can, in principle, be filed later during the proceedings (except at the 'first day of appearance').

32 Ciobanu *et al.* 2001, p. 17.

33 See 'The New Code of Civil Procedure' in Section 3. 8.

34 See, for some discussions, <http://www.avocatura.com/forum/administrarea-probelor-de-catre-avocati-t3199.html>, last consulted 15 October 2011.

35 Florea 2010 stated, 'Situations in which the judges recommend the parties ... to accept this procedure are not known. The predilection of the judges towards extrajudicial procedures they recommend and publicly support (pointing to mediators, to notaries) and the obvious repudiation of the application of procedures which implies the treatment of lawyers as effective partners of the judge remain without an explanation' (Mr. Florea is, currently, the President of the National Bar Association). It is also true that only the NCPC (Art. 234) institutes the obligation for the judge to 'advertise' these procedures to the parties.

(supposedly unable to insure the necessary personnel and technical means) and the parties (unable to hire a lawyer) were also mentioned. Finally, some elements of the design of the institution do not encourage its application (the fact that the court can re-administer any evidence induced the sense that following the procedure may prove futile and counterproductive).

3.2.3.3. Other Legal Rules

The ordinance also modified a text that allowed requests for evidence to be filed in a later stage of the proceedings on the grounds of ignorance or lack of instruction of the party, adding that such a request will be admissible only if the party is not assisted or represented by a lawyer.

3.3. *The Principle of the Active Role of the Judge*

Professor Eugen Herovanu wrote in 1932: 'The new laws everywhere are constantly extending the powers of the judge and his right to intervene in the proceedings. ... His freedom in appreciating and choosing solutions ... and means ... finds itself in a continuous advancement'.[36] This is an example of the theoretical reflection that substantiated the modifications of the procedural law brought by the law of 1900 and the Acceleration Laws. They introduced and reinforced, as already pointed out,[37] judicial activism in Romanian civil procedure.

The Socialist system nevertheless promoted the principle of the active role of the judge as its own revolutionary achievement.[38] After 1989, the principle was maintained in Romanian procedure, despite opinions considering it a Socialist principle that must be promptly discarded.[39]

The principle was conceived to impact on finding the truth, but its capacity to also have an influence on efficiency was discovered early.[40]

As for finding the truth, the Code of Civil Procedure states that 'the judge is entitled to require the parties to offer clarifications ... regarding the facts and legal

36 Herovanu 1932, p. 346.

37 See 'Acceleration Laws' in Section 3.2.1., and n. 21. See also Cădere 1928, p. 63-64, on the role of the judge during the proceedings.

38 Hilsenrad & Stoenescu 1957, p. 37: 'The principle of the passive role of the court was established in our Code of Civil Procedure too, in its version before the ... 1948 restructuring. In Socialist law, ... the judge ceases to be a passive arbitrator who collects and weighs, without intervening, the demands of the parties'. But see n. 40 above. See also Art. 95 of the CPC in its 1947 version (in Văiteanu 1947, p. 14), and Arts. 129 and 130 of the 1958 version of the CPC (Codul 1958). There is no essential difference.

39 Ciobanu 1997, p. 132, mentions this conception and offers arguments against it.

40 See, for example, Păduraru *et al.* 1943, p. 29: 'the function of the judge cannot be limited to that of being merely an arbitrator for the parties ... , he must do justice ... because the social interest demands that courts are not obstructed by endless lawsuits and economic opportunities are not held up for years'; and, they continue, the 1943 Acceleration Law introduced 'judge's prerogatives to organize/manage the course of the proceedings and the capacity to impose the obligation to carry on the legal action on the [reluctant] parties'.

grounds they assert for substantiating their demands and defences, and also to put in discussion any legal or factual circumstances ... The judges can order the taking of evidence they consider necessary, even if the parties oppose'.

On the other hand, 'the principle of the active role of the judge' also refers to the involvement of the judge in the expedient resolution of the case. Such an obligation is not specifically prescribed by the current Code of Civil Procedure but its existence proceeds from the purpose itself of the judicial activity'.[41] I would add that the obligation can be easily detected in various disparate rules in the Code.[42] The judge, indeed, conducts the proceedings, can order the parties[43] to accomplish procedural activities (e.g., delivering written submissions (arguments),[44] producing explanatory notes or various other documents - including written evidence, providing information and meeting the appointed experts) and sets conditions and time-limits for such actions. The judge may impose sanctions if someone fails to comply with legal prescriptions or court orders.[45] The judge also has the duty to attempt to reconcile the parties (settle).

The power of the court in Romania to boost efficiency through the management of the taking of evidence is obviously dependent on the legal framework, the whole structure of the process, and also the timing and the

41 Leş 2005, p. 42. The author also mentions the provisions of the 2003 revised Constitution, according to which (Art. 21(3)) 'the parties have the right to ... the resolution of cases in a reasonable time'.

42 See, e.g., Art. 129(1) CPC. The obligation was explicitly expressed by Ordinance No. 138/2000: 'the judge, during the whole trial, conducts the proceedings, watches that legal rules are observed and has the power to ... give the necessary orders for the lawsuit to be carried out'. Law No. 219/2005 removed the phrase, even though the rule was always practised in the courts (also after the removal of the text).

43 Or other persons or authorities.

44 Submissions or arguments can be oral and/or written, final (closing) or intermediate (the latter - usually on legal issues or any incidents appearing in the course of the proceedings).

45 Art. 108 CPC: 'The court may impose fines for a number of procedural violations, such as, among others: the calling into question, in bad faith, of the writing or signature on a document [when confronted with a document, a party must confirm or challenge the fact that the document is written and signed by him]; failure of the witness to appear in court; failure of the lawyer or representative of the party to appear in court, or their act of non-fulfilling their duties, if they cause the delay of proceedings; refusal of the appointed expert to accept the appointment, or the act of not submitting his/her opinion in the scheduled time-limit or refusing to present clarifications requested by the court; the act of the head of an institution assigned to deliver an expert opinion of not taking the necessary measures for its execution or for its completion on time; the act of the one that holds a document or an object of not presenting it in the time-limit set by the court; refusal or omission of an authority or another person to communicate the information requested by the court, within the time-limit which was established'. The judge (that is, the judge responsible for receiving and registering the statement of claim, who can be the president of the court or another appointed judge) can instruct the plaintiff to complete or modify the claim if it does not meet the legal requirements, and can order the stay of the proceedings if the plaintiff does not fulfil this duty (Art. 114(1)-(4) CPC). The stay of the proceedings ordered by the judge as a sanction will result in the putting aside, in the archives, of the case file and can eventually lead to the 'extinction' of the lawsuit - if the party does not take any action to carry it forward during a certain amount of time (six months in commercial matters, one year in other matters).

conditions of the admissibility of evidence[46] being predetermined by the law. The court enjoys only limited discretion in this field; it will mostly have to observe and enforce the rules. Knowing, sensing how to do this properly would nevertheless be quite consequential. The most important tool it possesses is the possibility to censor the requests for evidence of the parties or lawyers, dismissing whatever it considers illegitimate or unnecessary. It can also organise individualised schedules for the taking of complex evidence. It can impose (or rather certify) the forfeiture of the right to present evidence when the request is filed after the legal time-limits have expired. It can order the immediate production of evidence (after the party unjustifiably failed to do so at several court sessions) and impose forfeiture in case of noncompliance. It can reduce the number of proposed witnesses, and it can limit the duration of any oral argument.

3.4. *Adversarial Principle*

One of the first rules a trainee lawyer learns from his supervisor when he starts to practise his profession is that he has the responsibility, to his client, to direct and organise the course of the proceedings – that is, to interview the party, synthesise and present the facts to the court and administer the evidence. This becomes the way to deal with all cases in practice, which looks somewhat like a paradox, against the background of the existence of the principle of the active role of the judge, introduced in Romanian procedure as early as the 1920s, strongly emphasised for a long period of time (more than forty years) during the Socialist regime, and preserved all but unchallenged after the fall of totalitarianism.

A number of circumstances can explain this seeming paradox. First may be the legacy of the French model. One of the features of this model, also adopted in Romania, is the fact that a part of the evidentiary rules is to be found in the Civil Code. While some evidentiary rules in the Romanian Code of Civil Procedure were modified and new principles were introduced in the 1900s, an important Civil Code rule regarding evidence remained active: 'the party who makes an affirmation before the court must prove it'.[47] The text expresses almost literally the ancient rule *ei incumbit probatio qui dicit*. The same rule can be discovered in the way the pleading documents were regulated:[48] the statement of claim, answer and counterclaim had to include in their contents mention of the evidence offered in support of the

46 See, for the phase of the process when evidence requests are to be filed, n. 25; for the conditions of admissibility of evidence, see 'Rules regarding the admissibility of evidence' in Section 3.6.2.

47 Art. 1169 of the Romanian Civil Code (which has a different wording than the corresponding Art. 1315 of the French Civil Code: *Celui qui réclame l'exécution d'une obligation doit la prouver. Réciproquement, celui qui se prétend libéré doit justifier le paiement ou le fait qui a produit l'extinction de son obligation* – a person who claims the performance of an obligation must prove it. Reciprocally, a person who claims to be released must substantiate the payment or the fact which has produced the extinction of his obligation (Translation according to Legifrance – <http://195.83.177.9/code/liste.phtml?lang=uk&c=22&r=476#art4378>, last consulted in June 2012).

48 Since 1925 – see Cădere 1928, p. 262.

allegations of the parties.[49] It appears that the original adversarial character of the procedure was far from being relinquished. Instead, it was complemented with inquisitorial attributes.

What happened during the Socialist period and why such consistent adversarial traits did not disappear we can only postulate. It may be the old 'habits of the court'[50] that proved to be enduring: Socialist lawyers were never fully 'Socialist' in essence.[51] Courts may not have actually been quite so 'active' as was proclaimed, but many (most?) times 'passive and reactive'[52] (despite the fact that, for example, judicial inactivity represented grounds for appeal).[53] These all may also have a political explanation - a 'fracture' existed between Romania and the U.S.S.R. in the late 1960s and 1970s, hence a general tendency towards a reduction of any influence originating in that era.

However, it does not seem that introducing inquisitorial traits and maintaining adversarial ones was an accident of those earlier times when this evolution occurred. Ever since, Romanian civil procedure has developed and maintained combined features that may prove today an adequate mix - which may ensure a balance between the powers of the judge and those of the parties.[54]

As regards evidence, parties primarily have the duty to provide it. But the judge also has the authority to take measures for finding the truth. In recent years, case law on the principle of the active role of the judge actually shows a decisive detachment from the previous 'Socialist' spirit. Various decisions state today, for example, that: 'the active role of the court, prescribed by Article 130[55] of the Code of Civil Procedure, cannot justify the court in substituting itself in the procedural

49 The regulation of the pleading documents remained essentially unchanged. Another text (Art. 129-1 *in fine*) also states, somewhat redundantly, that 'parties have the duty ... to prove their claims and defenses'.

50 *Les habitudes du Palais* are mentioned by Vincent and Guinchard 1999 as factors leading to the modest results of the 1935, 1944 and 1958 French reforms tending to increase the powers of the judge (p. 480).

51 As Professor Alan Uzelac puts it in Uzelac 2010, p. 380. This may also mean that the new spirit of judicial activism did not find particularly fertile ground in 1920s Romania either.

52 Uzelac 2011.

53 Art. 304(2) point 2 of the Code of Civil Procedure, in its 1952-1993 wording: 'the judgment is not well founded when the court did not ascertain all the facts from which it could have drawn a just conclusion regarding the relations between the parties and their correlative rights'. Porumb 1962, p. 41: the appellate court could have 'examine[d] the well-founded character of the judgment brought in appeal. During the examination, the appellate court will [also] verify ... if the lower court exercised its active role'. Ciobanu 1986, p. 34: 'The establishment ... of the active role of the judge represents a safeguard for the finding of the truth, because, under the sanction of the quashing (cassation) of the decision in the appellate court', the judge has a number of [correspondent] duties. But legal theory pointed out that 'the active role does not deny the right of the parties to take the initiative'- see Hilsenrad & Stoenescu 1957, p. 37; Negru and Radu 1987, p. 37.

54 According to Deleanu 2005, p. 649, rules of evidence are characterised by liberalism (as an expression of the principle of party initiative, under the court's control and as far as the law provides), equality of the parties, loyalty (or good faith in finding the truth) and activism (of both the parties and the court, for the finding of truth and justice).

55 Currently, Art. 129 of the CPC.

position of the party and in defending its [i.e., the latter's] interests'; 'the civil lawsuit is, as a general rule, a suit of private interests; the active role of the judge must be understood' as 'ensuring a balance in association with the other principles of the civil process - party initiative and the adversarial principle'; 'the appellate court had the possibility, and not the duty, to order the taking of evidence, because its active role does not mean to transgress the principle of party initiative; the duty to prove the claims belonged to the plaintiff, according to Article 1669 of the Civil Code'.[56] Generally, it may be said that the parties have the (right and) duty to be actively involved in the proceedings: according to the CPC, 'parties have the duty ... to pursue the advancement and conclusion of the lawsuit'.[57]

This way of positioning the parties and the judge in litigation prevented situations that occurred in other ex-Socialist countries. In Croatia, for example, the active role largely obstructed efficiency: 'the collection of evidence was an inexhaustible source ... [of] delays', in the name of 'the sacred duty of the judge to find the "material truth"'.[58] 'The ... strengthening of the adversarial principle and the active roles of the parties ... has been regarded' in Croatia 'as the optimum means to achieve faster proceedings'.[59] On the contrary, in Romania (certainly in the years after 1989), whenever the court took, *sua sponte*, the initiative to order the taking of evidence, while parties were assisted by lawyers who already requested evidence, such an action looked (leastways for the lawyer) not necessarily illegitimate, but ostentatious and suspicious anyway.

3.5. *Means of Evidence*

The rules of evidence are governed by the postulate of 'legality' - in order to be admissible, any submitted evidence must be such as is prescribed by the law. The means of evidence are therefore delineated by the Code of Civil Procedure and the Civil Code:[60] written documents;[61] witness testimony; inspection by the judge 'on-site'; expert opinions (reports); interrogation/questioning by the opposing party.[62]

56 Boroi & Spineanu-Matei 2005, p. 236. It should be noted that the principle of the active role of the judge, at least the way it is seen today, raises a problem: if the court has the possibility, and not the duty, to be actively involved in the proceedings, it may do so in an arbitrary and partial manner, without the possibility of being challenged (see, for a similar observation, Van Rhee 2008b, p. 56; see also, for a critical comment on the possibility of the judge raising grounds for appeal *ex officio*, Spinei 2008, p. 217, n. 1.

57 Art. 129(1) CPC, *in limine*.

58 Uzelac 2010, p. 384 and *passim*.

59 *Ibidem*, p. 392.

60 In accordance with the French model.

61 In the same manner as in French law, there are two categories of documents that may certify the existence of rights and obligations - 'authentic documents' (drawn up by an authorised official, usually a notary public) and 'documents under private signature' (drafted or signed by the parties alone); electronic documents are mentioned in the NCPC.

62 The interrogation may lead to a 'confession' (a recognition of certain facts); the confession may also be spontaneous, that is, made in the absence of a formal interrogation. Interrogation was called *la preuve la plus inutile du monde* (the most useless means of evidence in the world) and a *gaspillage d'activité procesuelle* (waste of procedural activity) - Oberto 1997. In my →

The oath[63] was eliminated in 1950. The category of real (material, physical) evidence will be introduced by the New Code of Civil Procedure.[64]

3.6. *Efficiency-oriented Evidentiary Rules*

A number of legal prescriptions establish rules intended to secure a more efficient evidentiary procedure. These rules, most of them regularly employed in civil law systems, may regard the way various relations (transactions) must be documented at the very moment they are concluded, the way certain relations may be proved in court, or the procedure itself (time-limits for proposing and producing evidence, conditions for its admissibility).

3.6.1. Pre-action Rules

The Establishment of a Number of Legal (or Judicial) Presumptions

Certain facts are presumed by the law to be true and, therefore, no evidence is required to prove that fact (e.g., in family cases, the mother's husband is presumed to be the father of the child; the goods acquired by spouses during marriage are presumed to be common goods).[65] In certain cases, only particular means of evidence can overturn a presumption (e.g. the presumption that the debt is extinguished, generated by the act of the remission of the deed to the debtor, can only be overturned by way of confession).

opinion, such statements may be subject to discussion. It is true that in many cases, due to the position of the party (who is not a witness and cannot be prosecuted because of the way he answers when questioned in court), the party will not willingly 'confess'. But in some cases it may still contribute to the finding of truth. And, in principle, a recognised fact does not need to be proved.

63 The 'decisory' or 'decisive' oath is administered by one party to the opposing party as regards a specific fact; the case is concluded on the basis of the statement made under oath. The 'suppletory' oath may be ordered by the court to both parties to compensate for insufficient evidence.

64 The Code of Criminal Procedure has always contained rules on real evidence.

65 The 'community of goods' (joint ownership) was the only legal regime regarding the goods of the spouses under the Socialist Family Code. The new Civil Code, entered into force in October 2011, introduced alternative possibilities. Under the previous regulation, the case law also created a judicial presumption according to which the spouses, in case of the partition of the community of goods, owned equal shares of the 'community'. The presumption, however, could be overturned, producing evidence that the shares were different in size.

The Obligation of Constituting Written Documents to Prove the Existence of most Agreements (The Documents are required ad probationem)
The rationale behind this old rule is the fact that documents present a high degree of veracity and are easy to be presented in court as evidence. By organising such a pre-litigation documentary system, the work of the courts is obviously simplified in case of later disputes.

3.6.2. Pending Litigation Rules

Rules for Submitting Evidence
Already for a long time, the issue of the timeframe for presenting evidence has been governed by the principle that requests to submit evidence can only be made by the parties *in limine litis*, either through the pleading documents or no later than the 'first day of appearance'.[66] Failing to comply with this restriction is sanctioned with forfeiture of the right to present evidence.

Rules Regarding the Admissibility of Evidence
a) General conditions of admissibility. In order for a request for evidence to be granted, there are a number of general conditions to be fulfilled by any piece of evidence: legality (any piece of evidence must be prescribed by the law; it must not fall under a particular interdiction);[67] verisimility/credibility (the evidence must head towards proving possible, credible facts); pertinence (the evidence must tend to prove facts that present a connection with the case); and conclusiveness (the evidence must be able to lead to the resolution of the case).[68]
b) Particular conditions of admissibility. Special conditions govern particular means of evidence. Witness evidence, for example, is non-admissible if it aims to prove a legal act (transaction) which has a value of more than the equivalent of €60 or if it aims to prove against the content of a written document.[69]

Rules Regarding the Taking of Evidence
a) General rules:[70]
Evidence must be taken before any arguments on the merits of the claim. All evidence will be taken, as a general rule, in the order established by the court. Proof and counter proof must be produced, as far as possible, at the same time.

66 See n. 24.
67 See 'Particular conditions of admissibility' in Section 3.6.2.
68 There may be evidence that, even if it is 'pertinent', it is not 'conclusive'. For example, when an introductory claim is filed for *ex-delictu* damages, the defendants's request for evidence will be dismissed as 'inconclusive' (even if it is 'pertinent') if it tends to prove that the wrong was committed by him together with other persons, because in delictual matters parties have joint liability.
69 This is the sanction for failing to fulfil the obligation to pre-constitute documents for transactions. There are several exceptions: witness evidence is allowed when writings are impossible to be drafted.
70 Arts. 167 and 168 CPC.

b) Specific rules:
Documents must be presented together with the written introductory pleadings. The court can order the presentation of a document that relates to the case if it is held by a party. If the party refuses to answer questions about documents held by him, or if it is proved that a party has hidden or destroyed documents or holds documents and refuses to present them, the court may consider as proven the allegations of the party that requested the production of the document. If another person or institution holds the document and does not send it if required, the court can impose fines and order compensation for delay.[71]
Witnesses'[72] names and addresses must be included in the written introductory documents.[73] The court can limit the number of proposed witnesses. The witness who fails to appear in court can be brought in by agents of the police, based on an order issued by the judge. The proceedings can ultimately continue without the witness if it is impossible for the witness to be present.
Expert opinion. The issues to be addressed by the expert are proposed by the party and approved (ordered) by the court. The expert will present the conclusions in a report submitted to the court. Any objections a party would raise to the conclusions are to be exposed no later than the first hearing following the delivery of the report to the party.

3.7. *Means of Evidence and Incidents Susceptible to Cause Delay*

a) The expert's report.
According to some scholars, there are a number of reasons why experts 'are trouble'.[74] The experts in civil law systems are not the same as the 'expert witnesses' in the common law systems; nevertheless, they can cause trouble. One of the problems both categories can generate is the fact that they 'make mistakes'. The 'Continental' expert may not be, due to the legal 'shape' of his office, predisposed to make mistakes of the same nature as his common law counterpart,[75] but he may nevertheless be wrong. If the mistake is not corrected, it leads to a wrong court decision, which is a question of the quality of justice. If the mistake is corrected, this will cause delay. If a significant number of mistakes occur,[76] this denotes a problem that is structural, but it does not pertain to procedural rules.

71 Arts. 172-176 CPC.

72 See Arts. 186-188 CPC.

73 The Legislator's action was well intended: this way, it supposedly would already be possible to summon witnesses for the first hearing. This is impossible, though, because the court must verify, at the first hearing, the conditions of admissibility of the evidence. This, and any other issues, must also be brought into the arguments of the parties.

74 Fenner 1996 identifies 'The top ten reasons expert witnesses are trouble'.

75 *Ibidem.*

76 It is my opinion, based strictly on personal experience in courts, that too many mistakes appear in expert reports in Romania.

There is also another way expert opinions generate problems for the judicial system - they cause delay.[77] This is independent of the quality of the expert's work. If an expert opinion is ordered, it will take months for the report to be submitted. This circumstance does not pertain to procedural rules either. In order to overcome delays, measures should be taken to increase the number of the members of the expert corps. The possibility to achieve this is dependent on the existence of qualified and available personnel and the degree of reward they may find in this line of work. But the amount of the fees they can charge depends, in turn, on the general level of income of the population.

b) A cause for delay may also be found in the way the questioning of witnesses is conceived: the questions can be asked only by the judge;[78] the answers are rephrased by the judge and, in this 'remodelled' form, dictated to the clerk. This is a long-established pattern which is difficult to tackle: facing a similar problem, Croatian legal theory considered an alternative, but noticed it also generates inconvenience.[79]
c) If the previously mentioned issues are structural, a number of incidents can also arise, disrupting the linear course of the proceedings and generating delay. This is the case with the various motions challenging evidence, such as the request for investigating the authenticity of a document (relatively rare), motions challenging the procedure of producing the expert report, the inspection on-site, etc.[80]

Replacing witnesses or experts if necessary will also significantly prolong the proceedings.[81]

3.8. *The New Code of Civil Procedure (NCPC)*[82]

A new Romanian Code of Civil Procedure is expected to come into force; the latest official predictions indicating sometime in 2012. The new code is expected by many to eliminate a number of asserted problems of Romanian justice: the incoherence of

77 This seems to be a problem in many justice systems. In Austrian civil procedure, for example, one 'of the most significant reasons for delay' is 'the necessity to employ experts' - Oberhammer & Domej 2008, p. 62.

78 In practice, the party or the lawyer always formally solicits from the judge that he address the question the party or the lawyer expressed; most of the time, the judge does not repeat the question to the witness, unless he wants to rephrase it; the Code provides that, if requested, the judge can also allow the questions to be directly addressed to the witness.

79 In Croatia, fragments of the 'protocol' of the hearing are 'dictated by the judge ... every few minutes'. It was suggested that this technique should be replaced by an audio-visual record of the trial. But extracting transcripts of the records 'requires more time and expense' (Uzelac 2008, p. 89-90).

80 See Deleanu 2005, p. 673-680.

81 Sixty to one hundred wasted days to replace a witness (this includes all the procedural activity employed to bring to the court both the initially proposed witness and the replacement).

82 See, for further information on the new code, Spinei 2012.

case law and therefore the lack of predictability of judgments; the lack of speed in litigation and in enforcement proceedings; the overburdening of the courts; and others. Many (or most) provisions of the current code regarding evidence are maintained. A number of new ideas and rules are also introduced.

Statement of principles. Right from the outset, the NCPC enunciates that any person has, *inter alia,* the right to have his case judged 'within an optimal and predictable time. ... To this end, the court has the duty to take all measures allowed by the law and to ensure the expeditious advancement of the procedure'.[83]

Evidentiary rules will be unified. Currently, rules of evidence are provided for by the Code of Civil Procedure but also by the Civil Code, and some by the Commercial Code. In the future, the New Code of Civil Procedure will be the only legislative instrument to regulate evidence. The NCPC mentions electronic documents[84] and regulates material evidence as means of proof.

Ensuring speed; case-management elements.[85] On the first hearing date, the judge will estimate, after listening to the parties, the duration of the instruction phase. He will also inform the parties of the possibility of employing the procedure of the taking of evidence by the lawyers. Short intervals (even of a single day only) will be granted between hearing dates. The judge can impose duties[86] on the participants in the trial, and he can perform any action necessary for resolving the case. The participants can be informed of the measures ordered by means of, among other possibilities, telephone, fax and email.

The 'instruction' phase will take place in the judge's chambers and not in a public hearing in open court.[87]

The complaint for delaying the proceedings is a new procedure established by the NCPC in case procedural duties regarding the expeditious advancement of the procedure are not fulfilled. The complaint will be judged by another panel or a single judge of the same court that judges the delayed case. If the complaint is admitted, the court will immediately have to take the necessary measures to eliminate the circumstances that caused the delay. The judgment that dismisses the complaint can be challenged before the superior court.

83 Art. 6. The duties of the parties are no different when compared with the current system (see Art. 10 NCPC and the current Art. 129 CPC). The new text adds one phrase: 'parties have the duty ... to pursue the advancement *without delay* and the conclusion of the lawsuit'. The current content of the principle of the active role of the judge can be found almost identically in the phrasing of Art. 22 NCPC, but this time under the marginal title 'The role of the judge in finding the truth'. This is probably due to the fact that the active duty of the judge regarding the expeditious development of the procedure is distinctly provided by Art. 6 NCPC.

84 Electronic documents are presently, and will continue to be, regulated by other legislative acts.

85 Arts. 233-234, 236 NCPC.

86 Regarding the presentation of written evidence; providing information or a written answer to an interrogation; assistance, and support for timely producing an expert opinion.

87 See 'Conclusions' in Section 4.

4. Conclusions

It appears that the Romanian NCPC does not bring essential changes to the way the system of procedure was shaped during previous stages. Most provisions of the current code regarding evidence and the roles of the judge and the parties during the lawsuit were actually maintained. Objectively, there may not be much room for fundamental transformation[88] here, since the principle of responsibility and collaboration of the various participants towards finding the facts and the advancement of the proceedings is long established, and also there are a number of other rules.[89] But it seems that, for example, at least the notion of case-management will have to be further explored. As regards the new rules of the NCPC, they are reduced in number and their impact on efficiency will still have to be assessed. The provision, for example, that the judge will estimate the duration of the instruction phase may prove quite ineffective, since such an estimate can be reconsidered during the proceedings. On the other hand, it can only be assumed that the judge will also have to draft an actual detailed calendar of the activities.[90]

One of the most revolutionary ideas in the NCPC is the change of the structure of the instruction phase of the trial. Personally, I fail to understand how simply transforming one public and 'common' court session,[91] where a number of cases are heard successively, into the same number of non-public (series of) sessions, where each case is heard 'individually' *in camera*,[92] would be more efficient - at least so long as no improvement is also brought into the logistics of the judicial system. The number of cases assigned per judge (too high), the number of chambers (too small), the number (and role) of judicial clerks, the role of the judge[93] and of the lawyers,[94]

88 As happened, for example, in Croatia, where the adversarial principle replaced the active role of the judge (see Uzelac 2010, p. 384, 392 and *passim*).

89 The rules regarding the structure of the procedure (a written introductory phase, a preliminary hearing); the rule that all the claims, evidence and exceptions can be brought at the beginning of the proceedings only; etc.

90 See, for some considerations on the complaint for delaying the proceedings, Spinei 2012.

91 A case is, traditionally, judged in a series of court sessions (hearings). There is a time interval of two, three or more weeks between the sessions. At every session a number of cases (up to several dozen, even around one hundred occasionally - before first instance courts) are heard. At every session (or exceptionally between the sessions - in the event of inspections on-site) some parts of the procedural activity of various cases takes place (documents are submitted, witnesses or parties questioned, etc.).

92 The NCPC plans to change the traditional pattern regarding the arguments, providing that sessions will be non-public and will take place in chambers, which is supposed to provide a closer connection between the judge and the parties, and to make the intervals shorter (even of a single day only).

93 The (same) judge 'prepares' the case (takes evidence, decides the exceptions and incidents), hears the closing arguments and makes the final decision.

94 The taking of evidence by lawyers remains optional.

and the way the court archives are organised are currently unchanged,[95] and I do not see much chance that this situation will immediately become different.

95 This is why 'amendments of procedural law are ... a welcome opportunity to give a signal that something is being done against procedural delay – without having to spend more money on the judicial system', as noted by Oberhammer & Domej 2008, p. 62.

Bibliography

Boroi & Spineanu-Matei 2005
Boroi, G. & Spineanu-Matei, O., *Codul de procedură civilă - adnotat*, Bucureşti: All Beck, 2005.

Cădere 1928
Cădere, V.G., *Tratat de procedură civilă*,: Cultura Naţională, 1928.

Ciobanu 1986
Ciobanu, V.M., *Drept procesual civil*, I, Bucureşti: Universitatea din Bucureşti, 1986.

Ciobanu 1997
Ciobanu, V.M., *Tratat teoretic şi practic de procedură civilă*, Bucureşti: Naţional, 1997.

Ciobanu *et al.* 2001
Ciobanu, V.M., Boroi, G. & Nicolae, M., 'Modificările aduse Codului de procedură civilă prin Ordonanţa de urgenţă a Guvernului No. 138/2000', *Dreptul*, 2001, No. 1, p. 3-22.

Codul 1958
Codul de procedură civilă - text oficial, Bucureşti: Editura Ştiinţifică, 1958.

Deleanu 2005
Deleanu, I., *Tratat de procedură civilă*, I, Bucureşti: All Beck, 2005.

Fenner 1996
Fenner, G.M., 'Here's the Real Trouble with Experts!', <http://papers.ssrn.com/sol3/papers.cfm?abstract_id=1739866> (last consulted 15 October 2011).

Fix-Fierro 2003
Fix-Fierro, H., *Courts, Justice and Efficiency: a Socio-legal Study of Economic Rationality in Adjudication*, Oxford/Portland/Oregon: Hart Publishing Ltd., 2003.

Florea 2010
Florea, Gh., 'Exigenţe ale conduitei părţilor şi avocaţilor în asigurarea duratei rezonabile a proceselor', < www.juridice.ro/104695/exigente-ale-conduitei-partilor-si-avocatilor-in-asigurarea-duratei-rezonabile-a-proceselor.html>, last consulted 15 October 2011.

Herovanu 1932
Herovanu, E., *Principiile procedurii judiciare*, I, Bucureşti: Lupta, 1932.

Hilsenrad & Stoenescu 1957
Hilsenrad, A. & Stoenescu, I., *Procesul civil în R.P.R.*, Bucureşti: Editura Ştiinţifică, 1957.

Jean 2007
Jean, J.-P., 'La qualité des décisions de justice au sens du Conseil de l'Europe', in: Mbongo, P. (ed.), *La qualité des décisions de justice*, Éditions du Conseil de l'Europe, p. 30-47, <www.coe.int/t/dghl/cooperation/cepej/quality/Poitiers2007final.pdf>, last consulted 15 October 2011.

Leş 2002
Leş, I., *Drept procesual civil*, Bucureşti: Lumina Lex, 2002.

Leş 2004
Leş, I., 'Examen de drept comparat asupra sistemelor moderne de autoguvernare a magistraturii şi cu privire la noile reglementări adoptate de Parlamentul României', *Dreptul*, 2004, No. 11, p. 5-31.

Leş 2005
Leş, I., *Tratat de drept procesual civil*, Bucureşti: All Beck, 2005.

Negru & Radu 1987
Negru, V. & Radu, D., *Drept procesual civil*, Bucureşti: Editura Didactică şi Pedagogică, 1987.

Oberhammer & Domej 2008
Oberhammer, P. & Domej, T., 'Improving the efficiency of civil justice. Some remarks from an Austrian perspective', in: Van Rhee, C.H. & Uzelac, A. (eds.), *Civil Justice between Efficiency and Quality: From Ius Commune to the CEPEJ*, Antwerp/Oxford/Portland: Intersentia, 2008, p. 61-69.

Oberto 1997
Oberto, G., 'Les éléments de fait réunis par le juge: l'administration judiciaire de la preuve dans le procès civil italien', <http://www.giacomooberto.com/enm/-paris1997/frame.htm> (last consulted 15 October 2011).

Păduraru *et al.* 1943
Păduraru, Gh.D., Stoenescu, I.I., Protopopescu, G.V., *Accelerarea judecăților*, Bucureşti: Tiparul Românesc S.A.R., 1943.

Porumb 1962
Porumb, Gr., *Codul de procedură civilă comentat şi adnotat*, II, Bucureşti: Editura Ştiinţifică, 1962.

Shetreet 2011
Shetreet, S., 'Fundamental Values of the Justice System', <http://ssrn.com/-abstract=1837486>, last consulted 15 October 2011.

Spinei 2008
Spinei, S., *Recursul în procesul civil*, Bucureşti: Hamangiu, 2008.

Spinei 2012
Spinei, S., 'Romanian Civil Procedure. The Reform Cycles', in: Kramer, X.E. & Van Rhee, C.H. (eds.), *Civil Litigation in a Globalising World*, The Hague: T.M.C. Asser Press, 2012, p. 363-378.

Uzelac 2008
Uzelac, A., 'Reforming Mediterranean Civil Procedure: Is there a Need for Shock Therapy?', in: Van Rhee, C.H. & Uzelac, A. (eds.), *Civil Justice between Efficiency and Quality: From Ius Commune to the CEPEJ*, Antwerp/Oxford/Portland: Intersentia, 2008, p. 71-99.

Uzelac 2010
Uzelac, A., 'Survival of the Third Legal Tradition?', in: Walker, J. & Chase, O.G. (eds.), *Common Law, Civil Law and the Future of Categories*, Markham, Ontario: LexisNexis Canada Inc., 2010, p. 377-396.

Uzelac 2011
Uzelac, A., '"Material Truth" versus Fair Trial within a Reasonable Time: The Fight Continues?', presentation at the Public and Private Justice course and conference, Dubrovnik, 24 May 2011.

Văiteanu 1947
Văiteanu, Em. R., *Codul de procedură civilă de la 1900 cu modificările la zi*, Bucureşti: R. Cioflec, 1947.

Van Rhee 2008a
Van Rhee, C.H., 'The Development of Civil Procedural Law in Twentieth-century Europe: From Party Autonomy to Judicial Case-management and Efficiency', <http://arno.unimaas.nl/show.cgi?fid=14848>, last consulted 15 October 2011.

Van Rhee 2008b
Van Rhee, C.H., 'Dutch Civil Procedure: Reform and Efficiency', in: Van Rhee, C.H. & Uzelac, A. (eds.), *Civil Justice between Efficiency and Quality: From Ius Commune to the CEPEJ*, Antwerp/Oxford/Portland: Intersentia, 2008, p. 47-60.

Vincent & Guinchard 1999
Vincent, J. & Guinchard, S., *Procédure civile*, Paris: Dalloz, 1999.

V. Rijavec

EFFICIENCY VERSUS FAIRNESS IN CIVIL PROCEDURE IN SLOVENIA

1. Introduction

One of the goals of rules of civil procedure is to manage a litigation system well. But the design of procedural rules does present difficult questions of policy that at times implicate deep philosophical matters. There is a close and inescapable relationship between procedural and substantive law and every system of procedure must make normative trade-offs between fairness to the parties and economic efficiency. Substantive rights are only as good as the procedure available to enforce them. People can rely on others to use reasonable care, abide by their promises, respect privacy and avoid injury in large part because of the deterrent force of the substantive law, and that deterrence depends on a properly functioning procedural system.[1] One of the essential requirements is efficiency that enables adjudication within a reasonable time. The challenge for procedural law is to find the right balance between economics and protection of the rights of parties, the balance between benefit and cost. In Slovenia, procedural reform in its broader sense has been particularly focused on efficiency, due to extensive backlogs at the courts that arose while Slovenia was a part of Yugoslavia. Slovenia gained its independence in 1991 when the current legal system was instituted by the modern Constitution.[2] Like most of Europe, Slovenia has a codified system of law and a system of civil procedure similar to that of Austria and Germany, due to common historical roots[3] based on the Roman law tradition within the German circle. However, at the same time it is a specific national system of justice that is adversarial rather than inquisitorial and provides for judicial review.[4] The Constitutional Court is

1 Bone 2003, p. 2.

2 Ustava RS (the Constitution of the Republic of Slovenia, referred to herein as the Constitution), Official Gazette of the Republic of Slovenia/I, Nos. 33/1991, 42/97, 66/2000, 24/03, 69/04 and 68/06.

3 Ivanič 1999, p. 17 *et seq.*

4 The principle of judicial review is explicitly a part of the modern Slovenian Constitution. A core concept is that of the rule of law, a government based on law, in which citizens are guaranteed equality and in which government decisions may be challenged in court (Arts. 2, →

Slovenia's highest body for the protection of constitutionality, legality and human rights. The Constitution declares Slovenia as a social state and a state based on the principle of law.[5]

The Slovenian rules governing civil procedure,[6] like their counterpart in other countries, set out how a civil action is to proceed. They explain how a lawsuit must be commenced,[7] what kind of service of documents is required,[8] the types of pleadings and motions permitted[9] and provide for appropriate court orders.[10] The rules also denote the timing and manner of depositions and discovery,[11] the conduct of trials[12] and the process for issuing judgment.[13] In addition, procedure in Slovenia

22 and 23). The Constitutional Court of the Republic of Slovenia focuses on judicial review and constitutional interpretation. It deals with constitutional matters and plays a vital role through its interpretative rulings on the Basic Law.

5 This principle requires the clear division of competences between state authorities; Constitutional Court Decision U-I-98/95, Official Gazette of the Republic of Slovenia 44/96; see more Jambrek 2002, p. 53 *et seq.*

6 The principal Act is the Civil Procedure Act, *Zakon o pravdnem postopku* – ZPP, which replaced the old Yugoslav Civil Procedure Act of 1977 that remained in force after the independence of Slovenia until 1999; Official Gazette of the Republic of Slovenia 26/1999, amendments: 83/2002, 12/2003, 36/2004, 73/2007, 101/2007, 102/2007, 45/2008, 45/2008, 62/2008, 111/2008, 116/2008, 121/2008, 47/2009, 57/2009, 12/2010, 49/2010, 50/2010, 107/2010, 43/2011, 58/2011.

7 Civil proceedings shall be initiated by the plaintiff. The filing of the complaint is deemed to commence the action; Art. 179 ZPP. There are three essential elements that the complaint must contain: 1. statement of the grounds upon which the court's jurisdiction depends; 2. statement of claim showing that the plaintiff is entitled to relief; and 3. relief – demand for judgment which the plaintiff seeks.

8 The service of the complaint, of all court decisions, where a legal remedy is foreseen, and of the extraordinary remedies has to be performed personally to the addressee (Art. 142/1 ZPP). The service of documents in judicial matters is organised by the court.

9 Either in the answer or by separate motion the defendant may attack the validity of the complaint in a number of ways. But he can also acknowledge the claim or abstain from filing the answer. The plaintiff can file a change of his action (of the complaint), he can dismiss the action or he can even denounce his claim completely. The parties can settle the claim (judicial settlement).

10 The judge has to govern the proceedings by issuing procedural court orders as preliminary rulings, the orders dealing with the taking of evidence, with procedural prerequisites, etc. to enable clearing up the facts through his formal guidance.

11 The principle of concentration of the proceedings became very much accentuated with the last reform; see below.

12 Civil proceedings in the court of original jurisdiction shall be conducted by a professional judge based on the principle of substantive and formal guidance of the process. The present code defines the cases when the court shall sit in a panel (Art. 15 ZPP). The proceedings in disputes under the jurisdiction of district courts shall be conducted by a single judge (Art. 31 ZPP). The proceedings in disputes under the jurisdiction of circuit courts shall be conducted by a single judge, except when the statute provides that such proceedings be conducted by a panel of judges (Art. 33 ZPP). The proceedings before the high court shall be conducted by a panel consisting of three judges (Art. 36 ZPP).

13 See below.

governs available remedies.[14] In appropriate cases, the rules provide for special types of procedures.[15] The Slovenian legal system belongs to the Continental tradition and therefore in many respects, procedural as well as substantive, it falls within the German legal tradition.

2. Efficiency and Fair Trial

2.1. *General*

Efficiency is an important part of any system of adjudication; it is certainly not the only relevant value. The goal of civil litigation is implementation of the rights of the substantive law, in a manner expressed in the Slovenian Constitution and in relevant Conventions. Thus, the European Convention on Human Rights[16] and the Constitution guaranty the right to an independent and impartial judge,[17] to the public nature of court proceedings,[18] to a legal remedy,[19] to equal treatment in any proceeding before a court[20] and the right to be heard[21] with all its derivations (e.g. the right to present evidence, the right of civil litigants to the assistance of counsel at state expense).[22 23]

One major goal of the Slovenian legislator with the first Act and all later amendments was to streamline the Slovenian judicial system and improve judicial efficiency, but in practice it is not always easy to implement new rules in accordance with the fair trial principle. However, it can be said that the current Civil Procedure Act (ZPP) provides a solid procedural basis for the resolution of individual disputes.

14 Remedies are divided into ordinary (appeal) and extraordinary remedies (Revision, Petition for Protection of Legality, Re-opening of Proceedings, Action for Annulment of a Court Settlement and Action for Annulment of an Arbitration Award). Arts. 333, 367, 385, 392, 394 ZPP.

15 According to the ZPP, special types of procedures are: proceedings in matrimonial actions and actions concerning the relations between parents and children, proceedings in disputes for disturbance of possession, issue of payment order, small-claims procedure, arbitration proceedings and proceedings in commercial litigations. Arts. 406-497 ZPP.

16 Right to a fair trial, Art. 6, EU Convention on Human Rights, Official Gazette of the Republic of Slovenia (13.6.1994) MP 7-41/1994 (RS 33/1994).

17 Art. 23 of the Constitution.

18 Art. 24 of the Constitution.

19 Art. 25 of the Constitution.

20 Art. 22 of the Constitution.

21 Art. 22 of the Constitution, Art. 5 ZPP.

22 The Constitution of the Republic of Slovenia does not expressively regulate the right to free legal assistance, but it can be derived from the constitutional principles as: equality before the law (Art. 14), the right to judicial protection (Art. 23), the right to a legal remedy (Art. 25) and even from the principle of the rule of law. The unified system of free legal assistance was instituted by *Zakon o brezplačni pravni pomoči* (Free Legal Aid Act; Official Gazette of the Republic of Slovenia 96/04); see more Kežmah 2004, p. 380.

23 Galič 2000, p. 25-26.

Of course, rules of procedure are only one component of any judicial system's efficiency. The very structure of the courts also contributes to or interferes with judicial efficiency. One example is the possibility that judicial specialisation, advanced through courts of specialised subject-matter jurisdiction, might improve efficiency. It is possible that further reform of the Slovenian system of justice, but particularly through a better organisation of judicial services, might provide for further efficiency while preserving other values. The current situation is still far from optimal.

2.2. *Measures to Accelerate Procedure*

Among a number of important efficiency-oriented provisions under the ZPP, special instructions for the promotion of alternative dispute resolution proceedings (court settlement, mediation, arbitration), all of which tend to have relatively simple rules of procedure in comparison to the highly formalised procedures seen in the courts, have been particularly emphasized in the last amendments to the Act from 1999.[24] The first hearing is devoted to the attempt to achieve a court settlement or to attempt mediation.[25] Greater emphasis has been placed on the preliminary examination of the action and preparation of a main hearing by the judge and clerks. Special effort was devoted to the rules for better discipline of the parties and concentration of proceedings, including rules limiting the introduction of new facts, evidence and allegations to the first motions and to the first hearing, as well as the provisions for judgment without a trial (e.g. default judgments)[26] and legal sanctions when a party is too passive. The objectives can also be reached by other traditional rules for accelerating and facilitating litigation, including those concerning burdens of pleading and proof, summary judgment, prevention from frivolous litigation, rules on joinder of parties and claims, rules on summary proceedings as a small-claims procedures and rules on proceedings to issue and enforce a payment order based on an authentic document,[27] etc. Economics and efficiency should generally find more expression in every feature of the procedural system.

2.3. *General Principles of Procedure*

On the other hand, the procedural mechanisms and methods must also provide appropriate legal protection and fair access to justice. To this end, the general principles of fair trial, as mentioned earlier, are derived from the Constitution as the building blocks of the ZPP. One of the most important ones is the principle that both parties should be heard: each party to the action should be granted at least the

24 See n. 6.

25 Mediators appointed in this system are mostly retired judges.

26 Art. 318 ZPP.

27 Enforcement based on an authentic document, Art. 23 Civil Enforcement Act, *juncto* Arts. 431-441 ZPP.

opportunity to be heard on the opposing party's claims and assertions.[28] The Civil Procedure Act provides the system of service of process and other requisites of reasonable notification.[29] The cause of concern within the system of notification is usually the substituted service. In cases of deficient service or other deprivation of opportunity to be heard, legal remedies are provided, among them also the re-opening of the procedure.

The parties are the masters of the process, which is commenced, conducted and terminated by them, but the judge still plays an active role. He manages the case and issues rulings that determine the matters on which he will decide. At the same time, he is not allowed to consider any facts or proof that have not been asserted or proposed by one or the other party.

2.3.1. Limitation of *Ius Novorum*

Parties are bound to state all the facts upon which their motions are based, to adduce evidence required to establish the truth of their statements, and to produce declarations regarding the statements and evidence adduced by the opposing party at the opening hearing.[30]

At later hearings, the parties are allowed to present new facts and new evidence only if at the opening hearing they were prevented from presenting them by reasons beyond their control (due to no fault of their own). Facts stated and evidence adduced contrary to this rule must be ignored.[31] The parties are also entitled to adduce new facts and evidence even on appeal under the condition that, due to no fault of their own, this was not possible in time.

This legal institute (which has been enacted and abolished many times in the past) was in the stricter manner introduced into Slovenian civil procedural law by the Code of Civil Procedure of 1999, although some legal scholars had emphasised its controversial nature.[32] It is considered a method of making civil proceedings faster, because the possibilities for the parties to delay the procedure by stating new facts and presenting new evidence are restricted now. Consequently, it imposes some discipline on litigants.

This legal institute continues to be controversial. Because parties can introduce new facts and present new evidence subsequent to the opening hearing only in limited circumstances, they adduce all kinds of facts and evidence (important and not important to the litigation) to ensure that they have missed nothing on which they may later need to rely. Moreover, ascertaining who is responsible for the

28 Art. 5 ZPP.

29 After becoming a Member State of the EU, Regulation 1348/2000 on Service in Member States of Judicial and Extrajudicial Documents in Civil or Commercial Matters also became internal law of the Republic of Slovenia; as a successor state of Yugoslavia, Slovenia signed the Hague Convention on the Service Abroad of Judicial and Extrajudicial Documents in Civil or Commercial Matters of 1969.

30 Art. 286 ZPP.

31 *Ibidem.*

32 Juhart 1961, p. 74 and 75; same also Ude 1998, p. 971; Wedam 1996, p. 15; Butala 1999, p. 1159.

delayed stating of facts or presenting of evidence is an additional burden on the court. In addition, given that this rule is subject to varying interpretations, there is inevitably some uncertainty in the parties' and in the court's actions. Also, parties are often, in cases where representation by an attorney is not mandatory, not capable of making a legal analysis of their case and consequently not capable of stating all the relevant facts and presenting all the relevant evidence at the opening hearing. In the Slovenian system, the parties are in general not allowed to claim that they did not know the law, and accordingly a party not represented by an attorney cannot justify a delayed adducing of facts and evidence by saying that he was not aware of the limitation of *ius novorum*.[33]

On the one hand, the limitations imposed by *ius novorum* prevent the parties from acting negligently or deceptively. The late submission of facts and evidence can be admitted if the evidence was collected during the proceedings. The concept 'without fault' needs to be adjudicated thoroughly. As a result, the judge who conducts the trial has to help the parties with questions to adduce all relevant facts and evidence at the opening hearing or even earlier in the stage of the preparation of the hearing.[34] On the other hand, a party cannot justify his delayed adducing of facts and evidence by claiming that the judge failed to ensure that the party brought them forward. Since the limitation imposed by the *ius novorum* rule is binding, courts have to plan and organise the opening hearing thoroughly. Postponements of the opening hearing sessions should become exceptions and no longer usual events at courts as it has been up to now. Despite these modern rules, the standard of a single hearing is still far from being reached.

2.3.2. Fact-finding Methods

The Civil Procedure Act charges a judge to conduct the trial actively, to take testimony as an oral deposition using trial techniques of examination. The judge asks questions first, then he permits questioning by the parties.

2.3.3. Principle of Free Evaluation of Evidence

The decision whether or not the parties have proven their case shall be based upon the opinion of the court after careful and thorough evaluation of every piece of evidence in and of itself, and of the evidence as a whole, and considering the outcome of the entire proceedings.[35] The fact-finding body in the Slovenian system is a single first instance judge and in certain cases a panel. The appellate court decision only exceptionally can rely on facts different from the ones found as proven by the court of original jurisdiction.

33 Rijavec 1999, p. 393-410.
34 Butala 1999, p. 1161-1162.
35 Art. 8 ZPP.

2.3.4. Iura Novit Curia

The role of a judge is in the first place supplying a legal qualification of the case and deciding on legal questions. In their pleadings the parties can present their legal statements, but the court is not bound by them.

2.4. *Rendering Decisions*

2.4.1. General

Under Slovenian law, decisions rendered in civil proceedings take the form either of a judgment or of a decree. A claim is in principle decided by a judgment, while an action for disturbance of possession (a special civil proceeding) is determined by a decree. A payment order issues in the form of a decree as well. On the other hand, procedural decisions and decisions relating to costs are always made by decree.[36] The traditional and still most common form of judgment in trials is the general one, by which the court finds for either the plaintiff or the defendant after an adversarial process. The ZPP requires the trial judge to evaluate findings of fact and make conclusions of law when entering judgment. The judgment must be supported by grounds for the particular decision in order to enable the appellate court to control the process of decision-making. Summary judgment without detailed explanation is only provided in small-claims procedure.[37]

2.4.2. Default Judgments

2.4.2.1. Mandatory Written Answer

An action that fulfils all formalities (Article 180 ZPP) and in respect of which the required court fee has been paid shall be served by the court on the defendant to permit the defendant to make a defence plea in the form of a written answer delivered to the court within thirty days after regular service. The action shall be served on the defendant personally together with the relevant documents.[38] The defence plea has to be supported by grounds - well substantiated. The defendant has to adduce the objections which would cause a dismissal of the claim if they were proven as correct. The omission of this requirement causes the court to regard the defence plea as non-existent.[39] The purpose of this rule is to force the defendant to play an active and constructive role in the trial. The documents and proposed other evidence for the asserted facts have immediately to be attached to the defence plea.

The requirement for a substantiated defence plea is not known in German and Austrian legislation. It did not exist in the previous Code of Civil Procedure (ZPP

36 Art. 128 ZPP.

37 Arts. 457, 496 ZPP.

38 Art. 276 ZPP.

39 Art. 278 ZPP.

1977). Any kind of objection by the defendant to the action used to successfully prevent the issuing of a default judgment (also in Germany and in Austria). The courts interpreted any answer by the defendant that did not contain an admission of the claim as an objection to the claim. In fact, courts interpreted many other written responses by defendants, especially those requesting postponement of the (opening) hearing session, as objections to the claim. It was held that due to the immense consequences of a default judgment the defendant needed a better opportunity to be heard in court.[40]

However, the introduction of the previously mentioned restriction brought positive results. Parties in the modern process have to be charged with more responsibility for focused proceedings, and they need understandable and exact instructions in this respect when the summonses are served.

2.4.2.2. *Requirements for Validity of the Default Judgment*

If the defendant fails to file the defence plea within thirty days of being served with the action, under current law the court shall render a judgment granting the claim (default judgment), provided that:

1. the action has been duly served on the defendant;
2. the action does not contain a claim based on rights that the parties may not dispose with[41] (contradiction to mandatory legal and ethical rules);
3. the claim is legally substantiated as regards the facts; and
4. the facts upon which the claim is based do not conflict with the evidence adduced by the plaintiff or with facts of which the court may take notice *ex officio*.

a) Substantiated Claim

For a default judgment to be issued the court must be able to conclude that, assuming all the facts asserted in the action are true, the proposed relief is legally well founded.[42]

b) Contradictions between Statements in the Complaint and Adduced Evidence

The court may base its decision to issue a default judgment only on facts that are generally known or adduced in the action. The latter are presumed to be admitted by the defendant, because he has not objected to them in due time, although he had the opportunity to do so. The court does not test whether the facts adduced in the action are true; it only puts to the test whether the claim is well founded if the facts adduced in the action are presumed to be true.[43] However, when evidence accompanies the action (e.g. documents), the court needs to examine whether there is any contradiction between the adduced evidence and asserted or generally

40 Juhart, Ude & Wedam-Lukić 1974, p. 371-372.

41 Art. 3/3 ZPP.

42 Ude 2002, p. 308; Galič 2003, p. 165.

43 Galič 2003, p. 165.

known facts. If a contradiction exists, the court will not issue a default judgment.[44] If the court does not find any contradiction between the facts asserted in the action and adduced evidence, it must issue the default judgment regardless of the nature or the quality of the adduced evidence. It must do so even if the adduced evidence would not be adequate to prove the claim if a trial were held.[45]

c) Forbidden Dispositions
If the substance of the claim in the action is in contradiction with mandatory statutes or moral rules,[46] the default judgment will not be issued.[47] When the court issues it anyway and an appeal is filed, then the appellate court has the official duty to annul the judgment of the lower court.[48]

2.4.2.3. *Legal Nature of the Default Judgment*

As mentioned earlier, the court does not test whether the facts adduced in the action are true; it only puts to the test whether the claim is founded upon the law under the presumption that the facts adduced in the action are true.[49] Therefore, default judgments fall into the category of so-called one-sided judgments. A partial default judgment is also possible because in his defence plea the defendant can object to the claim in whole or in part. When the defendant does not object to some claim among several independent claims or to some part of the claim that can be adjudicated separately, then, provided that all other legal prerequisites are met, a partial default judgment can be issued.[50] Omission of an objection presumes that the defendant acknowledged the facts substantiating the specific claim or specific part of the claim.

2.4.2.4. *Claimant's Request*

A court must issue a default judgment when the relevant legal conditions are met.[51] A request by a claimant for such a judgment is not required. A claimant's request for a default judgment is considered to be implicitly included in the plaintiff's action, i.e. in the part of the action where the claimant requests legal protection. If the court does not issue a default judgment even though all conditions for its issuance have been met, the claimant can request the judgment's issuance.[52]

44 Art. 318/1, fourth point ZPP.
45 Supreme Court of the Republic of Slovenia, No. III Ips 31/94; Supreme Court of the Republic of Slovenia, No. II Ips 154/95 VS RS in conjunction with the decision of the Higher (Appeals) Court in Maribor, No. Cp 1245/94-3; Rijavec 1998, p. 1005.
46 Art. 3/3 ZPP.
47 Betetto 2002, p. 39.
48 Art. 339/2, sixth point ZPP; Rijavec 1998, p. 1005-1006; Tekavc 2001, p. 1501.
49 Galič 2003, p. 165.
50 Rijavec 1998, p. 1001; Tekavc 2001, p. 1497.
51 Požun 2000, p. 5.
52 Rijavec 1998, p. 1003-1004.

2.4.2.5. *Legal Remedies against the Default Judgment*

The default judgment can be attacked (challenged) through appeal, which is a regular legal remedy, on the grounds of severe violation of civil procedural provisions or on the grounds of violation of substantive law.[53] However, it is not possible to attack the default judgment on the grounds of false or incomplete determination of the facts.[54] A default judgment, in accordance with the claim, is passed without any hearing, as it is irrefutably presumed that the defendant has with his passivity implicitly admitted the facts alleged in the action. Therefore, the court passes the default judgment dismissing the claim without ascertaining the facts.[55] On the other hand, the law has to be applied by the court *ex officio*. Consequently, the false application of law is a reason for appeal.[56]

2.4.3. Default Judgment Dismissing a Claim

When the defendant does not produce the defence plea within thirty days after the correct service of the action and the judge in preliminary examination of this action establishes that the facts stated in the action do not provide an adequate basis for the asserted claim, the court has to give the plaintiff the possibility to rectify the action/claim. If he does not follow the request, the court has to pass a default judgment dismissing the claim.[57] Thus, the plaintiff has to be very careful when filing the action/claim to ensure that the facts stated in the action form a sufficient basis for the claim.[58]

2.4.4. Judgment on the Basis of Abandoning the Claim

If the plaintiff abandons his claim before the main hearing is over, the court shall pass, without further consideration, a judgment dismissing the claim.[59]

2.4.5. Judgment on the Basis of Acknowledgment

If the defendant acknowledges the claim before the main hearing is over, the court shall pass, without further consideration, a judgment satisfying the claim.[60]

53 Art. 338/1 ZPP.
54 Art. 338/2 ZPP.
55 Rijavec 1998, p. 1007; Galič 2003, p. 171.
56 Rijavec 1998, p. 1005.
57 Art. 318/3 ZPP.
58 Zobec 2002, p. VII.
59 Art. 317/1 ZPP.
60 Art. 316 ZPP.

2.5. *Judgment on the Basis of Substantial Adjudication of the Claim*

2.5.1. Final Judgment

By passing a judgment, the court shall decide on the relief claimed, and determine the collateral claims.[61]

2.5.2. Partial Judgment

Of great importance for efficiency is the duty of the court to decide immediately after fulfilment of the conditions for a decision. If only one of several claims or only one part of a particular claim is ripe for decision, the court should close the hearing in respect of such claim, or of such part of the claim, and render judgment (partial judgment).[62]

2.5.3. Interlocutory Judgment

An interlocutory judgment is commonly entered for the purpose of procedural economy. If the defendant has challenged the grounds as well as the amount of the claim, and if the case is only ripe for decision regarding the grounds, the court may render an interlocutory judgment in respect of the grounds of the claim only when this is reasonable or convenient. The court shall stay the hearing in respect of the amount of the claim until the interlocutory judgment becomes binding.[63] The Slovenian ZPP contains another specific rule in that the court may issue an interlocutory judgment upon agreement of the parties when there is no disagreement on the grounds of the claim (Article 315/3 ZPP).

2.6. *Effects of Judgments*

In Slovenia as well as in other states peace in the community is a public concern. The dispute must be ended in a reasonable time. The concept of *res iudicata* aims toward this goal.[64] The judgment symbolises the final termination of a lawsuit when appeal is no longer admissible. Judgments awarding compensation acquire enforceability if the claim is not paid voluntarily within the appointed time.[65] Enforceable titles are not only judgments, but also court settlements and notary acts.

61 Art. 301/1 ZPP.

62 Art. 314 ZPP.

63 Art. 315 ZPP.

64 Art. 319 ZPP.

65 Art. 17 Civil Enforcement Act, *Zakon o izvršbi in zavarovanju* – ZIZ (Execution of Judgments in Civil Matters and Insurance of Claims Act), Official Gazette of the Republic of Slovenia, No. 51/98, 75/02, 16/04.

2.7. *Court Settlement*

At all times during the proceedings before a court of first instance the parties may voluntarily settle the matter in dispute. The court does not allow the settlement if the parties seek to dispose with their claim in contradiction to mandatory statutes or moral rules.[66] The court settlement is granted with the effect of *res transacta* immediately with its conclusion. The only remedies are an action for annulment of the settlement and a petition for protection of legality. Settlement is an important economic component of dispute resolution.[67]

2.8. *Ordinary Legal Remedies*

Fair process in reasonable time also depends on a balanced system of legal remedies against court decisions. The Slovenian Constitution guarantees to everybody the right of appeal against court decisions.[68] This guarantee does not embrace all decisions but only first instance judgments.

2.8.1. Appeal

The courts of second instance are called upon to review the first instance judgment.[69]

2.8.2. Grounds of Appeal

A judgment may be appealed on the grounds of:

1. severe violation of the rules of civil procedure;
2. erroneous or incomplete determination of the facts; and
3. violation of substantive law.[70]

2.9. *Extraordinary Legal Remedies*

2.9.1. Revision

The reform in 2008 changed the concept of this legal remedy.[71] The Supreme Court adjudicates only on legal issues of considerable importance, the existence thereof being a prerequisite for the Supreme Court accepting an appeal on points of law. The parties have to plead the importance of the legal problem dealt with by the

66 Art. 306 ZPP.
67 For a more complete discussion of the economic impact of court settlements, see Keresteš 2004, p. 385-386.
68 Art. 25 of the Constitution.
69 Art. 35 ZPP.
70 Art. 338 ZPP.
71 Amendments ZPP-D.

lower court or they have to prove an unjustified change of court practice. No filtering procedure for admission of revision against second instance judgments is in place if the disputed part of the claim exceeds €40,000. Consequently, the application for revision can be submitted directly to the court. Supreme Court appeals are not allowed at all below a certain value in small-claims disputes (€2,000).[72]

Judgments of courts of second instance may only be challenged through an appeal on points of law. However, the Supreme Court decides only on asserted legal issues and is therefore bound in its judgment by the facts previously established. The Supreme Court not only performs an appellate function, it may also decide on the matter itself (to confirm or amend the judgment), vacate the previous decisions and instruct the courts of first or second instance to retry the matter, or dismiss the action.[73]

2.9.2. Petition for Protection of Legality

This specific instrument used to be a parallel remedy introducing appeal to the Supreme Court by the State Prosecutor. It was supposed to be abolished with the last changes of ZPP 2008 as a relic of the past but it remained nevertheless, to a very limited extent. The opinion prevailed that the petition for protection of legality should remain for the procedures where revision is not foreseen. These are small-claims procedures, enforcement procedures and most non-contentious civil procedures for which the law does not provide revision at all. The legislator estimated also that the petition shall stay for protection against the abuse of law when the process is terminated by the will of the parties without a decision on the merits (such as settlement, default judgment, judgment on acknowledgment).

In these limited cases the State Prosecutor is still authorised to submit a petition against any final judicial decision within a period of three months to guarantee the same *acquis* of law in all the courts of the state.[74] The Supreme Court is the only court competent to decide on such a petition.[75]

2.10. *Re-opening of Proceedings*

Proceedings may be re-opened only under extraordinary, specially determined circumstances.[76]

The trial judge may grant a new trial mostly because of newly discovered evidence. The person seeking the re-opening must show that: 1) the evidence was discovered subsequent to the end of the trial on facts which existed at the time of the trial; 2) the petitioner was reasonably diligent in his search for evidence before and during the trial, and could not reasonably have found the evidence before the

72 Arts. 367 and 370 ZPP.

73 Arts. 378-381 ZPP.

74 Ude 2009, p. 569.

75 Arts. 385-391 ZPP.

76 Art. 394 ZPP.

end of the trial; and 3) the evidence is material, and in fact likely to produce a different result for the party requesting re-opening.

2.11. *Action for Annulment of a Court Settlement or Action for Annulment of an Arbitration Award*

The other two remedies against final decisions or settlements are the Action for Annulment of a Court Settlement[77] and the Action for Annulment of an Arbitration Award.[78]

3. Special Procedures

The nature of certain disputes does not require a complete array of procedural rules. Therefore, the second part of the ZPP contains the rules for some special civil procedures as for example the Procedure regarding Disturbance of Possession, the Small Claims Procedure, the Order for Payment, and the so-called Summary Proceedings. These rules, adapted to the nature of specific matters should lead to more effective adjudication.

Besides the rules of civil litigation, Slovenia knows one more sectoral jurisdiction under special rules of non-contentious civil procedure (*iurisdictio voluntaria*), mostly regulated in the Non-Contentious Civil Procedure Act[79] but also in some substantive law statutes (e.g. probate procedure).

A significant share in backlogs appertains to cases in enforcement procedure. The reform of this field cannot be dealt with in this contribution. Here, it is only necessary to indicate that civil enforcement is regulated under the special Civil Enforcement Act.[80]

4. Conclusion

Slovenia continues to seek ways to improve the speed and efficiency of its judicial system. It is making a special effort to diminish the backlog of unresolved civil cases. This includes the introduction of practical measures on the operational level, including better implementation of procedural rules and better case-management. The principle of the autonomy of the parties has already been very much emphasised, but the judge has continued to play an active role. There is still a lot of open space in the field of pre-trial negotiations and ADR.

Upon leaving Yugoslavia, Slovenia had a substantial backlog of civil cases. In order to efficiently dispose of this backlog, as well as future legal cases, Slovenia

77 Art. 392 ZPP.

78 Art. 476 ZPP.

79 *Zakon o nepravdnem postopku*, (Non-Contentious Civil Procedure Act), Official Gazette of the Republic of Slovenia 30/86 in 20/88, 87/02.

80 *Zakon o izvršbi in zavarovanju* (Execution of Judgments in Civil Matters and Insurance of Claims Act), Official Gazette of the Republic of Slovenia, Nos. 51/98, 75/02, 16/04.

incorporated new features along with an adversarial process. The Slovenian efficiency procedures include:

1. Limitation of *ius novorum*, essentially an early or opening hearing that freezes the factual context of the lawsuit;[81]
2. The authority, indeed mandate, for judges to actively participate in determining, *ab initio*, whether the lawsuit has sufficient merit to continue;
3. Trial before a single professional judge as a rule and a panel of judges, with the assistance of lay assessors only in specified cases, but without a jury; and finally
4. Encouragement of alternative systems of dispute resolution, such as mediation and arbitration.

Efficiency is not the only goal of Slovenian civil procedure, but it is a central concern. However, an efficient system also has to guarantee the equality of the parties before the law.

81 Art. 286 ZPP.

Bibliography

Betetto 2002
Betetto, N., *'Zamudna sodba (Default Judgment)', Pravosodni bilten* (Jurisdictional Bulletin), Ljubljana: CIP, 2002, 3.

Bone 2003
Bone, R.G., *Civil Procedure: The Economics of Civil Procedure,* New York: Foundation Press New York, 2003.

Butala 1999
Butala, A., *'Pravdni postopek brez nepotrebnega odlašanja* (Civil Procedure without Unnecessary Delay)', *Podjetje in delo* (Company and Labour), Ljubljana: GV, 1999, 6-7.

Galič 2000
Galič, A., *'Pravica do tožbe - pravica* do sodnega varstva kot pravica do meritorne odločitve v ustavnoskladnem postopku (Right to Civil Action -Access Court as a Right for Decision Making in a Procedure in Conformity with the Constitution)', *Zbornik znanstvenih razprav,* (Miscellany of Scholarly Papers), Ljubljana: Pravna fakulteta Univerze v Ljubljani, 2000, 2.

Galič 2003
Galič, A., 'Sankcije za neaktivnost strank v pravdem postopku (Sanctions against the Passivity of the Parties in Civil Procedure)', *Zbornik znanstvenih razprav* (Miscellany of Scholarly Papers), Ljubljana: Pravna fakulteta Univerze v Ljubljani, 2003, 5.

Ivanič 1999
Ivanič, M., *Kratka ilustrirana zgodovina Slovencev* (Short Illustrated History of the Slovenian People), Ljubljana: Mladinska knjiga, 1999.

Jambrek 2002
Jambrek, P., in Šturm, L., *Komentar Ustave RS* (Commentary on the Constitution of the Republic of Slovenia), Ljubljana: Dignitas, 2002.

Juhart, Ude & Wedam-Lukić 1974
Juhart, J., Ude, L. & Wedam-Lukić, D., *Komentar Zakona o pravdnem postopku* (Commentary on the Civil Procedure Act), Ljubljana: ČGP Delo, 1974.

Keresteš 2004
Keresteš, T., *'Ekonomsko vrednotenje v pravu* (Economic Evaluation in Law)', *Pravnik,* Ljubljana: Uradni list RS, 2004, 7-9.

Kežmah 2004
Kežmah, U., *Free Legal Assistance, Pravo - družina - civilna družba* (Law - Family - Civil Society), Maribor: Pravna fakulteta, UM, 2004.

Požun 2000
Požun, J., '*Sklepčnost tožbe - zamudna sodba - pravna sredstva* (Legally Unfounded Action - Default Judgment - Legal Remedies)', *Pravna Praksa* (Legal Practice), Ljubljana: GV Založba, 2000, 4.

Rijavec 1999
Rijavec, V., '*Posledice pasivnosti strank v pravdnem postopku* (The Consequences of the Passivity of the Parties in Civil Litigation)', *Pravnik (Lawyer)* Ljubljana: Uradni list RS, 1999, 54(6-8).

Rijavec 1998
Rijavec, V., '*Zamudna sodba* (Default Judgment)', *Podjetje in delo* (Company and Labour), Ljubljana: GV Založba, 1998, 6.

Tekavc 2001
Tekavc, J., '*Zamudna sodba* (Default Judgment)', *Podjetje in delo* (Company and Labour), Ljubljana: Gv Založba, 2001, 8.

Ude 2002
Ude, L., *Civilni pravdni postopek*, Ljubljana: Uradni list RS, 2002.

Ude 2009
Ude, L., in: Ude, L. *et al.*, *Pravdni postopek, zakon s komentarjem* (Civil Procedure Act with Commentary), Ljubljana: Uradni list and GV Založba, 2009.

Wedam-Lukić 1996
Wedam-Lukić, D., *Pravica do sodnega varstva civilnih pravic* (Access to Justice in Civil Matters) Zbornik znanstvenih razprav, Ljubljana: Pravna fakulteta Univerze v Ljubljani, 1996.

Zobec 2002
Zobec, J., 'Nesklepčnost tožbe in zamudna sodba (Legally Unfounded Action and Default Judgment)', *Pravna praksa* (Legal Practice), Ljubljana: GV Založba, 2002, 18.

D.Kh. Valeev
L.V. Fatkhullina
A.V. Valeeva

THE JURISDICTION OF RUSSIAN COURTS IN CIVIL MATTERS

1. Constitutional Foundations of the Court System

Modern Russian civil procedural law, in contrast to previous legislation (i.e. the 1964 Code of Civil Procedure of Soviet Russia), regulates jurisdiction in only one article - Article 22 of the Code of Civil Procedure of the Russian Federation (hereafter: CCP). However, other regulations governing this area of civil justice are extensive. In order to present them, we need to analyse - in addition to the CCP - the Federal Constitutional Law on the Judicial System of Russia, and various acts on substantive law, such as the Civil Code, the Family Code, the Labour Code and the Administrative Code.

The Constitution and federal constitutional laws of the Russian Federation contain basic principles regarding jurisdiction. For example, Article 10 of the Constitution establishes that state power in the Russian Federation is divided among three independent branches: the legislative, the executive and the judicial. Moreover, state protection of human rights and freedoms is guaranteed, and all are entitled to defend their rights and freedoms by every means not prohibited by law.[1]

There are various remedies in civil law that may serve as means of protection of individual rights, e.g. remedies for the recognition of a right, the restoration of the situation which existed before the violation of a right, suppression of the actions that violated or threatened a right to the nullification of a disputed transaction as invalid, etc.[2] The Constitution establishes the priority of the judicial protection of civil rights. For example, Article 46 of the Constitution stipulates that judicial protection of rights and freedoms shall be guaranteed to everyone, and Article 11 of the Civil Code states that 'the violated or disputed civil rights shall be protected by the courts of justice, the commercial courts and tribunals ... in conformity with the rules on jurisdiction, established by the procedural legislation'. Protection of civil rights in administrative procedure is carried out only in cases stipulated by law. Administrative acts may be appealed.

1 Art. 45 of the Russian Constitution.
2 See also Art. 12 of the Civil Code.

Judicial power in Russia is exercised through constitutional, civil, administrative and criminal proceedings.[3] Pursuant to Article 4 of the Federal Constitutional Law on the Judicial System of the Russian Federation (hereafter: FCL), under the heading 'Courts in the Russian Federation', the Russian judicial system comprises the federal courts, constitutional courts and magistrates courts (justices of the peace). Federal courts are the Constitutional Court of the Russian Federation and the Supreme Court of the Russian Federation; the supreme courts of the republics; courts of territories and regions; courts of more important federal cities; courts of autonomous regions and autonomous districts; district courts; and military and specialised courts. The system of federal commercial courts (in Russia for historical reasons referred to as 'Arbitration Courts') consists of the Supreme Commercial Court of the Russian Federation, the federal commercial courts of districts and the commercial courts of one of the 89 constituent units of the Russian Federation.

2. The Jurisdiction of Russian Courts

The competence of individual courts is regulated by the FCL in the following way:

1. The Supreme Court of the Russian Federation hears cases as a court of second instance, as a supervisory court and when new evidence is discovered, and also hears cases as a court of first instance when so provided by a federal law. The Supreme Court is a superior court in relation to other courts – the supreme courts of the republics, courts of territories and regions, courts of more important federal cities, courts of autonomous regions and autonomous districts, and the military courts of military districts, fleets and divisions of the military forces;[4]
2. The supreme court of a republic, a court of a territory and a court of a region, a court of a more important federal city, a court of an autonomous region and a court of an autonomous district hear cases as a court of first and second instance, as a supervisory court and when new evidence is discovered. They are superior to district courts;[5]
3. A district court adjudicates cases as a court of first and second instance, and performs other duties stipulated by federal constitutional law. The district court is itself a higher court with respect to the magistrates acting within the territory of the judicial district;[6]
4. Magistrates' courts deal in the first instance with civil, administrative and criminal cases. The powers of the magistrates and procedural rules of magistrates' courts are regulated by the Federal Law of 17 December 1998 No. 188-FL 'On the Magistrates in the Russian Federation';[7]

3 Art. 118 of the Russian Constitution.
4 Art. 19 FCL.
5 Art. 20 FCL.
6 Art. 21 FCL.
7 Art. 28 FCL.

5. The establishment of military courts is based on a territorial principle. They are located in the place of the deployment of troops and fleets for the purpose of exercising judicial power in the armed forces, their agencies and units. Military courts hear cases as a court of first and second instance, as a supervisory court and when new evidence is discovered. Competence, establishment and rules of procedure of military courts are regulated by the Federal Constitutional Act of 23 June 1999 No. 1-FCL 'On Military Courts of the Russian Federation';[8]
6. Specialised federal courts for civil and administrative cases may be established by amendments to the FCL. The authorities, rules on establishment and activity of specialised federal courts may be established by federal constitutional law.[9] However, no such laws have yet been adopted. The State Duma of the Russian Federal Assembly is currently examining a draft law 'On Administrative Courts'.

Part 1 of Article 22 of the Code of Civil Procedure lists the categories of civil cases and the courts which are competent to consider and resolve them. Six types of civil proceedings are listed: civil actions; payment orders; cases arising from public legal relations; special procedures; cases challenging the decisions of commercial courts and requests to enforce them; and cases challenging foreign judgments and requests to enforce foreign judgments and foreign arbitral awards. In our view, there is an additional form of civil proceedings which is not directly identified in the article – legal proceedings regarding issues arising from enforcement proceedings.

Courts decide claims involving citizens, organisations, government bodies and local authorities. Claims to be adjudicated deal with the protection of the violated or disputed rights, freedoms and legitimate interests in the area of civil law, family law, work, housing and land law, environmental law and other legal relations. It is noteworthy that the legislator abandoned the traditional principle of determining court jurisdiction. Under Article 25(1) of the former Code of Civil Procedure of Soviet Russia, a court had jurisdiction when at least one of the parties to the dispute was a Russian citizen. The absence of such a rule in the present Article 22 can be explained by the fact that the level and quality of existing legislation allow that exclusive jurisdiction of various governmental and non-governmental organisations be specifically and exhaustively provided, failing which the courts should be competent.

3. Jurisdiction in Labour Disputes

Civil legal relationships are regulated by many acts and regulations. All of them have provisions regarding the right to judicial protection.[10] Courts of general

8 Art. 22 FCL.

9 Art. 26 FCL.

10 For example, Arts. 17, 40-46 Federal Law 'On Protection of Consumers' Rights'; Arts. 136-142 Federal Law titled 'Transport Charter of Railways of the Russian Federation'; Arts. 15-19 Federal Law 'On Obligatory Social Insurance against Industrial Accidents and Professional Diseases'; Arts. 14-18 Federal Law 'On Protection of Rights and Legitimate Interests of →

jurisdiction hear cases arising from employment relationships. The courts can resolve individual labour disputes involving claims brought by (a) an employee, employer or trade union defending the interests of employees when they disagree with the decision of the committee on labour disputes, (b) when an employee goes to court, bypassing the committee on labour disputes or (c) by the prosecutor, if the committee's decision on the labour dispute does not comply with the law or other legal acts.[11]

Individual labour disputes should be submitted directly to the court when the following claims are concerned:

- Claims of an employee for reinstatement to work regardless of the grounds for dismissal; for change of the date of a dismissal and the reasons for dismissal; challenging a change of the type of work to be executed; for payment during a period of involuntary unemployment, or with regard to higher payment for work performed outside ordinary working hours; concerning an employment contract contravening the law; and when the employee believes that he or she has been discriminated against;
- Claims of an employer for damages caused by an employee, unless otherwise stipulated by federal law.

In judicial practice, while labour disputes were resolved in the courts, some questions appeared because of the participation of shareholder companies and other business partnerships and companies. Therefore, the Plenum of the Supreme Court had to provide special explanations and instructions[12] regarding cases instituted by the former management of companies and other organisations: members of the collegial executive bodies of the organisations (general managers of joint-stock companies and other business partnerships and companies), and also members of boards of directors (supervisory boards). The opinion of the Plenum also dealt with the decisions of various authorities or the owners of companies regarding dismissal of executive personnel of the companies. It was contested whether or not such matters should be within the jurisdiction of courts of general jurisdiction.[13]

Article 292 of the Labour Code establishes the limitation period for applying to a court for the resolution of an employment dispute. The employee has the right to apply to the court for the resolution of an individual labour dispute within three months from the date of the violation of his rights. For dismissal disputes, the limitation period is one month from the date of receipt of the dismissal order or

Investors on Capital Markets'; Arts. 37 and 38 Federal Law 'On Postal Communications', and others.

11 See Art. 391 of the Labour Code.

12 See the explanation of the Plenum dated 20 November 2003, No. 17: 'On some issues that have arisen in judicial practice in cases involving labour disputes, shareholder companies and other business partnerships and companies'.

13 *Cf.* Arts. 11, 273-281, 391 Labour Code; Art. 33 Commercial Procedure Code (hereafter: CPC); Art. 22 CCP; paras 4 and 5, Regulation of the Plenum of the Supreme Court of the Russian Federation of 20 January 2003, No. 2, 'On some issues arising in connection with the adoption and enactment of the Code of Civil Procedure of the Russian Federation'.

from the date of the returning of the work book. The employer has the right to resort to the court with regard to disputes on compensation for damages caused by the employee within one year after the discovery of the tortuous action. That deadline can be extended by the court.

4. Jurisdiction in Family Cases

Another large group of cases processed by the courts involve disputes regarding family relationships. Under applicable legislation, the protection of family rights is provided by the courts and by state bodies or bodies of trusteeship and guardianship.[14] In comparison to all other proceedings, judicial relief is common and universal. Cases dealt with by the courts of general jurisdiction include:

- divorce proceedings, if the spouses have common minor children, or when there is no consent of one spouse to divorce;[15]
- challenge of paternity (or maternity);[16]
- deprivation of parental rights;[17]
- adoption of a child;[18]
- residence of a child when the parents live apart;[19]
- parents' contacts with their children;[20]
- communication of relatives with a child;[21]
- return of an abducted child to the parents[22] or foster parents;[23]
- restoration of parental rights;[24]
- limitation of parental rights[25] and their termination;[26]
- termination of adoption;[27]
- payment of support to illegitimate children;[28]
- annulment of marriage;[29]

14 See Art. 8(1) of the Family Code (FC).
15 Art. 21(1) FC.
16 Art. 52 FC.
17 Art. 70 FC.
18 Art. 125 FC.
19 Art. 65(3) FC.
20 Art. 66(2) FC.
21 Art. 67(3) FC.
22 Art. 68(1) FC.
23 Art. 153(3) FC.
24 Art. 72(2) FC.
25 Art. 73(1) FC.
26 Art. 76 FC.
27 Art. 140 FC.
28 Art. 38 FC.
29 Art. 27 FC.

- payment of maintenance in case of a dispute;[30]
- payment of maintenance to disabled parents;[31] and
- payment of maintenance to one's spouse.[32]

5. Payment Orders

Payment orders are regulated by the provisions of the CCP.[33] Payment order proceedings have some similarities with simplified proceedings before commercial courts.[34] However, the simplified proceedings in its essence is a kind of ordinary proceedings, whereas the order for payment presents an independent form of civil proceedings provided for only in civil procedural law. A court order is issued by a single judge on an application for the recovery of money or for the recovery of movable property of the debtor.

In particular, payment orders are issued if the claim is based on:

- a notarised transaction;
- a transaction made in writing or a notarised protest of non-payment of bills;
- non-acceptance and undated acceptance;
- a claim for support to minors;
- cases in which paternity or maternity are not challenged;
- a claim for a penalty of back taxes, levies and other mandatory payments;
- a claim for a penalty of awarded but unpaid wages to the employee;
- a claim by the office investigating criminal and administrative offenses committed by state employees, by the federal tax service or by a local division of bailiffs;
- expenses caused by the search for the defendant or the debtor and his property; and
- costs associated with the storage of property seized from a debtor and the debtor's eviction from his premises.

6. Public Law Cases

The courts of general jurisdiction also hear cases arising from public law relations.[35] The Code of Civil Procedure[36] contains a list of such cases:

- challenge of government regulations in whole or in part, if consideration of these cases is not attributed by federal law to the jurisdiction of other courts;

30 Art. 80 FC.
31 Art. 87 FC.
32 Art. 89 FC.
33 See Art. 22(2) Part 1 of the CCP.
34 See Chapter 29 of the CPC.
35 See Art. 22 Part 1 CCP.
36 Art. 245 CCP.

- challenge of the decisions and actions (or inactions) of government bodies, local government officials, and state and municipal employees;
- protection of voting rights or rights to participate in a referendum for the citizens of the Russian Federation; and
- other categories of cases arising from public law relations.

There is also a need to consider jurisdiction with regard to cases brought before the commercial courts and the Constitutional Court. These cases[37] include for example:

- secondary appeals against decisions, actions or the inaction of customs authorities of the Russian Federation and their officials during customs control and customs clearance;
- the control of proceedings examining violations of customs regulations;[38] and
- other matters which do not affect the economic policy of the Russian Federation.

These cases are within the territorial competence of the district (municipal) court in the area where customs authorities are located or, alternatively, in the area where an officer of the customs authorities of the Russian Federation, whose decisions, acts or inaction are challenged, usually works.

Repeated appeals against decisions, actions or inactions of customs authorities of the Russian Federation and their officials are under the jurisdiction of the commercial court in accordance with federal laws. Repeated appeals against the general regulations of the State Customs Committee of the Russian Federation or against law enforcement practices that affect the economic policy of the Russian Federation should be addressed to the Constitutional Court. Other secondary appeals against decisions, actions or inactions of the State Customs Committee of the Russian Federation and its officials are within the competence of the General Prosecutor of the Russian Federation.

7. Special (extra-contentious) Proceedings

Russian courts also hear and decide cases in special (extra-contentious) proceedings listed in Article 262 CCP.[39] These cases include, among other things:

- establishment of legally significant facts;
- adoption of a child;
- recognition of a citizen as missing or the declaration of a citizen as deceased;
- limitation of capacity of a citizen, or the recognition of a citizen as incapable;
- limitation or deprivation of a minor between fourteen and eighteen years of age of the right to dispose of his income;

37 See Art. 416 of the Customs Code of 18 June 1993, No. 5221-I (amended in 2002).

38 Except the appeal against the decisions and penalties imposed by customs authorities in simplified proceedings.

39 See Art. 22(4) Part 1 CCP.

- declaration of a minor as fully capable (emancipation);
- declaring movables as ownerless and awarding of the right of ownership to the state;
- involuntary hospitalisation of a citizen in a psychiatric hospital and forced psychiatric examination; and
- corrections or changes in official documents regarding the civil status of persons.

The Code of Civil Procedure added new categories of cases, unknown in the former law of the Russian Soviet Federative Socialist Republic (RSFSR):[40] cases challenging the decisions of the commercial courts, and the enforcement of such decisions (Section VI CCP); and cases on the recognition and enforcement of foreign judgments and foreign arbitral awards.[41]

8. Cases Involving Foreigners, Foreign States and International Organisations

Courts also have jurisdiction to hear and decide cases against foreign citizens, stateless persons, foreign organisations, organisations with foreign investments, and international organisations.[42] In return, foreign citizens, stateless persons, foreign organisations and international organisations are eligible to apply to the courts in the Russian Federation to protect their violated or disputed rights, freedoms and legitimate interests.

The government of the Russian Federation may impose retaliatory restrictions on foreign persons of those states whose courts restrict the procedural rights of Russian citizens and organisations.[43] However, filing a claim in Russia against a foreign state is allowed only with the consent of the competent authorities of that state, unless otherwise provided by an international treaty or a federal law. The same applies to the participation of a foreign state as a third party, to seizure of the foreign state's property, and to the use of provisional measures for security. International organisations are under the jurisdiction of Russian courts within the limits set by international treaties and by federal law. Diplomatic representatives of foreign governments accredited in the Russian Federation and similar foreign personnel are under the jurisdiction of courts in the Russian Federation within the limits of norms and principles of international law.[44]

9. Jurisdiction of Commercial Courts

Economic disputes and other matters specifically defined in federal constitutional law are within the jurisdiction of commercial courts.[45]

40 See Art. 22(5) and (6) CCP.
41 See Chapter 45 CCP.
42 Art. 22 Part 2 CCP.
43 See Art. 398 CCP.
44 Art. 401 CCP.
45 See Art. 22 Part 3 CCP.

Commercial courts deal with cases related to business and other economic activities.[46] There are two types of proceedings before the commercial courts: the first is associated with business disputes, and the second concerns non-contentious matters related to business and other economic activities. The cases within the jurisdiction of commercial courts should arise from civil, administrative and other public relations.[47]

Under current laws and practices, the jurisdiction of commercial courts includes the following categories of cases:

1. Disputes regarding agreements that need to comply with specific criteria (e.g. agreements that need to be in writing);[48]
2. Disputes regarding modification or termination of contracts. The request for making an amendment to or to terminate a contract can be made to the court only if the proposal to change or terminate the contract was refused by the other party or if the other party did not reply within a court-ordered or statutory time-limit.[49] In order to change the terms of the contract, an additional agreement might be needed. In this case, there is also the possibility of requesting court intervention;[50]
3. Disputes regarding non-performance or improper performance of obligations;[51]
4. Disputes on the recognition of rights to property;[52]
5. Disputes regarding recovery of property by the lawful owner when illegally possessed by a third party (vindication claims);
6. Disputes regarding violation of ownership rights not associated with dispossession;
7. Claims for damages;[53]
8. Disputes regarding the protection of honour, dignity and business reputation,[54] unless the damaging information has been disseminated by the claimant himself;[55]

46 Art. 27(1) CPC.
47 Arts. 28 and 29 CPC.
48 For example, Art. 11(3) of the Federal Law 'On State Defence Orders'.
49 Art. 452(2) CCP.
50 A suitable example would be disputes relating to the conditions of additional agreements for the purchase of government (municipal) property which has been used under a lease agreement. These disputes are under the jurisdiction of the commercial courts (para 8 of the Presidential Decree 'On regulation of the lease and the privatisation of rented state and municipal enterprises').
51 For example, Art. 24(1) of the Federal Law 'On Information and the Protection of Information'.
52 Para 19 of the Supreme Commercial Court decision 'On certain issues concerning the settlement of disputes which relate to the protection of property rights and other rights'.
53 See e.g. Art. 78(3) of the RSFSR law 'On the protection of the environment'; Art. 2(2) of the RSFSR law 'On the national economy'.
54 For example, under Art. 8(2) of the Federal Law 'On Advertising', a natural or legal person who has learned about advertising containing information discrediting his honour, dignity or business reputation has the right to seek protection of his rights in court in accordance with →

9. Disputes concerning agreements regarding the compulsory supply of goods to the State Reserve;[56]
10. Disputes on the liquidation of legal entities.[57]

In administrative proceedings arising from administrative and other public law relations, and in economic disputes and other matters related to business activities, commercial courts hear the following cases:

1. Challenges to regulations affecting the rights and legitimate interests of the applicant in the field of business and other economic activities;[58]
2. Challenges to non-legislative acts of the government of the Russian Federation, the state authorities of the Russian Federation, local authorities' decisions and the actions (or inactions) of state bodies, local authorities, other agencies and officials concerning the rights and legitimate interests of the applicant in business and other economic activities;[59]
3. Administrative offences. Cases where a business party is answerable for committing an administrative offence are under the jurisdiction of commercial courts;[60]

the law. He also has the right to force the advertiser to rectify the advertisement if the advertiser does not act on a voluntary basis.

55 See para 10 of the Information Letter of the Presidium of the Supreme Commercial Court of 23 September 1999 No. 46 'Commercial courts' review of the practice of dispute settlement connected with the protection of business reputation'.

56 Art. 9(5) of the Federal Law 'On the State Reserve of Material Resources'.

57 Para 27 of the Resolution of the Plenum of the Supreme Court and the Plenum of the Supreme Commercial Court of 9 December 1999 No. 90/14 'On some issues caused by the application of the Federal Law "On Limited Liability Companies"'.

58 These cases, including those on the jurisdiction of the Supreme Commercial Court under Art. 34(2) and Art. 192, are to be resolved in commercial courts only if such jurisdiction is expressly provided by federal law. See *inter alia* Art. 138 of the Tax Code, Art. 13 of the Federal Law 'On State Regulation of Tariffs for Electricity and Heat', and Art. 43 of the Federal Law 'On the Securities Market'.

59 Thus, in accordance with Art. 31 of the Federal Law 'On Protection of Competition on the Market for Financial Services', federal executive bodies, executive bodies of entities of the Russian Federation and local government (their officials), financial organisations (their leaders) and citizens, including individual entrepreneurs, may apply to a court or commercial court to invalidate all or part of the decisions and orders of the federal anti-monopoly body, or to repeal or modify regulations regarding the imposition of administrative liability in the form of a warning or a fine. An individual entrepreneur, who has been subject to administrative punishment, may appeal to a commercial court and challenge the act of punishment. See Letter of the Supreme Commercial Court of 12 May 1999 No. 40 'On jurisdiction of commercial courts if cases involve appeals against decisions of administrative commissions'.

60 See Art. 23(1) Part 3 of the Code of Administrative Offences. Resolution of the Plenum of the Supreme Commercial Court of 27 January 2003 No. 2 'On some issues relating to the enactment of the Administrative Code' noted that only if the offences are committed by legal entities or individual entrepreneurs (even when administrative investigation took place) would administrative offences be under the jurisdiction of the commercial courts (para 9 of the Resolution).

4. Recovery of mandatory payments and penalties from entrepreneurs, organisations and individuals.[61]

Some other cases which arise from administrative and other public law relations should also be resolved under federal law by the commercial courts.

Under a broad interpretation of Article 29 of the Commercial Procedure Code, commercial courts should deal with appeals against the refusal of registration or evasion by the state authorities of registration of an organisation or of a citizen in the public registers before a deadline, and in other cases where such registration is provided by law.[62] In some cases, the state registry must obtain the consent of the relevant public authority. The refusal to grant consent by the relevant authority may also be challenged before the Commercial Court.[63]

Cases which are dealt with by the commercial courts in special (non-contentious) proceedings include the following:

1. Establishing the facts relevant to the accrual or termination of the rights of organisations and citizens in the sphere of entrepreneurial and other economic activities;[64]
2. Insolvency (bankruptcy) of legal entities and citizens.

Under new rules on special jurisdiction,[65] the competence of the commercial courts is also provided for disputes between shareholders and shareholding companies and other members of business partnerships and societies arising from the activities of business partnerships and companies (except for labour disputes); and also for other matters arising from the implementation of entrepreneurial and other economic activities, if so stipulated by federal law.

61 For example, antitrust authorities may apply to the court for the collection of fines from offenders for unfair advertising (Part 1, Information Letter of the Presidium of the Supreme Commercial Court of the Russian Federation of 25 December 1998 No. 37 'Overview of practices dealing with disputes arising from the application of legislation on advertising'). A request for the collection of tax sanctions from business organisations or individual entrepreneurs should be submitted to the commercial court, whereas for other persons a court of general jurisdiction should be approached (Art. 104 Part 2 of the Tax Code).

62 For example, in accordance with Art. 16(3) of the Federal Law of 3 February 1996 No. 17-FZ 'On Amendments and Additions to the RSFSR Law "On Banks and Banking Activity in the RSFSR"', the refusal of registration and licensing of a credit institution by the Bank of Russia can be challenged in a commercial court. The refusal to register a Chamber of Commerce can also be appealed to the Commercial Court - see Art. 10(3) of the Federal Law of 7 July 1993 No. 5340-1 'On Chambers of Commerce in the Russian Federation'.

63 For example, the refusal to grant consent for the registration of associations of insurers may be appealed to the Commercial Court (clause 7, Order of the State Committee for Anti-monopoly Policy (GKAP) of 29 April 1994 No. 50 'On approval of the regulations on examining the applications for consent of GKAP to state registration of insurers' associations').

64 Art. 218 CPC and para 2, Plenum of the Supreme Commercial Court of 31 October 1996 No. 13 'On the application of the CPC in cases before the Court of First Instance'.

65 See Art. 33 CPC.

10. Resolving Conflicts of Jurisdiction

The Constitutional Court of the Russian Federation has paid attention to the problems of jurisdictional demarcation between the Constitutional Court and other courts. Under its interpretation of Article 127 of the Russian Constitution, courts of general jurisdiction and commercial courts cannot declare that certain legal acts are null and void due to their inconsistency with the Constitution of the Russian Federation. If such courts come to the conclusion that an act of law is contrary to the constitutional rules and principles, they should notify the Constitutional Court, which will examine the constitutionality of the legal act. The duty to apply to the Constitutional Court exists regardless of whether the case was already resolved or not. The courts of general jurisdiction and commercial courts are not entirely precluded from the possibility of independently checking the compliance of legal acts with the Constitution, federal laws and other regulations. But, these powers of the courts have to be established specifically and in detail by federal constitutional law, failing which they do not have the right to nullify unconstitutional acts.

When there is a conflict of jurisdiction between a court of general jurisdiction and a commercial court which cannot be resolved by dividing the claims between these courts, litigation will take place in a court of general jurisdiction.[66]

66 See Art. 22 Part 4 of the Code of Civil Procedure.

V. Abolonin
G. Abolonin

TRUTH AND EFFICIENCY IN RUSSIAN CIVIL PROCEDURE

1. Introduction

The very word 'truth' in English is often used with the definite article 'the' as something which is one of a kind. This seems to imply that there must be one and only one truth in the world and that the truth as an everyday occurrence is material and quite comprehensible.

The Russian language has no articles in its grammar at all; instead, it achieves a similar effect through, among other means, word order. There is an idiomatic expression in Russian which says that 'everyone has his own truth'.

The more we consider the notion of truth in civil procedure, the more we are inclined to think that Russians are quite right in speaking of the multiplicity and subjectivity of the truth. The reason for saying this is that for several years now a discussion has taken place over what the truth to be ascertained by the court is. Shall it be a total reflection of the events which occurred in the past and which must be determined by the court on the basis of requested additional evidence and special independent enquiry? Or, perhaps, would it be enough for the court to declare as solemn truth some circumstances which may be ascertained purely on the basis of the evidence that was presented by the parties to the litigation even if there is a high risk of distortion between the facts established by the court and reality?

2. Objective Truth and Formal Truth – The Theoretical Dualism of Russian Civil Procedure

It should be noted that the truth and its role in civil procedure is always a matter of sharp debate between lawyers, and this is so in many countries. Russia is no exception. In spite of considering the court's duty to ascertain the truth as one of the underlying principles of civil justice,[1] the Russian legal theory of civil procedure

1 Shakaryan 2004, p. 59.

contains several approaches to the question of what the court shall establish as the truth. It is generally accepted to contrast objective truth with formal truth.[2]

Objective truth is understood as real, corresponding to the facts, to the actual circumstances of the case established by the court on the basis of an all-round and full examination of the relevant and admissible evidence, which was verified as reliable and sufficient in the 'furnace' of adversary trial.[3] The doctrine of objective truth is associated with the active role of the court in the trial and the collection of evidence as well as with the principle of limitation inherent in adversary trial. The establishment of the objective truth is a main task of the court. In order to reach this goal, the court may collect evidence *ex officio* and facilitate the submission of evidence by the parties.

Formal truth means that the court renders judgment with a certain degree of conviction regarding the correctness of the decision based upon its reliance on the rightness of testimonial evidence and the confession of a party.[4] The judge, therefore, does not need to fully investigate whether the testimonial evidence or the confession of the party conform to reality. What is important is that the court could believe that submitted evidence is credible. The formal truth doctrine is related to the principle of adversarial litigation. It is also related to the trial court's passiveness.[5] The court only accepts and considers the evidence presented by the parties; it does not care much about establishing the veracity of the evidence and its relevance to the real facts and circumstances of the case.

A good example of the difference between objective truth and formal truth can be shown by a contract of loan dispute: Article 168 of the Civil Code of the Russian Federation makes it obligatory that all transactions exceeding 1,000 rubles (RUB) be in written form.[6] A failure to observe the written form requirement may lead to the disregarding of any other evidence offered by the parties as to the existence of the loan agreement.

For example, if an individual lent money to another individual and the loan amount exceeded RUB 1,000, the lender could either require a receipt or decide not to demand a receipt. In the event of a dispute regarding the loan agreement, the court is under the obligation to establish the contractual relationship between the plaintiff and the defendant. Where there is a receipt signed by the defendant, the receipt can be presented in court as evidence. But it would be impossible to establish the fact of a contractual relationship where the plaintiff failed to introduce a receipt. That would create the problem of how an evident wrong could be rectified by the court, as – failing to introduce proper written evidence – the plaintiff's action should be dismissed on the grounds of lack of evidence.

Based on the (non)existence of adequate written evidence, the court could reach two different conclusions in two essentially similar cases. In the first case – if a

2 Osokina 2008, p. 616; Sakhnova 2008, pp. 104–05.

3 Kleinman 1954, p. 269.

4 Sakhnova 2008, p. 105.

5 Vaskovsky 2003, p. 101.

6 The Russian Central Bank official exchange rate is approximately €1 to RUB 40 at the time of writing.

receipt were presented - the court would establish the objective truth, i.e. the truth based on the real facts. In the second case, due to the lack of prescribed evidence, the court would establish the formal truth.

3. The Modern Doctrine of Civil Procedure and the Concept of Truth

The modern doctrine of civil procedure has evolved in comparison with the earlier concepts of objective truth. The change of attitude was caused by changes in procedural legislation. The main changes took place during the 1995-96 period, when the principle of the adversarial trial process was introduced. The new rules also introduced changes as to the collection, presentation and evaluation of evidence.[7]

The deletion of direct reference to 'objective truth' from the Code caused a new theoretical dispute.[8] As a result of this change, a polarisation of Russian scholars in the field of civil procedure took place. Some scholars[9] began to consider the common law system as a model for reforms of Russian civil procedure, advocating the formal truth concept as an integral part of it. These scholars supported the idea of embracing the common law tradition, ignoring the fact that Russian law traditionally was under the strong influence of Continental law.

The formal truth principle is often imagined as giving rise to an extremely adversarial process which allows the parties at trial to engage in a sort of gladiatorial match before the judge who is just a passive observer waiting to see who the winner of the contest will be. The role of the judge – let us call him a formal-truth judge – under this concept is that of a mere calculator and evaluator of the evidence presented. The judgment, accordingly, depends on the result of a competition. The judge, as an unbiased referee of the match, shall deliver a decision in favour of the party whose evidence is better. The judge shall not even bother himself with questioning the parties as long as their clever lawyers can do this instead of him. The same lawyers will do a lot of work in preparing the litigation. They will spoon-feed the judge with evidence, offering conclusions which will rain down in abundance while the trial goes on. The parties' lawyers, just like Roman gladiators, shall use all possible means in order to be victorious and win the case.

At the present time, a number of Russian scholars believe that the effectiveness of the adversarial trial process shall be the criterion of primary importance.[10] In their opinion, effectiveness must prevail even over the key aim of any civil litigation - the correct settlement of a civil dispute in conformity with factual circumstances, and in strict compliance with the law.[11]

The adversarial trial process system, in the opinion of these Russian scholars, is capable of providing the fairness of the judgment for the following reasons. First,

7 Zhuykov 2006, p. 61.

8 Afansyev 2006, p. 195; Plyuchina 2002, p. 330.

9 Reshetnikova 1997, p. 23; Bernam, Reshetnikova & Yarkov 1996, p. 26; Vershinin 1995, p. 66-67; Reznichenko 1998, p. 389-391; Plyuchina 2002, p. 332-336.

10 Reshetnikova 2006, p. 198.

11 *Ibidem.*

since the court does not itself collect evidence, no one could accuse the court of being partial or biased. Second, the parties have every prospect of success if they collect the necessary evidence and properly present it in court. For this reason, the parties should have well-founded confidence in the fair and adequate representation of their interests.[12] Third, as long as the parties collect the evidence on their own, they will collect all the possible evidence which supports their respective interests.[13] Fourth, whatever the judgment may be, the fact that a party on its own signed an agreement with an attorney and followed the course of the trial should help the party calmly accept the outcome, even in case of failure.[14]

In this way, the adversarial trial process becomes a key aim of civil procedure and replaces the true initial aim of any civil procedure, which is the correct substantive settlement of civil disputes according to the law.

Should we consider this uncontrolled adversarial trial process as a fair one? No, we do not think we should. The party that has a right to judicial protection in accordance with the law is not obliged 'to accept calmly the failure of its case' being, for example, the victim of the plaintiff's unfair abuse of process. The party should not be happy with the unfair result of the trial just by reason of having signed an agreement with an attorney or having spent its time and efforts in following the course of the trial for several years. The state is constitutionally under an obligation to award judicial protection precisely to those individuals who really need it. Otherwise, the state would be in violation of the litigants' rights and lawful interests. The judicial protection owed by the state to the litigants implies the introduction of all the necessary measures for a complete understanding of the matter in dispute. The state should not be content only with the evidence presented by the parties, but should take additional evidence on its own motion and independently investigate the case. That is what the supporters of the concept of objective truth say as well.[15]

The main idea of the concept of objective truth is that a judge shall do his best to find the truth or discover by means of judicial investigation the real and actual state of affairs. The basic objection to such an ambitious task for the judge is whether he is really capable of finding the one and only truth about facts or events which he did not witness himself. Russian supporters of the objective truth concept answer this question affirmatively.[16] For a judge, it does not really matter whether it is feasible or not to find the truth: he must at least have this aim and try to achieve it, because it would be good for the parties, for the state and for the entire system of Russian law.[17]

Under the concept of objective truth the judge should not have a passive role. He should not be disinterested in the realities of the case. Quite the contrary: he

12 Reshetnikova 1997, p. 23; Bayles 1984, p. 34-35.
13 Reshetnikova 1997, p. 23.
14 *Ibidem.*
15 Sakhnova 2008, p. 105; Treushnikov 2003, p. 76; Bonner 2000, p. 51-53; Muradyan 2002, p. 20; Afanasyev 2006, p. 207-208, and others.
16 See n. 15.
17 Sakhnova 2008, p. 105; Muradyan 2002, p. 91.

should be eager to know the truth, to play an active role and to take any measures necessary for discovering the truth. Supporters of the objective truth concept argue that this doctrine is also officially approved by the state.[18] In support of this argument, they refer to Article 12 of the Code of Civil Procedure of the Russian Federation which states that the court, while preserving its independence, objectivity and impartiality, needs to actively manage the trial, explaining their rights to the participants in the litigation; warning them about the consequences of their procedural actions or omissions; assisting them in the exercise of their rights; creating conditions for comprehensive and thorough assessment of evidence, the ascertainment of the real facts and circumstances of the case; and correctly applying the positive law while examining and resolving civil cases.

Alexander Melekhin makes the following statement in his book *Theory of State and Law*:

> 'Public law regulates administrative relations based on the enforcement mechanisms of power and obedience. It is mandatory law, which cannot be altered by the subjects of legal relationships. The subjects of public law are not equal. For example, in Russian administrative law the state bodies have regulatory authority and citizens must follow their directions in matters which are within their competence'.[19] (our translation)

Private law is different. It is a field of law where the subjects of legal relationships are equal. They cannot order each other to do something, unless it is a result of their mutual agreement, or a result of the application of mandatory provisions of civil law.

Thus, for civil law countries – the peoples of which are used to thinking of the state not as something that belongs to them (as in the United States), but as something that stands above them and is separate from the people – the concept of objective truth is an indispensable key feature. The court procedures of any kind – civil, criminal or administrative – belong to the area of public law. When someone talks about formal truth and the necessity for the court to stay away from the private affairs of the parties, it means that the time of uncertainty and of lack of social understanding has arrived. It is doubtful whether procedure should become a private matter and the court a state-supported corporation which provides services of private dispute resolution. Were this the case, this would automatically mean that the state should stay away from the control of the compliance with its laws, disregarding the ideals of the state based on the rule of law, as they are understood in civil law countries.

The state and the court, as the body vested with official powers, could hardly ever be compared with private corporations rendering dispute resolution services. However, in the next section we will discuss whether modern Russian legislation on civil procedure and current case law of Russian courts follow this theoretical understanding, and consider that the objective truth should prevail over the formal

18 Bonner 2000, p. 111-122.

19 Melekhin 2007, p. 13.

truth. In order to answer this question, we must first give a short survey of the modern Russian law of evidence.

4. Russian Law of Evidence

4.1. *Burden of Proof*

The law of civil procedure imposes on the parties an obligation which is called 'burden of proof'. Each party shall prove the facts it refers to as grounds for its respective claims and objections (Article 56 Code of Civil Procedure). The court shall determine which facts are relevant to the case, and which party needs to prove them. But, even if none of the parties raised a particular factual point relevant for the case, the court should take this point into account and discuss it with the parties. Evidence has to be submitted by the parties and other persons participating in the proceedings. The court may, however, suggest that they should submit additional evidence. If the submission of additional evidence is complicated for the parties and other actors in the proceedings, then the court should assist them on its own motion, and obtain the missing evidence *ex officio*.

The decisive facts and circumstances which are the most important for consideration of the case shall be determined by the court on its own on the basis of the arguments of the parties and their objections in conformity with rules of law. In addition, the court decides which party shall present evidence and facts to be proved.

The Code provides various exceptions from the general burden of proof rule. Facts that need not be proven encompass, besides the facts admitted by the opposing party (and accepted by the court), several other situations provided by Article 61 of the Code, e.g. facts that are generally known ('notorious facts'), and facts which were established by a court in a previously adjudicated case between the same parties ('pre-adjudicated facts').[20] The latter exception is quite similar to the *res judicata* rule in common law countries. Also, so-called procedural presumptions and fictions are considered by the theory of civil procedure as grounds for exclusion from the burden of proof rules.[21] An example is a presumption of exercising civil rights in good faith. As argued by Y.A. Serikov, pursuant to Articles 35 and 99 of the Code, it is supposed that parties to a civil dispute enjoy their procedural rights in good faith unless it is proved otherwise.[22]

4.2. *Collection and Adduction of Evidence*

On the basis of legal rules on distribution of the burden of proof, the parties are under an obligation to adduce their evidence in court. In accordance with Article 57 of the Code of Civil Procedure, the court may allow the parties to adduce additional

20 Yarkov 2005, p. 216.
21 Serikov 2006, p. 131.
22 *Ibidem*, p. 132-133.

evidence. If obtaining certain evidence is difficult for a party, upon its application the court may assist that party in obtaining such evidence. The requesting party should specify what evidence is needed, and what facts should be proven by such evidence. The reasons why that evidence cannot be adduced without court assistance should be specified as well. In the event the court grants the application, the party may request that evidence be submitted directly to the court. If the opposing party has the evidence in its possession, it shall present it in court or hand it over to the requester. The party which is legally bound to present the evidence may be subject to a fine if it fails to hand the evidence over to the court or to the opposing party. Imposition of a fine does not release the party from the duty to hand over the evidence within a renewed time-limit established by the court. Repeated failure to hand over evidence by a party causes imposition of another fine. It should also be mentioned that facilitating the collection and adduction of evidence by the court is a power, and not a duty, of the court.[23]

At the same time, the court should take into account the provisions of Article 12 of the Code regarding the chief tasks of the court. Under this article, the court shall create conditions for comprehensive and complete examination of the evidence, accurately establishing the facts of the case, and correctly applying the law. If the court groundlessly ignores a party's request for assistance in the collection of evidence, this may be grounds for appeal, consisting in incomplete establishment of the facts of the case and, consequently, in incorrect adjudication.[24]

4.3. *Evaluation of Evidence by the Court*

The court shall evaluate the evidence according to its conviction, based on a comprehensive, complete, objective and immediate examination of the evidence. No evidence is pre-established for the court, and no evidence has a prevailing evidentiary force in comparison to other evidence. This is true also in regard to written evidence (including notarial deeds), which was in history sometimes preferred to oral testimony. However, there are some exceptions provided in substantive law, according to which adducing particular kinds of evidence in court is not allowed. An example is the previously mentioned written form requirement for some transactions provided by Article 168 of the Civil Code. If this requirement needs to be met, this prevents parties from using witnesses and other oral testimony to prove the existence of a contract, but it will not disable them from making reference to written evidence regarding the relevant facts.

In evaluating the evidence, the court shall proceed on the basis of the following four criteria:[25]

23 Yarkov 2005, p. 248.

24 Korshunov & Mareev 2004, p. 190.

25 See also Yarkov 2005, p. 223-230; Treushnikov 2004, p. 110-139.

1. *Relevance of evidence* – that the evidence is important for the case (Article 59 Code of Civil Procedure);
2. *Admissibility of evidence* – that the facts of the case may be proved with particular kinds of evidence acceptable to the court (Article 60 Code of Civil Procedure);[26]
3. *Reliability of evidence* – that the evidence accurately and correctly represents the circumstances aimed at proving the ultimate fact.[27] If false or fake evidence is used by the court and such falsity is not established by the final court judgment, that would be a ground for re-opening the case (a special case of discovery of new facts; see Article 392 of the Code of Civil Procedure); and,
4. *Sufficiency of evidence* – that the court, in evaluating the evidence and establishing the facts on the basis of adduced evidence, should have enough evidence in order to come to an unambiguous decision on the events that took place.[28] For example, in evaluating written evidence, the court cannot consider as an established matter a fact which is proved solely by a copy of a written document if the original of the document was lost, and the copies of the document presented by the parties are not identical.

The results of the evaluation of evidence shall be explained by the court in the reasons of the judgment, with reference to the adduced evidence. The grounds for acceptance and rejection of any of the evidence adduced by the parties have to be elaborated in the judgment as well.

4.4. *The Role of the Court with Respect to Taking Evidence and the Truth*

Pursuant to Article 12 of the Code of Civil Procedure, we may conclude that the role of the court with respect to the taking of evidence is to make sure that the parties may effectively exercise their rights and duties, and thus satisfy their obligation to bear the burden of proof. In this connection, the court is not only obliged to explain to the parties their procedural rights and duties, but it should also warn them about the possible consequences of their procedural actions. The court should also assist the parties in collecting evidence, allocating the burden of proof between the parties and correctly evaluating the evidence adduced by the parties.

It should be noted that the court in principle does not collect evidence on its own motion; it only facilitates the evidentiary activities of the parties to the case. The court should take evidence only if a party has difficulties in obtaining it. The Supreme Court of the Russian Federation has held that difficulties in the introduction of evidence by the parties involved in litigation may occur for various reasons.[29] Among the reasons are: ill health, age, secluded place of residence, poor transportation facilities, and storage of the documents by bodies and offices of the

26 Sakhnova 2008, p. 370-373.

27 Yarkov 2005, p. 227.

28 *Ibidem*, p. 229.

29 Art. 10 of the Resolution of the Plenum of the Supreme Court of the Russian Federation, 31 November 1995, Section 8, 'On some matters of applying the Constitution by the courts of the Russian Federation in the exercise of the administration of justice'.

state, which makes it difficult to obtain a document.[30] For example, under Article 5 of the Fundamental Principles of the Legislation of the Russian Federation Concerning Notarial Services, a certificate on notarial acts may be issued by the notary only on the basis of a proper court order.[31]

Furthermore, some kinds of evidence, such as expert testimony, cannot be obtained without an order of the court.[32] Therefore, despite the fact that the burden of proof lies with the parties to the litigation, the Russian court today still retains a significant amount of power with respect to establishing the facts. It includes its role in facilitating the process of collection of evidence, and in assisting the parties in obtaining the evidence that the parties would otherwise not be able to collect on their own.

At the same time, if the parties fail to make an application regarding the collection of evidence through the court and thereby are in breach of their procedural duty of introducing evidence, the court is authorised to confine itself only to the evidence actually presented by the parties.[33] In such a case, there is a risk of the establishment of the formal truth by the court, provided the evidence is not sufficient for making conclusions that correspond to the real facts of the case.[34]

As a sort of safeguard for the objective truth in this particular situation, Article 327 of the Code of Civil Procedure allows the court of appeal to establish the real facts of the case by considering the evidence on its own. In such a way, a so-called second attempt is granted to the parties to introduce evidence which might convince the court of the real factual circumstances and permit it to establish the objective truth. In addition, both the court of appeal and the court of cassation have the authority to repeal a decision of the inferior court either if facts have been erroneously established, or if they were not sufficiently proven (Article 362 Code of Civil Procedure).[35]

5. The Russian Judicial System – Efficient and Advanced

What is the principal criterion allowing us to judge whether the civil procedure of a country is efficient or not? As is rightly pointed out by Alan Uzelac, any attempt to judge the efficiency of a judicial system usually draws criticism of the legal community.[36] Nevertheless, the European Commission for the Efficiency of Justice regularly makes efforts at conducting such research: the latest review based on data from 2010 may be found on the website of the Commission.[37]

Civil procedure, in our opinion, shall be considered efficient if it provides timely, inexpensive and proper adjudication of civil cases, in accordance with rules

30 Postanivlenie Plenuma Verkhovnogo Suda RF 31.11.1995, No. 8.
31 Cheremnykh & Cheremnykh 2006, p. 405-413.
32 Sakhnova 1999, p. 123; Osokina 2008, p. 649.
33 Osokina 2008, p. 649.
34 Treushnikov 2003, p. 76.
35 Yarkov 2005, p. 229.
36 Uzelac 2005, p. 14.
37 <www.coe.int/T/dghl/cooperation/cepej/default_en.asp>, last consulted in October 2012.

of substantive and procedural law. Assessing today's judicial system and civil procedure of the Russian Federation we may come to the conclusion that they are quite efficient and advanced. According to the official Judicial Department statistics for 2010, more than 14 million civil cases were commenced before the first instance courts of the Russian Federation, and more than 80 per cent of these cases were adjudicated by the courts.[38]

Furthermore, the Russian judicial system and civil procedure in comparison to those of other countries have some interesting peculiarities, which reinforce our assessment of the system as an efficient one. Here are some of them:

1) Consideration and Resolution of Civil Cases in a Reasonable Time

Civil disputes are resolved in Russia in a comparatively short period of time. As contrasted with many European countries, the time-limits with respect to the consideration and resolution of civil cases are directly set by the Code of Civil Procedure. Under Article 154, civil cases shall be examined and resolved by the court within two months from the date a statement of claim has been filed with the court, and by a justice of the peace within one month from the receipt of a statement initiating the proceedings.

In some cases it is permissible for a judge to exceed these time-limits. For example, in accordance with Article 152 of the Code, the judge, taking into account the points of view of the parties, may schedule preliminary hearings exceeding the period provided by the Code. Once the court has completed its consideration of the case, it shall immediately issue the operative part of the decision and within five-days time complete its reasoning, and send the entire written judgment by post to the parties.

The general attitude towards the time-limits provided by the Code is divided. On the one hand, the law does not provide any sanctions to be imposed on judges for failure to meet the target dates set by the legislation. On the other hand, a gross breach of procedural time-limits and delay of process means that the judge is in breach of the parties' right to trial within a reasonable time, and that is grounds for bringing legal action at the European Court of Human Rights in Strasbourg.

In order to reduce the pressure from the European Court of Human Rights, in 2010 the Code was supplemented with Article 22.1. This article introduced a separate kind of proceedings regarding complaints about undue delays and requests for awarding compensation for the breach of the right to trial within a reasonable time. It goes without saying that a judge who is in systematic and gross breach of the time-limits for the consideration and resolution of civil cases provided by the Code is to face disciplinary action, although it must be added that judicial practice regarding the matter is currently scarce.

At the same time, according to the official Judicial Department statistics, in 2010 a breach of procedural time-limits took place only in 0.8 per cent of civil cases considered by justices of the peace and in 4.1 per cent of civil cases considered by

[38] <www.cdep.ru/>, last consulted in June 2012.

district courts.[39] Thus it should be concluded that Russian judges for the most part are in conformity with the procedural time-limits provided by the Code.

2) Access to Justice

Access to justice is guaranteed due to the relatively low costs of litigation, including the amount of court fees, which are specified in the Tax Code of Russia. Article 333.19 of the Tax Code provides the following fees to be paid at the courts of general jurisdiction for filing a monetary claim: the minimum amount is RUB 400 while the maximum amount is RUB 73,200, i.e. no more than €1,080. The court fee for the action on divorce is equal to RUB 400. All the actions of a non-pecuniary nature amount to court fees of RUB 200 for individuals and RUB 4,000 for legal entities. To file a complaint regarding the non-conformity of a state body's regulations with Russian law, individuals have to pay a court fee of RUB 200, and legal entities of RUB 4,000. A petition for supervisory review would require a payment of RUB 200 for individuals and only RUB 3,000 for legal entities. Revision of a civil case by a court of appeal is even cheaper: it is one-half of the sum of the court fees for a non-pecuniary, non-monetary lawsuit: it is only RUB 200 for individuals and only RUB 2,000 for legal entities.

One may say that justice in Russia for the most part inherited the Soviet tradition of the people's courts. It is available to all citizens regardless of their material wealth. This accounts for the large number of civil cases considered by Russian courts annually.

3) Appealing Court Decisions in a Multilevel System

Russia has a remarkable multilevel system of appeal. Parties to a trial in Russia have the inalienable right to appeal to second instance and third instance courts. Consequently, the Russian model of civil procedure offers every citizen the opportunity to get at least one superior instance court's reconsideration of the first instance court's judgment in the case.

Parties involved in a civil dispute adjudicated before the courts of general jurisdiction have the right to file an application for judicial review by a higher tribunal. If there is an ambiguity in the law which does not allow a party to obtain a legally correct judgment, the party is entitled to have two or three instances of hearings and an opinion of the Supreme Court of the Russian Federation.

If the appeal raises an issue of great public importance or discloses a gross violation of substantive or procedural law, then the party is entitled to hearings at the highest instance. As Dmitry Maleshin rightly mentioned in a recent report, the supervisory court may render a new judgment when it is not necessary to consider additional facts or evidence. If the party fails with the reconsideration of its case by the highest instance court and its petition is denied, even this is not the end yet.[40] There is still a possibility for the party to address the Constitutional Court of the Russian Federation with a complaint based on ambiguous rules in the law which

39 See <www.cdep.ru/>, last consulted in June 2012.

40 Maleshin 2007, <www.law.msu.ru/file/7352/download/7352>, last consulted in June 2012.

cause trouble and a number of mistaken judicial decisions. If the Constitutional Court supports the complaint of the party, it will schedule hearings; if it rejects the complaint, it will provide the party with a written opinion on the matter of law.

Following that, if the decision of the Constitutional Court grants a new clarification of law in favour of the party, the party is entitled to file an application on the re-opening of the entire case on the grounds of newly-discovered evidence and at the end of the day get a correct decision from the court.

4) Relative Uniformity in Interpreting the Law

A big step forward has been made with regard to the uniformity of case law. There is no precedent system in Russia as it is a country with roots in the civil law tradition. In spite of this, in the last decade the courts of general jurisdiction have gradually moved towards uniformity in the application and interpretation of the law.

Judges of the courts of general jurisdiction are not officially under the obligation to observe the views on points of law expressed by other courts, but in order to avoid mistakes in complicated matters of law, they customarily follow the instructions of the Supreme Court of the Russian Federation.[41]

In Russia, the highest judicial instance may issue specific forms of legal acts, which contain instructions for inferior courts. These documents are called Regulations of the Plenary Session of the Supreme Court. The Regulations describe in detail important aspects of law and draw the attention of the Russian Judiciary to the recommendations of the courts of the highest instances regarding particular kinds of cases. The Regulations are extremely popular among Russian judges, and in fact in Russia they play a role as a source of law which to some extent may be considered as one having some features similar to a common law precedent.

6. Conclusion

The peculiarities of the Russian judicial system influence the concept of truth in civil proceedings. Wide accessibility of Russian courts for the vast majority of individuals and organisations causes a steady annual increase in the number of civil suits, and the scope of work for the courts constantly grows. Relatively short legislative time-limits for processing civil cases force judges to observe these time-limits even if it means decreasing the quality of judgments. For the most part, 'speedy justice' unavoidably turns out to be inconsistent with the objective truth concept, which is in contradiction to the prevailing doctrine in civil procedure scholarship.

At the same time, Russian civil procedural law, while requiring correctness in establishing the factual background of a civil case, does not demand that judges be proactive in finding the truth and in verifying that established facts correspond to reality. In this way, provisions of the Code of Civil Procedure conflict with the objective truth doctrine advocated by the Russian theory of civil procedure. Another

41 Fetisov 2002-2003, p. 25; Tumanov 2008, p. 133.

conflict is the one between the duty of the court to fully establish the facts by examination of all evidence, and the short time-limits for the court to consider and resolve civil cases. The latter happens under the heavy burden of a constantly increasing influx of cases, which has enormously increased the workload of the Russian Judiciary.

A guarantee that civil disputes are resolved in the general interest (i.e. in the interest of the parties, the Judiciary and the State) consists in an opportunity to review each civil case before at least two higher courts. In any event, whether a court judgment will be based on establishing the objective truth or the formal truth is entirely up to the discretion of Russian judges. They still have broad powers granted by the Code of Civil Procedure with respect to the taking of evidence. Russian judges can always choose whether the truth they establish shall be an objective or formal one. They may also independently decide how much time it should take to consider a concrete civil case.

All the components which we have mentioned in this paper make the Russian system of civil procedure unique, and - for the time being - quite efficient. In our opinion, contemporary Russian civil procedure is moving in the right direction, which is quite the same as that of other jurisdictions. And, who knows - maybe Russian civil procedure will be the first to arrive at the final destination of procedural efficiency.

Bibliography

Afanasyev 2006
Afanasyev, S.F., 'Kratkiy obzor problemy istiny v grazhdanskom processualnom prave i sudoproizvodstve', *Rossiiskiy Ezhegodnik Grazhdanskogo i Arbitrzhnogo Processa*, 2006, No. 4, p. 175–208.

Bayles 1987
Bayles, M.D., *Principles of Law: A Normative Analysis*, Dordrecht: Kluwer Academic Publishers, 1987.

Bernam, Reshetnikova & Yarkov 1996
Bernam, Y., Reshetnikova, I.V. & Yarkov, V.V., *Sudebnaja reforma: problemi grazhdanskoy yurisdiktzii*, Yekaterinburg: USLA Publishing House, 1996.

Bonner 2000
Bonner, A.T., *Ustanovlenie obstoyatelstv grazhdanskikh del*, Moscow: Gorodets, 2000.

Cheremnykh & Cheremnykh 2006
Cheremnykh, G.G. & Cheremnykh, I.G., *Notarialnoe pravo Rossiyskoy Federatsii*, Moscow: Eksmo Education, 2006.

Fetisov 2002-2003
Fetisov, A.K., 'Opravdanie "precedentnogo" bytiya', *Rossiysiy Ezhegodnik Grazhdanskogo i Arbitrazhnogo Processa*, 2002-2003, No. 2, p. 20-30.

Kleinman 1954
Kleinman, A.F., *Sovietsky grazhdansky process*, Moscow: Moscow State University Press, 1954, partly republished in: Treushnikov, M.K., *Grazhdanskiy process. Khrestomatiya*, Moscow: Gorodets, 2005, p. 269-270.

Korshunov & Mareev 2004
Korshunov, M.K. & Mareev, Y.L., *Grazhdanskiy process*, Moscow: Norma, 2004.

Melekhin 2007
Melekhin, A.V., *Theory of State and Law*, Moscow: Market DC, 2007.

Muradyan 2002
Muradyan, E.M., *Istina kak problema sudebnogo prava*, Moscow: Bylina, 2002.

Osakina 2008
Osokina, G.L., *Grazhdansky process. Obschaya chast*, 2nd edn., Moscow: Norma, 2008.

Plyuchina 2002
Plyuchina, M.A., 'Istina v grazhdanskom sudoproizvodstve', *Rossiiskiy Ezhegodnik Grazhdanskogo i arbitrzhnogo processa*, 2002, No. 1, p. 329-336.

Reshetnikova 1997
Reshetnikova, I.V., *Dokazatelstvennoe pravo Anglii I SSHA,* Yekaterinburg: USLA Publishing House, 1997.

Reshetnikova 2006
Reshetnikova, I.V., 'Sostyzatelniy rossiyskiy arbitrazhniy process: problemy razvitiya', *Rossiyskiy Ezhegodnik Grazhdanskogo i Arbitrazhnogo Processa,* 2006, No. 5, p. 187-199.

Reznichenko 1998
Reznichenko, I.M., 'Prinzip formalnoy istiny - prozessualnaya realnost', in: Shevchenko, A.S. (ed.), *Aktualnye problemy gosudarstva i prava na rubezhe vekov,* Vladivostok: Far Eastern State University, 1998, p. 389-391.

Sakhnova 1999
Sakhnova, T.V., *Sudebnaya ekspertiza,* Moscow: Gorodets, 1999.

Sakhnova 2008
Sakhnova, T.V., *Kurs grazhdanskogo processa. Teoreticheskie nachala i osnovniye instituty,* Moscow: Wolters Kluwer, 2008.

Serikov 2006
Serikov, Y.A., *Prezumptsii v grazhdanskom sudoproizvodstve,* Moscow: Wolters Kluwer, 2006.

Shakaryan 2004
Shakaryan, M.S. (ed.), *Grazhdanskoe processualnoe pravo,* Moscow: Prospekt Publisher, 2004.

Treushnikov 2003
Treushnikov, M.K. (ed.), *Grazhdansky process,* Moscow: Gorodets, 2003.

Treushnikov 2004
Treushnikov, M.K., *Sudebniye dokazatelstva,* Moscow: Gorodets, 2004.

Tumanov 2008
Tumanov, D.A., *Probely v grazhdanskom processualnom prave,* Moscow: Norma, 2008.

Uzelac 2005
Uzelac, A., 'Mozhno li izmerit effectivnost sudebnoi sistemi?', *Rossiyskiy Ezhegodnik Grazhdanskogo i Arbitrazhnogo Processa,* 2005, No. 4, p. 14-42.

Vaskovsky 2003
Vaskovsky, E.V., *Uchebnik grazhdanskogo processa,* Moscow: Zertsalo, 2003.

Vershinin 1995
Vershinin, A.P., 'Dokazivannie v grazhdanskom prozesse: novie pravila', *Pravovedenie*, 1995, No. 6, p. 66-67.

Yarkov 2005
Yarkov, V.V. (ed.), *Grazhdanskiy process,* 5th edn., Moscow: Wolters Kluwer, 2005.

Zhuykov 2006
Zhuykov, V.M., *Sudebnaya reforma: problemy dostupa k pravosudiyu,* Moscow: Statut, 2006.

TRANSNATIONAL PERSPECTIVE: TRUTH-FINDING AT INTERNATIONAL TRIBUNALS

J. Sladič

TAKING AND ADMINISTERING EVIDENCE BEYOND THE STATE - SOME REFLECTIONS ON PROCEDURAL ISSUES BEFORE THE COURT OF JUSTICE OF THE EUROPEAN UNION

1. Introduction

In practice, two issues, namely truth and efficiency, in any judicial proceedings affect the core notion of taking and administering evidence and then assessing this evidence in rulings of different judicial or even quasi-judicial bodies.[1] Truth, efficiency, evidence and the taking of evidence and even in broader terms the relationship between law and facts correspond to modern practices of efficient processing of data and information.[2] Confidence in the justice system would be seriously impaired if it were ineffective.[3] These findings also apply to the international and European judiciaries. This paper does not deal with civil proceedings *stricto sensu,* although the elasticity of rules on the gathering of facts and therefore establishing the judicial truth[4] provided for in the procedural law of European courts allows us to draw some conclusions on the efficiency of any judicial procedure.

Since the end of the Second World War Western Europe has seen unprecedented development, namely the phenomenon of European integration be it in the form of the Council of Europe (intergovernmental form) or in the form of what is today referred to as the European Union (supranational form). Both forms

1 I define as 'quasi-judicial bodies' especially the institutions of the Austrian *Unabhängige Verwaltungssenate* and the Belgian *Conseil du Contentieux des Étrangers/Raad voor Vreemdelingenbetwistingen*. Both bodies do actually perform tasks of judicial review of administrative action (unilateral administrative acts and omissions to act by several agencies of the executive branch).

2 An interesting observation can be made when studying German legal writing. German authors are starting to introduce terms such as 'gathering of information' (*Informationsbeschaffung*) together with rules on evidence (Rosenberg, Schwab & Gottwald 2004, p. 737-738).

3 Rijavec 2009, p. 227.

4 The term 'judicial truth' shall be construed as the truth by facts that could be established by definitive judicial rulings having acquired *res judicata* effect (*res judicata pro veritate habetur*).

of integration have developed a highly sophisticated system of judicial bodies which offer judicial protection and dispute resolution to private parties and states. Whereas the Council of Europe has developed a system for the protection of individual rights that has evolved into the current European Court of Human Rights, the Treaty establishing the European Coal and Steel Community (1952) and the Treaties of Rome (1958) instituted a Court of Justice of the European Communities that has seen its name changed by the Treaty of Lisbon (2009). Today it is referred to as the Court of Justice of the European Union (hereinafter, the CJEU).[5] This court has developed highly sophisticated techniques in dealing with issues such as truth and efficiency in judicial proceedings.

This contribution is based on the assumption that European, international and supranational judicial bodies apply a separation between substantive and procedural law,[6] as the gathering of facts and information in any judicial proceedings also concerns the application of substantive law. As far as the proceedings in the judicial system of the European Union (EU) are concerned, their object is not only the discussion of points of law. Especially in the so-called direct administration of the EU,[7] the gathering and submitting of facts is essential for legal remedies provided by EU law.[8]

In this Chapter, I shall examine some procedural issues of the CJEU[9] related to truth and efficiency in judicial proceedings. EU judicial bodies rarely engage directly in civil proceedings as judicial authorities or even as litigants.[10] This is not to say that their contribution to the development of civil procedure in Europe is not important; indeed, their influence is significant through the adoption of preliminary rulings that may completely change the structure of national procedural law (the so-

5 I first served as legal secretary (*référendaire*) to the judge and then Advocate-General at the Court of Justice of the European Communities Madame Verica Trstenjak and afterwards pleaded as advocate before the Court of Justice of the European Union. Therefore, I was able to gather direct experience on both sides of the bar of the European Union.

6 It should be stressed that such a separation – although natural in national legal orders – is not accepted as such without reservation in international law (Kolasa 2000, p. 185 *et seq.* and Sladič 2008, p. 66). The reason probably being that in international law there is no enforcement of the judicial award rendered by an international judicial body. Enforcement of a judicial decision is an act *jure imperii*. International judicial bodies lack such competence *ratione personae*. See also for other opinions Benzing 2010, p. 31-35.

7 See, e.g., Ziller 2004, p. 13.

8 Biavati 2005, p. 198.

9 Today the CJEU is composed of the Court of Justice, the General Court (formerly the Court of First Instance (CFI)) and the Civil Service Tribunal. In this text the term CJEU is used both for the institution comprising three courts and the Court of Justice itself. Decisions of the Civil Service Tribunal can be appealed on points of law before the General Court and decisions of the General Court delivered in first instance can be appealed on points of law before the Court of Justice. The term 'appeal' in the English version of the TFEU and the Statute of the Court is misleading. The Spanish version uses a better term, 'el recurso de casación'.

10 If one examines the case law of the Luxembourg courts, one can sometimes find rulings concerning the CJEU as a litigant. These cases mainly concern public procurement and other service contracts entered into by the CJEU.

called *Factortame effect*). Nevertheless, the core tasks of the CJEU can be compared more to those of an administrative or constitutional court.[11]

In the first part (Sections 2-5) I shall address the issue of fundamental rules on the gathering of facts and information before the CJEU.[12] In the second part (Section 6) I shall address the difference between the measures of organisation of procedure as a very efficient and flexible tool of gathering data, on the one hand, and the normal ordinary procedure of the gathering of facts, on the other. Then I shall try to link the aforementioned measures of organisation of procedure to the terms known in civil law jurisdictions such as the principle of the concentration of submitting pleas, facts and evidence (*Konzentrationsmaxime*), the restriction of written submissions and the active role of the judge in conducting the procedure (*materielle Prozessleitung*).[13] The expedited procedure should expressly be mentioned as a solution offering the highest degree of efficacy.

2. Lack of National and European Rules on the Gathering of Facts, Evidence and Information

It might be interesting to start with the brief observation that there are extremely few codified rules on the gathering of facts or information of relevance for proceedings[14] in the procedure before the CJEU. The next observation is that the evidence is seldom taken under the principle of immediacy.

It should be stressed that national rules on the gathering of facts are not applicable in proceedings before the CJEU.[15] However, 'given that there is no legislation at the EU level governing the concept of proof, any type of evidence admissible under the procedural law of the Member States in similar proceedings is in principle admissible'.[16] Where EU law fails to lay down requirements of proof, the parties are free to use any conclusive means of proof.[17] However, the issue gets even more complicated. 'If the evidence of the existence of a right granted by a

11 The application for annulment (Art. 263 TFEU) and the application for failure to act are typical remedies for judicial review of administrative action.

12 I shall use the English translations of German and French terms found in English language versions of CJEU decisions and opinions.

13 This term originating in German legal terminology refers to the active role performed by a (civil) court when gathering, segmenting and preparing facts and evidence for a concrete case or litigation, elaborating the *thema probandi* and tenders of evidence (see, e.g., Rechberger & Simotta 2010, paras 606-610, and Fasching 1990, p. 414-418). For historical reasons, it is also known in current Slovenian (*materialno procesno vodstvo*) and Croatian Civil Procedure (*materijalno upravljanje postupkom*) (on the historical influence, see, e.g., Rijavec 2009, p. 219).

14 In the sense of *jus positum*. One should note that the principle *actori incumbit probatio* is somehow rudimentarily codified in Art. 38 of the old Rules of Procedure and identical text in Art. 120 of the new Rules of Procedure (published in *OJ* EU L 265 of 29 September 2012 p. 1 *et seq.*).

15 Lenaerts 2007, p. 477.

16 CJEU, Joined Cases C-310/98 *Hauptzollamt Neubrandenburg* and C-406/98, *Sagpol SC Transport Miedzynarodowy i Spedycja* [2000] ECR I-01797, para 29.

17 Plender 1997, p. 165 with reference to CJEU, Joined Cases 225/81 and 241/81 *Toledano Laredo and Mario Garilli v Commission* [1983] p. 347, para 13.

provision of ... [EU] law is governed by the national law to which the person concerned is subject [for example maintenance payable as a result of divorce], it is ... , in the case of an action before the CJEU[,] for that Court ... to consider, in order to ensure a correct application of the said provision, whether the conditions required by the national law are satisfied'.[18]

The nature of the procedure before the CJEU also explains the failure to elaborate legal provisions on the gathering of facts. There are essentially two types of procedure before the CJEU. For lawyers of common law jurisdictions, it might be interesting to observe that the Anglo-American rules concerning the competence, relevance and materiality of evidence built up around the jury have found no counterpart in the CJEU.[19]

Quantitatively more important are the preliminary rulings as special proceedings which are by their very nature limited to points of law. Under Article 267 of the Treaty on the Functioning of the European Union (TFEU) a national court submits questions to the CJEU about the interpretation or validity of a provision of EU law.[20]

> 'That article establishes the framework for a relationship of close co-operation between the national courts or tribunals and the CJEU based on the assignment to each of different functions.[21] In the context of that co-operation, it is the national court seized of the dispute which alone has direct knowledge of the facts of the main action.[22] Where the CJEU receives a request for interpretation of EU law under Article 267 TFEU which is not manifestly unrelated to the reality or the subject-matter of the main proceedings and it has the necessary information in order to give appropriate answers to the questions put to it in relation to the applicability of EU law to those proceedings, it must reply to that request and is not required to consider the facts as presumed by the referring court or tribunal, a presumption which it is for the referring court or tribunal to verify subsequently if that should prove to be necessary'.[23]

The importance of gathering information in preliminary rulings is therefore somewhat different. However, legal writers referring to Advocate-General Warner's opinion in the *EMI Records* case[24] and case law[25] continue to stress the importance of the burden of proof and of the adducing of facts in preliminary rulings.[26] Indeed,

18 CJEU, Case 24-71 *Meinhardt v Commission* [1972] ECR 269, para 12.

19 Plender 1997, p. 165.

20 <http://curia.europa.eu/jcms/jcms/Jo2_7024/#procedures>, last consulted in June 2012.

21 See CJEU, Case C-303/06 *S. Coleman* [2008] ECR I-5603, para 29; Joined Cases 36/80 and 71/80 *Irish Creamery Milk Suppliers Association and Others* [1981] ECR 735, para 5, and Case C-236/98 *JämO* [2000] ECR I-2189, para 30.

22 CJEU, Case C-152/03 *Ritter-Coulais* [2006] ECR I-1711, para 14, and Van Raepenbusch 2011, p. 542.

23 See, to that effect, CJEU, Case C-127/92 *Enderby* [1993] ECR I-5535, para 12, and Case C-303/06 *S. Coleman* [2008] ECR I-5603, para 31.

24 Opinion of Advocate-General Warner delivered on 31 March 1976, Joined Cases 51/75, 86/75 and 96/75 *EMI Records* [1976] ECR 853, 855-857.

25 See to that effect in the circumstances of doubts on the validity of the Commission's decision CJEU, Case C-269/90 *Technische Universität München* [1991] ECR I-5469, paras 21-22.

26 Biavati 2005, p. 199.

the CJEU may *ex officio*, after hearing the Advocate-General, 'request clarification' from the national court.[27] Such requests are not very frequent and do not always concern only facts; they refer to any information the CJEU considers necessary for the procedure.[28] The CJEU may in proceedings for preliminary rulings also require the parties to produce all documents and to supply all information which it considers desirable.[29]

Nevertheless, the general rule in preliminary rulings is that the CJEU is interpreting and not applying the law. Facts must be gathered only for the application of law in a particular case.

The second set of proceedings are referred to as 'direct actions' (in practice the most common being the application for annulment (Articles 263-264 TFEU),[30] actions for failure to fulfil obligations (Articles 258-260 TFEU)[31] and actions for damages (Article 340 TFEU), and appeals procedures (Articles 56-61 Statute of the Court of Justice of the European Union[32])).

> 'In direct actions the CJEU must only rule on the application of the parties. It is for them to define the framework of their dispute, and the CJEU cannot, as a matter of principle, rule on matters other than the claims made, nor, of course, rule in complete disregard of the dispute as defined in the application initiating proceedings. Nevertheless, the role of the court is not a passive one and it cannot be expected to be merely 'the mouthpiece of the parties'. Its task of *juris dictio* requires it to be able to apply to the facts put before it by the parties the relevant rules of law for the solution of the dispute. It cannot confine itself to the arguments put forward by the parties in support of their claims or it may be forced to base its decision on erroneous legal considerations'.[33]

The low importance of rules on adducing information and the gathering of facts for the CJEU compared to national legal systems is explained by the limited priority given to rules on evidence in the proceedings before the CJEU. There is seldom litigation on the veracity of the adduced facts.[34] Instead, parties litigate about facts

27 Art. 104(5) of the old Rules of Procedure and Art. 101 of the new Rules of Procedure.

28 Naômé 2010, p. 199-202, lists a short and non-exhaustive list of requests for clarification. It would appear that the requests mainly concern clarifications on issues such as the exact framework of national substantive law, national procedural law and factual issues.

29 Naômé 2010, p. 202-204, with reference to the CJEU Joined Cases C-329/06 and C-343/06 *Wiedemann v Land Baden-Württemberg* (C-329/06) and *Funk v Stadt Chemnitz* (C-343/06) [2008] ECR I-4635, paras 42-43.

30 By an action for annulment, the applicant seeks the annulment of a measure (in particular a regulation, directive or decision) adopted by an institution, body, office or agency of the European Union (<http://curia.europa.eu/jcms/jcms/Jo2_7024/#procedures>, last consulted in June 2012).

31 These actions enable the Court of Justice to determine whether a Member State has fulfilled its obligations under European Union law. The action may be brought by the Commission – as, in practice, is usually the case – or by a Member State (<http://curia.europa.eu/jcms/-jcms/Jo2_7024/#procedures>, last consulted in June 2012).

32 Protocol (No. 3) on the Statute of the Court of Justice of the European Union.

33 Opinion of Advocate-General Léger delivered on 2 April 1998, Case C-252/96 P *Parliament v Gutiérrez de Quijano y Lloréns* [1998] ECR I-7421, paras 35-36.

34 The CJEU is a judge of law and of fact.

which have already been established in previous administrative proceedings that are not contested before the CJEU.[35] If one speaks of administrative proceedings, one speaks, as far as truth and efficiency are concerned, of the 'principle of official inquiry'.[36] The majority of procedures before the CJEU could be compared to the judicial review of administrative action. By taking over the French tradition[37] and the elements of administrative doctrine the CJEU elaborated the two rebuttable presumptions (*praesumptio juris tantum*), namely the presumption of legality[38] and the presumption of validity of any measure adopted by EU bodies.[39] This situation creates a position of substantive inequality between the parties in terms of their inability to prove the necessary facts.[40]

However, the body of case law on the gathering of information in proceedings with direct actions is today firmly established. German and Italian legal doctrine noticed this particular situation and started elaborating principles of procedure before the CJEU, including the principles on the gathering of facts and information.[41] The main scientific interest lies in the judicial creation of a body of case law that is neither civil nor common law.[42] However, it is unfortunately true that the rules governing procedure in the CJEU attract less attention than those governing procedure in domestic courts.[43] Although it is well known in all legal systems, the term 'burden of proof' does not have the same meaning in civil law systems as it does in common law systems. Such a finding complicates work in

35 Hackspiel 2003b, p. 435-436.

36 This term is the translation used by the CJEU for the French term *principe inquisitoire* and the German term *Untersuchungsgrundsatz*. As far as the importance of that principle is concerned, see Opinion of Madame Advocate-General Trstenjak, Case C-1/06 *Bonn Fleisch* [2007] ECR I-5609, paras 56 *et seq*. It should be noted that Austrian, Slovenian and Croatian legal writers also stress the importance of the *principle of the search for the material truth* (*Grundsatz der Erforschung der materiellen Wahrheit*) as a consequence of the principle of official inquiry and of the principle of the unfettered adduction and evaluation of evidence (see, e.g., Antoniolli & Koja 1996, p. 608-609; Rijavec 2003, p. 55, 59).

37 Historically in common law jurisdictions it was up to juries to decide on questions of fact. However, such a limitation of the role of the judge is not known in civil law jurisdictions. Especially in the 'Latin part' of civil law jurisdictions (France, Italy) one can therefore still encounter the system of legal proof in civil procedure.

38 CJEU, Joined Cases 42 and 49/59 *S.N.U.P.A.T. v High Authority* [1961] ECR English special edition p. 53; CFI, Case T-34/92 *Fiatagri and New Holland Ford v Commission* [1994] ECR II-905, para 27, and Sladič 2008, p. 33. However, legal writers sometimes claim that there is no assumption of legality of EU acts (Schermers & Waelbroek 2001, p. 730).

39 CJEU, Case 101/78 *Granaria* [1979] ECR 623, para 4. Any measure which is brought into force in accordance with the Treaty must be presumed to be valid so long as a competent court has not made a finding that it is invalid.

40 Lenaerts, Arts & Maselis 2006, p. 556.

41 Biavati 2005, p. 200-202 and Hackspiel 2003b, p. 434-435.

42 See, e.g., CJEU, Case C-550/07 P *Akzo Nobel Chemicals and Akcros Chemicals v Commission* [2010] ECR I-8301, concerning the autonomous European notion of 'legal professional privilege' that is today (at least in European competition law) a mixture of the *in rem* common law approach and the *in personam* civil law approach applied *ratione personae* only to independent lawyers (see to that effect Baudesson & Rosher 2006, p. 37 *et seq.*; Ronzi 2008, p. 680-681, and Magnus 2010).

43 Plender 1997, p. 31.

international judicial bodies.[44] Even if terms such as 'proof', 'evidence', 'taking of evidence', etc. might be familiar to lawyers worldwide, they will not necessarily have the same meaning. Indeed, according to the CJEU,

> 'the need for a uniform application of European Union law and the principle of equality require that the terms of a provision of European Union law which make no express reference to the law of the Member States for the purpose of determining its meaning and scope must normally be given an independent and uniform interpretation throughout the European Union; that interpretation must take into account the context of the provision and the objective of the relevant legislation'.[45]

Distinguished legal writers refer to this issue as the independence of European law of evidence.[46] However, the issue of the gathering of facts has a different meaning for preliminary rulings than it has for direct actions.[47]

It is of interest that the CJEU performs only a marginal review on questions of evidence and fact-gathering.

> 'Provided that the evidence has been properly obtained and the general principles of law and the rules of procedure in relation to the burden of proof and the taking of evidence have been observed, it is for the General Court alone to assess the value which should be attached to the evidence produced to it. Save where the clear sense of the evidence has been distorted, that appraisal does not therefore constitute a point of law which is subject as such to review by the Court of Justice'.[48]

A sharp distinction between questions of law and questions of fact - as in other legal systems - is well established.[49] 'A notice published in the Official Journal of the European Union cannot be regarded as a mere piece of evidence, but forms part of the dispute's legal background which the Court not only may but, as the case may be, must take into consideration of its own motion and to which the parties may

44 See Grando 2006, p. 615, who explains that 'the concept of the burden of proof has evolved differently in the civil law and the common law legal systems. In contrast to the common law, in the civil law system the phrase "burden of proof" has only one meaning. It refers to the duty of each party to prove their claims. In the common law system, the concept has been divided into two ideas. The "burden of going forward" refers to the burden of producing evidence that would allow the court to consider the proponent's case and possibly rule in its favour. The "burden of persuasion" refers to the idea of actually persuading the court to find in favour of the proponent of the evidence. The distinction developed in the common law finds no place in international law'. It should be added that the last finding also applies to the CJEU. 'The classic apportionment of the burden of proof, whereby each party proves the facts on which the claim or defence is based, applies' also in EU procedural law (Lenaerts, Arts & Maselis 2006, p. 556).

45 CJEU, Case 327/82 *Ekro* [1984] ECR 107, para 11; Case C-287/98 *Linster* [2000] ECR I-6917, para 43; and Case C-523/07 *A* [2009] ECR I-2805, para 34.

46 Lenaerts 2007, p. 478.

47 Biavati 2005, p. 198.

48 CJEU, Case C-551/03 P *General Motors v Commission* [2006] ECR I-3173, paras 51-52.

49 The crucial point emerging from the rigid separation between law and facts was the founding of a system of proof that emphasised judicial discretion (Giuliani 2009, p. 33).

also refer at any stage of the proceedings'.[50] One finds similarities with the principle *jura novit curia*. It should be stressed that the legality of a contested act that has been adopted by EU institutions, with the exception of very few infringements of essential procedural requirements,[51] is never reviewed of its own motion.[52] The review is essentially limited to the pleas in law submitted by the applicant. However, in direct actions questions of national law are questions of fact.[53] The principle *da mihi facta, dabo tibi jus* is as such not wholly applicable in the procedural law of the CJEU.[54]

3. Principle of Unfettered Adduction and Evaluation of Evidence

As far as the procedure before the CJEU is concerned, rules on the gathering of facts and information are based on general principles of law, common to all Member States of the EU.[55] According to Advocate-General Mengozzi,

> 'a particular fact may be proved by any form of evidence (freedom as to the form of evidence adduced) and determination of the probative value of an item of evidence is a matter for the EU judicature,[56] not for legislation (unfettered evaluation of evidence), it cannot on the other hand, in my view, be maintained that every item of evidence produced is usable and has to be evaluated as to its merits by the EU Institutions or the EU judicature'.[57]

In practice, due to the internal (though unofficial) working language (namely French) a very strong resemblance to French and Belgian law can be seen.[58]

50 CJEU, Case C-373/07 P *Mebrom v Commission* [2009] ECR I-54* (summary publication), para 80.

51 Namely lack of competence, lack of statement of reasons and certain procedural rights like consultation in various administrative and legislative procedures. The Court can raise pleas of its own motion only where those pleas relate to public policy. The pleas concerning the substance of the case are not pleas relating to public policy (GC Case T-44/00 *Mannesmannröhren-Werke v Commission* [2004] ECR II-2223, para 126; see also Sladič 2005, p. 127 and Lenaerts, Arts & Maselis 2006, p. 287-288).

52 See to that effect Sachs 2010, p. 10.

53 This is especially true in the framework of actions for failure to fulfil obligations. The theoretical reasoning is that the CJEU shall according to Art. 19 of the Treaty on European Union (TEU) ensure that in the interpretation and application of the treaties the law is observed.

54 Lenaerts, Arts & Maselis 2006, p. 557 and Hackspiel 2003b, p. 434.

55 Biavati 2005, p. 198, as far as the rule *actori incumbit probatio* is concerned.

56 The principle *quaestio facti est in arbitrio judicis*.

57 Opinion of Advocate-General Mengozzi delivered on 6 November 2008, Case C-511/06 P *Archer Daniels Midland v Commission* [2009] ECR I-5843, para 114.

58 Hackspiel 2003a, p. 370. Such a solution implies a strong civil law influence. However, there are important differences between civil law jurisdictions. For example, the interdiction of *reformatio in pejus* is considered to be a general principle in any judicial proceedings in Germany, Austria, Slovenia and Croatia. Advocate-General Trstenjak considered this principle to be a general principle of EU law (see Opinion of Madame Advocate-General Trstenjak delivered on 29 November 2007, Case C-16/06 *Les Éditions Albert René v OHIM and Orange* [2008] I-10053, paras 35-36). However, the CJEU left this issue open as far as →

The main principle concerning the law of evidence (standard of proof) is the 'principle of the unfettered adduction and evaluation of evidence',[59] which is known in some form in every civil law jurisdiction.[60] The CJEU has to assess the facts adduced by the parties or gathered on its own motion (*principe inquisitoire*) and its assessment is not covered by any system of law of evidence (*quaestio facti est in arbitrio judicis*).[61] Evidence is therefore a term used by the CJEU.[62] However, before the CJEU evidence and facts seem to be interchangeable items. The Full Court has stressed that 'the General [C]ourt has exclusive jurisdiction to establish and assess the relevant facts and to assess the value which should be attached to the items of evidence produced to it, unless there has been distortion of such facts or evidence'.[63] The English version of that ruling does not actually match its French original. Legal experts at the CJEU deduced from this ruling that evidence shall be considered as important as facts.[64]

As far as the gathering of facts is concerned, I would also like to mention the difficulties experienced with the common law institute of pre-trial discovery, as the procedural law of the CJEU is something very different compared to civil trials in common law jurisdictions.[65]

proceedings for the review of legality of contested EU administrative measures are concerned (see CJEU, Case C-16/06 *Les Éditions Albert René v OHIM and Orange* [2008] ECR I-10053, para 49).

59 This is the English translation offered by the CJEU for the French term *la libre administration de la preuve* or in German *die freie Beweiswürdigung*. For an explanation, see Joined Opinions of Judge Vesterdorf acting as Advocate-General delivered on 10 July 1991, Joined Cases T-1/89 *Rhone-Poulenc v Commission;* T-2/89 *Petrofina v Commission;* T-3/89 *Atochem v Commission;* T-4/89 *Basf v Commission;* T-6/89 *Enichem Anic v Commission;* T-7/89 *Hercules Chemicals v Commission;* T-8/89 *DSM v Commission;* T-9/89 *Huels v Commission;* T-10/89 *Hoechst v Commission;* T-11/89 *Shell v Commission;* T-12/89 *Solvay v Commission;* T-13/89 *Imperial Chemical Industries v Commission;* T-14/89 *Montedipe v Commission;* T-15/89 *Chemie Linz v Commission* [1991] ECR II-867, at II-869 and at II-954 and Opinion of Advocate-General Geelhoed delivered on 12 September 2006, Case C-411/04 P *Salzgitter Mannesmann v Commission* [2007] ECR I-959, para 65.

60 See to that effect Legal 2007, p. 186. Referring to French *la doctrine*, it has been asserted in the cited article by the former French judge at the CFI that there is a casual link between the terms 'standards of proof' and 'standard of review'. If the standard of review to be adopted in the case is that of a manifest error of assessment, the defendant is subject to a lighter standard of proof (*la prevue allégée*), whereas the applicant is still subject to the normal unfettered adduction of evidence.

61 Biavati 2005, p. 202. See to that effect also CFI, Case T-324/05 *Estonia v Commission* [2009] ECR II-3681, paras 51-52, 54-55.

62 Mehdi 2007, p. 165.

63 CJEU, Case C-488/01 P *Martinez v Parliament* [2003] ECR I-13355, para 53.

64 Naômé 2011, p. 91. The author would like to thank Mrs. Caroline Naômé for allowing him to use her publication for the purpose of this conference.

65 See to that effect Kleyr 2011, p. 16–17, regarding difficulties encountered in Luxembourg civil procedure with the notion of pre-trial discovery.

4. Principle *Actori Incumbit Probatio* and Exceptions

The basic principle in procedural law concerning the gathering of facts is *actori incumbit probatio*. It is normal for the person alleging facts in support of a claim to adduce proof of such facts.[66] 'The fact that the CJEU has the power to order measures of organisation of procedure to be carried out does not release the parties from their obligation to prove their assertions'.[67] Facts asserted and evidence submitted must be detailed and specific. According to case law, 'a party may only put forward, in support of its claims, facts which are sufficiently specific and detailed for the CJEU to regard them, at the very least, as credible and to enable the opposing party to contest them in an effective manner and, if appropriate, to submit evidence in rebuttal'.[68]

Essential points of law and of fact on which an action is based must be indicated coherently and intelligibly in the application itself.[69] The submissions must be sufficiently clear and precise to enable the defendant to prepare a defence and the Court to rule on the application, if necessary, without any further information.[70] In order to satisfy those requirements, an application (seeking compensation for damage caused by an EU institution) must state the evidence from which the conduct which the applicant alleges against the institution can be identified, the reasons for which the applicant considers that there is a causal link between the conduct and the damage it claims to have suffered, and the nature and extent of that damage.[71] It also follows from the provisions mentioned above that any plea which is not adequately articulated in the application initiating the proceedings must be held to be inadmissible.[72]

Although an applicant cannot generally transfer the burden of proof to the defendant by relying on circumstances which it is not in a position to establish, the

66 Order of the CJEU of 25 January 2008, Case C-461/07 P(I) *Provincia di Ascoli Piceno and Comune di Monte Urano v Sun Sang Kong Yuen Shoes Factory and Council* [2008] ECR I-11 summary publication, para 9. See also GC, Case T-222/07 P *Kerstens v Commission*, <http://www.curia.europa.eu>, paras 73-75, not available in English (last consulted in June 2012). The French text states: 'Il appartient, en principe, aux parties d'apporter les éléments de preuve à l'appui de leurs assertions. Ceux-ci doivent toutefois pouvoir faire l'objet d'un débat contradictoire'.

67 Lenaerts, Arts & Maselis 2006, p. 557.

68 Order of the CFI of 29 September 1999, Joined Cases T-148/98 and T-162/98 *Evans and Others v Commission* [1999] ECR II-2837, para 41.

69 CJEU, Case C-165/08 *Commission v Poland* [2009] ECR I-6843, para 42, and Case C-375/10 *Commission v Spain* [2011], not reported and not available in English at <http://www.curia.-europa.eu>, para 10 (last consulted in June 2012).

70 CFI, Case T-113/96 *Dubois et Fils v Council and Commission* [1998] ECR II-125, para 29, and order of the CFI, Case T-294/04 *Internationaler Hilfsfonds v Commission* [2005] ECR II-2719, para 23.

71 CFI, Case T-113/96 *Dubois et Fils v Council and Commission* [1998] ECR II-125, para 30, and order of the CFI, Case T-294/04 *Internationaler Hilfsfonds v Commission* [2005] ECR II-2719, para 24.

72 CFI, Case T-209/01 *Honeywell v Commission* [2005] ECR II-5527, para 54, and CG Case T-303/08 *Tresplain Investments v OHIM* [2010] not yet reported in the ECR, para 37.

concept of burden of proof cannot be applied to the defendant's advantage if the defendant is an EU institution, authority or body. In some exceptional circumstances it is for the EU body to adduce the evidence.[73] In early case law, the transfer of the burden of proof was even clearer. 'When a decision of the High Authority is contested, the High Authority must transmit to the ... [CJEU] its minutes relating to the decision' if such minutes are relevant for deciding the case.[74]

The principle of official inquiry cannot be considered as a remedy against failure to put forward the facts and submissions. In actions for compensation by an EU institution, the applicant has to plead the unlawful conduct of the institution. 'In an action for compensation, the illegality of the conduct of an institution is not presumed nor can it be investigated at the motion of the CJEU. The CJEU's task is to determine whether such allegations are substantiated'.[75]

Although the rule *actori incumbit probatio* is derogated from when the allegation concerns facts which are well known, the finding that the facts concerned are well known or are not well known is the task of the General Court and constitutes a finding of fact which, save where the facts or evidence is distorted, is not subject to review on appeal.[76]

The EU authority or body must prove the infringement of EU law that it has found and adduce evidence capable of demonstrating to the requisite legal standard the existence of circumstances constituting an infringement.[77] Any doubt in the mind of the Court must operate to the advantage of the undertaking to which the decision finding an infringement was addressed (principle *in dubio pro reo*). The Court cannot therefore conclude that the relevant EU body has established the infringement at issue to the requisite standard of proof if it still entertains any doubts on that point, in particular in proceedings for annulment of a decision imposing a fine.[78] However, it is not necessary for every item of evidence produced by the EU body to satisfy the criteria mentioned above in relation to every aspect of the infringement. It is sufficient if the body of evidence relied on by the institution, viewed as a whole, meets that requirement.[79] However, the evidence on which a party relies may be of such a kind as to require the other party to provide an

73 CFI, Case T-44/00 *Mannesmannröhren-Werke v Commission* [2004] ECR II-222, paras 261-263.

74 CJEU, Case 2/54 *Italy v High Authority* [1954] ECR English special edition 37 at 54 and 55.

75 Opinion of Advocate-General Ruiz-Jarabo Colomer delivered on 23 February 1999, Case C-64/98 P *Petrides v Commission* [1999] ECR I-5187, para 21.

76 Order of the CJEU of 25 January 2008, Case C-461/07 P(I) *Provincia di Ascoli Piceno and Comune di Monte Urano v Sun Sang Kong Yuen Shoes Factory and Council* [2008] ECR I-11 summary publication, para 9.

77 CJEU, Case C-185/95 P *Baustahlgewebe v Commission* [1998] ECR I-8417, para 58, and Case C-49/92 P *Commission v Anic Partecipazioni* [1999] ECR I-4125, para 86.

78 CFI, Case T-38/02 *Groupe Danone v Commission* [2005] ECR II-4407, para 215.

79 CFI, Joined Cases T-67/00, T-68/00, T-71/00 and T-78/00 *JFE Engineering* (T-67/00), *Nippon Steel* (T-68/00), *JFE Steel* (T-71/00) and *Sumitomo Metal Industries* (T-78/00) *v Commission* [2004] II-02501, para 180.

explanation or justification, in case of failure of which it is permissible to conclude that the rules on the burden of proof have been satisfied.[80]

At the end, the treatment of confidential documents must also be addressed. Neither the fact that the documents may be confidential nor the fact that they may have been obtained improperly precludes their remaining in the case file. There is no provision at the EU level that expressly prohibits evidence obtained unlawfully from being taken into account. Secondly, the CJEU has not excluded the possibility that even internal documents may, in certain cases, be lawfully placed in a case file.[81]

The limits of adducing confidential documents are to be found in legal advice given by the internal legal service. It would be contrary to public policy, which requires that institutions can receive the advice of their legal service, given independently, to allow such internal documents to be produced in proceedings before the Court unless such production has been authorised by the institution concerned or ordered by the Court.[82]

5. Principle under which the Parties Delimit the Scope of Proceedings (*le principe dispositif*) and the Principle of Official Inquiry (*Untersuchungsgrundsatz, le principe inquisitoire*)

An active role by the judge in the gathering of facts and in conducting proceedings is not deemed to be necessary by lawyers originating from legal systems where a judge plays a more passive role. An active role by the judge is considered to be the rejection of the principle under which the parties delimit the scope of proceedings (*le principe dispositif*).[83] It is uncontested that the procedural law of the CJEU is covered more by the principle under which the parties delimit the scope of proceedings than by the principle of official inquiry.[84] This, however, does not mean that the principle under which the parties delimit the scope of proceedings applies

80 CJEU, C-413/08 P *Lafarge v Commission* [2010], not yet reported, <http://curia.europa.eu>, paras 29 and 33 (last consulted in June 2012).

81 GC Case T-149/09 *Dover v Parliament* [2011] not yet reported in the ECR, paras 61-62.

82 Order of the CJEU of 23 October 2002, Case C-445/00 *Austria v Council* [2002] I-9151, para 12, and CFI, Case *Greece v Commission* [2007] ECR II-63, para 134. The most interesting judgment concerning the publication of legal opinions from the point of view of comparative law is the order of the CFI of 8 November 2000 Case T-44/97 *Ghignone and Others v Council* [2000] ECR-SC I-A-223; II-1023, paras 47-48. However, this order is not translated in English. The French text 'il est nécessaire d'accorder une protection particulière à des avis du service juridique d'une institution' underscores the special nature of legal advice given by the legal service of an EU institution without recognising legal professional privilege to in-house lawyers working in the legal service.

83 See to that effect Van Drooghenbroeck 2007, p. 241.

84 Biavati 2005, p. 201 and Hackspiel 2003a, p. 372.

without any limits.[85] The CJEU can play an active role in taking evidence and in search of evidence.[86]

The role of the *principe dispositif* in CJEU procedural law has been examined by Advocate-General Ruiz-Jarabo Colomer in his opinion in the *Vedial* case.[87] At paragraph 33 the Advocate-General concluded that 'plainly ... the EU judicature is also bound by the factual framework and legal grounds established by the parties'. However, also at paragraph 33 the Advocate-General concluded that 'the Rules of Procedure only exclude the general application of this principle in actions for annulment or in actions for a declaration that an institution has failed to act, specifically because of the objective approach taken to the action'.[88]

This means that in the framework of judicial review of EU decisions and legislative measures the CJEU can proceed in accordance with the principle of official inquiry. In doing so, it shall not serve as a tool for repairing the lack of facts and information in the parties' written submissions.[89] However, this principle is to be applied according to the rule *exceptiones non sunt extendendae*. The limits of the principle of official inquiry as far as the gathering of information is concerned are to be found in the general principles of (criminal) law such as the principle of presumption of innocence,[90] principle *in dubio pro reo*,[91] and principle *nemo tenetur se ipsum accusare*.[92]

It should be stressed that in direct actions the *principe dispositif* at the CJEU has two meanings. It actually comprises two components, namely the component under which the parties delimit the legal scope of proceedings (*Dispositionsgrundsatz*) and the component under which the parties delimit the factual scope of proceedings (*Beibringungsgrundsatz*). The parties themselves delimit the legal and factual scope of proceedings. The CJEU cannot raise pleas in law concerning the substantive legality of a contested measure of its own motion.[93] Before the CJEU the first part (*Dispositionsgrundsatz*) does not only concern the form of order sought, but also concerns the legal background of the case.[94] The second component

85 The most important limit being the principle *ne ultra petita* (*Ne eat judex ultra et extra petita partium*). See to that effect Castillo de la Torre 2005, p. 448.

86 Civil Service Tribunal, Case F-105/05 *Wils v Parliament*, <http://www.curia.europa.eu>, para 77 (last consulted in June 2012).

87 See Opinion of Advocate-General Ruiz-Jarabo Colomer delivered on 15 July 2004, Case C-106/03 P *Vedial v OHIM* [2004] ECR I-9573, para 32.

88 It should be mentioned that the CJEU left this issue open as far as proceedings for the review of the legality of contested EU administrative measures are concerned (CJEU, Case C-106/03 P *Vedial v OHIM* [2004] ECR I-9573, para 26.

89 Castillo de la Torre 2005, p. 447.

90 Lenaerts 2007, p. 483.

91 *Ibidem.*

92 CJEU, Case C-407/04 P *Dalmine v Commission* [2007] ECR I-829, para 34.

93 See CJEU, Case C-367/95 P *Sytraval and Brink's France v Commission* [1998] ECR I-1719, para 67, and Pechstein 2011, para 524. See, however, an exception to that rule in CFI, Joined Cases T-576/93 to T-582/93 *Browet and Others v Commission* [1994] ECR-SC II-619, ECR II-677; SC-I-A-191.

94 However, there are exceptions in proceedings in which the CJEU has unlimited jurisdiction (French: *la pleine juridiction*). See to that effect Castillo de la Torre 2005, p. 446, and CJEU, Case →

(*Beibringungsgrundsatz*) concerns the gathering of facts and information on which the application is based.

It should be stressed that in the CJEU the ultimate goal of the *principe dispositif* is the establishment of truth. Therefore, the difference between formal truth, which should be contained in the principle under which the parties delimit the scope of proceedings, as opposed to material truth, which should be contained in the principle of official inquiry (*Untersuchungsgrundsatz, le principe inquisitoire*), is only gradual, as the CJEU also depends on the co-operation of the parties when establishing the facts.[95]

The principle of official inquiry can serve as a powerful tool to aid judicial efficiency if interpreted in such a way that it is only a secondary principle to the principle under which the parties delimit the scope of proceedings and that it concerns the conduct of procedure and does not replace the parties as *domini litis*. At the EU level, the combination of both principles, namely the principle under which the parties delimit the scope of proceedings (*le principe dispositif*) and the principle of official inquiry (*Untersuchungsgrundsatz, le principe inquisitoire*) are therefore extremely efficient. The principle of official inquiry implies an active role by the judge in conducting the procedure.

6. Active Role of the European Judge: Measures of Organisation of Procedure or Measures of Inquiry

The peculiar structure of the European Judiciary with the CJEU as the highest court, the General Court hearing complex competition cases and the Civil Service Tribunal complex staff cases comes as a consequence of criticism that the CJEU did not devote sufficient time to establishing the facts.[96] The CJEU may and has to play an active role in fact-finding provided, however, that the right to be heard on a piece of evidence has been respected.[97] One could describe the active role played by the CJEU with the German term *richterliche Aufklärungspflicht*.[98] To that extent the principle *lex de futuro, judex de praeterito* also applies in the procedural law of the CJEU.

However, the essence of the active role for a judge in Europe has been developed by the other European court, namely the European Court of Human Rights in cases concerning the right to a judicial decision within a reasonable time.[99]

24/79 *Oberthür v Commission* [1980] ECR 1743, para 14: 'since this case involves proceedings in which the Court has unlimited jurisdiction it has, even in the absence of proper conclusions to that effect, the power not only to annul but also, if need be, of its own motion to order the defendant to pay compensation for the non-material damage caused by a wrongful act or omission on its part'.

95 See for German law Rosenberg, Schwab & Gottwald 2004, p. 483.

96 Edward 2007, p. 2.

97 Lenaerts, Arts & Maselis 2006, p. 556.

98 Rechberger & Simotta 2010, para 606.

99 See the analysis in Van Drooghenbroeck 2007, p. 247.

6.1. *Measures of Inquiry*

The classic and burdensome means of the gathering of facts are measures of inquiry. The CJEU, after hearing the Advocate-General, shall prescribe the measures of inquiry[100] that it considers appropriate *by means of an order setting out the facts to be proved*.[101] Before the CJEU decides on such measures the parties shall be heard.[102] Measures of inquiry are intended to prove the veracity of the facts alleged by one of the parties in support of its pleas in law.[103] The solution adopted in the Rules of Procedure clearly demonstrates the civil law origin of the rules on the gathering of facts before the CJEU. The case law concerning such measures is also similar to civil procedure as applied in the majority of civil law jurisdictions.[104] For example, an application for the adoption of measures of inquiry made by a party cannot be accepted if that party offers no evidence whatever to justify such measures.[105] It is for the EU judicature to decide, in the light of the circumstances of the case and in accordance with the provisions of the Rules of Procedure on measures of inquiry, whether it is necessary for a document to be produced.[106] However, in the context of interlocutory proceedings, a request for the adoption not of interim measures but of a measure of organisation of procedure or of inquiry falling within the jurisdiction

100 Measures of inquiry are: personal appearance of the parties; a request for information and production of documents; oral testimony; the commissioning of an expert's report and an inspection of the place or thing in question (Art. 45 of the old Rules of Procedure of the CJEU and Art. 64 of the new Rules of Procedure of the CJEU; Art. 65 of the Rules of Procedure of the General Court and Art. 57 of the Rules of Procedure of the Civil Service Tribunal). It would seem that one measure does not exclude or preclude the others (see to that effect CFI, Joined Cases T-33/89 and T-74/89 *Blackman v Parliament* [1993] ECR II-249, para 18, not available in English).

101 On the importance of the order, see also CJEU, Case C-113/07 P *SELEX Sistemi Integrati v Commission* [2009] ECR I-2207, para 51.

102 Art. 65 of the old Rules of Procedure of the CJEU; the new Rules seem not to address this issue, Art. 66 of the Rules of Procedure of the General Court and Art. 58(2) of the Rules of Procedure of the Civil Service Tribunal.

103 Lenaerts, Arts & Maselis 2006, p. 560. The authors refer to CFI, Case T-175/97 *Bareyt and Others v Commission* [2000] ECR-SC I-A-299 and II-1053, para 90. The text of this judgment is not available in English. The French text states: 'Les mesures d'instruction au titre des articles 65 à 67 du règlement de procédure visent à permettre de prouver la véracité des allégations factuelles faites par une partie à l'appui de ses moyens'.

104 Even though a high degree of flexibility can be observed. The classic civil law position of the commissioning and obtaining of an expert's report would be an order by the CJEU. The order appointing the expert shall define his task and set a time-limit within which he is to make his report (Art. 49 of the old Rules of Procedure of the CJEU, Art. 70 of the new Rules of Procedure of the CJEU and Art. 70 of the Rules of Procedure of the General Court). *Prima facie* there would be no possibility of inducing new means of measures of inquiry. However, after having heard the defendant and the expert statement produced by the applicant, it seems that the Court of First Instance accepted this as a statement by an *expert witness* without any measure of inquiry (see CFI, Case T-128/01 *DaimlerChrysler v OHIM* [2003] ECR II-701, paras 5, 22 and 42).

105 CJEU, Case 51/65 *ILFO v High Authority* [1966] ECR English special edition 87 at 96.

106 See also CJEU, Joined Cases C-189/02 P; C-202/02 P; C-205/02 P to C-208/02 P and C-213/02 P *Dansk Rørindustri and Others v Commission* [2005] ECR I-5425, paras 68-71.

of the General Court must be dismissed as inadmissible since it does not seek to prevent serious and irreparable harm pending a decision on the merits.[107]

A request for the production of documents is a measure of inquiry which the CJEU may order at any stage of the proceedings if it deems them necessary to ascertain the truth.[108] When it concerns the main proceedings and not the proceedings in an application for interim measures, a measure of inquiry falls within the jurisdiction of the Court and not within that of the President ruling on the application for interim measures.[109]

If a document was apparently material to the outcome of the case and had stated the author, the addressee and the date of the document in question, the General Court cannot reject a request for the production of the document on the grounds that this document had not been produced and there was nothing to confirm its existence. It could not simply reject the parties' allegations on the grounds of insufficient evidence when it was up to the Court, by granting the appellants' request to order the production of documents, to remove any uncertainty there might be as to the correctness of those allegations.[110]

6.2. *Measures of Organisation of Procedure*

The burdensome and inflexible structure of measures of inquiry caused by a requirement for a formal order to be adopted and the enumeration of facts in such an order prompted the EU judicature to request amendments to the Rules of Procedure to be made in such a way that measures of organisation of procedure or preparatory measures be introduced as complementary to the measures of inquiry.[111] Until September 2012 Article 54a of the old Rules of Procedure of the CJEU states, 'The Judge-Rapporteur and the Advocate-General may request the parties to submit within a specified period all such information relating to the facts, and all such documents or other particulars, as they may consider relevant'. The General Court and the Civil Service Tribunal have adopted a slightly different approach *ab initio*. Under Article 64(1) of the Rules of Procedure of the General Court[112] the 'purpose of measures of organisation of procedure shall be to ensure that cases are prepared for hearing, procedures carried out and disputes resolved under the best possible conditions'. This approach was then also followed by the

107 Order of the President of the CFI of 3 March 1997, Case T-6/97 R *Comafrica and Dole Fresh Fruit Europe v Commission* [1997] II-291, para 27.

108 CJEU, Case C-182/99 P *Salzgitter v Commission* [2003] ECR I-10761, paras 41-44.

109 Order of the President of the Court of 14 February 1990, CJEU, Case C-358/89 R *Extramet v Council* [1990] ECR I-431, para 26.

110 CJEU, Case C-119/97 P *Ufex, DHL International and Service CRIE v Commission* [1999] ECR I-1341, paras 110-111.

111 Rideau & Picod 2002, p. 800.

112 Art. 55 of the Rules of Procedure of the Civil Service Tribunal is a shortened version of Art. 64(1) of the Rules of Procedure of the General Court.

CJEU in the new Rules of Procedure. The aims of measures of organisation of procedure are:[113]

a. to ensure efficient conduct of the written and oral procedure and to facilitate the taking of evidence;
b. to determine the points on which the parties must present further argument or which call for measures of inquiry;
c. to clarify the forms of order sought by the parties, their pleas in law and arguments and the points at issue between them; and
d. to facilitate the amicable settlement of proceedings.

The purpose of measures of organisation of procedure is severalfold, in particular, to ensure the efficient conduct of written and oral procedure[114] and to facilitate the taking of evidence,[115] to clarify the forms of order sought by the parties, their pleas in law and arguments, and the points at issue.[116] To that extent, these measures can be described as a very efficient way of case-management. Measures of organisation of procedure are relatively informal. They do not have the compelling nature of measures of inquiry and are not prescribed by an order but notified by letter from the Registrar.[117] It is considered that these measures are particularly well adapted to deal with complex factual situations where the establishing of facts is quite complicated.[118] In order to facilitate the procedure, an informal meeting with the parties can be organised.[119] It is considered that informal meetings are particularly well suited for clarifying the obstacles causing complex issues which result in

113 Art. 64(3) of the Rules of Procedure of the General Court states that measures of organisation of procedure may, in particular, consist of putting questions to the parties, inviting the parties to make written or oral submissions on certain aspects of the proceedings, asking the parties or third parties for information or particulars, asking for documents or any papers relating to the case to be produced and summoning the parties' agents or the parties in person to meetings.

114 This finding is of extreme importance especially since lawyers coming from the 'third legal tradition' used to having a fear of decision-making, and were used to 'de-concentrated' proceedings, excessive formalism, lack of procedural discipline, and impersonal, anonymous and disproportionate efforts for reaching ephemeral and socially insignificant results (see to that effect Uzelac 2010, especially p. 390).

115 CFI, Joined Cases T-45/98 and T-47/98 *Krupp Thyssen Stainless and Acciai speciali Terni v Commission* [2001] II-3757, para 30. However, to enable the Court to determine whether it is conducive to the proper conduct of the procedure to order the production of certain documents, the party requesting production must not only identify the documents requested but also provide the Court with at least minimum information indicating the utility of those documents for the purposes of the proceedings.

116 CFI, Case T-234/95 *DSG v Commission* [2000] ECR II-2603, para 65.

117 Lenaerts, Arts & Maselis 2006, p. 559.

118 Rideau & Picod 2002, p. 800.

119 CFI, Joined Cases T-132/96 and T-143/96 *Freistaat Sachsen, Volkswagen and Volkswagen Sachsen v Commission* [1999] ECR II-3663, para 53.

inefficiencies in the case.[120] However, measures of organisation of procedure shall not be used as a fishing expedition.[121]

The assessment of the appropriateness of adopting a measure of organisation of procedure or a measure of inquiry is a matter for the General Court, not the parties. Although it is true that a party cannot require the courts of the European Union to adopt a measure of inquiry, it is nonetheless true that the court cannot draw inferences from the absence of certain items in the file until it has exhausted all the means provided for in its rules of procedure to obtain production of those items from the relevant party.[122]

As far as the efficient conduct of the oral procedure is concerned and in compliance with the principle of hearing both parties and the rights of the defence, which are also enshrined in Article 6 of the European Convention on Human Rights, the General Court may thus invite the parties to submit collectively their common pleas in law in order to avoid repetition of identical arguments, with each party continuing to have the opportunity to submit its own arguments in a complementary manner.[123]

The issue of non-compliance with the measures of organisation of procedure is not so easy to understand. When a party informs - the CJEU that it is not able to comply with measures of organisation of procedure since some of the requested documents are confidential, the CJEU can order that party to produce the requested documents and ensure that they will not be communicated to the other party at that stage.[124] The consequences of such a radical solution are then levelled by the supranational or international nature of the CJEU. That Court has no power to order coercive measures or to impose sanctions in the case of refusal to comply with such an order.[125]

A direction to the European Commission to allow an applicant to consult the file in which it is involved falls, in principle, within the scope of measures of organisation of procedure or measures of enquiry, which are within the jurisdiction

120 See *per analogiam* Rideau & Picod 2002, p. 802.

121 CFI, Case T-175/97 *Bareyt and Others v Commission* [2000] ECR-SC I-A-299 and II-1053, para 91. The text of this judgment is not available in English. The French text states: 'En l'espèce, la mesure proposée par les requérants n'a pas pour objet de préciser les griefs qu'ils ont soulevés ou de prouver la véracité de leurs allégations factuelles. Leur proposition se présente plutôt comme une tentative d'obtenir de nouveaux éléments permettant de mettre en doute la validité des coefficients correcteurs litigieux. Or, en l'absence de reproches concrets, susceptibles d'être vérifiés ou précisés par une demande de renseignements ou de documents spécifiques, il n'y a pas lieu d'ordonner la mesure proposée par les requérants'.

122 GC, Case T-560/08 P *Commission v Meierhofer* [2010] not yet reported in the ECR, paras 61-62.

123 CJEU, Joined Cases C-238/99 P; C-244/99 P; C-245/99 P; C-247/99 P; C-250/99 P to C-252/99 P and C-254/99 P *Limburgse Vinyl Maatschappij and Others v Commission* [2002] ECR I-8375, para 348.

124 GC Case T-560/08 P *Commission v Meierhofer* [2010] ECR 2010 II-1739, para 72.

125 GC Case T-560/08 P *Commission v Meierhofer* [2010] ECR 2010 II-1739, para 73.

of the General Court and not within the scope of interim measures adopted in proceedings for interim relief.[126]

6.3. *Principle of the Concentration of Pleas in Law and Facts Alleged (Konzentrationsmaxime)*

The spirit and purpose of the principle of the concentration of pleas in law and facts alleged (*Konzentrationsmaxime*) is simple: the parties shall perform all necessary procedural acts as soon as possible and as fast as possible and shall omit all acts not having any influence on the issue under litigation.[127] An application of this principle is also the reduction in the number of written submissions. In direct actions the application initiating the proceedings and the defence may be supplemented by a reply from the applicant and by a rejoinder from the defendant.[128]

In accordance with Article 42(1) of the old Rules of Procedure of the CJEU, Article 128(1) of the new Rules of Procedure of the CJEU and Article 48(1) of the Rules of Procedure of the General Court, while the parties may offer further evidence in support of their arguments in reply or rejoinder, the CJEU allows the lodging of evidence offered after the rejoinder only in exceptional circumstances, that is, if the person offering the evidence was unable, before the end of the written procedure, to obtain possession of the evidence in question, or if evidence produced belatedly by the other party justifies completing the file so as to ensure observance of the rule that both parties should be heard.[129] In any case, both provisions provide that the parties must give reasons for the delay in submitting further evidence. If the applicant admitted at the hearing that it had not referred to those circumstances in the written procedure, it would not provide any justification for that delay. Consequently, offers of further evidence cannot be taken into account.[130] However, *a fortiori*, the fact that a party became aware of the legal position only in the course of the procedure cannot constitute a new matter of law or of fact.[131]

The direct consequence of the principle of the concentration of pleas in law and facts alleged is a restrictive admission once the oral procedure has been closed. In general, a measure of inquiry may be ordered by the CJEU at any stage of the proceedings.[132] However, 'as regards the request for measures of inquiry, if made after the oral procedure is closed, such a request can be admitted only if it relates to

126 Order of the President of the Court of First Instance of 4 June 1996, CFI Case T-18/96 R *Stichting Certificatie Kraanverhuurbedrijf and Federatie van Nederlandse Kraanverhuurbedrijven v Commission* [1996] II-407, para 41.

127 Willmann 2004, p. 27.

128 Art. 41(1) of the old Rules of Procedure of the CJEU, Art. 126(1) of the new Rules of Procedure of the CJEU and Art. 47 of the Rules of the Procedure of the General Court.

129 CFI, Case T-172/01 *M v Court of Justice* [2004] ECR II-1075, para 44, and CFI, Case T-51/07 *Agrar-Invest-Tatschl v Commission* [2008] ECR II-2825, para 57.

130 CFI, Case T-51/07 *Agrar-Invest-Tatschl v Commission* [2008] ECR II-2825, para 57.

131 CG Case T-303/08 *Tresplain Investments v OHIM* [2010] not yet reported in the ECR, para 167.

132 CJEU, Joined Cases C-287/95 P and C-288/95 P *Commission v Solvay* [2000] ECR I-2391, para 54.

facts which may have a decisive influence on the outcome of the case and which the party concerned could not put forward before the close of the oral procedure'.[133]

6.4. *Expedited Proceedings on the Merits of the Case*

As this is the last point concerning efficiency one should mention the expedited procedure.[134] Under Article 133 of the new Rules of Procedure of the CJEU (old Article 62a), at the request by the applicant or the defendant the President may exceptionally decide, on the basis of a recommendation by the Judge-Rapporteur and after hearing the other party and the Advocate-General, that a case is to be determined pursuant to an expedited procedure derogating from the provisions of these Rules, where the particular urgency of the case requires the Court to give its ruling with the minimum of delay. Under Article 76a(1) of the Rules of Procedure of the General Court, that Court may, on application by the applicant or the defendant, after hearing the other parties and the Advocate-General, decide, having regard to the particular urgency and the circumstances of the case, to adjudicate under an expedited procedure.[135]

For the time being, the expedited procedure is the most effective way of achieving efficient and quick decisions on the merits. The historical origins of that procedure are to be found in the requirement of efficient judicial protection that also involves rapid judicial response. In the *Coget* case (T-95/01)[136] the Court of First Instance offered, in a hearing on interim measures on 29 May 2001, a rapid ruling provided *inter alia* that the applicants withdraw their request for interim measures. The judgment was delivered on 12 September 2001 (after a two-month period of annual judicial recess in summer). This characteristic is still visible today. An expedited procedure requires concentration on the short presentation of the main pleas in law and facts. Its price is then a rapid decision on the merits of the case.

Unfortunately, the expedited procedures are linked to a special form of urgency, which makes them unusable for ordinary proceedings.

7. Conclusion

The CJEU is a court not subject to any national procedural law. However, issues such as truth and efficiency are very much at the core of its activity. Therefore, the CJEU has developed highly sophisticated means to ensure truth and efficiency in judicial proceedings. The best way of dealing with the gathering of facts in judicial proceedings is by means of the principle of unfettered adduction of evidence, the

133 CJEU, Case C-234/92 P *Shell v Commission* [1999] ECR I-4501, para 63.

134 Barbier de la Serre 2006, p. 783 and Sladič 2008, p. 160 *et seq*.

135 The urgent procedure for references for a preliminary ruling relating to the areas of freedom, security and justice under Art. 23a of the Statute of the CJEU (Council Decision 2008/79/EC, *Euratom* of 20 December 2007 amending the Protocol on the Statute of the Court of Justice) is by its very nature limited to the points of law.

136 CFI, Case T-95/01 *Coget and Others v Court of Auditors* [2001] ECR-SC I-A-191, II-879, especially para 27.

principle *actori incumbit probatio,* and the principle under which the parties delimit the scope of the proceedings mixed with the principle of official inquiry. Those principles allow the parties to be *domini litis,* while the judge retains his own power to intervene in the gathering of facts. The efficient intervention of the judge in reviewing the acts of the parties is necessary today for the smooth conduct of judicial proceedings.

Bibliography

Antoniolli & Koja 1996
Antoniolli, W. & Koja, F., *Allgemeines Verwaltungsrecht, Lehr- und Handbuch*, 3rd edn., Vienna: Manz, 1996.

Barbier de la Serre 2006
Barbier de la Serre, E., 'Accelerated and Expedited Procedures before the EC Courts: A Review of the Practice', *Common Market Law Review*, 2006, Vol. 43, p. 783-815.

Baudesson & Rosher 2006
Baudesson, T. & Rosher, P., 'Le secret professionnel face au legal privilege = Professional Secrecy Versus Legal Privilege', *Revue de droit des affaires internationales*, 2006, Vol. 22, p. 37-66.

Benzing 2010
Benzing, M., *Das Beweisrecht vor internationalen Gerichten und Schiedsgerichten in zwischenstaatlichen Streitigkeiten*, Heidelberg: Springer, 2010.

Biavati 2005
Biavati, P., *Diritto processuale dell'Unione europea*, 3rd edn., Milano: Giuffrè Editore, 2005.

Castillo de la Torre 2005
Castillo de la Torre, F., 'Le relevé d'office par la juridiction communautaire', *Cahiers de droit européen*, 2005, Vol. 50, p. 395-463.

Edward 2007
Edward, D., 'The Court of First Instance – the Beginnings', in: Baudenbacher, C., Gulmann, C., Lenaerts, K., Coulon, E. & Barbier De La Serre, E. (eds.), *Liber Amicorum en l'honneur de/in honour of Bo Vesterdorf*, Brussels: Bruylant, 2007, p. 1-11.

Fasching 1990
Fasching, H.F., *Zivilprozeßrecht. Lehr- und Handbuch*, 2nd edn., Vienna: Manz, 1990.

Giuliani 2009
Giuliani, A.G., 'Civilian Treatises on Presumptions, 1580–1620', in: Helmholz, R.H. & Sellar, W.D.H., *The Law of Presumptions: Essays in Comparative Legal History*, Berlin: Duncker & Humblot, 2009, p. 21-73.

Grando 2006
Grando, M.T., 'Allocating the Burden of Proof in WTO Disputes: A Critical Analysis', *Journal of International Economic Law*, 2006, Vol. 9, p. 615-656.

Hackspiel 2003a
Hackspiel, S., 'Allgemeines und Verfahrensgrundsätze', in: Rengeling, H.-W., Middeke, A. & Gelermann, M. (eds.), *Handbuch des Rechtsschutzes in der Europäischen Union*, 2nd edn., Munich: C.H. Beck, 2003, p. 368-386.

Hackspiel 2003b
Hackspiel, S., 'Beweisrecht', in: Rengeling, H.-W., Middeke, A. & Gelermann, M. (eds.), *Handbuch des Rechtsschutzes in der Europäischen Union*, 2nd edn., Munich: C.H. Beck, 2003, p. 434-447.

Kleyr 2011
Kleyr, M., 'La production forcée de pièces par voie de référé dans un contexte international: la pre-trial document discovery à la luxembourgeoise', *Journal des tribunaux Luxembourg*, 2011, Vol. 3, p. 16-25.

Kolasa 2000
Kolasa, J., 'Origins and Sources of Procedural Law of International Courts - Ubi jus, ibi remedium', in: Epping, V., Fischer, H. & Heintschell Von Heinegg, W. (eds.), *Brücken bauen und begehen, Festschrift für Knut Ipsen zum 65. Geburtstag*, Munich: C.H. Beck, 2000, p. 185-196.

Legal 2007
Legal, H., 'Commentaire', in: Ruiz Fabri, H. & Sorel, J.-M. (eds.), *La preuve devant les juridictions internationales*, Paris: Pedone, 2007, p. 183-188.

Lenaerts 2007
Lenaerts, K., 'Réflexions sur la preuve et sur la procédure en droit communautaire de la concurrence', in: Baudenbacher, C., Gulmann, C., Lenaerts, K., Coulon, E. & Barbier De La Serre, E. (eds.), *Liber Amicorum en l'honneur de/in honour of Bo Vesterdorf*, Brussels: Bruylant, 2007, p. 475-507.

Lenaerts, Arts & Maselis 2006
Lenaerts, K., Arts, D. & Maselis, I., *Procedural Law of the European Union*, London: Sweet & Maxwell, 2006.

Magnus 2010
Magnus, R., *Das Anwaltsprivileg und sein zivilprozessualer Schutz. Eine rechtsvergleichende Analyse des deutschen, französischen und englischen Rechts*, Tübingen: J.C.B. Mohr, 2010.

Mehdi 2007
Mehdi, R., 'La prevue devant les juridictions communautaires', in: Ruiz Fabri, H. & Sorel, J.-M. (eds.), *La preuve devant les juridictions internationales*, Paris: Pedone, 2007, p. 165-181.

Naômé 2010
Naômé, C., *Le renvoi préjudiciel en droit européen, guide pratique,* 2nd edn., Brussels: Larcier, 2010.

Naômé 2011
Naômé, C., *Guide du pourvoi devant le juge de l'Union européenne,* update: 1 January 2011, internal document of the CJEU.

Pechstein 2011
Pechstein, M., *EU-Prozessrecht,* 4th edn., Tübingen: J.C.B. Mohr, 2011.

Plender 1997
Plender, L., 'Procedure in the European Courts: Comparisons and Proposals', *Collected Courses of the Hague Academy of International Law,* 1997, Vol. 267, p. 9-343.

Rechberger & Simotta 2010
Rechberger, W.H. & Simotta, D., *Zivilprozessrecht. Erkenntnisverfahren,* 8th edn., Vienna: Manz, 2010.

Rideau & Picod 2002
Rideau, J. & Picod, F., *Code des procédures juridictionnelles de l'Union européenne,* Paris: Litec, 2002.

Rijavec 2003
Rijavec, V., *Civilno izvršilno pravo,* Ljubljana: GV Založba, 2003.

Rijavec 2009
Rijavec, V., 'The Recovery of Debts Secured by Mortgage or Pledge in Slovenia', in: Uzelac, A. & Van Rhee, C.H. (eds.), *Access to Justice and the Judiciary: Towards New European Standards of Affordability, Quality and Efficiency of Civil Adjudication,* Antwerp: Intersentia, 2009, p. 219-228.

Ronzi 2008
Ronzi, C., 'The AKZO Nobel Case and the Reiterated Denial of Legal Privilege for In-House Counsels under EC Law', in: De Walsche, A. & Levi, L. (eds.), *Mélanges en hommage à Georges Vandersanden. Promenades au sein du droit européen,* Brussels: Bruylant, 2008, p. 677-706.

Rosenberg, Schwab & Gottwald 2004
Rosenberg, L., Schwab, K.H. & Gottwald, P., *Zivilprozessrecht,* 16th edn., Munich: C.H. Beck, 2004.

Sachs 2010
Sachs, B., *Die ex-officio-Prüfung durch die Gemeinschaftsgerichte,* Tübingen: J.C.B. Mohr, 2010.

Schermers & Waelbroek 2001
Schermers, H.G. & Waelbroek, D., *Judicial Protection in the European Union*, 6th edn., Deventer: Kluwer, 2001.

Sladič 2005
Sladič, J., 'Die Begründung der Rechtsakte des Sekundärrechts der EG in Rechtsprechung des EuGH und des EuG', *Zeitschrift für Rechtsvergleichung, Internationales Privatrecht und Europarecht*, 2005, Vol. 46, p. 123-134.

Sladič 2008
Sladič, J., *Einstweiliger Rechtsschutz im Gemeinschaftsprozessrecht - Eine Untersuchung der Rechtsprechung des EG/EU-Prozessrechts*, Baden-Baden: Nomos, 2008.

Uzelac 2010
Uzelac, A., 'Survival of the Third Legal Tradition', *Supreme Court Law Review*, 2010, Vol. 49, p. 377-396.

Van Drooghenbroeck 2007
Van Drooghenbroeck, J.-F., 'Le nouveau droit judiciaire, en principes', in: De Leval, G. & Georges, F. (eds.), *Le droit judiciaire en mutation, en hommage à Alphonse Kohl*, Commission Université - Palais, Université de Liège, Vol. 95, Liège: Anthemis, 2007, p. 213-331.

Van Raepenbusch 2011
Van Raepenbusch, S., *Droit institutionnel de l'Union européenne*, Brussels: Larcier, 2011.

Willmann 2004
Willmann, P., *Die Konzentrationsmaxime: eine Untersuchung des heutigen und früheren Rechts*, Berlin: Duncker & Humblot, 2004.

Ziller 2004
Ziller, J., 'L'autorité administrative dans l'Union européenne', <http://cadmus.eui.eu/handle/1814/2829>, 2004.

PURSUIT OF TRUTH AND THE HISTORY OF CIVIL PROCEDURE: ROMAN LAW PERSPECTIVE

I. Milotić

THE PURSUIT OF TRUTH AND EFFICIENCY IN ROMAN ARBITRATION PROCEEDINGS

1. Introduction

In certain circumstances, arbitration was considered to be a preferable means of dispute resolution in Roman law.[1] Substantial evidence on Roman arbitration indicates important reasons that stimulated the disputing parties to go beyond the boundaries of ordinary jurisdiction in order to resolve their disputes and other conflicts. Roman arbitration was inherently flexible in the determination of the decisive facts. It was an informal and generally private means of dispute resolution which was not bound by the constraints of ordinary jurisdiction. Its practical operation depended entirely on the arbitral agreement which signified the consent of the disputing parties to whatever award the arbiter might make. If the arbitral tribunal was composed of magistrates, the arbiter was authorised by the state to make the award and the parties were, consequently, bound to accept it. The use of arbitration was a reaction to the disadvantages of Roman civil litigation which was often *de facto* inaccessible to non-Roman citizens, risky, expensive, full of formalities and procedural situations that a disputing party should take his opponent through.[2] Thus, civil litigation was often beyond the power of many Roman citizens. For this reason, arbitration was not an alternative to ordinary jurisdiction, but rather a necessity, i.e. the means reserved for the resolution of particular types of disputes.[3] Roman law took an interest in arbitration to ensure that the litigation was indeed ended by the arbiter's decision. The decision of the arbiter was adjudication - the final and binding determination of the parties' rights and obligations. It had to finally end all disputes, differences and uncertainties between the disputing parties that had been mentioned in the arbitral agreement. No other result of the arbitration proceedings was sustainable.[4]

1 Seneca, *De beneficiis*, III.7.5.
2 Harries 2004, p. 173.
3 Stein 1995, p. 215-216.
4 Paulus, D.4.8.1.

Arbitration in Roman law was primarily a comprehensive pursuit of truth. This paper will analyse the values, guidelines, tendencies and techniques in the pursuit of truth in Roman arbitration proceedings and their relation to the idea of efficient justice as Roman jurists perceived it in their practical considerations.

2. The Arbiter's Role in the Pursuit of Truth

The choice of arbiters in Roman law was neither conditional nor accidental. Among other goals, their choice facilitated the pursuit for the truth by ensuring that a skilled person, a knowledgeable individual, an expert, a person who knew the disputing parties and their positions from before[5] or understood the dispute would resolve it. Arbiters in Roman law were expected to use their relevant background experience for the purpose of making decisions. They were not necessarily professionals although they were given the task of providing certainty on the decisive facts of the dispute.[6] If arbiters could not provide certainty by themselves, they might summon the assistance of an expert.[7] Roman law paid considerable attention to the choice of arbiters due to their specific role in fact-finding. This approach increased confidence in the arbitration process as a whole, and especially in the person of the arbiter and in the final decision.[8] It guaranteed a higher standard of the arbiter's formal and *de facto* competence, more accurate perceptions of what the truth actually was and the reliability of decision-making (this was directly reflected in the area of the enforcement of the award, which in Roman law depended upon the good will of the parties only).[9] The arbiter of Roman law is denoted as a moderator of the legal cause.[10] He balanced the different interests and goals that the disputing parties wanted to achieve in arbitration without exposing them to the risk of losing the case because of making excessive claims (*pluspetitio*).[11]

Roman arbitration was an adversarial proceeding with the arbiter playing an active role. The immediacy and orality of the procedure allowed the arbiter to participate actively: to ask questions, to make demands for explanations, to indicate disputed questions, to make expert (technical) determinations,[12] to make demands

5 Nehlsen von Stryk 1981, p. 258 on Horatius, *Epistolae*, I, 16, 40; Roebuck & De Loynes De Fumichon 2004, p. 56-57; Greenidge 1901, p. 39.

6 Roebuck & De Loynes De Fumichon 2004, p. 82-86; Campbell 2000, p. 476; Matthews 1921, p. 253, 267.

7 Scaevola, D.4.8.44; *Tabulae Herculanenses* No. 79.

8 On the confidentiality of Roman arbitration proceedings, see Ulpianus, D.4.8.17.1; Ulpianus, D.4.8.11pr.; Ulpianus, D.4.8.9.5.

9 Justinian reformed this rule in AD 530 (a series of imperial constitutions preserved in C.I.2.55). The Reform of 530 was abandoned in 539 by constitution No. 82. c. 11. in Justinian's Novels.

10 Cicero, *De partitione oratoria*, 10.

11 In judicial proceedings *per formulas*, the function of the judge (*iudex*) was to decide whether the defendant (*reus*) was liable. He had no powers to balance the different legal interests of the plaintiff and the defendant.

12 Cato, *De agri cultura*, 144-149.

for documents,[13] to issue warnings, requests and commands, to make interlocutory decisions,[14] etc. Due to his expert position, he was also obliged to conduct investigations, and to respond to the requests and questions of the disputing parties. Arbitral practice recorded cases where the arbiter made inquiry into and studied registers of land property rights. The powers of the arbiter in the pursuit of truth were even wider when he acted as mediator.[15]

The number of arbiters was left to the discretion of the disputing parties. By convention, they were allowed to designate multiple arbiters. Most evidence on how arbitration operated in practice indicates a tendency to appoint a single arbiter, however this was not a rule, but rather a trend in legal practice.[16] The designation of multiple arbiters was related to problems with decision-making,[17] but in the field of the pursuit of truth it facilitated fact-finding and truth-seeking, and provided multiple controls over truth-seeking and the determination of the facts.

3. Concentrated Proceedings and Immediacy

Once the procedure and the arbiter(s) were agreed, the pursuit of the material and immaterial aspects of the truth was modelled on three main principles: concentrated proceedings; immediacy; and, orality (hearings) and expert determinations.

Concentrated proceedings were a distinctive feature of Roman arbitration. Files documenting its operation in practice indicate the arbiter's duty to schedule hearings frequently and continuously. This (trend) was an intentional procedural method which supported an integrated and concentrated debate, and permanent awareness of the decisive facts in dispute and of the evidence presented, giving reliable insight into the procedural state of affairs. This facilitated an efficient and cost-effective sequence of procedural stages that ended with decision-making. Concentration could be arranged voluntarily by the parties. Texts of the *Tabulae Pompeianae Sulpiciorum* record arbitrations in which the parties probably had given instructions to the arbiter to resolve their disputes immediately - at one hearing held in a single day.[18] In such procedural circumstances, the disputing parties had to present all the evidence at one time. They had to discuss the decisive facts immediately while the arbiter made his decision as soon as he thought the legal cause was elaborated and clear enough.

We share the opinion that arbitration proceedings in Roman law were guided by the standard of *reasonable time* (*modicum tempus*). This standard is explained by the Roman jurist Ulpian, who claimed that the disputing parties should execute an

13 Campbell 2000, p. 475-477.

14 Iavolenus, D.4.8.39pr.; Celsus, D.4.8.37; Roebuck & De Loynes De Fumichon 2004, p. 143-144.

15 Cicero, *De partitione oratoria*, 17, 39.

16 *Lex duodecim tabularum*, VII, 5b; Cicero, *De legibus*, I, 21, 55; Plinius, *Epistula*, V, 1, 6, (Annio Severo).

17 Ulpianus, D.4.8.17.6.

18 *Tabulae Pompeianae Sulpiciorum*, Nos. 35-37; Camodeca 1999, p. 106-109. The inscriptions belong to a Pompeian banker's archive. They record credit affairs and disputes arising out of them, resolved exclusively by arbitration *ex compromisso*. Wolf & Crook 1989, p. 9-23.

arbitral decision within a reasonable time.[19] We believe that *modicum tempus* was also a guideline for the arbiter's decision-making in case the time to end the arbitration was not specified by the arbitral agreement between the disputing parties. In that case, the arbiter would set a period of time which was convenient to conduct the proceedings and to make a decision. The period was not defined by a hypothetical legal rule or determined in practice. Its determination should conform to the general perceptions of what was practical, expedient and reasonable in the actual case considering the circumstances and position of both parties. Once the arbiter accepted his duty and set the necessary period of time, he was bound by it, and his duty was enforceable by public authorities, i.e. by the praetor.[20]

The trend toward the concentration of proceedings promoted immediacy. There are several points, one related to the other, which supported immediacy:

1. The subjects in the proceedings were bound to be present at each procedural act and hearing.[21] The absence of (*a*) the arbiter, (*b*) one or more arbiters of the arbitral commission, or (*c*) any of the disputing parties stopped the proceedings and the sequence of the procedural phases. The liable party would be imposed a penalty that had previously been arranged in the arbitral agreement. This rule was softened by the provision that the parties could be legally represented in arbitration proceedings[22] or, exceptionally, make observations and claims in a letter.[23] Subsequently, no absence excuses were sustainable.
2. Inspection was an important method of fact-finding. The subjects in the proceedings were bound to attend the inspection which was conducted at the disputed place. The disputing parties could be legally represented.[24]
3. The identity of Roman arbitration was determined by the person of the arbiter.[25] He could not be substituted. If there were multiple arbiters, none of them could be excluded or substituted by another. The parties could neither add additional arbiters nor make reselections.
4. All arbiters were equal, and they participated in the discussion at the hearing and in decision-making equally. They decided together on an equal footing. Only those arbiters who participated in the hearings could make the decision.[26] Under this rule, it is a virtue for a decision to be made by the very person who considers the proof and hears the parties. This rule tries to preserve the integrity of arbitration by ensuring that arguments and proofs are put to the arbiter directly.
5. The decision had to be made by the arbiter himself or by his delegate. It had to be proclaimed orally in the presence of both parties or, if they were absent, in the

19 Ulpianus, D.4.8.21.12. See Zimmermann 1996, p. 111.

20 Ziegler 1971, p. 84 *et seq.*; Roebuck & De Loynes De Fumichon 2004, p. 96 *et seq.*, 145-147.

21 *Tabulae Pompeianae Sulpiciorum*, Nos. 35-39; Camodeca 1999, p. 106-111; Ulpianus, D.4.8.27.4.

22 Roebuck & De Loynes De Fumichon 2004, p. 159.

23 Iulianus, D.4.8.49.1.

24 Scaevola, D.4.8.44; La Pira 1932, p. 216.

25 Martino 1986, p. 28-29; Ziegler 1971, p. 5.

26 Ulpianus, D.4.8.17.2; Ziegler 1971, p. 123.

presence of their legal representatives. Otherwise, the decision had no legal effect.
6. Succession in the position of the disputing parties was possible only if it had been previously explicitly foreseen and determined in the arbitral agreement. The successor had to be identified by his name and/or his relation to his predecessor without leaving any doubt as to his identity.[27] Procedural succession in arbitration was very rare, which supports the views on immediacy as regards the disputing parties.

Immediacy should be understood as a working principle of Roman arbitration. 'That the Romans themselves did not speak of an idea does not mean we cannot profitably observe the idea in Roman procedure and give our own name to it'.[28] Etymological and terminological concepts for the final decision support this view. The technical term for the arbitral decision was *sententia* (sentence, in English). It derives from the verb *sentio* which means to feel or to perceive the nature of a certain thing directly through the senses.[29] *Sententia* is the legal realisation of *sentire*. It should be understood as the arbiter's proclamation of what he had noticed through his senses and how he noticed it, taken altogether with what the disputing parties requested and claimed during the hearings.

4. Orality and Hearings

Orality is closely related to immediacy. E. Metzger has noted that 'it lessened the complexity and secrecy of a procedure dominated by writing'.[30] Orality made the procedure accessible, understandable and adaptable to the needs and desires of the disputing parties. It affirmed the active role of the parties and arbiters in the proceedings. The core of the pursuit of truth in Roman arbitration was contradictory debate and the presentation of evidence (the statements of the disputing parties, witnesses and experts, and written instruments, etc.). Epigraphic evidence suggests the main purpose of the procedure: to hear all the arguments and claims and to discuss the legal matter comprehensively. In the technical terminology of Roman law such an imperative is indicated as duty *ad audiendum* and was set very wide. It allowed the disputing parties to ask questions, make statements and comments on what the arbiter(s) or counterparty had previously said, make counterclaims, and to seek explanations.[31] The duty *ad audiendum* could only be exercised if the disputing parties, or their legal representative, were personally present at each procedural act. If the right to hear and to be heard was neglected, such a situation would make

27 *Tabulae Herculanenses,* No. 79.
28 Metzger 2004, p. 23.
29 Lewis & Short 1879; Lewis 1890.
30 Metzger 2004, p. 22.
31 *Tabulae Herculanenses,* Nos. 53, 77, 78, 80, 92. See Camodeca 1994, p. 137-146.

legal grounds for actions on fraud, which subsequently meant that the arbitral decision was not sustainable.[32]

5. Exclusion of Publicity

Exclusion of publicity in private dispute resolution has a long tradition in Roman law. There is a considerable number of authorities who claim that the archaic tribal communities of Italy insisted on resolving their disputes within the community and before the personal authorities they already knew.[33] Tribal communities took an interest in disputes and considered them as something that should not be exposed to third persons. J. Harries explained such views as efforts by rural communities to prevent divisions and conflicts among their members as a result of the dispute.[34] In the first century AD the practice of exclusion of publicity from private dispute resolution is best recorded in the early Christian communities. From its very beginnings, Christianity had an important role in supplementing the justice organised by the Roman State with lay justice. The earliest leaders of Christian communities gave advice to their members not to resolve their disputes before public authorities, but rather before private individuals of the Christian religion.[35] The rationale for this attitude was the protection of secrecy, confidentiality and an intention to have the dispute settled *sine strepitu forensi*.

Exclusion of publicity was a distinctive attractiveness of Roman arbitration which facilitated the pursuit of truth in many ways. Arbitration was conducted in private. In the famous hereditary dispute of Asudius Curianus, decided before three arbiters who should be considered 'good men' (*arbitri boni viri*), which is recorded by Pliny the Younger in his *Letters*, one reads of an arbitral commission that conducted the proceedings in private and summoned the party to the hearing before making a decision. After the commission had heard the arguments, the decision was made immediately and proclaimed orally to the single party only.[36]

Arbitration intended to avoid the publicity which regularly attended the hearings that were part of ordinary judicial proceedings.[37] The reason for this was to protect two major interests: (*a*) the parties' intention to reach a final resolution of their dispute; and (*b*) confidentiality. In order to achieve this, it was necessary that during arbitration the secrets of business transactions (*secreta negotii*) and the personal identities of the disputing parties (*intima*) were kept from public view.[38] Otherwise, during arbitration, the disputing parties would not reveal all the details of their legal relations. Consequently, the pursuit of truth would be constrained in its method and result. Exclusion of publicity lessened the parties' risk and fears regarding the presentation of evidence, and it facilitated deeper insight into the

32 Roebuck & De Loynes De Fumichon 2004, p. 165.
33 Martino 1986, p. 27-28; Broggini 1957, p. 40; Kaser 1949, p. 208, 213, 337.
34 Harries 1999, p. 173.
35 St. Paul, *First Letter to the Corinthians*, 6, 1-6.
36 Plinius, *Epistulae*, V, 1 (Annio Severo).
37 Stein 1995, p. 215.
38 Papinianus, D.36.3.5.1.

state of affairs and the disputed legal relation. Above all, it was an indirect instrument that provided effective fact-finding. Exclusion of publicity reflected the confidentiality of the relationship between the arbiter and the disputing parties, and their mutual trust.

The trend toward exclusion of publicity was, consequently, a trend toward the prevention of public disgrace as a result of the arbitration proceedings. Exclusion of publicity in arbitration meant that neither party risked the sanction of loss of reputation (*infamia*) as a result of the proceedings.[39] The qualification of being infamous in Roman law meant not only the diminution of a person's honour and credibility in society, but also legal disabilities and exclusions from certain aspects of the legal system.[40] Nothing that the arbiter did could affect the reputation of the disputing parties. But there were disputes in Roman law whose resolution in the regular legal process was related to the emergence of *infamia* for the convicted party. An arbitral decision never resulted in *infamia*,[41] which made it attractive in those disputes whose resolution in the regular judicial process could end with *infamia* for the defendant. Perquisite of *infamia* in ordinary judicial proceedings was publicity, i.e. that everyone was or could be informed of what was proclaimed in the judicial decision (*iudicium*). Exclusion of publicity in arbitration meant avoiding the appearance of *infamia* and its legal consequences. Arbitration diminished the risk of social exclusion as well as the risk that the arbitral decision would not be sustainable.[42]

6. Importance of Language

Though Latin was an official language of the Roman State, it cannot be denied that Roman society was *de facto* highly multilingual. Latin was the language of Rome and the western part of the Empire while the eastern cities and provinces mostly used Greek or other mother tongues in their legal activity or even when they formally addressed Roman provincial administrative authorities. Court proceedings regularly took place in Latin. Arbitration had no constraints regarding the language, which is considered one of arbitration's advantages. D. Roebuck and B. de Loynes de Fumichon have stated that some papyri show that all the stages of the arbitral process were recorded in Greek, and some in Coptic and other provincial languages.[43] With a high degree of certainty one can conclude that numerous arbitrations in the Roman province of Dalmatia between different Liburnic and Dalmatian communities which took place during the first half of the first century AD were conducted at least partially or simultaneously in the provincial languages of the local tribal communities.[44] There is a substantial amount of evidence on arbitrations conducted in Greece during Roman rule that were exclusively recorded

39 Roebuck & De Loynes De Fumichon 2004, p. 173.
40 Berger 1953, p. 500.
41 Ulpianus, D.3.2.13.5.
42 Roebuck & De Loynes De Fumichon 2004, p. 165.
43 Roebuck & De Loynes De Fumichon 2004, p. 177.
44 Wilkes 1976, p. 258-274.

in the Greek language.[45] The arbitral files written exclusively in Greek show a general trend toward the usage of the Greek language in arbitration proceedings as well.

On the other hand, the *Tabula Contrebiensis*, a famous epigraphic record of the arbitration between tribal communities in Spain in the first century BC, shows an opposite example. The disputing parties agreed not to use their provincial languages in dispute resolution but to use the technical Roman legal language and concepts of Roman law.[46] The parties were familiar with Roman law and its technical legal terminology in the Latin language. At a certain point they realised they could profit from the application of Roman law and Latin legal terminology in their dispute (the case was not a matter of Roman law at all). That is why the style and the language are entirely Roman and reflect Roman legal thinking.[47] One may not exclude the possibility that *in concreto* certain procedural acts for the pursuit of the truth were executed in their tribal mother tongue - Celtiberian.

Arbitration in Roman law gave the opportunity to the parties to have their dispute resolved in a language they understood. On the question of language, arbitration was fully adapted to the needs and desires of the disputing parties which essentially facilitated the reliable and effective pursuit of truth. The parties could choose the language they found convenient and understandable for their mutual procedural communications. Selection of the language could be intentional with regard to the sustainability of the result of dispute resolution as well. There were no constraints on the parties in the provinces or in those territories where Roman government was not fully established to selecting the Latin language and to resolving their dispute following Roman legal and terminological standards.

7. Constraints on the Pursuit of Truth

There are references to Roman arbitration stating that it was a more expedient means of dispute resolution than the regular judicial process.[48] The pursuit of truth set the limits. The main purpose of arbitration *ex compromisso* is excellently described in the interpolated fragment of the Roman jurist Paul wherein he says that it should bring controversies to an end.[49] The Romans were in permanent search for a balance between two procedural extremes: the absolute pursuit of truth, on the one hand, and what was expedient, practical, economical and effective, on the other. These trends and values of arbitral procedure were in perpetual tension,

45 See for a comprehensive study with epigraphic documents: Ager 1997.

46 Richardson 1983, p. 36, 41.

47 Birks, Rodger & Richardson 1984, p. 48.

48 P. Stein stated that arbitration might have been speedier because the parties did not have to wait until the court was ready and because it was less beset by formalities. Stein 1995, p. 215. J. Harries considered arbitration as an affordable means of dispute resolution which was not beyond the power of ordinary citizens. Harries 1999, p. 173.

49 'Compromissum ad similitudinem iudiciorum redigitur et ad finiendas lites pertinet'. Paulus, D.4.8.1; La Pira 1932, p. 202, 207, 217 *et seq.*; Talamanca 1958, p. 21-23; Ziegler 1971, p. 19-20; Weizsäcker 1879, p. 71.

which did not go unnoticed in Roman jurisprudence. The arbiter had to finally resolve the dispute by his decision (he could not just give his opinion on the dispute, his advice or directions to the disputing parties).[50] His decision was not subject to appeal.[51] Paul identified the final arbitral decision as the means by which unreasonable prolongations of arbitral procedure were prevented. The function of the arbitral award was explained, in Latin, considering its goal: *ne propagentur arbitria*.[52] As mentioned in Section 3 above, the proceedings had to be completed within *modicum tempus*.[53]

Low cost-effectiveness was a fundamental advantage of arbitration. This was not a goal that the disputing parties might reach as a long-term result of the proceedings, but primarily a comparative and direct advantage of arbitration embodied in its proceedings as well as in its long-term result. Cicero made contrary comments on the pursuit of truth in arbitration. His definition of arbitration by good men favoured an absolute pursuit of truth. Whenever this absolute principle was reasonably narrowed with what was practical, reasonable and expedient, Cicero refused to define such a mechanism as arbitration by good men. In Ciceronian thinking, a person whose aim was to settle the legal matter quickly and practically while disregarding the truth and morality could not be considered a good man-arbiter.[54]

Arbitration *prima facie* paid attention to the interests of the disputing parties which could narrow the pursuit of truth. Arbitration ended with the decision of the arbiter, which was the adjudication by a person whose authority was accepted by the disputing parties.[55] The framework of arbitration differed from the regular judicial process because in its concept it stimulated negotiated justice: bargaining, mediation, levelling the parties' interests and the moderation of the claims of the parties in dispute.[56]

The technical legal term that Roman jurists used to denote arbitration was *arbitrium* or *arbitratus*. This term and institute of Roman law was the basic and senior generic term which signified a general concept of dispute resolution which

50 Even if the arbiter made an obvious mistake, he could not correct it later or revise his decision. Gaius, D.4.8.20.

51 When the disputing parties made an agreement to have their dispute resolved in arbitration, they were aware that the arbitral decision was final. Arbitration in Roman law did not favour the absolute pursuit of truth, but was primarily modelled to achieve the goal of low cost-effectiveness. On the other hand, this concept favoured and affirmed the person of the arbiter and his authority.

52 '[N]ot to prolong arbitrations', Paulus, D.4.8.32.16.

53 See n. 19.

54 Cicero, *Pro Quinto Roscio Comoedo*, IV, 10-11; Kaser 1966, p. 256-259; Broggini 1957, p. 199-210. Cicero's views should necessarily be perceived as extreme and generally not accepted by Roman jurisprudence.

55 Exceptionally, the *arbiter* could be authorised by the public authorities, which qualified the arbitration as mandatory.

56 Cicero, *ibidem*; Cicero, *De fato*, 17, 39. Cicero suggests that an *arbiter ex compromisso* is a moderator of the legal matter and of the final arbitral decision. He makes the decision after moderating the legal interests of the disputing parties and bringing them into harmony. See Cicero, *De partitione oratoria*, III, 10.

was different from the judicial process. Deeper insight into the sources suggests there were different types of arbitration in Roman law with different functions, mechanisms of dispute resolution and methods for the pursuit of the truth. Roman law *in concreto* knew nothing of a universal concept of arbitration.[57] The previously mentioned values and trends of arbitration were common to all, but their significance and importance were distributed according to each type. Arbitration conducted by good men (*arbitrium boni viri*) was grounded merely on negotiated justice while arbitration *ex compromisso* was predominately an adversarial proceeding slightly modelled with the values of negotiated justice and the arbiter's powers to moderate the legal matter. In many cases, seeking the truth in arbitration was modelled on the technical (expert) judgments of the arbiters which was reflected in the arbitral decision that was *de iure* adjudication, but an expert judgment in its *de facto* content and nature.[58] In the classical period of Roman law, different types of arbitration existed together and the disputing parties who made an arbitral agreement could choose the type they wanted. The method of truth-seeking and its constraints could be the decisive point in deciding which type of arbitration the disputing parties might select.

Throughout the provinces, epigraphic evidence documents attest of one specific kind of arbitration which was not voluntarily selected by the disputing parties, but imposed as obligatory by military officials or magistrates. It was a mandatory type of arbitration whose framework was private, and the process of dispute resolution and the pursuit of truth itself were greatly influenced by local customs, traditional legal rules, local laws, the legal substrate of local origin and *de facto* conditions,[59] although the constitution of the arbitral tribunal and decision-making were not controlled by the disputing parties at all.[60] Mandatory arbitrations of this kind facilitated real fact-finding within categories which were irrelevant from the Roman point of view, or sometimes even contrary to the main principles of Roman law. On the other hand, the pursuit of truth was constrained because the parties had no control over the proceedings. Such mechanisms tended to resolve

57 The medieval development of arbitration, which was firmly grounded on principles of Roman law, confirms its conceptual diversity. Works of Roman-canon procedure regularly had a separate chapter entitled 'de arbitro et arbitratore' suggesting there were at least two different types of arbiters and arbitrations. See Ziegler 1967.

58 Cato's models of agricultural contracts are the most representative examples (Cato, *De agricultura*, 144-149). Technical arbitrations are best documented in disputes over the valuation of property, technical features of merchandise, determinations of quality and quantity of goods, characteristics of certain things, etc. See Matthews 1921, p. 253, 257; Nehlsen-von Stryk 1981, p. 260-261; Lübtow 1957, p. 379, 399.

59 T. Elliot defined them as proceedings whose *modus operandi* was private although they had a distinctive, obligatory character. Because of the obligatory character, the parties did not have control over the proceedings at all or the proceedings were partially controlled by their arrangements. Elliot 2004, p. 20. Especially see Wilkes 1976, p. 258 *et seq.*

60 F.F. Abott and A. Chester Johnson denoted them as *administrative arbitrations*. They considered them as a mechanism of resolution of those disputes which had appeared before the Roman conquest, during Roman rule or where the dispute was the result of incomplete or partial determinations of boundaries or real property rights in the provinces between neighbouring tribal communities. Abott & Chester Johnson 1926, p. 158.

disputes by taking into account the interests of both parties as well as to result in a decision which was sustainable cumulatively for the disputing parties and the Roman State.

D. Roebuck and B. De Loynes De Fumichon noted that the appropriateness of private arbitration, which included different techniques from which the disputing parties could choose whatever was appropriate for their dispute, was a central issue.[61] The selection of certain techniques, especially those that favoured negotiated justice and bargaining, constrained the pursuit of truth. If the parties wanted the arbiter primarily to pay attention to their interests, positions and conditions or to mediate, then fact-finding was limited and sacrificed for the superior goal - the final resolution of the dispute acceptable to both disputants. In private arbitrations, the parties could arrange such a concept of dispute resolution which did not always favour an absolute pursuit of truth.

Appeals were excluded from arbitration, which was analogous to civil litigation in Roman law (process *per formulas*). The case once decided before the arbitral tribunal could not be reheard or revised on the grounds of arbitral appeal. D. Roebuck and B. De Loynes De Fumichon have stated that appeal was possible only if the disputing parties provided in their agreement that a disappointed party could appeal.[62] Such a view, however, cannot be verified in Roman legal sources or in documents that record arbitral practice. Recourse to another arbitral tribunal on the grounds of the same arbitral agreement was also not allowed. In the late classical period of Roman law, the emperors enacted rules that no arbitral decision could be contested at a state court (previously it was possible, but a penalty - *poena compromissa* - was imposed on the party who initiated the court proceedings),[63] though legal practice indicates this was not always or consistently followed.[64]

The nonexistence of a second instance and the legal impossibility to rehear or revise the decision of an arbiter meant that there was no senior control on the reliability of the facts determined in arbitration. The exclusion of appeals in arbitration can be explained as an ultimate effort to facilitate expedient and efficient private justice. On the other hand, the exclusion of appeals could be appreciated from the point of view of the methods of fact-finding and the nature of the facts that an arbiter took into account. Especially in the provinces, these facts could be irrelevant from the point of view of civil litigation and the Roman legal system as a whole. How could the hypothetical second instance arbitral tribunal appreciate those facts which were, for example, strictly local, contrary to Roman law, traditional or the result of customs that were unknown to Roman society?

61 Roebuck & de Loynes de Fumichon 2004, p. 194.

62 Roebuck & de Loynes de Fumichon 2004, p. 186-187.

63 C.I.2.55.1. from AD 213 proclaimed this principle following some earlier decisions of the emperors on the same matter.

64 Paul says that there were different views on this problem. Paulus, D.4.8.30. See *Consultatio veteris cuiusdam iurisconsulti*, 9.17.

8. Role of the Public Authorities

The Roman State had no interest in the pursuit of truth in arbitration proceedings even in those types of arbitration where the arbitral tribunal was constituted by decree (*ex decreto*) or edict (*ex edictu*) or command (*iussu*) issued by magistrates or military officials and/or when the proceedings were in some way controlled by public authorities.[65] The interest of the Romans in arbitration was manifested through its purpose (*ad finiendas lites pertinet*) and the final result (*sententia*). The practice of arbitration *ex compromisso* suggests the quality and the content of the final decision were not considered to be a part of the praetor's jurisdiction (unless they were excessively wrong or unlawful, or unless fraudulent acts occurred in the proceedings).[66] The praetor did not concern himself with *arbitration of good men* (*arbitrium/arbitratus boni viri*) at all, except where fraud was committed and an action on fraud (*actio doli*) arose out of it.[67]

9. Conclusion

The pursuit of truth in Roman law was a complex activity which had to satisfy different interests, appreciate many values and reach diverse goals. Often, only the extremes of the pursuit of truth are observed: (*a*) an absolute pursuit of truth which coincides with the absolute - only hypothetically reachable - accuracy of determinations and decisions; and (*b*) the efficiency and effectiveness of private justice. An arbiter in Roman law was a *moderator* of the different interests of the disputing parties and of various procedural values which were in perpetual tension. He had to find the right way - a specific point of balance of the parties' interests and values which would cause harm to no one. The balance reached as a result of the arbiter's activity was fundamentally important. In particular legal and social surroundings, within the existing circumstances and state of affairs, the appropriate balance of different values qualified arbitration as a preferable means of dispute resolution.

Good mechanisms to determine the truth were never fully exploited in Roman arbitration. The determination of the truth and the trend toward accuracy should be perceived as very important goals of arbitration, but not as something that should endanger or marginalise other values of arbitration in Roman law by which it was a distinctive mechanism of dispute resolution.

65 Wilkes 1976, p. 258 (No. 1); p. 259 (No. 3); p. 262 (No. 10); p. 265 (No. 16); CIL III, 3167; CIL III, p. 1515, No. 8663; CIL III, p. 2326, No. 14239; CIL III, No. 9973; CIL III, No. 2883; CIL III, No. 15045.

66 Ulpianus, D.4.8.3.1.

67 Roebuck & de Loynes de Fumichon 2004, p. 146.

Bibliography

Abott & Chester Johnson 1926
Abott, F.F. & Chester Johnson, A., *Municipal Administration in the Roman Empire*, Princeton: Oxford University Press, 1926.

Ager 1997
Ager, S., *Interstate Arbitrations in the Greek World, 337–90 B.C.*, Berkeley/Los Angeles: University of California Press, 1996.

Berger 1953
Berger, A., 'Encyclopedic Dictionary of Roman Law', *Transactions of the American Philosophical Society*, n. s., 1953, Vol. 43, No. 2, p. 333-809.

Birks, Rodger & Richardson 1984
Birks, P., Rodger, A. & Richardson, J.S., 'Further Aspects of the Tabula Contrebiensis', *The Journal of Roman Studies*, 1984, Vol. 74, p. 45-73.

Broggini 1957
Broggini, G., *Iudex Arbiterve: Prologomena zum Officium des römischen Privatrichters*, Köln/Graz: Böhlau, 1957.

Camodeca 1994
Camodeca, G., 'Riedizione del trittico Ercolanese: Th 77+78+80+53+92 del 26 gennaio 69', *Cronache Ercolanesi*, 1994, No. 24, p. 137-146.

Camodeca 1999
Camodeca, G., *Tabulae Pompeianae Sulpiciorum: Edizione critica dell'archivio puteolano dei Sulpicii*, Rome: Quasar, 1999.

Campbell 2000
Campbell, B., *The Writings of the Roman Land Surveyors – Introduction, Text, Translation and Commentary*, London: The Society for the Promotion of Roman Studies, 2000.

Elliot 2004
Elliot, T., *Epigraphic Evidence for Boundary Disputes in the Roman Empire*, doctoral thesis (unpublished), Chapell Hill: University of North Carolina, 2004.

Greenidge 1901
Greenidge, A.H.J., *The Legal Procedure of Cicero's Time*, Oxford: Clarendon Press, 1901.

Harries 1999
Harries, J., *Law & Empire in Late Antiquity*, Cambridge: Cambridge University Press, 1999.

Kaser 1949
Kaser, M., *Das altrömische ius*, Göttingen: Vandenhoeck & Ruprecht, 1949.

Kaser 1966
Kaser, M., *Das Römische Zivilprozessrecht*, München: C.H. Beck'sche Verlagsbuchhandlung, 1966.

La Pira 1932
La Pira, G., '"Compromissum" e "litis contestatio" formulare', in: *Studi in onore di S. Riccobono*, 1932, No. II, Palermo: Castiglia, p. 189-226.

Lewis 1890
Lewis, C.T., *An Elementary Latin Dictionary*, New York/Cincinnati/Chicago: American Book Company, 1890.

Lewis & Short 1879
Lewis, C.T. & Short, C., *A Latin Dictionary*, Oxford: Clarendon Press, 1879.

Lübtow 1957
Lübtow, U., 'Catos leges venditioni et locationi dictae', *Symbolae Raphaeli Taubenschlag dedicatae*, 1957, No. 2, p. 226-441.

Martino 1986
Martino, P., *Arbiter: Biblioteca di ricerche linguistiche e filologiche*, Vol. 17, Roma: Universitá 'La Sapienza', 1986.

Matthews 1921
Matthews, N., 'The Valuation of Property in the Roman Law', *Harvard Law Review*, 1921, Vol. 34, No. 3, p. 229-259.

Metzger 2004
Metzger, E., 'Roman Judges, Case Law, and Principles of Procedure', *Law and History Review*, 2004, Vol. 22, No. 2, para 39, 10 July 2011, available at: <http://www.historycooperative.org/journals/lhr/22.2/metzger.html>.

Nehlsen-Von Stryk 1981
Nehlsen-Von Stryk, K., *Die boni homines des frühen Mittelalters*, Berlin: Verlag von Duncker & Humblot, 1981.

Richardson 1986
Richardson, J.S., 'The Tabula Contrebiensis: Roman Law in Spain in the Early First Century B.C.: I', *The Journal of Roman Studies*, 1983, Vol. 73, p. 33-41.

Roebuck & De Loynes De Fumichon 2004
Roebuck, D. & De Loynes De Fumichon, B., *Roman Arbitration*, London: Holo Books, 2004.

Stein 1995
Stein, P., 'Roman Arbitration: an English Perspective', *Israel Law Review*, 1995, Vol. 29, p. 215-227.

Talamanca 1958
Talamanca, M., *Ricerche in tema di 'compromissum'*, Milano: Giuffrè, 1958.

Weizsäcker 1879
Weizsäcker, C., *Das Romische Schiedsrichteramt Unter Vergleichung mit dem Officium Judicis*, Tübingen: Laupp, 1879.

Wilkes 1976
Wilkes, J.J., 'Boundary Stones in Roman Dalmatia (I. Part: The Inscriptions)', *Arheološki vestnik*, 1976, Vol. 25, p. 258-274.

Wolf & Crook 1989
Wolf, J.G. & Crook, J.A., *Rechtsurkunden in Vulgärlatein aus den Jahren 37-39 n. Chr.*, Heidelberg: C. Winter, 1989.

Ziegler 1967
Ziegler, K.-H., 'Arbiter, arbitrator und amicabilis compositor', *Zeitschrift der Savigny-Stiftung für Rechtsgeschichte*, Romanistische Abteilung, 1967, Vol. 94, p. 376-381.

Ziegler 1971
Ziegler, K.-H., *Das private Schiedgericht im antiken römischen Recht*, München: C.H. Beck'sche Verlagsbuchhandlung, 1971.

Zimmermann 1996
Zimmermann, R., *The Law of Obligations: Roman Foundations of the Civilian Tradition*, Oxford: Oxford University Press, 1996.

T. Karlović

PROPTER CELERITATEM DIRIMENDARUM LITIUM - PRESUMPTIONS AND STIPULATIO IN ROMAN LAW

1. Generally on Presumptions in Roman Law

Two systems of civil procedure, *per legis actiones* and *per formulas*, were successively used during the greater part of Roman history, approximately from the time of the enactment of the *Leges XII tabularum* to the third century AD.[1] Their common and main feature was the division of proceedings into two parts: the first part (*in iure*) took place before the *praetor*, who decided on the admissibility of a case, i.e. whether the alleged conduct constituted a violation of a legally recognised right; the second part (*apud iudicem*) took place before a judge, whose primary role was to rule on the matter of facts.[2] This judge, before whom the case was discussed and evidence was produced, was a layman. Also, the advocates acting on behalf of the parties were predominantly orators, not jurists. Furthermore, there were no special procedural rules or separate law of evidence.[3] In the classical period, there existed only the general principle regarding the burden of proof with the primary, relative meaning,

1 For a detailed overview of the development of Roman civil procedure, see Bethmann-Hollweg 1865; Bekker 1871; Sohm 1886, p. 130-196; Wenger 1925; Buckland 1932, p. 604–673; Kaser 1966; Metzger 2009.

2 In textbooks, the first part is referred to as the preliminary hearing and the second part as the full trial. See Buckland 1932, p. 608; Borkowski & Plessis 2010, p. 66-73. A reservation must be made regarding the second part in that the judge had the authority as well to decide on questions of law, especially in case of *bonae fidei iudicia*, and was not limited to the investigation of facts. See Kaser 1966, p. 273.

3 Although the proceedings *in iudicio* during the system of *legis actiones* were in a certain measure regulated by law, e.g. the sequence *causae coniectio* and *peroratio* in Gai. Inst. 4,15, it can be said that only the broadest outlines of the process of presenting evidence were marked. Later on, in the formulary procedure, even these general precepts were gradually abandoned. It can be said that apart from the special cases in the earliest period, like *furtum conceptum*, evidence mainly remained outside the scope of interest of jurists until the classical period. See Greenidge 1901, p. 270-275; Steinwenter 1947, p. 84-92; Kaser 1954, p. 225-227; Pugliese 1960, p. 395-404.; Kaser 1966, p. 83-88, 272-284.

as Levy and Kaser have suggested,[4] that the plaintiff had to prove his allegations made in the *intentio*,[5] while the defendant had to produce evidence to corroborate the contents of the *exceptio*.[6]

The judge was free to consider all the evidence equally, without restrictions, and to make an appraisal of its probative value.[7] Also, if the evidence was not clear enough, he could decide on the basis of presumptions. However, initially, in the formulary procedure, *praesumptiones* rarely had the significance of legal rules.[8] At this stage, in connection with the common understanding of the verb *praesumere*, *praesumptiones* represented the arguments relying on generally accepted conclusions from certain facts. The procedural, technical legal meaning of presumption was developed only later by the Stoics. As evidence was the area of expertise of orators, it is generally accepted that the Stoics transposed the meaning of the corresponding Greek term *πρόληψις* from their theory of evidence onto *praesumptio*.[9] That is to say, the Stoics developed an earlier idea of Aristotle's distinguishing between *probationes inartificiales* and *artificiales*, as Quintilian translated the Greek terms, where the second group, in Roman texts also denoted *argumentationes*, was further divided into *probabiles* and *necessariae*, *praesumptiones* being equivalent to the first group - *argumentationes probabiles*.[10]

This form of argumentation based on the *communis opinio* with regard to the probability of the existence of one uncertain fact assumed from the fact that is certain was called, in postclassical terminology, *praesumptio facti* or *praesumptio hominis*, because it was founded solely on probability or on the persuasiveness of

4 See Levy 1952; Kaser 1954. The opposite opinion expressed by Pugliese and Wacke is that these rules on burden of proof were stricter and obliged the judge. See Pugliese 1956; Wacke 1992. See also Musielak 1975, p. 196-198.

5 The principle embodied in the maxim *Actori incumbit probatio* is derived from several texts, such as D. 6,1,24 (Gaius 7. *ad ed. provinc.*); D. 12,2,30pr. (Paulus 18. *ad ed.*); D. 22,3,2 (Paulus 69. *ad ed.*); D. 22,3,21 (Marcianus 6. *inst.*).

6 D. 22,3,12 (Celsus 17. *dig.*); D. 22,3,19pr. (Ulpianus 1. *disp.*); D. 44,1,1 (Ulpianus 4 *ad ed.*).

7 The issue of the judge's duties was primarily elaborated within Stoic philosophy, not in law. As an exception, Aullus Gellius, 14,2,20, informs us on the *libri de officio iudicis* written by Q.A. Tubero, Stoic and jurist, but these were not preserved. See Broggini 1957, p. 219; Kaser 1966, p. 272, 278.

8 The only undisputed exception represents the *praesumptio Muciana* as a legal presumption, while the other cases of alleged presumptions were convincingly refuted as rules of interpretation. The problem is that in the classical Roman sources it is sometimes very difficult to draw the line between rules of interpretation and presumptions since there was no systematic division of substantive and procedural law in this area. See Donatuti 1931, p. 15-19; Donatuti 1933, p. 177-183; Kaser 1954, p. 232-241; Martinez de Morentín Llamas 2007, p. 43-44.

9 Gradenwitz defined the role of presumptions in classical law by stating that they did not represent an order to the judge to rule in a certain way, but they merely reminded him that he would do the right thing by accepting the option indicated by the presumption as true. The first use of the term *πρόληψις* in the given meaning is attributed to Chrysippus, while the Latin translation *praesumptio* is known from Seneca, *Epistulae*, 117,6. See Gradenwitz 1886, p. 70; Donatuti 1933, p. 165-166.

10 Aristotle, *Rhetoric*, 1,2, 1355 b. 36-40; Cicero, *Libri rhetorici*, 1, 29, 44; Quintilian, *Institutiones oratoriae*, 5,1. See Donatuti 1933, p. 164-167. See also Giuliani 2009, p. 39-40.

the facts.[11] On the contrary, *praesumptio iuris* represented a legally binding rule according to which the judge had to take certain facts as proven from presumption unless the other party produced suitable counter-evidence.[12]

The *praesumptio iuris* was introduced with the development of the *cognitio extraordinaria*, the third system of procedure in Roman law, which was characterised by its unitary structure and conducted by a professional judge. The prominent feature of this procedure, facilitating the creation of presumptions, was the establishment of strict rules regarding the burden of proof.[13] In this context, presumptions are mostly recognised in the sources of Roman law by the phrase *nisi specialiter adprobetur*, or a similar appendix added by the postclassical writers or compilators,[14] according to which it is often stated that they are used to reverse the burden of proof. Nevertheless, it should be stressed that this is only the secondary effect of presumptions as it is always necessary to prove the basis of a presumption in the first place.[15] The difference between evidence (*probatio*) and presumptions, more exactly *praesumptiones iuris* as the only truly legally relevant presumptions, thus became perceptible in the postclassical sources while the recognition of presumption as an element of procedure could be clearly seen from the heading of Book 22, Title 3 of Justinian's *Digest*, 'De probationibus et praesumptionibus'.[16] Although there are only three presumptions in this title,[17] this is understandable as the title in itself represented an innovation and the other presumptions, concerning the problems of *commorientes*, paternity, inheritance, etc., were left in the appropriate titles where their *sedes materiae* was situated.[18]

2. *Stipulatio* and the 'Stipulation Clause'

One of the issues resolved by the use of presumptions, which are preserved in different parts of the *Corpus Iuris Civilis*, was the relationship between *stipulatio*, one of the Roman verbal contracts, and the written instrument, *cautio*, which was used as proof of a concluded contract. The development and the effects of these

11 For postclassical sources, see Donatuti 1933, p. 168. Considering the nature of this presumption, Kaser described it, with notice of Steinwenter's reserved commentary, as based on 'Erfahrungswissen'. See Steinwenter 1947, p. 88, No. 66; Kaser 1954, p. 236.

12 The difference between *praesumptiones hominis* and *iuris* was further developed in the Middle Ages with the addition of the *presumptio iuris et de iure* by the Glossators, viz. Accursius' glossa *ad Tit.* 22,3. See Burckhard 1866, p. 11-15; Giuliani 2009, p. 44-51.

13 See Levy 1952, p. 172-177; Kaser 1966, p. 339-518.

14 In earlier works, these interpolations were exclusively attributed to Justinian's compilators, but Donatuti demonstrated that some of them were the result of earlier postclassical interventions by which *praesumptiones facti* from classical law were transformed into *praesumptiones iuris*. See Donatuti 1931, p. 20-56.

15 See Donatuti 1933, p. 172.

16 See Burckhard 1866, p. 67-74.

17 D. 22,3,9; D. 22,3,24; D. 22,3,25pr. See Gradenwitz 1886, p. 73, 75; Donatuti 1931, p. 45-46, 49, 90.

18 See Lemosse 1984, p. 333.

presumptions followed the general pattern and are thus illustrative of the progress made in this area of the law of evidence.

In classical law, *stipulatio* was a unilateral verbal contract that consisted of a formal promise made in answer to a formal question.[19] The prerequisites for its validity were (*a*) the oral form, (*b*) the question and the answer had to be congruent, (*c*) it had to be made *inter praesentes*, i.e. the parties had to be present at the same place and at the same time (what also constituted the following requirement), and (*d*) there had to be *unitas actus*.[20] All these elements had to be proven if contested in court, but the proof was made easier by the composition of a written instrument that recorded the object of the obligation and that the *stipulatio* was concluded, as made clear by the finishing words *stipulatus spopondit*.[21]

The formulation *quae supra scripta sunt* followed by *stipulatus spopondit* and the names of the parties, called in Romanist literature 'general stipulation' or 'stipulation clause', was already to be found in documents from the first century AD excavated in Italy,[22] but appeared more frequently in Greek translation on Graeco-Egyptian papyri from the third century onwards.[23] This confirmed that everything written in the document prior to the clause was encompassed by the *stipulatio* and was accordingly actionable. In this manner, to guarantee judicial enforcement, the clause was already used in classical law for situations in which it was indeed superfluous to make a *stipulatio* or even for some in which it could not be properly made.[24] Later in Egypt, after the enactment of the *Constitutio Antoniniana,* it was added to secure the legal validity of all the elements of the existing contracts recorded in the papyri, whereby it is questionable whether the words of the *stipulatio* were ever pronounced.[25] With regard to the wide and pre-existing practice of written contracts and the composition of legal documents by notaries, it is generally accepted that the parties dispensed with the oral form in the eastern part of the empire and in Egypt. Additionally, especially after Levy's work on the Roman vulgar law of obligations, it is commonly assumed that the oral form gradually became unnecessary also in the western part of the empire in the postclassical period.[26] However, the pace of this development is uncertain as the written form was never manifestly accepted in official decisions as sufficient without the oral form of the concluded contract.

19 From the abundant literature on *stipulatio,* see Liebe 1840; Riccobono 1957; Sacconi 1989; Pastori 1994.

20 See Buckland 1932, p. 434-435; Nicholas 1953; Zimmerman 1990, p. 68-75.

21 There were also other similar compositions corresponding to the verbs used in the *stipulatio.* See further Pringsheim 1961; Simon 1964; Diosdi 1981, p. 41, 51-53.

22 See Camodeca 1999, p. 133-150.

23 See further Pringsheim 1961, p. 222-229; Simon 1964, p. 26-27, 41-51.

24 E.g. the contract concluded with *ordo decurionum.* See Simon 1964, p. 28; Diosdi 1981, p. 52.

25 See Pringsheim 1961, p. 250-251; Simon 1964, p. 44.

26 This view became dominant as early as the nineteenth century after Gneist, but for the writers of the second part of the twentieth century it is mainly represented by Levy. Also, the critics primarily directed their objections towards Levy's thesis. See Archi 1946 (1981), p. 1809-1810; Levy 1956, p. 39-42; Kaser 1975, p. 373-378; Van Oven 1958; Diosdi 1982, p. 59-62.

3. 'Defective' *cautiones* in Late Classical Law

The lawyers and the emperors already discussed the problem of correspondence between the oral *stipulatio* and the written form at the end of the classical period, but they went only so far as to give probative effect to 'defective' *cautiones*, the instruments lacking some of the elements identifying the valid *stipulatio*. They were confronted with the cases where either the answer or the question was missing from the document, so the question arose whether these *cautiones* represented sufficient evidence. With regard to the absence of the answer, the position was that its existence could not be argued from the question, but the opposite situation, where the question was omitted, would have been taken as the question having really preceded the answer.[27]

The existence of the verbal question could be inferred from the recorded answer, so it can be said that this presented a *praesumptio facti*, as the plaintiff did not have to present additional evidence to prove the full execution of the spoken formula.[28] The judge was advised to accept the instrument as legitimate proof of the *stipulatio*, but the important prerequisite stressed in the texts was that both parties had to be present.[29] This, however, raises the question of whether the presence of the parties had to be specially proven by the plaintiff, or was supposed to be clearly demonstrated by the *instrumentum*.

27 This attitude was clear from the writings of the late classical jurists Paulus, D. 45,1,134,2, Sent. V,7,2, and Ulpianus, D. 45,1,30, and in the response given by Emperors Severus and Antoninus, C. 8,37(38),1 (*Licet epistulae, quam libello inseruisti, additum non sit stipulatum esse eum cui cavebatur, tamen si res inter praesentes gesta est, credendum est praecedente stipulatione vocem spondentis secutam*). Regarding Paul. D. 24,1,57, accepting that the letter is not interpolated, it can be concluded that the document had to be composed in words proving the oral stipulation, not purporting to substitute it. See Riccobono 1957, p. 1-2, 66 (especially Beinart's overview of later opinions and his personal remarks regarding D. 2,14,7,12 in n. 22a), 150-151; Pringsheim 1961, p. 208-209; Sacconi 1989, p. 169-173.

28 According to the sources, this presumption could also be understood as *praesumptio iuris*, especially in case of the *constitutio*, but the words used still do not create a strict rule. Furthermore, the main objection would be that these texts deal with the evidence and its value in establishing facts, not with the existence of facts. However, as the difference is very subtle considering the different interpretations of the texts, it is easy to see why Nicholas rejected the differentiation *praesumptio facti* and *praesumptio iuris* and adopted, at that time rather new, Lord Denning's division between provisional and compelling presumptions. Thus, it is understandable that Brandileone spoke about the issue generally as pertaining 'nel campo del diritto probatorio', while Donatuti, in a commentary to the redacted Ulp. D. 2,14,7,12, claimed it created a *praesumptio iuris*, but could not be sure precisely when it was elevated to that rank. In his commentary to the texts, Nicholas said that they created a rebuttable presumption, while Pringsheim generically called it 'Vermutung' (exceptionally, raised by later compilators in the case of P.S. V,7,2 to the level of fiction), the understanding also accepted by Martini. See Brandileone 1928, p. 16-19, 44-59; Donatuti 1930, p. 50-51; Nicholas 1953, p. 237, 244-247; Pringsheim 1961, p. 218; Martini 2001, p. 246.

29 Doubts were raised about the authenticity of the *inter praesentes* requirement by Riccobono and Levy, but Pringsheim suggested, considering its overall appearance in classical texts, that it should be taken as a doctrinal, not practical instruction. See Riccobono 1957, p. 63, 72-73; Levy 1956, p. 36; Pringsheim 1961, p. 210, 215-216.

From the preserved documents recording the *stipulatio* composed in this period, it can be seen that the parties mentioned the date and the place of the conclusion of the contract, but the special indication of their being present there at the same time was not to be found. This is easily understandable as it would be deemed superfluous to specifically write down something that was obvious considering the nature of the contract. In the same manner, as was argued by Nicholas, it can be concluded that the presence of the parties was not supposed to be additionally examined by the court.[30] Its indication in these texts merely pointed to the most frequent counter-evidence - that the parties were not present at the alleged place simultaneously and consequently could not have uttered the words of the *stipulatio*. Only if the document was imperfect, as in the cases elaborated by Paulus, Ulpianus, and Severus and Antoninus, in the preceding period, would the parties most likely be requested to introduce additional evidence to prove the presence of both parties and the exchange of the formula, but the presumption set aside this additional burden for the creditor. By accepting the natural inference of the question from the answer in the case of an 'elliptical' stipulatory clause, it was up to the defendant to prove to the contrary that there was no *stipulatio* in order to contest the existence of the obligation.

4. Justinian and the Presumption from *instrumentum*

During the postclassical period, besides the confirmation made early on by Diocletian that the oral form was essential for the *stipulatio*,[31] there is no evidence of greater change with regard to the role of the *cautio*. Nevertheless, the *stipulatio* was undergoing some other important changes, especially significant being the decision by emperor Leo in AD 472 allowing for the informal *stipulatio* without the need for specific and congruent words.[32] Although Levy considered that this *constitutio* sanctioned the written form as equal to the oral, there is no substantial evidence for this.[33] The effect of giving the document form prevalence over the oral form, by procedural means, had to wait for Justinian's constitution of 531, C. 8,37(38),14.[34]

30 See Nicholas 1953, p. 235-239, 244.

31 E.g. C. 4,12,12, C. 4,64,3, etc. See Riccobono 1957, p. 42-44.

32 C. 8,37(38),10: *Omnes stipulationes, etiamsi non sollemnibus vel directis, sed quibuscumque verbis pro consensu contrahentium compositae sint, legibus cognitae suam habeant firmitatem.* For the interpretation, see Riccobono 1957, p. 51-52; Nicholas 1953, p. 77-79; Sacconi 1989, p. 152-154.

33 Regarding the verb *componere*, used as a main argument for the written form, Van Oven did not analyse its use more specifically as he concentrated on the wider picture. However, the use of this verb in Iulianus D. 45,1,53 indicates its application for the oral *stipulatio* as well as for documents. Also, even earlier Archi suggested that the Legislator could have had in mind more frequent cases of documented stipulations, but this would not necessarily imply the equality of the forms. Later, both Diosdi and MacCormack adhered to the oral conception of the *stipulatio* in the constitution. See Archi 1946 (1981), p. 1832-1833; Levy 1956, p. 39; Van Oven 1958, p. 416; Diosdi 1981, p. 60; MacCormack 1983, p. 99.

34 Justinian's constitution represents the essential part of all the discussions about the relationship between *verba* and *scriptura*, and all the other sources on the topic are usually interpreted in relation to it. The text is accordingly analysed by all the aforementioned authors writing on the *stipulatio*.

In this decision, Justinian dealt with three cases that had caused many disputes before the courts, especially, as the emperor stated, because unscrupulous men used the classical prerequisites of the *stipulatio* as an excuse not to pay, but to go to court. The first two cases related to stipulations evidenced by a document and made by slaves - the owners claimed that the slave did not belong to them or that he was not present at the conclusion of the contract. The third concerned the case where the defendant himself was named in the document, but he claimed that he was not present. The problem was whether the presence stated in the document needed to be proved by the plaintiff, or was to be presumed.

Justinian addressed, in the first paragraph, the first two questions concerning the use of slaves in concluding a *stipulatio*. He decided that the presumptions of the presence and of the ownership of slaves from the document could not be rebutted. The phrasing which was used, 'credi omnimodo et servum adesse et fecisse stipulationem et eam esse scripto domino adquisitam et non dubitari, si servus ipse praesto fuerit vel eius domini fuit is, pro quo scriptus est fecisse stipulationem', shows that conclusive presumptions are concerned, or in continental European legal language, *praesumptiones iuris et de iure*.[35] [36]

The other situation, where the document testified to the conclusion of a contract between free persons and in their presence, was decided differently. The counter-evidence was admitted to rebut the presumption raised by the document, but it was limited concerning the object of proof and the allowed forms of evidence. Namely, the defendant had to prove that one of the alleged contracting parties was not in the same city on the same day. Furthermore, he had to prove this using only the easily attestable and clearest evidence (*liquidis ac manifestissimis probationibus*). It was suggested that the defendant should procure another written instrument to the contrary, but witnesses could be admitted as well, although only those of high esteem or the most credible. Considering these propositions, in the second paragraph the constitution raised only a *praesumptio iuris* or a compelling presumption, according to the terminology used by Nicholas.[37] From the fact that the document recorded the contract being created in the presence of the parties, the

35 Riccobono generally claimed that both paragraphs created a *praesumptio iuris et de iure*, what is rightly observed by Nicholas as a mistake for the second paragraph and also followed by MacCormack. Pringsheim spoke about the fiction of presence ('die fingiert werden sollte'), but it is questionable whether he had in mind fiction as a legal figure or just used the usual term, because the text does not correspond to the meaning of fiction. Kaser, however, does not mention the constitution in the context of presumptions, but only when considering the evidentiary function of documents. See Nicholas 1953, p. 247-249; Riccobono 1957, p. 58; Pringsheim 1961, p. 219; Kaser 1966, p. 487, 489; MacCormack 1983, p. 104, No. 32.

36 This statement holds true only if the first paragraph is considered as a separate regulation. If, on the other hand, Pringsheim's suggestion, accepted and further elaborated by Martini, is true that the text of the constitution was the result of merging two similar constitutions in the second Codex, and the counter-evidence of its absence from the second paragraph was admitted here as well, it would merely constitute a *praesumptio iuris*. However, without additional evidence as to how these two paragraphs would be connected, it is safer to follow the preserved division of the text. See Pringsheim 1961, p. 219; Martini 1983, p. 249-251.

37 See Nicholas 1953, p. 249.

judge was explicitly instructed to accept as proved the same presence and, consequently, the formation of a contract.

The presumptive nature of the document was stressed by Vinnius in his commentary on Justinian's *Institutes* where the second paragraph was recapitulated in Inst. III,19(20),11(12).[38] The *Institutes* only reiterated the second paragraph of the constitution, but the text revealed in very direct words the motivation behind its enactment, 'propter celeritatem dirimendarum litium', to swiftly resolve disputes before the courts. The purpose of the presumption was to hasten the procedure and to relieve the courts of excessive litigation by strictly prescribing what counter-evidence would be admitted.[39] This was especially important considering the variety of applications of the *stipulatio,* e.g. surety and *novatio;* and a further reflection of Justinian's reform can be recognised in Inst. III,20,8, the text dealing with *fideiussio,* where the idea of supplementing the elliptical clause was combined with the notion that the document equalled a performed act. Already in its first part, 'quodcumque scriptum sit quasi actum, videatur etiam actum', Theophilus recognised that the document created a *praesumptio iuris,*[40] the effect given to the *instrumentum* specifically by the constitution.[41]

5. Conclusion

The developments in the relationship between the *stipulatio* and the *cautio* up to AD 531 and Justinian's constitution introducing the *praesumptio iuris* regarding the regular *cautio* composed *inter praesentes* are indicative of the changes in the law of presumptions in Roman law. During the classical period, the written form had become the standard means of proving the *stipulatio,* so the jurists and the emperors tried in their responses to extend the probative force of documents based on common reasoning that the answer was preceded by the question, to uphold defective *cautiones.* In line with the nature of the formulary procedure and in the absence of strict rules on the burden of proof, their responses corresponded to the *praesumptio facti* in advising the judges to accept the 'elliptical' stipulatory clause as

38 Vinnius declares that this was not a *praesumptio iuris et de iure,* but a *praesumptio iuris tantum.* Furthermore, regarding the probative value of the document, it is called *praesumptio veritatis,* meaning that the content corresponds to the recorded facts and is thus believed to be true. The other, the *praesumptio solennitatis,* in which the form of question and answer was upheld, was discussed in relation to Inst. III,19,17. See Vinnius 2005, p. 243 (the numbers in brackets are Vinnius' reading, while the first numbers represent the usual numbering from Krüger's edition of the *Institutes*).

39 Considering the difference between Thayer-Wigmore's and Morgan-McCormick's concepts of presumptions, Justinian's constitution should be understood in the latter sense, as the defendant needed to show (*ostenderit*) that he was absent.

40 Theophilus, *Paraphrasis* III,20,8.

41 MacCormack interpreted the text along the same lines, especially in contrast to Inst. III,19,17, but expressed reservations regarding the applicability of the constitution with respect to a document composed along the lines of the *Institutes* without the apparent indication of presence. However, it should be noted that the *Institutes* represented a textbook, so it would not be necessary to repeat continuously all the details. See MacCormack 1983, p. 101-103.

complete in proving the oral *stipulatio*. Further developments brought a more extensive use of documents, especially in the East, but it took a much longer time for the *cautio* to receive legal sanction (almost) equal to the oral form. This was accomplished indirectly by Justinian's giving the document presumptive force without expressly renouncing the need for the spoken exchange of question and answer.[42]

Justinian raised the presumption of *stipulatio* in the document to the level of a legal rule, *praesumptio iuris*, in reaction to the frequency of litigation initiated regarding a specific problem, the claim that the party was not present when the contract was formed, entailing prolonged proceedings, considering the examination of probable witnesses that the parties would present. Decreeing that the presumption could be rebutted only by qualified evidence, the constitution was intended to increase the efficiency of the courts and suppress the fraudulent behaviour of the debtors. Its secondary effect was the influence on substantive law, as the stipulatory document composed in the presence of the parties became *de facto* equal to the oral *stipulatio*.

42 This conforms with Justinian's overall efforts to preserve classical law and at the same time acknowledge existing practice. See Pringsheim 1961, p. 199.

Bibliography

Archi 1946 (1981)
Archi, G.G., 'Indirizzi e problemi del sistema contrattuale nella legislazione da Costantino a Giustiniano', in: Archi, G.G. (ed.), *Scritti in onore di Contardo Ferrini*, Milano: Hoepli, 1946, p. 661-727 (*cit.* = Archi, G.G., *Scritti di diritto romano*, III, Milano: Giuffrè Editore, 1981, p. 1779-853).

Bekker 1871
Bekker, E.I., *Die Aktionen des römischen Privatrechts*, Vols. I & II, Berlin: Franz Vahlen, 1871, 1873.

Bethmann-Hollweg 1865
Bethmann-Hollweg, A. von, *Der Civilprozeß des Gemeinen Rechts in geschichtlicher Entwicklung*, 2nd edn., Bonn: Adolph Marcus, 1865.

Borkowski & du Plessis 2010
Borkowski, A. & Plessis, P. du, *Textbook on Roman law*, 4th edn., Oxford: Oxford University Press, 2010.

Brandileone 1928
Brandileone, F., 'La stipulatio nell'età imperiale e durante il medio evo', *Rivista di storia del diritto italiano*, 1928, Vol. I, No. 1, p. 7-73, 270-310 (= Brandileone, F., *Scritti di storia del diritto privato italiano*, II, Bologna: Zanichelli, 1931, p. 421-528).

Broggini 1957
Broggini, G., *Iudex arbiterve. Prolegomena zum Officium des römischen Privatrichters*, Köln/Graz: Böhlau Verlag, 1957.

Buckland 1932
Buckland, W.W., *A Text-book of Roman law from Augustus to Justinian*, Cambridge: Cambridge University Press, 1932.

Burckhard 1866
Burckhard, H., *Die Civilistischen Präsumtionen*, Weimar: Landes-Industrie-Comptoir, 1866.

Diósdi 1981
Diósdi, G., *Contract in Roman Law*, Budapest: Akadémiai Kiadó, 1981.

Donatuti 1931
Donatuti, G., 'Le praesumptiones iuris in diritto romano', *Annali della Facoltà di Giurisprudenza dell'Universitá di Perugia*, 1931, Vol. 42, p. 1-112.

Donatuti 1933
Donatuti, G., 'Le "praesumptiones iuris" come mezzi di svolgimento del diritto sostanziale romano', *Rivista di diritto privato*, 1933, Vol. III, No. 1, p. 161-206.

Giuliani 2009
Giuliani, A., 'Civilian Treatises on Presumptions, 1580-1620', in: Helmholz, R.H. & Sellar, W.D.H. (eds.), *The Law of Presumptions: Essays in Comparative Legal History*, Berlin: Duncker & Humblot, 2009, p. 21-71.

Gradenwitz 1886
Gradenwitz, O., 'Interpolationen in den Pandekten', *Zeitschrift der Savigny-Stifung für Rechtsgeschichte, Romanistische Abteilung*, 1886, Vol. 7, p. 45-84.

Greenidge 1901
Greenidge, A.H.J., *The Legal Procedure of Cicero's Time*, Oxford: Clarendon Press, 1901.

Kaser 1954
Kaser, M., 'Beweislast und Vermutung im römischen Formularprozeß', *Zeitschrift der Savigny-Stifung für Rechtsgeschichte, Romanistische Abteilung*, 1954, Vol. 71, p. 221-241.

Kaser 1966
Kaser, M., *Das römische Zivilprozessrecht*, Munich: C.H. Beck'sche Verlagsbuchhandlung, 1966.

Kaser 1975
Kaser, M., *Das Römische Privatrecht*, II, Munich: C.H. Beck'sche Verlagsbuchhandlung, 1975.

Lemosse 1984
Lemosse, M., 'Onere della prova e procedura classica', *Labeo*, 1984, Vol. 30, No. 3, p. 329-333.

Levy 1956
Levy, E., *Weströmisches Vulgarrecht. Das Obligationenrecht*, Weimar: Böhlau Verlag, 1956.

Liebe 1840
Liebe, F., *Die Stipulation und das einfache Versprechen*, Braunschweig: Verlag von Meyer, 1840.

MacCormack 1983
MacCormack, G., 'The Oral and Written Stipulation in the Institutes', in: Stein, P.G. & Lewis, A.D.E. (eds.), *Studies in Justinian's Institutes in memory of J.A.C. Thomas*, London: Sweet & Maxwell, 1983, p. 96-108.

Martini 2001
Martini, R., 'Sulla presenza delle parti alla "stipulatio" nel diritto giustinianeo', *Labeo*, 2001, Vol. 47, No. 2, p. 245-252.

Metzger 2009
Metzger, E., 'An Outline of Civil Procedure in Roman Law' (draft 5 September 2009), in: Johnston, D. (ed.), *Cambridge Companion to Roman Law*, available at SSRN: <http://ssrn.com/abstract=1588142>.

Martinez De Morentín Llamas 2007
Martínez de Morentín Llamas, M.L., *Régimen jurídico de las presunciones*, Madrid: Librería-Editorial Dykinson, 2007.

Musielak 1975
Musielak, H.-J., *Die Grundlagen der Beweislast im Zivilprozess*, Berlin: Walter de Gruyter, 1975.

Nicholas 1953
Nicholas, B., 'The Form of the Stipulation in Roman Law', *Law Quarterly Review*, 1953, Vol. 69, p. 63-79, 233-252.

Pastori 1994
Pastori, F., *Il negozio verbale in diritto romano*, Bologna: Cisalpino, 1994.

Pringsheim 1961
Pringsheim, F., 'Stipulationsklausel', in: Pringsheim, F. (ed.), *Gesammelte Abhandlungen*, Bd. II, Heidelberg, Carl Winter Universitätsverlag, 1961, p. 194-256.

Pugliese 1956
Pugliese, G., 'L'onere della prova nel processo romano *per formulas*', *Revue internationale des droits de l'antiquité*, 1956, Vol. 3, p. 350-422.

Pugliese 1960
Pugliese, G., 'La prova nel processo romano classico', *Jus*, 1960, Vol. 11, p. 386-424.

Riccobono 1957
Riccobono, S., *Stipulation and the Theory of Contract*, trans. Kerr Wylie, J., revised by B. Beinart, Amsterdam-Cape Town, A.A. Balkema, 1957 (= 'Stipulatio ed instrumentum nel Diritto Giustinianeo', *Zeitschrift der Savigny-Stiftung für Rechtsgeschichte, Romanistische Abteilung*, 1914, Vol. 35, p. 214-305, and 1922, Vol. 43, p. 262-397).

Sacconi 1989
Sacconi, G., *Ricerche sulla stipulatio*, Camerino: Jovene Editore, 1989.

Simon 1964
Simon, D., *Studien zur Praxis der Stipulationsklausel*, München: C.H. Beck'sche Verlagsbuchhandlung, 1964.

Sohm 1886
Sohm, R., *Institutionen des römischen Rechts*, Leipzig: Duncker & Humblot, 1886.

Steinwenter 1947
Steinwenter, A., 'Rhetorik und römischer Zivilprozeß', *Zeitschrift der Savigny-Stifung für Rechtsgeschichte, Romanistische Abteilung*, 1947, Vol. 65, p. 69-120.

Van Oven 1958
Van Oven, J.C., 'La stipulation a-t-elle dégénéré? ', *Tijdschrift voor Rechtsgeschiedenis*, 1958, Vol. 26, p. 409-436.

Vinnius 2005
Vinnius, A., *Institutionenkommentar Schuldrecht: Text und Übersetzung*, trans. Wille, K., Heidelberg: C.F. Müller Verlag, 2005.

Wacke 1992
Wacke, A., 'Zur Beweislast im klassischen Zivilprozeß', *Zeitschrift der Savigny-Stifung für Rechtsgeschichte, Romanistische Abteilung*, 1992, Vol. 109, p. 411-449.

Wenger 1925
Wenger, L., *Institutionen des römischen Zivilprozessrechts*, München: Max Hueber, 1925.

Zimmermann 1990
Zimmermann, R., *The Law of Obligations. Roman Foundations of the Civilian Tradition*, Cape Town: Juta & Co., 1990.

EXPERIMENTAL APPROACH TO TRUTH-FINDING

R. Bloemink
S.P.W. v. Dooren
L.I.M. Entjes
S.A.H. v. Gompel
F. Fernhout

IMMEDIATE JUDGMENTS IN CIVIL PROCEEDINGS IN THE NETHERLANDS - AN EXPERIMENT

1. Introduction

Former British Prime Minister William Ewart Gladstone once said: 'Justice delayed is justice denied'.[1] The background of this statement is clear. The parties to a civil dispute certainly want to win the case, but when judgment fails to be pronounced, both parties lose. Delaying justice, in addition to creating unnecessary uncertainty and prolonged stress pending the decision of the court, amounts to denying justice.

Inefficiency and injustice go hand in hand in this matter. Sadly, court proceedings in many cases are inefficient indeed. Let us take a look at a random case brought before a Dutch cantonal court (*kantonrechter*).[2] The case is about a dispute between a private individual and an insurer.[3] The individual's automobile had collided with a company's automobile. The latter automobile's driver had clearly acted negligently and the employer was liable under vicarious liability. The claim for damages amounting to €1,500 was brought directly against the insurance company (*action directe*). At the hearing after the submission of the statement of defence (*comparitie na antwoord*, post-defence hearing or 'hearing after submission of the statement of defence'),[4] which was conducted thoroughly and took more than

1 Subramanian 2004, p. 151.

2 For reasons of legibility, we refer to the relevant type of court as the 'cantonal court', although this is somewhat anachronistic. The cantonal court became a division of the District Court under the 2002 amendments to the Dutch Judiciary Act (*Wet op de rechterlijke organisatie*). The judges of this division have exclusive jurisdiction in labour cases, rent cases, tenancy cases, consumer cases and all cases in which no value higher than €25,000 is disputed. In this respect, these judges can be seen as forming a court distinct from other courts.

3 The case was brought before the Cantonal Court of Heerlen, a division of the District Court of Maastricht. The judgment, which is of 3 August 2011, was not published. The case number is 423594 CV EXPL 11-3657.

4 A post-defence hearing is a personal appearance of the parties only (and their lawyers, if any). If necessary, witnesses are heard at separate hearings. Hereafter, this post-defence hearing is simply referred to as 'hearing'.

an hour, it became clear that the case was clear-cut, most notably because the sitting judge held that she found the insurance company liable to pay the damages. Although this preliminary view did not yet deal with the defence of comparative negligence (*eigen schuld*), the judge actually gathered enough information to form an opinion on the full case during the hearing. Nonetheless, it took about five weeks – from 30 June to 3 August – to get her opinion (awarding the full amount) on this clear-cut case on paper. Worse, this was done much too elaborately, as the judgment took four and a half pages (A4 size), clearly written by some official, most probably a court clerk, who must have spent at least half a working day writing the judgment.

Was this delay inevitable? Admittedly, in the Netherlands all judgments have to be delivered in writing and need to give the grounds for the decision. On the other hand, these grounds can be succinct and modern technology allows the production of written judgments without much delay. This would certainly serve the judge, who would not run the risk of forgetting essential parts of the hearing.

Starting from the idea that current practice is largely due to tradition and habit, we designed a simulation to test whether cantonal judges would be capable of changing actual practice into a much faster and much more efficient way of working. This contribution describes the results of this simulation. First, we explain current practice in more detail. Next, we go into the proposed alternative approach and its advantages. This leads to a brief description of the experiment and its results. We conclude with some recommendations based on our observations and findings.

2. Production of Cantonal Judgments in the Netherlands

The procedure applicable to civil cantonal cases in the Netherlands is based on the procedure for regular civil cases. A case is brought to court by means of a writ of summons that is served on the defendant.[5] Exchange of pleadings takes place in a cause-list sitting. Before the cantonal court, the defence may also be presented orally by the defendant in person[6] (which frequently happens as became apparent from a qualitative field inquiry into current practice).[7] After this sitting, an interim judgment sets a date for the post-defence hearing referred to above. During this hearing, which on average takes about forty-five minutes, parties are usually given some time to present their opinions, information is gathered and attempts are made to reach a settlement.

After the hearing, the court is supposed to give a judgment. Several options are open, such as ordering a witness hearing (*enquête* or *getuigenverhoor*) or a site

5 The analysis is restricted to cases which are commenced by a writ of summons, as opposed to cases which are commenced by a petition.

6 In sub-district cases, legal representation is not obligatory.

7 Most empirical remarks in this paragraph are based on a field inquiry at the Heerlen Cantonal Court, including numerous observations of cantonal court hearings and interviews with court clerks and a cantonal judge. Additional information was provided by the District Court in Maastricht.

inspection (*descente* or *plaatsopneming*), but more often than not a final judgment can be given. Accordingly, at the end of the hearing a date is set for the pronouncement of this judgment.[8] This date is noted in the records of the hearing, of which a copy is sent to the parties. After the hearing, the file is sent to the registry, and the registry then sends it to a court clerk (we refer to this type of clerk, schooled in the law, as a 'judicial clerk').[9] For the clerk, it usually takes between four hours and a full working day to write a draft of the judgment. After finishing the draft, it is sent to the sitting judge, in most cases some weeks after the hearing, who then usually comments on it and sends it back to the clerk. The clerk then corrects his draft, after which the draft is again sent to the judge, and so on. When the judgment is finally approved, it is sent to the registry, which converts the judgment into the correct format and sends it to the parties involved. In Figure 1, we present this practice visually.

The current practice of adjudication in civil cantonal cases in the Netherlands is suboptimal and unnecessarily complicated: (i) the hearings are usually rather long, (ii) the judgment is usually drafted and rendered quite a long time after the hearing, (iii) the judgment is usually not very accessible, even to the well-educated consumer of adjudication, which is especially problematic in cases in which the consumer does not enjoy the assistance of a lawyer, and (iv) the long period between the hearing and the pronouncement of the judgment probably results in a lower level of consumer satisfaction. Most notable, however, is that (v) a lot of time is usually spent on writing a judgment.

With regard to issue (i) above, we observed two possible causes for long hearings: (1) generally, the judge does not fully use the hearing as an information gathering tool and (2) quite a lot of time is spent on trying to reach a court settlement starting from the *ex ante* expectation that this will save time, since writing a judgment is in the event of a settlement obviously not needed. Reducing the time needed to write a judgment may therefore help to eliminate most of the fruitless attempts to reach a settlement aimed at preventing the need to write a judgment. As to issue (ii), firstly, the judgment is usually written by a judicial clerk (*gerechtssecretaris*) who was not present at the hearing, which may very well lower the quality of the judgment, and, secondly, since the court report is usually written months after the hearing, valuable information and insights may already be lost by then. Issue (iii) is largely related to the formal, legal language that is inevitably used to draft judgments. Immediate adjudication would offer the advantage of an oral explanation of the grounds of the judgment, thus motivating the judge to use terms that are comprehensible for his audience.

Although not all of these issues will be fully remedied, immediate adjudication would remove most of the drawbacks of current practice. We therefore set out to show that immediate post-hearing judicial decision making in cantonal

[8] In fact, the judgment is not pronounced but only mentioned during a cause-list sitting. The judgment is sent to the parties immediately after the date on which it is considered to be pronounced.

[9] This type of court clerk is usually *not* present at any hearing.

court proceedings (i) is feasible and (ii) does improve the efficiency of such proceedings (iii) without a significant loss of quality.

Figure 1. A Flowchart of Judgment Production by the Cantonal Court

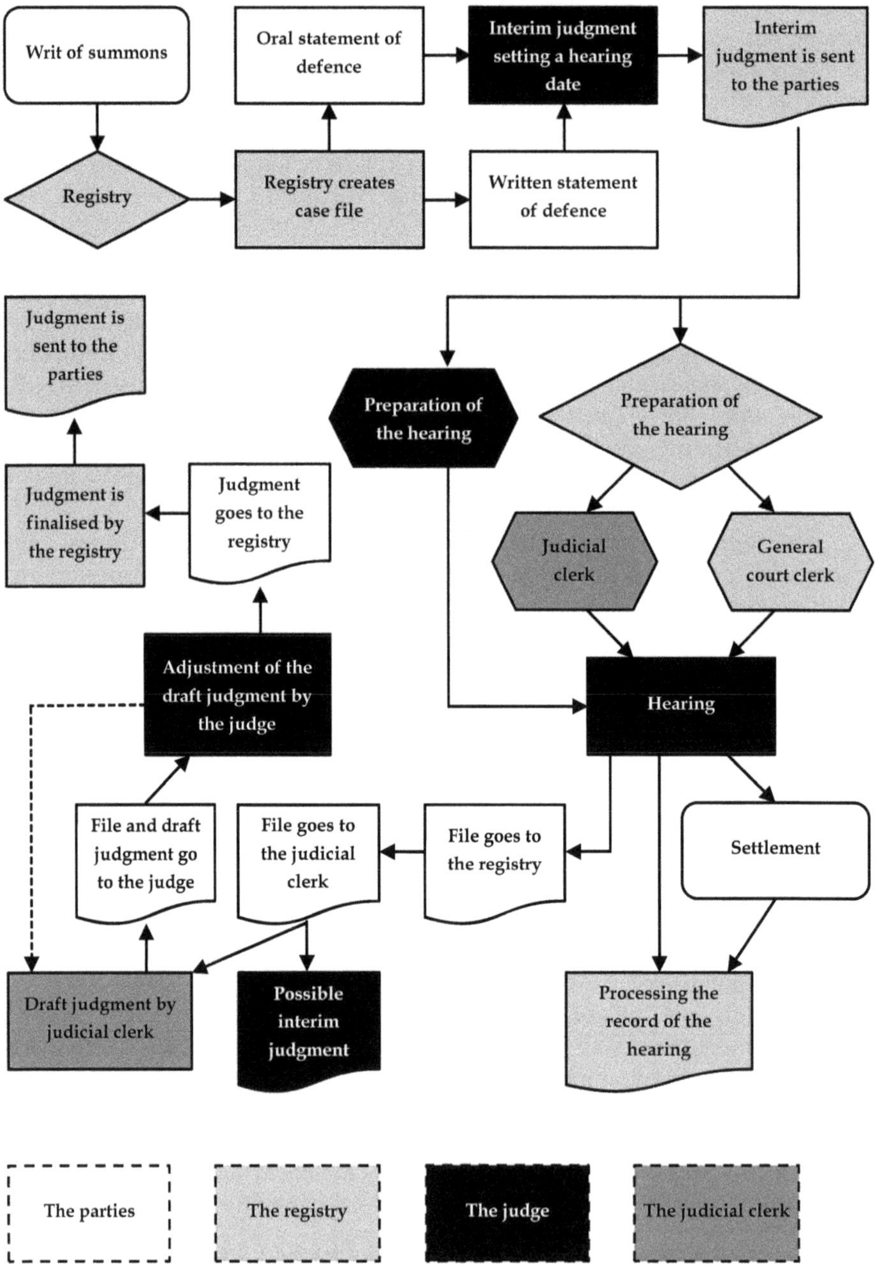

3. Outline of the Alternative Approach

As noted, the core of the alternative approach is that, as a guiding principle, the judge issues the judgment immediately after the hearing. This is not, however, an obligation. Cases which are not suitable for an immediate judgment can be dealt with in the traditional way.

The alternative approach mainly changes the procedure from the moment of the hearing. Proceedings preceding the hearing will not change radically. However, a draft skeleton judgment (not containing any grounds) and a tailor-made template for the record of the hearing will have to be prepared, as this will facilitate rendering the judgment immediately after the hearing. After the hearing, five to ten minutes should be allocated to finalise the record of the hearing and the judgment.

The hearing itself can be limited to fact finding and giving room to the parties to put forward their views on the claim and the defences raised by the defendant. 'Mediating' between the parties and motivating them to reach an agreement will only be rational when the parties clearly indicate that an agreement can be reached. This will avoid the loss of time spent in the usually idle hope of saving time in the future.

Figure 2. A Flowchart of the Alternative Approach

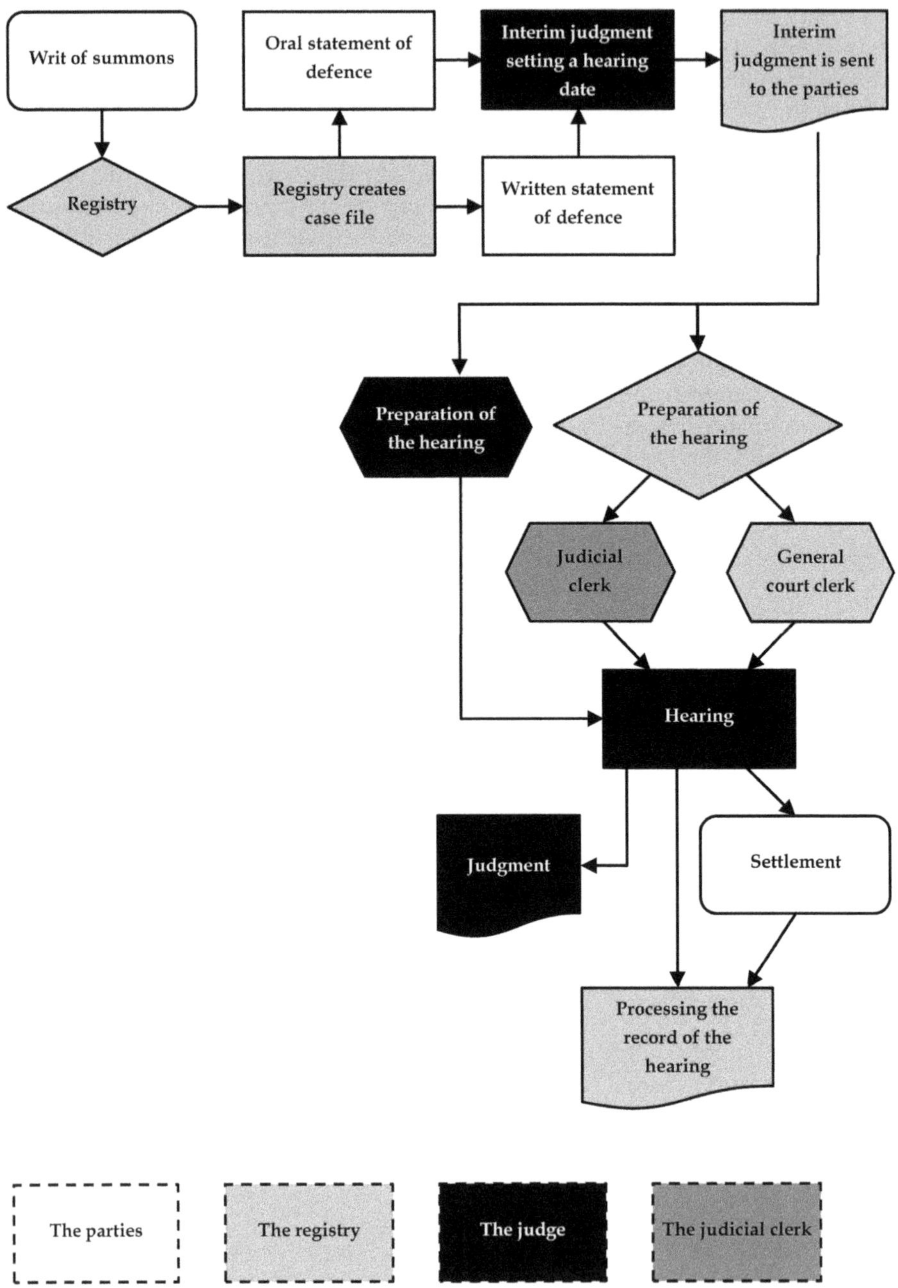

At the end of the hearing the judgment can be given, including the grounds for it. The grounds will have to be succinct, but adequate. To comply with the existing legal framework, best practice will be to write down the orally given grounds of the judgment into the record of the hearing. These grounds can then be copied into the actual judgment. Judgments will, accordingly, change radically as regards their content, since the position of the parties will only be hinted at instead of being elaborated in full as is current practice. Record and judgment can be submitted to the administration directly after the hearing to be copied and sent to the parties.

From the above, the potential benefit is immediately apparent. The judicial clerk and/or the judge no longer have to write a long and overly elaborate judgment. In addition, the number of administrative and physical operations with the case file is greatly reduced. Figure 2 shows the differences with current practice.

4. Simulation of Immediate Post-Hearing Adjudication

The assumptions set out above were tested by means of an experimental simulation to find out whether the alternative approach, which is, as is made plausible in paragraphs 2 and 3, more efficient, would actually work in practice and not result in an apparent loss of quality. Empirical, non-simulation research would have enhanced the validity of the research results, but time was too short to convince the District Court Governing Board to allow such an experiment in the court's courtrooms. Nonetheless, the experimental simulation did provide enough data to reach conclusions with regard to our assumptions.

The simulation took the form of a series of simulated post-defence hearings, all scheduled in one afternoon, as is current practice. The experiment was conducted with a professional judge and a professional court clerk in a setting that was similar to an ordinary courtroom, including the portrait of the Queen. The parties and their legal representatives were played by about fifteen actors. Adjusted models for the records of the oral hearing and adjusted models for the written judgment were drafted beforehand.

Files from real court cases were used to approximate reality as closely as possible, changing the original names to fictitious ones. These files were provided by the District Court of Maastricht. The files used were selected to provide a broad range of different types of cases. This deliberate selection bias, in view of the small number of cases used, enhanced the validity of the research. As to the ecological validity, there were no deficiencies, as we approximated reality very closely by using a real sub-district court judge, a real clerk, real cases, actors who were not schooled in the law and a realistic courtroom which is normally used for moot court purposes.[10] The recording of the simulation and the presence of the researchers, however, might raise validity issues, although we do not think these factors significantly influenced the outcome.[11]

10 *Cf.* Lawless, Robbenholt & Ulen 2010, p. 110.

11 *Cf.* Lawless, Robbenholt & Ulen 2010, p. 110-111.

To ensure that the simulation hearing was as realistic as possible we used actors unknown to the judge and the clerk. The actors were cast for their roles by matching gender and age. Each individual party was given client instructions that contained a description of the case, the facts that were disputed and the claims that were brought. The actors did not know about the alternative approach and were only told that they would participate in a simulation of a court hearing. The judge and the clerk received the new, adapted forms for the record of the hearing and the judgment and verbal instructions on how to use these new forms. We chose to give verbal instructions to the judge and the clerk to afford them the opportunity to directly ask for clarification if some aspect was unclear. In the morning, two test hearings took place to make the judge and the clerk familiar with the new approach. After this test, the actual simulation was carried out. Five cases were scheduled with thirty minutes for each case.

The simulation was very successful. The judge handled the cases swiftly and was able to reach and pronounce a judgment – final or interim – on the spot. The thirty minutes allotted were more than sufficient, although one of the cases required a bit more time.[12] On average, the time required for post-defence hearings was shorter than is actually the case, particularly as a result of the judge's judgment-directed approach,[13] mainly aimed at gathering enough information to reach a decision. This leaves little room for the parties to submit information that is irrelevant. The greatest time savings, however, are achieved by not writing an elaborate judgment, as is done in the current procedure.

The judge had no difficulty in giving grounds for his decision. In cases like this, the legal issues are usually rather basic and the debate is more about the facts than the law. That also enabled the judge to give the parties a clear picture of the legal background of his rulings. The judgments themselves were drafted during breaks and after the hearing. They were printed out immediately after the hearing and signed by the judge and the clerk, thus delivering a completed product.

In a post-simulation interview, the judge declared being very satisfied with the way he had worked that afternoon. According to him, his simulation judgments met all the standards that apply to judgments according to Dutch law. He did not have the feeling that he had been under particular pressure to come up with a decision when he felt the case needed a bit more consideration than was possible in the simulation setting.[14]

12 For the five hearings the judge needed 10, 24, 20, 35 and 19 minutes, respectively, including the time used by the parties during a break to try to reach a settlement.

13 There are no comparable data available, but from a national survey of 150 post-defence hearings it can be concluded that the simulation hearings were really very short. The mentioned survey registered an average hearing length of 2 hours and 11 minutes (Van der Linden, Klijn & Van Tulder 2009, p. 30).

14 Actually, the same judge later revealed that he is using the proposed method in his everyday work now, with very satisfying results.

5. Concluding Remarks

As noted, there are no legal difficulties concerning the alternative approach. As a result of running the simulation session, it also became clear that this new and efficient way of operating functions as it should and does not result in an apparent loss of quality. The alternative approach is therefore compatible with Dutch procedural law and is much more efficient than current practice. It could therefore be used in practice when sub-district court judges and clerks are willing to give up their current *modus operandi*.

Bibliography

Lawless, Robbenholt & Ulen 2010
Lawless, R.M., Robbenholt, J.K. & Ulen, T.S., *Empirical Methods in Law*, New York: Aspen Publishers, 2010.

Subramanian 2004
Subramanian, V.K., *The Great Ones in Public Life*, Vol. 2, New Delhi: Abhinav Publications, 2004.

Van der Linden, Klijn & Van Tulder 2009
Van der Linden, J., Klijn, A. & Van Tulder, F., *Meesterlijk gedrag: leren van compareren*, Rechtstreeks 2009, No. 3, The Hague: SDU, 2009.

IUS COMMUNE EUROPAEUM

A peer-reviewed book series in which the common foundations of the legal systems of the Member States of the European Community are the central focus.

The *Ius Commune Europaeum* series includes horizontal comparative legal studies as well as studies on the effect of treaties within the national legal systems. All the classic fields of law are covered. The books are published in various European languages under the auspices of METRO, the Institute for Transnational Legal Research at the Maastricht University.

Recently published:

Volume 95: *The Landscape of the Legal Professions in Europe and the USA: Continuity and Change*, A. UZELAC and C.H. VAN RHEE (eds.)
Volume 96: *Constitutional Constraints on Ad Hoc Legislation. A Comparative Study of the United States, Germany and the Netherlands*, A. JASIAK
Volume 97: *The Social Security Position of Irregular Migrant Workers. New Insights from National Security Law and International Law*, K. KAPUY
Volume 98: *Educating European Lawyers*, A.W. HERINGA and B. AKKERMANS (eds.)
Volume 99: *The Draft Common Frame of Reference: A National and Comparative Perspective*, E. TERRYN, V. SAGAERT and M.E. STORME (eds.)
Volume 100: *Does Law Matter? On Law and Economic Growth*, M. FAURE and J. SMITS (eds.)
Volume 101: *The Power of Punitive Damages. Is Europe Missing Out?*, L. MEURKENS and E. NORDIN (eds.)
Volume 102: *The Changing Role of the European Council in the Institutional Framework of the European Union*, F. EGGERMONT
Volume 103: *Linked Contracts*, I. SAMOY and M.B.M. LOOS (eds.)
Volume 104: *Constitutions Compared* (3rd ed.), A.W. HERINGA and PH. KIIVER
Volume 105: *Alternative Ways to Ius Commune*, A.L.M. KEIRSE and M.B.M. LOOS (eds.)
Volume 106: *Property Law Perspectives*, B. AKKERMANS and E. RAMAEKERS (eds.)
Volume 107: *Constitutional Conversations*, C. VAN DE HEYNING and M. DE VISSER (eds.)
Volume 108: *Enforcing Health and Safety Regulations. A Comparative Economic Approach*, L. TILINDYTE
Volume 109: *Administrative Law of the European Union, its Member States and the United States. A Comparative Analysis*, R. SEERDEN (ed.)
Volume 110: *Market Integration through 'Network Governance': The Role of European Agencies and Networks of Regulators*, M. ZINZANI

www.ingramcontent.com/pod-product-compliance
Ingram Content Group UK Ltd.
Pitfield, Milton Keynes, MK11 3LW, UK
UKHW051925100926
8556IPUK00022B/1380

9 781780 681337